Drawn by W.H. Bartlett. Engraved by [illegible] in the possession of [illegible]

BLACK'S
PICTURESQUE TOURIST

OF

SCOTLAND.

FIFTH EDITION.

EDINBURGH:

ADAM AND CHARLES BLACK, 27, NORTH BRIDGE,

BOOKSELLERS AND PUBLISHERS TO THE QUEEN.

MDCCCXLVII.

EDINBURGH : PRINTED BY T. CONSTABLE,
PRINTER TO HER MAJESTY.

PREFACE

TO THE FIFTH EDITION.

THE plan and execution of the present volume will be found, in an important respect, to differ from any other work devoted to the same object. In the compilation of Guide-Books, it appears to the Publishers that much eloquence is often needlessly expended in ambitious eulogiums on the beauty or grandeur of natural scenery, of which no adequate idea can be conveyed to the mind by any written description, however graphic and minute. In the present work, such attempts have been studiously avoided. A plain and intelligible account has been given of the scenery most worthy of the attention of strangers, without dictating the amount of admiration with which any given scene is to be contemplated. By adopting this course, space has been found for the incorporation of a large amount of Traditionary, Historical, and Literary illustration, by which it is conceived a recollection of the scenery will be more permanently fixed in the memory of the tourist, than by any original description of its features which the author could himself have given.

Neither labour nor expense has been spared to give the work the greatest possible degree of accuracy. To secure this object, the several sheets, in their progress through the press, have been transmitted to individuals conversant with the topography of the respective districts ; while the descriptions of Edinburgh, Glasgow, and Aberdeen, have been wholly contributed by natives of these cities.

The expense of travelling, and the gratuities paid to servants at hotels, are subjects so materially influenced by the habits of the traveller, and the style of the establishment at which he sojourns, that it is difficult to afford precise information in regard to them. At the same time, the Publishers have reason to believe that a few particulars on these heads will be generally acceptable to tourists, and they have accordingly embodied, in the following note, the result of the enquiries which they judged it proper to make upon the subject.

The improvements made upon every edition since the work first appeared, have been numerous and important. The present has been enlarged, as well as corrected in its information, a description of Skye and of Arran having been introduced into the text, and several new engravings having been added to the list of Illustrations. Among these, the view of Loch Scavaig, forming the Frontispiece to the volume, may be referred to as a work of art which would do honour to any publication, however high its pretensions.

For the favourable reception of former editions the Publishers return their best thanks. They, at the same time, express their acknowledgments to the public press for numerous laudatory notices, which, if not unmerited by the *four former* editions, will be found to be still better deserved by the *present.*

TRAVELLING EXPENSES.

THE expense necessarily attendant upon travelling must be admitted to be a considerable drawback from its pleasures. Still
the evil is inevitable; and it may be satisfactory to tourists to
be able to estimate the price to be paid for their enjoyment.

The following scale shows the average charge for the several
items which enter into the traveller's bill. The prices in the *first*
division of the scale are rarely exceeded in any of the Inns in
the smaller towns in Scotland; while in some villages, charges
even more moderate may sometimes be met with. The prices
in the *second* division show the charges in Hotels of the highest
class in Edinburgh.

Breakfast, 1/6 to 2/	2/ to 3/
Dinner, 2/ to 3/	3/ to 4/
Tea, 1/6 to 2/	2/ to 3/
Supper, 1/6 to 2/	According to what is ordered.
Port or Sherry, per bottle, 5/	6/
Porter or Ale, per bottle, /6 to 1/	1/
Brandy, per gill, 1/6	2/
Whisky, per gill, /9	1/
Bed, 1/6 to 3/	3/6 to 4/

. If the Traveller require his table to be furnished beyond the ordin-
ary scale of comfort, he must be prepared for a proportionate increase of
charge.

In the inferior country Inns, Wine, Brandy, and Malt Liquor
are frequently not to be met with, or, if kept, will probably be
of indifferent quality.

Posting, 1s. 6d. per mile; postboy, 3d. per mile.
A one-horse four-wheeled carriage, 1s. per mile, or 15s. per day.
A gig, 10s. 6d. to 12s. per day.
A riding-horse, 6s. or 7s. ; a pony, 5s. per day.
. In large towns the charges for carriages and riding-horses are about 20 per cent.
above those here quoted. Where the hire is for several successive days, an abate-
ment may be expected. The posting is the same in town and country.

The payment of the gratuities to servants at Inns is a source
of great annoyance to travellers. It would very largely contri-

bute to the tourist's comfort were the charges under this head included among the other items of the landlord's bill. Although this practice has been adopted by a few Hotel-keepers in other parts of the kingdom, it is believed that it has not yet been introduced into any of the Inns in Scotland.

To enable them to furnish tourists with some information on this subject, the publishers have applied to two Hotel-keepers of the first respectability (the one in Dublin, the other in Liverpool) by whom the practice of charging for servants is adopted, and the following are averaged from the rates charged in their establishments :—

1.

A single gentleman, taking the general accommodation of the Hotel for one or two meals as a passing traveller, Waiter, 6d. ; Chambermaid, 6d. ; Porter or Boots, 6d. This includes the removal of any reasonable weight of luggage; but extra messages and parcels are charged separately.

2.

A single gentleman, staying a day and night, and taking his meals in the hotel, 1s. 6d. or 2s. for servants, and if he stays several days, 1s. or 1s. 6d. per day.

3.

A gentleman and his wife, occupying a sitting-room and bedroom, 2s. 6d. to 3s. 6d. per night for servants. If accompanied by sons or daughters, or other relatives, half this rate from each; but no charge for children under nine years of age.

4.

A party of four or six for one night, about 1s. 6d. each.

Upon submitting this scale to several of the most respectable Hotel-keepers in Edinburgh, they consider the rates to be a fair average. In country and village inns, even the lowest of the payments above quoted may be unnecessarily liberal, while in some of the fashionable hotels in London the highest may be considerably under par.

CONTENTS.

SIXTH TOUR.

SEVENTH TOUR.

EIGHTH TOUR.

NINTH TOUR.

TENTH TOUR.

ELEVENTH TOUR.

TWELFTH TOUR.

THIRTEENTH TOUR.

FOURTEENTH TOUR.

FIFTEENTH TOUR.

SIXTEENTH TOUR.

ROAD AND RAILROAD ITINERARY.

₊ The Railways are distinguished by *Italics.*

ILLUSTRATIONS

I. MAPS, PLANS, AND RAILWAY CHARTS.

II. VIEWS OF SCENERY, &c.

*** The Engravings on wood are distinguished by *Italics.*

THE

PICTURESQUE TOURIST

OF

SCOTLAND.

ORIGIN OF THE NAME—EXTENT—GENERAL ASPECT—NATURAL DIVISIONS—MOUNTAINS—VALES—RIVERS—LAKES—MINERAL PRODUCE AND SPRINGS—CLIMATE—AGRICULTURE—ANIMAL KINGDOM—FISHERIES—MANUFACTURES—COMMERCE—INTERNAL COMMUNICATION—REVENUE—CONSTITUTION—RELIGIOUS INSTITUTIONS—UNIVERSITIES AND SCHOOLS—ADMINISTRATION OF JUSTICE—POPULATION.

SCOTLAND is the northern and smaller division of the Island of Great Britain. The origin of the term is involved in much obscurity. That part of the country which lies beyond the Firths of Forth and Clyde received from the Romans the appellation of Caledonia, and its inhabitants were denominated Caledonians. They were afterwards known by the name of Picts, and from them the country was for some centuries called Pictland. The term Scotland began to come into use, for the first time, in the eleventh century, and this name is supposed to have been derived from a colony of Scots, who had previously left Ireland, and planted themselves in Argyleshire and the West Highlands.

EXTENT.—The longest line that can be drawn in Scotland, is from its most southerly point, the Mull of Galloway, in lat. 54° 38′ N., long. 4° 50′ W., to Dunnet Head, its most northerly point, in lat. 58° 40′ 30″ N., long. 3° 29′ W., or about 285 miles; but the longest line that can be drawn in about the same parallel of longitude, is from the former point to Cape Wrath, in lat. 58° 36′ N., long. 4° 56′ W., a distance of 275 miles. The breadth is extremely various. From Buchanness point to the point of Ardnamurchan in Argyleshire, the distance is 160 miles; but from the bottom of Loch Broom to the Firth of Dornoch, it is only twenty-four miles. The whole coast is so much penetrated by arms of the sea, that there is only one spot throughout its whole circuit upwards of forty miles from the shore. The area of the mainland is computed at 25,520 square miles of land, and 494 of fresh water lakes; the islands are supposed to contain about 4080 square miles of land, and about 144 of water.

GENERAL ASPECT.—The surface of the country is distinguished for variety, and, compared with England, it is, generally speaking, rugged and mountainous. It is supposed, that estimating the whole extent of the country, exclusive of lakes, at 19,000,000 acres, scarcely so many as 6,000,000 are arable—that is, less than one-third; whereas in England, the proportion of arable land to the entire extent of the country exceeds three-fourths. With the exception of a few tracts of rich alluvial land along the courses of the great rivers, Scotland has no extensive tracts of level ground, the surface of the country being generally varied with hill and dale.

· NATURAL DIVISIONS.—Scotland is naturally divided into Highlands and Lowlands. The former division comprehends, besides the Hebrides, the Orkney and Shetland islands, the counties of Argyle, Inverness, Nairn, Ross, Cromarty, Sutherland, and Caithness, with parts of Dumbarton, Stirling, Perth, Forfar, Kincardine, Aberdeen, Banff, and Moray or Elgin. The Highlands, again, are divided into two unequal portions, by the chain of lakes occupying the Glenmore-nan-albin, or "Great glen of Caledonia," stretching north-east and south-west across the island, from Inverness to Fort-William, now connected together, and forming the Caledonian Canal. The northern division of the Highlands is decidedly the more barren and unproductive of the two, though the other division contains the highest mountains. In the eastern parts of Ross and Cromarty there are level tracts of considerable fertility. The Lowland division of the kingdom, though comparatively flat, comprises also a great deal of mountainous country.

MOUNTAINS.—Of the Highland mountains, the most celebrated is the chain of the Grampians. It commences on the south side of Loch Etive in Argyleshire, and terminates between Stonehaven and the mouth of the Dee on the eastern coast. The most elevated part of this range lies at the head of the Dee. Ben Macdui, the highest mountain in Scotland, rises to the height of 4418 feet, and the adjoining mountains of Cairngorm, Cairntoul, and Ben Avon, are respectively 4050, 4245, and 3967 feet high. The other principal summits of the Grampian chain are, Schehallion, near the east end of Loch Rannoch, 3613 feet above the level of the sea ; Ben Lawers, on the north side of Loch Tay, 3945 ; Ben More, at the head of Glendochart, 3818 ; Ben Lomond, on the side of Loch Lomond, 3191 ; and Ben Cruachan, at the head of Loch Awe, 3390. Ben Nevis, till recently reputed the highest of the British mountains, lies immediately to the east of Fort-William, being separated from the Grampians by the moor of Rannoch ; it rises 4416 feet above the mean level of the sea,* and its circumference at the base is supposed to exceed twenty-four miles. To the south of the Grampians, and running parallel to them across the island, there is a chain of hills divided by the valleys of the Tay and Forth into three distinct portions, and bearing the names of the Sidlaw, Ochil, and Campsie hills. The low country between them and the Grampians is called the valley of Strathmore. In the Lowland division of the country, the Cheviots form the principal range. These hills are situated partly in England and partly in Scotland. They separate Northumberland from Roxburghshire, stretch through the latter county in a westerly direction, keeping to the north of Liddesdale, then bending north-west towards

* The height of Ben Nevis, as here given, was obtained by Mr. David Stevenson, civil engineer, from careful barometric observations made simultaneously on the top of Ben Nevis and at Corpach Loch on 15th August 1844, and the calculations were made by Mr. William Swan, teacher of mathematics, Edinburgh.

the junction of the counties of Roxburgh, Selkirk and
Dumfries, they unite with the Lowther Hills. This extensive group, which, near the above-mentioned junction, has
Ettrick water for its eastern boundary, spreads over the
southern portion of the counties of Selkirk, Peebles, and
Lanark, and the north of Dumfries-shire, and in the west of
the latter county joins the ridges, which, passing through
Kirkcudbrightshire, Wigtonshire, and the south of Ayrshire,
terminate at Loch Ryan in the Irish Channel. Of these
hills the highest lie on the confines of the counties of Dumfries, Peebles, Lanark, and Selkirk ; Broadlaw, in the parish
of Tweedsmuir, the most elevated mountain in the south of
Scotland, is 2741 feet above the level of the sea ; Hartfell,
contiguous to Broadlaw, is 2635 feet above the level of the
sea, and several of the neighbouring hills rise to the height
of about 2000 feet.

VALES.—The most important level tracts in Scotland are,
the Carse of Stirling and Falkirk, which occupies the country
on both sides the Forth, from Borrowstounness on the south,
and Kincardine on the north, westward to Gartmore ; the
tract between Dundee and Perth, bounded by the Sidlaw
hills on the north, and the Tay on the south, denominated
the Carse of Gowrie ; the Merse of Berwickshire, extending
from Leader water along the Tweed to Berwick ; and the
valley of Strathmore, which comprises a considerable portion of the counties of Perth and Angus, stretching from
Methven in the former to the vicinity of Laurencekirk in
Kincardineshire, and from thence, under the name of *the
How of the Mearns*, to within a short distance of Stonehaven.
Besides these, there are several smaller straths, such as
Teviotdale in Roxburghshire, Tynedale in East-Lothian, and
the How of Fife.

RIVERS.—The principal rivers of Scotland are, the Tweed,
the Forth, the Tay, the Spey, and the Clyde. The Tweed
rises in Tweedsmuir about six miles from Moffat. It runs
first north-east to Peebles, then east, with a little inclination
to the south, to Melrose ; it next passes Kelso and Coldstream, and pursuing a north-easterly direction, falls into
the sea at Berwick. During the latter part of its course, the

Tweed forms the boundary between England and Scotland. The descent from its source to Peebles is 1000 feet, and thence to Berwick about 500 feet more. Including windings, its length is reckoned at rather more than 100 miles. Its principal tributaries are, the Ettrick, which it receives near Selkirk ; the Gala a little above, and the Leader a little below Melrose ; the Teviot at Kelso ; the Till at Tillmouth ; and the Adder near Berwick. The salmon fisheries at Berwick are very productive. The extent of country drained by the Tweed is 1687 square miles.

The Forth rises on the east side of Ben Lomond, and runs in an easterly direction, with many windings, till it unites with the Firth of Forth at Kincardine. Its most important tributary is the Teith, which it receives a short way above Stirling. It drains 793 square miles.

The Tay conveys to the sea a greater quantity of water than any other river in Britain. It has its source in the western extremity of Perthshire, in the district of Breadalbane, on the frontiers of Lorn in Argyleshire. At first it receives the name of the Fillan. After a winding course of eight or nine miles it spreads itself out into Loch Dochart, and, under the appellation of the Dochart, flows in an easterly direction through the vale of Glendochart, at the eastern extremity of which, having previously received the waters of the Lochy, it expands into the beautiful long narrow lake, called Loch Tay. Issuing thence, it speedily receives a great augmentation by the river Lyon, and running north and east at Logierait, about eight miles above Dunkeld, it is joined by the Tummel. It now takes a direction more towards the south, to Dunkeld, where, on its right bank, it receives the beautiful river Bran. On leaving Dunkeld, it runs east to Kinclaven, and after receiving a considerable augmentation to the volume of its waters by the accession of the Isla, the Shochie, and the Almond, it flows in a southwesterly course to Perth. At the foot of the vale of Strathearn, it receives on its right bank its last great tributary, the Earn, and gradually expanding its waters, it flows in a north-easterly direction past Newburgh, where it assumes the appearance of a Firth or estuary. Ten miles from the

German ocean it passes Dundee, and finally unites its waters to the sea, between Tentsmoor Point and Buttonness. The Tay is celebrated for its salmon fisheries, the value of which is between £10,000 and £11,000 per annum. The river is navigable for vessels of 400 tons burden, as far as Perth, thirty-two miles from the German ocean. Its drainage is 2283 square miles, and its mean discharge below the junction of the Earn, has been ascertained by Mr. David Stevenson, to be 273,117 cubic feet per minute. That of the Thames is stated at only 80,220 cubic feet per minute, or less than one-third that of the Tay.

The Spey is the most rapid of the Scottish rivers, and, next to the Tay, discharges the greatest quantity of water. It has its source in Loch Spey, within about six miles of the head of Loch Lochy. It runs in a north-easterly direction through Badenoch and Strathspey to Fochabers, below which it falls into the Moray Firth, at Garmouth. During its course, it receives numerous mountain streams, but no important tributary. From its source to its mouth, the distance is about seventy-five miles; but following its windings, its course is about ninety-six miles. Owing to the origin and course of its tributary waters, the Spey is very liable to sudden and destructive inundations. It flows through the best wooded part of the Highlands, and affords a water-carriage for the produce of the extensive woods of Glenmore and Strathspey, large quantities of which are floated down to the seaport of Garmouth. It drains 1234 square miles.

The Clyde is, in a commercial point of view, the most important river of Scotland. It has its origin in the highest part of the southern mountain land, at no great distance from the sources of the Tweed and the Annan. It flows at first in a northerly direction, with a slight inclination to the east, as far as Biggar. Being joined by the Douglas, near Harperfield, it takes a north-west course by Lanark, Hamilton, and Glasgow, falling into the Firth of Clyde below Dumbarton. Following its windings, the course of the Clyde, from its source to Dumbarton, is about seventy-three miles, but the length of the river, in a direct line, is only about fifty-two miles. Its principal tributaries are the Douglas, Nethan, Avon, Mouse, Kelvin, Cart, and Leven. The extent of its drainage, exclusive of the Leven, is 945 square miles. Of the celebrated falls of the Clyde, two are above, and two below Lanark; the uppermost is Bonnington Linn, the height of which is about thirty feet; the second fall is Corra Linn, where the water dashes over the rock in three distinct leaps; Dundaff Fall is ten feet high, and at Stonebyres there are three distinct falls, altogether measuring about seventy-six feet in height. At high water the Clyde is navigable for the largest class of merchant vessels as far as Glasgow, and large sums of money have been expended, especially of late, in improving and deepening the channel. The Forth and Clyde Canal falls into the latter river, at Dunglass, a little above Dumbarton.

LAKES.—The chief lakes of Scotland are—Loch Lomond, lying between Dumbartonshire and Stirlingshire; Loch Ness, in Inverness-shire; Loch Maree, in Ross-shire; Loch Awe, in Argyleshire; Lochs Tay, Rannoch, and Erich, in Perthshire, &c.

MINERAL PRODUCE.—The minerals of Scotland are numerous and valuable. The great coal-field of Scotland extends, with little interruption, from the eastern to the western coast. The most valuable part of this field is situated on the north and south sides of the Forth, about the average breadth of ten or twelve miles on each side, and on the north and south sides of the Clyde, ranging through Renfrewshire, part of Lanarkshire; and the north of Ayrshire. Detached coal-fields have also been found in various other parts of Scotland. Lime is very generally diffused throughout the country. Iron abounds in many parts, particularly in the coal-field. Lead-mines are wrought to a great extent at Leadhills and Wanlockhead, in Dumfries-shire. In the soil which covers these fields, particles of gold have occasionally been found; copper-ore is found at Blair Logie, Airthrie, and at Fetlar, in Orkney; antimony at Langholm; manganese in the neighbourhood of Aberdeen; silver has been wrought at Alva in Stirlingshire, in Clackmannanshire, and at Leadhills in Lanarkshire; there are extensive slate-quarries in Aberdeenshire, Argyleshire, Perthshire, and Peebles-shire; marble is found in Argyleshire, Sutherland, and the Hebrides; sandstone abounds generally throughout the country; and granite, and other primitive rocks, within the limits of the Grampians.

MINERAL SPRINGS.—There are numerous medicinal mineral springs in various parts of Scotland. " The most remarkable of these are—the sulphurous waters of *Strathpeffer*, near Dingwall, Ross-shire; *Muirtown*, in the same neighbourhood; *Moffat*, in Dumfries-shire; and *St. Bernard's*, at Stockbridge, a suburb of Edinburgh: the chalybeates of *Hartfell*, near Moffat; *Vicar's Bridge*, near Dollar, Stirlingshire; and *Bonnington*, near Edinburgh: the saline waters of *Dunblane*, near Stirling; *Airthrie*, also near Stirling; *Pitcaithly*, near Perth; and *Innerleithen*, near Peebles. At *St. Catherine's*, in the parish of Liberton, near Edinburgh, there is a spring which yields asphaltum in considerable quantities." *

CLIMATE.—The climate of Scotland is extremely variable. Owing to its insular situation, however, neither the cold in winter, nor the heat in summer, is so intense as in similar latitudes on the continent. The annual average temperature may be estimated at from 44° to 47° of Fahrenheit. The quantity of rain which falls on the east coast of Scotland varies from 22 to 26 inches, while on the west coast, and in the Hebrides, it ranges from 35 to 46 inches. The average number of days in which either rain or snow falls in parts situated on the west coast, is about 200; on the east coast, about 145. The winds are more variable than in England, and more violent, especially about the equinoxes. Westerly winds generally prevail, especially during autumn and the early part of winter, but north-east winds are prevalent and severe during spring and the early part of summer.

AGRICULTURE.—The soils of the various districts of Scotland are exceedingly diversified. The general average is inferior to that of England, although many of the valleys

* Malte Brun and Balbi Abridged. *Second Edition.* Edin. 1844.

are highly productive. In Berwickshire, the Lothians, Clydesdale, Fifeshire, the Carses of Stirling, Falkirk, and more particularly in the Carse of Gowrie, Strathearn, Strathmore, and Moray, there are tracts of land not inferior to any in the empire. The inferiority of the climate and soil, as compared with England, is exhibited by contrasting the phenomena of vegetation in the two countries. Notwithstanding the very advanced state of agriculture, in many districts of Scotland, the crops are not reaped with the same certainty as in England, nor do the ordinary kinds of grain arrive at the same perfection. Thus, although Scotch and English barley may be of the same weight, the former does not bring so high a price ; it contains less saccharine matter, and does not yield so large a quantity of malt. Various fruits, also, which ripen in the one country, seldom arrive at maturity in the other, and never reach the same perfection ; while different berries acquire in Scotland somewhat of that delicious flavour which distinguishes them in still higher parallels.

ANIMAL KINGDOM.—The domestic animals common to Scotland are the same as those of England, with some varieties in the breeds. Among the wild animals, the roe and the red-deer are most worthy of notice. The golden eagle, and other birds of prey, are found in the mountainous districts, and the country abounds with all kinds of moor-game, partridges, and water-fowl.

FISHERIES.—There are many valuable fisheries in Scotland ; the salmon fisheries, especially, produce a large revenue to their owners, but, during late years, they have experienced an extraordinary decline.

The herring fishery is carried on to a considerable extent on the east coast of Scotland, and there are most productive and valuable fisheries of ling and cod in the neighbourhood of the Shetland and Orkney Islands.

MANUFACTURES.—The manufactures of Scotland, especially those of linen and cotton, are extensive and flourishing. The woollen manufacture, compared with that of England, is inconsiderable. The making of steam-engines, and every other description of machinery, as also the building of steam-boats, both of wood and iron, is carried on to a great extent, especially on the Clyde ; and vast quantities of cast-iron goods are produced at Carron, Shotts, and other works.

COMMERCE.—The commerce of Scotland has increased with astonishing rapidity, especially within a comparatively recent period, and a vast trade is now carried on, particularly with America and the West Indies. It is supposed, that since 1814, the increase in the principal manufactures and trades carried on in the country, and in the number of individuals employed in them, amounts to at least 30, or 35 per cent.

INTERNAL COMMUNICATION.—Carriage roads extend over every part of the country ; and " in consequence of the excellent materials which abound in all parts of Scotland, and of the greater skill and science of Scottish trustees and surveyors, the turnpike roads in Scotland are superior to those in England." * The irregularity of surface is not favourable to artificial inland navigation. Among the most important Canals are the *Caledonian Canal*, connecting the Lakes Ness, Oich, and Lochy, with the Beauly Firth on the north, and with Loch Eil on the south ; the *Forth and Clyde* or *Great Canal*, extending from the Firth of Forth at Grangemouth, to Bowling Bay on the Firth of Clyde ; and the *Union Canal*, commencing at Edinburgh, and terminating in the Great Canal at Port Downie near Falkirk. Besides these, there are several others which may be noticed in describing the localities through which they pass. Among the Railways of Scotland, completed, or in progress, the most important are—the *Edinburgh and Glasgow*, the *Caledonian*, the *North British*, the *Scottish Central*, the *Edinburgh and Northern*, the *Aberdeen*, and the *Dundee and Perth*. There are many other undertakings of this kind completed, in progress, or projected, but limited space prevents our noticing them more particularly.

REVENUE.—The increase in the revenue has fully kept pace with the increasing prosperity of the country. At

---

* Sir H. Parnell on Roads, p. 313.

the period of the Union, the revenue amounted only to £110,696; in 1788, it was £1,099,148; in 1813, (when the Income Tax was at its height,) it amounted to £4,204,097; in 1831, notwithstanding the repeal of the Income Tax, and many other taxes, the gross revenue amounted to £5,254,624; and in 1840, although there was a farther reduction of taxation, it amounted to £5,231,727. The returns since this period, with the exception of the year 1842, have continued to exhibit a progressive increase in amount.

CONSTITUTION.—Under the Reform Act of 1832, Scotland returns fifty-three members to the Imperial Parliament, of whom thirty are for the shires, and twenty-three for the cities, boroughs, and towns; twenty-seven counties return one member each, and the counties of Elgin and Nairn, Ross and Cromarty, and Clackmannan and Kinross, are combined in pairs, each of which returns one member. Of the cities, boroughs, and towns—seventy-six in number— Edinburgh and Glasgow return two members each; Aberdeen, Paisley, Dundee, Greenock, and Perth, one each; the remaining burghs and towns are combined into sets or districts, each set, jointly, sending one member. The Scottish Peers choose sixteen of their number to represent them in the House of Lords. These representative Peers, like the Commoners, hold their seats for only one Parliament.

RELIGIOUS INSTITUTIONS.—Scotland is divided into 1023 parishes, (including parishes *quoad sacra*,) each of which is provided with one minister, or, in a few instances in towns, with two. The number of parishes, *quoad sacra*, has, however, been increased of late. The stipends of the endowed clergy, with the glebe and manse, probably average from £260 to £300 a-year. The government of the Church is vested in kirk-sessions, presbyteries, synods, and the General Assembly. The number of churches belonging to Dissenters, of all denominations, amounts to 1500, besides a considerable number of missionary stations. Of this number about 730 belong to the Free Church of Scotland, which separated from the Establishment in 1843. The incomes of the Dissenting clergy are wholly derived from their congregations; they average, probably, from £120 to £130 a-year, including a house and garden. In many cases, however, the income is considerably larger.

UNIVERSITIES AND SCHOOLS.—Scotland has four Universities, that of St. Andrews, founded by Papal authority in 1413; that of Glasgow, by the same authority, in 1450; that of Aberdeen, also, with the sanction of the Pope, in 1494, though education did not commence there till 1500; and that of Edinburgh, the only one instituted since the Reformation, in 1582. None of these colleges or universities can be said to be liberally endowed. St. Andrews has eleven professorships; Glasgow twenty-two; King's College, Aberdeen, nine; Marischal College, twelve; and Edinburgh thirty-one. The aggregate number of students in these universities is at present about 2593, of which Edinburgh has 1050, Glasgow 843, Aberdeen about 550, and St. Andrews 150. In every parish there is at least one school, for teaching the ordinary branches of education. The emoluments of the schoolmaster are derived from a small annual salary, with a free house and garden, provided by the landed proprietors, and moderate school fees. Private schools, also, are very numerous, and it is supposed, on good authority, that the total number of schools of every kind in Scotland amounts to about 5500.

ADMINISTRATION OF JUSTICE.—The supreme *civil* court of Scotland, is called the Court of Session. It holds, in Edinburgh, two sessions annually. The number of judges was formerly fifteen, but is now thirteen; they are styled Lords of Session, and sit in two courts or chambers, called the first and second divisions, which form in effect, two courts of equal and independent authority. The Court of Justiciary, the supreme *criminal* court of Scotland, consists at present of six judges, who are also judges of the Court of Session. The president of the whole Court is the Lord Justice-General. The Court holds sittings in Edinburgh during the recess of the Court of Session; and twice a year, in the spring and autumn vacations, the judges hold circuits in the chief provincial towns, two going each circuit. The Court of Exchequer, for the trial of cases connected with the revenue, is now held as a separate establishment, and the duties are devolved on two of the judges of the Court of Session. There are also inferior courts of law, viz. the courts of the boroughs, of the justices of the peace, and of the sheriffs.

POPULATION.—The population of Scotland at the period of the Union, in 1707, is supposed not to have exceeded 1,050,000. In 1755, it amounted to 1,265,380 ; in 1831, it had increased to 2,365,114 ; and in 1841, to 2,628,957 ; of which 1,246,427 were males, and 1,382,530 females. The average population per square mile is 88.5. During the ten years ending with 1820, the increase was 16 per cent. ; during the ten years ending with 1830, 13 per cent. ; and during the ten years ending with 1840, 11 per cent. The population of Scotland has increased less rapidly than that of England, and much less so than that of Ireland ; and, in consequence, the Scotch have " advanced much more rapidly than the English or Irish, in wealth, and in the command of the necessaries and conveniences of life. Their progress in this respect has indeed been quite astonishing. The habits, diet, dress, and other accommodations of the people, have been signally improved. It is not too much to affirm, that the peasantry of the present day are better lodged, better clothed, and better fed, than the middle classes of landowners a century ago." *

THE approach to Scotland by Tourists from other countries must, of course, be determined by the particular views and circumstances of individuals. Those who enter the kingdom by the western road may either proceed to Glasgow, and assume it as their starting point, or to Edinburgh, visiting, on the way, the classic banks of the Tweed, Teviotdale, the valleys of Ettrick and Yarrow, with Melrose, Dryburgh, and Abbotsford. The great majority of Tourists come at once to the metropolis ; and to all who, for the first time, approach Scotland on the east coast, this plan

* Encyclopædia Britannica, Seventh Edition.

possesses many advantages.   Edinburgh is not only easily
reached from London, Hull, and Newcastle, but is in itself,
with its environs, an object of very great interest and
curiosity, and, by the increased facilities of travelling, is
placed cheaply within from one to two days' journey of the
finest scenery of Perth, Stirling, Dumbarton, and Argyle-
shires ; while the approach to all of these scenes lies through
those lowland districts which abound the most in landscape
beauty, and in historical and traditionary interest.   We
shall therefore assume Edinburgh as our first great starting
point, and commence our description with a notice of that
city and its interesting environs.

EDINBURGH.

SITUATION—ARCHITECTURE—POPULATION—LEGAL PROFESSION—
MANUFACTURES—SOCIAL ADVANTAGES.

THE metropolis of Scotland is situated in the northern part
of the County of Mid-Lothian, and is about two miles distant from the Firth of Forth.*   Its length and breadth
are nearly equal, measuring about two miles in either direction.   In panoramic splendour, its site is generally admitted to be unequalled by any capital in Europe, and the
prospect from the elevated points of the city and neighbourhood is of singular beauty and grandeur.   The noble
estuary of the Forth, expanding from River into Ocean ;
the solitary grandeur of Arthur's Seat ; the varied park
and woodland scenery which enrich the southward prospect ; the pastoral acclivities of the neighbouring Pentland
Hills, and the more shadowy splendours of the Lammer-
moors, the Ochils, and the Grampians, form some of the
features of a landscape combining, in one vast expanse, the
richest elements of the beautiful and the sublime.

* The precise geographical position of the centre of the city is 55° 57′ 20″
north latitude, and 3° 10′ 30″ west longitude.

EDINBURGH OLD TOWN
FROM PRINCE'S STREET

observed, that while the greater number are distinguished by chaste design and excellent masonry, there are some of those sumptuous structures, described wholly, like St. Paul's, or Westminster Abbey, York Minster, and some few of the English Provincial Cathedrals, astonish the observer alike by their magnitude and their architectural grandeur. But in no city of the kingdom is the general style of excellence so well maintained. If there be no building of exceeding the impression by its magnitude, there is comparatively few to which, seen by their, would be instances of design. Almost any Londoner, if wanting a series from such examples of, to, London, or in London, may be seen a range of, as to, give a most graceful appearance to, and, the Regent Park.

" Traced like a map the landscape lies
    In cultured beauty stretching wide;
  There Pentland's green acclivities;
    There Ocean, with its azure tide;
  There Arthur's Seat; and, gleaming through
  Thy southern wing, Dunedin blue!
  While in the orient, Lammer's daughters,
    A distant giant range, are seen,
      North Berwick-Law, with cone of green,
  And Bass amid the waters." *

To most of the great cities in the kingdom the approaches
lie through mean and squalid suburbs, by which the stranger
is gradually introduced to the more striking streets and
public edifices. The avenues to Edinburgh, on the contrary, are lined with streets of a highly respectable class,
the abodes of poverty being, for the most part, confined to
those gigantic piles of building in the older parts of the
city, where they so essentially contribute to the picturesque
grandeur of the place.

The general architecture of the city is very imposing,
whether we regard the picturesque disorder of the buildings in the Old Town, or the symmetrical proportions of
the streets and squares in the New. Of the public edifices
it may be observed, that while the greater number are distinguished by chaste design and excellent masonry, there
are none of those sumptuous structures which, like St.
Paul's or Westminster Abbey, York Minster, and some
other of the English Provincial Cathedrals, astonish the
beholder alike by their magnitude and their architectural
splendour. But in no city of the kingdom is the general
standard of excellence so well maintained. If there be no
edifice to overwhelm the imagination by its magnificence,
there are comparatively few to offend taste by their deformity or meanness of design. Above all, Edinburgh is
wholly exempt from such examples of ostentatious deformity as, in London, may be seen to mingle with some
of the most graceful specimens of domestic architecture in
the Regent Park.

* Delta.

The resemblance between Athens and Edinburgh, which has been remarked by most travellers who have visited both capitals, has conferred upon the Scottish Metropolis the title of " The Modern Athens."* Stuart, author of " The Antiquities of Athens," was the first to draw attention to this resemblance, and his opinion has been confirmed by the testimony of many later writers. Dr. Clarke remarks, that the neighbourhood of Athens is just the Highlands of Scotland enriched with the splendid remains of art ; and Mr. W. H. Williams observes, that the distant view of Athens from the Ægean Sea is extremely like that of Edinburgh from the Firth of Forth, " *though certainly the latter is considerably superior.*"

Nor are the natural or artificial beauties of the place its only attractions, for many of its localities teem with the recollections of " the majestic past," and are associated with events of deep historical importance. Other of its localities have been invested with an interest no less engrossing by the transcendent genius of Sir Walter Scott, whose novels have not only refreshed and embellished the incidents of history, but have conferred on many a spot, formerly unknown to fame, a reputation as enduring as the annals of history itself.

In literary eminence, also, Edinburgh claims a distinguished place. At the commencement of the present century, its University displayed an array of contemporaneous talent unequalled by any similar institution either before or since,† and the present professors continue honourably to maintain its scientific and literary reputation.

The population of Edinburgh and Leith, at the Union in 1707, was estimated at 35,000 ; in 1755, at 57,195 ; and in

* In one of those altercations with which Lords Brougham and Campbell occasionally enliven the discussions in the Upper House of Parliament, it was stated by the former that the epithet "Modern Athens" was resented by the inhabitants of Edinburgh as a mockery or an insult. So far as our own experience goes, we have never heard of any of our townsmen quarrelling with the epithet.

† We have only to remind our readers of the names of Robertson, Playfair, Black, Cullen, Robison, Blair, Dugald Stewart, Gregory, and Monro, to vindicate what otherwise might appear a sweeping assertion.

1775, at 70,430.   The population of the city and suburbs, *exclusive of Leith*, according to the decennial census since 1801, has been—in 1801, 66,544; in 1811, 81,784; in 1821, 112,235; in 1831, 136,301; and in 1841, 138,182.*

POPULATION RETURNS OF 1841 FOR EDINBURGH AND ITS SUBURBS.				
	MALES.		FEMALES.	
OCCUPATIONS.	20 years of age and upwards.	Under 20 years of age.	20 years of age and upwards.	Under 20 years of age.
Persons engaged in professions, commerce, trade, and agriculture,	30,431	6,476	16,016	4,990
Persons of independent means,	1,013	74	5,127	241
Alms-people, pensioners, paupers, and beggars,	431	239	710	186
Persons in barns, boats, and barges; lunatics, and prisoners in gaol,	255	147	299	85
Residue of population,	691	21,556	24,790	24,425
TOTAL POPULATION,	32,821	28,492	46,942	29,927

Distinguishing males from females, the above table shows an excess of the latter amounting to 15,556. Probably no great city in the kingdom exhibits such a numerical disproportion in the sexes. This circumstance is mainly to be attributed to the stationary or retrograde state of industrial occupation in the town, the young men being obliged to seek for employment in other fields of enterprise, while the females, less adventurous, and less able to indulge the spirit of adventure where it exists, are compelled to remain ' cabin'd, cribb'd, confin'd,' in their native town. The numerical preponderance of the gentler sex may further be accounted for by the fact that an unusually large proportion of the inhabitants of Edinburgh are in circumstances enabling them to employ one or more domestic servants, of whom the great proportion are females.

A comparison of the population returns of Edinburgh, with those of five other of the large towns of the kingdom, will enable the reader to form some idea of the proportions which the professional and other liberally educated classes bear to the other orders of society. The returns for 1831 admitting of a more accurate classification than those of

* These are the numbers according to the *Parochial* enumerations. Within the *Parliamentary* boundary the population is 140,241.

1841, we adopt the former as being more convenient for our present purpose.

NAMES of TOWNS AND THEIR SUBURBS.	TOTAL POPU- LATION.	MALES TWENTY YEARS OF AGE.					MALE SERVANTS.	FEMALE SERVANTS.
		Employed in Manu- factures, or in making Manufacg. Machiny.	Employed in Retail or Handi- craft Trades.	Capitalists, Bankers, Profession- al, and other liberally educated Men.	Labourers employed in Labour not Agri- cultural.	Other Males (except Ser- vants.)		
EDINBURGH and Leith.	161,909	792	19,764	7463	4448	2296	1422	12,429
GLASGOW.	202,426	19,913	18,832	2723	574	4012	946	8006
LIVERPOOL and Toxteth Park.	189,242	359	21,208	5201	16,095	1214	363	9033
MANCHEST. and Salford.	182,812	15,342	17,931	2821	7629	1695	398	3965
BRISTOL and Barton-Regis.	103,886	415	11,270	2654	7312	1867	814	5702
BIRMING- HAM.	146,986	5028	19,469	2388	5292	1371	966	5233

This table, compiled from parliamentary documents, not only demonstrates the large proportion borne by the educated ranks to the general mass of the population, but from the number of male and female domestic servants, it is also obvious that the average number of families in comfortable circumstances must exceed that of any of the other large towns of the empire.* It must not, however, be concluded that there are many of the inhabitants of Edinburgh in circumstances of great opulence ; in this respect it proba- bly cannot vie with the other towns in the table, but com- petence is as generally possessed and comfort as widely diffused as in any other community of like magnitude.

The prosperity of the city essentially depends upon its College and Schools, and still more essentially upon the Courts of Judicature. The former attract many strangers

---

* According to the census of 1841, the number of domestic servants was 14,381, of whom 1614 were males, and 12,767 females. The increase in the number of this class during the ten years, therefore, appears to be 503—or considerably more than one-fourth of the entire increase in the population of the city.

who desire to secure for their families a liberal education at a moderate expense; the latter afford employment for the gentlemen of the Legal Profession, whose number is so great that they may be said to form at least one-third of the population in the higher and middle ranks of society.*

As it has no very extensive manufactures, the city is exempt from those sudden mercantile convulsions productive of so much misery in many other of the great towns

---

* The great family of Lawyers may be divided into the following classes. The first class consists of the Judges of the Court of Session, generally styled LORDS OF SESSION. Their nomination is with the Crown: they are now invariably chosen from among the Advocates, and, before their appointment, they must have been practising at the bar for at least five years. Their number was formerly 15, but is now reduced to 13. The salaries of the ordinary judges are £3000 a-year each, and those of the Lord Justice-Clerk and Lord President are £4000 and £4500 respectively. The ADVOCATES (*Anglice* Barristers) form the second class. They are united into a Society or Incorporation called the *Faculty of Advocates*, and possess the privilege of pleading before every Court in Scotland, and also in Scotch appeals before the House of Lords. The present number of the body is about 440, but there are not one-third of them in practice, and probably not one-sixth of them subsist solely by their professional gains. A considerable number of them are gentlemen wholly independent of their profession, who have joined the body on account of the status which they acquire from the learning and accomplishment of its members. The next class consists of the WRITERS TO THE SIGNET, who also form an Incorporation. They were originally called *Clerks to the Signet*, from their having been employed in the Secretary of State's office in preparing summonses, and other writs which received the Royal Signet, and they have still the sole privilege of preparing such writs. They are in other respects similar to the English Attorneys or Solicitors, and they are the oldest, most numerous, and most wealthy body of Law Practitioners in Scotland. Before admission to the body, an apprenticeship of five years is required, and an attendance of two Sessions at one of the Universities, independently of the Law Classes. The number of the Society is at present about 650, of whom about 400 are in practice. The SOLICITORS BEFORE THE SUPREME COURT, and ADVOCATES' FIRST CLERKS, form another section of this class, their duties being the same as those of Writers to the Signet, with the exception of their not being entitled to sign writs passing the Signet. These three classes, along with certain functionaries connected with the Court, form the College of Justice, which possesses certain privileges, the members being, until lately, exempted from most of the local taxes, and they are still exempt from the annuity levied for payment of the stipend of the Clergy of Edinburgh. They are not amenable to the jurisdiction of any inferior Court, excepting the Small Debt Court held by the Sheriff. The Solicitors at Law, (who practise before the inferior Courts,) the Accountants, and others, who pass under the more general name of Writers, are also included in the great family of Lawyers, but their distinctive peculiarities we think it unnecessary to mention here.

of the kingdom. Printing and publishing are carried on to a large extent. In this department of industry Edinburgh far surpasses all the towns of the kingdom, London only excepted ; many of the most valuable and popular works of the age emanating from the Edinburgh press.* Printing papers are manufactured to a large extent in the neighbourhood, but none of the mills are in the immediate vicinity of the city. Although there are some other branches of manufacture, they are, for the most part, on an insignificant scale.

As a place of family residence, Edinburgh possesses many advantages. The climate, although it cannot be called mild or genial, is yet eminently salubrious ; and favourable, not only to longevity, but to the development of the mental and physical powers. The annual quantity of rain is moderate, compared with the fall upon the western coast ; for while the average in Edinburgh is about 23½, in Glasgow it is about 29.65. The violent winds, to which the city is exposed by its elevated situation, are by no means unfavourable to general health, as they carry the benefit of a thorough ventilation into the close-built lanes and alleys of the Old Town. The facilities of education, and the advantages of cultivated society, have been already alluded to. In the former of these particulars, we believe it to be unequalled in the kingdom, and in the latter it can be surpassed by London alone.

The markets are liberally supplied with all the necessaries and luxuries of the table. White fish are more especially abundant, cod, haddocks, and, at certain seasons, herrings, being sold at a very low price. Coal of good quality is found in the immediate neighbourhood of the city, and

---

* The Edinburgh Review, the North British Review, Blackwood's Magazine, Tait's Magazine, the Medical Journal, the Journal of Agriculture, and the Philosophical Journal, are some of the more important periodical publications. In circulation, it is worthy of remark, that both Blackwood's and Tait's Magazines far exceed any of their London contemporaries.

Chambers's Journal is also deserving of notice, as being the first and most extensively circulated of the periodicals of its class.

There are eleven newspapers, of which one is published thrice a-week, five twice a-week, and the rest weekly.

PLAN
OF
EDINBURGH

Road to London by Haddington, &c.

LONDON ROAD

Holyrood Palace

G. Aikman

although the supply of water is at present inadequate to the wants of the community, arrangements are in progress for increasing it. Upon the whole, it would be difficult to name a city which unites so many social advantages, and where a person of cultivated mind and moderate fortune could pass his time more agreeably.

The most convenient mode of imparting information to strangers, is to select a particular district of the city to be perambulated, describing the objects of interest on the way. With this view, we shall visit all the more important public buildings and institutions in successive walks, adding in notes such collateral or subordinate information, as may appear necessary to convey a more accurate idea of the city and its institutions, as well as other matter which may tend to enliven the dulness of dry topographical details.

WALK FIRST.*

REGISTER HOUSE—THEATRE-ROYAL— STAMP-OFFICE— POST-OFFICE— PRISON—BRIDEWELL—CALTON HILL—STEWART'S MONUMENT—OB-SERVATORY—PLAYFAIR'S MONUMENT—CAMERA OBSCURA—NELSON'S MONUMENT—NATIONAL MONUMENT—HIGH SCHOOL—BURNS'S MO-NUMENT—HOLYROOD PALACE AND ABBEY—ARTHUR'S SEAT—HOUSE OF JOHN KNOX—NORTH BRIDGE.

THE central situation of the building, and the large number of hotels in its neighbourhood, points out

THE REGISTER HOUSE

as an appropriate starting point. This handsome edifice, designed by the celebrated Robert Adam, is the Depository of the Public Records.† It forms a square of 200 feet,

* The several Walks are indicated by different colours on the Map of the City prefixed. Walk First is coloured *Red*. When the *continued* line of colour is exchanged for a *dotted* line, it is to be understood that tourists who cannot accomplish the whole distance may omit the dotted portion of the Walk.

† This important establishment includes various offices, such as the offices of the Clerks and Extractors of the Court of Session, of the Jury Court, and of the Court of Justiciary, the office of the Great and Privy Seal, of the Chancery, the Lord Lyon's office, the Bill-Chamber, &c. But it is most celebrated for the

surmounted by a dome of fifty feet diameter. It contains
upwards of 100 apartments for the transaction of public

different Registers which are there kept, and from which it derives its name.
The most important and useful of these are the Registers of Sasines, of Inhibitions, and of Adjudications.

When a person wishes either to dispose absolutely of a landed estate in Scotland, or to grant a security over it (such as an heritable bond), it is necessary
for him not only to grant a conveyance of the property to the purchaser or
creditor, as the case may be, but also to give him Infeftment or Sasine, which
is a symbolical delivery of the land. An instrument of Sasine is then written
out by a notary-public, which must be recorded in the Register of Sasines. The
date of recording is held to be the date of the Sasine, and the party whose Sasine is *first recorded* is preferred to the property. The Sasine may be recorded
either in the General Register for all Scotland, which is kept in the Register
House at Edinburgh, or in the particular Register for the County where the
lands lie. These County Registers are transmitted at stated periods to the
Keeper of the Records in Edinburgh.

This is the manner in which a person *voluntarily* divests himself of his
lands; but there are also two kinds of diligence—Inhibition and Adjudication—
by which an individual's heritable property may be affected without his consent.
By the former, a debtor is prohibited from conveying or burdening his property
to the prejudice of the creditor using the inhibition; by the latter, he is divested
of the property, which, by a decree of the Court, is declared to belong to his
creditor, in satisfaction of his debt. An inhibition must be executed, and with
the execution of it recorded within forty days of its date, either in the General
Register of Inhibitions at Edinburgh, or in the particular Register for the
County, which, like the County Registers of Sasines, are transmitted at stated
periods to the Keeper of the Records at Edinburgh. An abbreviate of a decree
of adjudication must be recorded within sixty days of its date, in a register kept
in the Register House for that purpose, called the Register of Abbreviates of
Adjudication.

A person, therefore, who wishes either to purchase a property, or make a
loan over it, may, by a search of the Register of Sasines, Inhibitions, and Adjudications, ascertain whether there has been any previous sale or conveyance
of it by the proprietor or his predecessors—to what extent it may be burdened
with debts—whether the proprietor has been prohibited by inhibition from
granting any voluntary conveyance—or whether there has been any judicial
assignation of it by adjudication. It is a principle of the Scotch law, that no
party who has possessed a property upon an heritable title for forty years shall
be disquieted in his possession thereafter; and, also, that any party who may
have possessed a title to a property without insisting in or prosecuting it for a
period of forty years shall be held to have abandoned his right. A forty years'
search of the records, showing that no incumbrances exist, is therefore generally
considered sufficient evidence that the property is not liable to any burden or
ground of eviction, and that any one may with safety either purchase it or lend
money on its security. No such assurance of the safety of a transaction, relative to landed property, can be obtained in England, nor probably in any other
country in Europe. The consequence is, that Scotch mortgages form a very
favourite investment with those capitalists who are more anxious to secure the
safety of the capital itself, than a high rate of interest.

business. Among these the great room, in which the older records are deposited, is distinguished for its handsome proportions. Admission can only be obtained by an introduction to some of the public officers.

Directly opposite the east end of the Register House, stands

THE THEATRE-ROYAL.

Its exterior is plain almost to meanness, but its internal accommodation is excellent. Its management is unexceptionable, the manager, Mr. W. H. Murray, being equally esteemed for his distinguished ability in his profession, and for the virtues and accomplishments of his private life.*

Proceeding due east, we enter Waterloo Place, and on the right pass successively the STAMP OFFICE and the POST OFFICE. The lightness of the open colonnades on either side of the street are generally much admired by English strangers. It was upon entering this street, and contemplating the Calton Hill before him, that George IV. exclaimed, in royal rapture, "How superb!" Still advancing in the same direction, we reach the stair leading to the Calton Hill, from the top of which may be seen, in the churchyard across the street, the circular tower erected as a monument to David Hume the Historian. In the same churchyard stands an obelisk erected in 1845 to the memory of Muir, Palmer, Skirving, Gerrald, and Margarot, who suffered banishment for their efforts in the cause of popular freedom in 1794. However worthy the object, it may well be questioned whether human ingenuity could have devised a structure worse fitted for such a site, or more uncongenial to the surrounding architecture. The GAOL is immediately to the east of the churchyard, and a little farther along, in the same direction, is BRIDEWELL. These institutions are now consolidated into one prison. Strangers are admitted only when accompanied by a member of the Prison-Board.

* A smaller theatre, under the same management, is open during the summer months. It stands at the head of Leith Walk, but possesses no architectural attraction.

Upon the left hand, in ascending the second flight of
steps to the hill, is the graceful MONUMENT TO DUGALD
STEWART, a reproduction, with some variations, of the
Choragic monument of Lysicrates.   For the design of this
monument, Edinburgh is indebted to the classical taste of
Mr. Playfair.   Close by are THE OBSERVATORY, and MONU-
MENT to PROFESSOR PLAYFAIR.   The unshapely building,
occupying a prominent position a little to the west, is the
OLD OBSERVATORY.   Upon the summit of the hill stands
NELSON'S MONUMENT, a structure more ponderous than elegant, "modelled exactly after a Dutch skipper's spy-glass,
or a butter-churn,"* but which, though wholly destitute
of grandeur of design, becomes impressive from its magnitude and elevated site.   The prospect from the top of the
monument is very fine; the admission-fee is threepence.
Near Nelson's Monument are the twelve columns of the
NATIONAL MONUMENT, a structure intended to commemorate the heroes who fell at Waterloo.   The splendour of
the projected building (which was to be a literal reproduc-

tion of the Parthenon) was worthy of so patriotic a cause,
but, unfortunately, the architectural ambition of the pro-
jectors was far in advance of the pecuniary means at their

* The Modern Athens.   By a Modern Greek.   London, 1825.

YALE COLLEGE. NEW HAVEN.

disposal, and the monument consequently remains unfinished. It cannot fail to be lamented, not only by all Scotsmen, but by every man of taste, that this attempt to restore one of the " glories of the antique world," upon a site worthy of its fame, should thus be defeated by the want of funds. So far as the building has proceeded, the workmanship is masterly, affording a very fine example of Edinburgh masonry. The view with which our text is illustrated represents the existing condition of this modern ruin.

On the southern slope of the hill, overlooking the buildings of the Old Town,

THE HIGH SCHOOL

occupies a site worthy of its architectural beauty. The business of the school is conducted by a Rector, four Classical Masters, Teachers of French and German, of Writing, Arithmetic, and Mathematics, and of Fencing and Gymnastics. Of these the first five have a small endowment from the city, in addition to the Class-fees. Although essentially a classical seminary, due consideration is given to those collateral branches of learning which form a necessary part of a liberal education. The extent of the building affords ample accommodation for conducting the business of instruction upon the most approved principles; and the play-ground, extending to nearly two acres, commands a fine prospect of the Old Town, Arthur's Seat, and the adjacent country.* Opposite the High School, close upon

* In 1823, the increasing population of the city appeared to demand the institution of another seminary for the same branches of learning as the High School. THE NEW ACADEMY was accordingly then founded in the northern suburbs of the city by an influential body of the inhabitants, and its situation renders it more convenient for those residing in that neighbourhood. In both institutions the instruction of the pupils is conducted with the utmost zeal and success, many of them, after completing their curriculum of study, carrying off the highest honours in the Universities of Oxford and Cambridge. Still more recently has been instituted THE SOUTHERN ACADEMY, for the convenience of the inhabitants of that quarter of the city. Here also the instruction of the pupils is most judiciously superintended. To the admirable mental culture these institutions afford may principally be imputed the advanced intelligence which distinguishes the great body of the inhabitants of the Scottish Metropolis, a large proportion of the children of the higher and middle classes receiv-

the road side, stands Burns's Monument. The statue of
the Poet by Flaxman, which for some time adorned the
interior, has now been placed in the University Library.

From this point a descent may be made by a footpath to
the North Back of the Canongate, at the Lower end of which
the stranger will reach

HOLYROOD PALACE.

This ancient residence of Scottish Royalty is a handsome
building of a quadrangular form, with a central court
ninety-four feet square. Its front is flanked with double
castellated towers, imparting to the building that military
character which the events of Scottish History have so
often proved to have been requisite in her Royal residences.

The changes which from time to time the edifice has
undergone render it a matter of difficulty to affix a precise
date to any part of it. The towers of the north-west corner, built by James V., are understood to be the most
ancient portion of the present building. In 1822, previous
to the visit of George IV., some improvements were made
in its internal accommodation, and since that time its walls
have undergone a thorough repair at the expense of the
Crown. The most interesting relic is the Bed of Queen
Mary, which remains in the same state as when last occupied by that unhappy Princess. The Closet, where the
murderers of Rizzio surprised their victim, is also an object
of interest to visiters. This bloody tragedy was acted on
the 9th of March 1566. "The Queen was seated at supper
in a small cabinet adjoining to her bedroom, with the
Countess of Argyle, Rizzio, and one or two other persons.
Darnley suddenly entered the apartment, and, without addressing or saluting the company, gazed on Rizzio with a
sullen and vindictive look ; after him followed Lord Ruthven, pale and ghastly, having risen from a bed of long

---

ing their education in one or other of these seminaries. Besides the public
Institutions, there are many admirably conducted private schools. Those interested in the instruction of the humbler ranks would do well to visit Dr. Bell's
School in Niddry Street, where a very large number of children of both sexes
receive the benefit of a useful education.

sickness to be chief actor in this savage deed; other armed men appeared behind. Ruthven called upon Rizzio
to come forth from a place which he was unworthy to hold.
The miserable Italian, perceiving he was the destined victim
of this violent intrusion, started up, and seizing the Queen
by the skirts of her gown, implored her protection. Mary
was speedily forced by the King from his hold. George
Douglas, a bastard of the Angus family, snatched the King's
own dagger from his side, and struck Rizzio a blow; he
was then dragged into the outer apartment, and slain with
fifty-six wounds. The Queen exhausted herself in prayers
and entreaties for the wretched man's life; but when she
was at length told that her servant was slain, she said, 'I
will then dry my tears, and study revenge.' During the
perpetration of this murder, Morton, the chancellor of the
kingdom, whose duty it was to enforce the laws of the
realm, kept the doors of the Palace with 160 armed men,
to ensure the perpetration of the murder."*

Stains are still shown at the door of the apartment, said
to be produced by the blood of the murdered man.† The

* SCOTT'S *Scotland,* vol. ii., p. 105.

† A pleasant story, suggested by these reputed blood-marks, occurs in the
introductory chapter to the Second Series of Chronicles of the Canongate. Our
readers, we are assured, will thank us for enlivening our narrative by here in-
troducing it.

" My long habitation in the neighbourhood," says Mr. Chrystal Croftangry,
" and the quiet respectability of my habits, have given me a sort of intimacy
with good Mrs. Policy, the housekeeper in that most interesting part of the
old building, called Queen Mary's Apartments. But a circumstance which
lately happened has conferred upon me greater privileges; so that, indeed, I
might, I believe, venture on the exploit of Chatelet, who was executed for being
found secreted at midnight in the very bedchamber of Scotland's mistress.

" It chanced, that the good lady I have mentioned, was, in the discharge of
her function, showing the apartments to a Cockney from London;—not one of
your quiet, dull, commonplace visitors, who gape, yawn, and listen with an
acquiescent *umph,* to the information doled out by the provincial cicerone. No
such thing—this was the brisk alert agent of a great house in the city, who
missed no opportunity of doing business, as he termed it—that is, of putting off
the goods of his employers, and improving his own account of commission. He
had fidgeted through the suite of apartments, without finding the least opportunity to touch upon that which he considered as the principal end of his
existence. Even the story of Rizzio's assassination presented no ideas to this
emissary of commerce, until the housekeeper appealed, in support of her narrative, to the dusky stains of blood upon the floor.

largest apartment in the Palace is the Picture Gallery,
which measures 150 feet long, by 27 broad.   Upon the walls
of this room are suspended the portraits of 106 Scottish
Kings, in a style of art truly barbarous.   They appear to
be " mostly by the same hand, painted either from the ima-

" ' These are the stains,' she said : ' nothing will remove them from the place
—there they have been for two hundred and fifty years—and there they will
remain while the floor is left standing—neither water nor any thing else will
ever remove them from that spot.'

" Now, our Cockney, amongst other articles, sold Scouring Drops, as they are
called, and a stain of two hundred and fifty years' standing was interesting to
him, not because it had been caused by the blood of a Queen's favourite, slain
in her apartment, but because it offered so admirable an opportunity to prove
the efficacy of his unequalled Detergent Elixir.   Down on his knees went our
friend, but neither in horror nor devotion.

" ' Two hundred and fifty years, ma'am, and nothing take it away ?   Why,
if it had been five hundred, I have something in my pocket will fetch it out in
five minutes.   D'ye see this elixir, ma'am ?   I will show you the stain vanish
in a moment.'

" Accordingly, wetting one end of his handkerchief with the all-deterging spe-
cific, he began to rub away on the planks, without heeding the remonstrances
of Mrs. Policy.   She, good soul, stood at first in astonishment, like the Abbess
in St. Bridget's, when a profane visitant drank up the vial of brandy which had
long passed muster among the relics of the cloister for the tears of the blessed
saint.   The venerable guardian of St. Bridget probably expected the interference
of her patroness—She of Holy Rood might, perhaps, hope that David Rizzio's
spectre would arise to prevent the profanation.   But Mrs. Policy stood not long
in the silence of horror.   She uplifted her voice, and screamed as loudly as
Queen Mary herself, when the dreadful deed was in the act of perpetration—

' Earrow now out ! and walawa !' she cried.

" I happened to be taking my morning walk in the adjoining gallery, ponder-
ing in my mind why the kings of Scotland, who hung around me, should be
each and every one painted with a nose like the knocker of a door, when lo !
the walls once more re-echoed with such shrieks, as formerly were as often
heard in the Scottish Palaces as were sounds of revelry and music.   Somewhat
surprised at such an alarm in a place so solitary, I hastened to the spot, and
found the well-meaning traveller scrubbing the floor like a housemaid, while
Mrs. Policy, dragging him by the skirts of the coat, in vain endeavoured to
divert him from his sacrilegious purpose.   It cost me some trouble to explain
to the zealous purifier of silk stockings, embroidered waistcoats, broad cloth,
and deal planks, that there were such things in the world as stains which ought
to remain indelible, on account of the associations with which they are connected.   Our good friend viewed every thing of the kind only as the means of
displaying the virtue of his vaunted commodity.   He comprehended, however,
that he would not be permitted to proceed to exemplify its powers on the present occasion, as two or three inhabitants appeared, who, like me, threatened
to maintain the housekeeper's side of the question.   He therefore took his
leave, muttering that he had always heard the Scots were a nasty people, but

gination, or porters hired to sit for the purpose."*   In the olden time, many a scene of courtly gaiety has enlivened this gloomy hall ; among the last were the balls given by Prince Charles Edward in 1745.   The election of the representative Peers of Scotland and the levees and entertainments given by the Lord High Commissioner to the General Assembly of the Church of Scotland, are now the only ceremonies performed within its walls.   In the south side of the quadrangle is the Hall of State fitted up for the levees of George IV. in 1822 ; and in the eastern side is the suite of apartments occupied by Charles X. (of France) and his family in 1830-3.   The Palace is shown to strangers by the domestics of the Duke of Hamilton, hereditary keeper.   Three different persons are employed in exhibiting the Palace and Abbey, the gratuities being left to the discretion of visitors.   Various attempts have been made by the Magistrates and Council of the city to induce the Duke of Hamilton to sanction the exaction of a stated fee of small amount, or to make some other arrangement by which the exhibition should be placed on a more satisfactory footing. These attempts having been unsuccessful, the Municipal body passed a resolution expressive of their opinion, that the payment of 1s. by each party not exceeding six, to each of the exhibitors, should be regarded as adequate remuneration.   It may at the same time be observed, that the payment of even this sum is wholly dependent on the pleasure of visitors, as Mr. Hume, when referring in the House of Commons to the estimate for the repairs of the Royal Palaces in Scotland, observed, that " he held in his hand a letter from the Duke of Hamilton, stating that orders had been given for the opening of Holyrood Palace free of charge to the public."

On the north side of the Palace are the ruins of the

---

had no idea they carried it so far as to choose to have the floors of their palaces blood-boltered, like Banquo's ghost, when to remove them would have cost but a hundred drops of the Infallible Detergent Elixir, prepared and sold by Messrs. Scrub and Rub, in five shilling and ten shilling bottles, each bottle being marked with the initials of the inventor, to counterfeit which would be to incur the pains of forgery."

* Humphrey Clinker.

ABBEY OF HOLYROODHOUSE.

This Abbey was founded in 1128, by David I., a prince whose prodigal liberality to the clergy drew from James VI. the pithy observation that he was "a sair sanct for the Crown."* Of this building nothing now remains but the mouldering ruins of the chapel, situated immediately behind the palace. " It was fitted up by Charles I. as a chapel royal, that it might serve as a model of the English form of worship, which he was anxious to introduce into Scotland. He was himself crowned in it in 1633. James II. (VII. of Scotland) afterwards rendered it into a model of Catholic worship, to equally little purpose. Since the fall of the roof in 1768, it has been a ruin."† In the south-east corner are deposited the remains of David II., James II., James V., and Magdalen his Queen, Henry Lord Darnley, and other illustrious persons. The precincts of the Abbey, including Arthur's Seat and Salisbury Crags, are a sanctuary for insolvent debtors. The limit of the privileged territory, on the side next the town, extends to about a hundred yards from the Palace.‡

The immediate proximity of Arthur's Seat may induce many tourists to ascend the hill.§ Its height is 822 feet

* The legend connected with its foundation is as follows:—The pious David, while hunting in the forest of Drumsheuch, was placed in the utmost peril by the attack of a stag. When defending himself from his assailant, a cross miraculously descended from heaven into his hand, upon seeing which the stag fled in dismay. The sequel is more credible. In a dream which visited the slumbers of the monarch, he was commanded to erect an abbey on the spot of his remarkable preservation; and, in obedience to the heavenly mandate, he founded the Abbey of Holyroodhouse.

† CHAMBERS' *Picture of Scotland.*

‡ In Croftangrie, a narrow lane close by the Abbey, is a house said to have been occupied by the Regent Murray.

§ " A nobler contrast there can hardly exist than that of the huge city, dark with the smoke of ages, and groaning with the various sounds of active industry or idle revel, and the lofty and craggy hill, silent and solitary as the grave; one exhibiting the full tide of existence, pressing and precipitating itself forward with the force of an inundation; the other resembling some time-worn anchorite, whose life passes as silent and unobserved as the slender rill, which escapes unheard, and scarce seen, from the fountain of his patron saint. The city resembles the busy temple, where the modern Comus and Mammon hold their

above the level of the sea. The ascent, which is neither difficult or dangerous, may be made either by the footpath leading past St. Anthony's well, with St. Anthony's Chapel on the left ; or by following the new road, commencing at the northern base of the hill, to the point presenting the easiest access to the summit. This point is reached immediately after passing the pond on the left of the road, a spot as sequestered as if there were no such city as Edinburgh within a distance of 50 miles. Descending again to the road, the tourist may prosecute the beautiful walk round the hill, and return to the city by the south side ; or he may retrace his steps and proceed up the Canongate from Holyrood.

If the footpath ascent be preferred, the pedestrian proceeds up the face of the hill, passing on the left the ruins of St. Anthony's Chapel,* while upon the right is the semicircular ridge of bold and precipitous rocks known by the name of Salisbury Crags. The walk along the top of these Crags commands beautiful prospects of the city, as also

court, and thousands sacrifice ease, independence, and virtue itself, at their shrine; the misty and lonely mountain seems as a throne to the majestic but terrible genius of feudal times, where the same divinities dispensed coronets and domains to those who had heads to devise, and arms to execute, bold enterprises.—SIR WALTER SCOTT—*Introduction to the Chronicles of the Canongate.*

* The spot where Jeanie Deans is represented to have met with the ruffian Robertson may be seen in ascending the hill, although no remains of the cairn are now visible. "It was situated," says the novelist, "in the depth of the valley behind Salisbury Crags, which has for a background the north-western shoulder of the mountain, called Arthur's Seat, on whose descent still remain the ruins of what was once a chapel, or hermitage, dedicated to Saint Anthony the Eremite. A better site for such a building could hardly have been selected: for the chapel, situated among the rude and pathless cliffs, lies in a desert, even in the immediate vicinity of a rich, populous, and tumultuous capital; and the hum of the city might mingle with the orisons of the recluses, conveying as little of worldly interest as if it had been the roar of the distant ocean. Beneath the steep ascent on which these ruins are still visible was, and perhaps is still pointed out, the place where the wretch Nicol Muschat had closed a long scene of cruelty towards his unfortunate wife, by murdering her with circumstances of uncommon barbarity. The execration in which the man's crime was held extended itself to the place where it was perpetrated, which was marked by a small *cairn,* or heap of stones, composed of those which each passenger had thrown there in testimony of abhorrence, and on the principle, it would seem, of the ancient British malediction, 'May you have a cairn for your burial-place.' "—*Heart of Mid-Lothian.*

does the promenade immediately below.*   From this walk may be seen the site of the cottage of Davie Deans, and other objects rendered imperishably interesting by the novels of Sir Walter Scott.

Retracing our steps to Holyrood, and proceeding up the Canongate, we reach, upon the right, a narrow archway conducting to a court known by the name of the WHITE HORSE CLOSE, a singular looking group of houses, which, in ancient times, was a well-frequented *hostelrie*.†   The White Horse Inn is understood to be the oldest place of the kind in the city, of which the premises preserve, in any measure, their original integrity.   It is now partitioned into dwelling-houses of the lowest class.   A little further up the street, on the opposite side, is QUEENSBERRY HOUSE, a large dull looking structure, erected by William, first Duke of Queensberry. The building is now converted into a hospital.   Continuing to ascend the street, we pass, upon the right hand, the un-

* " If I were to choose a spot from which the rising or setting sun could be seen to the greatest possible advantage, it would be that wild path winding around the foot of the high belt of semi-circular rocks, called Salisbury Crags, and marking the verge of the steep descent which slopes down into the glen on the south-eastern side of the City of Edinburgh. The prospect, in its general outline, commands a close-built, high-piled city, stretching itself out in a form which, to a romantic imagination, may be supposed to represent that of a dragon; now a noble arm of the sea, with its rocks, isles, distant shores, and boundary of mountains; and now a fair and fertile champaign country, varied with hill, dale, and rock, and skirted by the picturesque ridge of the Pentland mountains. But as the path gently circles around the base of the cliffs, the prospect, composed as it is of these enchanting and sublime objects, changes at every step, and presents them blended with, or divided from each other, in every possible variety which can gratify the eye and the imagination.   When a piece of scenery so beautiful, yet so varied—so exciting by its intricacy, and yet so sublime—is lighted up by the tints of morning or of evening, and displays all that variety of shadowy depth, exchanged with partial brilliancy, which gives character even to the tamest of landscapes, the effect approaches near to enchantment. This path used to be my favourite evening and morning resort when engaged with a favourite author or new subject of study."—*Heart of Mid-Lothian.*

The solid and commodious pathway which has now superseded the winding footpath above described was suggested by this glowing eulogy of the surrounding landscape.

† A modern proprietor has had the singularly bad taste to change the name of this antique court to *Davison's Close.* Surely the Antiquarian Society, or some other competent tribunal, should be armed with power to avenge such affronts upon antiquity.

gainly fabric called the CANONGATE KIRK, and next reach
the Court-Room and Jail of the Canongate. In a niche of
the latter building are painted the arms of the Canongate,
with the motto, " *Sic itur ad astra*," as if the worthy inhabitants of this ancient burgh regarded the prison as the
surest avenue to heaven. A little farther up the street, on
the left, is MORAY HOUSE, the ancient mansion of the Earls
of Moray, erected in 1618. From the balcony in front of
the building, the Marquis of Argyle and his family saw the
Marquis of Montrose conducted to prison, from whence he
was shortly afterwards led to execution. Still ascending
the street, we pass, upon the right and left, Leith Wynd
and St. Mary's Wynd, two narrow Streets, dedicated to the
sale of old clothes. At the head of the Netherbow, where
it expands into the High Street, stands the HOUSE OF JOHN

KNOX, represented in the accompanying woodcut. Over
the door is an inscription, at present totally eclipsed by the

numerous signboards of the inhabitants, but which, if visible, would run thus :

LUFE.GOD.ABOVE.AL.AND.YOUR.NICHBOUR.AS.YOUR.SELF.

Close beneath the window, from which Knox is said to have preached to the populace, there has long existed a rude effigy of the Reformer stuck upon the corner in the attitude of addressing the passers by.* After having sufficiently admired this grotesque specimen of sculpture, the stranger will pursue his way up the High Street. The stupendous height of many of the houses, and the air of antique majesty, which, in spite of some modern innovations, still distinguishes the street, cannot fail to strike the attention of visiters. From either side descend numerous lanes or *closes*, of a width frequently limited to six

* "Of this no features were, for a long time, discernible, till Mr. Dryden,† about three years ago, took shame to himself for the neglect it was experiencing, and got it daubed over in glaring oil-colours at his own expense. Thus a red nose, and two intensely black eyes, were brought strongly out upon the mass of the face; and a pair of white iron Geneva bands, with a new black gown, completed the resuscitation. A large canopy of Chinese fashion, hung at the edges with tassels, was spread over the preacher's head, making him look much finer than he had ever done in his lifetime, and a demure precentor was placed underneath his yellow pulpit, in order to prevent strangers from taking up an idea that our great Reformer, like the poor itinerant Methodists of modern times, had to direct the singing as well as the doctrine of his hearers. The precentor, however, was not very well used in his station; for, provoking only the laughter of the spectators, while the preacher excited their veneration, he was soon after taken down. There is a stone in the building, at a little distance from the diminutive pulpit, and pointed at by the preacher, bearing the name of the Deity in Greek, Latin, and English, carved upon it, from which rays seem to diverge upon the side next the effigy, and clouds upon the side most remote from his irradiating finger. Some ingenuity seems to have been exercised here, in painting the radiance of a bright saffron, while the reprobate clouds are treated with a villanous dark green—a distinction of wonderful delicacy, considering what the rays and the clouds are intended to emblematize. The modern possessor, to whom the general thanks of Scotland are due, takes care to paint the whole piously over every second of May."—*Traditions of Edinburgh*, vol. i., p. 243.

† An intelligent tonsor, occupying the house at the time Mr. Chambers visited the premises. The house is now possessed by a member of the same family, who cherishes the effigy of the Reformer with similar affection, and displays a more classical taste in its colouring and decorations; but the Free Church having purchased this house and some of the neighbouring property, that they may erect places of worship on the ground, this interesting relic of the great Reformer will very speedily be swept away.

feet, and so steep as to be of very laborious ascent. In these closes are the squalid abodes of some of the lowest of the population.

Upon reaching the North Bridge, our first walk will terminate by returning to the Register Office. If the stranger desires to prolong it, he will continue to ascend the High Street, commencing with the Tron Church. For the sake of arrangement, however, we must designate the next division of his progress the Second Walk.

WALK SECOND.*

TRON CHURCH—ROYAL EXCHANGE—ST. GILES'S CATHEDRAL—PARLIAMENT HOUSE—ADVOCATES' LIBRARY—SIGNET LIBRARY—COUNTY HALL — BANK OF SCOTLAND — CASTLE — GEORGE IV. BRIDGE — HERIOT'S HOSPITAL.

PROCEEDING as before from the Register Office, the stranger will now walk along the North Bridge. This bridge was founded in 1763, and completed in 1769. On the 3d of August in the latter year, the arches of three vaults in the south abutment, in consequence of an error in construction, gave way with a tremendous crash, and filled the whole city with alarm. Five persons were killed by the accident. There is a floating prediction that a similar catastrophe is once more destined to occur. From the parapet, on each side, is an extensive view of the city towards the east and the west. For architectural effect, the buildings upon the Calton Hill are perhaps more advantageously grouped in the view from the northern end of the open space of this bridge, than from any other point, although the most prominent deformity on the hill—the Martyrs' Monument—is offensively conspicuous. In the spacious area seen immediately below, when looking over the western parapet,

* This Walk is coloured *green* on the Map.

are the termini of the Edinburgh and Glasgow and of the
Edinburgh, Leith, and Granton Railways. The same area
also contains the fruit and vegetable markets. From these,
an ascent by stairs conducts to the fish, butcher, and poultry markets, which are situated upon successive terraces
communicating with each other. The terminus of the
North British Railway occupies the area on the east side
of the bridge. Proceeding to the upper end of the North
Bridge, the stranger again reaches the High Street, part
of which he traversed in the preceding walk. Its length
from the Castle to Holyrood Palace is about a mile.* At
the point where the High Street and the North and South
Bridges cross each other, stands the Tron Church, an edifice
of no architectural pretension. It derived its name from a
tron or weighing beam in its immediate neighbourhood, to
which, in former times, it was customary to nail false
notaries and other malefactors by the ears. Its clock is
provided with a dial plate of dimmed glass, which is lighted
with gas from the inside after nightfall.

Ascending the High Street,

THE ROYAL EXCHANGE BUILDINGS

stand upon the right hand side of the way, opposite St. Giles's
Cathedral. The Council Chamber for the meetings of the
Magistracy, and various other apartments for the transaction of municipal business, occupy the side of the quadrangle opposite the entrance. Parties proposing to visit
the Crown Room in the Castle, will here obtain orders of
admission on the terms mentioned on page 50 of the present work. The spot where the city Cross formerly stood

---

* Although we have here given the general designation of High Street to this
imposing line of buildings, its various divisions, commencing at the Castle, are
severally known by the names *Castle Hill*, *Lawnmarket*, *High Street*, *Netherbow* and *Canongate*. A more stirring spectacle can scarcely be imagined than
the progress of Her Majesty along this street, from Holyrood to the Castle.
From ground to roof the windows of these gigantic dwellings were crowded with
fair and happy faces, while the advance of the Royal Pair was heralded by the
waving of thousands of white handkerchiefs, and by the enthusiastic cheering
of the populace, who lined the street on either side, and of the various public
bodies who occupied the temporary platforms along the line of progress.

is now indicated by a radiated pavement about twenty-five yards from the entrance to the Exchange. It was demolished in 1756. On the morning of the day when the workmen began their labours, "some gentlemen who had spent the night over a social bottle, caused wine and glasses be carried thither, mounted the ancient fabric, and solemnly drank its dirge."*

ST. GILES'S CATHEDRAL

is nearly opposite the Royal Exchange. It derives its name from its patron, St. Giles, abbot and confessor, and

* " Dun-Edin's Cross, a pillar'd stone,
   Rose on a turret octagon;
   But now is razed that monument,
      Whence royal edict rang,
   And voice of Scotland's law was sent
      In glorious trumpet clang.
   O! be his tomb as lead to lead;
   Upon its dull destroyer's head.
   A minstrel's malison is said."—
                    Marmion, canto v., st. 25.

tutelar saint of Edinburgh.*   The date of its foundation is
unknown.   It is first mentioned in the year 1359, in a charter
of David II.   In 1466, it was made a collegiate church,
and no fewer than forty altars were at this period supported
within its walls.   The Scottish poet, Gavin Douglas, (the
translator of Virgil,) was for some time Provost of St. Giles.
After the Reformation it was partitioned into four places
of worship, and the sacred vessels and relics which it contained, including the arm-bone referred to in the preceding
note, were seized by the Magistrates of the City, and the
proceeds of their sale applied to the repairing of the building.   In 1603, before the departure of James VI. to take
possession of the throne of England, he attended divine
service in this church, after which he delivered a farewell
address to his Scottish subjects, assuring them of his un-
alterable affection.   " His words were often interrupted by
the tears of the whole audience, who, though they exulted
at the King's prosperity, were melted into sorrow by these
tender declarations."†   On the 13th October 1643, the
Solemn League and Covenant was sworn to and subscribed
within its walls by the Committee of Estates of Parliament,
the Commission of the Church, and the English Commission.   The Regent Murray and the Marquis of Montrose are
interred near the centre of the south side of the church,

* Mr. Stark, in his very accurate work, relates that the legend regarding St.
Giles, describes him as " a native of Greece, born in the sixth century.   On the
death of his parents, he gave all his estate to the poor, and travelled into France,
where he retired into the deep recess of a wilderness, near the conflux of the
Rhone with the sea, and continued there for three years, living upon the spontaneous produce of the earth and the milk of a doe.   Having obtained the
reputation of extraordinary sanctity, various miracles were attributed to him;
and he founded a monastery in Languedoc, long after known by the name of
St. Giles.   In the reign of James II., Mr. Preston of Gourton, a gentleman
whose descendants still possess an estate in the county of Edinburgh, procured
a supposed arm-bone of this holy man, which relic he most piously bequeathed
to the Church of St. Giles in Edinburgh.   In gratitude for this invaluable dona-
tion, the magistrates of the city, in 1454, considering that the said bone was
' freely left to oure moyer kirk of Saint Gele of Edinburgh, withoutyn ony condition makyn,' granted a charter in favour of Mr. Preston's heirs, by which the
nearest heir of the name of Preston was entitled to the honour of carrying it in
all public processions.   This honour the family of Preston continued to enjoy
till the Reformation."—*Picture of Edinburgh*, p. 217.
     † ROBERTSON's *History of Scotland*.

ST. MICHAEL'S CHURCH, DUBLIN.

and on the outside of its northern wall is the monument of Napier of Merchiston, the inventor of logarithms.

·The cathedral is now divided into three places of worship, viz. the High Church, the Tolbooth Church, and a Hall, originally intended for the meetings of the General Assembly, but which, after its completion, was found to be unfit for the purpose. In the High Church the Magistrates of the City, and the Judges of the Court of Session, attend divine service in their official robes. The patronage of these, as well as of all the other city parish churches, is vested in the Magistrates and Town Council. The remains of John Knox, the intrepid Ecclesiastical Reformer, were deposited in the cemetery of St. Giles, which formerly occupied the ground where the buildings of the Parliament Square now stand.

So lately as the year 1817, all the spaces between the buttresses of the church were occupied by small shops called the *krames*, grafted upon the walls of the building ; the unholy fires of the shopkeepers begriming with their smoke the whole external surface of the sacred edifice. The annexed engraving represents this curious alliance between the sacred and profane, while the wood-cut introduced into the text exhibits the building in its present state. With the exception of the spire, the whole of the external walls of the Cathedral have in recent years been renovated—a circumstance which has materially impaired the venerable aspect of the building.

In the centre of the Parliament Square, of which the Cathedral just described may be said to form the northern side, stands THE EQUESTRIAN STATUE OF CHARLES II., which, in vigour of design and general effect, still maintains its rank as the best specimen of bronze statuary which Edinburgh possesses.

The Chambers of the Court of Exchequer, the Parliament House, and the Libraries of the Faculty of Advocates and of the Writers to the Signet, form the eastern, western, and southern sides of the Square.

THE PARLIAMENT HOUSE

is situated in the south-west angle. The large hall, now

known by the name of the *Outer-House*, is the place in which the Scottish Parliament met before the Union. This hall is 122 feet long by 49 broad. Its roof is of oak, arched and handsomely finished. It contains two statues—one of Henry Dundas, the first Lord Melville, and the other of that eminent lawyer, Lord President Blair, who died in 1811. At the south end of the Outer-House are four small chambers or Courts, in which the Lords Ordinary sit. Entering from the east side, are two larger Courts of modern and elegant structure, appropriated to the First and Second Divisions of the Court, before whom are tried those cases which are of unusual importance or difficulty, or where the judgment of a Lord Ordinary has been brought under review of the Court by a reclaimer or appeal. Adjoining to the Court-Rooms of the Divisions is another Court-Room of nearly similar appearance, in which sits the High Court of Justiciary, the supreme criminal tribunal of Scotland.

In session time, and during the hours of business, the Outer-House presents a very animated scene. As all the Courts open into it, it affords a very convenient promenade or lounging place for those counsel or agents whose cases are not then actually going on in Court. The well-employed advocates may be seen flitting from bar to bar, or Court to Court, while agents whose causes have just been called, may be observed pressing through the crowd, with anxious face and hurried step, looking out for the counsel, whose absence from the debate might be fatal to their clients. Occasionally may be seen some unfortunate litigant, listening with all reverence and humility, to an opinion on the merits of his case from one of the fathers of the bar, his countenance unequivocally expressing the hopes or fears engendered by the communication. The less employed and unemployed counsel and agents, and a number of loungers who make this hall a place of resort, may be seen in groups conversing together, in every variety of tone and manner, from the gravity of consultation to the gaiety of uncontrolled merriment.*

* For an account of the various classes of Law Practitioners, see the footnote, page 19.

THE ADVOCATES' LIBRARY

adjoins the Parliament House, with which it has a communication. It contains the most valuable collection of books in Scotland, the printed works amounting to 150,000 volumes, and the manuscripts to 1700. The collection of Scottish poetry is exceedingly rare and curious. The volumes in this department amount to nearly 400, and the number is likely to be still further increased by the zeal and research of Dr. Irving, the present librarian, who devotes unremitting attention to augment its treasures. Of the manuscripts, the most valuable are those relating to the civil and ecclesiastical history of Scotland. The funds of the Library are chiefly derived from the fees paid by each advocate, upon his entering as a member of the Faculty. It is also one of the five libraries which receive from Stationers' Hall a copy of every new work published in Great Britain or Ireland. No public institution in Great Britain is conducted with greater liberality. Strangers are freely admitted without introduction ; and no one who is at all known, is ever denied the privilege of resorting to, and of reading or writing in the library. The members are entitled to borrow twenty-five volumes at one time, and to lend any of the books so borrowed to their friends. The literary wealth of the library is at present deposited in a suite of apartments neither spacious, elegant, nor commodious. It is proposed to build a new library in the neighbourhood for their reception. The office of principal librarian has been held by men eminently distinguished in the world of letters, Thomas Ruddiman, David Hume, and Adam Ferguson, having honoured the institution by filling this situation ; and David Irving, LL.D., who at present holds the appointment, is an accomplished scholar, a learned civilian, and eminently skilled in ancient Scottish history, biography, and poetry.

THE SIGNET LIBRARY

is also immediately adjoining to the Parliament House. It

possesses two handsome rooms, one of which was acquired a few years ago from the Advocates' Library. These rooms, more especially the upper one, are well worthy the attention of strangers. This library is peculiarly rich in the department of history, more especially in British and Irish history. The total number of volumes it contains may be estimated at 50,000. It is supported exclusively by the contributions of the Writers to Her Majesty's Signet, and the same liberality which distinguishes the Advocates' Library, also prevails in the management of its affairs. The present librarian, Mr. David Laing, is distinguished by the extent and accuracy of his bibliographical knowledge. He also possesses that general acquaintance with literature which forms one of the most valuable qualifications for the office which he holds.

THE COUNTY HALL stands at the western termination of the Libraries above described. The general plan is taken from the Temple of Erectheus at Athens, and the principal entrance, from the Choragic Monument of Thrasyllus. The Hall is decorated with a statue of Lord Chief Baron Dundas, by Chantrey.

THE OLD TOLBOOTH, sometimes called by the inhabitants

"The Heart of Mid-Lothian," and which, under this name, has become so renowned in the novel of Sir Walter Scott, formerly stood in the middle of the High Street, at the north-west corner of St. Giles's Church.* This gloomy looking building was built in 1561. From that period till the year 1640, it served for the accommodation of Parliament and the Courts of Justice, as well as for the confinement of prisoners; but after the erection of the present Parliament House, it was employed only as a prison. Its situation, jammed as it was into the middle of one of the chief thoroughfares of the city, was signally inconvenient, and in 1817, when the New Prison was prepared for the reception of inmates, the ancient pile of the Tolbooth was demolished. The great entrance-door, with its ponderous padlock and key, were removed to Abbotsford, the seat of Sir Walter Scott, where they are now to be seen, with the other curiosities of the place.†

Proceeding up the High Street, we pass, upon the left, George the Fourth's Bridge, and on the right, Bank Street, at the foot of which stands THE BANK OF SCOTLAND, an edifice of high architectural merit, erected at an expense of £75,000.‡ The fine gothic building on the left, the

---

* A few years ago a chartist orator, in addressing an audience upon the Calton Hill, commenced with the inauspicious phrase, "Men of the Heart of Mid-Lothian!" The compliment, which unquestionably belongs to the class called "left-handed," was, of course, acknowledged by an unanimous burst of laughter from the crowd.

† Alluding to the removal of these relics, Sir Walter observes, "It is not without interest, that we see the gateway through which so much of the stormy politics of a rude age, and the vice and misery of later times, had found their passage, now occupied in the service of rural economy. Last year, to complete the change, a tom-tit was pleased to build her nest within the lock of the Tolbooth—a strong temptation to have committed a sonnet, had the author, like Tony Lumpkin, been in a concatenation accordingly."

‡ The Bank of Scotland has the merit of having originated and established the distinctive principles of the Scottish Banking System. It is the earliest establishment of the kind in Scotland, having been incorporated by Act of the Scottish Parliament in 1695. The capital of the Bank—originally £100,000—is now £1,500,000; of which sum £1,000,000 has been paid up. In the year 1704, it commenced the issue of £1 notes—a practice universally adopted by Scottish Banks till the passing of Sir Robert Peel's bill of 1844, which limits the number of banks privileged to issue notes to those established at the period of the enactment.

foundation stone of which was laid during the recent visit of Her Majesty, is VICTORIA HALL, erected as a place of meeting for the General Assembly of the Church of Scotland, and also used as one of the city churches. The noble spire of this building, which rises to the height of 241 feet, is one of the finest modern ornaments of the city, and from its commanding position there is scarcely any point from which it is not conspicuously seen. The length of the building from east to west is 141 feet. The design is by Mr. Gillespie Graham. At the head of the High Street, upon a precipitous rocky eminence, stands

THE CASTLE,

the most prominent building in the city, and one of the four fortresses which, by the Articles of Union, are to be kept constantly fortified.* The period of its foundation is unknown. There is no doubt, however, that it can boast a more remote antiquity than any other part of the city, and that it has formed the nucleus around which Edinburgh has arisen. The earliest name by which it is recognised in history, is *Castrum Puellarum,* or " The Camp of the Maidens," from the daughters of the Pictish kings being educated and brought up within its walls. It consists of a series of irregular fortifications, and although, before the invention of gunpowder, it might be considered impregnable, it is now a place of more apparent than real strength.

With the exception of the *Bank of Scotland,* the *Royal Bank of Scotland,* and the *British Linen Company,* all of which possess large capitals, there are no chartered banking associations in Scotland *with limited responsibility.* In all the other institutions of the kind, *the partners are jointly and severally liable for the debts of the company, to the whole extent of their fortunes.* And when, in addition to this security, it is considered that there is no limitation to the number of partners of which a banking company of Scotland may consist, and that the public records afford the means of ascertaining with absolute certainty, the real and heritable estate of which the partners may be possessed, it is obvious that the banking establishments of the country possess a solidity of basis highly advantageous to the community at large. " Whatever may be the defects of the Scotch Banking System," says Mr. M'Culloch, " it is probably superior to every other system hitherto established."

* The other fortresses included in this provision, are the Castles of Dumbarton, Blackness, and Stirling.

It can be approached only upon the eastern side. The other three sides are very precipitous ; some parts, as an English friend of our own observed, being *more than perpendicular.* Its elevation is 383 feet above the level of the sea, and, from various parts of the fortifications, a magnificent view of the surrounding country may be obtained. It contains accommodation for 2000 soldiers, and its armoury affords space for 30,000 stand of arms. Facing the north-east is the principal or Half-Moon Battery, mounted with twelve, eighteen, and twenty-four pounders, the only use of which, in these piping times of peace, is to fire on holidays and occasions of public rejoicing. The architectural effect of the Castle has been much marred by a clumsy pile of barracks on its western side, which, observes Sir Walter Scott, would be honoured by a comparison with the most vulgar cotton-mill.

In the earlier periods of Scottish history, this fortress experienced the vicissitudes common to the times, and was frequently taken and re-taken by various conflicting parties. In the present work, we can only advert to one or two of the more striking events in its annals.

In 1296, during the contest for the crown between Bruce and Baliol, it was besieged and taken by the English. It still remained in their possession in 1313, at which time it was strongly garrisoned and commanded by Piers Leland, a Lombard. This governor, having fallen under the suspicion of the garrison, was thrown into a dungeon, and another appointed to the command, in whose fidelity they had complete confidence. It has frequently been remarked, that in capturing fortresses, those attacks are generally most successful which are made upon points where the attempt appears the most desperate. Such was the case in the example now to be narrated. Randolph, Earl of Moray, was one day surveying the gigantic rock, and probably contemplating the possibility of a successful assault upon the fortress, when he was accosted by one of his men-at-arms with the question, " Do you think it impracticable, my lord ?" Randolph turned his eyes upon the querist, a man a little past the prime of life, but of a firm, well-knit figure, and bearing in his bright eye, and bold and open brow, indications of an intrepidity which had already made him remarkable in the Scottish army.

" Do you mean the rock, Francis ?"* said the earl; " perhaps not, if we could borrow the wings of our gallant hawks."

" There are wings," replied Francis, with a thoughtful smile, " as strong, as buoyant, and as daring. My father was keeper of yonder fortress."

" What of that ? you speak in riddles."

" I was then young, reckless, high-hearted ; I was mewed up in that convent-like castle ; my mistress was in the plain below—"

" Well, what then ?"

" 'Sdeath, my Lord, can you not imagine that I speak of the wings of love ? Every night I descended that steep at the witching hour, and every morning before the dawn I crept back to my barracks. I constructed a light twelve-foot ladder, by means of which I was able to pass the places that are perpendicular ; and so well, at length, did I become acquainted with the route, that in the darkest and stormiest night, I found my way as easily as when the moonlight enabled me to see my love in the distance, waiting for me at her cottage door."

" You are a daring, desperate, noble fellow, Francis ! However, your motive is now gone ; your mistress—"

" She is dead : say no more ; but another has taken her place."

" Ay, ay, it's the soldier's way. Women will die, or even grow old ; and what are we to do ? Come, who is your mistress now ?"

" My Country ! What I have done for love, I can do again for honour ; and what I can accomplish, you, noble Randolph, and many of our comrades, can do far better.

---

* The soldier's name was William Frank. Mr. Leitch Ritchie here uses the novelist's license in dealing with the name, and in throwing the story into the form of a dialogue, but the events are strictly in accordance with the historical narrative.

Give me thirty picked men, and a twelve-foot ladder, and the fortress is our own ! "

The Earl of Moray, whatever his real thoughts of the enterprise might have been, was not the man to refuse such a challenge. A ladder was provided, and thirty men chosen from the troops ; and in the middle of a dark night, the party, commanded by Randolph himself, and guided by William Francis, set forth on their desperate enterprise.

By catching at crag after crag, and digging their fingers into the interstices of the rocks, they succeeded in mounting a considerable way ; but the weather was now so thick, they could receive but little assistance from their eyes ; and thus they continued to climb, almost in utter darkness, like men struggling up a precipice in the nightmare. They at length reached a shelving table of the cliff, above which the ascent, for ten or twelve feet, was perpendicular ; and having fixed their ladder, the whole party lay down to recover breath.

From this place they could hear the tread and voices of the " check-watches" or patrol above ; and surrounded by the perils of such a moment, it is not wonderful that some illusions may have mingled with their thoughts. They even imagined that they were seen from the battlements ; although, being themselves unable to see the warders, this was highly improbable. It became evident, notwithstanding, from the words they caught here and there, in the pauses of the night-wind, that the conversation of the English soldiers above, related to a surprise of the castle ; and, at length, these appalling words broke like thunder on their ears : " Stand ! I see you well !" A fragment of the rock was hurled down at the same instant ; and, as rushing from crag to crag, it bounded over their heads, Randolph and his brave followers, in this wild, helpless, and extraordinary situation, felt the damp of mortal terror gathering upon their brow, as they clung, with a death-grip, to the precipice.

The startled echoes of the rock were at length silent, and so were the voices above. The adventurers paused, listening breathless ; no sound was heard but the sighing of the

wind, and the measured tread of the sentinel, who had re-
sumed his walk. The men thought they were in a dream,
and no wonder; for the incident just mentioned, which is
related by Barbour, was one of the most singular coinci-
dences that ever occurred. The shout of the sentinel, and
the missile he had thrown, were merely a boyish freak; and
while listening to the echoes of the rock, he had not the
smallest idea that the sounds which gave pleasure to him,
carried terror, and almost despair, into the hearts of the
enemy.

The adventurers, half uncertain whether they were not
the victims of some illusion, determined that it was as safe
to go on as to turn back ; and pursuing their laborious and
dangerous path, they at length reached the bottom of the
wall. This last barrier they scaled by means of their ladder; and leaping down among the astonished check-watches,
they cried their war-cry, and, in the midst of answering
shouts of " treason ! treason !" notwithstanding the desperate resistance of the garrison, captured the Castle of
Edinburgh.*

Robert Bruce then entirely demolished its fortifications,
that it might not again be occupied by a hostile power.
The wisdom of this policy was subsequently proved by the
conduct of Edward III. who, on his return from Perth,
caused it to be rebuilt and strongly garrisoned. But his
possession of it was destined to be of short duration. One
of those stratagems characteristic of the adventurous spirit
of the times, was successfully resorted to for its deliverance.
In 1341, Sir William Douglas, with three other gentlemen,
waited upon the governor. One of them, professing to be
an English merchant, informed him that he had a vessel
in the Forth richly laden with wine, beer, and biscuits exquisitely spiced, and produced at the same time samples of
the cargo. The governor, pleased with their quality, agreed
for the purchase of the whole, which the pretended captain
requested permission to deliver early next day, to avoid interruption from the Scots. He accordingly arrived at the

* HEATH'S Picturesque Annual. *Scott and Scotland*, pp. 174-7.

time appointed, attended by a dozen of armed followers, disguised as seamen, and the gates being opened for the reception of the provisions, they contrived, just in the entrance, to overturn one of the carriages, thus effectually preventing the closing of the gates. The porter and guards were then put to the sword, and the assailants being reinforced by Douglas and his party, who lay in ambush near the entrance, the English garrison was overpowered, and expelled from the castle.

During the reign of Queen Mary, when the country was distracted by intestine wars, this fortress was gallantly defended for the Queen by Kirkaldy of Grange. The rest of Scotland had submitted to the authority of Morton the Regent, Kirkaldy alone, with a few brave associates, remaining faithful to the cause of his Royal Mistress. Morton was unable, with the troops at his command, to reduce the garrison, but Elizabeth having sent Sir William Drury to his aid with 1500 foot, and a train of artillery, trenches were opened, and approaches regularly carried on against the castle. For three and thirty days Kirkaldy gallantly resisted the combined forces of the Scots and English, nor did he demand a parley till the fortifications were battered down, and the wells were dried up or choked with rubbish. Even then, with a heroism truly chivalrous, he determined rather to fall gloriously behind the ramparts, than surrender to his enemies. But his garrison were not animated with the same heroic courage. Rising in a mutiny, they compelled him to capitulate. Drury, in the name of his mistress, engaged that he should be honourably treated; but Elizabeth, insensible alike to the claims of valour, and to the pledged honour of her own officer, surrendered Kirkaldy to the Regent, who, *with her consent*, hanged the gallant soldier and his brother at the Cross, on the 3d of August 1573.

In 1650, the castle was besieged by the Parliamentary army under Cromwell; and capitulated on honourable terms. In 1745, although Prince Charles Stuart held possession of the city, he did not attempt the reduction of the castle. In modern times, some of the prisoners, during the

D

French war, were confined within its walls. The SCOTTISH

REGALIA are exhibited in the Crown Room every day from twelve till three o'clock. Visitors are gratuitously admitted by an order from the Lord Provost, which may be obtained by applying at the City Chambers between twelve and three o'clock. Persons procuring orders are required to sign their names and places of residence in a book kept in the City Chambers for this purpose, and the order is available only upon that day on which it is dated. These insignia of Scottish Royalty consist of a Crown, a Sceptre, and a Sword of State.* Along with them is also shown the Lord Trea-

---

* "Taking these articles in connection with the great historical events and personages that enter into the composition of their present value, it is impossible to look upon them without emotions of singular interest, while, at the same time, their essential littleness excites wonder at the mighty circumstances and destinies which have been determined by the possession or the want of possession of what they emblematize and represent. For this diadem did Bruce liberate his country; with it, his son nearly occasioned its ruin. It purchased for Scotland the benefit of the mature sagacity of Robert II.—did not save Robert III. from a death of grief—procured, perhaps, the assassination of James I.—instigated James IV. to successful rebellion against his father, whose violent death was expiated by his own. Its dignity was proudly increased by James V. who was yet more unfortunate, perhaps, in his end, than a long list of unfortunate predecessors. It was worn by the devoted head of Mary, who found it the occasion of woes and calamities unnumbered and unexampled. It was placed

surer's Rod of Office, found deposited in the same strong oak chest in which the Regalia were discovered. The room where Queen Mary gave birth to James VI., in whom the crowns of England and Scotland were united, will be an object of interest to many strangers. The gigantic piece of artillery, called MONS MEG, from being cast at Mons in Flanders, is mounted on an elegant carriage on the Bomb Battery. It was employed at the siege of Norham, and afterwards burst when firing a salute to the Duke of York in 1682, since which time it has never been repaired. On the north side of the esplanade stands the Statue of the late Duke of York, erected to commemorate his services as Commander-in-Chief of the Forces. A cannon-ball, said to have been shot from the castle in 1745, may be seen sticking in the gable wall of the house on the south side of the entrance to the esplanade.

In returning from the Castle, an opening upon the left, immediately upon leaving the esplanade, conducts to the house of Allan Ramsay, the author of "The Gentle Shepherd," a pastoral drama of charming simplicity, and still highly popular among the rural population of Scotland.

The stranger will now retrace his steps to

GEORGE IV. BRIDGE,

which spans the Cowgate, and forms an important feature in the modern improvements of the city. At its northern end is the WEST BOW, which, before the erection of this bridge, presented an aspect highly interesting to the lover

upon the infant brow of her son, to the exclusion of herself from all its glories and advantages, but not the conclusion of the distresses in which it had involved her. Her unfortunate grandson, for its sake, visited Scotland, and had it placed upon his head with magnificent ceremonies; but the nation whose sovereignty it gave him was the first to rebel against his authority, and work his destruction. The Presbyterian solemnity with which it was given to Charles II. was only a preface to the disasters of Worcester; and afterwards it was remembered by this monarch, little to the advantage of Scotland, that it had been placed upon his head with conditions and restrictions which wounded at once his pride and his conscience. It was worn by no other monarch, and the period of its disuse seems to have been the epoch from which we may reckon the happiness of our monarchs, and the revival of our national prosperity."—CHAMBERS' *Walks in Edinburgh*, p. 49.

of antique buildings. Although now a place of small consideration, it is not 100 years since the Assembly Rooms of Edinburgh were situate within its precincts. Before the erection of the North and South Bridges, it was also the principal avenue by which wheel-carriages reached the more elevated streets of the city. It "has been ascended by Anne of Denmark, James I., and Charles I., by Oliver Cromwell, Charles II., and James II. How different the avenue by which George IV. entered the city!"* But the West Bow has also been the scene of many more mournful processions. Previous to the year 1785, criminals were conducted through the Bow to the place of execution in the Grassmarket, and the murderers of Porteous, after securing their victim, hurried him down this street to meet the fate they had destined for him.† The spot where the city gibbet stood is now indicated by a cross upon the causeway of the

* CHAMBERS' *Traditions of Edinburgh*, vol. i., p. 140.

† The murder of Captain Porteous forms an event so memorable, not only in the annals of the city, but in what may be termed the philosophy of mobs, that a brief account of the event may not be unacceptable. We need hardly remind our readers that it forms one of the most striking incidents in the Heart of Mid-Lothian.

John Porteous was the son of a tailor in Edinburgh; his father intended to breed him up to his own trade, but the youthful profligacy of the son defeated the parent's prudent intention, and he enlisted into the Scotch corps at that time in the service of the States of Holland. Here he learned military discipline, and upon returning to his own country in 1715, his services were engaged by the magistrates of Edinburgh to discipline the City Guard. For such a task he was eminently qualified, not only by his military education, but by his natural activity and resolution; and, in spite of the profligacy of his character, he received a captain's commission in the corps.

The duty of the Edinburgh City Guard was to preserve the public peace when any tumult was apprehended. They consisted principally of discharged veterans, who, when off duty, worked at their respective trades. To the rabble they were objects of mingled derision and dislike, and the numerous indignities they suffered, rendered them somewhat morose and austere in temper. At public executions they generally surrounded the scaffold, and it was on an occasion of this kind that Porteous, their captain, committed the outrage for which he paid the penalty of his life.

The criminal, on the occasion in question, had excited the commiseration of the populace by the disinterested courage he displayed in achieving the escape of his accomplice. At this time it was customary to conduct prisoners under sentence of death to attend divine service in the Tolbooth Church. Wilson, the criminal above alluded to, and Robertson, his companion in crime, had reached the church, guarded by four soldiers, when Wilson suddenly seized one of the

market-place, in the middle of the street, between No. 104 on the one side, and No. 123 on the other; the centre of

guards in each hand, and a third with his teeth, and shouted to his accomplice to fly for his life. Robertson immediately fled and effected his escape. This circumstance naturally excited a strong feeling of sympathy for Wilson; and the magistrates, fearing an attempt at rescue, had requested the presence of a detachment of infantry in a street adjoining that where the execution was to take place, for the purpose of intimidating the populace. The introduction of another military force than his own into a quarter of the city where no drums but his were ever beat, highly incensed Captain Porteous, and aggravated the ferocity of a temper naturally surly and brutal. Contrary to the apprehension of the authorities, the execution was allowed to pass undisturbed; but the dead body had hung only a short time upon the gibbet when a tumult arose among the multitude—stones and other missiles where thrown at Porteous and his men, and one of the populace, more adventurous than the rest, sprung upon the scaffold, and cut the rope by which the criminal was suspended.

Porteous was exasperated to frenzy by this outrage on his authority, and leaping from the scaffold, he seized the musket of one of the guards, gave the word to fire, and discharging his piece, shot the man dead upon the spot. Several of his soldiers also, having obeyed his order to fire, six or seven persons were killed, and many others wounded. The mob still continuing their attack, another volley was fired upon them, by which several others fell, and the scene of violence only closed when Porteous and his soldiers reached the guard-house in the High Street. For his reckless and sanguinary conduct in this affair, Captain Porteous was arraigned before the High Court of Justiciary, and sentence of death was passed upon him. His execution was appointed to take place on the 8th of September 1736.

The day of doom arrived, and the ample area of the Grassmarket was crowded in every part with a countless multitude, drawn together to gratify their revenge or satisfy their sense of justice by the spectacle of the execution. But their vengeance met with a temporary disappointment. The hour of execution was already past, without the appearance of the criminal, and the expectant multitude began to interchange suspicions that a reprieve might have arrived. Deep and universal was the groan of indignation which arose from the crowd, when they learned that such was indeed the fact. The case having been represented to her Majesty Queen Caroline, she intimated her royal pleasure that the prisoner should be reprieved for six weeks. The shout of disappointed revenge was followed by suppressed mutterings and communings among the crowd, but no act of violence was committed; they saw the gallows taken down, and then gradually dispersed to their respective homes and occupations.

Night ushered in another scene of the drama. A drum was heard beating to arms, and the populace promptly answered its summons by turning out into the streets. Their numbers rapidly increased, and, separating into different parties, they took possession of the city gates, posting sentinels for their security. They then disarmed the City Guard, and, having thus possessed themselves of weapons, they were the uncontrolled masters of the city. During the progress of the riot, various efforts were made to communicate with the castle, but the vigilance of the insurgents defeated all such attempts. The Tolbooth was now invested, and a strong party of the rioters having surrounded it, another party proceeded to break up the doors. For a considerable time the

the cross covering the precise spot in which the socket-stone of the gallows-tree was sunk. About the middle of the Bow, where the roadway now passes, stood the House of Major Weir, the celebrated necromancer, who, along with his sister, suffered death for witchcraft in 1670. The fate of Weir is chiefly remarkable from his being a man of some condition, (the son of a gentleman, and his mother a lady of family in Clydesdale,) which was rarely the case with those who were the victims of such accusations. Whether the crimes which he confessed were the diseased fancies of a mind labouring under temporary insanity, or whether he was in reality a man of atrociously depraved life, does not very clearly appear. After his condemnation, he doggedly refused to have recourse to prayer, " arguing, that as he had no hope whatever of escaping Satan, there was no need

great strength of the place rendered their efforts fruitless, but, having brought fire to their aid, they burned the door and rushed into the prison.

Porteous, elated with his escape from the sentence he so richly merited, was regaling a party of his boon companions within the building, when the assault was made upon its gates. The wretched man well knew the hatred with which he was regarded by the populace, and was at no loss to comprehend the motive for their violence. Escape seemed impossible. The chimney was the only place of concealment that occurred to him, and scrambling into it, he supported himself by laying hold of the bars of iron with which the chimneys of a prison-house are crossed to prevent the escape of criminals. But his enemies soon dragged him from his hiding-place, and, hurrying him along the streets, they brought him to the very spot, where, that morning, he ought to have paid the forfeit of his life. The want of a rope was now the sole obstacle to the accomplishment of their purpose, and this want was soon supplied by breaking open a shop where the article was sold; a dyer's pole served in room of a gallows, and from it they suspended the unhappy man. Having thus propitiated the spirit of offended justice, they threw down the weapons of which they had possessed themselves, and quietly dispersed to their respective homes.

It has been justly observed, that the murder of Porteous has more the character of a conspiracy than of a riot. The whole proceedings of the insurgents were marked by a cool and deliberate intrepidity, quite at variance with the accustomed conduct of rioters. No violence was perpetrated either upon person or property, save the single act of vengeance executed upon Porteous. So studious were the insurgents to avoid every appearance of prædial outrage, that a guinea was left upon the counter of the shop from which they took the rope to hang their victim. None of the offenders were ever discovered, although Government made the most strenuous exertions, and offered large rewards for their apprehension. There can be little doubt, however, that many of the participators in that night's transactions were of a class unaccustomed to mingle in scenes of vulgar tumult.

of incensing him by vain efforts at repentance."* The modern improvements in this part of the city have now swept away all vestiges of the house, which, ever after the death of Weir, enjoyed the reputation of being haunted. So general was the horror entertained for the crimes of the man and the terrors of his abode, that no family was ever found hardy enough to occupy the house as a residence.

In the Grassmarket—situated, as we have already mentioned, at the foot of the Bow—a weekly market is held on Wednesday for grain, horses, cattle, and sheep. At its south-west corner it is entered by the WEST PORT, the scene of the appalling atrocities of the monster Burke. As the name of this wretched man has now become the current term to distinguish the crime for which he suffered, we need scarcely remind our readers that his victims were destroyed by strangling, and that his object was not to possess himself of their property, for they were all of a humble rank in life, but to convert their bodies into a source of gain by selling them to the anatomist.

Proceeding along the Bridge, Heriot's Hospital will be seen occupying a fine situation on the right. At the southern end of the Bridge, upon the right hand, is the entrance to THE GREYFRIARS' CHURCHYARD, in ancient times the garden belonging to the monastery of Greyfriars, which was situated in the Grassmarket. In this churchyard are interred George Buchanan, the accomplished Latin poet, and preceptor of James VI., Allan Ramsay, the Scottish poet, Principal Robertson, the historian, Dr. Black, the distinguished chemist, Dr. Hugh Blair, Colin Maclaurin, Dr. M'Crie, the biographer of Knox, and other eminent men. The two Churches in the burying-ground, known by the name of Old Greyfriars, and New Greyfriars, were completely destroyed by fire in January 1845. Of the former, Principal Robertson was pastor for many years. Leaving the churchyard, and advancing a few yards up the Candlemaker Row, a broad road will be seen upon the right conducting to the CHARITY WORKHOUSE. The grounds around the house are laid out as a kitchen garden for the establish-

* SIR WALTER SCOTT'S *Letters on Demonology and Witchcraft*, p. 330.

ment, and the inmates are frequently employed in its cultivation. The house itself is a large building of the plainest
description. The funds by which the institution is supported are derived from an assessment on house property,
collections at the church-doors, and occasional donations
and voluntary contributions from the citizens. The average
number of inmates is about 750.*

After passing the Work-House the stranger will take the
road to the right, and in a few minutes he will reach the
gate of

HERIOT'S HOSPITAL.

This handsome edifice, one of the proudest ornaments of
the city, owes its foundation to George Heriot, jeweller to
James VI., whose name will probably be more familiar to
the ear of strangers as the "jingling Geordie" of "The
Fortunes of Nigel."† The design, which is attributed to
Inigo Jones, is in that mixed style which dates its origin
from the reign of Elizabeth, examples of which are afforded
by Drumlanrig Castle in Dumfries-shire, Northumberland
House in the Strand, and many other edifices throughout
the kingdom. Its form is quadrangular, the sides each
measuring 162 feet, and enclosing a court of 92 feet square.
The building was commenced in 1628, and completed in
1660, and the erection is said to have cost £27,000. The
chapel, occupying the south side of the quadrangle, a few
years ago presented nothing but a clay floor and bare walls,
round which there was a stone seat, to accommodate the
boys when assembled for morning and evening service.
It is now fitted up in a very different style, and with its
splendid pulpit, fine oaken carvings, richly adorned ceiling,
and beautifully stained glass windows, forms one of the
principal attractions of the place. The object of this splen-

---

* Besides this institution, the parish of St. Cuthberts and the Canongate
have each a house for the reception of paupers, with peculiar funds, and separate boards of management.

† "For the wealth God has sent me, it shall not want inheritors while there
are orphan lads in Auld Reekie."—*Fortunes of Nigel, Chapter IV.*

A brief outline of the benevolent founder's history is given in the Note to
Chapter II. of the same work.

HERIOT'S HOSPITAL, FROM THE GRASSMARKET.

FREDERICK MAGISTRATE GRAND HOTEL OF A.D. 1500

G. Aikman

did institution is the maintenance and education of " poor and fatherless boys," or boys whose parents are in indigent circumstances, " freemen's sons of the town of Edinburgh," of whom 180 are accommodated within its walls. The course of instruction consists of English, Latin, Greek, Writing, Arithmetic, Book-keeping, Mathematics, and Geography. To these branches have recently been added French, Drawing, the Elements of Music, and Practical Mechanics. Boys are admitted between the age of seven and ten, and generally leave at fourteen, unless superior scholarship appears to fit them for prosecuting some of the learned professions, in which case the period of their stay is extended, with the view of preparing them for the studies of the University. All the boys, upon leaving the hospital, receive a bible, and other useful books, with two suits of clothes of their own choice. Those going out as apprentices are allowed £10 annually for five years, and £5 at the termination of their apprenticeship. Those destined for any of the learned professions are sent to college for four years, during which period they receive £30 a-year. In 1836, an act was obtained from Parliament, empowering the Governors to extend the benefits of the Institution, and employ their surplus funds in establishing Free Schools in the different parishes of the city. Ten of these schools are already in full operation, in which very nearly 3000 children, of both sexes, are instructed in the usual branches of a parochial education, the females being, in addition, taught sewing and knitting. This great scheme of instruction, when complete, must prove of incalculable benefit to the community, as the advantages of a substantial education will be brought within the reach of every citizen, however humble. In addition to these liberal provisions for the instruction of youth, there are also ten bursaries, or exhibitions, open to the competition of young men not connected with the institution. The successful competitors for these bursaries receive £20 *per annum*, for four years. The princely provision thus made for the welfare of his countrymen, amply justifies the sentiment put into the mouth of the founder by Sir Walter Scott, " I think mine own estate and memory, as I shall order it, has a fair chance of outliving those of greater men." The management is vested in the Town Council and Clergy of the City, and visitors are admitted by an order from any of the Governors.

Retracing our steps to the entrance of the Charity Work-House, the Meadow Walk will be seen exactly opposite. In a field, upon the right hand, a short way down the walk, stands

GEORGE WATSON'S HOSPITAL.

This hospital is for the benefit of the children and grand-children of decayed merchants of the city of Edinburgh. The building is plain, but commodious. Boys are received into this hospital between seven and ten, and remain till fifteen years of age. The number of boys amount to about eighty, and the education they receive very much resembles that of Heriot's Hospital. Each boy, after leaving the hospital, receives £10 a-year for five years ; and, upon attaining the age of twenty-five, if unmarried and well-conducted, he receives a further sum of £50. Such as evince " an extraordinary genius for letters," receive £20 a-year, for four years, and £17 a-year, during the two succeeding years. The management is vested in the Master, Assistants, and Treasurer of the Merchant Company of Edinburgh, the ministers of the Old Church, and five members of the Town Council. A little to the west of George Watson's Hospital, stands the Merchant Maiden Hospital, but as it does not come within the scope of any of our walks, we think it better to include the description of it, and of the other more important hospitals which we do not pass in our progress, in a foot-note.*

* *The Merchant Maiden Hospital* was founded in 1695, for the maintenance and education of the daughters of merchant burgesses in the city. Nearly 100 girls are maintained in this hospital. They are admitted between seven and eleven years of age, and leave at seventeen. The course of instruction includes English, Writing, Arithmetic, Geography, French, Music, Drawing, Dancing, and Needle-work. Upon leaving the hospital, each girl receives £9, 6s. 8d. The original edifice stood in Bristo Street; the present building is agreeably situated in Lauriston, a little to the west of George Watson's Hospital.

The Trades' Maiden Hospital stands on the south side of Argyle Square. The girls eligible for admission into this institution, are the daughters of decayed

Immediately adjoining to the Meadows, on the south-west, are Bruntsfield Links (*Anglice* Downs), where many of the inhabitants are accustomed to amuse themselves with

tradesmen. It supports about 50 girls, who are admitted at the same age, and instructed in the same branches as in the Merchant Maiden Hospital. They go out at the age of seventeen, each girl receiving £5, 11s. and a bible.

The Orphan Hospital maintains and educates about 100 children of both sexes. The old building, situated near Trinity College Church, was abandoned as unhealthy, and a handsome new edifice was erected in 1833, on the property of Dean. The benefits of the institution are extended to the whole of Scotland.

John Watson's Institution is a spacious and showy edifice, also situated on the property of Dean. The purpose of the endowment, is the maintenance and education of destitute children. About 120 children are maintained in it. They are admitted between the ages of five and eight, and leave at fourteen.

Cauvin's Hospital is pleasantly situated at Duddingston, a village about a mile and a half to the east of Edinburgh. The children enjoying the benefit of this institution are " the sons of respectable but poor teachers," and " of poor but honest farmers ;" whom failing, " the sons of respectable master printers or booksellers," and " of respectable servants in the agricultural line." Twenty boys are maintained in it. They are admissible from six to eight years of age, and are retained in the hospital for six years.

Trinity College Hospital, the oldest charitable institution in the city. Was founded in 1461 by Mary of Gueldres. It stood at the foot of the lane called Leith Wynd, but the ground being purchased by the North British Railway Company, the inmates have been removed to Moray House, which has been comfortably fitted up for their reception. Its benefits are conferred on " burgesses, their wives or children not married, nor under the age of fifty years." Forty persons are maintained within the walls of the hospital, and about ninety out-pensioners receive £6 a-year.

Gillespie's Hospital enjoys a fine situation on the south-west confines of the city. The founder was a tobacconist in Edinburgh, who devoted the greater part of his property to endow an hospital for the maintenance of indigent old men and women, and for the elementary education of 100 poor boys. The number of the aged inmates is between thirty and forty. None are admitted under the age of fifty-five, a preference being given to servants of the founder, or persons of his name.

Donaldson's Hospital—probably the finest building in Scotland, certainly the finest of modern date—stands on a piece of ground to the westward of the city, about half a mile along the Glasgow Road from the Edinburgh and Glasgow Railway Station at the Hay-Weights. The founder was a printer in Edinburgh, who died in 1830, and bequeathed the greater part of his estate, amounting to nearly £200,000, for the purpose of building and maintaining an hospital for poor boys and girls. Of these there will be accommodation for about 300. The building is from the design of Mr. W. H. Playfair, whose reputation would securely rest on this structure alone, if Scotland were not fortunate enough to possess numerous other examples of his taste and genius.

Fettes' Endowment.—Another institution for the maintenance of poor boys and girls, not yet erected, but for which Sir W. Fettes, Bart., who died in 1836, left the greater part of his large fortune.

the national game of golf. The game is played with a club and ball. The club is formed of ash, flexible and finely

tapered, measuring from three to four feet long, according to the player's height or length of arm. The head is faced

Chalmers' Hospital.—For the erection and endowment of an hospital under this name, "for the sick and hurt," Chalmers, a plumber, who died in 1836, has left the sum of £30,000.

Besides the endowments for the relief of the destitute, there are many other charitable associations maintained by private subscription. Among them may be mentioned, The House of Refuge—The House of Industry—The Strangers' Friend Society—The Blind Asylum—The Deaf and Dumb Institution—The Night Asylum for the Houseless—The Society for Relief of the Destitute Sick —The Society for the Relief of Indigent Old Men, and two similar institutions for the Relief of Indigent Old Women—The Seamen's Friend Society—and the Society for Clothing the Industrious Poor.

There are also many public Dispensaries, and a Lying-in Hospital, where medicines and medical attendance are gratuitously afforded to the poor; but a further enumeration of such institutions does not appear to be required for the purposes of the present work.

with horn and loaded with lead. The ball is about the size of a common tennis ball, made of feathers, compressed very firmly into a hard and slightly elastic leathern cover. The game consists in striking the ball successively into a certain number of small holes, about a quarter of a mile apart, the player who does so in the smallest number of strokes being the victor. Each player carries an assortment of clubs varying in elasticity, and thus adapted to the distance the ball is to be driven, the best club for a long stroke being laid aside for one less elastic when the distance becomes shortened. An expert player will strike a ball from 130 to 200 yards.* The *Thistle Golf Club of Edinburgh* have their arms, crest, and uniform. The last consists of a single-breasted scarlet coat, with green collar, and plain gilt buttons, white trousers, and a badge bearing the device of the thistle upon the left breast.

Returning from the Links to that point of the Meadows where the walks cross each other, the stranger will be in the immediate neighbourhood of

GEORGE'S SQUARE.

This is the only large square in the Old Town. Towards the close of the last century, it was the principal place of residence of the higher ranks; the Duchess of Gordon, the Countess of Sutherland, the Countess of Glasgow, Viscount Duncan, the Hon. Henry Erskine, and many other persons of rank, residing there. The house of Walter Scott, Esq., W.S., father of the novelist, was on the west side of the Square.

Passing along Charles Street and Bristo Street, and turning to the right into Lothian Street, two places of worship will be observed upon the left hand—the one a Roman Catholic and the other a Baptist Chapel—the two being built upon a mutual gable. Proceeding along Lothian

---

* Among the most memorable feats in the annals of golfing is that of a player who struck a ball over the top of St. Giles's steeple from a point within the Parliament Square. Another player, still alive, struck his ball over Melville's Monument, which, from the ground to the head of the statue, measures 150 feet.

Street and South College Street, and then turning to the right a short distance along Nicolson Street, the stranger will arrive in front of the fine portico of

THE ROYAL COLLEGE OF SURGEONS.

In classic elegance, few buildings will be found to surpass this handsome structure, although its effect is much impaired by the uncongenial architecture of the surrounding houses. The principal portion of the building is occupied with an extensive museum of anatomical and surgical preparations. The arrangement is, in every respect, admirable, and a praiseworthy liberality is exhibited in the admission of strangers. Although, by the strict letter of the regulations, a member's order is requisite, yet even this form is, in most cases, dispensed with. A little further south, on the same side of the street, is the Asylum for the Industrious Blind.

Returning northward, the next object of importance is

THE UNIVERSITY.

No regular University existed in Edinburgh till the year 1582, although, long previous to this period, teachers of philosophy and divinity had been established in the city. On the 24th of April of that year, King James VI. issued the charter for its foundation, and in the following year the course of instruction was commenced. By the liberality of James, and private benefactions, the University rapidly advanced in importance, and, as its revenues increased, its sphere of usefulness was extended by the addition of new professorships, till, in the 18th century, it attained a celebrity unsurpassed by any academical institution in Europe.

The present structure is of modern erection. The old buildings were both unsightly and incommodious, and a subscription having been set on foot, the foundation of the present handsome and spacious edifice was laid in 1789. The local subscriptions, however, were insufficient to accomplish the object; and, upon the case being brought before Parliament, an annual grant of £10,000 was obtained to complete the undertaking. The plan is by Mr.

Robert Adam, with some subsequent modifications, principally in the internal arrangement, by Mr. W. H. Playfair. The buildings are of a quadrangular form, the sides measuring 358 by 255 feet, with a spacious court in the centre. The eastern front is adorned with a portico, supported by Doric columns, twenty-six feet in height, each formed of a single block of stone.

No test of any description is required from the students; they are not resident within the College, nor are they distinguished by any peculiarity of dress. In pursuing their studies they are at perfect liberty to select the classes they attend—a certain curriculum of study is, however, requisite in taking degrees in Medicine and Art, those who intend to qualify for a degree in the latter being required to attend the Classes of Humanity, Greek, Logic, Rhetoric, Moral Philosophy, Natural Philosophy, and Mathematics. The number of students attending the University during the present session (1844-45,) is 1050.

There are 34 foundations for bursaries, the benefit of which is extended to 80 students. The greater number of these bursaries do not exceed in value £10 per annum, their aggregate amount being only £1172 a-year.

The Museum contains a large collection of specimens in the various departments of Natural History. The Ornithological department is peculiarly valuable, both from its extent and admirable classification. Visiters are admitted upon payment of one shilling each. There is also an Anatomical Museum, where the professional visiter will be highly interested by the variety and beauty of the preparations.

The Library occupies the south side of the building. The principal apartment is equally distinguished by the symmetry of its proportions, the chasteness of its decorations, and its admirable adaptation to the purpose for which it is intended. It is incomparably the finest library-room in Scotland—measuring 187 feet in length, by 50 in breadth, with an arched roof from 50 to 58 feet high. The monument of Burns by Flaxman graces the west end of the room.

Proceeding northward, upon leaving the University,

THE ROYAL INFIRMARY

is situated in the first street upon the right. A detailed account of this institution does not appear to be necessary in the present work. Besides the relief afforded to patients, clinical lectures, or discourses on the cases in the several wards, are delivered within the walls by certain Professors of the University. The professor of clinical surgery also lectures upon the more important surgical cases in the wards under his inspection. Besides the professorial lectures, the ordinary physicians and surgeons of the institution deliver clinical discourses on the cases under their immediate care. Journals are regularly kept, recording the symptoms, progress, and result of the cases, with the various remedies employed. To these journals the students have access.

The fees paid by students for the right to attend the medical and surgical practice in the Hospital, are five guineas for an annual, or twelve guineas for a perpetual ticket.

Proceeding along the South Bridge, an open railing, for a short distance on either side, affords a view of the Cowgate, with which the tourist will, in all probability, have no wish to cultivate a closer acquaintance. The Register House will again come into view on reaching the Tron Church, thus terminating our Second Walk.

WALK THIRD.*

SCOTT MONUMENT—ROYAL INSTITUTION—NEW CLUB—ST. JOHN'S CHAPEL—ST. CUTHBERT'S CHURCH—CHARLOTTE SQUARE—ST. GEORGE'S CHURCH—DEAN BRIDGE—AINSLIE PLACE—MORAY PLACE—HERIOT ROW—PITT MONUMENT—GEORGE FOURTH'S MONUMENT—ASSEMBLY ROOMS—PHYSICIANS' HALL—ST. ANDREW'S SQUARE—MELVILLE MONUMENT—ROYAL BANK.

In this walk we shall conduct the stranger through the principal streets of the New Town, adverting to all the more striking objects in our progress.

* This Walk is coloured *yellow* on the Map.

THE SCOTT MONUMENT

Proceeding to the westward, the buildings of the High Street will be seen upon the left, towering to the heavens like the habitations of a race of Titans. These buildings, standing upon a steep and lofty ridge, with tributary lanes or closes descending abruptly to the valley beneath, produce an effect highly picturesque and majestic. The interjacent valley, extending westward to the end of Princes Street, along which the Edinburgh and Glasgow Railway now passes, was formerly a stagnant pond or marsh, known by the name of the Nor-Loch. The

MONUMENT TO SIR WALTER SCOTT,*

of which an engraving illustrates our text, will be observed within the railing of the pleasure-grounds opposite the foot of St. David Street. The design was furnished by George M. Kemp, an architect wholly unknown to fame until declared the successful competitor for this honour, and who died before the structure was completed. The foundation was laid on the 15th of August 1840, and the building was finished in 1844. Its height is 200 feet 6 inches, and its cost was £15,650. A stair of 287 steps conducts to the gallery at the top. In each front of the Monument, above the principal arch, are six small niches, making a total of 24 in the main structure, besides 32 others in the piers and abutment towers. These niches are to be occupied by sculptural impersonations of the characters, historical and fanciful, pourtrayed in the writings of Sir Walter. The following statues fill the four principal niches which crown the four lowest arches. In the northern niche facing Princes Street is the statue of Prince Charles (from *Waverley*) drawing his sword. In the eastern niche, on the side next the Calton Hill, is Meg Merrilees (from *Guy Mannering*) breaking the sapling over the head of Lucy Bertram. In the southern niche, next the Old Town, is the statue of the *Lady of the Lake* stepping from a boat to the shore ; and, in the western niche, is the *Last Minstrel* playing on his harp. Other statues

* To the different galleries of the Scott Monument, there is admission by tickets, price one shilling each; to be had at 39, Princes Street.

for the remaining niches are in progress. The following is the inscription on the plate placed under the foundation-stone :—

THIS GRAVEN PLATE,
DEPOSITED IN THE BASE OF A VOTIVE BUILDING
ON THE FIFTEENTH DAY OF AUGUST IN THE YEAR OF CHRIST 1840,
AND NEVER LIKELY TO SEE THE LIGHT AGAIN
TILL ALL THE SURROUNDING STRUCTURES ARE CRUMBLED TO DUST
BY THE DECAY OF TIME, OR BY HUMAN OR ELEMENTAL VIOLENCE,
MAY THEN TESTIFY TO A DISTANT POSTERITY THAT
HIS COUNTRYMEN BEGAN ON THAT DAY
TO RAISE AN EFFIGY AND ARCHITECTURAL MONUMENT

TO THE MEMORY OF SIR WALTER SCOTT, BART.,

WHOSE ADMIRABLE WRITINGS WERE THEN ALLOWED
TO HAVE GIVEN MORE DELIGHT AND SUGGESTED BETTER FEELING
TO A LARGER CLASS OF READERS IN EVERY RANK OF SOCIETY
THAN THOSE OF ANY OTHER AUTHOR,
WITH THE EXCEPTION OF SHAKSPEARE ALONE :
AND WHICH WERE THEREFORE THOUGHT LIKELY TO BE REMEMBERED
LONG AFTER THIS ACT OF GRATITUDE,
ON THE PART OF THE FIRST GENERATION OF HIS ADMIRERS,
SHOULD BE FORGOTTEN.

HE WAS BORN AT EDINBURGH 15TH AUGUST 1771 ;
AND DIED AT ABBOTSFORD 21ST SEPTEMBER 1832.

Fine though the structure be, it may be questioned whether the site is the best that could have been chosen ; and whether the Old Town would not have been a more congenial atmosphere for such a memorial. In its present situation, the effect of its mass is to depress and overpower every surrounding object, the Castle Rock itself not excepted. A marble statue of Scott, by Steele, for which the sculptor is to receive £2000, is about to be placed in the Monument.

The Earthen Mound, formed by the deposition of the rubbish accumulated in digging the foundations of the houses in the New Town, is a convenient avenue between the New Town and the Old. Had circumstances admitted of the communication being effected by a handsome arched bridge instead of this shapeless accumulation of earth, another fine feature might have been added to the architecture of the city. Sir Walter Scott, in his "Provincial Antiquities," bitterly denounces the narrowness of spirit

G. M. Kemp

ROYAL INSTITUTION.

which led to the formation of this Mound, speaking of it as "that huge deformity which now extends its lumpish length betwixt Bank Street and Hanover Street, the most hopeless and irremediable error which has been committed in the course of the improvements of Edinburgh, and which, when the view which it has interrupted is contrasted with that which it presents, is, and must be, a subject of constant regret and provocation." At the time Sir Walter penned this invective, the rubbish of which the Mound is composed met the eye in all its naked deformity. The shrubbery which now adorns the slopes has deprived the censure of much of its force, although it can never cease to be lamented that such an opportunity to add another grace to the architecture of the city should be for ever lost. The southern end of this mound is disfigured by wooden structures of all shapes and sizes, erected for exhibitions, dioramas, and panoramas; while the recent establishment of various workshops forbids any present hope that these temporary erections will soon be removed. The Free Church College will occupy a very commanding position beyond these, and it is to be hoped that the design will be worthy of the situation. At the northern extremity of the Mound stands

THE ROYAL INSTITUTION,

one of the handsomest modern buildings of which Edinburgh can boast. The expense of driving the piles upon which this fine structure is built, exceeded £1600. The Royal Society, the Royal Institution for the Encouragement of the Fine Arts in Scotland, and the Board of Trustees for the Improvement of Manufactures, have apartments within its walls. The paintings of the Scottish Artists are exhibited in the Institution during the spring months,* and

---

* The Scottish School of Painting is at present in a most prosperous condition. Two associations have been formed in Edinburgh, by means of which many members of the community, who could in no other way be expected to contribute to the support of Art, are rendered willing and efficient patrons. These associations each possess a numerous body of subscribers. The amount of the annual subscriptions is expended in the purchase of pictures, which are distributed among the members by lottery. The only essential distinction between these two Associations, consists in the purchase of pictures, in the one

the native manufactures are also exhibited here for a short period during the same season. The Royal Society holds its meetings once a fortnight during the winter months, when papers connected with the varied departments of science and learning, falling within the scope of the Society's plan, are read by the several members.

Continuing our walk towards the west, we pass on the right THE NEW CLUB, an association of Noblemen and Gentlemen, partaking of the character of a joint-stock Hotel and Reading Room, for the exclusive accommodation of members. These are elected by ballot, the number being limited to 660. The entrance-money is thirty-five guineas, and the annual subscription five guineas.

The frowning grandeur of the Castle Rock now becomes very imposing, and presents a striking contrast to the tranquil beauty of the green sward and shrubberies of the valley beneath. These pleasure grounds, endowed with natural features of the most varied character, and improved by all the resources of modern horticulture, form one of the chief ornaments of the City.

Upon reaching the west end of Princes Street, ST. JOHN'S CHAPEL and ST. CUTHBERT'S CHURCH will be seen upon the left, the former an elegant structure of the florid Gothic order, the latter an unsightly pile of huge dimensions, with

---

case, being made by a Committee; while, in the other, the purchase is made by the prize-holders themselves.

The advantage of the former plan, appears to consist in the encouragement which it holds out to Artists to devote their talents to the production of works in the higher walks of Art, for which private purchasers are necessarily few in number. The advantage of the second scheme consists, in the first place, in the choice of pictures being devolved upon the prize-holders themselves, whereby each individual is enabled to gratify his personal taste; and, secondly, in the protection it affords to the subscribers, from the danger of unreasonable prices being affixed to their pictures by those Artists who have personal friends on the Committee of Management.

A very general impression prevails, that the prices which, in some instances, have been paid by the Committee of the former Association, are altogether disproportioned to the merit of the pictures bought; and it may reasonably be questioned, whether such liberality is not in effect injurious to the very parties deriving the temporary advantage, by encouraging an exaggerated view of their merit, and a false notion of the value of their works, which must ultimately be highly prejudicial to their professional success.

a double gallery.* St. John's is one of the places of worship belonging to the Scottish Episcopal Communion, and is embellished with all those graces of internal and external architecture, by which the English Church usually distinguishes the edifices dedicated to her religious service.†

Turning to the north, the stranger will now enter Charlotte Square, a spacious quadrangle of excellent houses. In the centre of its western side stands ST. GEORGE'S CHURCH, the handsomest modern place of worship in the Scotch Establishment. Its erection cost £33,000.

After passing along the narrow lane by the side of St. George's, and through Charlotte Place, the stranger will turn to the right, and proceed by Melville Place, Randolph Crescent, and Lynedoch Place, to

THE DEAN BRIDGE.

For this fine bridge Edinburgh is principally indebted to the enterprise of one individual, who contributed largely to the expense of its erection, for the improvement of his property on the northern side of the river. The road-way passes at the great height of 106 feet above the bed of the stream.‡ The arches are four in number, each 96 feet span,

* " A circumstance happened with respect to this Church, and to more than one besides, which singularly illustrates the proverb, that Scotsmen are ever wise behind the hand. When the heritors had chosen the cheapest, or at least the ugliest, plan which was laid before them, had seen it executed, and were at leisure to contemplate the ground cumbered with a great heavy oblong barn, with huge disproportioned windows, they repented of the enormity which they had sanctioned, and endeavoured to repair their error by building a steeple, in a style of ornamented and florid architecture; as if the absurd finery of such an appendage could relieve the heaviness of the principal building, which it only rendered more deformed by the contrast."—SIR WALTER SCOTT's *Provincial Antiquities.*

† The other Episcopal Chapels in Edinburgh are, St. Paul's, York Place, a Gothic structure of singular elegance; St. George's, also in York Place, a small but commodious place of worship; St. James's, Broughton Place; St. Paul's, Carrubber's Close; St. Peter's Roxburgh Place; Trinity Chapel, near the Dean Bridge, and St. Thomas's, Rutland Street.

‡ This is the stream which Richie Moniplies, in the Fortunes of Nigel, represents as a navigable river, superior to the Thames. Strangers, who have seen both, will be enabled to estimate how far Richie's patriotism had obscured his power of memory.

" I suppose you will tell me next," (said Master Heriot) " that you have at Edinburgh as fine a navigable river as the Thames, with all its shipping ?"—" The

the breadth between the parapets being 39 feet, and the total length of the bridge 447 feet.   The design was furnished by the late Mr. Telford.

As no object of any interest occurs on the river side, the stranger may retrace his steps to Randolph Crescent, through which he will pass to Great Stuart Street, Ainslie Place, and

MORAY PLACE.

This is the quarter of the city most celebrated for the architectural magnificence of its buildings.   The ground is the property of the Earl of Moray, and the various streets, squares, and crescents erected upon it, are in accordance with a uniform plan designed by Mr. Gillespie Graham, architect.*   By some persons it has been objected that the simplicity of style, and massiveness of structure, which particularly distinguish these buildings, impart an aspect of solemnity and gloom repugnant to the character of domestic architecture.   Even the harmony of design and uniformity of plan have offended some critics.   " The New Town of Edinburgh," says Dr. James Johnson, in his work entitled ' The Recess,' " is beautifully monotonous, and magnificently dull."   Until philosophers shall succeed in establishing a uniform standard of taste, it will be vain to contend with such cavillers ; we may only observe, that the massive dignity of the architecture in this quarter of the city, has called forth the admiration of the large majority of intelligent visiters.   Nor is the substantial comfort of the dwellings to be overlooked.   The walls are of the most solid and durable masonry ; both the building materials and workmanship being of the best description.   The house, No. 24, which the stranger passes in following the line of route we have adopted, is the residence of Lord Jeffrey.

The rent of the houses in Moray Place, varies from £140 to £160, and in Ainslie Place, from £100 to £130.

Thames !" exclaimed Richie, in a tone of ineffable contempt, " God bless your honour's judgment, we have at Edinburgh the Water of Leith and the Nor-Loch !"

* The annual *feu-duty* or ground-rent of the houses, in this quarter of the city, varies from 20s. to 40s. per foot of frontage.

Leaving Moray Place by Darnaway Street, the stranger is introduced to another *suite* of those pleasure grounds, which tend so much to beautify the city. Ascending the first opening on the right (Wemyss Place), we reach Queen Street, which overlooks the pleasure grounds. Through the openings formed by the streets running to the north, a noble prospect is obtained of the Firth of Forth, the shores of Fife, and the Ochil Hills, and in some states of the atmosphere, the peaks of the Grampians may be seen in the distance. Proceeding eastward along Queen Street, the first opening on the right is Castle Street, in which street the house numbered 39, was the town residence of Sir Walter Scott. The house is now occupied by Professor Napier, editor of the Edinburgh Review. Continuing his progress up Castle Street, the stranger reaches George's Street, and looking eastward, he will observe

THE PITT STATUE

occupying the spot where George's Street is intersected by Frederick Street. The statue is executed by Chantrey, and is regarded as a very favourable specimen of his bronzes. Still continuing to proceed eastward, THE ASSEMBLY ROOMS will be seen upon the right. Their external appearance is plain and unpretending, the only approach to ornament being the four Doric columns, doing duty as a portico in the front of the building. In these Rooms are held the public Assemblies and Concerts,* and other meetings of

---

* Although there is no want either of taste or capacity for music in Scotland, the inhabitants of Edinburgh cannot be said to be distinguished for their practical devotion to the art. Vocal music in parts, or concerted instrumental music, is rarely met with in private society; the Glee Club, and the associations formed from time to time, for orchestral music, being almost wholly dependent upon the professional musicians. The higher styles of ecclesiastical music may be said to be unknown, except from the performances at the three musical festivals held at the distant intervals of 1815, 1824, and 1844. The organ is excluded both from the churches of the Establishment and from the chapels of the most numerous of the Dissenting bodies, and in few congregations is there even a band of professional singers. The psalmody is, for the most part, led by the precentor alone, who is followed by the whole congregation, vociferating the melody, "without remorse or mitigation of voice." The want of chorus-singers, arising from the abject state of sacred music, is a formidable obstacle to holding a musical festival in the city; and although efforts have been making, by some

various kinds.   The Music-room, a recent addition to the
original edifice, forms the largest of the apartments, and is
fitted up in a style of great splendour.   It measures 108
feet long, by 9_ broad.   The courtesy of Messrs. Burn and
Bryce, the architects, has enabled us to give a ground plan,

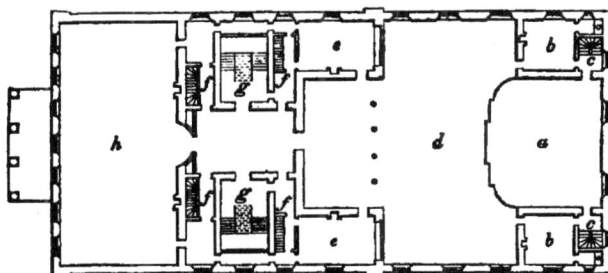

a, Orchestra.
b b, Musicians' Rooms.
c c, Staircases.
d, Music Hall.
e e. Ladies' Robing Room.
f f, Private Staircases.
g g g, Entrance Stairs and Lobby.
h, Assembly Room.

exhibiting the proportions of this noble room, the expense
of which, including the organ, exceeded £10,000.   The
principal Ballroom is 92 feet long, 42 feet wide, and 40
feet high.   There are also various other apartments of
smaller dimensions.   A little to the east, where Hanover
Street intersects George street, stands

GEORGE IV. STATUE,

also executed by Chantrey, but wholly unworthy of the

of the professional vocalists, to discipline a body of singers to supply this want,
by which a considerable measure of proficiency has been attained, Edinburgh
is still immeasurably behind the cathedral towns, and even some of the manufacturing towns of England, in that indispensable requisite of the oratorio—an
efficient chorus.

The introduction of the ' Wilhem *Method*,' and the ' Mainzerian *System*,'
must be admitted to have diffused, to a considerable extent, an elementary
knowledge of music among the middle and lower ranks; and so far, they are
deserving of praise.   Whether the temporary enthusiasm kindled by these in-
structors of " the million," will result in a real advance of musical skill and
science, is still to be determined.

The Professional Society of Edinburgh includes, among its members, many
highly respectable musicians; but the more liberal encouragement held out in
London, to the first order of talent, deprives the city of most of its best professors in this as well as other walks of art.

fame of that gifted artist.   There is gross affectation in the head, in the manner of extending the sceptre, and, in fact, in the whole air of the figure.   These defects, when named to him by a friend, were frankly acknowledged by Chantrey, who stated that, in his original design, both the head and the sceptred hand were in very different attitudes, but that he had been compelled to alter them to their present position by the express command of his sovereign.   The fine building forming the north-east corner of the intersecting streets is the Edinburgh and Glasgow Bank; and, on the opposite side of George's Street, in the house No. 24, is the Museum of the Antiquarian Society, to which strangers are admitted by an order from any of the members.   Among the relics of antiquity preserved in this collection may be mentioned the colours carried by the Covenanters during the civil war; the stool which Jenny Geddes, in her zeal against Prelacy, launched at the head of the Bishop of Edinburgh in St. Giles's Church; and the *Maiden,* or Scottish Guillotine, with which the Earl of Morton, the Marquis of Argyle, Sir Robert Spottiswood, and many other distinguished persons, were beheaded. *

Continuing our progress eastward, ST. ANDREW's CHURCH stands upon the left.   It possesses a portico, supported by four Corinthian columns, and a handsome spire rising to the height of 168 feet, remarkable for its lightness of design and elegance of proportion.   The showy building on the opposite side is the Commercial Bank of Scotland.

THE MELVILLE MONUMENT,

which graces the centre of St. Andrew's Square, was erected to the memory of the late Lord Melville.   It rises 136

* It is very generally believed that it was the Earl of Morton who introduced the Maiden into Scotland. This opinion, however, has been proved to be erroneous, entries in the Council Records showing that it was in use long before his time.   Michael Wing-the-wind, in " The Abbot," refers to this instrument during his conversation with Adam Woodcock in Holyrood Palace.   " Herod's daughter," says Michael, "who did such execution with her foot and ancle, danced not men's heads off more cleanly than this Maiden of Morton.   'Tis an axe, man—an axe, which falls of itself like a sash window, and never gives the headsman the trouble to wield it."

feet in height, to which the statue adds other 14 feet. The
design is that of the Trajan column, the shaft being fluted,
instead of ornamented with sculpture as in the ancient
model.

In the third flat (*Anglice* floor) of the house in the north-
west corner of the Square (No. 21), Lord Brougham was
born; and the house directly opposite, in the south-west
corner, with entrance from St. David Street, was the residence of David Hume.

In the centre of the east side of the Square, standing
apart from the other buildings, is the ROYAL BANK. In
front of the Bank is an equestrian STATUE of the EARL OF
HOPETOUN.

Passing through St. Andrew's Street, we again reach
Princes Street, and terminate our Third Walk by returning to the Register House.

WALK FOURTH.*

ROYAL TERRACE—LEITH WALK—(LEITH—NEWHAVEN)—INVER-LEITH ROW—EXPERIMENTAL GARDENS—BOTANIC GARDENS.

IN the three preceding Walks we have exhausted most of
the objects of interest in the city; and if the stranger
should with them close his perambulations, he sacrifices
very little worthy of notice. But in order to render our
Hand-book more complete, we find it necessary to give a
short description of Leith, and a passing notice of Newhaven. By omitting both of these places, the circuit of
the present walk is very materially abridged, without any
corresponding diminution of its interest. We shall therefore print the description of Leith and Newhaven in a
smaller type, that the reader may more readily distinguish
the portion of the text which relates to them, and which
may be read or passed over at pleasure.

Proceeding from the Register House down Greenside

* This Walk is coloured *blue* on the Map.

Street, nothing worthy of remark occurs till we reach the head of LEITH WALK, one of the most splendid roads in the kingdom. Turning to the right at this point, a noble range of buildings, called the ROYAL TERRACE, partly obscured by an unsightly church of recent erection, will be seen occupying the northern side of the Calton Hill. These buildings command a magnificent prospect of the Firth of Forth and the opposite shores, with all the interjacent country.

Tourists proposing to visit Leith will continue their progress down Leith Walk. Omnibuses ply between Edinburgh and Leith every quarter of an hour; and as there is nothing of peculiar interest to be seen upon the way, time will be saved by taking advantage of one of these vehicles as they pass.

LEITH,

The sea-port of Edinburgh, is distant about a mile and a half from the centre of the metropolis. It was not only the first, but, for several centuries, the only port in Scotland, traces of its existence being found in documents of the 12th century. During its early history, few places have so often been the scene of military operations. In 1313, all the vessels in the harbour were burned by the English, and in 1410 a similar act of vengeance was repeated. "In 1544, the town was plundered and burned, its pier destroyed, and its shipping carried off, by the Earl of Hertford, to avenge the insult which Henry VIII. conceived the Scotch had offered him by refusing to betroth their young queen, Mary, to his son Prince Edward. Three years subsequent to this, it was again plundered and burned by the English, under Hertford, then Duke of Somerset, and its whole shipping, together with all that in the Forth, entirely annihilated by the English admiral, Lord Clinton. Four years after this, the town was fortified by Desse, a French general, who came over with 6000 men to assist the Queen-Regent in suppressing the Reformation. On the completion of these fortifications, which consisted in throwing a strong and high wall, with towers at intervals, around the town, the Queen-Regent took up her residence there, and, surrounded with her countrymen, hoped to be able to maintain her authority in the kingdom. These measures, however, had only the effect of widening the breach between her and her subjects, till they finally took up arms, and besieged her in her stronghold. In October 1559, the

Lords of the Congregation invested Leith with an army, but, after various ineffectual attempts to gain access to the town by scaling the walls, they were driven back with great slaughter by a desperate sally of the besieged.

"In the month of April in the succeeding year, the forces of the Congregation again invested the town, being now aided by an army of 6000 men, under Lord Grey of Wilton, despatched to their assistance by Elizabeth. On this occasion, the contest was protracted and sanguinary. For two months, during which the town suffered dreadfully from famine, as well as from the more violent casualties of war, the struggle continued, without any decisive advantage being gained by either side; at the end of that period, both parties being heartily tired of the contest, a treaty was entered into, by which it was stipulated that the French should evacuate the kingdom, that they should be allowed to embark unmolested, and that the English army should, upon the same day, begin its march to England. Immediately after the conclusion of this treaty, the walls of Leith were demolished by order of the Town Council of Edinburgh, and no vestige of them now remains."* In 1561, when Queen Mary came from France to take possession of the throne of her ancestors, she landed upon the pier of Leith; but of this pier no vestiges now remain. In 1650, the town was occupied by Cromwell, who exacted an assessment from the inhabitants. In 1715, the citadel was taken by a party of the adherents of the Stuart family, but, upon being threatened by the Duke of Argyle, it was speedily evacuated. George IV., upon visiting Scotland in 1822, landed at a spot a little to the north of the New Drawbridge, where an inscribed plate has been inserted in the pavement to commemorate the event.

Leith presents few antiquities of any interest. Among those which remain, may be mentioned the Parish Church of South Leith, a Gothic edifice, built previous to the year 1496, and the old church of North Leith, founded in 1493. In the Links, upon the south-east side of the Town, may be seen several mounds, raised for the purpose of planting cannon, by the besieging army, in 1560.

The town "is for the most part irregularly and confusedly built, and a great portion of it is extremely filthy, crowded, and inelegant. Some parts of it, again, are the reverse of this, being spacious, cleanly, and handsome. Such are two or three of the modern streets, and various ranges of private dwellings, erected of late years on the eastern and western skirts of the town.

"The modern public buildings worthy of remark are the Exchange Buildings, a large and elegant structure in the Grecian style of architecture, containing a spacious and handsome assembly-room, a commodious hotel, and public reading-room. The expense of the

* *Encyclopædia Britannica*, Seventh Edition. Article LEITH.

erection was £16,000. The Custom-House, situated in North Leith, is also a very handsome building ; it was erected in 1812, at an expense of £12,000. The premises of the Leith branch of the National Bank occupy a neat little edifice, erected in 1805-6. The New Court House, by far the most elegant building in the town, forms altogether, whether the chasteness of the design or the neatness of the workmanship be considered, a very favourable specimen of modern architecture on a small scale." * The Parish Church of North Leith is a handsome though unpretending structure, surmounted by a tasteful spire ;—the living is one of the best in the Church of Scotland.

The chief manufactures are ropes and cordage, sail-cloth, bottles, soap, and candles. There are several breweries and a distillery, and ship-building is carried on to a considerable extent.

Leith is the most important naval station on the east coast of Scotland, and a considerable traffic is carried on at the port, the gross revenues of which average above £20,000 a-year: but " it is universally admitted that the harbour, in its present state, is very inadequate to the accommodation of the trade of Edinburgh and of the Firth of Forth, especially to the important branches of steam navigation and the ferry communication between the opposite shores of the Firth." † Large sums have been expended, from time to time, with the view of improving the harbour and docks, but they are still considered inadequate to the trade. Government, in the arrangement of the affairs of the City of Edinburgh, by an Act passed in July 1838, made provision for making extensive improvements in the harbour, a portion of which have been carried into effect. The pier, which is a fine work, forms an excellent promenade.

Leith, with Musselburgh, Portobello, and Newhaven, returns a Member to Parliament. The population amounted, in 1841, to 26,026.

NEWHAVEN

Is a small fishing village, situate about a mile farther up the Forth than Leith. It possesses a stone and a chain pier, but neither the one nor the other has sufficient depth of water to admit of the approach of steamers of large size. The London boats, accordingly, now land and take on board their passengers at Granton, a little farther up the Firth, where a low-water pier has recently been constructed by the Duke of Buccleuch. It was at this pier that Her Majesty, on her recent gracious visit, landed and re-embarked.

* *Encyclopædia Britannica.*
† Parliamentary Report, July 1835.

The inhabitants of Newhaven are a laborious and hardy race. They form a distinct community, rarely intermarrying with any other class. The male inhabitants are all almost fishermen, and the females are constantly occupied in vending the produce of their husbands' industry in the markets or streets of Edinburgh.

When provoked, the *fishwives* display resources of abuse quite equal to their Billingsgate contemporaries. They are also celebrated for the exorbitant prices they demand for their goods, not unfrequently asking three or four times the sum they finally consent to take. Other traders, when purchasers are cheapening their wares, or offering a price which they consider much below their value, are therefore in the habit of saying, "What! would you mak' a fishwife o' me?" Although a very hard-working people, they rarely indulge in an excessive use of ardent spirits. The quantity they consume is, indeed, very considerable, but the prodigious loads with which they are burdened, may be allowed to form some apology for the occasional use of such a stimulus, and their constant exercise in the open air appears to prevent any injurious effects from following the indulgence. They are for the most part, tidy in their habits, and, in these days, when one dull uniformity pervades the dress of all classes, it is refreshing to the lover of the picturesque to contemplate the gaudy garb of the rosy, hearty, mirth-making fishwife.

The Edinburgh, Leith, and Granton Railway affords the means of returning to Edinburgh in seven minutes. At the Newhaven end, the terminus is at Trinity, a little to the west of the village, and there is another at Granton pier. At Edinburgh, the temporary terminus is at the foot of Scotland Street. From this point, the tourist will proceed in a straight line by Dublin Street and Duke

Street to St. Andrew Square, where he may visit the statue of Sir Walter Scott, described on page 82, and conclude his walk as there pointed out.*

Returning to the head of Broughton Street, the neat Gothic front of the ROMAN CATHOLIC CHAPEL will be observed on the west side of the street, close by the Adelphi Theatre. At the end of York Place stands ST. PAUL'S CHAPEL, an elegant Gothic structure, one of the places of worship of the Episcopal Communion. Continuing to proceed down Broughton Street, the stranger will next pass the chapel of the sect called Rowites, whose vagaries made so much noise in the religious world some years ago. Immediately contiguous to this place of worship, is ALBANY STREET CHAPEL, belonging to the Independents. At the corner of Broughton Place is ST. JAMES'S CHAPEL, an Episcopal place of worship, and at the east end of the same street is the principal chapel of the United Secession, the most numerous dissenting body in Scotland, with the exception of the Free Church, which, although essentially a community of Dissenters, is not yet reconciled to the name. Continuing to proceed northwards, by Mansfield Place and Bellevue Crescent, ST. MARY'S CHURCH will be seen terminating the northern extremity of the latter street. It is one of the neatest of the Edinburgh Churches, possessing a portico and spire, respectable in design and of excellent masonry. Immediately beyond the Church is the entrance to the Newhaven Railway. At the northern end of Claremont Street—(the range of lofty houses opposite St. Mary's Church)—are the ZOOLOGICAL GARDENS. They are pleasantly situated, and laid out with good taste. Although the collection is only of recent formation, it is already con-

---

* Those tourists who visit Leith and Newhaven, and do not return by railway, will require to invert the order of the subsequent pages of this walk, so that the succession of the objects described may accord with the progress of their route. The following will be the order in which the objects will occur, supposing the stranger to return the direct road to Edinburgh :— BOTANIC GARDENS, CANONMILLS, ST. MARY'S CHURCH, ST. JAMES'S CHAPEL, ALBANY STREET CHAPEL, ST. PAUL'S CHAPEL, ROMAN CATHOLIC CHAPEL.

siderable, and is constantly receiving additions. The adventurous spirit which carries Scotsmen to the remotest corners of the globe, has tended in no small degree to enrich the collection, many of the fine specimens which it contains having been presented by natives of Scotland travelling, or permanently resident in foreign countries.

From St. Mary's Church the road now declines towards the village of Canonmills. After passing this squalid suburb, * the stranger crosses the Water of Leith, by Canonmills Bridge. Upon his left he will observe some massive and singular looking buildings, erected, some years ago, by an Oil Gas Company. The speculation was soon abandoned as an unprofitable one, and the buildings are now occupied as warehouses. At the further end of Howard Place is situated the CALEDONIAN HORTICULTURAL SOCIETY'S GARDEN, a beautiful and interesting piece of ground, containing 10 imperial acres, and commanding one of the finest views of Edinburgh from the north. Strangers are admitted by orders from members of the Society, or on application to Mr. James M'Nab, the Curator of the garden.†

* The general character of the place has one redeeming feature. Dr. Neill's pleasant suburban residence, "like a jewel of gold in a swine's snout," is situated on the confines of the village. The proprietor is a distinguished botanist and naturalist, his gardens displaying a variety of botanical rarities, as well as many choice living specimens of interesting objects in the animal kingdom.

† The Caledonian Horticultural Society was established in 1809, since which period large sums have been annually expended in the production of new fruits, flowers, and vegetables, and in perfecting and bringing to maturity those already introduced. In the centre of the garden stands a spacious and elegant hall for the meetings of the Society, adorned with a marble bust, by Steele, of the Secretary, Dr. Neill; and in front of the hall, a fine lawn is laid out, as a promenade ground; where several exhibitions of exotic plants annually take place, attended by all the beauty and fashion of the city. The garden is arranged into various compartments, having soils suited for the different collections placed in them. The raised belts which surround and intersect the garden are occupied as an Arboretum, and contain authentic named specimens of all the newer kinds of trees and shrubs. There is an Apple orchard containing specimens of upwards of 900 named varieties; and a pear orchard, containing upwards of 450 named varieties. The collections also contain 85 varieties of Plums, 25 of Cherries, 27 of Currants, and 30 of Raspberries. The kinds of Strawberries are very numerous, extending to no fewer than 120 sorts, and of Gooseberries the collection is still greater, exceeding 400 kinds. One of the chief objects of the garden is also to exhibit the most approved kinds of culinary vegetables in a growing state, duly tallied, so as to form a school for the infor-

Upon the same side of Inverleith Road, considerably farther along, is the ROYAL BOTANIC GARDEN. To this noble garden, strangers are freely admitted, but the hot-houses are open to the public only on Saturday, between the hours of twelve and four.

The garden embraces an extent of 14½ English acres, and presents every facility for prosecuting the study of Botany.*

It is surrounded by trees on the west, south, and eastern

mation of those visiting the garden; and to test such novelties or rarities as may from time to time be recommended, to make trial of various manures, and to exhibit different modes of culture.

* Immediately upon his entrance to the grounds, the stranger is struck with the luxuriance and vigour of the evergreens, to the cultivation of which Mr. Wm. M'Nab, the able curator, has devoted much attention. On the southern side of the garden there is a large collection of hardy plants arranged according to the Natural System of Jussieu, such as *ferns, grasses, labiate, cruciform, leguminous, umbelliferous,* and *composite plants, &c.* Close to this collection is a small pond containing rushes, water lilies, &c., and a ditch containing those plants which thrive best in such a situation. To the north of this arrangement is a collection of British plants, arranged according to the Linnæan or artificial system, with the name attached to each species. On the eastern side are the plants indigenous to Scotland, and on the west, a few which are found in England and Ireland but not in Scotland. A little to the east of this British arrangement, is a collection of roses. Proceeding northwards, we come to a general collection of hardy evergreens, chiefly exotic; to the east of which is a collection of Medical plants, with the names and natural orders attached. We then reach the Greenhouses. These contain a large collection of exotics, which thrive admirably. The western division contains *heaths, epacrideæ, dryandras, proteas, grevilleas, diosmas, &c.,* while in the eastern division, we have a stove with a northern exposure, in which *epiphytes* are cultivated with great success. The peculiar forms of these plants, and their remarkable mode of growth, attract the attention of all.

In the other greenhouses of the front range, there are many interesting plants; among these may be noticed *Plantains,* which bear fruit well, *Papaw tree, Pitcher-plant, Papyrus, Indian rubber fig, cacti, cinnamon, tea plants, camphor tree, Astrapæa,* some of the *Fig* tribe growing suspended in the air, *amaryllides, arums, euphorbias, &c.* In front of this range of houses is a piece of ground on which many of the plants of warmer regions, such as *palms, acacias, &c.,* are cultivated in the open air, being carefully protected during winter. Behind these houses is a smaller range in which numerous seedlings are cultivated, and a large Palm-house, about 45 feet high, in which are found *Plantains* and *Bananas, Sago Palms, Fan Palms, European Palms, Cabbage Palms, Date Palms, Coco Nut Trees, Sugar Cane, Bamboos, Screw Pine, &c.* The houses are heated partly by hot water and partly by steam. From the top of the boiler-house there is a very fine view of Edinburgh. Against the high northern wall of the garden, having a south aspect, many valuable exotics are trained, as, *Magnolias, Acacias, Edwardsias, Camellias, Myrtles, Eucalypti, &c.* On the north aspect of the south boundary wall, the Damask Rhododendrons are trained, and flower freely every year.

F

sides, and among these, there are some of considerable interest. Many of them were removed, in their full grown
state, from the former garden in Leith Walk, and under
the judicious management of Mr. M'Nab, they have all
succeeded. To the west of the general European collection
is an old Yew, which has been twice transplanted, having
been transferred, first, from the Old Physic Gardens, below
the North Bridge, to the garden in Leith Walk, and afterwards removed to its present situation. Beside the collection of British plants is a magnetic observatory, superintended by the Professor of Natural Philosophy. The
class-room of the Professor of Botany, and the house of the
superintendent, are situated on the right-hand side of the
entrance. A little further down the road, on the opposite
side, is the entrance to the burying-ground of the Edinburgh Cemetery Company. The grounds are laid out with
much taste, and the company has conferred an important
benefit on the community by affording the means of sepulture in such a spot at extremely moderate charges.

In returning, the stranger may vary his route by turning
to the right, immediately after recrossing Canonmills
Bridge, and proceeding by Huntly Street, Brandon Street,
Pitt Street, and Dundas Street, to Queen Street. Turning
to the left along Queen Street, he will pass St. David's
Street on the right, and proceed up St. Andrew's Street, the
next opening on the same side of the way. On the left hand,
upon entering St. Andrew's Square, he may step into the
passage No. 31, at the end of which, immediately in front
of the door to the premises of Mr. Cadell the publisher, is
placed a statue of Sir Walter Scott cut in freestone by
Greenshields, a self-taught Lanarkshire artist. The like-
ness is very striking, and the unaffected character and
homely manner of the great novelist are so faithfully expressed, that a friend of Sir Walter's, upon seeing it, exclaimed, " This is not a statue of the man, but his petri-
faction."

Resuming his progress along the side of the Square, the
stranger will again reach Princes Street, and, turning to
the left, will regain the Register House, thus terminating
our Fourth Walk.

Map of the
NS OF EDINBURGH
Comprehending the Country
TEN MILES ROUND.

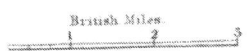

British Miles
1   2   3

The objects of interest in the City being now exhausted, we proceed to introduce the tourist to some spots in the vicinity more particularly worthy of notice. Among these we may observe that Roslin is regarded as the most attractive, although we have commenced with Habbie's Howe, as the best geographical arrangement.

ENVIRONS OF EDINBURGH.

HABBIE'S HOWE.

A VERY delightful excursion may be made from Edinburgh to Newhall, distant about twelve miles, supposed, with great probability, to be the scene of Allan Ramsay's celebrated pastoral, "The Gentle Shepherd."

Leaving Edinburgh by Bruntsfield Links, the tourist passes on the right MERCHISTON CASTLE, the birth-place of the celebrated Napier, the inventor of Logarithms. A little further on is the village of Morningside, and a number of villas and country boxes. Two miles from Edinburgh is the Hermitage of Braid, (J. Gordon, Esq. of Clunie,) situated at the bottom of a narrow and thickly wooded dell, through which a small rivulet, called the Braid Burn, strays. Braid once belonged to a family called Fairly, and the Laird of Braid, during the Reformation, was a personal friend and zealous defender of John Knox. The road now skirts the rocky eminences called the Hills of Braid, which command a most beautiful view of the Scottish metropolis, with the Firth of Forth, its islands, and the shores of Fife in the background. The more northern side, called Blackford Hill, the property of Richard Trotter, Esq. of Mortonhall, is the spot mentioned in "Marmion."

> " Still on the spot Lord Marmion stay'd,
> For fairer scene he ne'er survey'd," &c.

The space of ground which extends from the bottom of Blackford Hill to the suburbs of Edinburgh was formerly denominated the Borough Moor. We are informed by historians that it was studded with magnificent oaks at the time when James IV. arrayed his army upon it, previous to his departure on the fatal expedition which terminated in the Battle of Flodden. The HARE STONE, in which the Royal Standard was fixed, is still to be seen built into the wall, which runs along the side of the footpath at the place called Boroughmoor-head. At about half a mile's distance to the southward, there is another stone called the Buck Stone, upon which the proprietor of the barony of Penny-cuik is bound, by his charter, to place himself, and to wind three blasts of a horn, when the king shall visit the Borough Moor. On the right, at some distance, are Dreghorn, (A. Trotter, Esq.,) the village of Colinton, delightfully situated at the bottom of the Pentland Hills, and Colinton House, (Lord Dunfermline.) About five miles from Edinburgh, on the southern slope of the Pentland Hills, is WOODHOUSELEE, the seat of James Tytler, Esq., surrounded by fine woods. The ancient house of the same name, once the property of Bothwellhaugh, the assassin of the Regent Murray, was four miles distant from the present site. Woodhouselee had been bestowed upon Sir James Ballenden, one of the Regent's favourites, who seized the house, and turned out Lady Bothwellhaugh naked, in a cold night, into the open fields, where, before next morning, she became furiously mad.* The ruins of the mansion are still to be seen in a hollow glen beside the river. Popular report tenants them with the restless ghost of the lady. The road now passes the hamlet of Upper Howgate, and a little farther on Glencorse Church, embosomed in a wood. On the right is the vale of Glencorse, watered by a little rill, called Logan Water, or, more commonly, Glencorse Burn. The head of this valley is supposed by some to be the scene of Allan Ramsay's pastoral drama, " The Gentle Shepherd," but the appearance of the scenery, as well as the absence of all the

* This event forms the subject of Sir Walter Scott's fine ballad of " Cadyow Castle," which will be found quoted entire in the SEVENTH TOUR.

localities noticed by Ramsay, render this opinion extremely improbable. The sequestered pastoral character of this valley, however, renders it well worthy of a visit. After crossing Glencorse Burn, the road passes House-of-Muir, in the neighbourhood of which is the place where the Covenanters were defeated, 28th November 1666. The insurrection, which ended in this skirmish, began in Dumfries-shire, where Sir James Turner was employed to levy the arbitrary fines imposed for not attending the Episcopal churches. The people rose, seized his person, disarmed his soldiers, and, having continued together, resolved to march towards Edinburgh, expecting to be joined by their friends in that quarter. In this they were disappointed, and being now diminished to half their numbers, they drew up on the Pentland Hills, at a place called Rullion Green. They were commanded by one Wallace, and here they waited the approach of General Dalziel of Binns, who, having marched by Calder to meet them on the Lanark road, and finding that, by passing through Colinton, they had got to the other side of the hills, crossed the mountains, and approached them. The Covenanters were drawn up in a very strong position, and withstood two charges of Dalziel's cavalry, but upon the third shock they were broken, and utterly dispersed. There were about fifty killed, and as many made prisoners. Passing through the village of Silver Burn, the road reaches

NEWHALL,

on the banks of the North Esk, about three miles from Pennycuik House, and twelve south-west from Edinburgh. Newhall is now the property of Robert Brown, Esq. At the era of Ramsay's drama, it belonged to Dr. Alexander Pennycuik, a poet and antiquary. In 1703, it passed into the hands of Sir David Forbes, a distinguished lawyer; and, in Ramsay's time, was the property of Mr. John Forbes, son to Sir David, and cousin-german to the celebrated President Forbes of Culloden. The scenery around Newhall answers most minutely to the description in the drama. Near the house, on the north side of the vale, there is a

crag (called the Harbour Crag, from having afforded refuge
to the Covenanters,) which corresponds exactly with the
first scene of the first act:

" Beneath the south side of a craggy bield,
   Where crystal springs the halesome waters yield."

Farther up the vale, and behind the house, there is a
spot beside the burn, which corresponds to the description
of the second scene:

" A flowr'y howm between twa verdant braes,
   Where lasses used to wash and spread their claes ;
   A trottin' burnie wimplin' through the ground,
   Its channel pebbles shining smooth and round."

A little farther up the vale there is a place called the
Howe Burn, where the stream forms a small cascade, and
where the scenery in every respect corresponds with the
exquisite description of the spot called " Habbie's Howe."

" Gae farer up the burn to Habbie's Howe,
   Where a' the sweets o' spring and summer grow,
   There, 'tween twa birks, out ower a little linn,
   The water fa's and mak's a singand din ;
   A pule, breast deep, beneath as clear as glass,
   Kisses wi' easy whirls the bordering grass."

Still farther up the vale, at a place called the Carlops,*
a tall rock shoots up on each side. At this spot, near an
old withered solitary oak tree, is the site of Mause's cottage,
described in the second scene of the second act:

" The open field, a cottage in the glen,
   An auld wife spinnin' at the sunny end.
   At a sma' distance, by a blasted tree,
   Wi' faulded arms and half raised look, ye see
                    Bauldy his lane."

PENNYCUIK HOUSE, the seat of Sir George Clerk, Bart.,
is well worthy of a visit. The neighbouring scenery is extremely beautiful, and the pleasure-grounds are highly ornamented. The house contains an extensive and excellent
collection of paintings, with a number of Roman antiquities

---

* A contraction of Carline's Loups, in consequence, it is said, of a witch or
carline having been frequently observed to leap, by night, from the rock at one
side over to that at the other.

found in Britain, and, amongst other curiosities, the buff-coat worn by Dundee at the battle of Killiecrankie. The principal apartment, called Ossian's Hall, has a ceiling beautifully decorated with paintings by Runciman.

ROSLIN.

Another interesting scene, visited more frequently than any other by the inhabitants of Edinburgh, is ROSLIN CHAPEL, situated about seven miles from the city, on the banks of the North Esk. The vale of Roslin is one of those beautiful and sequestered dells which so often occur in Scotland, abounding with all the romantic varieties of cliff, copsewood, and waterfall. Its beautiful Gothic Chapel is one of the most entire and exquisitely decorated speci-mens of ecclesiastical architecture in Scotland. It was founded, in 1446, by William St. Clair, Earl of Orkney, and Lord of Roslin. At the Revolution of 1688, part of it was defaced by a mob from Edinburgh, but it was repaired in the following century by General St. Clair. The late Earl of Rosslyn, some years ago, undertook the restoration of its more dilapidated parts, and the present Earl still continues the repairs, with scrupulous attention to preserve the ori-ginal character of the structure. " This building," says Mr. Britton, " may be pronounced unique, and I am confi-dent it will be found curious, elaborate, and singularly in-teresting. The Chapel of King's College, St. George, and Henry VII., are all conformable to the styles of the respec-tive ages when they were erected ; and these styles display a gradual advancement in lightness and profusion of orna-ment : but the Chapel of Roslyn combines the solidity of the Norman with the minute decorations of the latest spe-cies of the Tudor age. It is impossible to designate the architecture of this building by any given or familiar term : for the variety and eccentricity of its parts are not to be defined by any words of common acceptation." The nave is bold and lofty, enclosed, as usual, by side aisles, the pil-lars and arches of which display a profusion of ornament, executed in the most beautiful manner. The " Prentice's Pillar" in particular, with its finely sculptured foliage, is a piece of exquisite workmanship. It is said that the master-builder of the Chapel, being unable to execute the design of this pillar from the plans in his possession, proceeded to Rome, that he might see a column of a similar description which had been executed in that city. During his absence, his apprentice proceeded with the execution of the design, and, upon the master's return, he found this finely ornamented column completed. Stung with envy at this proof of the superior ability of his apprentice, he struck him a blow with his mallet, and killed him on the spot. Upon the architrave uniting the Prentice's Pillar to a smaller one, is the following sententious inscription from the book of Apocryphal Scripture, called Esdras ;—" *Forte est vinum, fortior est rex, fortiores sunt mulieres ; super omnia vincit veritas.*" Beneath the Chapel lie the Barons of Roslin, all of whom, till the time of James VII., were buried in complete armour.*

* This circumstance, as well as the superstitious belief that, on the night before the death of any of these barons, the chapel appeared in flames, is beautifully described by Sir Walter Scott, in his exquisite ballad of Rosabelle :

O listen, listen, ladies gay !
　No haughty feats of arms I tell ;
Soft is the note, and sad the lay,
　That mourns the lovely Rosabelle.

". Moor, moor the barge, ye gallant crew !
　And, gentle ladye, deign to stay !
Rest thee in Castle Ravensheuch,
　Nor tempt the stormy firth to day.

" The blackening wave is edged with white :
　To inch and rock the sea-mews fly ;
The fishers have heard the Water-Sprite,
　Whose screams forbode that wreck is nigh.

" Last night the gifted Seer did view
　A wet shroud swathed round ladye gay !
Then stay thee, Fair, in Ravensheuch ;
　Why cross the gloomy firth to day ?"—

" 'Tis not because Lord Lindesay's heir
　To-night at Roslin leads the ball,
But that my ladye-mother there
　Sits lonely in her castle-hall.

" 'Tis not because the ring they ride—
　And Lindesay at the ring rides well—
But that my sire the wine will chide,
　If 'tis not fill'd by Rosabelle."

O'er Roslin, all that dreary night,
　A wondrous blaze was seen to gleam ;

'Twas broader than the watch-fire's light,
　And redder than the bright moon-beam.

It glared on Roslin's castled rock,
　It ruddied all the copsewood glen ;
'Twas seen from Dryden's groves of oak,
　And seen from cavern'd Hawthornden.

Seem'd all on fire that chapel proud,
　Where Roslin's chiefs uncoffin'd lie,
Each baron, for a sable shroud,
　Sheathed in his iron panoply.

Seem'd all on fire within, around,
　Deep sacristy and altar's pale ;
Shone every pillar foliage bound,
　And glimmer'd all the dead men's mail.

Blazed battlement and pinnet high,
　Blazed every rose-carved buttress fair—
So still they blaze, when fate is nigh
　The lordly line of high St. Clair.

There are twenty of Roslin's barons bold
　Lie buried within that proud chapelle ;
Each one the holy vault doth hold—
　But the sea holds lovely Rosabelle.

And each St. Clair was buried there,
　With candle, with book, and with knell ;
But the sea caves rung, and the wild winds
　The dirge of lovely Rosabelle.　　　[sung,

...descendant of the old stock, the lineal de...
...of the high race who first founded the pile, and...
...the last of their long line. He was captain of the
...Company of Archers, and Hereditary Grand Master
...of the Masons, by his title; the male descended...
...James Sandilands, Clerk, father of the present Earl
of ..., worthily represents the family.

The ancient mansion of Roslin was the scene of a celebrated combat, on the 24th February 1302, in which the
gallant Sir John Comyn, the Guardian of the kingdom, and
Simon Fraser, attacked and defeated three divisions of the
English on the same day.

The following lines, which I venture only as a curiosity, the absence
of the subject of them scarcely affecting Pleasance and Bonnybog, Wednesday, being a day on which all the three character bemg, and written
and curiously hang up in the spot for the purpose.

        They bid me sit in thee
        Ere with a welcome to me...
        Their spirits round about me play
        Remind me of a former day
        Why pensive and thy solemn...
        No more among the buy...
        With power o'er thousand's own...
        Would spur the mind about...
        At last, a thought that most in trifle,
        Bore pleasure and ambition down...

There is no stated fee for admission to the Chapel, but the exhibiter expects a small gratuity.*

The mouldering ruin of ROSLIN CASTLE, with its tremendous triple tier of vaults, stands upon a peninsular rock, overhanging the picturesque glen of the Esk, and is accessible only by a bridge of great height, thrown over a deep cut in the solid rock, which separates it from the adjacent ground. This Castle, the origin of which is involved in obscurity, was long the abode of the proud family of the St. Clairs, Earls of Caithness and Orkney. In 1544, it was burned down by the Earl of Hertford; and, in 1650, it surrendered to General Monck. About sixty or seventy years ago, the comparatively modern mansion, which has been erected amidst the ruins of the old castle, was inhabited by a genuine Scottish laird of the old stamp, the lineal descendant of the high race who first founded the pile, and the last male of their long line. He was captain of the Royal Company of Archers, and Hereditary Grand Master of the Scottish Masons. At his death, the estate descended to Sir James Erskine St. Clair, father of the present Earl of Rosslyn, who now represents the family.

The neighbouring moor of Roslin was the scene of a celebrated battle, fought 24th February 1302, in which the Scots, under Comyn, then guardian of the kingdom, and Simon Fraser, attacked and defeated three divisions of the English on the same day.†

---

* Hawthornden being open to strangers *only on Wednesdays*, (as directed on page 90,) and Dalkeith Palace *only on Wednesdays and Saturdays*, Wednesday is the only day upon which *all the three places* can be seen, and tourists will, therefore, endeavour to devote this day to the purpose.

> † " Three triumphs in a day !
>   Three hosts subdued by one !
>   Three armies scattered like the spray
>   Beneath one summer sun.—
>   Who, pausing 'mid this solitude
>   Of rocky streams and leafy trees,—
>   Who, gazing o'er this quiet wood,
>   Would ever dream of these ?
>   Or have a thought that ought intrude,
>   Save birds and humming bees."

A

After leaving Roslin, we pass the caves of Gorton, situated in the front of a high cliff on the southern side of the stream. These caverns, during the reign of David II., while Scotland was overrun by the English, afforded shelter to the gallant Sir Alexander Ramsay of Dalwolsey, with a band of chosen patriots.

Passing through scenery of great natural beauty, the footpath down the river conducts the tourist to

HAWTHORNDEN,

the classical habitation of the poet Drummond, the friend of Shakspeare and Jonson; it is now the property of Sir James Walker Drummond. " This romantic spot seems to have been formed by nature in one of her happiest moments. All the materials that compose the picturesque seem here combined in endless variety: stupendous rocks, rich and varied in colours, hanging in threatening aspect, crowned with trees that expose their bare branching roots; here the gentle birch hanging midway, and there the oak, bending its stubborn branches, meeting each other; huge fragments of rocks impede the rapid flow of the stream, that hurries brawling along unseen, but heard far beneath, mingling in the breeze that gently agitates the wood." Being built with some view to defence, the house rises from the very edge of the grey cliff, which descends sheer down to the stream. An inscription on the front of the building testifies that it was repaired by the poet in 1638. It is well known that Ben Jonson walked from London, on foot, to visit Drummond, and lived several weeks with him at Hawthornden. Under the mansion are several subterraneous caves, hewn out of the solid rock with great labour, and connected with each other by long passages; in the courtyard there is a well of prodigious depth, which communicates with them. These caverns are supposed to have been constructed as places of refuge, when the public calamities rendered the ordinary habitations unsafe. The walks around the house are peculiarly fine, but free admission to them is limited to Wednesday of each week, unless by a special order from the proprietor, application for

MELVILLE CASTLE

which must be made at the office of Walker & Melville, Esquires, Writers to the Signet, 110, George Street.

Farther down the river is the pretty village of LASSWADE, the name of which is said to be derived from a *lass*, who, in former times, waded across the stream, carrying upon her back those whose circumstances enabled them to purchase the luxury of such a conveyance. In a cottage in the vicinity Sir Walter Scott spent some of the happiest years of his life. At a short distance is

MELVILLE CASTLE,

the seat of Viscount Melville. The building was erected by the celebrated Harry Dundas, first Viscount Melville. The park contains some fine wood. Two miles farther is the town of DALKEITH, in which is held the most extensive grain market in Scotland. In its immediate neighbourhood, situated on an overhanging bank of the North Esk, a little to the east of the town, stands

DALKEITH PALACE,

a seat of the Duke of Buccleuch. It is a large, but by no means elegant, structure, surrounded by an extensive park, through which the rivers of North and South Esk flow, and unite their streams a short way below the house. The first proprietors of Dalkeith upon record are the Grahams; from them it passed, in the reign of David II., by a daughter, into the possession of Sir William Douglas, ancestor of the Earls of Morton. In the reign of Queen Mary, Dalkeith was the head-quarters of the celebrated Regent Morton, and, after resigning his regency, he retired to this stronghold, which, from the general idea entertained of his character, acquired, at that time, the expressive name of the Lion's Den. In the year 1642, the estate was purchased from the Earl of Morton by Francis, Earl of Buccleuch. Anne, Duchess of Buccleuch and Monmouth, after the execution of her unhappy husband, substituted the modern for the ancient mansion, and lived here in royal state, and, for more than a century, it has formed the residence of the Buccleuch family. Since the union of the crowns, Dalkeith

House has thrice been the temporary residence of royalty,
—namely, of King Charles, in 1633, of George IV., in 1822,
and of her present Majesty, in 1842.   It is worthy of notice,
that Froissart, the historian of chivalry, visited the Earl of
Douglas, and lived with him several weeks at the Castle of
Dalkeith.   There is a popular belief current, that the
treasure unrighteously amassed by the Regent Morton lies
hidden somewhere among the vaults of the ancient building; but Godscroft assures us, that it was expended by the
Earl of Angus in supporting the companions of his exile in
England, and that, when it was exhausted, the Earl generously exclaimed, "Is it, then, all gone? let it go; I never
looked it should have done so much good!"   Dalkeith
Palace is shown to strangers, when the family is not residing there, on Wednesday and Saturday.   The environs of
Dalkeith are interesting, and the tourist may be conveyed
thither from Edinburgh, by the railroad, in a short space
of time, and at a very low rate.*

About a mile south-west from Dalkeith, on the northern
bank of the South Esk, is

NEWBATTLE ABBEY,

a seat of the Marquis of Lothian.   This mansion stands on

* The beautiful scenes through which the North and South Esk flow, and
the various seats that adorn the banks of these streams, are very happily described by Sir Walter Scott in his ballad of the Grey Brother :—

> "Sweet are the paths,—Oh, passing sweet!
>   By Esk's fair streams that run,
>   O'er airy steep, through copsewoods deep,
>   Impervious to the sun.
> There the rapt poet's step may rove,
>   And yield the Muse the day,
> There Beauty, led by timid Love,
>   May shun the tell-tale ray.
> From that fair dome where suit is paid, †
>   By blast of bugle free,
> To Auchindinny's hazel glade,
>   And haunted Woodhouselee.
> Who knows not Melville's beechy grove,
>   And Roslin's rocky glen,
> Dalkeith, which all the virtues love,
>   And classic Hawthornden?"

† Pennycuik. See ante, p. 84.

the spot formerly occupied by the Abbey of Newbattle, founded by David I. for a community of Cistertian monks. An ancestor of the present noble proprietor was the last abbot, and his son, Mark Ker, got the possessions of the abbey erected into a temporal lordship in the year 1591. The house contains a number of fine paintings and curious manuscripts, and the lawn is interspersed with some straggling trees of great size.

About two miles farther up the South Esk is

DALHOUSIE CASTLE,

a modernized building in the castellated form. The original structure was of vast antiquity and great strength. The present possessor, the Earl of Dalhousie, is the lineal descendant of the celebrated Sir Alexander Ramsay. The scenery around Dalhousie is romantic and beautiful.

Passing ARNISTON, the residence of the celebrated family of Dundas, the tourist, at the distance of about eleven miles from Edinburgh, comes in sight of BORTHWICK CASTLE, an ancient and stately tower, rising out of the centre of a small but well cultivated valley, watered by a stream called the Gore. This interesting fortress is in the form of a double tower, seventy-four feet in length, sixty-eight in breadth, and ninety feet in height from the area to the battlements. It occupies a knoll, surrounded by the small river, and is enclosed within an outer court, fortified by a strong outward wall, having flanking towers at the angles. The interior of the castle is exceedingly interesting. The hall is a stately and magnificent apartment, the ceiling of which consists of a smooth vault of ashler work. Three stairs, ascending at the angles of the building, gave access to the separate stories; one is quite ruinous, but the others are still tolerably entire. The license for building Borthwick Castle was granted by James I. to Sir William Borthwick, 2d June 1430. It was to Borthwick that Queen Mary retired with Bothwell, three weeks after her unfortunate marriage with that nobleman, and from which she was obliged, a few days afterwards, to flee to Dunbar in the disguise of a page. During the civil war, Borthwick held out gallantly against the victorious Cromwell, and surrendered at last upon honourable terms. The effect of Cromwell's battery still remains, his fire having destroyed a part of the freestone facing of the eastern side of the castle. Borthwick is now the property of John Borthwick, Esq. of Crookstone, a claimant of the ancient peerage of Borthwick, which has remained in abeyance since the death of the ninth Lord Borthwick, in the reign of Charles II. The valley of Borthwick is a sober, peaceful, sequestered, and exquisitely rural spot, and its manse and church, farm-houses and cottages, are in complete harmony with its prevailing character. In the manse of Borthwick, Dr. Robertson, the historian, was born.

A mile and a quarter to the eastward of Borthwick Castle, and within sight of its battlements, stands CRICHTON CASTLE, on the banks of the Tyne, twelve and a half miles south from Edinburgh, and about two miles above the village of Pathhead, on the Lauder road. The footpath which leads from Borthwick to Crichton meanders delightfully through natural pastures and rushy meadows, among dwarf hazel, and alder and blackthorn bushes, broom and brackens, till walled in by a nearly impenetrable wilderness of furze roughly clothing the bank. The waters divide hereabouts, —the infant Tyne running eastward, while Borthwick burn, descending from the southward heights, flows west till it falls into the Esk. Crichton Castle was built at different periods, and forms, on the whole, one large square pile, enclosing an interior court-yard. A strong old tower, which forms the east side of the quadrangle, seems to have been the original part of the building. The northern quarter, which appears to be the most modern, is built in a style of remarkable elegance. The description of the castle given by Sir Walter Scott, in his poem of Marmion, is so minutely accurate, that we transcribe it in preference to any remarks of our own.

> That Castle rises on the steep
>   Of the green vale of Tyne;
> And, far beneath, where slow they creep
> From pool to eddy, dark and deep,

Where alders moist, and willows weep,
  You hear her streams repine.
The towers in different ages rose;
Their various architecture shows
  The builders' various hands;
A mighty mass, that could oppose,
When deadliest hatred fired its foes,
  The vengeful Douglas' bands.

Crichtoun ! though now thy miry court
  But pens the lazy steer and sheep,
  Thy turrets rude, and totter'd Keep,
Have been the minstrel's loved resort.
Oft have I traced within thy fort,
  Of mouldering shields the mystic sense,
  Scutcheons of honour, or pretence,
Quarter'd in old armorial sort,
  Remains of rude magnificence.
Nor wholly yet hath time defaced
  Thy lordly gallery fair;
Nor yet the stony cord unbraced,
Whose twisted knots with roses laced,
  Adorn thy ruin'd stair.
Still rises, unimpair'd, below,
The court-yard's graceful portico;
Above its cornice, row and row
  Of fair-hewn facets richly show
    Their pointed diamond form,
  Though there but houseless cattle go,
    To shield them from the storm.
  And, shuddering, still may we explore,
    Where oft whilom were captives pent,
  The darkness of thy Massy More;*
    Or, from thy grass-grown battlement,
May trace in undulating line,
The sluggish mazes of the Tyne.

Crichton was the patrimonial estate and residence of the
celebrated Sir William Crichton, Chancellor of Scotland,
whose influence during the minority of James II., contributed so much to destroy the formidable power of the
Douglas family. On the forfeiture of William, third Lord
Crichton, the castle and barony of Crichton was granted to
Sir John Ramsay, a favourite of James III. The defeat

* The pit or prison vault.

and death of James involved the ruin of Ramsay. He in his turn was proscribed, exiled, and his estate forfeited, and the castle and lordship of Crichton were granted anew to Patrick Hepburn, third Lord Hales, who was created Earl of Bothwell. He was ancestor of the infamous James Earl of Bothwell, who exercised such an unhappy influence over the fortunes of Queen Mary. On his outlawry, Crichton was conferred by James VI. on his kinsman Francis Stewart, Earl of Bothwell, so noted for the constant train of conspiracies and insurrections in which he was engaged. Since that period, Crichton has passed through the hands of about a dozen proprietors, and is now the property of William Burn Callender, Esq. The ancient church of Crichton still exists, at the distance of half a mile to the north of the castle. It is a small but venerable building in the shape of a cross, with a low and truncated belfry. The west end has been left unfinished.

Returning to the road, about half a mile from Pathhead, stands OXENFORD CASTLE, a residence of the Earl of Stair. It is situate on the north bank of the Tyne, in the midst of an extensive park.

About three miles south from Edinburgh are the ruins of CRAIGMILLAR CASTLE, situate on the top of a gentle eminence, and surrounded with some fine old trees. "There is nothing to show at what age or by what hand it is built;"* but the rampart wall which surrounds the castle appears, from a date preserved on it, to have been built in 1427. Craigmillar, with other fortresses in Mid-Lothian, was burned by the English after Pinkey fight in 1555, and Captain Grose surmises, with great plausibility, that much of the building, as it now appears, was erected when the castle was repaired after that event.

In point of architecture and accommodation, Craigmillar surpasses the generality of Scottish Castles. It consists of a strong tower, flanked with turrets, and connected with inferior buildings. There is an outer court in front, defended by the battlemented wall already mentioned, and beyond these there was an exterior wall, and in some places

* CHALMERS's *Caledonia*, vol. ii. p. 570.

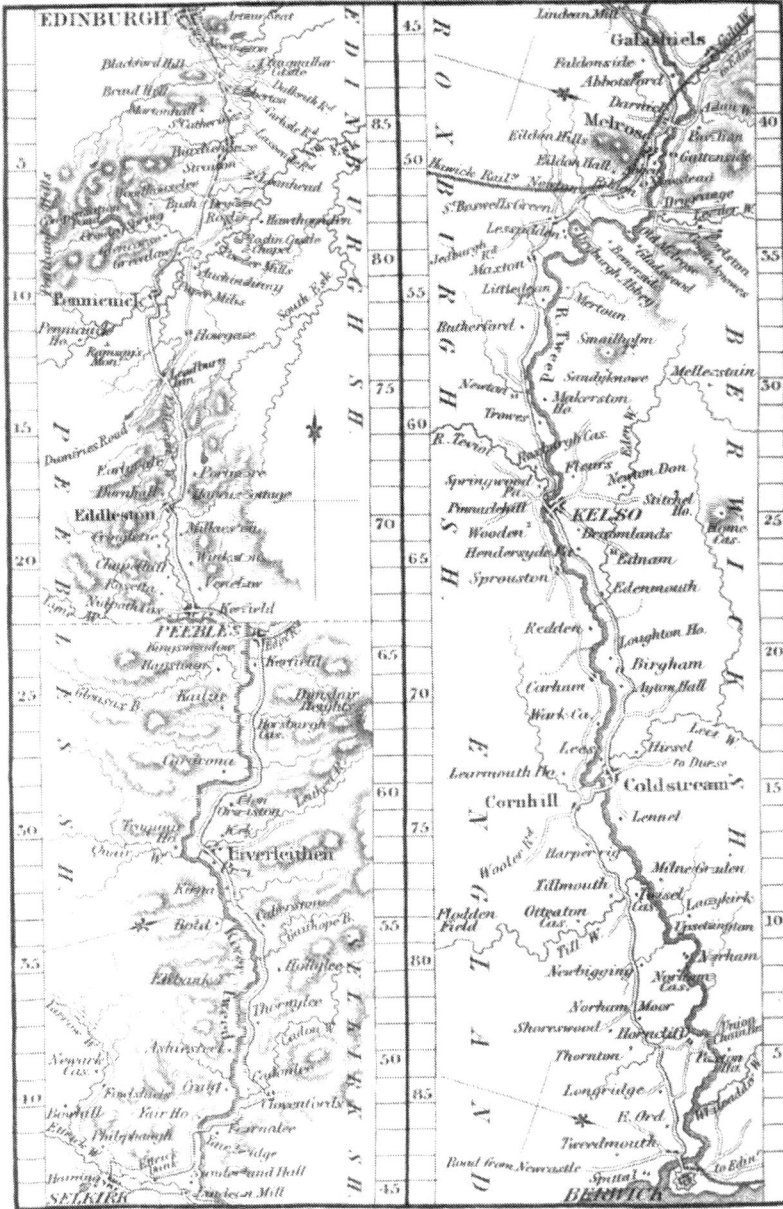
EDINBURGH to PEEBLES, SELKIRK, MELROSE, KELSO & BERWICK.

a deep ditch or moat. In 1813, a human skeleton was found enclosed, in an upright position, in a crevice of the vaulting of the castle. Upon being exposed to the air, it shortly crumbled to dust.

Being so near Edinburgh, Craigmillar was often occupied as a royal residence. Here John Earl of Mar, younger brother of James III., was imprisoned in 1477. James V. occupied it occasionally during his minority, and it was so often the residence of Queen Mary, that the adjacent village acquired the name of Little France, from her French guards being quartered there.

The castle and estate of Craigmillar were acquired by Sir Simon Preston in 1374, from John de Capella, and they continued in the possession of the Preston family till about the period of the Revolution, when they were purchased by Sir Thomas Gilmour, the great lawyer, to whose descendant, Walter Little Gilmour, Esq., they still belong.

FIRST TOUR.

EDINBURGH TO PEEBLES — INNERLEITHEN — SELKIRK — (VALES OF ETTRICK AND YARROW) — MELROSE — KELSO — COLDSTREAM AND BERWICK.

LEAVING Edinburgh by Nicolson Street, the tourist sees on an eminence, a short distance to the left, the ruins of CRAIGMILLAR CASTLE, an interesting edifice, of which a description is given on the preceding page. A little farther on, and nearer the road, stand the village and church of Libberton, pleasantly situated on a rising ground, and commanding a splendid view of Edinburgh and the surrounding scenery. Passing on the right, Morton Hall, (Richard Trotter, Esq.,) and upon the left, Gracemount, (Mrs. Hay,) and St. Catherine's, (A. Wright, Esq.,) we reach the small village of Burdiehouse, a corruption of Bourdeaux House, the name conferred on it by a native of that port in France. A little farther on is the village of Straiton, near which was

fought the second of three conflicts which took place in one
day, in 1302, styled the battle of Roslin. Six miles from
Edinburgh we pass Bilston toll-bar, where a road strikes
off on the left to Roslin. About a mile farther the tourist
passes Greenlaw, built as a depôt for the French prisoners
during the late war, and on the right, Glencorse House and
Church. A little beyond are Auchindinny House, once the
residence of Henry Mackenzie, author of the Man of Feeling;
and Auchindinny paper-mill. At the distance of other two
miles the road enters PENNYCUIK VILLAGE, ten miles distant
from Edinburgh. In the immediate vicinity are the extensive paper-mills of Messrs. Cowan and Sons. On the right
stands Pennycuik House, the seat of Sir George Clerk,
Bart., a fine specimen of modern architecture, surrounded
by beautiful woods. At the top of the hill, south of Pennycuik, a new road has been opened, leading to Linton and
Biggar. Three miles from Pennycuik the tourist enters
Peebles-shire, where the direct road to Dumfries parts off
on the right. The tract of country around is bleak and
moorish. Three miles from Kingside Edge is The Cottage,
(W. F. Mackenzie, Esq. of Portmore, M.P.,) and a mile beyond this, Eddlestone village. Passing in succession, Dam-
hall, (Lord Elibank,) Cringletie, (Murray, Esq.,) Winkstone,
(M'Gowan, Esq.,) Rosetta, (Dr. Young,) and Venelaw,
(Erskine, Esq.,) the tourist enters the royal burgh of

PEEBLES,

the county town, beautifully situated on the Tweed, twenty-
two miles distant from Edinburgh. Peebles is a town of
great antiquity, and must, from a very early period, have
been a seat of population, as is indicated by its name, which,
in British, signifies shielings or dwelling places; it is certain that at the end of the 11th century there were at this
place, a village, a church, a mill, and a brewhouse. The
population of the burgh within the Royalty, at last census,
was 1908. Owing to its situation in the midst of a fine
hunting country, and on the direct road to the royal forest
of Ettrick, it became at an early period the occasional residence of the Kings of Scotland, and is the scene of the

celebrated poem of James I., entitled "*Peblis to the Play.*" On account of its sequestered situation, this town figures little in Scottish history, and seems to have taken no part in any great historical event. It was, however, burnt and laid waste oftener than once during the invasions of the English. Peebles is divided into two districts — the old and new town. A bridge of great antiquity, consisting of five arches, connects the town with an extensive suburb on the opposite bank. The appearance of the whole is very pleasing, and the surrounding scenery is extremely beautiful. Peebles is a town possessed of very little commerce or manufacture. It has a weekly market, and seven annual fairs. At the end of the fifteenth century Peebles possessed no fewer than eleven places of worship, out of which the remains of only two are now visible. There is a large edifice of a castellated appearance still existing, known to have belonged to the Queensberry family, which is believed to be the scene of a highly romantic incident thus related by Sir Walter Scott. There is a tradition in Tweeddale, that when Nidpath Castle, near Peebles, was inhabited by the Earls of March, a mutual passion subsisted between a daughter of that noble family, and a son of the Laird of Tushielaw, in Ettrick forest. As the alliance was thought unsuitable by her parents, the young man went abroad. During his absence the young lady fell into a consumption, and at length, as the only means of saving her life, her father consented that her lover should be recalled. On the day when he was expected to pass through Peebles, on the road to Tushielaw, the young lady, though much exhausted, caused herself to be carried to the balcony of a house in Peebles, belonging to the family, that she might see him as he rode past. Her anxiety and eagerness gave such force to her organs, that she is said to have distinguished his horse's footsteps at an incredible distance. But Tushielaw, unprepared for the change in her appearance, and not expecting to see her in that place, rode on without recognizing her, or even slackening his pace. The lady was unable to support the shock, and, after a short struggle, died in the arms of her attendants.

The vale of the Tweed, both above and below Peebles,
contained a chain of strong castles to serve as a defence
against the incursions of English marauders.   These castles
were built in the shape of square towers, and usually consisted of three stories—the lower one on the ground floor
being vaulted, and appropriated to the reception of horses
and cattle in times of danger.   They were built alternately
on both sides of the river, and in a continued view of each
other.   A fire kindled on the top of these towers was the
signal of an incursion, and, in this manner, a tract of
country seventy miles long, from Berwick to the Bield, and
fifty broad, was alarmed in a few hours.

> " A score of fires, I ween,
> From height, and hill, and cliff were seen,
> Each with warlike tidings fraught,
> Each from each the signal caught;
> Each after each they glanced in sight,
> As stars arise upon the night;
> They gleam'd on many a dusky tarn,
> Haunted by the lonely earn,*
> On many a cairn's grey pyramid,
> Where urns of mighty chiefs lie hid."
>
> *Lay of the Last Minstrel.*

The strongest and the most entire of these fortresses is
NIDPATH CASTLE, situated about a mile west from the town
of Peebles, on a rock projecting over the north bank of the
Tweed, which here runs through a deep narrow glen, once
well wooded on both sides.   Nidpath was at one time the
chief residence of the powerful family of the Frasers, from
whom the families of Lovat and Salton in the north are
descended.   The last of the family in the male line was Sir
Simon Fraser, the staunch friend of Wallace, who, in 1302,
along with Comyn, then guardian of the kingdom, defeated
three divisions of the English on the same day, on Roslin
Moor.   Sir Simon left two daughters co-heiresses, one of
whom married Hay of Yester, an ancestor of the Marquis
of Tweeddale.   The second Earl of Tweeddale garrisoned
Nidpath, in 1636, for the service of Charles II., and it held
out longer against Cromwell than any place south of the

---

* The Scottish Eagle.

Forth. The Tweeddale family were so much impoverished
by their exertions in the royal cause, that they were obliged,
before the end of the reign of Charles II., to dispose of their
barony of Nidpath to William, first Duke of Queensberry,
who purchased it for his son the first Earl of March. On
the death of the last Duke of Queensberry in 1810, the
Earl of Wemyss, as heir of entail, succeeded to the Nidpath
estate. The castle is now falling fast to decay. It was
formerly approached by an avenue of fine trees, all of which
were cut down by the late Duke of Queensberry to impo-
verish the estate before it descended to the heir of entail.
The poet, Wordsworth, has spoken of this conduct with
just indignation in the following sonnet :—

> " Degenerate Douglas ! oh, the unworthy Lord !
> Whom mere despite of heart could so far please,
> And love of havoc, (for with such disease
> Fame taxes him,) that he could send forth word
> To level with the dust a noble horde,
> A brotherhood of venerable Trees,
> Leaving an ancient dome, and towers like these,
> Beggar'd and outraged !—Many hearts deplored
> The fate of those old Trees; and oft, with pain,
> The traveller, at this day, will stop and gaze
> On wrongs which Nature scarcely seems to heed :
> For shelter'd places, bosoms, nooks, and bays,
> And the pure mountains, and the gentle Tweed,
> And the green silent pastures, yet remain."

Leaving Peebles, the tourist proceeds along the northern
bank of the Tweed, and passing in succession Kerfield
(Gillespie, Esq.) on the opposite bank of the river, King's
Meadows and Hayston, (Sir Adam Hay, Bart.)—the ruins
of Horsburgh Castle, the property of the ancient family of
the Horsburghs now resident at Pirn— Kailzie, (R. N.
Campbell, Esq.) Nether Horsburgh (Campbell, Esq.) Car-
drona, the seat of the old family of Williamson, and Glen-
ormiston House (Stewart, Esq. ;) six miles below Peebles
reaches the village of

INNERLEITHEN,

situated about a quarter of a mile from the mouth of
Leithen water. It occupies a pleasant situation at the bot-

tom of a sequestered dell, environed on the east and west
by high and partially wooded hills, and having the Tweed
rolling in front.　Till little more than thirty years ago,
Innerleithen was one of the smallest and most primitive
hamlets in this pastoral district.　But about the beginning
of the present century, its mineral spring began to attract
notice, and it has now become a favourite watering-place,
much frequented in the summer and autumn by visiters
from Edinburgh.　The healthiness of the climate —the
beauty of the situation—its proximity to St. Mary's Loch
in Yarrow, the Tweed, and various trouting streams, as well
as other advantages connected with its locality, render
Innerleithen a very delightful residence.　A handsome
wooden bridge leads across the Tweed to the hamlet of
Traquair and Traquair House, the seat of the Earl of
Traquair.　At a short distance, at the base of a hill overlooking the lawn, a few birch trees may be seen, the scanty
remains of the famed "Bush aboon Traquair."　A few
years ago an association was instituted at Innerleithen,
called the St. Ronan's Border Club, consisting of a number
of gentlemen connected with all parts of the country, who
hold an annual festival for the performance of games and
gymnastic exercises.

Leaving Innerleithen, at a short distance upon the right,
is Pirn ; and three miles farther on, the road enters Selkirkshire, passing, on the left, Holylee (Ballantyne, Esq.)　A
mile beyond, on the opposite side of the river, are the ruins
of Elibank Tower, from which Lord Elibank takes his title.
Two miles farther on is Ashiestiel (Col. Russell,) once the
residence of Sir Walter Scott.　A mile beyond this the road
crosses Caddon Water, and at the village of Clovenfords,
joins the road from Edinburgh to Selkirk.　Two miles
beyond, it passes the old mansion-house of Fairnielee, now
almost in ruins, and Yair, the seat of Alexander Pringle,
Esq., of Whytbank, one of the loveliest spots in Scotland,
closely surrounded by hills most luxuriantly wooded.　The
road then crosses the Tweed at Yair Bridge, and, two miles
farther on, crosses the Ettrick, and enters the royal burgh of

SELKIRK,

situated on a piece of high ground overhanging the Ettrick. Selkirk is a town of neat appearance, and the beautiful woods surrounding the Haining, the seat of the late Robert Pringle, Esq., of Clifton, now belonging to his sister, Mrs. Douglas of Edderstone, form an excellent background to it. The population of the burgh is 2593. It gives the title of Earl to a branch of the Douglas family.

A party of the citizens of Selkirk, under the command of their town-clerk, William Brydone, behaved with great gallantry at the battle of Flodden, when, in revenge for their brave conduct, the English entirely destroyed the town by fire. A pennon, taken from an English leader by a person of the name of Fletcher, is still kept in Selkirk by the successive Deacons of the weavers, and Brydone's sword is still in the possession of his lineal descendants. The well-known pathetic ballad of "The Flowers of the Forest," was composed on the loss sustained by the inhabitants of Ettrick Forest at the fatal battle of Flodden. The principal trade carried on in Selkirk at the time of the battle, and for centuries afterwards, was the manufacture of thin or *single-soled* shoes.* Hence, to be made a sutor of Selkirk is the ordinary phrase for being created a burgess, and a *birse* or hog's bristle is always attached to the seal of the ticket. Of late the manufactures of Galashiels have found their way to Selkirk. Large mills have been erected on the Ettrick; the old decaying burgh seems to have revived its youth; new buildings are seen rising in and around a town which was long thought to have been in a hopeless state of decay, and the population has greatly increased.

[Those tourists whose time does not admit of their visiting the vales of Ettrick and Yarrow, may pass over the following chapter, which, forming a sort of episode in the tour, we have printed in a smaller type.]

* Up wi' the Souters o' Selkirk,
    And down wi' the Earl o' Hume;
  And up wi' a' the braw lads
    That sew the single-soled shoon.

ETTRICK AND YARROW.

" By Yarrow's stream still let me stray,
  Though none should guide my weary way ;
  Still feel the breeze down Ettrick breaks,
  Though it should chill my wither'd cheeks."
                                        SCOTT.

Leaving Selkirk, the tourist will retrace his steps to the bridge
over the Ettrick, and turn up the north bank. The plain on the
northern side of the river is Philiphaugh, the scene of the defeat of
Montrose, by General Leslie, 13th September 1645. Montrose himself had taken up his quarters, with his cavalry, in the town of Selkirk, while his infantry, amounting to about twelve or fifteen hundred men, were posted on Philiphaugh. Leslie arrived at Melrose
the evening before the engagement, and next morning, favoured by
a thick mist, he reached Montrose's encampment without being
descried by a single scout. The surprisal was complete, and when
the Marquis, who had been alarmed by the noise of the firing,
reached the scene of the battle, he beheld his army dispersed in
irretrievable rout. After a desperate but unavailing attempt to re-
trieve the fortune of the day, he cut his way through a body of
Leslie's troopers, and fled up Yarrow and over Minchmoor towards
Peebles. This defeat destroyed the fruit of Montrose's six splendid
victories, and effectually ruined the royal cause in Scotland. The
estate of Philiphaugh is the property of Colonel Murray, the descendant of the " Outlaw Murray," commemorated in the beautiful ballad
of that name. At the head of Philiphaugh the Yarrow comes out,
from Newark's " birken bower" to join the Ettrick. At the confluence of these streams, about a mile above Selkirk, is Carterhaugh,
the supposed scene of the fairy ballad of " Tamlane." The vale of
Yarrow parts off from the head of Philiphaugh towards the right,
that of Ettrick towards the left. The whole of this tract of country
was, not many centuries ago, covered with wood, and its popular
designation still is " the Forest." A native of Selkirk, who died
about eighty years ago at an advanced age, used to tell that he had
seen a person older than himself who said he had in his time walked
from that town to Ettrick, a distance of eighteen miles, and never
once all the way escaped from the shadow of trees. Of this primeval
forest no vestige is now to be seen.

"The scenes are desert now, and bare,
  Where flourished once a forest fair,
  Up pathless Ettrick and on Yarrow,
  Where erst the outlaw drew his arrow."
                                        SCOTT.

Turning up the vale of Ettrick, the first object of interest that
occurs is Oakwood, the residence of the hero of the ballad called

" The Dowie Dens of Yarrow," and, from time immemorial, the property of the Scotts of Harden ; it is supposed, also, to have been the mansion of the famous wizard Michael Scott. Two or three miles farther up the glen is the village of Ettrick-brig-end, and about six miles above, the remains of the Tower of Tushielaw may be discerned upon the hill which rises from the north bank of the river. Tushielaw was the residence of the celebrated freebooter Adam Scott, called the King of the Border, who was hanged by James V. in the course of that memorable expedition in 1529, which proved fatal to Johnnie Armstrong, Cockburn of Henderland, and many other marauders; the elm tree on which he was hanged still exists among the ruins. Opposite to Tushielaw the Rankleburn joins the Ettrick. The vale of Rankleburn contains the lonely farm of Buccleuch, supposed to have been the original property of the noble family of that name. There are remains of a church and burial ground, and of a kiln and mill in this district, but no traces of a baronial mansion. Farther up are the ruins of Thirlestane Castle, and close by, the modern mansion of Thirlestane, the seat of Lord Napier, the lineal descendant of the old family of the Scotts of Thirlestane, as well as of the still more famous one of the Napiers of Merchiston. Sir John Scott of Thirlestane, his paternal ancestor, was the only chief willing to follow James V. in his invasion of England, when the rest of the Scottish nobles, encamped at Fala, obstinately refused to take part in the expedition. In memory of his fidelity, James granted to his family a charter of arms, entitling them to bear a border of fleurs-de-luce similar to the tressure in the royal arms, with a bundle of spears for the crest, motto, " ready, aye ready."—(See *Lay of the Last Minstrel*, canto iv.) Thirlestane is surrounded with extensive plantations, and its late noble and benevolent owner employed for many years his whole time and talents in carrying on, at great expense, important improvements in this district. About a mile farther up stand the kirk and hamlet of Ettrick. A cottage near the sacred edifice is pointed out as the birth-place of the Ettrick Shepherd. The celebrated Thomas Boston was minister of Ettrick, and, in the church-yard, a handsome monument has been erected to his memory, since the commencement of the present century.

Crossing the hills which bound the vale of Ettrick on the right, the tourist descends into the celebrated vale of Yarrow. At the head of the vale is the solitary sheet of water called ST. MARY'S LOCH, four miles long, and nearly one broad.

> ——" lone St. Mary's silent lake.
> ———————— nor fen nor sedge
> Pollute the pure lake's crystal edge.
> Abrupt and sheer the mountains sink,
> At once upon the level brink ;
> And just a trace of silver sand
> Marks where the water meets the land.

Far in the mirror bright and blue
Each hill's huge outline you may view;
Shaggy with heath, but lonely bare,
Nor tree, nor bush, nor brake, is there,
Save where of land yon slender line
Bears 'thwart the lake the scatter'd pine.
Yet even this nakedness has power,
And aids the feeling of the hour;
Nor thicket, dell, nor copse you spy,
Where living thing concealed might lie;
There's nothing left to fancy's guess,
You see that all is loneliness;
And silence aids—though the steep hills
Send to the lake a thousand rills;
In summer tide so soft they weep,
The sound but lulls the ear asleep;
Your horse's hoof-tread sounds too rude,
So stilly is the solitude." *

The river Yarrow flows from the east end, and a small stream connects the Loch of the Lowes with its western extremity. In the
winter it is still frequented by flights of wild swans; hence Wordsworth's lines:

"The swans on sweet St. Mary's Lake
Float double—swan and shadow!

In the neighbourhood is the farm of Blackhouse, adjacent to which
are the remains of a very ancient tower in a wild and solitary glen,
upon a torrent named Douglas Burn, which issues from the hills
on the north, and joins the Yarrow, after passing a craggy rock,
called the Douglas-craig. This wild scene, now a part of the
Traquair estate, formed one of the most ancient possessions of the
renowned family of Douglas, and is said by popular tradition to be
the scene of the fine old ballad of "The Douglas Tragedy." Near
the eastern extremity of St. Mary's Loch are the ruins of Dryhope
Tower, the birth-place of Mary Scott, famous by the traditional name
of the "Flower of Yarrow," and a mile westward is the ancient
burying-ground of St. Mary's Kirk, but the Church has long ago
disappeared.

"Though in feudal strife, a foe
Hath laid Our Lady's chapel low,
Yet still beneath the hallow'd soil
The peasant rests him from his toil,
And, dying, bids his bones be laid
Where erst his simple fathers pray'd."†

A funeral in a spot so very retired has an uncommonly striking
effect. At one corner of the burial-ground, but without its precincts, is a small mound, said by tradition to be the grave of Mass
John Birnam, the former tenant of the chaplainry.

* *Marmion.*   Introduction to Canto II.
† *Marmion.*   Introduction to Canto II.

"That wizard priest, whose bones are thrust
From company of holy dust."

In the adjacent vale of Megget is Henderland Castle, the residence of Cockburn, a border freebooter, who was hanged over the gate of his own tower by James V. Tradition says that Cockburn was surprised by the king while sitting at dinner. A mountain torrent, called Henderland Burn, rushes impetuously from the hills through a rocky chasm, named the Dow-glen, and passes near the site of the tower. To the recesses of this glen the wife of Cockburn is said to have retreated during the execution of her husband, and a place, called the *Lady's Seat*, is still shown, where she is said to have striven to drown, amid the roar of a foaming cataract, the tumultuous noise which announced the close of his existence. The beautiful pathetic ballad, entitled "The Lament of the Border Widow," was composed on this event. On the south side of St. Mary's Loch is a hill called the Merecleuchhead, over which there is a scarcely visible track, termed the King's Road, leading over the hills into Ettrick.* At the head of the Loch of the Lowes, on the east, is Kirkenhope, and on the west Chapelhope, the scene of the tale of "The Brownie of Bodsbeck." A few miles farther on through the hills is a small house, formerly an inn, called Birkhill, opposite the door of which Claverhouse shot four Covenanters, whose grave-stones were discernible in Ettrick churchyard a few years ago. Opposite the house at Birkhill is a hill called the Watch Hill, from the circumstance of the Covenanters stationing one of their number there, to give notice of the approach of the soldiers; and a little below is a hideous gully, containing a waterfall, called Dobbs Linn, and a cave which served as a place of retreat for the persecuted remnant. Near the head of Moffat Water is the "dark LOCH SKENE," a mountain lake of considerable size, pre-eminent over all lakes of the south of Scotland for the impressive gloom and sterility that surround it. The stream which forms its outlet, after a short and hurried course, falls from a cataract of immense height, and gloomy grandeur, called from its appearance THE GREY MARE'S TAIL. The water is precipitated over a dark rugged precipice, about 300 feet high. A little way from the foot of the cataract is a sort of trench, called "The Giant's Grave," which has evidently been a battery designed to command the pass. The character of the surrounding scenery is uncommonly savage and gloomy, and the *earn*, or Scottish eagle, has for many ages built its nest yearly upon an islet in Loch Skene. This rude

---

* An old song opens with this stanza:—
"The King rade round the Merecleuchhead,
Booted and spurr'd, as we a' did see;
Syne dined wi' a lass at Moesfennan yett,
A little below the Logan Lee.

and savage scene is well described in the introduction to the second
canto of Marmion.

> " There eagles scream from isle to shore;
> Down all the rocks the torrents roar;
> O'er the black waves incessant driven,
> Dark mists infect the summer heaven;
> Through the rude barriers of the lake
> Away its hurrying waters break
> Faster and whiter, dash and curl,
> Till down yon dark abyss they hurl.
> Rises the fog-smoke, white as snow,
> Thunders the viewless stream below.
>
>   *   *   *
>
> ———————— the bottom of the den,
> Where, deep deep down and far within,
> Toils with the rocks the roaring linn;
> Then issuing forth one foamy wave,
> And wheeling round the Giant's Grave
> White as the snowy charger's tail,
> Drives down the pass of Moffatdale."

The vale of Moffat, although less celebrated for its literary associations, is by no means inferior in picturesque attraction to its
more favoured rivals, the Ettrick and Yarrow. To within a short
distance from the village of Moffat the valley is strictly pastoral; and
although its upper extremity, from its great elevation, is not unfrequently shrouded in mist, a day of sunshine discloses scenery of a
highly pleasing and romantic character.

The Grey Mare's Tail is ten miles north-east from the village of
Moffat, noted for its mineral well.

Returning to the vale of Yarrow, a short way below St. Mary's
Loch, is MOUNT BENGER, at one time occupied by the Ettrick Shepherd; and "The Gordon Arms" Inn, about thirteen miles from Selkirk, where a bridge over the Yarrow leads to ALTRIVE, near the
east end of the lake, where the poet died. The next object of interest that occurs is the Church of Yarrow, a neat little edifice, erected about the time of Cromwell. On the moor, a little way west
from the kirk, two tall unhewn masses of stone, about eighty yards
apart from each other, mark the scene of the duel fought between
John Scott of Tushielaw and his brother-in-law, Walter Scott, third
son of Robert Scott of Thirlestane, in which the latter was slain.
The proposal of the lady's father to endow her with half his property,
upon her marriage with a warrior of such renown, is alleged to have
been the cause of this unnatural quarrel. The incident has given
rise, directly or indirectly, to ballads, songs, and poems innumerable.
The most famous are, the old ballad called "The Dowie Dens of
Yarrow," and those composed by Hamilton of Bangour and Logan;
and, more recently, the three charming poems of Wordsworth,—
Yarrow Unvisited, Yarrow Visited, and Yarrow Revisited. A few

verses of Yarrow Visited may here be quoted, as, in addition to the beauty of the poetry, they give an excellent description of the scenery.

" And is this—Yarrow ?—*This* the stream
　Of which my fancy cherish'd
So faithfully a waking dream ?
　An image that hath perish'd !
O that some minstrel's harp were near
　To utter tones of gladness,
And chase this silence from the air
　That fills my heart with sadness.

Yet why ?—a silvery current flows
　With uncontroll'd meanderings;
Nor have these eyes by greener hills
　Been soothed in all my wanderings.
And, through her depths, St. Mary's Lake
　Is visibly delighted ;
For not a feature of those hills
　Is in the mirror slighted.

Where was it that the famous Flower
　Of Yarrow Vale lay bleeding ?
His bed, perchance, was yon smooth mound
　On which the herd is feeding :
And, haply, from this crystal pool,
　Now peaceful as the morning,
The water-wraith ascended thrice,
　And gave his doleful warning.

Delicious is the lay that sings
　The haunts of happy lovers ;
The path that leads them to the grove,
　The leafy grove that covers ;
And pity sanctifies the verse
　That paints, by strength of sorrow,
The unconquerable strength of love ;
　Bear witness, rueful Yarrow !

But thou, that didst appear so fair
　To fond imagination,
Dost rival in the light of day
　Her delicate creation :
Meek loveliness is round thee spread,
　A softness still and holy ;
The grace of forest charms decay'd,
　And pastoral melancholy.

That region left, the vale unfolds
　Rich groves of lofty stature,
With Yarrow winding through the pomp
　Of cultivated nature ;
And, rising from these lofty groves,
　Behold a Ruin hoary !
The shatter'd front of Newark's Tower,
　Renown'd in Border story."

Farther down the vale is the village of Yarrowford, near which are the remains of the strong and venerable Castle of Hangingshaw, one of the possessions of the outlaw Murray, and, till within these few years, of his descendants. It stood in a romantic and solitary situation, and was the scene of the beautiful old ballad called " The Sang of the Outlaw Murray." * When the mountains around Hangingshaw were covered with the wild copse which constituted a Scottish forest, a more secure stronghold for an outlawed baron can hardly be imagined. A little beyond is the modern mansion of Broadmeadows (John Boyd, Esq.), commanding a delightful view; and a mile below are the romantic ruins of NEWARK CASTLE, standing on an eminence overhanging the Yarrow, with dark wooded hills rising closely around on both sides. It is scarcely necessary to remind the tourist that this is the mansion in which Anne Duchess of Buccleuch and Monmouth is made to listen to the " Lay of the Last Minstrel." At Newark, Leslie, after the battle of Philiphaugh, caused a number of his prisoners to be executed in

* The scene is, by the common people, supposed to have been the Castle of Newark, but this is highly improbable, as Newark was always a royal fortress; and Mr. Plummer, who, at one time, held the office of sheriff-depute of Selkirkshire, assured Sir Walter Scott that he remembered the *insignia* of the unicorns, &c., so often mentioned in the ballad, in existence upon the old tower at Hangingshaw. The house was burnt down by accident, about seventy or eighty years ago, to the great grief of the people, who loved the proprietor on account of his numerous virtues. As a trait of the hospitality practised at Hangingshaw, it is recorded by tradition, that whosoever called at the house was treated with a draught of stout ale from a capacious vessel, called " the Hangingshaw Ladle.

cold blood. The spot where this atrocious deed was perpetrated is still called the "Slain-men's-lee." Opposite Newark is the farm of Foulshiels, where Mungo Park, the celebrated African traveller, was born. Farther down, at the mouth of the vale on the right, is Bowhill, a summer residence of the Duke of Buccleuch, standing on the face of an eminence, embowered amidst its beautiful new woods; and on the left Philiphaugh House, (Colonel Murray,) situated on a hill overlooking Carterhaugh and the confluence of the Ettrick and Yarrow. The road now passes Philiphaugh and enters the town of Selkirk.

Leaving Selkirk for Melrose, the road leads along the south bank of the Ettrick, and at a distance of about a mile enters Roxburghshire. Near this spot is the secluded burying-ground of Lindean, with the ruins of its church. Here the body of the "dark Knight of Liddisdale" rested on its way from Ettrick Forest, where he was murdered, to Melrose Abbey, where he was interred. The old parish of Lindean is now annexed to Galashiels. Three miles from Selkirk, the Ettrick flows into the Tweed at Sunderland Hall, where bridges have lately been thrown over both rivers. Proceeding along the banks of the Tweed, the tourist, at the distance of a mile and a half, reaches

ABBOTSFORD,

the seat of Sir Walter Scott, Bart., situated on a bank overhanging the south side of the Tweed, which at this place

CHART OF THE VALES OF TEVIOT AND TWEED.

makes a beautiful sweep around the declivity on which the house stands. Further up the Tweed, on the opposite bank, venerable trees, scattered over a considerable space, indicate the site of the old mansion and village of Boldside, of which a fisherman's cottage is now the only representative. Below the Selkirk road may be seen the site of its Church, and the haunted Churchyard extended along the face of the bank. Immediately opposite, at the extremity of his property, Sir Walter had a bower overhanging the Tweed, where he frequently sat musing during the heat of the day. Boldside is referred to in Lockhart's Life of Scott.

Abbotsford is a house of very extraordinary proportions, and though irregular as a whole, it produces a very striking

effect. The entrance to the house is by a porchway, adorned
with petrified stags' horns, into a hall, which is perhaps the
most interesting of all the apartments. The walls are pan-
nelled with richly carved oak from the palace of Dunfermline, and the roof consists of painted arches of the same
material. Round the cornice there is a line of coats-armo-
rial richly blazoned, belonging to the families who kept the
borders—as the Douglasses, Kers, Scotts, Turnbulls, Maxwells, Chisholms, Elliots, and Armstrongs. The floor is of
black and white marble from the Hebrides, and the walls
are hung with ancient armour, and various specimens of
military implements. From the hall you proceed to the
armoury, a narrow low-arched room, which runs quite across
the house, having a blazoned window at either extremity,
and filled with smaller pieces of armour and weapons. This
apartment communicates with the drawing-room on the
one side, and the dining-room on the other. The former is
a lofty saloon with wood of cedar. Its antique ebony furniture, carved cabinets, &c., are all of beautiful workmanship. The dining-room is a very handsome apartment, with
a roof of black oak richly carved. It contains a fine collection of pictures ; the most interesting of which are the
head of Queen Mary in a charger the day after she was beheaded, and a full length portrait of Lord Essex, of Oliver
Cromwell, Claverhouse, Charles II., Charles XII. of Sweden,
and, among several family pictures, one of Sir Walter's
great-grandfather, who allowed his beard to grow after the
execution of Charles I. The breakfast parlour is a small
and neat apartment, overlooking the Tweed on the one
side, and the wild hills of Ettrick and Yarrow on the other.
It contains a beautiful and valuable collection of water-
colour drawings, chiefly by Turner and Thomson of Dud-
dingstone, the designs for the magnificent work entitled
" Provincial Antiquities of Scotland." The library, which
is the largest of all the apartments, is a magnificent room,
fifty feet by sixty. The roof is of carved oak, chiefly after
models from Roslin. The collection of books in this room
amounts to about 20,000 volumes, many of them extremely
rare and valuable. From the library there is a communi-

cation with the study, a room of about twenty-five feet
square by twenty feet high, containing of what is properly
called furniture nothing but a small writing-table in the
centre, a plain arm-chair covered with black leather, and a
single chair besides. There are a few books, chiefly for reference, and a light gallery of tracery work runs round
three sides of the room, which contains only one window,
so that the place is rather sombre. From this room you
enter a small closet, containing what must be viewed by
all with the deepest interest—the body-clothes worn by Sir
Walter previous to his decease.* The external walls of the
house, as well as those of the adjoining garden, are enriched
with many old carved stones, which have originally figured
in other and very different situations. The door of the old
tolbooth of Edinburgh, the pulpit from which Ralph Erskine preached, and various other curious and interesting
relics, may also be seen. Through the whole extent of the
surrounding forests there are a number of beautiful winding walks, and near the waterfalls in the deep ravines are
benches or bowers commanding the most picturesque views.
The mansion of Abbotsford and its woods have been entirely created by its late proprietor, who, when he purchased
the ground about thirty years ago, found it occupied by a
small onstead called "Cartley Hole." The first purchase
was made from the late Dr. Douglas of Galashiels. It is
said that the money was paid by instalments, and that the
letter enclosing the last remittance contained these lines :

> " Noo the gowd's thine,
> And the land's mine."

Various other "pendicles" were purchased at different times
from the neighbouring bonnet-lairds, at prices greatly above

* " After showing us the principal rooms, the woman opened a small closet
adjoining the study, in which hung the last clothes that Sir Walter had worn.
There was the broad-skirted blue coat with large buttons, the plaid trowsers,
the heavy shoes, the broad-rimmed hat, and stout walking-stick,—the dress in
which he rambled about in the morning, and which he laid off when he took
to his bed in his last illness. She took down the coat, and gave it a shake and
a wipe of the collar, as if he were waiting to put it on again !"—WILLIS's Pen-
cillings by the Way.

their real value.   In December 1830, the library, museum,
plate, and furniture of every description, were presented to
Sir Walter as a free gift by his creditors, and he afterwards
bequeathed the same to his eldest son, burdened with a
sum of £5000 to be divided among his younger children.
The proceeds of a subscription set on foot in London a considerable time ago, have been applied to the payment of this
debt, thus enabling the trustees to entail the library and
museum as an heir-loom in the family ; and it is expected
that the mortgage on the lands will be liquidated by the
profits·of the new edition of Sir Walter's works, and thereby enable the executors to complete an entail of the entire
property.

A little to the east of Abbotsford, and on the opposite
bank of the river, the Allan or Elwand water runs into the
Tweed.   There can be little doubt that the vale of the
Allan is the true " Glendearg" of the Monastery.*   The
banks on each side are steep, and rise boldly over the
eccentric stream which jets from rock to rock, rendering it
absolutely necessary for the traveller to cross and recross it,
as he pursues his way up the bottom of the narrow valley.
" The hills also rise at some places abruptly over the little
glen, displaying at intervals the grey rock overhung with
wood, and farther up rises the mountain in purple majesty

---

* " When we had ridden a little time on the moors, he said to me rather
pointedly, ' I am going to show you something that I think will interest you ;'
and presently, in a wild corner of the hills, he halted us at a place where stood
three small ancient towers, or castellated houses, in ruins, at short distances
from each other.   It was plain, upon the slightest consideration of the topography, that one (perhaps any one) of these was the tower of Glendearg, where
so many romantic and marvellous adventures happen in the Monastery.   While
we looked at this forlorn group, I said to Sir Walter that they were what Burns
called ' ghaist-alluring edifices.'   ' Yes,' he answered carelessly, ' I dare say
there are many stories about them.'   As we returned, by a different route, he
made me dismount and take a footpath through a part of Lord Somerville's
grounds, where the Elland runs through a beautiful little valley, the stream
winding between level borders of the brightest green sward, which narrow or
widen as the steep sides of the glen advance or recede.   The place is called the
Fairy Dean, and it required no cicerone to tell, that the glen was that in which
Father Eustace, in the Monastery, is intercepted by the White Lady of Avenel.
—Letter of Mr. Adolphus—LOCKHART'S Life of Scott, vol. v.

—the dark rich hue contrasting beautifully with the thickets of oak and birch, the mountain ashes and thorns, the alders and quivering aspens which chequered and varied the descent, and not less with the dark green velvet turf which composed the level part of the narrow glen." At a short distance from Abbotsford is the small village of Bridgend, which received its name from a bridge erected over the Tweed by David I., to afford a passage to the Abbey of Melrose. It consisted of four piers, upon which lay planks of wood ; and in the middle pillar was a gateway large enough for a carriage to pass through, and over that a room in which the toll-keeper resided. It was at a ford below this bridge that the adventure with the White Lady of Avenel befell Father Philip, the sacristan of the Monastery. (See Monastery, vol. i.) From this bridge the Girthgate, a path to the sanctuary of Soutra, runs up the valley of Allan Water, and over the moors to Soutra Hill. Between Bridgend and Darnick is a place called Skinnersfield (a corruption of Skirmishfield,) where a battle was fought in 1526 between the Earl of Angus and the Laird of Buccleuch, for possession of the person of James V., which terminated in favour of Angus.* The road now passes the village of Darnick, in which there is an ancient tower, built during the fifteenth century, and a little farther on reaches

MELROSE,

situated on the south side of the Tweed, near the base of

* The Earl of Angus, with his reluctant ward, had slept at Melrose, and the clans of Home and Kerr, under the Lord Home, and the barons of Cessford and Fairnihirst, had taken their leave of the king, when, in the grey of the morning, Buccleuch and his band of cavalry, comprehending a large body of Elliots, Armstrongs, and other broken clans, were discovered, hanging like a thunder cloud upon the neighbouring hill of Haliden. The encounter was fierce and obstinate, but the Homes and Kerrs returning at the noise of the battle, bore down and dispersed the left wing of Buccleuch's little army. The hired banditti fled on all sides, but the chief himself, surrounded by his clan, fought desperately in the retreat. The Laird of Cessford, chief of the Roxburgh Kerrs, pursued the chase fiercely, till, at the bottom of a steep path, Elliot of Stobbs, turned and slew him, with a stroke of his lance. When Cessford fell, the pursuit ceased, but his death, with those of Buccleuch's friends who fell in the action, to the number of eighty, occasioned a deadly feud betwixt the clans of Scott and Kerr, which cost much blood upon the marches.—See *Introduction to Minstrelsy of the Scottish Border*, and *Lay of the Last Minstrel*.

the Eildon Hills. It is thirty-six miles from Edinburgh,
twelve from Jedburgh, and fourteen from Kelso. " The
vale of the Tweed is everywhere fertile and beautiful, and
here grandeur is combined with beauty and fertility. The
eye is presented with a wide range of pleasing and impressive scenery—of villages and hamlets—the river winding
rapidly among smiling fields and orchards, the town with
its groves, and gardens, and neat rural church, wooded acclivities, and steep pastoral slopes crowned with the shapely summits of majestic hills, forming a richly diversified
and striking panorama, not to speak of the elegant and
graceful remains of the ancient Abbey, the sight of which
conveys a deep interest to the mind, carries it back through
ages and events long past, and leads to sober reflections
on the vicissitudes of human affairs, and the instability of
human institutions." *   Near the village are the remains
of the famous Abbey, which affords the finest specimen of
Gothic architecture and Gothic sculpture ever reared in
this country. The stone of which it is built, though it has
resisted the weather for so many ages, retains perfect sharp-
ness, so that even the most minute ornaments seem as entire as when newly wrought. The other buildings being
completely destroyed, the ruins of the church alone remain
to attest the ancient magnificence of this celebrated monastery. It is in the usual form of a Latin cross, with a square
tower in the centre, eighty-four feet in height, of which
only the west side is standing. The parts now remaining
of this structure are the choir and transept—the west side,
and part of the north and south walls of the great tower,
part of the nave, nearly the whole of the southmost aisle,
and part of the north aisle. The west gable being in ruins,
the principal entrance is by a richly moulded Gothic portal
in the south transept. Over this doorway is a magnificent
window, twenty-four feet in height and sixteen in breadth,
divided by four bars or mullions, which branch out or in-
terlace each other at the top in a variety of graceful curves.
The stone work of the whole window yet remains perfect.
Over this window are nine niches, and two on each buttress,

* *Monastic Annals of Teviotdale*, p. 196.

which formerly contained images of our Saviour and his
Apostles. Beneath the window is a statue of John Baptist,
with his eye directed upward, as if looking upon the image
of Christ above. The carving upon the pedestals and
canopies of the niches exhibits a variety of quaint figures
and devices. The buttresses and pinnacles on the east and
west sides of the same transept present a curious diversity
of sculptured forms of plants and animals. On the south-
east side are a great many musicians admirably cut. In
the south wall of the nave are eight beautiful windows,
each sixteen feet in height and eight in breadth, having
upright mullions of stone with rich tracery. These windows light eight small square chapels of uniform dimensions, which run along the south side of the nave, and are
separated from each other by thin partition walls of stone.
The west end of the nave, and five of the chapels included
in it, are now roofless. The end next the central tower is
arched over—the side aisles and chapels, with their original
Gothic roof, and the middle avenue with a plain vault
thrown over it in 1618, at which time this part of the
building was fitted up as a parish church. The choir or
chancel, which is built in the form of half a Greek cross,
displays the finest architectural taste. The eastern window
in particular is uncommonly elegant and beautiful. Sir
Walter Scott, in describing this part of the building, says—

> " The moon on the east oriel shone
> Through slender shafts of shapely stone
>   By foliaged tracery combined :
> Thou would'st have thought some fairy's hand
> 'Twixt poplars straight the osier wand
>   In many a freakish knot had twined ;
> Then framed a spell when the work was done,
> And changed the willow wreaths to stone."

The original beautifully fretted and sculptured stone roof
of the east end of the chancel is still standing, and rises
high

> " On pillars lofty, and light, and small,
> The keystone that lock'd each ribbed aisle,
> Was a fleur-de-lys or a quatre-feuille :
> The corbells were carved grotesque and grim,

H

> And the pillars with cluster'd shafts so trim,
> With base and with capital flourished around,
> Seemed bundles of lances which garlands had bound."

The outside of the fabric is everywhere profusely embellished with niches having canopies of an elegant design exquisitely carved, and some of them still containing statues.

The cloisters formed a quadrangle on the north-west side of the church. The door of entrance from the cloisters to the church is on the north side, close by the west wall of the transept, and is exquisitely carved. The foliage upon the capitals of the pilasters on each side is so nicely chiselled, that a straw can be made to penetrate through the interstices between the leaves and stalks. Through this door the "monk of St. Mary's aisle," in the Lay of the Last Minstrel, is said to have conducted William of Deloraine to the grave of Michael Scott, after conducting him through the cloister. The best view of the Abbey is obtained from the south-east corner of the churchyard; but

> " If thou would'st view fair Melrose aright,
> Go visit it by the pale moonlight;
> For the gay beams of lightsome day
> Gild, but to flout, the ruins grey.
> When the broken arches are black in night,
> And each shafted oriel glimmers white;
> When the cold light's uncertain shower
> Streams on the ruin'd central tower;
> When buttress and buttress, alternately,
> Seem framed of ebon and ivory;
> When silver edges the imagery,
> And the scrolls that teach thee to live and die;
> When distant Tweed is heard to rave,
> And the owlet to hoot o'er the dead man's grave,
> Then go—but go alone the while—
> Then view St. David's ruin'd pile;
> And, home returning, soothly swear,
> Was never scene so sad and fair!"

Within the Abbey lie the remains of many a gallant warrior and venerable priest. A large slab of polished marble, of a greenish-black colour, with petrified shells imbedded in it, is believed to cover the dust of Alexander II., who was interred beside the high altar under the east

MELROSE ABBEY.

Drawn by W. H. Townsend.

Engraved by W. Chapman.

window. Here, also, the heart of King Robert Bruce is supposed to have been deposited, after Douglas had made an unsuccessful attempt to carry it to the Holy Land. Many of the powerful family of Douglas were interred in this church—among these were William Douglas, " the dark knight of Liddisdale," who tarnished his laurels by the barbarous murder of his companion in arms, the gallant Sir Alexander Ramsay, and was himself killed by his god-son and chief, William Earl of Douglas, while hunting in Ettrick Forest; and James, second Earl of Douglas, who fell at the celebrated battle of Otterburn. Their tombs, which occupied two crypts near the high altar, were de-faced by the English, under Sir Ralph Evers and Sir Brian Latoun—an insult which was signally avenged by their descendant, the Earl of Angus, at the battle of Ancrum Moor.

Melrose Abbey was founded by David I., by whom it was munificently endowed. The foundation was laid in 1136, but the building was not completed till 1146, when it was dedicated to the Virgin Mary. The monks were of the re-formed class called Cistertians. They were brought from the Abbey of Rievalle, in the North Riding of Yorkshire, and were the first of this order who came into Scotland. It was destroyed by the English in their retreat under Edward II. in 1322, and, four years after, Robert Bruce gave £2000 sterling to rebuild it. This sum, equal to £50,000 of the money of the present day, was raised chiefly from the baronies of Cessford and Eckford, forfeited by Sir Roger de Mowbray, and the lands of Nesbit, Longnewton, Maxton, and Caverton, forfeited by William Lord Soulis. The present beautiful fabric, which is still the object of general admiration in its ruins, was then raised in a style of graceful magnificence, that entitles it to be classed among the most perfect works of the best age of that description of ecclesiastical architecture to which it belongs. In 1385, it was burnt by Richard II.; in 1545, it was despoiled by Evers and Latoun; and, again, in the same year, it was destroyed by the Earl of Hertford. At the period of the Reformation it suffered severely, from the misdirected zeal of the Reformers.* Its chief dilapidations, however, must be attributed to the hostile incursions of the English, and to the wanton mischief or sordid utilitarianism of later times.† The estates of the abbey were granted by Queen Mary in 1566 to James Hepburn, Earl of Bothwell, by whose forfeiture in 1567, they reverted again to the Crown, and the usufruct, with the title of Commendator, was conferred, the following year, upon James Douglas, second son to Sir William Douglas of Lochleven.‡ In 1609, the abbey and its possessions were erected into a temporal lordship for Sir John Ramsay, who had been created Viscount Haddington, for his service in preserving James VI. from the treasonable attempt of the Earl of Gowrie. Lord Haddington, who was afterwards created Earl of Holderness, appears to have disposed of the possessions belonging to the lordship of Melrose, since we find that they were granted by charter to Sir Thomas Hamilton, ("Tam o' the Cowgate,") a celebrated lawyer, who was created Earl of Melrose in 1619, and afterwards Earl of Haddington. Part of the lands were granted to Walter Scott, Earl of Buccleuch; and his descendants, about the beginning of the eighteenth century, acquired by purchase the remainder of the Abbey lands included in the lordship of Melrose, which still form a part of the extensive possessions of the same noble family.

At the abolition of heritable jurisdictions in 1747, the Lady Isabella Scott was allowed the sum of £1200 sterling, as compensation for her right to the bailiery of Melrose.

---

* The following verse, from a once popular ballad, shows that, at the time of the Reformation, the inmates of this Abbey shared in the general reproach of *sensuality* and *irregularity* thrown upon the Romish churchmen :—

> " The monks of Melrose made gude kail
> On Fridays when they fasted ;
> Nor wanted they gude beef and ale,
> As lang's their neighbours' lasted."

† The same remark is applicable to the dilapidations of the other monasteries of Teviotdale. In some instances the heritors seem to have availed themselves of the venerable ruins as a quarry for materials to build or repair modern churches and schools. Fragments of sculptured stones frequently occur in private dwellings. A better spirit now generally prevails.

‡ *Monastic Annals of Teviotdale*, p. 245.

When King David I. laid the foundations of Melrose Abbey, the ground on which Melrose now stands was occupied by a village called Fordel. The present village is an extremely curious and antique place, and has evidently been, in a great measure, built out of the ruins of the abbey. In the centre of the village stands a cross, about twenty feet high, supposed to be coeval with the abbey. There is a ridge in a field near the town, called the Corse-rig, which the proprietor of the field holds upon the sole condition that he shall keep up the cross.

In the vicinity of Melrose are the Eildon hills, the *Tremontium* of the Romans.* Opposite to the village, a wire bridge leads across the Tweed, to the scattered little village of Gattonside, with its numerous orchards. A short way farther down the river, on a peninsula formed by a remarkable sweep of the Tweed, stood the ancient monastery of Old Melrose. The estate of Old Melrose was long possessed by a family of the name of Ormestoun. It is now the property of William Elliot Lockhart, Esq., who has a house there delightfully situated. Two miles below Melrose, the Leader pours its waters from the north, through a beautiful wooded vale, to join the Tweed. The view from the Bemerside road, near Gladswood, is one of the most beautiful and interesting in the south of Scotland. From no other point can the eye command with equal advantage the whole vale of Melrose, and the tourist should by no means neglect to take this view on his way to Dryburgh—by this road, which, although not the most direct, is by far the most picturesque. In the immediate vicinity is Drygrange, (John Tod, Esq.) beautifully situated. About a mile and a half from Drygrange is the house of Cowdenknowes, (Dr. Home), situated on the east bank of the Leader, at the foot of the hill of Cowdenknowes, celebrated in song for its " bonny, bonny broom." A mile farther up the Leader is the village of Earlstoun, anciently Erceldoune, the dwelling of Thomas Learmont,

* It is said that Eildon hills were once an uniform cone, and that the summit was formed into the three picturesque peaks, into which it is now divided, by the spirit, for whom Michael Scott was under the necessity of finding constant employment. See *Lay of the Last Minstrel*, Canto ii., stanza 13.

commonly called Thomas the Rhymer, in whom, as in the mighty men of old,

—————————— the honour'd name
Of prophet and of poet was the same.

The remains of the Rhymer's Tower are still pointed out, in the midst of a beautiful haugh, on the east side of the Leader. About four miles from Melrose, on the north bank of the Tweed, within the county of Berwick, stand the picturesque ruins of

DRYBURGH ABBEY,

on a richly wooded haugh, round which the river makes a fine circuitous sweep. The situation is eminently beautiful, and both the abbey, and the modern mansion-house of the proprietor, are completely embosomed in wood. The finest view of the ruins is from the "Braeheads," behind the village of Lessuden. Dryburgh Abbey was founded in 1150, during the reign of David I., by Hugh de Moreville, Lord of Lauderdale, Constable of Scotland, upon a site which is supposed to have been originally a place of Druidical worship. The monks were of the Premonstratensian order, and were brought from the abbey founded at Alnwick a short time before. Edward II., in his retreat from the unsuccessful invasion of Scotland in 1322, encamped in the grounds of Dryburgh, and setting fire to the monastery, burnt it to the ground. Robert I. contributed liberally towards its repair, but it has been doubted whether it was ever fully restored to its original magnificence. In 1544, the abbey was again destroyed by a hostile incursion of the English, under Sir George Bowes and Sir Brian Latoun. The principal remains of the building are, the western gable of the nave of the church, the ends of the transept, part of the choir, and a portion of the domestic buildings. In St. Mary's aisle, which is by far the most beautiful part of the ruin, Sir Walter Scott was buried, 26th September 1832, in the burying-ground of his ancestors, the Haliburtons of Newmains, the ancient proprietors of the abbey. The ruins of the abbey are almost completely overgrown with foliage, and a number of fine trees have sprung up among the rubbish.

In 1604, James VI. granted Dryburgh Abbey to John Earl of Mar, and he afterwards erected it into a temporal lordship and peerage, with the title of Lord Cardross, to the same Earl, who made it over to his third son, Henry, ancestor of the Earl of Buchan. The abbey was subsequently sold to the Haliburtons of Mertoun, from whom it was purchased by Colonel Tod, whose heirs sold it to the Earl of Buchan in 1786. The Earl, at his death, bequeathed it to his son, Sir David Erskine, at whose death, in 1837, it reverted to the Buchan family.

In the immediate vicinity of the abbey is the neat mansion-house of Dryburgh, surrounded by stately trees. At a short distance, is a chain suspension-bridge over the Tweed, erected in 1818, at the expense of the late Earl of Buchan, but rendered impassable by a storm in January 1840, and never since repaired. On a rising-ground, at the end of the bridge, is a circular temple dedicated to the Muses, surmounted by a bust of Thomson, the author of the "Seasons." Farther up, on a rocky eminence overlooking the river, is a colossal statue of the Scottish patriot Wallace. The whole prospect around is eminently beautiful, embracing both wood and water, mountain and rock scenery.*

---

* Connected with Dryburgh is the following story, told by Sir Walter Scott in his Border Minstrelsy:—"Soon after the Rebellion in 1745, an unfortunate female wanderer took up her residence in a dark vault among the ruins of Dryburgh Abbey, which, during the day, she never quitted. When night fell, she issued from this miserable habitation, and went to the house of Mr. Haliburton of Newmains, or to that of Mr. Erskine of Shielfield, two gentlemen of the neighbourhood. From their charity she obtained such necessaries as she could be prevailed on to accept At twelve, each night, she lighted her candle and returned to her vault, assuring her neighbours that, during her absence, her habitation was arranged by a spirit, to whom she gave the uncouth appellation of Fatlips, and whom she described as a little man, wearing heavy iron shoes, with which he trampled the clay floor of the vault, to dispel the damps. This circumstance caused her to be regarded, by the well-informed, with compassion, as deranged in her understanding, and, by the vulgar, with some degree of terror. The cause of her adopting this extraordinary mode of life she would never explain. It was, however, believed to have been occasioned by a vow, that, during the absence of a man to whom she was attached, she would never look upon the sun. Her lover never returned. He fell during the civil war of 1745-6, and she never more would behold the light of day. The vault, or rather dungeon, in which this unfortunate woman lived and died, passes still by the

On the opposite bank of the Tweed lies St. Boswell's
Green, near the village of Lessuden, formerly a place of
some importance, for when burned by the English in 1544,
it contained sixteen strong towers.*   On the Green is held
the fair of St. Boswell's, the principal market for sheep and
lambs in the south of Scotland.   Near this place a bridge
has lately been erected across the Tweed, opening up a
desirable communication between the north and south sides
of the river.   Two miles from St. Boswell's is the village of
Maxton, and, on the opposite side of the river, in a delightful situation, is Mertoun House, the seat of Scott of Harden, who has lately established his claim to the title of
Lord Polwarth.   Near to Maxton, on the south bank of the
river, are the ruins of Littledean Tower, formerly a place
of great note, and long the residence of the Kers of Littledean and Nenthorn, a branch of the Cessford family.   It is
now the property of Lord Polwarth.   Six miles from St.
Boswell's Green is Makerstoun, the lovely residence of Sir
Thomas Makdougal Brisbane, Bart., surrounded by luxuriant woods.   To the north, a view may be obtained of
Smailholm Tower, the scene of Sir Walter Scott's ballad of
the "Eve of St. John."   The poet resided for some time,

name of the supernatural being with which its gloom was tenanted by her disturbed imagination."

In the vicinity of Dryburgh is the mansion of Bemerside, the lands and barony of which have been in the possession of the Haigs since the time of Malcolm IV.   The following rhyme respecting this family is ascribed, by tradition,
to Thomas the Rhymer :—

"Tide, tide, whate'er betide,
There 'll ay be Haigs in Bemerside."

The above rhyme, which testifies the firm belief entertained by the country
people in the perpetual lineal succession of the Haigs, is ascribed to no less
venerable and infallible authority than that of Thomas the Rhymer, whose
patrimonial territory was not far from Bemerside.   The great-grandfather of the
present Mr. Haig had twelve daughters, before his wife brought him a male-
heir.   The common people trembled for the credit of their favourite soothsayer.
But at length the birth of a son confirmed their belief in the prophecy beyond
a shadow of doubt.—*Minst. Scot. Bord.*, iii., 209.

* The village of St. Boswell's appears to have stood in the vicinity of the
Church, where the foundations of houses are occasionally discovered in the
operations of agriculture.   In the banks are many copious springs, and several
of them form beautiful petrifactions.

while a boy, at the neighbouring farm-house of Sandy-knowe, then inhabited by his paternal grandfather, and he has beautifully described the scenery in one of his preliminary epistles to Marmion.* The Tower is a high square building, surrounded by an outer wall, now ruinous. The circuit of the outer court being defended, on three sides, by a precipice and morass, is accessible only from the west by a steep and rocky path. The apartments are placed one above another, and communicate by a narrow stair. From the elevated situation of Smailholm Tower, it is seen many miles in every direction. It formerly belonged to the Pringles of Whytbank, and is now the property of Lord Polwarth. Continuing along the road, amidst the richest scenery, the tourist passes on the right, the scanty remains of the famous CASTLE OF ROXBURGH, situated near the junction of the Tweed and Teviot, which here approach so close as to form a narrow isthmus. Roxburgh Castle was formerly a fortress of great extent and importance ; but having been dismantled about 400 years ago, a few fragments of walls are all that now remain to attest its former strength. A deep moat, filled with water from the Teviot, formed part of its defences. In 1460, when in possession of the English, it was besieged by James II., and, after his death, it was

---

* " It was a barren scene, and wild,
  Where naked cliffs were rudely piled ;
  But, ever and anon, between
  Lay velvet tufts of loveliest green ;
  And well the lonely infant knew
  Recesses where the wall-flower grew,
  And honeysuckle loved to crawl
  Up the low crag and ruin'd wall.
  I deem'd such nooks the sweetest shade
  The sun in all its round survey'd ;
  And still I thought that shatter'd tower
  The mightiest work of human power ;
  And marvell'd, as the aged hind
  With some strange tale bewitch'd my mind,
  Of forayers, who, with headlong force, ·
  Down from that strength had spurr'd their horse
  Their southern rapine to renew,
  Far in the distant Cheviots blue,
  And, home returning, fill'd the hall
  With revel, wassel-rout, and brawl."

taken by his army, under the direction of his widow. The spot where James was killed, by the bursting of a cannon, is marked by a holly tree, which grows upon the opposite bank of the Tweed. Nearly opposite to the ruins of the Castle, on the left bank of the river, is FLEURS CASTLE, the seat of the Duke of Roxburghe, commanding a fine view of the surrounding country. Extensive alterations and repairs have lately been made on this building, which render it one of the most stately specimens of the Tudor style in Scotland. On the Haugh, upon the south side of the river, is held, on the 5th of August, St. James's Fair, the greatest fair, next to St. Boswell's, in the south of Scotland. Proceeding onward, the tourist crosses the Teviot, and shortly after, the Tweed, and enters the town of

KELSO,

occupying a beautiful situation on the north margin of the Tweed. It consists of four principal streets, and a spacious square or market-place, in which stand the town-hall, erected in 1816, and many well-built houses, with elegant shops. Kelso is the residence of a number of people in easy circumstances, who live in a style of considerable elegance. It carries on a good inland trade, and has a weekly market and four annual fairs.* Its population is 5328. The most prominent object in Kelso is the venerable abbey, a noble specimen of the solid and majestic style of architecture called the Saxon or early Norman. The monks were of a reformed class of the Benedictines, first established at Tiron in France, and hence called Tironenses. David I., when Earl of Huntingdon, introduced the Tironenses into Scotland, and settled them near his castle at Selkirk, in the year 1113. The principal residence of the kings of Scotland, at this period, was the Castle of Roxburgh; and when David succeeded to the Scottish crown, after the death of his brother, in 1124, he removed the convent from Selkirk to Kelso, within view of his royal castle. The foundation of the

---

* Kelso is a burgh of barony, governed, under the general police Act, by a bailie and sixteen Commissioners. It is one of the cleanest and best lighted towns in Scotland.

church was laid on the 3d of May 1128. In consequence of its vicinity to the English border, Kelso suffered severely during the wars between the two countries, and the monastery was frequently laid waste by fire. It was reduced to its present ruinous state by the English, under the Earl of Hertford, in 1545. The only parts now remaining are the walls of the transepts, the centre tower, and west end, and a small part of the choir. After the Reformation, a low gloomy vault was thrown over the transept, to make it serve as a parish church, and it continued to be used for this purpose till 1771, when one Sunday, during divine service, the congregation were alarmed by the falling of a piece of plaster from the roof, and hurried out in terror, believing that the vault over their heads was giving way; and this, together with an ancient prophecy, attributed to Thomas the Rhymer, "that the kirk should fall when at the fullest," caused the church to be deserted, and it has never since had an opportunity of tumbling on a full congregation. The ruins were disencumbered of the rude modern masonry, by the good taste of William Duke of Roxburghe, and his successor Duke James, and, in 1823, the decayed parts were strengthened and repaired by subscription. After the Reformation, the principal part of the estates of this rich abbey were held *in commendam* by Sir John Maitland, the ancestor of the Earl of Lauderdale, who exchanged it with Francis Stewart, afterwards Earl of Bothwell, for the priory of Coldinghame. This nobleman, for his repeated treasons, was attainted in 1592, and the lands and possessions of Kelso abbey were finally conferred upon Sir Robert Ker of Cessford, and they are still enjoyed by his descendant, the Duke of Roxburghe.

The environs of Kelso are singularly beautiful. They are thus described by Leyden, in his *Scenes of Infancy*:

" Bosom'd in woods where mighty rivers run,
  Kelso's fair vale expands before the sun,
  Its rising downs in vernal beauty swell,
  And, fring'd with hazel, winds each flowery dell,
  Green spangled plains to dimpling lawns succeed,
  And Tempe rises on the banks of Tweed,
  Blue o'er the river Kelso's shadow lies,
  And copse-clad isles amid the waters rise."

The most admired view is from the bridge, looking up the river. In this view is comprehended the junction of the rivers—the ruins of Roxburgh Castle; in front, the Palace of Fleurs, with its lawns sloping to the margin of the Tweed, and sheltered by lofty trees behind. On the south bank of the river are the woods and mansion of Springwood Park, (Sir George Douglas, Bart.,) with the elegant bridge of the Teviot. On the right is the town, extended along the bank of the river; nearer is Ednam House, and immediately beyond are the lofty ruins of the Abbey. In the background are the hills of Stitchel and Mellerstain—the castle of Home—the picturesque summits of the Eildon Hills, Penielheugh, &c. An excellent view may also be obtained of the district around Kelso, from the top of an eminence, on the south bank of the river, called Pinnaclehill; and a third, equally interesting, from the building appropriated as a Museum and Library, situated on an elevation termed the Terrace.*

About two miles north from Kelso, on the banks of the Eden, is the village of EDNAM, the birth-place of the poet Thomson, near to which a monument has been erected to his memory. A little to the west, is Newton-Don, the seat of Sir William Don, Bart.; and two miles farther to the north is Stitchel, the mansion of Sir John Pringle, Bart. A short way beyond, on a considerable eminence, commanding a view of the whole Merse and a great deal of Roxburghshire, is Home Castle, once the residence of the ancient and powerful family of that name. After the battle of Pinkie, 1547, it was taken by the English, under the Duke of Somerset, and again, during the time of the Commonwealth, it was besieged and taken by Oliver Cromwell. Three miles to the west is Mellerstain House, the seat of George Baillie, Esq., of Jerviswood, surrounded by extensive plantations.

Leaving Kelso, the road proceeds by Hendersyde Park,

* From Kelso a road leads to Jedburgh, by the villages of Maxwellheugh and Heaton, the beautiful banks of the Kale, Grahamslaw, where there are some remarkable caves, the villages of Eckford and Crailing, Crailing house, (J. Paton, Esq.,) formerly the seat of the noble family of Cranstoun, and Bonjedward, (Archibald Jerdon, Esq.)

(John Waldie, Esq.,) along the north banks of the Tweed. At the distance of two miles, is the village of Sprouston, on the south bank of the river. A mile beyond this the Eden joins the Tweed, and, half a mile farther, the tourist enters the Merse, or Berwickshire. The Tweed now forms the boundary between England and Scotland. On its south bank is Carham Church, with Carham Hall. A mile and a half farther, on the same side, are the ruins of Wark Castle, celebrated in Border history. A mile farther, on the left, is the Hirsel, the seat of the Earl of Home; the park contains some fine preserves. The road now crosses the water of Leet, and, nine miles from Kelso, enters the thriving town of

COLDSTREAM,

occupying a level and elevated situation on the north bank of the Tweed, which is here crossed by a handsome bridge. The population of the town is about 3000. In consequence of its proximity to England, Coldstream, like Gretna Green, is celebrated for its irregular marriages. In the principal inn Lord Brougham was married. General Monck resided in Coldstream during the winter of 1659-60, before he marched into England to restore Charles II., and here he raised a horse regiment, which is still denominated the Coldstream Guards. On the bank of the Tweed, to the west of the town, is Lees, the beautiful seat of Sir William Marjoribanks, Bart. About a mile and a half to the east of the town are the ruins of the Church of Lennel, which was the name of the parish before Coldstream existed. Near it is Lennel House, (Earl of Haddington,) in which the venerable Patrick Brydone, author of "Travels in Sicily and Malta," spent the latter years of his long life.* Following the course of the river, we come to Tillmouth, where the Till, a deep, dark, and sullen stream, flows into the Tweed.† On its banks stands Twisel Castle, (Sir Francis

* There are two roads from Coldstream to Berwick, one along the north bank and one along the south bank of the Tweed. The latter is the more interesting, and is generally preferred.

† The different characteristics of the two rivers are pointed out in the following rhyme :—

Blake, Bart.) Beneath the castle, the ancient bridge is
still standing by which the English crossed the Till before
the battle of Flodden.* The glen is romantic and delightful, with steep banks on each side, covered with copsewood. On the opposite bank of the Tweed is Milne-Graden,
(the late Admiral Sir David Milne, Bart.,) once the seat of
the Kerrs of Graden, and, at an earlier period, the residence
of the chief of a Border clan, known by the name of Graden.† A little to the north-east is the village of Swinton.
The estate of Swinton is remarkable, as having been, with
only two very brief interruptions, the property of one family
since the days of the Anglo-Saxon monarchy. The first of
the Swintons acquired the name and the estate, as a reward
for the bravery which he displayed in clearing the country
of the wild swine which then infested it. The family have
produced many distinguished warriors. At the battle of
Beaugé, in France, Thomas Duke of Clarence, brother to
Henry V., was unhorsed by Sir John Swinton of Swinton,
who distinguished him by a coronet of precious stones
which he wore around his helmet.‡ The brave conduct of
another of this warlike family, at the battle of Homildon
Hill, in 1402, has been dramatized by Sir Walter Scott,

> Tweed said to Till,
>   " What gars ye rin sae still ?"
> Till said to Tweed,
>   " Though ye rin wi' speed,
> And I rin slaw,
>   Yet, where ye drown ae man
>   I drown twa !"

*—————— " They cross'd
    The Till, by Twisel Bridge.
High sight it is, and haughty, while
They dive into the deep defile;
Beneath the cavern'd cliff they fall,
Beneath the castle's airy wall.
  By rock, by oak, by hawthorn tree,
Troop after troop are disappearing;
Troop after troop their banners rearing,
  Upon the eastern bank you see,
Still pouring down the rocky den,
  Where flows the sullen Till,
And, rising from the dim wood glen
Standards on standards, men on men,
  In slow succession still,
And sweeping o'er the Gothic arch,
And pressing on, in ceaseless march,
  To gain the opposing hill."
                    Marmion, c. vi.

† SIR WALTER SCOTT'S *Border Antiquities,* p. 152.
‡ " And Swinton laid the lance in rest
    That tamed, of yore, the sparkling crest
    Of Clarence's Plantagenet."
                    Lay of the Last Minstrel, c. v., s. 4.

whose grandmother was the daughter of Sir John Swinton of Swinton. Three miles eastward is Ladykirk, nine miles from Berwick, at which place a new bridge has lately been erected across the Tweed. The church of this parish is an ancient Gothic building, said to have been erected by James IV., in consequence of a vow made to the Virgin, when he found himself in great danger while crossing the Tweed, by a ford in the neighbourhood. By this ford the English and Scottish armies made their mutual invasions, before the bridge of Berwick was erected. The adjacent field, called Holywell Haugh, was the place where Edward I. met the Scottish nobility, to settle the dispute between Bruce and Baliol, relative to the crown of Scotland. On the opposite bank of the Tweed, stands the celebrated Castle of Norham. The description of this ancient fortress, in the poem of Marmion, is too well known to require to be quoted here. About four miles from Berwick, is Paxton House, the seat of Forman Home, Esq., which contains a fine collection of pictures. In the immediate neighbourhood, the Tweed is crossed by the Union Wire Suspension Bridge, constructed in 1820, by Captain Samuel Brown. Its length is 437 feet ; width, eighteen ; height of piers above low water-mark, sixty-nine ; and is one of the finest structures of that kind in this part of the island. Near Paxton, the Tweed is joined by the Whitadder, the principal river which flows through Berwickshire ; on its banks, a few miles to the north-west, is Ninewells, the paternal seat of David Hume. Before entering Berwick, we pass Halidon Hill, the scene of a battle in 1333, between the English and the Scots, in which the latter were defeated. The town of Berwick is more remarkable for its historical recollections than for its present importance. It is twenty-three miles distant from Kelso, and fifty-eight from Edinburgh, and is a respectable looking town, containing about 9000 or 10,000 inhabitants.

SECOND TOUR.

LEAVING Edinburgh by the great south road through the centre of Newington, the tourist passes on the right Grange House, (Sir T. Dick Lauder, Bart.) Three miles from the city, the village and kirk of Liberton will be seen at a short distance on the right. A mile farther the tourist passes Moredun (Anderson, Esq.) on the right, and a short distance beyond the road passes through the village of Gilmerton. On the right, five and a half miles from Edinburgh, is MELVILLE CASTLE, (Lord Melville.) After crossing the Esk, the tourist passes in succession NEWBATTLE ABBEY,* (Marquis of Lothian,) on the left, and Dalhousie Castle,* (Earl of Dalhousie,) on the right. Eleven miles distant from Edinburgh the tourist reaches Fushie Bridge Inn. On the left, half a mile before reaching Fushie, are the oldest powder-mills in Scotland. Immediately after passing Fushie Bridge, a view is obtained of BORTHWICK CASTLE,† and Borthwick Kirk, standing in the midst of a valley on the left. Passing Middleton Inn, the road now crosses a bleak upland, called Heriot Muir, and a few miles farther on, descends into the vale of Gala. Sixteen miles from Edinburgh is Heriot House, and on the right, at the distance of a mile, Heriot Kirk. Three miles beyond on the left, is Crookston, (Borthwick, Esq.) A little farther on, Pirntaiton, (Innes, Esq.) on the right, Burn House, (Thom-

---

* Described on pages 92, 93.
† For a description of this Castle, see page 93.

son, Esq.,) Pirn, (Tait, Esq.,) and Torquhan, (Colvin, Esq.,) on the left. On the right, the comfortable inn of Torsonce, and a short way beyond, the ancient and irregular village of Stow, situated in the middle of a district, which formerly bore the name of We-dale, (the vale of Woe.) The whole of this territory belonged at one time to the Bishops of St. Andrews, and many of their charters are dated from We-dale. Proceeding onwards, with the Gala on the right, the tourist reaches Crosslee, on the confines of the county of Roxburgh. The river now forms the boundary between the counties of Roxburgh and Selkirk, and the alder, birch, and hazel are found in abundance on its banks. The "Braw lads of Gala water," are celebrated in Burns's well-known beautiful lyric of that name. A short way farther on is TORWOODLEE, the fine mansion of Pringle of Torwoodlee, situated in the midst of stately trees, upon a fine terrace overhanging the Gala. A few hundred yards to the west of the modern mansion are the ruins of the old house, jut-ting out from the side of a hill. At a little distance to the west of the ruin, lies the family burying-ground, embower-ed in the midst of a dark grove. The Pringles of Torwood-lee are a very old family, and celebrated in Border story. Their representative, in the reign of Charles II., was pecu-liarly obnoxious to Government, on account of his exertions in the cause of the covenant, and his concern in Argyle's rebellion. Within a mile of his house, on different sides of the vale of Gala, were two old towers, called Buckholm and Blindlee, occupied by two of his inveterate enemies, who are said to have kept continual watch over his motions, in order to find occasion to accuse him to Government. A short way beyond, at the distance of 32 miles from Edin-burgh, the tourist reaches

GALASHIELS,

a thriving town, finely situated on the banks of the Gala, which joins the Tweed about a mile below. It contains about 4000 inhabitants, principally engaged in the produc-tion of woollen cloths. About sixty years ago, Galashiels was only a small village occupying part of the higher ground

I

near the church, and extending within the park, where the
ruins of the old court-house still remain, towards the baronial mansion of Gala. A few weavers contented themselves
with exercising their individual industry; but by degrees
union and enterprise enlarged the demand, and devised
new means of meeting it. Mills were built—at first on a
small scale, but by increasing prosperity were enlarged and
multiplied, and a populous town soon covered the green
fields beside the Gala. Originally the only species of manufacture was a coarse woollen cloth, called "Galashiels
gray," the wool employed being the produce of the surrounding hills; but now the goods manufactured chiefly consist
of fancy articles, such as tartans, tweeds, and shawls of the
finest texture and most brilliant colours, while the wool is
principally imported from Van Diemen's Land. Within the
last few years the town and its manufactures have increased
with even greater rapidity than at any former period. The
mills have grown to four times their original size; large
new premises have been erected; the water-force of the
Gala has been exhausted, and, though the distance from
coal is great, recourse has been had to the aid of steam;
whilst some of the inhabitants have sought larger scope for
their exertions at Selkirk and Innerleithen.

In a place where some hundreds have been suddenly
drawn together from all quarters, we may naturally expect
to find a considerable share of the evils incident to a manufacturing population; but of the masters, and generally of
the workmen, natives or long resident in the place, it may
be safely said that there does not exist, in any trade or employment a more intelligent, moral, and industrious class
of men.

The town is partly in Selkirkshire, and partly in Roxburgh. Galashiels proper is a burgh of barony, under the
family of Gala, which now bears the name of Scott though
representing the ancient Pringles, the ancestor of Mr. Scott
having married the heiress of that baronial house, and succeeded to its fortunes in 1623. An old pear tree exists
near the house, on which the destined bride is said to have

been amusing herself in youthful frolics whilst the marriage contract was signed.

In 1813, Mr. Richard Lees, manufacturer, assisted by a blacksmith, constructed a wire bridge over the Gala, being the first specimen of this American invention erected in the old world. It was destroyed by a flood in autumn 1838, but another has been erected in its place. The higher ground of the parish is traversed by the remains of an ancient wall, supposed to be the Catrail, and near it at Rink, on an eminence, is an old British Camp.

Leaving Galashiels, a fine view is obtained of the vale of the Tweed, and a passing glance of the towers of Abbotsford on the right, overtopping the surrounding trees. On the left is Langlee, (Bruce, Esq.) Farther on is Allan Water, already described in page 114, and, soon after, the road crosses the Tweed, passes the village of Darnick, and two miles beyond it, reaches

MELROSE,

with the magnificent ruins of its Abbey, for a full description of which the reader is referred to page 115. Three miles from Melrose is Newton-Dryburgh. Half a mile further a beautiful view is obtained of Dryburgh Abbey and the course of the Tweed. A few miles farther on, the road passes ANCRUM MOOR, where the Earl of Angus routed the English in 1545. During the year 1544, Lord Evers and Sir Brian Latoun committed the most dreadful ravages upon the Scottish frontiers. As a reward for their services, the English monarch promised to the two barons a feudal grant of the country which they had thus reduced to a desert; upon hearing which, Archibald Douglas, the seventh Earl of Angus, is said to have sworn to write the deed of investiture upon their skins, with sharp pens, and bloody ink, in resentment for their having defaced the tombs of his ancestors at Melrose. In 1545, Lord Evers and Latoun again entered Scotland with an army of upwards of 5000 men, and even exceeded their former cruelty. As they returned towards Jedburgh, they were overtaken by Angus at the head of 1000 horse, who was shortly after joined by the famous Norman Lesley with a body of Fife-men. While the Scottish general was hesitating whether to advance or retire, Sir Walter Scott of Buccleuch came up at full speed with a small but chosen body of his retainers, and by his advice, an immediate attack was made. The battle was commenced upon a piece of low flat ground, near Peniel-heugh,* and, just as it began, a heron, roused from the marshes by the tumult, soared away betwixt the encountering armies. " O !" exclaimed Angus, "that I had here my white gosshawk, that we might all yoke at once !" The Scots obtained a complete victory, and Lord Evers and his son, together with Sir Brian Latoun, and 800 Englishmen, many of whom were persons of rank, fell in the engagement. A mile beyond this, on the right, the road passes Ancrum House, (Sir William Scott, Bart.,) and on the opposite bank of the Ale, is the village of Ancrum.† At the manse of Ancrum, Thomson the poet spent much of his time with Mr. Cranstoun, the clergyman of the parish. A short way beyond, at some distance on the left, is Mount Teviot, a seat of the Marquis of Lothian, whose second title is Earl of Ancrum. On the right, two miles up the Teviot, is Chesters, (W. Ogilvie, Esq.) The tourist now crosses the Teviot by Ancrum Bridge. A short way beyond, on the right, is Tympandean, with the ruins of an ancient tower, and a mile farther on the left is Bonjedward, an ancient Roman station.‡ The Roman road here crossed the Jed, and is still in a state of preservation from the Jed to the Border hills. At the distance of another mile, in the deep vale of the sylvan Jed, the tourist enters the royal burgh of

JEDBURGH,§

romantically situated in the midst of gardens and venerable

* Penielheugh is the hill upon which the Waterloo Monument is built.

† Ancrum is situated near a bend of the Ale ; and derives its name (Alncrum) from that circumstance.

‡ "Beanjeddard, Hundlie, and Hunthill,
        Three, on they laid weel at the last."
                        Raid of Reidswire.

§ Jedburgh is vulgarly called Jethart, a corruption of its former name Jedworth ; from Jed, and the Saxon "*weorth,*" a hamlet.

orchards, and environed with wooded and precipitous banks. This is a place of great antiquity ; the village of old Jedworth, about four miles above the present town, having been founded by Ecgred, Bishop of Lindisfarn, A.D. 845. St. Kenoch was Abbot of Jedburgh, A.D. 1000, and its royal castle is mentioned in the earliest Scottish annals. It appears to have been a royal burgh even in the time of David I. It was the chief town on the middle marches. Defended by its castle and numerous towers, and, surrounded by the fastnesses of its forest, it was frequently the rendezvous of the Scottish armies, and was as frequently assailed, pillaged, and burnt, by the English.

Its importance declined from the union of the two crowns, and though it has in modern times revived, it has never reached any great extent either in population or trade. The population within the Parliamentary boundary in 1841, was 3277, being about 300 less than in 1831. It is the county town of Roxburghshire, the seat of the circuit court of justiciary and of a presbytery. Its weekly market is on Tuesday, and it has besides several good annual fairs and monthly markets for cattle.

Many interesting objects of antiquity were destroyed during the last century, such as St. David's tower—the gateway of the ancient bridge of the Canongate—and the cross, an interesting edifice, on which, according to Bannatyne, the magistrates, having espoused the cause of James VI., compelled the heralds of Mary, after suffering unseemly chastisement, to eat their proclamation. The principal object of curiosity is the remains of the Abbey. It was enlarged and richly endowed by David I., and other munificent patrons about the year 1118, or 1147. At one period, its powerful abbots disputed, though unsuccessfully, the jurisdiction of the Bishops of Glasgow, who generally resided at Ancrum in the neighbourhood. It suffered frequently in the English wars, especially from the invasions of Edward I. and Edward III. It sustained a siege of two hours under the artillery of the Earl of Surrey, at the storming of Jedburgh, in the reign of Henry VIII., and the traces of the flames are still visible on its ruined walls. It suffered sub-

sequent dilapidation from the forces of the Earl of Hertford ; and in common with the other monasteries of Teviotdale, does not appear to have been inhabited at the time of
the Reformation. The monks were Canons regular or Augustine friars, brought from Beauvais in France.

At the Reformation, the lands of the Abbey were converted into a temporal lordship, with the title of Lord
Jedburgh, in favour of Sir Andrew Ker of Ferniehirst, and
they are now possessed by his descendant, the Marquis of
Lothian. It is a magnificent ruin, and is considered the
most perfect and beautiful specimen of the Saxon and early
Gothic in Scotland. The principal parts now remaining
are, the nave, nearly the whole of the choir, with the south
aisle, the centre tower, and the north transept, which is
entire, and has long been set apart as a burial-place for the
family of the Marquis of Lothian. In the western gable is
a door of exceedingly beautiful workmanship. But the
most curious and interesting part of it is the Norman
door, which entered from the cloisters on the south, of exquisitely delicate and beautiful workmanship : the finer portions of sculpture are rapidly decaying. Over the intersec-
tion of the nave and transept, rises a massive square tower,
with irregular turrets and belfry, to the height of 100 feet.
The west end is fitted up as a parish church, in a most barbarous and unseemly style. Some public-spirited individuals have lately expended a considerable sum in repairing
the decayed parts of the building, so as to prevent farther
dilapidation.

The best view of the Abbey is obtained from the banks
of the river. The Castle of Jedburgh, situated on an eminence at the town head, was a favourite residence of our
early Scottish kings, from the time of David I. to Alexander
III.* Malcolm the fourth died there—Alexander III. married there, with unusual pomp, October 14, 1285, Jolande,
daughter of the Count de Dreux, on which occasion the
festivities of the evening are said to have been interrupted
by the sudden and ominous appearance of a spectre, which,

* " Jeda's ancient walls, once seat of kings."
                                        HAMILTON of Bangor.

entering the dance, filled the gay company with consterna-
tion. The importance of this castle may be estimated from
the circumstance of its always ranking in the treaties with
England, along with Roxburgh, Edinburgh, and Stirling,
and from the fact, that when the Scottish government determined to destroy it, it was meditated to impose a tax of
two pennies on every hearth in Scotland, as the only means
of accomplishing so arduous an undertaking. The site of
this ancient fortress is now occupied by a new jail, from
the top of which there is a beautiful view of the town and
neighbourhood.

In the lower part of the town, may be still seen the old
mansion occupied by Queen Mary, and where she lay sick
for several weeks after her visit to Bothwell, at Hermitage.
She rode from Jedburgh to Hermitage, and returned on
the same day, a distance of about 40 miles; she was in
consequence thrown into a violent fever, and her life for
some time despaired of.

The rich soil and mild climate of Jedburgh renders it
peculiarly congenial to horticulture; delicate plants and
fruits succeeding in the open air, which in other places require to be placed under glass. Many of the pear trees
are of great size and antiquity, and bear immense crops,
which are disposed of through an extensive district. The
best kinds are French, and may probably have been planted
by the Monks.

The inhabitants of Jedburgh, in ancient times, were a
warlike race, and were celebrated for their dexterity in
handling a particular sort of partisan; which, therefore,
got the name of the " Jethart staff." Their timely aid
is said to have turned the fortune of the day at the skirmish of Reidswire. Their proud war-cry was, " Jethart's
here."* Their arms are a mounted trooper advancing to
the charge, with the motto, " Strenue et prospere." They
have still in preservation some ancient trophies taken from
the English, particularly a flag or pennon taken at Bannockburn. The ordinary proverb of " Jethart justice,"

* " Then raise the slogan with ane shout,
" Fy, Tindaill to it! Jedbrugh's here."
Raid of Reidswire.

where men were said to be hanged first and tried afterwards, appears to have taken its rise from some instances
of summary justice executed on the Border marauders.*

In the south aisle of the Abbey, then used as the Gram-
mar School, the poet Thomson, whose father was translated
from Ednam to Southdean on the Jed, when the poet was
only two years old, received the rudiments of his education.
It is not generally known that when he attended Edinburgh
University, he did so as the bursar of the Presbytery of
Jedburgh. The celebrated Samuel Rutherford is also said
to have been educated here. Dr. Somerville, historian of
William and Anne, was upwards of fifty years minister of
Jedburgh, and in the manse was born the amiable and
highly gifted Mrs. Somerville. Sir David Brewster is also
a native of Jedburgh.

The environs of Jedburgh abound in rich woodland scenes,
and the walk through the picturesque woods and groves
which adorn the precipitous banks of the winding Jed,
is especially delightful.† On the banks of the Jed, at
Hundalee, Lintalee, and Mossburnford, are caves dug cut
of the rock, supposed to have been used as hiding-places in
ancient warfare. In the neighbourhood are the remains of
numerous camps; but the most remarkable is the camp of
Lintalee, little more than a mile from the town, where
Douglas, as described in Barbour's Bruce, lay for the defence of Scotland, during the absence of the king in Ireland,
and where in a desperate personal encounter he slew the
English commander the Earl of Brittany, at the head of
his army, and routed the whole with great slaughter—an
achievement commemorated in the armorial bearings of the
Douglas family. Jed forest was conferred on Douglas by
Bruce, the regality of which was sold to the crown by the
Duke of Douglas. The forest lands still belong to Lord
Douglas. A short distance from the town, the half ruinous

* There is a similar English proverb concerning Lydford :—
　　" I oft have heard of Lydford law,
　　Where in the morn men hang and draw,
　　And sit in judgment after."
　　　　　　　　　　BROWN'S *Poems.*

† " Eden scenes on crystal Jed."
　　　　　　　　　　BURNS.

castle of Ferniehirst, the ancient seat of the Kerrs, occupies a romantic situation on the right bank of the river. It was built by Sir Thomas Kerr in 1490, and was taken by the English in 1523, and again, after the battle of Pinkie. The family of Kerr settled at Kerrsheugh in the 13th century, and from this place the Marquis of Lothian takes his title as a British Peer. About a mile northward from the castle grows a large oak tree, called, on account of its great size, " the king of the wood," and at the side of the ruin stands another, equally large, called " the capon tree." Both trees are noticed in Gilpin's Forest Scenery.

From Jedburgh to Hawick there is a fine walk of about ten miles along the bank of the Teviot. The vale of the Rule intervenes, as also the chief hills of Teviotdale, the Dunian, and Ruberslaw. The whole course of the Teviot between these towns is studded on each side with cottages and mansions, the most distinguished of which is Minto House, the residence of the Earl of Minto. The grounds are ample and varied. In the immediate vicinity of the house are Minto crags, a romantic assemblage of cliffs which rise suddenly above the vale of Teviot. A small platform on a projecting crag, commanding a most beautiful prospect, is termed *Barnhill's Bed*. This Barnhill is said to have been a robber or outlaw. There are remains of a strong tower beneath the rocks, where he is supposed to have dwelt, and from which he derived his name. On the summit of the crags are the fragments of another ancient tower in a picturesque situation.* Nearly opposite

* " On Minto crags the moon-beams glint,
  Where Barnhill hew'd his bed of flint,
  Who flung his outlaw'd limbs to rest,
  Where falcons hang their giddy nest,
  'Mid cliffs from whence his eagle eye
  For many a league his prey could spy,
  Cliffs, doubling, on their echoes borne,
  The terrors of the robber's horn;
  Cliffs which for many a later year
  The warbling Doric reed shall hear,
  When some sad swain shall teach the grove,
  Ambition is no cure for love." †
                    Lay of the Last Minstrel.

† Sir Gilbert Elliot, grandfather to the present Lord Minto, was the author of the beautiful pastoral song, beginning, " My sheep I neglected," &c.

to Minto House lies the pleasant village of Denholm, the
birthplace of Dr. John Leyden.

HAWICK

is a thriving town, situated upon a haugh at the junction
of the Slitterick and Teviot. It is a burgh of regality, and
is of considerable antiquity. Its inhabitants are principally engaged in manufactures, and are remarkable for
their industry and intelligence. Hawick has made a considerable figure in Border history, and from its proximity to
the Border, has frequently suffered severely from the inroads
of the English. The Slitterick is crossed by a bridge of peculiarly antique construction, and at the head of the town is
a moat-hill, where the brave Sir Alexander Ramsay was
acting in his capacity of Sheriff of Teviotdale, when he was
seized by Sir William Douglas, the " dark knight of Liddisdale," and plunged into one of the dungeons of Hermitage
Castle, where he perished of hunger. Hawick is noted
among topers for its " gill." A *Hawick gill* is well known
in Scotland to be half a mutchkin, equal to two gills.* On
the right bank of the Teviot, about two miles above Hawick,
stands the ancient tower of Goldielands, one of the most
entire now extant upon the Border. The proprietors of this
tower belonged to the clan of Scott. The last of them is
said to have been hanged over his own gate, for march
treason. About a mile farther up the river, on the opposite
bank, stands the celebrated tower of Branxholm, the principal scene of the " Lay of the Last Minstrel," and during
the 15th and 16th centuries the residence of the Buccleuch
family. Branxholm was famous of yore for the charms of
a *bonnie lass*, whose beauty has been celebrated by Ramsay
in a ballad beginning

> " As I came in by Teviot side,
>   And by the braes o' Branksome,
> There first I saw my bloomin' bride,
>   Young, smiling, sweet, and handsome."†

---

* " Weel she loo'ed a Hawick gill,
        And leuch to see a tappit hen."
                        Andrew and his Cuttie Gun.
        [A tappit hen is a frothing measure of claret.]
    † The bonnie lass was daughter to a woman nicknamed Jean the Ranter, who

Nearly opposite Goldielands Tower the Teviot is joined by Borthwick water. In a narrow valley formed by this stream, stands Harden Castle, an interesting specimen of an ancient Border fortress. The carved stucco work upon the ceiling of the old hall is well worth attention. The lobby is paved with marble; and the mantel-piece of one of the rooms is surmounted with an earl's coronet, and the letters, W. E. T. wreathed together, signifying " Walter Earl of Tarras," a title which, in 1660, was conferred for life upon Walter Scott of Highchester, the husband of Mary Countess of Buccleuch. In front of the house there is a dark precipitous dell, covered on both sides with beautiful trees; in the recesses of which the freebooting lairds of former times were said to have kept their spoil.*

kept an ale-house at the Hamlet, near Branxholm Castle. A young officer named Maitland, who happened to be quartered somewhere in the neighbourhood, saw, loved, and married her. So strange was such an alliance deemed in those days, that it was imputed to the influence of witchcraft.

* " Where Bortho hoarse, that loads the meads with sand,
    Rolls her red tide to Teviot's western strand,
    Through slaty hills whose sides are shagged with thorn,
    Where springs in scatter'd tufts the dark green corn,
    Towers wood-girt Harden, far above the vale,
    And clouds of ravens o'er the turrets sail;
    A hardy race who never shrunk from war,
    The *Scott* to rival realms a mighty bar,
    Here fix'd his mountain home, a wide domain,
    And rich the soil had purple heath been grain;
    But what the niggard ground of wealth denied,
    From fields more bless'd his fearless arm supplied."
                LEYDEN'S *Scenes of Infancy.*

" Wide lay his lands round Oakwood tower
  And wide round haunted Castle Ower ;
  High over Borthwick's mountain flood,
  His wood-embosomed mansion stood,
  In the dark glen so deep below,
  The herds of plunder'd England low."
            Lay of the Last Minstrel, c. iv.

THIRD TOUR.

*** The North British Railway affords the most rapid means of making this Tour. A topographical and descriptive chart of this Railway is given in the Itinerary at the end of the volume.

EDINBURGH—HADDINGTON—DUNBAR—BERWICK.

LEAVING Edinburgh by Waterloo Bridge, and the south side of the Calton Hill, the tourist obtains a fine view of Salisbury Crags, Arthur's Seat, and St. Anthony's Chapel. Passing Jock's Lodge and Piershill Barracks, the road enters

PORTOBELLO,

a favourite summer residence of the citizens of Edinburgh. Tradition asserts that the first house in this village was built by a retired sailor, who had been with Admiral Vernon in his celebrated South American expedition of 1739, and therefore named it "Portobello," in commemoration of the capture of that town. A great number of elegant new streets have been built in the village, and hot and cold baths were erected in 1807. About two miles farther, the road enters Fisherrow, and on the opposite bank of the Esk, the town of

MUSSELBURGH,

connected with Fisherrow by three bridges, the oldest of which is supposed to have been built by the Romans. Musselburgh, including Fisherrow, is an ancient burgh of regality,* and unites with Portobello, Leith, and Newhaven

> * "Musselburgh was a burgh
> When Edinburgh was nane,
> And Musselburgh 'll be a burgh,
> When Edinburgh's gane."
> *Old Rhyme.*

in returning a member to Parliament. The population of the town, within the Parliamentary boundary, is 6366. The lordship and regality of Musselburgh were granted by James VI. to his chancellor, Lord Thirlestane, an ancestor of the Earls of Lauderdale. From them it was purchased in 1709 by Anne, Duchess of Buccleuch and Monmouth, and it still continues in the family of Buccleuch, along with the superiority of the burgh. The great Randolph, Earl of Moray, the nephew of Bruce, and regent of the kingdom, died, it is supposed of poison, in Musselburgh, in 1332. On Musselburgh links, an extensive plain between the town and the sea, the Edinburgh races, formerly held at Leith, are run. On this plain, in 1658, the Marquis of Hamilton, representing Charles I., met the Covenanting party ; and here Oliver Cromwell, in 1650, quartered his infantry, while the cavalry were lodged in the town. In a garden, at the east end of Musselburgh, is a small cell, covered by a mound, the only remains now existing of a religious establishment, called the chapel of Loretto. After the Reformation, the materials of the ruined chapel were employed in building the present jail. For this sacrilegious act, it is said the inhabitants of Musselburgh were annually excommunicated at Rome till the end of the last century. At the east end of Musselburgh is Pinkie House, the seat of Sir John Hope, Bart., interesting for its many historical associations. It was originally a country mansion of the Abbot of Dunfermline, but was converted into its present shape at the beginning of the seventeenth century by Alexander Seton, Earl of Dunfermline. About half a mile southward of Pinkie House, on the east side of the Esk, is the spot where, in 1547, the battle of Pinkie was fought, in which the Scottish army was defeated by the English, commanded by the Duke of Somerset. Southward of Inveresk is Carberry Hill, where, in 1567, Queen Mary surrendered to the insurgent nobles.*

---

* In the year 1728, a woman named Maggy Dickson, resident in Inveresk, was tried and condemned for child-murder, and duly (as was thought) executed in the Grassmarket of Edinburgh. When the dreadful ceremony was over, poor Maggy's friends put her body into a chest, and drove it away, in a cart, to

Leaving Musselburgh, the road passes Drummore, (W. Aitchison, Esq.) on the left; and St. Clement's Wells Distillery, and Wallyford, (—— Aitchison, Esq.) on the right. A short way beyond, on the left, is Preston Grange (Sir George Suttie, Bart.) and Dolphinton village, with its castle in ruins.

A little farther on, upon the left, is Preston Tower, formerly the residence of the Hamiltons of Preston. On the coast is the large village of Prestonpans. In this neighbourhood, 21st September 1745, was fought the memorable battle between the royal forces under Sir John Cope and the Highland army under Prince Charles Stuart. Near Tranent is Bankton House, (—— M'Dowall, Esq.,) which belonged to Colonel Gardiner, who fell nobly fighting for his country close beside the wall of the park attached to his own residence. Tranent is a very ancient village, chiefly inhabited by colliers. It is mentioned in a charter of the 12th century under the name of Travernent. A short way farther on, to the left, is Seton House, which stands on the site of the once princely palace of Seton, for many centuries the seat of the Setons, Earls of Wintoun.* The last

---

Musselburgh. When about two miles from town, the cart was stopped at a place called Peffermill, and the relations adjourned to a tavern for refreshment. On coming out of the house, what was their astonishment to see Maggy sitting up in the chest, having been restored to life by the motion of the cart. They took her home to Musselburgh, and she was soon entirely recovered. Sir Walter Scott, in the "Heart of Mid-Lothian," makes Madge Wildfire speak of "half-hangit Maggie Dickson, that cried saut mony a day after she had been hangit; her voice was roupit and hoarse, and her neck was a wee agee, or ye wad hae ken'd nae odds on her, frae ony other sautwife."—*Waverley Novels,* vol. xiii. p. 26.

* The Setons were one of the most distinguished Scottish families, whether in respect of wealth, antiquity of descent, or splendour of alliance. They took their original name from their habitation, Seaton, "the dwelling by the sea," where, it is said, their founder was settled by King David I. About the middle of the fourteenth century, the estate descended to Margaret Seton, who married Allan de Wyntoun, a neighbouring baron. This match was so displeasing to her own relations, that it occasioned a deadly feud, in consequence of which, we are assured by Fordun, no fewer than a hundred ploughs were put off work. George, the fifth Lord Seton, who lived in the time of Queen Mary, was one of her most attached friends, and it was to his castle of Niddry that she repaired, after her escape from Lochleven. He was grand-master of the household, in which capacity he had a picture painted of himself, with his official baton, and the following motto :—

Earl was attainted on account of his concern in the rebellion of 1715. After his attainder the furniture of the palace was sold by the Commissioners of Enquiry, and, about forty years since, the building itself was removed, and the present mansion erected on its site. At a little distance from the house stands the Collegiate Church of Seton, which is now all that remains to attest the splendour of the family. It is a handsome little Gothic edifice, still nearly entire. There are also visible some monuments of the ancient lords of Seton fast mouldering into decay. Near Seton is Long Niddry, the laird of which was a zealous reformer, and had John Knox for the tutor of his children. The ruins of the family chapel, in which Knox preached, are still pointed out. Northward, near the coast, is Gosford House, a mansion of the Earl of Wemyss. About three miles from Tranent the road passes Gladsmuir, noted

> In adversitate patiens;
> In prosperitate benevolus.
> Hazard, yet forward.

He declined to be promoted to an earldom, which Queen Mary offered him. On his refusing this honour, Mary wrote, or caused to be written, the following lines :—

> Sunt comites, ducesque, alii sunt denique reges;
> Sethoni dominum sit satis esse mihi.

Which may thus be rendered :—

> Earl, duke, or king, be thou that list to be;
> Seton, thy lordship is enough for me.

After the battle of Langside, Lord Seton was obliged to retire abroad for safety; and was in exile for two years, during which he was reduced to the necessity of driving a waggon in Flanders for his subsistence. His picture in this occupation, and the garb belonging to it, was painted at the lower end of the gallery in the ancient palace of Seton. In the time of James VI. the Seton family attained the dignity of Earl of Wintoun, and continued to flourish until the time of George, the fifth and last who enjoyed that dignity, and the large fortune which was annexed to it. In 1715, this unfortunate nobleman entered into the rebellion, and joined the Viscount of Kenmore with a fine troop of horse. He behaved with spirit and gallantry in the affair of the barricades at Preston; and afterwards, when waiting his fate in the Tower, made his escape by sawing through, with great ingenuity, the bars of the windows. He ended his motley life at Rome, in 1749, and with him closed the long and illustrious line of Seton, whose male descendants have, by intermarriage, come to represent the great nouses of Gordon, Aboyne, and Eglinton. Their estate was forfeited, and has since passed through several hands.—*Provincial Antiquities*, by SIR WALTER SCOTT, p. 97. See also *The Abbot*, vol. i., p. 277.

The Earl of Eglinton was lately served heir to the title of Earl of Wintoun.

as the birth-place of George Heriot, founder of the Hospital at Edinburgh.   Dr. Robertson was clergyman of this
parish, and here he composed his History of Scotland.   As
the tourist leaves this hamlet, he sees a column in the distance rising conspicuously from the top of the highest of
the Garleton Hills.   It is a monument raised by his grateful tenantry to commemorate the virtues of the fourth Earl
of Hopetoun.   Passing on the right Woodside, (J. Veitch,
Esq.,) and successively on the left, Elvington, (R. Ainslie,
Esq.,) Huntington, (J. Ainslie, Esq.) ; and Alderston, (J.
Aitchison, Esq.) ; and on the right Letham, (Sir T. B. Hepburn, Bart.,) and Clerkington, (General Sir Robert Houston,
Bart.,) the tourist is met with a chaste and beautiful monument of granite, raised as a tribute of regret and affection
to the late Robert Ferguson of Raith.

HADDINGTON

is the county town of East Lothian, distant seventeen miles
from Edinburgh.   It occupies an agreeable situation on the
north bank of the Tyne, the burgh, within the parliamentary
boundary, containing 3777 inhabitants.   The precise period
at which Haddington became a royal burgh is unknown, its
ancient records being lost; but it is known to be of very
great antiquity, and is supposed to have received its name
from Ada Countess of Northumberland, who founded a
nunnery here in 1178.   It has been several times burnt by
the English or by accident, and has twice suffered greatly
from an inundation of the Tyne.   On the south side of the
town is the Franciscan Church, a noble old Gothic building,
partly in ruins.   Fordun says, that on account of its splendour it was called the "Lamp of Lothian."   The great
tower and choir are roofless, and fast falling into decay, but
the chancel is still in repair as a parish church.   It is
alleged that the celebrated John Knox was born in a house
about a hundred feet to the east of the church.   Haddington is chiefly remarkable in the present day for its grain
market, one of the most extensive in Scotland.   About a
mile to the south of Haddington is Lennoxlove or Lethington, a seat of Lord Blantyre.   It consists of a massive old

tower, erected by the Giffords, with a modern addition, and is surrounded by a grove of lofty aged trees. Lethington came into the possession of the Lauderdale family by purchase about the middle of the fourteenth century, and was for some time the chief residence of that family. It was there that the celebrated Secretary Lethington lived, and one of its alleys, which he frequented, is still called the Politician's Walk.* Within sight of Lethington stands the mansion-house of Coalstoun, a seat of the Earl of Dalhousie, whose mother was the heiress of the ancient family of Broun of Coalstoun.†

To the north of Haddington lies the little village of Athelstaneford, which, in the early part of the last century, had for its ministers successively two poets—Robert Blair, author of "The Grave," and John Home, the author of "Douglas."

Resuming from Haddington the eastward course of the London Road, and passing on the right Amisfield, and Stevenston House, (Sir J. G. Sinclair, Bart.,) the tourist perceives the ruins of Hailes Castle, (Sir C. Ferguson, Bart.,) overhanging the south bank of the Tyne. It formerly belonged to the Hepburns, and was the chief residence of Queen Mary during her union with Bothwell. South of the castle rises Trapraine Law, a rocky hill, anciently called

---

* Lethington contains several fine portraits, particularly a full-length, by Lely, of Frances Theresa Stuart, Duchess of Lennox, the most admired beauty of the court of Charles II. She was a daughter of Walter Stuart, M.D., a son of the first Lord Blantyre; and Lethington got the additional name of Lennoxlove, from being a compliment to her from her husband. It is stated by Grammont, that the King caused this lady to be represented as the emblematical figure *Britannia* on the coin of the realm.

† One of the Brouns of Coalstoun, about 300 years ago, married a daughter of John third Lord Yester, with whom he obtained in dowry a pear, with the assurance that, as long as the pear was preserved, the family would be attended with unfailing prosperity. This celebrated pear is still preserved in a silver box. At no great distance, in the neighbourhood of Gifford, is Yester House, the elegant seat of the Marquis of Tweeddale, the descendant of the wizard Lord who enchanted the Coalstoun pear. The ancient Castle of Yester stood nearer the Lammermuir Hills, and the remains of it are still to be seen on a peninsula, formed by two streams. It contained a capacious cavern, called in the country Bo' Hall, i. e. Hobgoblin Hall, supposed to have been formed by magical art. The reader will not need to be reminded of the use made of the Goblin Hall and the wizard Lord in the poem of "Marmion," canto iii.

K

Dunpender Law. The road now passes over the steep
ascent of Pincraig, from which the tourist sees on his right
Whittinghame, (Jas. Balfour, Esq.) ; on his left, Newbyth,
(Sir D. Baird, Bart.,) and, in the distance, on the same side,
North Berwick Law, North Berwick House, (Sir H. Dal-
rymple, Bart.,) the Bass, and Tantallon.* At the bottom

* About seven miles north-west of Dunbar, and two and a half eastward
from North Berwick, are the ruins of the famous Castle of Tantallon. From
the land side they are scarcely visible, till the visiter, surmounting a height
which conceals them, finds himself close under the external walls. The description of this castle given in the poem of Marmion, renders any account of our
own unnecessary.

————————————————" Tantallon vast
Broad, massive, high, and stretching far,
And held impregnable in war,
On a projecting rock it rose,
And round three sides the ocean flows,
The fourth did battled walls enclose,
          And double mound and fosse ;
By narrow drawbridge, outworks strong,
Through studded gates, an entrance long,
          To the main court they cross.
It was a wide and stately square,
Around were lodgings fit and fair,
          And towers of various form,
Which on the court projected far,
And broke its lines quadrangular ;
Here was square keep, there turret high,
Or pinnacle that sought the sky,
Whence oft the warder could descry
          The gathering ocean storm."
                              c. v., st. 33.

Tantallon was a principal stronghold of the Douglas family ; and when the
Earl of Angus was banished in 1526, it continued to hold out against James V.
The king went in person against it, and, for its reduction, borrowed from the
Castle of Dunbar, then belonging to the Duke of Albany, two great cannons,
whose names, Pitscottie informs us, were " Thrawn-mouth'd Mow and her
Marrow ;" also, " two great bocards, and two moyan, two double falcons, and
four quarter falcons," for the safe guiding and re-delivery of which three lords
were laid in pawn at Dunbar. Yet, notwithstanding all this apparatus, James
was forced to raise the siege, and only afterwards obtained possession of Tantallon by treaty with the governor, Simon Panango. Tantallon was at length
" dung down" by the Covenanters ; its lord, the Marquis of Douglas, being a
favourer of the royal cause. About the beginning of the eighteenth century,
the Marquis, afterwards Duke of Douglas, sold the estate of North Berwick,
with the castle of Tantallon, to Sir Hew Dalrymple, President of the Court of
Session, and they now remain in the possession of his descendant, Sir Hew H.
Dalrymple, Bart., of Bargeny and North Berwick.

Two miles north from Tantallon lies the Bass Island, or rather Rock, rising

of Pincraig, the road skirts the populous village of Linton, and crosses the Tyne there by an old, narrow, and very ugly bridge. The kirk of Preston, and its village, and Smeaton House, (Sir T. B. Hepburn, Bart.,) are now seen at a little distance on the left bank of the Tyne. About half a mile from Linton, the road runs close past Phantassie, (T. Mitchell Innes, Esq.,) so noted in the annals of agriculture as the residence of the late Mr. Rennie. The late John Rennie, the celebrated engineer, was born at Phantassie, and educated in this neighbourhood. At some distance, on the left, situate on the estuary of the Tyne, is Tyningham House, the noble mansion of the Earl of Haddington, surrounded by venerable woods and a spacious park.* To the south of the London Road, but not seen from it, is Biel, (Mrs. Ferguson), with its extensive plantations and charming walks. Immediately below the mansion-house, formerly the residence of Lord Presmennan, a beautiful sheet of water, called Presmennan Lake, has recently been formed, by throwing an artificial mound across a small rivulet which runs down from the Lammermuir Hills. The privilege of perambulating the grounds is permitted by the

---

400 feet sheer out of the sea. The Bass is about a mile in circumference, and is conical on the one side, presenting, on the other, an abrupt and overhanging precipice. It is remarkable for its immense quantities of sea-fowl, chiefly solan geese. Upon the top of the rock gushes out a spring of clear water, and there is verdure enough to support a few sheep. The Bass was long the stronghold of a family of the name of Lauder, one of whom distinguished himself as a compatriot of Wallace. The castle, situated on the south side of the island, is now ruinous. In 1671, it was sold by the Lauder family, for £4000, to Charles II., by whom it was converted into a royal fortress and state prison. Many of the most eminent of the Covenanters were confined here. At the Revolution, it was the last stronghold in Great Britain that held out for James VII.; but, after a resistance of several months, the garrison were at last compelled to surrender, by the failure of their supplies of provisions. The Bass is now the property of Sir Hew Hamilton Dalrymple, Bart. This remarkable rock is visited in summer by numerous pleasure parties. In order to perform the visit, it is necessary to apply for a boat either at North Berwick, or at Canty Bay, near Tantallon.

* In the Tyningham grounds are some magnificent holly hedges. "One of these hedges," says Mr. Miller, in his "Popular Philosophy," "is no less than twenty-five feet high and eighteen broad; and the length of what is denominated the Holly Walks, lying chiefly between two hedges of fifteen feet high and eleven broad, is no less than thirty-five chains eighty links, English measure."

kindness of the proprietrix, who also allows the use of a
boat upon the lake to the numerous summer parties who
visit it. Beyond, on the right, is Belton Place, (Captain
Hay, R.N.,) and on the left, Nineware House, (James Hamilton, Esq.) A short way farther on is the village of Belton-
ford, a mile farther West Barns, and half a mile beyond it
the beautifully situated village of Belhaven, from which
Lord Belhaven takes his title. Near the village is excellent
sea-bathing. It is much frequented during summer by
visiters from a distance, and a sulphurous Spa lately discovered in its neighbourhood is not the smallest of its
attractions. The road now passes on the left, Winterfield,
(Colonel Anderson,) Belhaven Church, and an old tower
called Knockenhair, used, during last war, as a signal
station. On the right the tourist sees at a little distance
Lochend House, (Sir George Warrender, Bart.) Still farther off, on the same side, are seen Bower House, (General
Carfrae,) and Spott, (James Sprott, Esq.,) their plantations
imparting a sylvan variety to a rich corn-field country.
Shortly after the tourist enters

DUNBAR,

a royal burgh and thriving sea-port, twenty-eight miles distant from Edinburgh and eleven from Haddington. The
name is supposed to be derived from two Celtic words,
signifying the Castle on the extremity. Its population was
3014 at last census. It was created a royal burgh by David
II., ostensibly to prevent English merchants from bringing
into and carrying out of the kingdom wool, hides, and other
commodities, without the payment of custom. The only
public building worthy of notice is the church, erected in
1819, on the site of the old collegiate church, the first of
the kind founded in Scotland. It contains a most splendid
marble monument to Sir George Home, created Earl of
Dunbar and March by James VI. At the entrance to the
town from the west, there are the remains of a monastery
of the Grey Friars. Dunbar could also boast of a convent
of the White Friars; but the record says they were *banished to Peebles* for their *immorality*. The coast in the neigh-

bourhood of Dunbar is remarkably perilous, and the entrance to the harbour is rocky and difficult. Oliver Cromwell contributed three hundred pounds towards the erection of the eastern pier; another pier on the west has been lately built, and a dry dock has also been constructed. A large addition has been made to the harbour, at the joint expense of the town and the Fishery Board. The cost has been about £14,000. A grain market is held every Monday, and a cattle market the first Monday of every month. Dunbar House, the residence of the Earl of Lauderdale, stands at the north end of the principal street. About two hundred yards north from Dunbar House stands the celebrated Castle of Dunbar. Its antiquity is unknown, but so early as 1070 it was given, with the adjacent manor, by Malcolm Canmore, to Patrick Earl of Northumberland, a princely noble, who fled from England at the Conquest, and became the progenitor of the family of Cospatricks, Earls of Dunbar and March. This once formidable fortress has passed through many varieties of fortune, but the most memorable incident in its history was the gallant and successful defence made by *Black Agnes*, Countess of March, against an English army under the Earl of Salisbury. When the battering engines of the besiegers flung massive stones on the battlements, she caused her maidens, as if in scorn, to wipe away the dust with their handkerchiefs; and when the Earl of Salisbury commanded a huge military engine, called a *sow*, to be advanced to the foot of the walls, she, in a scoffing rhyme, advised him to take good care of his sow, for she would make her farrow her pigs. She then ordered an enormous rock to be discharged on the engine, which crushed it to pieces.* On another occasion, an arrow shot by an

---

* A similar story is told of Judge Bankes's lady, while holding out Corffe Castle against the Parliament forces. The incident is thus alluded to by Mr. W. Stewart Rose, in his poem addressed to Corffe Castle:—

" 'Twas when you rear'd, 'mid sap and siege,
The banner of your rightful liege,
   At your she-captain's call;
Who, miracle of womankind!
Lent mettle to the meanest hind
   That mann'd her castle wall.   What

archer of her train struck to the heart an English knight, through his complete suit of armour,—"There goes one of my lady's tiring-pins," said the Earl of Salisbury, "the Countess' love-shafts pierce to the heart." After a successful defence, which lasted six weeks, the siege was abandoned by the English troops. George, tenth Earl of Dunbar and March, on a quarrel with Alexander, Duke of Albany, brother of James III., retreated into England. His large estate was thereupon forfeited, and, with Dunbar Castle, passed into the hands of the Duke of Albany, to whom on his memorable escape from Edinburgh Castle, it afforded shelter till he departed for France. In the year 1567, Queen Mary conferred the keeping of this important stronghold on the infamous Bothwell; and here she twice found shelter— once, after the murder of Rizzio; and a second time, when she made her escape from Borthwick Castle, in the disguise of a page. After her surrender at Carberry Hill, Dunbar Castle was taken, and completely destroyed by the Regent Murray. It is now the property of the Earl of Lauderdale, who is also superior, in right of the Earl of March.

Near the town of Dunbar were fought two battles, in both of which the Scots were defeated—one in 1296, when Baliol was defeated by the forces of Edward I.; the other in 1650, when the Scottish army, under General Leslie, was routed with great slaughter at Doonhill, by Cromwell. This battle is still remembered by the people of Scotland under the opprobrious epithet of "the race of Dunbar," or "the Tyesday's chase;" the engagement having taken place on a Tuesday. An eminence, lying about two miles south from the town, gives its name to the latter battle, and the former was in the same direction, but a little nearer.

Perhaps no part of the British coast affords a richer treat to the geologist, than that lying between Belhaven and St. Abb's Head. Over the whole of it, Hutton and Playfair,

What time the banded zealots swore,
Long foil'd thy banner'd towers, before
          Their fearful entrance made,
To rase thy walls with plough and harrow,
Yet oft the wild sow cast her farrow,
          And well the boar was bay'd."

and Sir James Hall, have very frequently wandered ; and, from its phenomena, some of their favourite theories derive their clearest illustrations. The Emperor of Russia, when he visited Dunbar as Prince Nicholas, was so charmed with a singularly beautiful formation of basalt that presents itself at the entrance of the harbour, as to direct that specimens of it should be conveyed to Russia.

Leaving Dunbar, the tourist passes, on the left, Broxmouth Park, formerly the head-quarters of Cromwell at the battle of Doonhill, but now the site of a large mansion belonging to the Duke of Roxburghe. The stream of Broxburn here crosses the road. A mile and a half farther, on the right, are Barnyhill, (Sandilands, Esq.,) and the village of East Barns. A mile to the south is Thurston, (Hunter, Esq.) A short way beyond, on the right, are the ruins of Innerwick Castle, situated on the edge of a precipitous glen; and, on the opposite side of the glen, stands Thornton Tower : the former the fortalice of a Hamilton, and the latter of a Hume. Innerwick was burnt by the English, and Thornton blown up with gunpowder, during Somerset's expedition. Dunglas House, the splendid mansion of Sir John Hall, embosomed amid beautiful plantations, is well deserving the tourist's notice;* and he should alight from his carriage, and look into that lovely glen, where the road, crossing the Dean Burn, enters Berwickshire. A mile farther on, is the village of Cockburnspath, (a corruption of Colbrandspath.) A mile beyond the village, and on the left, close to the road, is the ancient tower of Cockburnspath, now the property of Sir J. Hall of Dunglas. The tract of country through which the road now passes is high and flat, but broken at little distances by numerous deep and

---

* Dunglas House stands on the site of the old castle, which was originally a fortress of the Earls of Home, and still gives their second title to that family. After the attainder of the Earl of Home, in 1516, it passed into the hands of the Douglases. It was destroyed by Somerset, in 1548, but was again rebuilt and enlarged. It was finally destroyed in 1640, on which occasion the Earl of Haddington, and a number of other persons of distinction, were killed by the explosion of the powder magazine. The old parish church stands near Dunglas House. Great good taste is displayed in the manner the ruin is preserved as the family mausoleum.

narrow ravines, each of which has a small stream at the
bottom running towards the sea.   The most remarkable
of these ravines is the Peaths, over which the celebrated
Peaths or Pease bridge was thrown in 1786, when it was
the post road.   This singular structure is 123 feet in height,
300 feet in length, and sixteen feet wide.   The post road
now crosses the glen, about a quarter of a mile above the
bridge.   In former times, the Peaths was a most important
pass, and Oliver Cromwell describes it in his dispatch to the
Parliament, after the battle of Dunbar, as a place "where
one man to hinder, is better than twelve to make way."
The road now passes in succession, Grant's Inn, where the
Dunse road diverges to the right, and about three miles
farther, Houndwood Inn, Houndwood Church, and Houndwood House, (Mrs. Coulson.) Two miles farther, the tourist
passes, on the right, the village of Reston, and a road turns
off on the left to the beautiful village of Coldingham, distant
about three miles.* Proceeding along the banks of the Eye,

* Coldingham is situated upon a small eminence, in the centre of a fine valley,
at a short distance from the sea.   It is remarkable for the ruins of its priory,
so celebrated in Border history.   The monastery was established by St. Abb, in
the seventh century, and is said to have been the first in Scotland.   The buildings were once of great magnificence and extent, but, of late years, they have
been greatly dilapidated, by the rapacious license of the people in taking away
stones, for the purpose of building their own houses, so that only a few detached
fragments now remain.   About fifty years ago, in taking down a tower at the
south-west corner, the skeleton of a nun was found standing upright in a hollow
of the wall, no doubt a victim to a breach of her vows.

North-east of Coldingham about two miles, is the celebrated promontory
called St. Abb's Head.   It consists of two hills, the western of which is occupied
by an observatory; the eastern, called the Kirkhill, still exhibits the remains
of a monastery and a church.   The savage and dreary character of the scenery
is exceedingly striking.   The neighbouring promontory of Fast Castle derives
its name from an ancient baronial fortress, built upon the very point of the
precipitous headland.   Fast Castle is the Wolf's Crag of the " Bride of Lammermoor," and is thus described in that tragic tale :—" The roar of the sea had long
announced their approach to the cliffs, on the summit of which, like the nest
of some sea-eagle, the founder of the fortalice had perched his eyry.   The pale
moon, which had hitherto been contending with flitting clouds, now shone out,
and gave them a view of the solitary and naked tower, situated on a projecting
cliff, that beetled on the German Ocean.   On three sides, the rock was precipitous; on the fourth, which was that towards the land, it had been originally
fenced by an artificial ditch and drawbridge, but the latter was broken down
and ruinous, and the former had been in part filled up, so as to allow passage
for a horseman into the narrow court-yard, encircled on two sides with low

the tourist reaches the village of Ayton, pleasantly situated on its northern bank. Ayton House, (—Mitchell Innes, Esq.) stands to the east of the village. The banks of the Eye afford some fine scenery. At its confluence with the sea stands the sea-port and fishing town of Eyemouth. This town was formerly notorious for the smuggling carried on by its inhabitants, but of late years the contraband trade has been entirely suppressed.* About two miles from Ayton, at the bottom of a deep ravine, on the left of the road, is the romantic little fishing village of Burnmouth, the well-situated, and formerly well-frequented haunt of the smuggler. Ten miles farther, the tourist passes the ruins of Lamerton Kirk, where, in 1503, Margaret, daughter of

offices and stables, partly ruinous, and closed on the landward front by a low embattled wall, while the remaining side of the quadrangle was occupied by the tower itself, which, tall and narrow, and built of a greyish stone, stood glimmering in the moonlight, like the sheeted spectre of some huge giant. A wilder, or more disconsolate dwelling, it was perhaps difficult to conceive. The sombrous and heavy sound of the billows, successively dashing against the rocky beach, at a profound distance beneath, was, to the ear, what the landscape was to the eye—a symbol of unvaried and monotonous melancholy, not unmingled with horror." That castle was, in former days, a place of retreat of the great Earls of Home. Notwithstanding its strength, it was repeatedly taken and recaptured during the Border wars. About the close of the sixteenth century, it became the stronghold of the celebrated Logan of Restalrig, so famous for his share in the Gowrie Conspiracy; and it was to this place that the conspirators intended to convey the king, after getting possession of his person. There is a contract existing in the charter chest of Lord Napier, between this Logan and the celebrated Napier of Merchiston, setting forth, that, as Fast Castle was supposed to contain a quantity of hidden treasure, Napier was to make search for the same by divination, and, for his reward, was to have the third of what was found, and to have his expenses paid in whatever event. Fast Castle now belongs to Sir J. Hall of Dunglas. The precipitous rocks on this coast are inhabited by an immense number of sea-fowl, and a number of young men in the neighbourhood occasionally scale these dreadful and dizzy heights, in order to steal the eggs of the birds. Strange to say, an accident does not occur among them, perhaps, once in a century.

* " I stood upon Eyemouth fort,
    And guess ye what I saw?
Fairnieside and Flemington,
    Newhouses and Cocklaw.
The Fairy Folk o' Fosterland,
    The witches o' Edincraw,
The rye rigs o' Reston,
    And Dunse dings a'."
                                    Old Rhyme.

Henry VII., was married by proxy to James IV.,—a marriage which ultimately led to the union of the crowns.
Lamerton is now the property of Colonel Renton. At
Lamerton toll-bar, runaway lovers from England are frequently united in the bands of matrimony. At a distance
of three miles, the road enters the town of

BERWICK,

situated upon a gentle declivity close by the German ocean,
on the north side of the mouth of the river Tweed. It is
a well-built town, with spacious streets, and is surrounded
by walls which only of late ceased to be regularly fortified.
The population amounts to about 10,000. It is governed
by a mayor, recorder, and justices, and sends two members
to Parliament. The trade of the port is considerable. Berwick occupies a prominent place in the history of the Border wars, and has been often taken and retaken both by the
Scots and English. It was finally ceded to the English in
1482, and, since then, has remained subject to the laws of
England, though forming, politically, a distinct territory.
Its castle, so celebrated in the early history of these king-
doms, is now a shapeless ruin.

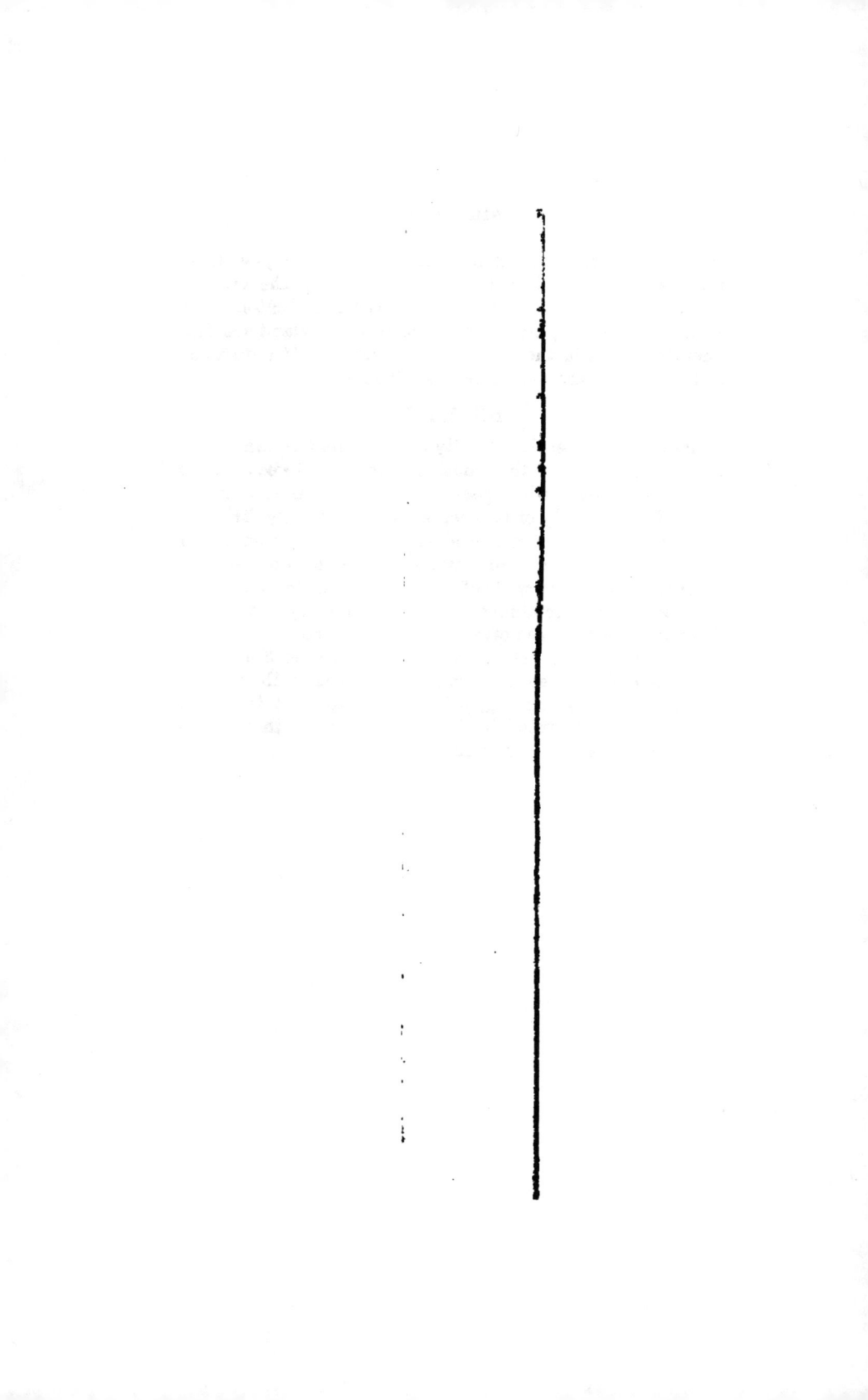

MAP
ILLUSTRATIVE OF THE
ROYAL PROGRESS
IN
Scotland
1842.

FOURTH TOUR.

₄ The Map of the Royal Progress annexed, exhibits the various routes from Edinburgh to Stirling. Of these the most expeditious is by the Edinburgh and Glasgow Railway to Falkirk, where coaches are in attendance to carry on passengers to Stirling. Tourists adopting this route may consult the Map of the Edinburgh and Glasgow Railway at the end of the volume, and the description of the Railway in the Itinerary.

It has not been deemed necessary to give a special description of the Royal Route, as the places visited by Her Majesty are all described in one or other of the Tours into which the work is subdivided. Her Majesty's Route is indicated on the Map by a conspicuous double line dotted in the centre; and by consulting the Index, the reader will be directed to the page of the volume where the several places of interest which she visited are described.

EDINBURGH—LINLITHGOW—FALKIRK—STIRLING.

LEAVING Edinburgh by Princes Street, the tourist passes along the side of Corstorphine Hill, richly wooded and studded with villas, and, three miles from Edinburgh, reaches the village of Corstorphine. At the seventh milestone the road crosses Almond water, and enters Linlithgowshire. A short way farther on is the village of Kirkliston. Near the village is Newliston, (Hog, Esq.) formerly the seat of the great Earl of Stair, who is said to have caused the woods around the house to be planted so as to resemble the position of the troops at the battle of Dettingen, where he commanded under George II.* A short dis-

---

* "During the rebellion of 1745, the route of the Highland army having brought them near Newliston, an alarm arose in the Councils of Prince Charles, lest the MacDonalds of Glencoe should seize the opportunity of marking their recollection of the massacre of Glencoe, by burning or plundering the house of the descendant of their persecutor; and it was agreed that a guard should be posted to protect the house of Lord Stair. MacDonald of Glencoe heard the resolution, and deemed his honour and that of his clan concerned. He demanded an audience of Charles Edward, and, admitting the propriety of placing a guard on a house so obnoxious to the feelings of the Highland army, and to those of his own clan in particular, he demanded, as a matter of right rather than of favour, that the protecting guard should be supplied by the MacDonalds of Glencoe. The request of the high-spirited chieftain was granted,

tance beyond, to the left, are the ruins of Niddry Castle, where Queen Mary passed the first night after her escape from Lochleven. It was at that time the property of the Earl of Seton—it now belongs to the Earl of Hopetoun. The road now passes through the village of Winchburgh, where Edward II. first halted in his flight from the battle of Bannockburn. About the sixteenth mile-stone, the road crosses the Union Canal, under an aqueduct bridge, and a short way farther on enters

LINLITHGOW.*

an ancient royal burgh, and the county town of Linlithgow-shire, situated in a hollow, along the borders of a beautiful lake. So early as the beginning of the twelfth century, Linlithgow was one of the principal burghs in the kingdom. It contains a considerable number of old fashioned houses, many of which belonged of old to the knights of St. John, who had their preceptory at Torphichen, in this county.

The most interesting object in Linlithgow is the Palace, a massive quadrangular edifice, situated upon an eminence which advances a little way into the lake. It occupies about an acre of ground, and, though in ruins, is still a picturesque and beautiful object.† The internal architecture is extremely elegant, but the exterior has a heavy appear-

---

and the MacDonalds guarded from the slightest injury the house of the cruel and crafty statesman who had devised and directed the massacre of their ancestor."—*Tales of a Grandfather*, vol. iv. p. 23.

It was in the family of the first Lord Stair, that the tragic incident occurred which forms the groundwork of Sir Walter Scott's tale of the " Bride of Lammermoor."

* Popularly denominated " the faithful town of Linlithgow."

   † " Of all the palaces so fair
      Built for the royal dwelling
      In Scotland, far beyond compare
      Linlithgow is excelling.
     And in its park in genial June,
     How sweet the merry linnet's tune,
      How blyth the blackbird's lay !
     The wild buck *bells* from thorny brake,
     The coot dives merry on the lake,—
     The saddest heart might pleasure take
      To see a scene so gay."
               Marmion, c. iv., st. 15.

LINLITHGOW CASTLE.

ance from the want of windows. Over the interior of the grand gate is a niche which was formerly filled by a statue of Pope Julius II., who presented James V. with the sword of state, which still forms part of the regalia. It was destroyed during the last century by a blacksmith, who had heard popery inveighed against in the neighbouring church. Above this entrance was the Parliament Hall, once a splendid apartment, with a beautifully ornamented chimney at one end, and underneath it, has been a magnificent piazza. This part of the palace is understood to have been begun by James IV., and finished and ornamented by his successor. The west side of the palace is the most ancient, and contains the room where the unfortunate Queen Mary was born.*

In one of the vaults below, James III. found shelter when he was in danger of assassination from some of his rebellious subjects. The north side of the quadrangle is the most modern, having been built by James VI. shortly after his visit to Scotland in 1617. In the centre of the court are the elaborately carved ruins of the Palace Well, a once beautiful and ingenious work, erected by James V. It was destroyed by the royal army in 1746.

The nucleus of the Palace seems to have been a tower or fort, first built by Edward I., who inhabited it in person a whole winter. It was taken and demolished by Bruce in 1307.† It appears, however, to have been rebuilt by the

---

* Her father, who then lay on his deathbed at Falkland, on being told of her birth, replied, "Is it so?" reflecting on the alliance which had placed the Stuart family on the throne, "then God's will be done! It came with a lass, and it will go with a lass." With these words he turned his face to the wall, and died of a broken heart.

† It was taken in the following remarkable way:—The garrison was supplied with hay by a neighbouring rustic, of the name of Binnock or Binning, who favoured the interest of Bruce. "Binnock had been ordered by the English governor to furnish some cart-loads of hay, of which they were in want. He promised to bring it accordingly; but the night before he drove the hay to the castle, he stationed a party of his friends, as well armed as possible, near the entrance, where they could not be seen by the garrison, and gave them directions that they should come to his assistance as soon as they should hear him cry a signal, which was to be,—'Call all, call all!' Then he loaded a great waggon with hay; but in the waggon he placed eight strong men, well armed, lying flat on their breasts, and covered over with hay, so that they could not be

English during the minority of David II., but was again
burnt down in 1424. The palace was finally reduced to its
present ruinous condition by Hawley's dragoons, who were
quartered in it on the night of the 31st of January 1746.
In the morning, when they were preparing to depart, the
dastardly scoundrels were observed deliberately throwing
the ashes of the fires into the straw on which they had lain.
The whole palace was speedily in a blaze, and it has ever
since remained an empty and blackened ruin.* A grant
has been made by Government to renew some of the stairs,
and to arrest the farther progress of dilapidation.

The Church, a venerable and impressive structure, stands
between the Palace and the town, and may be regarded as
one of the finest and most entire specimens of Gothic
architecture in Scotland. It was dedicated to the arch-
angel Michael, who was also considered the patron saint of

---

seen. He himself walked carelessly beside the waggon; and he chose the stout-
est and bravest of his servants to be the driver, who carried at his belt a strong
axe or hatchet. In this way Binnock approached the castle early in the morning; and the watchman, who only saw two men, Binnock being one of them,
with a cart of hay, which they expected, opened the gates, and raised up the
portcullis, to permit them to enter the castle. But as soon as the cart had gotten
under the gateway, Binnock made a sign to his servant, who, with his axe, suddenly cut asunder the *soam*, that is, the yoke which fastens the horses to the
cart, and the horses, finding themselves free, naturally started forward, the
cart remaining behind under the arch of the gate. At the same moment, Binnock cried, as loud as he could, 'Call all, call all!' and, drawing the sword
which he had under his country habit, he killed the porter. The armed men
then jumped up from under the hay where they lay concealed, and rushed on
the English guard. The Englishmen tried to shut the gates, but they could
not, because the cart of hay remained in the gateway, and prevented the fold-
ing-doors from being closed. The portcullis was also let fall, but the grating
was caught on the cart, and so could not drop to the ground. The men who
were in ambush near the gate, hearing the cry, 'Call all, call all!' ran to assist
those who had leapt out from amongst the hay; the castle was taken, and all
the Englishmen killed or made prisoners. King Robert rewarded Binnock by
bestowing on him an estate, which his posterity long afterwards enjoyed. The
Binnings of Wallyford, descended from that person, still bear in their coat
armorial a wain loaded with hay, with the motto, 'Virtute doloque.'—*Tales of
a Grandfather*, vol. i, p. 139.

* "They halted at Linlithgow, distinguished by its ancient palace, which,
sixty years since, was entire and habitable, and whose venerable ruins, *not quite
sixty years since*, very narrowly escaped the unworthy fate of being converted
into a barrack for French prisoners. May repose and blessings attend the
ashes of the patriotic statesman (President Blair) who, amongst his last services
to Scotland, interposed to prevent this profanation."—*Waverley*, vol. i, p. 92.

the town. The Church was founded by David I., but was ornamented chiefly by George Crichton, Bishop of Dunkeld. It is now divided by a partition wall, and the eastern half alone is used as a place of worship. It was in an aisle in this Church, according to tradition, that James IV. was sitting when he saw the strange apparition which warned him against his fatal expedition to England.* In front of the Town-house stands the Cross Well, a very curious and elegant erection. The present edifice was built in 1807, but it is said to be an exact fac-simile of the original, erected in 1620. The sculpture is very elaborate, and the water is made to pour in great profusion from the mouths of a multitude of grotesque figures. The vast copiousness of

---

* The story is told by Pitscottie with characteristic simplicity:—"The king came to Lithgow, where he happened to be for the time at the Council, very sad and dolorous, making his devotion to God to send him good chance and fortune in his voyage. In this meantime, there came a man, clad in a blue gown, in at the kirk door, and belted about him in a roll of linen cloth; a pair of brotikings (buskings) on his feet, to the great of his legs; with all other hose and clothes conformed thereto; but he had nothing on his head, but syde (long) red yellow hair behind, and on his haffits (cheeks) which wan down to his shoulders; but his forehead was bald and bare. He seemed to be a man of two-and-fifty years, with a great pike-staff in his hand, and came first forward among the lords, crying and speiring (asking) for the king, saying he desired to speak with him. While, at the last, he came where the king was sitting in the desk at his prayers; but, when he saw the king, he made him little reverence or salutation, but leaned down grofling on the desk before him, and said to him in this manner, as after follows:—' Sir king, my mother hath sent me to you, desiring you not to pass, at this time, where thou art purposed; for if thou does, thou wilt not fare well in thy journey, nor none that passes with thee. Further, she bade thee mell (meddle) with no woman, nor use their counsel, nor let them touch thy body, nor thou theirs; for if thou do it, thou wilt be confounded and brought to shame.'

" By this man had spoken thir words unto the king's grace, the evening song was near done, and the king paused on thir words, studying to give him an answer; but in the meantime, before the king's eyes, and in the presence of all the lords that were about him for the time, this man vanished away, and could no wise be seen or comprehended, but vanished away as he had been a blink of the sun, or a whip of the whirlwind, and could no more be seen. I heard say, Sir David Lindesay, lyon-herauld, and John Inglis, the marshal, who were, at that time, young men, and special servants to the king's grace, were standing presently beside the king, who thought to have laid hands on this man, that they might have speired further tidings at him; but all for nought, they could not touch him; for he vanished away betwixt them, and was no more seen." There can be little doubt that the supposed apparition was a contrivance of the queen to deter James from his impolitic warfare.

water at Linlithgow is alluded to in the following well-
known rhyme:—

> " Glasgow for bells,
> Lithgow for wells,
> Fa'kirk for beans and peas,
> Peebles for clashes and lees."

It was in Linlithgow that David Hamilton of Bothwellhaugh, on the 23d of January 1570, shot the Regent Murray,
when passing through the town, in revenge for a private
injury. The house from which the shot was fired belonged
to the Archbishop of St. Andrews. It was taken down a
number of years ago, and replaced by a modern edifice.

During the plague of 1645, Linlithgow happening to be
comparatively free of the infection, the Palace and Church
were used by the Courts of Justice and the members of the
University of Edinburgh as their meeting places. At the
Restoration, the inhabitants of Linlithgow burned the
Solemn League and Covenant amidst great rejoicing. The
ringleader in this affair was one Ramsay, the minister
of the parish, who had formerly been a zealous supporter
of the Covenant. In Linlithgow is still kept up the old
custom of riding the marches. The town has derived considerable advantage from the Union Canal, which passes
along the high grounds immediately to the south. Leather
is the staple commodity of the place; linen and woollen
manufactures are also carried on to a considerable extent.
The population of the burgh within the Parliamentary
boundary in 1841, was 3872.

Proceeding westward from Linlithgow, the road crosses
the Avon at Linlithgow Bridge, and enters Stirlingshire.
After this, nothing interesting occurs for some miles, till
the tourist passes, on the left, Callander House, (W. Forbes,
Esq.,) formerly the seat of the Earls of Callander and Linlithgow, and a short way farther on enters the town of

FALKIRK,

situated on the face of an eminence overlooking the
wide extent of country called the Carse of Falkirk. It
was a town of some note in the early part of the eleventh

century. The old church, which was demolished about thirty years ago, was erected in 1057. The original name of the town was *Eglishbreckk*, signifying "the speckled church," in allusion, it is supposed, to the colour of the stones. In the churchyard are shown the graves of two celebrated Scottish heroes—Sir John Graham, the friend of Wallace, and Sir John Stewart of Bonkill, both of whom fell fighting bravely against the English at the battle of Falkirk, in 1298. Over the former a monument was erected with an inscription, which has been renewed three times since his death. It at present stands thus :—

Mente Manuque Potens, et vallae Fidus Achates,
conditur Hic Gramus, Bello Interfectus ab Anglis.

TRANSLATION.

Here lyes Sir John the Grame, baith wight and wise,
Ane of the chiefs who rescewit Scotland thrise,
Ane better knight not to the world was lent,
Nor was gude Grame of truth and hardiment.

In the churchyard is also to be seen the monument of two brave officers, Sir Robert Monro of Foulis, and his brother, Dr. Monro, who were killed in the second battle of Falkirk, January 17, 1746. Falkirk is noted for its great cattle markets or *trysts*, held thrice a-year, to which a vast number of black cattle are brought from the Highlands and Islands.

About two miles north of the town are the celebrated Carron Iron Works, the largest manufactory of the kind in the world.

A short way from Falkirk is the village of Grahamston, near which, in 1298, was fought a battle between the forces of Edward I. and the Scots, under Wallace and Sir John Graham, in which the latter were defeated. The battle of Falkirk-muir, between the royal forces under General Hawley, and the Highlanders, in which the latter gained a complete victory, was fought on the high ground lying to the south-west of the town. Hawley had suffered himself to be detained at Callander House by the wit and gaiety of the Countess of Kilmarnock (whose husband was with the Prince's army,) until the Highlanders had taken up an advantageous position, and were ready to attack his army.

L

The consequence of this negligence, coupled with an incapacity to act, was, that his troops were thrown into confusion, and completely routed.*

The view from the eminence on which the battle was fought is remarkably extensive, varied, and beautiful.

Proceeding westward, the tourist, a short way from Falkirk, passes the village of Camelon, said to have been the situation of a Roman city built by Vespasian. A mile farther on, the road crosses the Carron. Near to this are the church and village of Larbert, and Larbert House. In Larbert Kirk, Bruce, the famous Abyssinian traveller, lies interred. Kinnaird, his patrimonial estate, is at no great distance. A mile and a half farther on, the road passes through the remains of the Torwood Forest, where Sir William Wallace is said to have found shelter in a tree when pursued by his enemies. At Torwood-head, Mr. Cargill, in 1680, excommunicated Charles II., the Duke of York, and the ministry. About four miles farther on, is the village of Bannockburn, remarkable for its manufac-

---

* "Hawley had not a better head, and certainly a much worse heart, than Sir John Cope, who was a humane, good-tempered man. The new general ridiculed severely the conduct of his predecessor, and remembering that he had seen, in 1715, the left wing of the Highlanders broken by a charge of the Duke of Argyle's horse, which came upon them across a morass, he resolved to manœuvre in the same manner. He forgot, however, a material circumstance—that the morass at Sheriffmuir was hard frozen, which made some difference in favour of the cavalry. Hawley's manœuvre, as commanded and executed, plunged a great part of his dragoons up to the saddle-laps in a bog, where the Highlanders cut them to pieces with so little trouble, that, as one of the performers assured us, the feat was as easy as slicing *bacon*. The gallantry of some of the English regiments beat off the Highland charge on another point, and, amid a tempest of wind and rain which has been seldom equalled, the field presented the singular prospect of two armies flying different ways at the same moment. The king's troops, however, ran fastest and farthest, and were the last to recover their courage; indeed, they retreated that night to Falkirk, leaving their guns, burning their tents, and striking a new panic into the British nation, which was but just recovering from the flutter excited by what, in olden times, would have been called the Raid of Derby. In the drawing-room which took place at Saint James's on the day the news arrived, all countenances were marked with doubt and apprehension, excepting those of George the Second, the Earl of Stair, and Sir John Cope, who was radiant with joy at Hawley's discomfiture. Indeed, the idea of the two generals was so closely connected, that a noble peer of Scotland, upon the same day, addressed Sir John Cope by the title of General Hawley, to the no small amusement of those who heard the *quid pro quo*."—SIR WALTER SCOTT'S *Prose Works*, vol. xix., p. 303.

tories of tartans and carpets. To the left of the road,
between Bannockburn and St. Ninians, and about a mile
distant from Stirling, is the scene of the famous battle, the
Marathon of the North, fought June 24th, 1314, between
the English army of 100,000 men, under Edward II., and
the Scottish army of 30,000, commanded by Robert Bruce,
in which the former were signally defeated, with the loss
of 30,000 men, and 700 barons and knights. The Scottish
army extended in a north-easterly direction from the brook
of Bannock, which was so rugged and broken as to cover
the right flank effectually, to the village of St. Ninians,
probably in the line of the present road from Stirling to
Kilsyth. The royal standard was pitched, according to
tradition, in a stone having a round hole for its reception,
and thence called the Bore-Stone. The remaining fragment of this stone, protected from the depredations of
strangers by a frame-work of iron, is still shown on the top
of a small eminence called Brocks Brae, to the south-west
of St. Ninians. To the northward, where there is a morass
called Halberd's Bog, Bruce fortified his position against
cavalry by digging a number of pits so close together as to
resemble the cells in a honeycomb. They were slightly
covered with brushwood and green sods, so as not to be
obvious to an impetuous enemy.* It was in the immediate

* On the evening before the battle a personal encounter took place between
Bruce and Sir Henry de Bohun, a gallant English knight, the issue of which had
a great effect upon the spirits of both armies. It is thus recorded by Sir Walter
Scott, in "The Lord of the Isles:"—

> "Dash'd from the ranks Sir Henry Boune,—
> He spurr'd his steed, he couched his lance,
> And darted on the Bruce at once.—
> As motionless as rocks that bide
> The wrath of the advancing tide,
> The Bruce stood fast. Each heart beat high,
> And dazzled was each gazing eye.—
> The heart had hardly time to think,
> The eye-lid scarcely time to wink,
> While on the king, like flash of flame,
> Spurr'd to full speed the war-horse came!—
> The partridge may the falcon mock,
> If that slight palfrey stand the shock.—
> But, swerving from the knight's career,
> Just as they met, Bruce shunn'd the spear;
> Onward the baffled warrior bore
> His course—but soon his course was o'er,—

High

neighbourhood of this spot that the heat of the contest took place. A short time ago one of the workmen employed in draining the moss discovered an old sword about three feet below the surface. Formerly there were two large stones, erected in the lower extremity of a lawn which fronts a villa near the village of Newhouse, about a quarter of a mile from the south part of Stirling, marking the spot where a skirmish took place between Randolph Earl of Moray, and a party of English commanded by Sir Robert Clifford.* The stones have been removed, but the place is still popularly called Randals-field.

> High in his stirrups stood the king,
> And gave his battle-axe the swing;
> Right on De Boune, the whiles he pass'd,
> Fell that stern blow—the first—the last!—
> Such strength upon the blow was put,
> The helmet crash'd like hazel-nut,
> The axe-shaft, with its brazen clasp,
> Was shiver'd to the gauntlet grasp;
> Springs from the blow the startled horse;
> Drops to the plain the lifeless corse,
> First of that fatal field, how soon,
> How sudden fell the fierce De Boune."

The Scottish leaders remonstrated with the king upon his temerity; he only answered, "I have broken my good battle-axe." The English vanguard retreated, after witnessing this single combat.

* Bruce had enjoined Randolph, who commanded the left wing of his army, to be vigilant in preventing any advanced parties of the English from throwing succours into the Castle of Stirling. Eight hundred horsemen, commanded by Sir Robert Clifford, were detached from the English army; they made a circuit by the low grounds to the east, and approached the Castle. The king perceived their motion, and coming up to Randolph, angrily exclaimed, "Thoughtless man! you have suffered the enemy to pass. Randolph hastened to repair his fault, or perish. As he advanced, the English cavalry wheeled to attack him. Randolph drew up his troops in a circular form, with their spears resting on the ground, and protended on every side. At the first onset, Sir William Daynecourt, an English commander of distinguished note, was slain. The enemy, far superior in numbers to Randolph, environed him, and pressed hard on his little band; Douglas saw his jeopardy, and requested the king's permission to go and succour him. "You shall not move from your ground," cried the king, "let Randolph extricate himself as he best may, I will not alter my order of battle, and lose the advantage of my position."—"In truth," replied Douglas, "I cannot stand by and see Randolph perish, and, therefore, with your leave, I must aid him." The king unwillingly consented, and Douglas flew to the assistance of his friend. While approaching, he perceived that the English were falling into disorder, and that the perseverance of Randolph had prevailed over their impetuous courage. "Halt!" cried Douglas, "those brave men have repulsed the enemy, let us not diminish their glory by sharing it."—DALRYMPLE'S *Annals of Scotland.*

About a mile from the field of battle, in another direction, is a place called the Bloody Folds, where the Earl of Gloucester is said to have made a stand, and died gallantly at the head of his own military tenants and vassals. There is also a place in this neighbourhood called Ingram's Crook, which is supposed to have derived its name from Sir Ingram Umfraville, one of the English commanders. In the rear of the position occupied by the Scottish army is the Gillies' Hill, which derived its name from the following circumstance :—In a valley westward of this hill, Bruce stationed his baggage, under the charge of the gillies or servants and retainers of the camp. At the critical moment when the English line was wavering, these gillies, prompted either by the enthusiasm of the moment, or the desire of plunder, assumed, in a tumultuary manner, such arms as they found nearest, and showed themselves on the hill like a new army advancing to battle. The English taking these for a fresh body of troops, were seized with a panic, and fled in every direction.

About a mile westward from the field of Bannockburn, was fought, in 1488, the battle of Sauchieburn, in which James III. was defeated and slain. The Barons of Scotland, being dissatisfied with the government of the king, rose in rebellion against him, and drew into their party the king's eldest son, then a youth of fifteen, afterwards James IV. The unfortunate monarch, with inferior numbers, attacked the army of the insurgents. The consequences proved most calamitous. The royal forces, after an obstinate struggle, gave way, and the king, flying from the field, fell from his horse as it started at a woman and water-pitcher near the village of Millton. He was carried into the mill in a state of insensibility by the miller and his wife, without being recognised. On recovering his senses he asked for a priest, to whom he might make confession. One of his pursuers coming up, exclaimed, " I am a priest," and, approaching the unfortunate monarch, who was lying in a corner of the mill, stabbed him several times to the heart. James IV. was seized with deep remorse for his conduct in this affair, which manifested itself in severe acts of penance, among others, in wearing a heavy iron belt, to the weight of which he added certain ounces every year as long as he lived.*

St. Ninians, or, as it is commonly called, St. Ringans, is a thriving village a short way south from Stirling. Its steeple stands separate from the church, which is in its immediate vicinity. The old church, being used as a powder magazine by the Highlanders in 1746, was accidentally blown up; but though the church was completely destroyed, the steeple remained uninjured. A mile farther on, the tourist enters the royal burgh of

STIRLING,

delightfully situated on an eminence near the river Forth, and bearing in its external appearance a considerable resemblance to Edinburgh, though on a smaller scale. The most interesting and conspicuous object in Stirling is the Castle, the first foundation of which is lost in the darkness of antiquity. It was frequently taken and retaken after protracted sieges, during the wars which were carried on for the independence of Scotland. It became a royal residence about the time of the accession of the house of Stuart, and was long the favourite abode of the Scottish monarchs. It was the birthplace of James II. and James V.; and James VI. and his eldest son Prince Henry were baptized in it. The palace, which was built by James V., is in the form of a quadrangle, and occupies the south-east part of the fortress. The buildings on the south side of the square are the oldest part of the Castle. One of the apartments is still called Douglas's Room, in consequence of the assassination of William Earl of Douglas by the hand of James II., after he had granted him a safe-conduct.†

On the west side of the square is a long low building, which was originally a chapel, and is now used as a store-

* So little had the prince been accustomed to his father's company, that he was almost a stranger to his person; for when Sir Andrew Wood appeared before him, a few days after the battle, struck with his stately appearance, or, perhaps, with some resemblance he bore to the late king, he asked him, "Sir, are you my father?" To which the admiral, bursting into tears, replied, "I am not your father, but I was your father's true servant."

† "Ye towers! within whose circuit dread,
   A Douglas by his sovereign bled."
                                   Lady of the Lake.

STIRLING CASTLE.

room and armoury. This building was erected by James VI., and was the scene of the baptism of his son Prince Henry. Underneath the exterior wall, on the west, a narrow road leads from the town, and descends the precipice behind the Castle. This is called Ballangeich, a Gaelic word signifying " windy pass," which is remarkable as having furnished the fictitious name adopted by James V. in the various disguises which he was in the habit of assuming, for the purpose of seeing that justice was regularly administered, and frequently also from the less justifiable motive of gallantry.* To the north of the Castle is a small

* The two excellent comic songs, entitled " The Gaberlunzie man," and " We'll gae nae mair a roving," are said to have been founded on the success of this monarch's amorous adventures, when travelling in the disguise of a beggar. The following anecdotes respecting this frolicsome prince, are given by Sir Walter Scott :—

" Another adventure, which had nearly cost James his life, is said to have taken place at the village of Cramond, near Edinburgh, where he had rendered his addresses acceptable to a pretty girl of the lower rank. Four or five persons, whether relations or lovers of his mistress is uncertain, beset the disguised monarch, as he returned from his rendezvous. Naturally gallant, and an admirable master of his weapon, the king took post on the high and narrow bridge over the Almond river, and defended himself bravely with his sword. A peasant, who was thrashing in a neighbouring barn, came out upon the noise, and whether moved by compassion or by natural gallantry, took the weaker side, and laid about with his flail so effectually, as to disperse the assailants, well threshed, even according to the letter. He then conducted the king into his barn, where his guest requested a bason and towel, to remove the stains of the broil. This being procured with difficulty, James employed himself in learning what was the summit of his deliverer's earthly wishes, and found that they were bounded by the desire of possessing, in property, the farm of Braehead, upon which he laboured as a bondsman. The lands chanced to belong to the Crown; and James directed him to come to the Palace of Holy-Rood, and inquire for the Guidman (i. e. farmer) of Ballangeich, a name by which he was known in his excursions, and which answered to Il Bondocani of Haroun Alraschid. He presented himself accordingly, and found with due astonishment that he had saved his monarch's life, and that he was to be gratified with a Crown-charter of the lands of Braehead, under the service of presenting an ewer, bason, and towel, for the king to wash his hands, when he shall happen to pass the Bridge of Cramond. In 1822, when George IV. came to Scotland, the descendant of this John Howison of Braehead, who still possesses the estate which was given to his ancestor, appeared at a solemn festival, and offered his Majesty water from a silver ewer."

Another of James's frolics is thus narrated by Mr. Campbell, from the Statistical Account. " Being once benighted when out a hunting, and separated from his attendants, he happened to enter a cottage in the midst of a moor, at the foot of the Ochil hills, near Alloa, where, unknown, he was kindly received. In order to regale their unexpected guest, the *gude-man* (i. e. landlord, farmer) desired the *gude-wife* to fetch the hen that roosted nearest the cock, which is

mount on which executions commonly took place.* On this eminence, and within sight of their Castle of Doune always the plumpest, for the stranger's supper. The king, highly pleased with his night's lodging, and hospitable entertainment, told mine host, at parting, that he should be glad to return his civility, and requested that, the first time he came to Stirling, he would call at the castle, and enquire for the *gude-man of Ballangeich*. Donaldson, the landlord, did not fail to call on the *gude-man of Ballangeich*, when his astonishment, at finding that the king had been his guest, afforded no small amusement to the merry monarch and his courtiers; and, to carry on the pleasantry, he was thenceforth designated by James with the title of King of the Moors, which name and designation have descended from father to son ever since; and they have continued in possession of the identical spot, the property of Mr. Erskine of Mar, till very lately, when this gentleman, with reluctance, turned out the descendant and representative of the King of the Moors, on account of his Majesty's invincible indolence, and great dislike to reform or innovation of any kind, although, from the spirited example of his neighbour tenants on the same estate, he is convinced similar exertion would promote his advantage."

The following anecdote is extracted from the genealogical work of Buchanan of Auchmar, upon Scottish surnames:—

" This John Buchanan of Auchmar and Arnpryor was afterwards termed King of Kippen,† upon the following account:—King James V., a very sociable, debonair prince, residing at Stirling, in Buchanan of Arnpryor's time, carriers were very frequently passing along the common road, being near Arnpryor's house, with necessaries for the use of the king's family, and he having some extraordinary occasion, ordered one of these carriers to leave his load at his house and he would pay him for it; which the carrier refused to do, telling him he was the king's carrier, and his load was for his majesty's use. To which Arnpryor seemed to have small regard, compelling the carrier, in the end, to leave his load; telling him, if King James was king of Scotland, he was king of Kippen, so that it was reasonable he should share with his neighbour king in some of these loads so frequently carried that road. The carrier representing this usage, and telling the story as Arnpryor spoke it, to some of the king's servants, it came at length to his majesty's ears, who, shortly thereafter, with a few attendants, came to visit his neighbour king, who was, in the meantime, at dinner. King James having sent a servant to demand access, was denied the same by a tall fellow with a battle-axe, who stood porter at the gate, telling there could be no access till dinner was over. This answer not satisfying the king, he sent to demand access a second time; upon which he was desired by the porter to desist, otherwise he would find cause to repent his rudeness. His majesty finding this method would not do, desired the porter to tell his master that the good-man of Ballangeich desired to speak with the King of Kippen. The porter telling Arnpryor so much, he in all humble manner, came and received the king, and having entertained him with much sumptuousness and jollity, became so agreeable to King James, that he allowed him to take so much of any provision he found carrying that road as he had occasion for; and, seeing he made the first visit, desired Arnpryor in a few days to return him a second at Stirling, which he performed, and continued in very much favour with the king, always thereafter being termed King of Kippen while he lived."

* " Thou, O sad and fatal mound,
  That oft has heard the death-axe sound.
                                     Lady of the Lake.

----

† A small district of Perthshire.

STIRLING CASTLE FROM THE LADY'S ROCK.

and their extensive possessions, Murdoch Duke of Albany, Duncan Earl of Lennox, his father-in-law, and his two sons, Walter and Alexander Stuart, were beheaded in 1424. The execution of Walter Stuart is supposed, with great probability, to be the groundwork of the beautiful pathetic ballad of "Young Waters." This "heading-hill" now commonly bears the name of Hurley-Hacket, from its being the scene of an amusement practised by James V. when a boy, and his courtiers, which consisted in sliding in some sort of chair from top to bottom of the bank. On the south side of the Castle Hill is a small piece of ground called the Valley, with a rock on the south side denominated the Ladies' Rock. On this spot tournaments used to be held. The view from the Castle Hill is remarkably magnificent. To the north and east are the Ochil hills, and the windings of the Forth through the Carse of Stirling, with its fertile fields, luxuriant woods, and stately mansions. On the west lies the vale of Menteith, bounded by the Highland mountains. The Campsie hills close the horizon to the south, and in the foreground, on the east, are the town, the Abbey Craig, and the ruins of Cambuskenneth Abbey, and, in a clear day, the Castle of Edinburgh and Arthur's Seat are seen. Stirling Castle is one of the four fortresses of Scotland, which, by the articles of the Union, are always to be kept in repair. It is now used as a barrack. South-west of the Castle lies the King's Park, and to the east of it are the King's Gardens, which, though now unenclosed, and reduced to the condition of a marshy pasture, still retain the fantastic forms into which they had been thrown by the gardeners of ancient times.

The Greyfriars or Franciscan church of Stirling was erected in 1494 by James IV., and some additions were made to it by Cardinal Beaton. It is a handsome Gothic building, and, since the Reformation, has been divided into two places of worship, called the East and West Churches. In this church the Earl of Arran, Regent of the kingdom, abjured Romanism in 1543 ; it was also the scene of the coronation of James VI., on the 29th July 1597, when John Knox preached the coronation sermon. The celebrated

Ebenezer Erskine, founder of the Secession Church, was one of the ministers of the West Church.

To the north of the church stand the ruins of a haggard-looking building called Mar's Work. It was built by the Earl of Mar out of the ruins of Cambuskenneth Abbey. This conduct excited much popular dissatisfaction, in allusion to which the Earl caused several inscriptions, in the form of distiches, to be affixed to his house. Three of these inscriptions may still be decyphered and severally run thus :—

> Speik forth aud spair nocht ;
> Consider weel, and cair nocht.
>
> The moir I stand in oppin hitht,
> My faultis more subject ar to sitht.
>
> I pray all luikars on this luging,
> With gentle e to gif their juging.

In the immediate neighbourhood of this building is a fine piece of architecture in the old Scottish style, called Argyle's Lodging, which was built by Sir William Alexander, the first Earl of Stirling, whose arms are elaborately sculptured above the door.* It afterwards passed into the hands of the Argyle family, and is now used as a military hospital.

Stirling has long been celebrated for its schools, and also for the number of its hospitals or residences for decayed persons. By an act of the Scottish Parliament in 1437, Stirling was appointed to be the place for keeping the Jug, or standard of dry measure, from which all others through-

---

* The Earl of Stirling was one of those men who, to literary habits, add a keen relish for the pursuits of active life. He was the originator of the project for the colonization of Nova Scotia, and had the entire management of the scheme. He was the author of several volumes of poetry, which at one time obtained considerable praise, Lithgow styling him " true castalian fire ;" Drayton, " my Alexander ; " and King James, " my philosophical poet. " Indeed, so great a favourite was he with the pedantic monarch, whose learning, doubtless, was not seldom the theme of his skilful flattery, that he obtained large grants of land and lordships both in North America and Scotland, as well as the privilege of coining for the latter country a species of base copper money called *turners*. It is said that when he inscribed the motto, *Per mare et terras*, upon his house in Stirling, his countrymen punningly read it, *Per metre et turners*, in allusion to his double capacity as maker of verses and coin.

out the country were appointed to be taken, while the Firlot was given to Linlithgow, the Ell to Edinburgh, the Reel to Perth, and the Pound to Lanark. The Stirling Jug is still preserved with great care. In 1841, the population of the town was 8029. Stirling Bridge was long a structure of great importance, having been, till lately, almost the only access into the northern part of Scotland for wheeled carriages. The old bridge is still standing, and viewed from the new bridge, by which it has been superseded, it forms a picturesque and interesting object. The erection of the new structure cost £17,000. The outside facing is of greenstone from the neighbouring cliff of Abbey Craig. At a very early period there was a wooden bridge over the Forth, about half a mile above the present structure, which was the scene of one of the most gallant achievements of Sir William Wallace, on the 13th of September 1297. An English army of 50,000 foot and 1000 horse, commanded by Cressingham, advanced towards Stirling in quest of Wallace, who, on his part, having collected an army of 40,000 men, marched southward to dispute the passage of the Forth. He posted his army near Cambuskenneth, allowing only a part of them to be seen. The English hurried across the river, to attack the Scots. After a considerable number of them had thus passed over, and the bridge was crowded with those who were following, Wallace charged those who had crossed with his whole strength, slew a very great number, and drove the rest into the river Forth, where the greater part were drowned. The remainder of the English army, who were left on the southern bank of the river, fled in great confusion, having first set fire to the wooden bridge, that the Scots might not pursue them. Cressingham himself was among the slain, and his rapine and oppression had rendered him so detestable to the Scots, that they are said to have flayed off his skin and cut it in pieces to make girths for their horses.

The Agricultural Museum of the Messrs. Drummond is well worthy of a visit. The extent of the collection would do credit to a town ten times the size of Stirling, and the

liberality with which it is exhibited is most creditable to
the proprietors.

The steel engraving of Stirling Castle, with which our
text is illustrated, represents the scene in Waverley, where
the party of Balmawhapple, upon passing the fortress, are
saluted by a bullet from its walls. The artist has selected
the moment when the valorous laird returns the compliment
by discharging his pistol at the inhospitable rock.

FIFTH TOUR.

₊ The Map of the Royal Progress facing page 159, illustrates this Tour.

FROM EDINBURGH TO STIRLING BY STEAMBOAT.*

LOOKING straight across the Firth, leaving Granton Pier,
the burgh of Burntisland may be observed directly opposite.
Shortly after leaving Granton, may be seen Lauriston Castle,
formerly the property of John Law, the projector of the
Mississippi scheme, and sold by his descendant Marshal
Lauriston about 30 years ago. On the north shore is the
village of Aberdour, and near it the seat of the Earl of Mor-
ton, who is known here by the title of " the Gudeman of
Aberdour." North of the Castle is the mansion-house of
Hillside. A little farther on is the island of Inch Colm,
with the remains of a monastery, founded, in 1123, by
Alexander I. To the north of this is Dalgetty Church,

• Steamboats sail for Alloa and Stirling every day from Granton Pier.
Coaches to the boat run from No. 10, Princes Street, where correct information
as to the hours of sailing may be obtained.

near which is Otterstoun Loch, with the mansion-houses of Otterstoun and Cockairney, the property of Sir Robert Moubray, on its sweetly-wooded banks. On the south shore, at the mouth of the river Almond, stand the village of Cramond, and Cramond House, (Lady Torphichen,) and a little farther west is Dalmeny Park, the seat of the Earl of Rosebery. Near it are the ruins of Barnbougle Castle, an ancient seat of the family of the Moubrays. Directly opposite is Donibristle, a seat of the Earl of Moray, the scene of the atrocious murder, by the Earl of Huntly, of the youthful Earl of Moray, son-in-law of the celebrated Regent Murray.* A short way to the westward lies the

---

* The Earl of Huntly, head of the powerful family of. Gordon, had chanced to have some feudal differences with the Earl of Murray, in the course of which John Gordon, a brother of Gordon of Cluny, was killed by a shot from Murray's castle of Darnaway. This was enough to make the two families irreconcilable enemies, even if they had been otherwise on friendly terms. About 1591-2, an accusation was brought against Murray, for having given some countenance or assistance to Stewart, Earl of Bothwell, in a recent treasonable exploit. King James, without recollecting, perhaps, the hostility between the two Earls, sent Huntly with a commission to bring the Earl of Murray to his presence. Huntly probably rejoiced in the errand, as giving him an opportunity of revenging himself on his feudal enemy. He beset the house of Donibristle, on the northern shore of the Forth, and summoned Murray to surrender. In reply, a gun was fired, which mortally wounded one of the Gordons. The assailants proceeded to set fire to the house; when Dunbar, sheriff of the county of Moray, said to the Earl, ' Let us not stay to be burnt in the flaming house : I will go out foremost, and the Gordons, taking me for your Lordship, will kill me, while you escape in the confusion.' They rushed out among their enemies accordingly, and Dunbar was slain. But his death did not save his friend, as he had generously intended. Murray, indeed, escaped for the moment, but as he fled towards the rocks of the sea-shore, he was traced by the silken tassels attached to his head-piece, which had taken fire as he broke out among the flames. By this means, his pursuers followed him down amongst the cliffs, near the sea ; and Gordon of Buckie, who is said to have been the first that overtook him, wounded him mortally. As Murray was gasping in the last agony, Huntly came up ; and it is alleged, by tradition, that Gordon pointed his dirk against the person of his chief, saying, ' By heaven! my Lord, you shall be as deep in as I ;' and so he compelled him to wound Murray whilst he was dying. Huntly, with a wavering hand, struck the expiring Earl on the face. Thinking of his superior beauty, even in that moment of parting life, Murray stammered out the dying words, ' You have spoiled a better face than your own.'

" After this deed of violence, Huntly did not choose to return to Edinburgh, but departed for the north. He took refuge, for the moment, in the castle of Ravenscraig, belonging to the Lord Sinclair, who told him, with a mixture of

ancient burgh of Inverkeithing. On the two coasts are the
towns of North and South Queensferry ; and, in the strait
between them, is the fortified islet of Inchgarvie. On a
rocky promontory, on the north shore, are the ruins of
Rosyth Castle, once the seat of the Stuarts of Rosyth, a
branch of the Royal House of Scotland, from whom it is
said the mother of Oliver Cromwell was descended. Half a
mile beyond Inchgarvie is Port Edgar, where George IV.
embarked, after a visit to the Earl of Hopetoun, 29th August
1822. On an eminence, beyond South Queensferry, is Dundas Castle, the original seat of the Dundas family before the
eleventh century, and still the residence of their lineal descendant, Dundas of that Ilk. Farther on, upon the same
side, and about a mile from the shore, is Hopetoun House,
the splendid mansion of the Earl of Hopetoun ; and on a
peninsula to the westward, stands Blackness Castle, one of
the four fortresses which, by the Articles of the Union, are
to be kept constantly garrisoned. Close by the village of
Charleston, on the north side of the Forth, stands Broomhall, the seat of the Earl of Elgin. Farther on is Crombie
Point and Crombie House, then the village of Torryburn,
next Torry House (Captain Erskine Wemyss of Wemyss
Castle) and Newmills village. Returning to the south coast,
and proceeding westward, may be seen in succession Carriden

Scottish caution and hospitality, that he was welcome to come in, but would
have been twice as welcome to have passed by. Gordon, when a long period
had passed by, avowed his contrition for the guilt he had incurred."—*Tales of a
Grandfather*, vol. ii., p. 191.

Upon this tragical circumstance, the following beautiful ballad is founded :—

" Ye Highlands and ye Lawlands,
   Oh, where have ye been ?
They hae slain the Earl o' Murray,
   And lain him on the green.

' Now, wae be to you, Huntly !
   And wherefore did ye sae ?
I bade you bring him wi' you,
   But forbade you him to slae.'

He was a braw gallant,
   And he rade at the ring ;

And the bonnie Earl o' Murray,
   Oh ! he micht ha' been a king.

He was a braw gallant,
   And he rade at the gluve ;
And the bonnie Earl o' Murray,
   Oh ! he was the Queen's luve !

Oh ! lang will his lady
   Look ower the Castle Doune,
Ere she see the Earl o' Murray
   Come sounding through the toun."

House,* (James Hope, Esq.,) Kirkgrange Salt Pans, Borrowstounness, Kinneil House, the property of the Duke of Hamilton, for some time the residence of the late Professor Dugald
Stewart; and Grangemouth, situated at the mouth of Carron
Water. On the north side is Valleyfield, (Lady Baird Preston,) and near it the ancient and decayed burgh of Culross,
(pronounced *Cooris*.)† The inhabitants are a remarkably
primitive set of people. Immediately behind it are the ruins
of a Cistertian abbey, founded in 1217 by Malcolm Earl of
Fife. At the Reformation, its possessions were conferred
upon Sir James Colville, who was created Lord Colville of
Culross. From the family of Colville it passed to the Earls
of Dundonald, who sold it to the late Sir Robert Preston,
Bart. A little farther on is Blair Castle, (Alison, Esq.,)
and about a mile beyond this is Sands House, (Johnstone,
Esq.,) after which the tourist reaches the town and shipping
port of Kincardine. Near it stand the ruins of the ancient
castle of Tulliallan, formerly the property of the knights of
Blackadder, and Tulliallan Castle, the residence of Baroness
Keith and Count Flahault, built by the late Admiral Lord
Keith, the father of the present proprietrix, who is also the
lineal representative of one of the most ancient families in
Scotland—the Mercers of Aldie. On the opposite side is
Higgin's Nook, (J. Burn Murdoch, Esq.,) and beyond it,
upon a height, Airth Castle, (Graham, Esq.,) near which
there is a square tower, built in 1298, previous to the battle

---

* In a house, close upon the shore, which now serves as a sort of lodge to
this property, the famous Colonel Gardiner, who fell at the battle of Prestonpans, was born.

† Culross was famous for the manufacture of *girdles*, the round iron plates
on which the people of Scotland bake their barley and oaten bread. "The
hammermen of Edinburgh are no' that bad at girdles for carcakes, neither,
though the Cu'ross hammermen have the gree for that."—*Heart of Mid-
Lothian*, vol. ii., p. 254.

Culross was also celebrated for its salt-pans and coal mines. In the reign of
James VI. the coal-mines were worked a great way under the bed of the Forth,
and the coals were shipped at a mound which defended from the water the
mouth of a subterraneous communication with the coal-pit. James VI., when
on a visit to the proprietor, Sir George Bruce, being conducted, by his own
desire, into the coal-pit, was led to ascend from it by the mound, when it was
high tide. Seeing himself surrounded, on all sides, by water, he apprehended a
plot, and bawled out "Treason," but Sir George soon dispelled his Majesty's
fears, by handing him into an elegant pinnace that was lying alongside.

of Falkirk. The castle contains original portraits of the
celebrated Graham of Claverhouse, Viscount Dundee; and
of the admirable Crichton. About a mile to the west is
Dunmore House, a castellated structure, the residence of
the Earl of Dunmore. Nearly opposite, upon the right, is
Kennet House, the seat of Robert Bruce, Esq. of Kennet.
Farther on, upon the same side, is Clackmannan, the capital of the small county of that name; and to the west of
the town, delightfully situated on an eminence, is Clackmannan Tower, said to have been built by Robert Bruce.
It is now the property of the Earl of Zetland. Close beside
the tower once stood the palace of Robert Bruce, and family
house of Bruce of Clackmannan, now demolished. This
was the residence of the old Jacobite lady, Mrs. Bruce of
Clackmannan, who is mentioned in Currie's Life of Burns
as having knighted that poet with a sword which belonged
to Bruce. The sword and a helmet which had also belonged to the hero are now in the possession of Lord Elgin,
who represents the family of Bruce, and are to be seen at
Broomhall, near Dunfermline. About a mile beyond Clackmannan, is the flourishing town of Alloa, in the neighbourhood of extensive collieries and distilleries. Near the town,
and in the midst of a fine park, stands Alloa House, the
ancient seat of the family of Erskine, Earls of Mar, and
the subject of a fine Scottish air. The principal part of
the building was destroyed by fire about twenty years ago,
but there is still standing the original tower, an erection
of the thirteenth century. It is ninety feet high, and the
walls are eleven feet thick. At Alloa commence those remarkable windings called the " Links of Forth." These
windings of the river form a great number of beautiful
peninsulas, which, being of a very luxuriant and fertile
soil, gave rise to the old rhyme,—

" The lairdship o' the bonnie Links o' Forth
  Is better than an earldom o' the North."

The distance by land from Alloa to Stirling Bridge is
only six miles, while by water it is twelve. On the same
side as Alloa, and a little to the westward, is Tullibody
House, a residence of the Abercromby family. The Ochil

hills, from their proximity, now assume an air of imposing grandeur, and Stirling Castle forms a magnificent feature in the landscape. Beyond Tullibody, on the same side, is Cambus village, at the mouth of the Devon. The vale of the Devon is famed for its romantic beauty, and for the striking cascades formed by the river. Nearly opposite Cambus is Polmaise, (Murray, Esq.) Farther on, upon the right, are the ruins of Cambuskenneth Abbey, situated on one of the peninsular plains formed by the windings of the river. It was founded by David I., in 1147, for canons regular of the order of St. Augustine, and was one of the richest and most extensive abbeys in Scotland. At the Reformation, its possessions were bestowed by James VI. on the Earl of Mar; but about the year 1737 it was purchased by the Town Council of Stirling, for the benefit of Cowan's Hospital. Of the once extensive fabric of the Abbey, nothing now exists except a few broken walls and a tower, which was the belfry. On the right is seen the Abbey Craig, and soon after the tourist reaches Stirling.

From Stirling a pleasant episodical tour may be made to Castle Campbell, the Rumbling Brig, and the Devil's Caldron.

Leaving Stirling, the tourist has on his left the soft green pastoral yet lofty hills of the Ochil range, with their magnificent wooded glades and warm sunward slopes, consisting of intermingling copse, cornfields, and meadows, while on the right is a rich and level country, bounded by the Forth, now entwining its silver links and spreading into a noble estuary. The most southerly of the Ochil hills is Damyat, famous for the extensive and splendid view obtained from its summit. In its neighbourhood is Bencleuch, which shoots up into a tall rocky point, called Craigleith, remarkable in ancient times for the production of falcons. In a hollow near this, the snow often lies far into the summer. The people give it the picturesque name of Lady Alva's Web. Three miles from Stirling the tourist reaches the beautiful village of Blairlogie, and four miles beyond it the village of Alva, which was formerly remarkable for its silver mines. Alva House, the residence of Johnstone of Alva, stands on an eminence projecting from the base of the Woodhill.* Three miles from Alva is Tilli-

* " Oh, Alva woods are bonnie,
    Tillicoultry hills are fair,
    But when I think o' the bonnie braes o' Menstrie,
    It mak's my heart aye sair."—*Fairy Rhyme.*
The village of Menstrie lies two miles west of Alva. Menstrie House was the seat of the Earl of Stirling.

M

coultry, and at the distance of other three miles is the village of Dollar, about thirteen miles from Stirling, and seven from Alva. At Dollar there is an extensive academy, founded by a person of the name of Macnab, a native of the parish, who had realized a large fortune in London. It is a handsome Grecian building, and is furnished with good masters for the various branches of education. In the neighbourhood is the remarkable ruin of Castle Campbell, occupying a wild and romantic situation on the top of a high and almost insulated rock. The only access to the castle is by an isthmus connecting the mount with the hill behind. The mount on which it is situated is nearly encompassed on all sides by thick bosky woods, and mountain rivulets descending on either side, unite at the base. Immediately behind rises a vast amphitheatre of wooded hills. Castle Campbell is a place of great antiquity. The precise period at which it came into the possession of the Argyle family is not certainly known. In 1493, an act of Parliament was passed for changing the name of " the castle called the Gloume,"* to Castle Campbell, and it continued to be a possession of the great clan family of Argyle, till about thirty years ago, upon the death of the late Duke, it was sold to the late Mr. Tait of Harvieston. It is said that John Knox resided in Castle Campbell, under the protection of Archibald, the fourth Earl, who was the first of the Scottish nobility that publicly embraced the Protestant religion. Castle Campbell was destroyed in 1645. " The feudal hatred of Montrose, and of the clans composing the strength of his army, the vindictive resentment also of the Ogilvies for the destruction of "the bonnie House of Airlie," and that of the Stirlingshire cavaliers for that of Menstrie, doomed this magnificent pile to flames and ruin. The destruction of many a meaner habitation by the same unscrupulous and unsparing spirit of vengeance has been long forgotten, but the majestic remains of Castle Campbell still excite a sigh in those that view them, over the miseries of civil war."† About two miles above Dollar is an interesting spot where the Devon forms a series of cascades, one of which is called the Caldron Linn.‡ The river here suddenly enters

---

* The ancient name of the castle, it is often said, was the Castle of Gloom. The mountain streams that flow on the different sides are still called, the one the Water of Care, the other the Burn of Sorrow; and, after the junction in front of the castle, they traverse the valley of Dollar, or Dolour. The proper etymologists, however, tell a different tale. The old Gaelic name of the stronghold was *Cock Leum*, or Mad Leap. The glen of Care, was the glen of *Caer* or castle, a British word; and Dollar is simply *Dalor*, the high field.—CHAMBERS' *Gazetteer*, vol i., 191.

† *Tales of a Grandfather*, vol. iii., p. 12.

‡ Instead of the usual route, pedestrians, in coming from Dollar, should strike off the high road soon after they get above *Vicar's Bridge*, and take along a path to the right, leading to *Cowden* and *Muckart Mill*, and from thence by

a deep gulf, where, finding itself confined, it has, by continual efforts against the sides, worked out a cavity resembling a large caldron. From this gulf the water works its way through an aperture beneath the surface into a lower cavity, where it is covered with a constant foam. The water then works its way into a third caldron, out of which it is precipitated by a sheer fall of forty-four feet. The best view of this magnificent scene is from the bottom of the fall. About a mile farther up the vale, the rocks on each side rise to the height of eighty-six feet, and the banks of the stream are contracted in such a manner, that a bridge of twenty-five feet span connects them. A handsome new bridge has lately been erected above the old one, from the bed of the stream a hundred and twenty feet. On account of the rocky nature of the channel, the river here makes a violent noise, hence the name of the Rumbling Bridge.* A few hundred yards farther up, there is another cascade, called the Devil's Mill, where the water vibrating from one side to another of the pool, and constantly beating against the sides of the rock, produces an intermittent noise like that of a mill in motion. The whole of the scenes around these remarkable cascades are of the most romantic kind, and strikingly different from all other Scottish scenery. "The clear winding Devon," as almost every reader will recollect, has been celebrated by Burns in his beautiful lyric, "The Banks of the Devon." Miss Charlotte Hamilton, (afterwards Mrs. Adair,) the lady on whom this song was composed, was at that time residing at Harvieston, near Dollar.

The tourist may, if he choose, proceed by the Crook of Devon to Kinross, and thence to Edinburgh,—a route which he will find described in the tour from Edinburgh to Perth ; or he may proceed to Dunfermline, and thence to North Queensferry, by a route much more agreeable, and only two miles longer.

A short but pleasant excursion may also be made from Stirling to Dunblane, distant six miles, and to the Roman Camp at Ardoch, twelve miles distant.

---

the *Blair Hill*, to the Caldron Linn. This is a short *cut*, which keeps near the river by a far more romantic line than the turnpike road.

* A short distance from the Rumbling Bridge is Aldie Castle, the ancient seat of the Mercers of Aldie, now represented by Baroness Keith. At Aldie, a man on being hanged for the slight offence of stealing a *caup fu' o' corn*, is said to have uttered a malediction upon the family, to the effect that the estate of Aldie should never be inherited by a male heir for nineteen generations. It is a somewhat singular coincidence, that this has already so far taken effect,—Lady Keith being the daughter of an heiress, who was the granddaughter and successor to another heiress, and being herself the mother of several daughters but of no male child. The slogan or war cry of the Mercers of Aldie, was "The grit pule."

Leaving Stirling, the tourist crosses the Forth by Stirling Bridge. A short way farther up the river is the Old Bridge, a very antique structure, narrow, and high in the centre. General Blakeney, the governor of the Castle, in 1745, caused the south arch to be destroyed, to interrupt the march of the Highlanders. On this bridge Archbishop Hamilton of St. Andrews, the last Roman Catholic Archbishop of Scotland, was hanged in 1571, in full pontificals, for his alleged accession to the assassination of Regent Murray. The tourist now passes, on the right, Airthrey Castle, (Lord Abercromby,) and afterwards the pretty little village of the Bridge of Allan, much resorted to in summer on account of a mineral well in the neighbourhood. In the vicinity is Keir, the seat of Archibald Stirling, Esq., and a mile and a half beyond it, the road passes Kippenross, the seat of Stirling of Kippendavie. In the lawn there is a remarkable plane-tree, supposed to be the largest in the kingdom. It is 42 feet in circumference at the ground, 27 where the branches shoot out, 100 feet high, and 467 years old. A little beyond Kippenross is

DUNBLANE,*

an ancient cathedral city, situated on the banks of the beautiful little river Allan. The cathedral, which was founded in 1142, and richly endowed by David I., is still tolerably entire. The east end is fitted up, in an elegant style, as a parish church. The prebendal stalls of richly carved dark oak, have fortunately been preserved. Several of the Bishops of Dunblane were distinguished persons, but the most celebrated of them was the good Bishop Leighton, afterwards Archbishop of Glasgow, who founded a library here, which has been greatly increased by subsequent literary donations. The mineral spring at Cromlix, in the vicinity of Dunblane, is frequented by many.

About two miles east by north of Dunblane is Sheriffmuir, the scene of the battle which was fought in 1715 between the Earl of Mar, and the royal forces under the Duke of Argyle. In this engagement the left wing of each army was defeated, and the right of each was victorious ; but the fruits of the victory remained with the Duke of Argyle.† Near the western extremity of the muir is

* Popularly characterized as " drucken Dumblane."

† Some person having remarked to the Duke of Argyle, that the rebels would probably claim the victory, his Grace replied,—

" If it wasna weel bobbit, weel bobbit, weel bobbit,
        If it wasna weel bobbit, we'll bobb it again ;"

alluding to the well known old song, called " The Bob of Dunblane."

A number of noblemen and gentlemen, on both sides, were slain in this engagement ; among others, the Earls of Forfar and Strathmore, the chieftain of Clanronald, &c. The body of the gallant young Earl of Strathmore was found on the field, watched by a faithful old domestic, who, being asked the name of

Kippendavie, (—Stirling, Esq.,) and four miles beyond is Green-leaning. A mile and a half farther on, the tourist reaches Ardoch House, the seat of Major William Moray Stirling. Within his parks is the celebrated Roman Camp of Ardoch, esteemed the most entire in the kingdom. General Wade's military road passes over one of its sides. The measure of the whole area is 1060 feet by 900, and it is calculated to have contained no fewer than 20,000 men. There appear to have been three or four ditches, and as many rampart walls surrounding the camp. The prætorium, which rises above the level of the camp, but is not precisely in the centre, forms a regular square, each side being exactly twenty yards. The camp is defended on the south-east side by a deep morass, and on the west side by the banks of the water of Knaick, which rises perpendicularly to the height of about fifty feet. In the immediate vicinity there are two other encampments more slightly fortified.

The tourist may proceed from Greenloaning to Perth, by Black-ford, Auchterarder, and Dalraich Bridge, passing on the road Braco Castle, Orchill, Gleneagles, Kincardine Castle, Strathallan Castle, Gask, and Dupplin Castle.

SIXTH TOUR.

STIRLING—DOUNE—CALLANDER—THE TROSACHS—LOCH KATRINE—
LOCH LOMOND.

THERE are two roads which lead from Stirling to Doune, the first stage on the way to Loch Katrine—one crosses the Forth by Stirling Bridge, and proceeds along the east bank of the Teith, passing, in succession, the beautiful village of Bridge of Allan, and the neat parish church of Lecropt,

the person whose body he waited upon with so much care, made this striking reply, " He was a man yesterday." " There was mair *tint* (lost) at Sheriff-muir," is a common proverb in Scotland. It is told, that a Highlander lamented that, at the battle of Sheriffmuir, he had " lost his father and his mother, and a gude buff belt, weel worth them baith." Burns has made this battle the subject of a song replete with humour.

built in the Gothic style; the other, proceeding up the valley of the Forth, passes the house of Craigforth, (Hon. C. F. Stuart,) and, two miles from Stirling, crosses the river at the bridge of Drip. At the distance of about four miles from Stirling, the road passes Ochtertyre, (Dundas, Esq.,) once the residence of Mr. J. Ramsay, the friend of Blacklock, of Burns, and of Scott; a mile and a half farther on, the road passes the mansion of Blair-Drummond, (Home Drummond, Esq.,) embosomed in fine woods and plantations. About sixty or seventy years ago, the celebrated Lord Kames became proprietor of this estate, and commenced that series of operations, by which what was once a bleak and marshy moor has been turned into rich corn-fields.* The road now crosses the Teith, by a fine old bridge built by Robert Spittal, tailor to Queen Margaret, widow of James IV., whence a fine view of Doune Castle is obtained; and, about nine miles from Stirling, enters the village of

DOUNE.

Just before crossing the bridge, and on the left hand, are Deanston Works, one of the most extensive cotton factories in Scotland. They are driven by the Water of the Teith, which is led for upwards of a mile in a capacious mill-lead, and propels four stupendous overshot wheels, 36 feet in diameter and 11 in breadth, which perform their stately revolutions under one spacious roof. The works are under

---

* The removal of Blair-Drummond Moss is probably the most extensive agricultural enterprise ever undertaken in this country. Underneath the moss, at a depth varying from six to sixteen feet, lay a stratum of fine clay of a most productive quality, if a plan could be devised for relieving it from the super-cumbent turf. This was accomplished by obtaining a command of water sufficient to wash the whole away into the river Forth. A wheel, twenty-eight feet in diameter and eight feet wide, propelled by a running stream, was employed to raise part of the water, by which it was driven to the level of the moss. This was accomplished by means of a simple mechanical arrangement, the water by driving the wheel being actually employed in raising itself, a duty which it performed at the rate of six and a half tons per minute. The water thus lifted was directed into channels cut in the moss, along the sides of which men were stationed, cutting the moss into pieces and tumbling it into the current of water, by which it was floated into the river. Fifteen hundred acres of fine land have thus been added to the estate of the present proprietor.

admirable regulation, and a visit to the clean village of Deanston, which is in their immediate neighbourhood, and inhabited entirely by the work people, may interest some tourists. These noble works owe their well merited celebrity to their late manager, Mr. James Smith. The village of Doune was, in former times, celebrated for the manufacture of Highland pistols. The ruins of Doune Castle, a massive and extensive fortress, supposed to have been built about the fourteenth century, are situated on the point of a steep and narrow green bank, washed on one side by the Teith, and on the other by the Ardoch. It was anciently the seat of the Earls of Monteith; but, about the beginning of the fifteenth century, it was forfeited to the Crown, and became the favourite residence of the two successive Dukes of Albany, who governed Scotland during the captivity of James I.; Queen Margaret, and the unfortunate Queen Mary, are also said frequently to have resided in this fortress. It was held for Prince Charles during the rebellion of 1745, and here he disposed his prisoners taken at Falkirk, and, among the rest, the author of the tragedy of Douglas.* Doune Castle has long been the

* "This noble ruin," says Sir Walter Scott, "holds a commanding station on the banks of the river Teith, and has been one of the largest castles in Scotland. Murdoch, Duke of Albany, the founder of this stately pile, was beheaded on the Castlehill of Stirling, from which he might see the towers of Doune, the monument of his fallen greatness. In 1745-6, a garrison, on the part of the Chevalier, was put into the castle, then less ruinous than at present. It was commanded by Mr. Stewart of Balloch, as governor for Prince Charles; who was a man of property, near Callander. This castle became, at that time, the actual scene of a romantic escape made by John Home, the author of Douglas, and by some other prisoners, who, having been taken at the battle of Falkirk, were confined there by the insurgents. The poet, who had, in his own mind, a large stock of that romantic and enthusiastic spirit of adventure which he has described as animating the youthful hero of his drama, devised and undertook the perilous enterprise of escaping from his prison. He inspired his companions with his sentiments, and when every attempt at open force was deemed hopeless, they resolved to twist their bed-clothes into ropes, and thus to descend. Four persons, with Home himself, reached the ground in safety. But the rope broke with the fifth, who was a tall, lusty man. The sixth was Thomas Barrow, a brave young Englishman, a particular friend of Home's. Determined to take the risk, even in such unfavourable circumstances, Barrow committed himself to the broken rope, slid down on it as far as it could assist him, and then let himself drop. His friends beneath succeeded in breaking his fall. Nevertheless he dislocated his ankle, and had several of his ribs broken. His com-

LOCH LOMOND AND THE TROSACHS.

property of the Earls of Moray, who derive it from their
second title of Lord Doune.   About a mile to the north-

panions, however, were able to bear him off in safety. The Highlanders next
morning sought for their prisoners with great activity. An old gentleman told
the author he remembered seeing the commander Stewart,

                ' Bloody with spurring, fiery red with haste,'

riding furiously through the country in quest of the fugitives."—*Note, Waverley*,
vol. ii., pp. 81, 82

west, the Earl of Moray has a mansion named Doune Lodge, formerly designated Cambus-Wallace, when it was the property of the Edmonstones. At the distance of three miles westward from Doune, on the opposite side of the river, is Lanrick Castle, (Jardine, Esq.,) formerly the seat of Sir Evan Murray M'Gregor, chieftain of Clan-Gregor, and three miles farther on is Cambusmore, (A. Buchanan, Esq.,) where Sir Walter Scott, in his juvenile days, spent some months, for several summers.* The village of

CALLANDER,

sixteen miles from Stirling, is situated at the foot of the chain of mountains which forms the Highland boundary. It is a neat and regular modern village, with a comfortable inn. Although not within the boundary of the Highlands, " yet, from having been so long in the near neighbourhood, it has caught much of the very best part of the Highland character. Few hills out of the Highlands, (if these, indeed, be out of it,) exhibit bolder bosoms of wooded crag

---

* He has given a striking sketch of the most interesting objects on his route, in his description of Fitzjames's ride, after the combat with Roderick Dhu :—

> They dashed that rapid torrent through,
> And up Carhonie's hill they flew;
> Still at the gallop prick'd the knight,
> His merry-men follow'd as they might.
> Along thy banks, swift Teith! they ride,
> And in the race they mock thy tide;
> Torry and Lendrick now are past,
> And Deanstoun lies behind them cast;
> They rise, the banner'd towers of Doune,
> They sink in distant woodland soon;
> Blair-Drummond sees the hoofs strike fire,
> They sweep like breeze through Ochertyre;
> They mark just glance and disappear
> The lofty brow of ancient Keir;
> They bathe their coursers' sweltering sides,
> Dark Forth! amid thy sluggish tides,
> And on the opposing shore take ground,
> With splash, with scramble, and with bound.
> Right-hand they leave thy cliffs, Craig-Forth!
> And soon the bulwark of the North,
> Grey Stirling, with her towers and town,
> Upon their fleet career look'd down."
>
> *Lady of the Lake*, c. v., st. 18.

and pastoral enclosure, than those which overhang the village, securing it from the blasts of the east and the north,

and receding in grand perspective far back in the sky."*
To the westward two little rivers, issuing respectively from
Loch Lubnaig and Loch Venachar, unite and form the
Teith. At the east end of the village there is a neat villa,
the property of Lady Willoughby D'Eresby. The Falls of
Bracklinn, about a mile to the north-east of the village,
form one of the most attractive objects in this vicinity.
They consist in a series of short falls, shelving rapids, and
dark linns, formed by the Keltie Burn. Above a chasm
where the brook precipitates itself from a height of at least

* CHRISTOPHER NORTH, in *Blackwood's Magazine.* Vol. xx., p. 402.

fifty feet, there is thrown a rustic foot-bridge, of about three feet in breadth, which is scarcely to be crossed by a stranger without awe and apprehension. The magnificent mountain Benledi, 3000 feet in height, which closes the prospect towards the west, forms the most striking feature of the scenery in this neighbourhood.*

There are two roads which lead from Callander to the Trosachs—the north and south roads; of these, the former is the more picturesque. Passing the valley of Bochastle, the house of Leny, (Hamilton, Esq.,) and the waterfalls of Carchonzie, the tourist reaches "Coilantogle Ford," about

* At Callander, a road much frequented by tourists, leads, in a northerly direction, to Lochearn-Head, (fourteen miles,) by the Pass of Leny, Loch Lubnaig, and Balquidder. At the distance of two miles from Callander, the river Leny forms several fine cascades which will well repay the tourist for the trouble of alighting from his vehicle and climbing the low wall on the road-side. The scenery of the Pass is very rich and beautiful. It is thus described in the opening scene of the Legend of Montrose:—" Their course had been, for some time, along the banks of a lake, whose deep waters reflected the crimson beams of the western sun. The broken path, which they pursued with some difficulty, was, in some places, shaded by ancient birches and oak-trees, and, in others, overhung by fragments of huge rock. Elsewhere, the hill, which formed the northern side of this beautiful sheet of water, arose in steep, but less precipitous acclivity, and was arrayed in heath of the darkest purple." The scenery in this district has been celebrated by the same illustrious pen, in the Lady of the Lake. It was up the Pass of Leny that the cross of fire was carried by young Angus of Duncraggan.

" Benledi saw the Cross of Fire;
It glanced like lightning up Strath-Ire;
O'er hill and dale the summons flew,
Nor rest, nor pause young Angus knew;
The tear that gathered in his eye
He left the mountain breeze to dry;
Until, where Teith's young waters roll,
Betwixt him and a wooded knoll,
That graced the sable strath with green,
The chapel of St. Bride was seen."

Here the cross is delivered to Norman of Armandave, who starts off with it along the shores of Loch Lubnaig, and away toward the distant district of Balquidder. The chapel of St. Bride stood on a small romantic knoll, between the opening of the Pass of Leny and Loch Lubnaig, and Strath-Ire is situated at the south end, and along the eastern side of Loch Lubnaig; Armandave is on the west side of the loch. By the side of Lubnaig is Ardhullary, a house built for a Highland retreat, by Bruce the Abyssinian traveller, in which it is said he wrote the account of his travels. In the churchyard of Balquidder Rob Roy was interred, beneath a stone, marked only with a fir-tree crossed by a sword, supporting a crown. " The braes of Balquither" have been celebrated in song.

two and a half miles from Callander. This is the scene of
the combat between Fitzjames and Roderick Dhu. Loch
Venachar is four miles long, Loch Achray a mile and a half,
the space between the lochs about half a mile, and from the
western extremity of the latter to Loch Katrine, one mile,
making the whole distance between Callander and Loch
Katrine from nine to ten miles. Lanrick Mead, the mus-
tering-place of Clan Alpin, lies on the north side of Loch
Venachar. Soon after, the tourist passes, a little to the
left, the hamlet of Duncraggan, the huts of which

> "Peep like moss-grown rocks half seen,
>   Half hidden in the copse so green."

In one of these a double bedded-room is fitted up for the
reception of tourists, and, if a humble scale of accommodation will satisfy the wayfarer, it may be prudent that he
should avail himself of its shelter, lest he should find the
inn full.

The Bridge of Turk* crosses the water, which, descending from Glenfinlas, joins the Teith between Lochs Venachar
and Achray ; and a mile and a half further on, is the
inn of Ardcheancchrochan, (Stewart's,) beautifully situate
on the side of Loch Achray.† The tourist is now in the
Trosachs, (*Troschen,* bristled territory,) the road which

---

* Here a path strikes off, on the right, to Glenfinlas, once a royal hunting
forest ; it is now the property of the Earl of Moray, and is inhabited by a primitive race of farmers, all Stewarts. In times of yore, it was chiefly inhabited
by the Macgregors. Glenfinlas is the scene of Sir Walter Scott's ballad entitled,
"Glenfinlas ; or, Lord Ronald's Coronach."

† The crowds of tourists visiting the Trosachs, during the summer months,
make it a matter of great uncertainty whether accommodation can be obtained
at the inn. The usual effects of monopoly will also be experienced, and the
civilities are nicely proportioned to the means the tourist is supposed to possess
for compensating them. The boats upon Loch Katrine belong to the inn, and
after paying the regular fare, (2s. 6d.,) the boatmen proceed to extort gratuities
from the passengers, which they state (with what truth we know not) to be the
only remuneration they receive for their services. The charge of these Highland
gillies, for conveying luggage from the inn to the loch, is also most extravagant.
The distance is about a mile, and three shillings have been occasionally extorted
for carrying a small parcel this trifling distance. These practices, it must be
admitted are calculated, in a high degree, to uphold the ancient reputation
of Loch Katrine, or, with more correctness of etymology, Loch Kateran, which
being interpreted, signifieth *The Loch of the Robbers.*

traverses them is rather more than a mile in length. The opening into the pass is flanked on the left by Benvenue, 2800 feet high, and on the right by Benan.

> " High on the south, huge Benvenue
> Down on the lake in masses threw
> Crags, knolls, and mounds confusedly hurled,
> The fragments of an earlier world ;
> A wildering forest, feather'd o'er
> His ruin'd sides and summit hoar ;
> While on the north, through middle air,
> Benan heav'd high his forehead bare."[*]

In the defile of Beal-an-Duine, (where Fitzjames lost his "gallant grey,") we are in the heart of the great gorge.[†] Then appears a narrow inlet, and a moment afterwards Loch Katrine itself bursts upon our view, the Alps of Ar-

---

[*] *Lady of the Lake, c. i., s.* 14.

[†] " A skirmish actually took place at a pass thus called, in the Trosachs, and closed with the remarkable incident mentioned in the ' Lady of the Lake.' It was greatly posterior in date to the reign of James V.

" In this roughly wooded island,[*] the country people secreted their wives and children, and their most valuable effects, from the rapacity of Cromwell's soldiers, during their inroad into this country in the time of the republic. These invaders, not venturing to ascend by the ladders along the side of the lake, took a more circuitous road, through the heart of the Trosachs, the most frequented path at that time, which penetrated the wilderness about half way between Binean and the lake, by a tract called Yea-chailleach, or the old Wife's Bog.

" In one of the defiles of this by-road, the men of the country at that time hung upon the rear of the invading enemy, and shot one of Cromwell's men, whose grave marks the scene of action, and gives name to that pass.[†] In revenge of this insult, the soldiers resolved to plunder the island, to violate the women, and put the children to death. With this brutal intention, one of the party, more expert than the rest, swam towards the island, to fetch the boat to his comrades, which had carried the women to their asylum, and lay moored in one of the creeks. His companions stood on the shore of the mainland, in full view of all that was to pass, waiting anxiously for his return with the boat. But, just as the swimmer had got to the nearest point of the island, and was laying hold of a black rock to get on shore, a heroine, who stood on the very point where he meant to land, hastily snatching a dagger from below her apron, with one stroke severed his head from the body. His party, seeing this disaster, and relinquishing all future hope of revenge or conquest, made the best of their way out of their perilous situation. This amazon's great-grandson lives at Bridge of Turk, who, besides others, attests the anecdote."—*Sketch of the Scenery near Callander.* Stirling, 1806, p. 20. I have only to add to this account, that the heroine's name was Helen Stuart.—*Notes to the Lady of the Lake,* p. 53.

---

[*] That at the eastern extremity of Loch Katrine, called " Ellen's Isle."

[†] Beallach-an-duine.

roquhar towering in the distance. Loch Katrine is of a ser-
pentine form, encircled by lofty mountains, and is ten miles
in length, attaining, in some places, a breadth of two miles.
The scenery which fringes it at its eastern extremity is precisely of the same wild character as the Trosachs. Near
the eastern shore there is an island exactly corresponding
with the description of the residence of Douglas, in the
Lady of the Lake. A cottage was erected upon it by Lady
Willoughby D'Eresby, which, a few years ago, was accidentally burnt down. Coir-nan-Uriskin, "the Den of the Goblin," is marked by a deep vertical gash in the face of one
of the extensive ramifications of Benvenue, overhanging the
lake. It is surrounded with stupendous rocks, and over-
shaded by birch trees, mingled with oaks, the spontaneous
production of the mountain, even where its cliffs appear
denuded of soil. Above the eastern hollow is the pass of
Beal-ach-nam-Bo, a magnificent glade overhung with birch
trees. By this pass, in the days of blackmail and reavers,
cattle were driven across the shoulder of the hill.

The following striking description of the Trosachs is given by Sir Walter
Scott, in the Lady of the Lake :—

"The western waves of ebbing day
Roll'd o'er the glen their level way;
Each purple peak, each flinty spire,
Was bathed in floods of living fire.
But not a setting beam could glow
Within the dark ravines below,
Where twined the path, in shadow hid,
Round many a rocky pyramid,
Shooting abruptly from the dell
Its thunder-splinter'd pinnacle;
Round many an insulated mass,
The native bulwarks of the pass,
Huge as the tower which builders vain
Presumptuous piled on Shinar's plain.
The rocky summits, split and rent,
Form'd turret, dome, or battlement,
Or seem'd fantastically set
With cupola or minaret,
Wild crests as pagod ever deck'd,
Or mosque of eastern architect.
Nor were these earth-borne castles bare,
Nor lack'd they many a banner fair:
For, from their shiver'd brows display'd,
Far o'er the unfathomable glade,
All twinkling with the dew-drops sheen,
The briar rose fell in streamers green,

And creeping shrubs of thousand dyes,
Waved in the west wind's summer sighs.

"Boon nature scatter'd free and wild,
Each plant or flower, the mountain's child.
Here eglantine embalm'd the air,
Hawthorn and hazel mingled there:
The primrose pale, and violet flower,
Found in each cliff a narrow bower;
Foxglove and nightshade, side by side,
Emblems of punishment and pride,
Group'd their dark hues with every stain
The weather-beaten crags retain.
With boughs that quaked at every breath,
Grey birch and aspen wept beneath;
Aloft, the ash and warrior oak
Cast anchor in the rifted rock:
And, higher yet, the pine-tree hung
His shatter'd trunk, and frequent flung,
Where seem'd the cliffs to meet on high,
His boughs athwart the narrow'd sky,
Highest of all, where white peaks glanced,
Where glist'ning streamers waved and danced,
The wanderer's eye could barely view
The summer heaven's delicious blue;
So wondrous wild, the whole might seem
The scenery of a fairy dream."

LOCH KATRINE.

The district of Menteith, only a few miles to the south of the Trosachs, comprehends a range of scenery little inferior in beauty. It contains the lake of Menteith, Aberfoyle, Loch Ard, and Loch Chon, and is approached from Stirling by Ochtertyre, Kincardine, and Ruskie. The lake of Menteith is a circular sheet of water, about five miles in circumference, adorned with ancient woods. It possesses an aspect of placid beauty rather than of grandeur, and the forms of the surrounding hills are neither bold nor striking, but present a gentle undulating line to the eye of the spectator. In the centre of the lake are two small islands called Inchmachome, or the Isle of Rest,* and Talla, or the Earl's Isle. The former, which is the larger and more easterly island, consists of about five acres, and contains the ruins of a Priory, where Queen Mary resided during the invasion of the English in 1547, before she was removed to France. This priory was founded, about the year 1238, by Walter Cumming, second son of William Cumming, Earl of Buchan. He obtained, by grant from the Crown, the extensive district of Badenoch, and by marriage with the Countess of Menteith, he became Earl of Menteith. After his death, Walter Stewart, brother of Alexander, High-Steward of Scotland, obtained a grant of the title and estates of Menteith, in right of his wife, the younger sister of the Countess of Menteith. His second son was Sir John of Ruskie, properly called Stewart, but usually Menteith, the betrayer of the patriot Wallace. In the choir of the church is an ancient tombstone, supposed to be that of Walter Stewart. A writ granted by Robert Bruce, at this place, in April 1310, is recorded in the Chartulary of Arbroath. The buildings connected with this monastery are supposed to have been destroyed at the Reformation. The island of Inchmachome is now the property of his Grace the Duke of Montrose. The principal proprietors around the lake are his Grace, General Graham Stirling, and Mr. Erskine of Cardross. The smaller island contains the remains of the Castle of the Grahams, Earls of Menteith, a race long extinct.† They

* " The world's gay scenes thou must resign,
    Stranger, when youth has past;
  Oh! were such bless'd asylum thine,
    As this—*The Isle of Rest!*"

† " The Earls of Menteith, you must know, had a castle, situated upon an island in the lake, or loch, as it is called, of the same name. But though this residence, which occupied almost the whole of the islet, upon which its ruins still exist, was a strong and safe place of abode, and adapted accordingly to such perilous times, it had this inconvenience, that the stables and other domestic offices were constructed on the banks of the lake, and were, therefore, in some sort defenceless.

" It happened upon a time that there was to be a great entertainment in the castle, and a number of the Grahams were assembled. The occasion, it is said, was a marriage in the family. To prepare for this feast, much provision was got ready, and in particular, a great deal of poultry had been collected. While the feast was preparing, an unhappy chance brought Donald of the

had their garden on the isle of the Priory, and their pleasure-
grounds on the neighbouring shore, which is still beautifully adorned
with oak, Spanish chestnut, and plane trees of ancient growth.
Some of the chestnuts are seventeen feet in circumference at six
feet above the ground, and must be above three centuries old.
Gartmore House, (Graham, Esq.,) lies to the west, and Rednock
House, the seat of General Graham Stirling, to the east of the lake.
Callander is distant seven miles. Proceeding westward, at the distance of four miles, the traveller reaches Aberfoyle, the scene of so
many of the incidents in the novel of Rob Roy,* where the tourist
will find a comfortable inn. At the Clachan of Aberfoyle is the
junction of the Duchray and Forth, here called Avondhu, or the Black
River. Under the rocky precipice on the north lies the Pass of
Aberfoyle, the scene of the defeat of a party of Cromwell's troops by
Graham of Duchray.† Loch Ard is a small lake, or rather two lakes,

Hammer to the side of the lake, returning at the head of a band of hungry followers, whom he was conducting homewards to the West Highlands, after some
of his usual excursions into Stirlingshire. Seeing so much good victuals ready,
and being possessed of an excellent appetite, the Western Highlanders neither
asked questions, nor waited for an invitation, but devoured all the provisions
that had been prepared for the Grahams, and then went on their way rejoicing
through the difficult and dangerous path which leads from the banks of the
Loch of Menteith, through the mountains, to the side of Loch Katrine.
"The Grahams were filled with the highest indignation. The company who
were assembled at the castle of Menteith, headed by the earl himself, hastily
took to their boats, and, disembarking on the northern side of the lake, pursued with all speed the marauders and their leader. They came up with
Donald's party in the gorge of a pass, near a rock, called Craig-Vad, or the
Wolf's Cliff. The battle then began, and was continued with much fury till
night. The Earl or Menteith, and many of his noble kinsmen, fell, while
Donald, favoured by darkness, escaped with a single attendant. The Grahams
obtained, from the cause of the quarrel, the nick-name of Gramoch-an-Garrigh,
or Grahams of the Hens."—*Tales of a Grandfather*, vol. ii., pp. 317-19.
    * "To the left lay the valley, down which the Forth wandered on its easterly
course, surrounding the beautiful detached hill, with all its garland of woods.
On the right, amid a profusion of thickets, knolls, and crags, lay the bed of a
broad mountain lake, lightly curled into tiny waves by the breath of the morning breeze, each glittering in its course under the influence of the sunbeams.
High hills, rocks, and banks, waving with natural forests of birch and oak,
formed the borders of this enchanting sheet of water; and, as their leaves
rustled to the wind and twinkled in the sun, gave to the depth of solitude a
sort of life and vivacity."—*Rob Roy*, vol. ii., p. 202.
    † "Our route, though leading towards the lake, had hitherto been so much
shaded by wood, that we only from time to time obtained a glimpse of that
beautiful sheet of water. But the road now suddenly emerged from the forest
ground, and, winding close by the margin of the loch, afforded us a full view
of its spacious mirror, which now, the breeze having totally subsided, reflected
in still magnificence the high, dark, heathy mountains, huge grey rocks, and
shaggy banks, by which it is encircled. The hills now sunk on its margin so
closely, and were so broken and precipitous, as to afford no passage except just

connected by a stream of 200 yards in length, beautifully situated in the middle of a fertile valley. The shores of the loch, though not remarkable for height, are so broken up into rocky and wooded eminences, here running into, and there retreating from each other, as to form some of the most beautiful landscape combinations of which Scotland can boast, and there is more than one spot which bears a striking resemblance to the Trosachs and Loch Katrine. A delightful view of the upper loch is obtained from a rising ground near its lower extremity. Looking westward, Ben Lomond is seen in the background. On the right is the lofty mountain of Benoghrie. In the foreground is Loch Ard itself, three miles in length, and one and an eighth in breadth. The road conducts along the verge of the lake, under a ledge of rock from thirty to fifty feet high. If a person standing immediately under this rock, towards its western extremity, pronounces with a firm voice a line of ten syllables, it is returned first from the opposite side of the lake, and then with equal distinctness from the wood on the east. But the day must be perfectly calm, and the lake as smooth as glass. A gnarled trunk of an oak overhanging the rock is that from which Bailie Nicol Jarvie was suspended by the skirts. In the upper loch is a rocky islet, on which are the mouldering ruins of a stronghold of Murdoch, Duke of Albany. Near the head of the lake, on the northern side, behind the House of Ledeard, is the romantic waterfall, thus accurately described in Waverley :—"It was not so remarkable either for great height or quantity of water, as for the beautiful accompaniments which made the spot interesting. After a broken cataract of about twenty feet, the stream was received in a large natural basin filled to the brim with water, which, where the bubbles of the fall subsided, was so exquisitely clear, that although it was of great depth, the eye could discern each pebble at the bottom. Eddying round this reservoir, the brook found its way as if over a broken part of the ledge, and formed a second fall, which seemed to seek the very abyss; then wheeling out beneath from among the smooth dark rocks, which it had polished for ages, it wandered murmuring down the glen, forming the stream up which Waverley had just ascended." A footpath strikes off towards Benlomond, by which the tourist may cross the hill and reach Rowardennan, on the banks of Loch Lomond; or he may proceed from Aberfoyle Inn, by Gartmore and Drymen, to Dumbarton, a distance of twenty-two miles. It is customary for travellers, after visiting the two lochs above named, to cross over the hill from Aberfoyle to the Trosachs, a distance of only five miles, but the pedestrian will do well to pursue the road along

upon the narrow line of the track which we occupied, and which was overhung with rocks, from which we might have been destroyed merely by rolling down stones, without much possibility of offering resistance."—*Rob Roy*, vol. ii., p. 208. A road has now been formed along the northern margin of the lake.

the margin of Loch Chon, a secluded sheet of water three miles in length, hemmed in by fine sloping hills feathered with natural coppice wood. This road will conduct him, after leaving the loch, into the pathway leading from Loch Katrine to Inversnaid on Loch Lomond.

A steamer now regularly plies on Loch Katrine during the summer months, sailing at such times as enables the passengers to meet the steamer on Loch Lomond. From June till the end of September, the boat generally makes two trips a-day from each end of the Loch, but as the hours of sailing, and the number of trips, are occasionally changed, we think it better to leave the tourist to obtain local information on the subject.*

" In sailing along you discover many arms of the lake—here a bold headland, where black rocks dip in unfathomable water—there the white sand in the bottom of a bay, bleached for ages by the waves. In walking on the north side, the road is sometimes cut through the face of the solid rock, which rises upwards of 200 feet perpendicular above the lake, which, before the rock was cut, had to be mounted by a kind of natural ladder. Every rock has its echo, every grove is vocal with the harmony of birds, or by the airs of women and children gathering nuts in their season. Down the side of the opposite mountain, after a shower of rain, flow an hundred white streams, which rush with incredible noise and velocity into the lake. On one side, the water-eagle sits in majesty undisturbed on his well-known rock, in sight of his nest on the top of Benvenue ; the heron stalks among the reeds in search of his prey, and the sportive ducks gambol in the waters or dive below. On the other, the wild goats climb where they have scarce room for the soles of their feet, and the wild birds, perched on exalted trees and pinnacles, look down with composed indifference on man. The scene is closed by a west view of the lake,

* An abortive attempt was made to establish a steamer on Loch Katrine in 1843. The enterprise naturally met with the strenuous opposition of the boat-men who row the oar-boats on the lake, and the steamer had plied only a few days when, during the night of the 18th July, it disappeared, and has never since been heard of. Although there can be no doubt that this daring outrage must have been the work of several accomplices, the perpetrators were never discovered.

which is ten miles long, having its sides lined with alternate clumps of wood and ample fields, and the smoke rising in spiral columns through the air from farm-houses, which are concealed by intervening woods, and the prospect is bounded by the towering Alps of Arrochar."*

Those conversant with the writings of Sir Walter Scott, will remember the spirited song, sung by the retainers of Roderick Dhu, while rowing down Loch Katrine :—

" Hail to the Chief, who in triumph advances !
　　Honour'd and bless'd be the ever-green Pine !
Long may the Tree, in his banner that glances,
　　Flourish, the shelter and grace of our line !
　　　　Heaven send it happy dew,
　　　　Earth lend it sap anew,
　　Gaily to bourgeon, and broadly to grow,
　　　　While every Highland glen
　　　　Sends our shout back agen,
　　' Roderigh Vich Alpine dhu, ho ! ieroe !'
" Ours is no sapling, chance-sown by the fountain,
　　Blooming at Beltane, in winter to fade ;
When the whirlwind has stripp'd every leaf on the mountain,
　　The more shall Clan-Alpine exhult in her shade.
　　　　Moor'd in the rifted rock,
　　　　Proof to the tempest's shock,
　　Firmer he roots him the ruder it blow ;
　　　　Menteith and Breadalbane, then,
　　　　Echo his praise agen,
　　' Roderigh Vich Alpine dhu, ho ! ieroe !'
" Proudly our pibroch has thrilled in Glen Fruin,
　　And Bannochar's groans to our slogan replied :
Glen Luss and Ross-dhu, they are smoking in ruin,
　　And the best of Loch-Lomond lie dead on her side.
　　　　Widow and Saxon maid,
　　　　Long shall lament our raid,
　　Think of Clan-Alpine with fear and with woe ;
　　　　Lennox and Leven-glen
　　　　Shake when they hear agen,
　　" Roderigh Vich Alpine dhu, ho ! ieroe !'
" Row, vassals, row, for the pride of the Highlands,
　　Stretch to your oars, for the ever-green Pine !
O ! that the rose-bud that graces yon islands
　　Were wreathed in a garland around him to twine !

* *Statistical Account of Scotland.*

O that some seedling gem,
Worthy such noble stem,
Honour'd and blest in their shadow might grow !
Loud should Clan-Alpine then
Ring from the deepmost glen,
'Roderigh Vich Alpine dhu, ho ! ieroe !' "

From the west end of the lake, a wild valley, traversed by a rugged pathway about five miles long, affords a communication with Loch Lomond, upon which it opens at Inversnaid Mill, where the steamboat, which every day plies along Loch Lomond, takes in the Loch Katrine tourists.* The small lake, Arklet, lies in the hollow near this pathway. In one of the smoky huts in the valley between Loch Katrine and Loch Lomond may be seen a long Spanish musket, six feet and a half in length, once the property of Rob Roy, whose original residence was in this lone vale. Near at hand is the hut where it is said Helen MacGregor, Rob Roy's wife, first saw the light. Beside the way are the ruins of Inversnaid Fort, erected by Government in 1713 to check the MacGregors. In descending to the margin of Loch Lomond, the stranger cannot fail to be struck with

* A flock of shaggy Highland ponies is in attendance, to convey travellers across this moorland region, and a pony cart to carry their luggage. The extortion and incivility to which tourists are subjected, at this stage of their progress, are a reproach to Scotland. A recent sufferer thus addresses the editor of a Glasgow paper on the subject :—

"On being landed at the hill of Inversnaid, we as usual took our departure for Loch Katrine, mounted on the Highland ponies which awaited us. I shall say nothing of the charge, (four shillings each,) which certainly appeared rather high for a ride of five miles on the back of such cattle ; but I feel bound to mention the conduct of the boatmen, and others, who formed an escort to our party. They came provided with a small pony cart, which carries the luggage across, and here their extortion began. On reaching the margin of Loch Katrine, one gentleman, who had not the precaution to make a bargain with them, was charged eight shillings for the carriage of a few articles; another party five shillings ; and so on in proportion. The sun was fast sinking, and, under the pretence of refreshing themselves, the whole party sat smoking and drinking for above an hour, deaf to all the entreaties which were made to them, and at length, with rudeness and extreme reluctance, at half-past five o'clock, set out : so that, by the time we reached the Trosachs, it was quite dark, and we reached the crowded inn, only to be obliged to take horses and hurry away ten miles to Callander. The consequence of this was, that we not only lost the view of the lovely scenery through which we passed, but the comfort, and even the health of our party, were endangered, by night travelling and its accompaniments."

Were this a solitary instance we should not have quoted it here ; but having personally experienced the annoyance, and many of our friends having suffered in the same way, we have no hesitation in cautioning travellers to make an express bargain before they avail themselves of either ponies or cart. For a pony, we regard 2s. 6d. a moderate, and 3s. 6d. a liberal hire.

BEN LOMOND & LOCH LOMOND.

admiration at the sublimity of the mountains which hang
over the opposite shore, and round the mouth of the narrow
glen of Inveruglas. While the tourist is in the midst of
the country of the MacGregors, he may be gratified by the
perusal of Sir Walter Scott's splendid lyric, "the Gathering
of Clan-Gregor :"

"The moon's on the lake, and the mist's on the brae,
And the clan has a name that is nameless by day;
    Then gather, gather, gather, Gregalich !

Our signal for fight, that from monarchs we drew,
Must be heard but by night in our vengeful haloo !
    Then haloo, Gregalich ! haloo, Gregalich !

Glen Orchy's proud mountains, Coalchuirn and her towers,
Glenstrae and Glenlyon no longer are ours ;
    We're landless, landless, landless, Gregalich !

But, doom'd and devoted by vassal and lord,
Macgregor has still both his heart and his sword !
    Then courage, courage, courage, Gregalich !

If they rob us of name, and pursue us with beagles,
Give their roofs to the flame, and their flesh to the eagles !
    Then vengeance, vengeance, vengeance, Gregalich !

While there's leaves on the forest, or foam on the river,
Macgregor, despite them, shall flourish for ever !
    Come then, Gregalich ! come then, Gregalich !

Through the depths of Loch Katrine the steed shall career,
O'er the peak of Ben Lomond the galley shall steer ;
And the rocks of Craig-Royston like icicles melt,
Ere our wrongs be forgot, or our vengeance unfelt !
    Then gather, gather, gather, Gregalich !"

It is said that General Wolf once resided in Inversnaid
Fort. At Inversnaid Mill there is a little rivulet and a
cataract, the scene of Wordsworth's beautiful poem to the
" Highland Girl."

Loch Lomond,* (" the lake full of islands,") is unquestionably the pride of Scottish lakes. "This noble lake,
boasting innumerable beautiful islands of every varying
form and outline which fancy can frame — its northern

* The tourist may proceed from the head of Loch Lomond, by Glenfalloch,
Orianlaroch, Tyndrum, and Glencoe, to Fort-William, (see Itinerary,) or by
Arroquhar, Glencroe, and Cairndow, to Inverary.

extremity narrowing until it is lost among dusky and retreating mountains, while, gradually widening as it extends
to the southward, it spreads its base around the indentures
and promontories of a fair and fertile land, affords one of
the most surprising, beautiful, and sublime spectacles in
nature.* Its upper extremity is not unworthy of comparison with the finest views on Loch Awe, while there are
points in the same division not dissimilar to the more striking parts of the Trosachs, and fully equal to them in wild
grandeur. Its length is about twenty-three miles, its
breadth, where greatest, at the southern extremity, is five
miles, from which it gradually grows narrower, till it terminates in a narrow prolonged stripe of water. The depth
varies considerably; south of Luss it is rarely more than
twenty fathoms, in the northern part it ranges from sixty
to 100, and, in the places where deepest, never freezes. The
total superficies of the lake is about 20,000 acres. About
two-thirds of the loch and most of the islands, are in the
county of Dumbarton, the rest, with the right bank, are in
the county of Stirling. After taking on board the tourists
from Loch Katrine, the steamboat visits the upper part
of the lake, which is there narrowed and hemmed in by the
neighbouring mountains. At the northern extremity of the
lake is a wide elevated valley called Glenfalloch. Sailing
southwards, three miles from the upper end, is a small
wooded island called Eilan Vhou, and, two miles farther,
another called Inveruglas, on each of which are the ruins
of a stronghold of the family of Macfarlane. The slogan
of this clan was "Loch Sloy," a small lake between Loch
Long and Loch Lomond. At the distance of other three
miles, Tarbet Inn is passed on the right, where there is a
ferry by which Ben Lomond may be approached. Farther
south, a projecting headland is seen on the right, where is
the ferry of Inveruglas to Rowardennan Inn, the usual
starting point for those who desire to ascend to the top of
Ben Lomond. This mountain is the property of the Duke
of Montrose. It rises 3210 feet above the level of the lake,
which is thirty-two feet above the level of the sea. The

* Rob Roy, vol. ii., p. 317.

distance from the inn to the top of the mountain is six miles of continued ascent. The view from the summit is varied and most extensive, comprehending the counties of Lanark, Renfrew, and Ayr, the Firth of Clyde, and the islands of Arran and Bute, to the south, and the counties of Stirling and the Lothians, with the windings of the Forth, and the Castles of Stirling and Edinburgh, to the east. About three and a half miles from Inveruglas, is Luss, a delightful little village, situated on a promontory which juts into the lake. One of the finest points for enjoying the scenery of Loch Lomond and the environs of Luss is Stonehill, to the north of the village. Near Luss is Rossdow, the splendid residence of Sir James Colquhoun, Bart. In the vicinity of the mansion is a tower of the ancient Castle of the family of Luss, the last heiress of which married Colquhoun of Colquhoun. A short way farther on are the ruins of the Castle of Banachra, overhanging the entrance to Glen Fruin.* This castle was anciently the residence of the Colquhouns, and here the chief of that clan was basely murdered, in 1640, by one of the Macfarlanes. Near it is the lofty hill of Dunfion, or the hill of Fingal, according to tradition one of the hunting-seats of that hero. From Luss southward, the breadth of the lake expands rapidly, and the surface of the water is studded with

> " All the fairy crowds
> Of islands that together lie
> As quietly as spots of sky
> Among the evening clouds."

* It was in Glen Fruin, or the Glen of Sorrow, that the celebrated battle took place between the Macgregors and Colquhouns, fraught with such fatal consequences to both parties. There had been a long and deadly feud between the Macgregors and the Laird of Luss, head of the family of Colquhoun. At length the parties met in the vale of Glen Fruin. The battle was obstinately contested, but in the end the Macgregors came off victorious, slaying two hundred of the Colquhouns, and making many prisoners. It is said, that after the battle the Macgregors murdered about eighty youths, who had been led by curiosity to view the fight. A partial representation of these transactions having been made to James VI., letters of fire and sword were issued against the Clan-Gregor. Their lands were confiscated, their very name proscribed, and, being driven to such extremity, they became notorious for acts of daring reprisal. Their legal rights were restored to them in 1755. For many interesting particulars in the history of the Macgregor clan, the reader may consult the Introduction to Rob Roy.

The islands of Loch Lomond are about thirty in number, and ten of these are of considerable extent.

After leaving Luss, the boat passes, in succession, Inch-Cruin, or the Round Island, (formerly a retreat for lunatics,) Inch Moan, or the Peat Island, Inch Fadn, (the long island,) Inch Tavanagh, to the south of which the ruins of Galbraith Castle start up from the water, Inch Lonaig, (used as a deer-park by the family of Luss,) Inch Carachan, Buck Inch, Inch Cardach, and Inch Cailliach, the Island of Women, so called from its having been the site of a nunnery. Inch Cailliach formerly gave name to the parish of Buchanan. The church belonging to the nunnery was long used as the place of worship for the parish of Buchanan, but scarcely any vestiges of it now remain; the burial-ground, which contains the family places of sepulture of several neighbouring clans, still continues to be used; the monuments of the Lairds of Macgregor, and of other families claiming a descent from the old Scottish King Alpine, are most remarkable.

> "The shafts and limbs were rods of yew,
> Whose parents, in Inch Cailliach, wave
> Their shadows o'er Clan-Alpine's grave,
> And, answering Lomond's breezes deep,
> Soothe many a chieftain's endless sleep."
>
> *Lady of the Lake*, c. iii., *and notes.*

At the north-east corner of Inch Cailliach, passengers are often landed at Beal'maha, a celebrated Highland pass.* Here some tourists choose to land, to pursue their journey through the pass, and along the banks of the loch to Rowardennan. The steamboat next approaches the little island of Clar-Inch, from which the Buchanans took their slogan or war-cry. The last island is a long narrow one, named Inch Murrin, the largest island in Loch Lomond. It is finely clothed with wood, and is employed as a deer-park by the Duke of Montrose. At its southern extremity there is an old ruined fortalice, called Lennox Castle, formerly a residence of the Earls of Lennox. Here Isabel Duchess of Albany, daughter of Duncan Earl of Lennox, resided after

---

* See *Lady of the Lake*, canto iv., st. 4.

the death of her husband, Murdoch, Duke of Albany, and of her two sons, and her father, who were executed after the restoration of James I., in 1424. See ante, p. 173. On the east side of the lake are the ruins of Buturich Castle, farther south is Balloch Castle, (Buchanan, Esq.) and near it, on the margin of the lake, stood the ancient castle of Balloch, a stronghold of the once powerful family of Lennox ; its site and moat are still visible. The steamboat now returns to Balloch, where a coach is waiting to convey the passengers to Dumbarton, and from thence a steamboat lands them in Glasgow the same evening.

GLASGOW.

SITUATION—HISTORICAL NOTICES—GENERAL STATISTICS OF POPULATION—COMMERCE AND MANUFACTURES—EDUCATION AND LITERATURE—CHARITABLE AND RELIGIOUS INSTITUTIONS, ETC.

GLASGOW, the commercial metropolis of Scotland, and, in wealth, population, and manufacturing and commercial importance, the third city in the United Kingdom, is situate in Lanarkshire, in the lower part of the basin of the Clyde ; about twenty miles from the Atlantic Ocean, and nearly double that distance from the German Sea. The fine range of the Campsie and Kilpatrick hills, forms a screen around it, from north-east to north-west, at the distance of eight to ten miles, and the uplands of Lanarkshire and Renfrewshire swell beautifully up on the east, south, and south-west. The climate is temperate, but, from its vicinity to the sea, and the high grounds in the neighbourhood, it is much subject to humidity. St. Mungo, or, as he has also been

styled, St. Kentigern, is the reputed founder of the city.
Somewhere about the year 560, he is supposed to have
founded the bishoprick of Glasgow, where the older and
upper part of the town still remains. In those rude times,
the vicinity of churches and churchmen was eagerly desired
from the comparative security they afforded; and thus, the
nascent elements of the future city, under the pastoral
protection of the good saint and his pious successors, had
leisure afforded them to extend and mature their natural
capacities for improvement. The annals of Glasgow, from
the period above mentioned to the early part of the twelfth
century, are involved in the obscurity which overshadows
nearly the whole contemporary history of those rude ages,
a fact we are disposed to acquiesce in rather cheerfully, as,
where little is known, little probably exists that it would
be useful to know. The first fact of any importance which
emerges from the clouds of its earlier history, is the erection of its noble Cathedral, which, for so many centuries,
has witnessed the growing prosperity and enlargement of
the city, forming a fine link between the past and the
present, and throwing the shadow of its venerable magnificence upon scenes memorable in Scottish history, but upon
which modern civilisation has impressed an entirely new
character. This fine old minster* was erected by John

* This venerable building contained formerly three churches, one of which,
the Old Barony, was situated in a vault,† but now there is only one, a new
church having recently been erected in a different part of the city, in place of
the second, the space occupied by which has been thrown into the choir, or
central part of the fabric. Having fallen, of late years, much into decay, the
Government, the custodiers of the cathedral, have agreed to repair and renew
certain parts of the building; and plans for its renovation having been prepared
by an eminent architect, the corporation of Glasgow has granted a thousand
pounds towards the object; other public bodies are expected also to contribute,
and a private subscription is in progress, for the same laudable purpose. For

† "Conceive an extensive range of low-browed, dark, and twilight vaults, such as are used
for sepulchres in other countries, and had long been dedicated to the same purpose in this,
a portion of which was seated with pews, and used as a church. The part of the vaults thus
occupied, though capable of containing a congregation of many hundreds, bore a small proportion to the darker and more extensive caverns which yawned around what may be termed
the inhabited space. In those waste regions of oblivion, dusky banners and tattered escut-
cheons indicated the graves of those who were once, doubtless, 'princes in Israel.' Inscriptions, which could only be read by the painful antiquary, in language as obsolete as the act
of devotional charity which they implored, invited the passengers to pray for the souls of those
whose bodies rested beneath."—*Rob Roy*, vol. ii., p. 267.

Achaius, Bishop of Glasgow, in 1133, or, according to M'Ure, in 1136, in the reign of David the First, whose pious largesses to the clergy obtained for him the name and honours of a saint, but drew from one of his impoverished successors the splenetic remark, that "he had been a sair saunct for the crown."

About forty years after the building of the Cathedral, William the Lion granted a charter to the bishop, to hold a "weekly mercat" in Glasgow, and a few weeks after, another was obtained for an annual fair. In these concessions of a despotic sovereign, we behold the rude and early germs of the future wealth and commercial greatness of Glasgow. The same indulgent sovereign completed the emancipation of the city, by erecting it into a burgh of regality, and thus placing its rights of independent traffic upon a broad and liberal basis. The new burgh was, however, unfortunately situated betwixt the more ancient royal burghs of Rutherglen and Renfrew, who beheld, with a jealous eye, its growing prosperity; and their rival exactions, and prescriptive immunities, for a time impeded the progress of the infant community, until the city obtained a charter of relief and independence, in 1242, from Alexander the Second.*

some time past a number of workmen have been employed in the repair and restoration of the Cathedral, making drains to carry off the surface water, and clearing out that fine old vault—the Old Barony Church. The appearance of this vault is now highly striking, exhibiting a vast chamber supported on a range of groined arches, many of them richly carved. Now that the subsoil, which had accumulated to the depth of several feet, is removed, these arches show to great advantage. Many curious ancient inscriptions, coats of arms, and other monumental devices, have been brought to light, whilst the taste exhibited in the restorations, has rendered this once gloomy receptacle for the dead, one of the most interesting portions of this time-honoured edifice, and one of the most impressive sights in the city. The revenues of the see of Glasgow were at one time very considerable, as, besides the royalty and baronies of Glasgow, eighteen baronies of land, in various parts of the kingdom, belonged to it, besides a large estate in Cumberland, denominated the spiritual dukedom. Part of these revenues have fallen into the University of Glasgow, and part to the crown.

* It is not a little curious to contemplate the "revenges which the restless whirligig of time" is sure to bring about. Whilst Glasgow has shot up into the third city of the British empire, Rutherglen and Renfrew, whose ancient importance is only to be traced in a few pages of Scottish history, have dwindled into absolute insignificance under the overshadowing influence of their ancient rival, whose commercial relations are now commensurate with the limits of civilisation and commerce.

Some of the details of the early history of Glasgow, after it had fairly started on its career as an independent community, are not a little curious and instructive, from their graphic simplicity and statistical interest ; but there is little to interest the general reader, till we turn the corner of the seventeenth century. It was ravaged by the plague no less than four times during the fourteenth, and five times during the seventeenth century. The loathsome disease of leprosy prevailed also for a long time, and, as late as 1589, some lepers were confined in a house in the suburbs of Gorbals. It is no wonder, indeed ; for, whatever might be the virtues of the citizens of Glasgow in these primitive times, cleanliness certainly was not one of them, as appears from sundry curious enough enactments by the city authorities. Previous to the seventeenth century, the principal part of the houses were built of wood, and the inhabitants lived chiefly in narrow lanes or closes, leading from the main streets. The population, in 1651, was about 14,000 ; in 1831, it amounted to 202,426 ; and according to the census of 1841, it had then reached 257,592.

Previous to 1775, the mercantile capital and enterprise of Glasgow were almost wholly employed in the tobacco trade. Large fortunes were made, and the city still exhibits evidences of the wealth and social importance of the " Tobacco Lords," as they were termed ; some of the finest private dwellings in the city, and several elegant streets, being the splendid relics of their former civic grandeur and importance. The interruption which the war of the American Revolution gave to this traffic, turned the attention* of the

---

* For more than forty years, however, previous to this period, there existed in Glasgow a considerable manufacture of linen, lawns, and cambrics, which ultimately merged in the cotton manufacture. Its progress was not very rapid till towards the close of the last century, when the wars which sprung out of the French Revolution, by suspending and limiting for a time the manufactures of the continental nations, gave a new impetus to this manufacture in Great Britain, in which impetus Glasgow largely partook. Of the extent of that branch of the cotton manufacture in which hand-loom weavers are employed, it is impossible to form any thing like an accurate estimate, from the absence of any ascertained data. It is supposed, but the calculation is necessarily loose and imperfect, that 40,000 hand-loom weavers are employed by Glasgow manufacturers, the produce of whose labour, including the additional value appended

citizens to the manufacture of cotton goods, then feebly developing its latent energies in Lancashire, and to this branch of manufacture Glasgow chiefly owes her pre-eminence as a commercial and manufacturing city.

In 1451, application was made to the Pope for a bull to

to it before it is brought to market, has been assumed to be about three millions sterling.

Power-loom weaving was introduced into Glasgow as far back as 1792, but until 1801, it may be considered as having been merely experimental. At present, there are from sixteen to seventeen thousand steam-looms set in motion by Glasgow capital. Each loom, on an average of the different kinds of work, produces about twenty-one yards daily, or 336,000 yards in all; and, in a year of 300 working days, 100,800,000 yards. Assuming sixpence per yard as the average value, this branch of the cotton manufacture in Glasgow amounts to £2,520,000,—a stupendous result, when it is considered that it is not quite forty years since its introduction.

The spinning of cotton yarn was begun in Glasgow in 1792, and has gradually and, of late years, rapidly increased. The total number of spindles in motion in Glasgow and belonging to Glasgow capitalists, has been calculated, by experienced persons to be about 1,100,000 at present. Of the value of the products, no estimate can be attempted with any certainty, but from three to four millions sterling have been assumed as the probable amount. In 1818, only 46,565 bales of cotton were consumed, and, in 1834, the consumption was 95,603 bales; since which it has considerably increased. Besides the spinning and weaving of cotton, the staple manufactures of Glasgow, silk has also become an extensive article of commerce and manufacture. This article, with various rich foreign wools, are now woven into cotton fabrics, with the most brilliant success. Calico printing is also carried on to a vast extent, especially since the abolition of the duty on printed goods. It was first attempted, in 1742, on a small scale at Pollockshaws, in the neighbourhood of Glasgow, and now there are few streams, in a vicinity of ten miles round the city, the waters of which do not carry abundant evidence of the printing establishments on their banks. The works of Henry Monteith and Company at Barrowfield, those on the Leven, belonging to James Black & Co., and of Messrs. Crum at Thornly Bank, are amongst the most noted and extensive. The establishment of the first mentioned house, from the perfection of their machinery and its close vicinity to Glasgow, has long been a point of interest to intelligent strangers.

Glasgow is the seat of various other extensive trades and manufactures, such as dying, bleaching, calendering, &c. The smelting of iron is also carried on to a vast extent in its neighbourhood, owing, in a great degree, to the adoption of the hot-blast, an improvement which, with less than one-half of fuel, produces one-third more of iron. In 1834, the whole produce of the iron-works of Scotland, (of which at least from two-thirds to three-fourths are carried on by Glasgow capital,) was 110,240 tons; and, although no accurate data are to be obtained as to the present amount of production, it cannot be far short of 150,000 tons. The coal trade is carried on to an enormous extent in the neighbourhood of Glasgow, chiefly for home consumption, though a considerable exportation takes place. In 1831, 561,049 tons passed into and through the city, of which 124,000 were exported, principally coastwise, since which a very large increase has taken place. The manufacture of machinery employs also a large capital and numerous work-people, especially the making of marine steam-

establish a university, and eight years afterwards a member of the illustrious house of Hamilton bequeathed four acres of ground, with a tenement of houses, for the same purpose; and thus this noble educational institution was established, and after encountering many difficulties arising from the unsettled character of the times, from its origin to near the end of the seventeenth century, rose into fame, importance, and utility. It is unnecessary here to state the many eminent names which adorn its annals, and which have shed a lustre over the literary and civil history of Scotland. It is a corporate body, and is governed by a chancellor, rector, and dean. The number of students is at present about 843. The Hunterian Museum, attached to the College, is one of the chastest buildings in Scotland, and is rich in various departments of natural history, particularly in anatomical preparations, and in coins and medals. The whole has been valued at £70,000. The Grammar or High School, for elementary classical education, is supported by the Corporation, on whom its superintendence devolves. It costs the city about £1000 per annum. Of late years, the range of elementary instruction has been extended, and various modern languages, besides drawing and mathematics, are taught. The number of scholars for the last year was 1357.

Anderson's University was founded about the middle of last century by Professor Anderson, chiefly for the promotion of physical science. Its lectures, particularly on medical and anatomical subjects, are well attended, and its

engines. Ship-building has been recently established in the vicinity, on the banks of the river Clyde, and is reported to be in a highly flourishing state, especially the building of steam-vessels, for which Glasgow and Greenock are celebrated all over the kingdom: as the deepening and improvement of the river and harbour proceed, the two latter branches of trade may be expected largely to increase. In this rough outline of the trade and manufactures of Glasgow, it would be unpardonable to omit the extensive chemical manufactory of Messrs. Charles Tennant and Company, at St. Rollox, near Glasgow, considered to be the largest in Europe, and covering nearly ten acres. As the situation is high, on the north side of the city, the numerous chimneys form a prominent feature in the general view of Glasgow. One of these is 440 feet from base to summit, forming a land-mark for thirty miles round the city. The bleaching-powder, sulphuric acid, and other chemical compounds, are manufactured to a large extent, and of the best quality, besides there being an extensive manufactory of soap.

professors are considered highly respectable. Its winter soirees have attracted much attention. There is an excellent museum attached to this institution. In Hanover Street, running from George's Square to the north, stands the Mechanics' Institution, the lectures of which are numerously attended; attached to it is an excellent library, with a valuable scientific apparatus; and they have, together with the Mechanic's class in Anderson's University, perhaps the most beautiful and extensive series of models of steam-engines and machines of various kinds to be found in any similar institution in the country. Besides these principal educational establishments, there are several others of an inferior, but respectable, description in the suburbs, which are well attended. Lectures upon a variety of important subjects—scientific, educational, and economical—are also delivered by various scientific and philanthropic individuals, at which great numbers attend. There is a Philosophical Society, two Statistical Societies, a Literary and Commercial Society, and various other Societies for mutual instruction, indicating the intelligent activity of mind and thirst for knowledge of the good citizens of Glasgow. The elementary schools are numerous, and are attended by great numbers of children, but no certain data exist from which to estimate the entire number of scholars. Nearly £30,000 sterling have been mortified by various worthy individuals, at different times, for educational purposes, in Glasgow. A normal seminary, the first of the kind in Scotland, and a handsome building, has recently been erected to the north of the city, and has proved eminently successful both as an elementary and a normal educational establishment. The Free Church of Scotland have recently erected another normal establishment in the close vicinity of the former one, which we learn is numerously attended by pupils. So that, on the whole, either in the amount or quality of its educational means, Glasgow is behind no city in the kingdom. In 1763, the illustrious James Watt began that memorable series of experiments in mechanical science which issued in the successful application of steam as a great motive power, and about fifty years after Mr. Henry Bell launched on the Clyde the first steam-vessel ever seen in this country. To the labours and discoveries of these eminent men, Glasgow may be said to owe her present eminent position as a manufacturing and commercial community. Monuments to perpetuate their memory have been erected by their grateful fellow-citizens. That of the former is placed in George's Square, in the centre of the city, and the latter at Dunglass, on the Clyde, eleven miles below the town, in a fine commanding situation.

Glasgow is also rich in religious, charitable, and philanthropic institutions of every variety of description, which are supported by annual donations to the extent of £50,000. To particularize these, would occupy far too much space, but two of the most recent establishments deserve especial notice, the Asylum for the Houseless Poor, and the House of Refuge for Indigent and Orphan Boys.* A similar institution to the latter, for the reception of Destitute Young Females, has also recently been erected. The former of these affords shelter during the night to above a hundred houseless creatures, who must otherwise lie in the streets, and the latter has from one hundred and thirty to one hundred and forty boys within its walls, learning some trade, and receiving the elements of a useful education. It is a fine building, in a prominent situation, to the north-east of the city.

In a commercial community like that of Glasgow, where the learned professions bear a small proportion to those engaged in the pursuits of trade and commerce, comparatively few individuals, not professional, are to be found of a purely literary character. Yet no city in the kingdom, the society of which is composed of similar elements, can exhibit a large number of enlightened and well-educated mercantile men ; and it may be said generally, that whilst the chief springs of action are to be found in the stimulants of commercial and manufacturing enterprize, the general character of the population is that of intellectual activity, and eagerness for the acquisition of general and available knowledge.

* A new edifice, on a large scale, is intended to be erected for the above establishment, on the north side of the city ; not far from which a large handsome building has been raised as an Asylum for Old Men, in the Rottenrow.

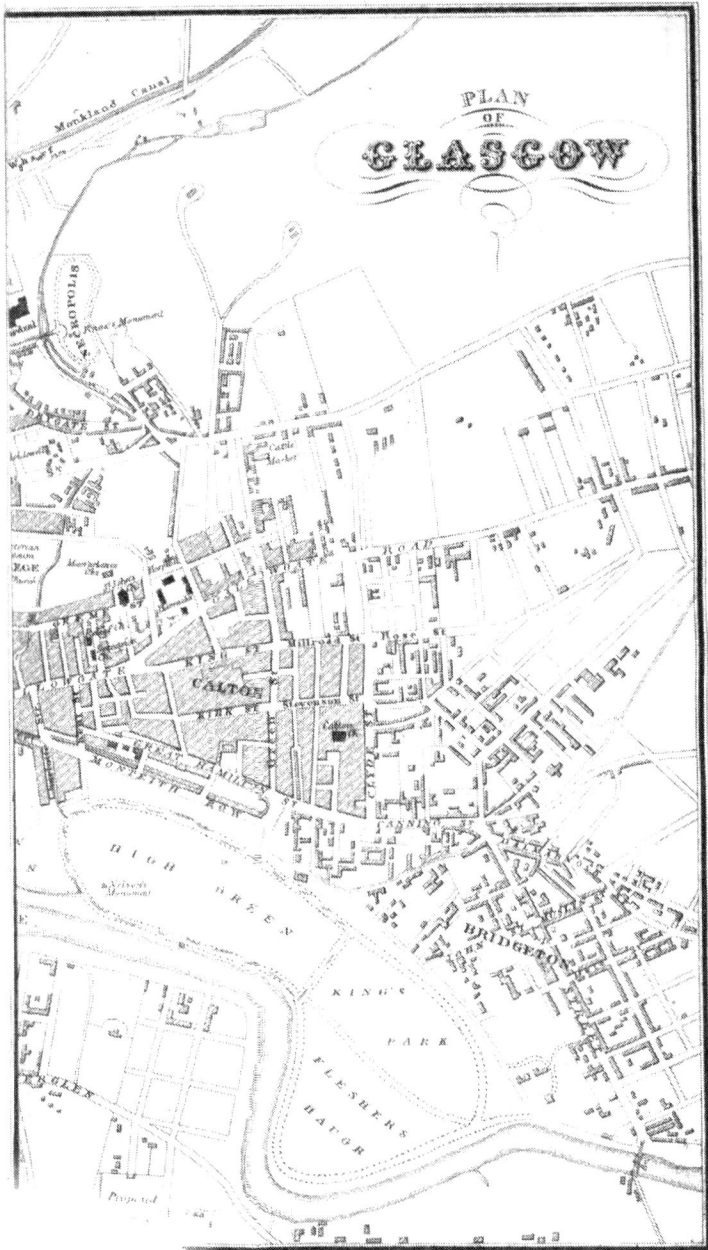

PLAN
OF
GLASCOW

Monkland Canal

METROPOLIS

Knox's Monument

Market

College

Exchange

CALTON

HIGH GREEN

Nelson's Monument

BRIDGETON

KING'S PARK

FLESHER'S HAUGH

GLEN

Projected

G. Aikman. Sc. Edin.

—

WALK FIRST.*

GEORGE'S SQUARE—MONUMENT TO SIR WALTER SCOTT—STATUES OF SIR
JOHN MOORE AND JAMES WATT—ROYAL EXCHANGE—EQUESTRIAN
STATUE OF THE DUKE OF WELLINGTON—ROYAL BANK—QUEEN
STREET—ARGYLE STREET—ARCADE—DUNLOP STREET—THEATRE-
ROYAL—MILLER STREET—GLASSFORD STREET—STOCKWELL—HUT-
CHESON'S HOSPITAL—CANDLERIGGS, AND BAZAAR—TRON STEEPLE
—CROSS—TONTINE BUILDINGS—EQUESTRIAN STATUE OF WILLIAM
THE THIRD—TOWN HALL—CROSS STEEPLE—SALTMARKET—ST. AN-
DREW'S SQUARE, AND CHURCH—BRIDGEGATE—COURTHOUSES AND
JAIL—HUTCHESON'S BRIDGE—GREEN—NELSON'S MONUMENT—LON-
DON STREET—HIGH STREET—COLLEGE BUILDINGS—BRIDEWELL—
BELL OF THE BRAE—INFIRMARY—CATHEDRAL—NECROPOLIS—ASY-
LUM FOR THE BLIND—GEORGE'S STREET.

IN point of picturesque situation Glasgow is far inferior to
Edinburgh. Whilst the latter stands upon a succession of
bold ridges, sloping finely down to the Firth of Forth; with
the rich indented coast of Fife, and the noble range of the
Ochils in the distance to the north, and on the south and
west, the green swelling outlines of the Pentlands—Glasgow is situate in the valley of the Clyde, and chiefly on the
levels along its banks, although some portions of the city
are located on acclivities to the north, which, by their commanding position, vary and enliven the monotony of an
otherwise nearly unbroken level. Neither can Glasgow exhibit the same rich and picturesque variety of surface within its limits proper, which Edinburgh presents. There is
no Castle-hill, with its summit bristling with the rude
fortifications of the middle ages, and an abrupt and lofty
mass of rock, sinking suddenly down into the bed of an
ancient lake, now transformed into pleasure gardens; or a

* In conformity with the plan adopted in our description of Edinburgh, the
reader will find that the several walks through Glasgow are each distinguished
by a different line of colour in the map of the city affixed. Walk First is
coloured *red*. Strangers whose time is limited may omit those parts of the
route indicated by a *dotted* line.

Calton-hill, rising boldly in the centre of the city, gorgeous
with splendid mansions, noble public buildings, and monuments to the illustrious dead ; nor has it the bold and
rough ridge of Salisbury Crags, diversifying the landscape,
and carrying the mind of the spectator away from the busy
hum and haunts of man, to the more still retreats, and the
solitary grandeur of nature.   So far, therefore, Glasgow
must suffer in the eye of the tourist on a comparison of its
natural advantages with those of Edinburgh, and not less
so, perhaps, when the general character and appearance of
the two cities are compared.   Edinburgh, with its Old
Town, still exhibiting in whole streets and divisions, the
irregular but striking style of architecture patronised by
our fathers, and teeming at every step with ancient buildings, associated with numberless historical reminiscences ;
and opposite to this, her New Town, with its splendid architectural vistas, and the chaste elegance of its general
exterior.   Glasgow has no such glowing and startling
contrasts to present ; yet, if the tourist will put himself
under our guidance for a short time, we promise to show
him one of the finest cities in the British dominions, and
even in a mere landscape point of view, presenting a series
of pictures of equal beauty and interest.   We shall adopt
the same method we have found so convenient in perambulating Edinburgh, and conduct the stranger in a succession of walks through the busy city.

Suppose the tourist, then, snugly deposited in one of the
excellent hotels in George's Square, one of the most central places in the city, and from which, as from a common
centre, we shall commence our examination of the memo-
rabilia of this great commercial emporium of the west.

Sallying from any of the various respectable hotels* in
this spacious and handsome square—which of itself, from
the elegance and agreeable bustle of its area, attracts attention from a stranger—the first object which strikes the

* There are five excellent hotels in George's Square — the George Hotel,
Comrie's, the Royal Hotel, the Star Hotel, and the Wellington Hotel ; at any of
which the stranger is sure of the best entertainment, as the old sign hath it, for
"man and horse." Besides these, there are various taverns and eating-houses
of the best description.

eye, is the monument recently erected to Sir Walter Scott. It is in the form of a fluted Doric column, about eighty feet in height, with a colossal statue of the great Minstrel on the top. The figure is half enveloped in a shepherd's plaid,* and the expression of the countenance is characterised by that air of *bonhommie* and shrewd sense which distinguished that illustrious individual. Directly in front of Sir Walter's pillar there is a fine pedestrian statue, in bronze, by Flaxman, of the lamented Sir John Moore, who was a native of Glasgow. To the right of Sir John Moore's statue, in the south-west angle of the square, there is also a noble figure of James Watt, in bronze, and of colossal magnitude. It is intended, as opportunity offers, to place the statues and monuments of other eminent men around the inclosed area of this handsome square, which is ornamented with shrubberies and walks, so that in process of time it will become a sort of open Pantheon, dedicated to the illustrious dead. Standing on the north side of the square, the spectator has before him one of the finest architectural vistas in the city. On the right, the bold spire of St. George's Church, 162 feet in height, catches the eye, surmounting a building, obviously too small for such a vast superstructure. Somewhat nearer, on the same side, is the Dissenting Chapel in which the celebrated Dr. Wardlaw officiates — an elegant building, of Grecian chasteness of conception. To the right and left a noble street, George's Street, extends for about half a mile, without presenting any other objects of especial interest. Looking to the south, the lofty colonnade of the Royal Exchange† appears, towards which imposing mass of building we shall now conduct the tourist. It stands in Queen Street, at the termination of Ingram Street, one of the finest openings in the city. This splendid fabric is built in the florid Corinthian

---

* It is somewhat unfortunate, that the plaid is placed on the wrong arm.

† The colonnade of the Royal Exchange is one of the boldest and most imposing architectural objects in the kingdom; and consists of a double range of fluted Corinthian pillars of great height. As a whole, the Royal Exchange of Glasgow is one of the most striking edifices in the empire, the general effect of which is grand and impressive, though some of the details may be liable to the objections of a refined criticism.

style of architecture, and is surmounted by a lantern, which forms one of the most conspicuous objects in the city. The News Room is one of the most striking apartments in the kingdom, about 100 feet long, by 40 broad, with a richly ornamented oval roof, supported by fluted Corinthian columns. The Royal Exchange is placed in the centre of a noble area, two sides of which are lined with splendid and uniform ranges of buildings, but simpler in design than the Exchange, and occupied as warehouses, shops, and counting-houses. Behind it is the Royal Bank, which is much admired by good judges, for the elegant simplicity and chasteness of its design. It is built after the model of a celebrated Greek temple. On each side of the Bank, two superb Doric arches, of bold and imposing character, afford access to Buchanan Street, also one of the principal streets in the city, in fact, the Regent Street of Glasgow. In front of the Royal Exchange has recently been placed, a colossal equestrian statue, in bronze, of the Duke of Wellington, executed by the Baron Marochetti, a French Artist. The countenance of the Duke, which is a portrait, possesses much calmness and dignity of expression. The head and neck of the charger are remarkably spirited, but the finest part of the performance consists of four elaborately finished alto relievos, representing the field of Waterloo, and three other designs which adorn the four sides of the pedestal. The work has been the subject of much controversy among critics, the hostile party charging it with a theatrical air inconsistent with true elevation of expression. It is, however, generally regarded as an effort of art, not unworthy of the hero and the achievements it is designed to commemorate.

Proceeding down Queen Street, one of the great thoroughfares and most animated avenues in the city, a noble square of buildings will be observed in course of erection for the proprietors of the National Bank of Scotland, who are to occupy part of it as an office. When completed, it will be one of the most imposing ranges of buildings in the city. At its northern extremity, in the north-west corner of George's Square, is the terminus of the Edinburgh and Glasgow Railway, where the stranger emerges into the main artery of Glasgow, here called Argyle Street, but which bears the names of the Trongate and Gallowgate, towards its eastern extremities. Taking in the whole extent of this noble avenue, from east to west, it exhibits a continuation of street of at least three miles in length.

Turning towards the east, the stranger finds himself involved in the bustle and animation of one of the most crowded thoroughfares in Europe, through which the stream of human existence flows at all hours of the day, and in all seasons, with undiminished volume and velocity. The general character of the buildings is plain, and there is no attempt at plan or uniformity of arrangement. An ancient tenement or two, with its narrow pointed gables and steep roofs, occasionally attracts the eye, and forms a fine contrast to the modern elegance of the shops below. On the left, a handsome entrance gives access to a covered Arcade, extending from this point to Buchanan Street, and containing numerous handsome shops, with a gay crowd of pedestrians at all hours. On the right, the first opening is Dunlop Street, containing the Theatre-Royal, a recent erection, but by no means very chaste or happy in its style. There was formerly a handsome theatre in Queen Street, which was destroyed by fire about ten years ago. Opposite is Miller Street, in which were formerly the stately mansions of the old Virginian merchants, but which are now occupied as places of business. Virginia Street, on the same side, is a narrow, but handsome thoroughfare, in which the City of Glasgow Bank, formerly occupied by the Union Bank of Scotland, is the most conspicuous building. It is built after the model of the Temple of Jupiter Stator at Rome, and is one of the most chaste and elegant buildings in the city. On the left, the next opening of any importance is Glassford Street, broad, and handsome in the style of its buildings, especially in that lately occupied as the Ship Bank. Here the new Post-Office is located, a plain but handsome structure, with no architectural pretensions, and greatly inferior in its public accommodations to the increasing wants of the community. In Wilson Street, one of the finest street vistas in the city, are located the New County Buildings, a splendid and imposing pile, of great extent, and of a character equally simple and majestic. Opposite Glassford Street, and

o

running to the right towards the river, is the Stockwell, one of the oldest streets in the city.   A few old tenements still show their venerable fronts here, but the remorseless march of improvement has recently swept away some of the finest. Sixty years ago, this was one of the chief avenues of the city, and the principal approach from the south, by the old bridge of Glasgow.   Excepting Hutcheson Street, with its fine hospital of that name, at the upper end surmounted by an elegant tapering spire,* and Candleriggs Street, terminated by St. David's Church and Tower, and containing the New City Hall, one of the largest rooms in the kingdom, and capable of containing 4000 persons, the Bazaar, a large general market, covered in, and containing extensive accommodation—the stranger will pass several other streets of no great importance, and observe, on the right, a rather puny but venerable-looking spire, the Tron Steeple, which finely breaks the monotony of the long line of street which he has just traversed.   On the right side, opposite the Candleriggs, is King Street, an old and well-frequented opening, containing the public markets for beef, mutton, fish, and vegetables, now nearly entirely disused.   It terminates in the Bridgegate, a fine old street, irregular in its appearance, and of considerable breadth in some parts.   An old steeple, of remarkably good proportions, rises up behind it, which anciently formed part of the building used as a hall for the merchants of Glasgow, but which has long ago been pulled down.   Eighty years ago, this street was inhabited by the most respectable classes of citizens, and contained many handsome buildings.   Many lanes or closes run off from it on either side, inhabited by a numerous and rather turbulent population, of the poorest classes.   Some very old buildings are still to be found in

---

* This building is erected on the site of the old hospital, founded by two brothers, whose statues are placed in the front of the edifice, and who left considerable property for its support, chiefly in ground on the south side of the river, and on which the extensive suburb of Hutchesontown is built.   A number of poor boys receive a gratis education from its funds, besides being supported otherwise.   In Candleriggs Street are situate also the extensive wholesale and retail warehouses of the Messrs. Campbell, said to be one of the largest commercial establishments in the kingdom, and worthy of a visit, from the excellence of its interior arrangements.

these closes, whose appearance tells a tale of other times, but the dun and squalid character of its present occupants, does not invite a lengthened examination of these remnants of antiquity. Returning to the Trongate, a little further on is the Cross of Glasgow, forming a centre and termination to the Trongate, the Gallowgate, (a continuation of this street,) the High Street, and the Saltmarket. There is an equestrian statue of William the Third placed here, of no great merit as a work of art.

A noble range of building, (represented in the above cut,) with a superb piazza under it, extends in front, denominated the Tontine, from having been built upon that principle. There is a fine large News Room here, which was formerly known by the appellation of the Coffee-Room, and, until the New Exchange was erected, was the great focus of business and politics. The ancient jail of the burgh stood exactly at the corner of the High Street and Trongate. Criminals were executed formerly in front of this building. On its site a heavy, tasteless pile of buildings has been erected, occupied by shops and warehouses. The old Court-houses also stood here, but they have been removed to the New Jail buildings, at the foot of the Saltmarket. The Town-Hall, however, a fine apartment, containing portraits of some of the Scottish and English sovereigns, besides a very fine marble statue of William Pitt, by Chantrey, still remains. The Cross Steeple, too, a relic of the ancient civic splendour of this part of the city, and in itself an interesting object, survives still. Leaving the ancient Cross of Glasgow we next enter the Saltmarket, not now, alas ! as in the palmy days of Bailie Nicol Jarvie, the domicile of bailies, and other civic dignitaries, but occupied with a busy population of inferior shopkeepers and trades-people. The lower part, and some portions of the neighbourhood, form the Monmouth Street and Rag Fair of Glasgow, being chiefly occupied with furniture brokers and old clothes dealers. On the left is St. Andrew's Square, the buildings of which are characterized by an elegant simplicity and chaste regularity of architecture. The greater part of the area of this square is occupied with St. Andrew's Church, the largest, and, in many respects, the finest Church in the city, the portico of which, for lightness and elevation, is much admired. On the right is the Bridgegate, of which notice has already been taken. Here stood anciently several fine old buildings of some historical note ; in one of them Cromwell is said to have lodged when in Glasgow ; but, with many other ancient tenements in this street, it has long since fallen a victim to the progress of time and improvement. The stranger now emerges into a fine broad esplanade, with the Public Park or Green stretching away to the left, and the imposing pile of buildings forming the

Court-houses and Jail, on the right. These elegant buildings are in the Grecian style of architecture. The front is chaste and simple, but thought rather low for its length. From the vast increase of the city and its population, these buildings are now found to be deficient in extent, and an extensive range of building, as already noticed, has been erected in Wilson Street, for the purpose of affording suitable accommodation to the County and City Courts. On the right of the Court-houses is the river Clyde, crossed at this point by Hutcheson's Bridge, commenced in 1829, and finished in 1833. The design was given by Mr. Robert Stevenson of Edinburgh, the distinguished engineer of the Bell Rock Lighthouse. At the time when it was built the arches were the flattest that had ever been executed, being segments of a circle whose radius is 65 feet. The erection cost £22,000. A carriage drive extends around the Green, which is about two miles and a quarter in circumference. Passing up the Green, on the left, is the fine column erected to the memory of Nelson, 143 feet in height, and modelled on the Trajan Pillar at Rome. When the tide is at the full, the brimming waters of the Clyde appear at this point to great advantage, and there is a fine landscape view down the river, with the four bridges in the distance, and the variety of buildings, public and private, on the opposite banks. On the south side, vast ranges of chimneys appear, indicating the *locale* of some of the largest spinning and weaving factories in the city. The same appearances are beheld to the northeast, whilst, on the south and south-east appear, at a few miles' distance, the beautiful slopes of the Cathkin Braes, adorned with fine plantations, and gentlemen's seats. The Green is diversified with walks, some of which are shaded by noble rows of trees, and being the common property of the inhabitants, and much used for the washing and bleaching of clothes, there are several fountains of fine spring water, round which abundance of damsels may be seen clustering with their *boynes* and pitchers. The north side of this fine pleasure-ground, termed the Calton Green, rises a little, and has a handsome row of dwelling-houses lining one side of it, called Monteith Row, which, from their elevation and beauty of situation, are amongst the pleasantest in the city.   Leaving the Green, (on the west and north surrounded for most of its length, by an iron railing,) by the North-west Gate, and crossing Charlotte Street, a quiet, dull-looking street, with some fine old mansions in ·it, we enter London Street, a broad and handsome avenue, but, considering its imme-diate vicinity to the Cross, the centre of the city, sorely bungled, being in a half-built and disgraceful state of dila-pidation.   Arrived again at the Cross, let us take a passing glance at the Gallowgate, the name of the eastern section of the main street of the city, which begins at this point. It is irregular, both in the appearance of its buildings and in its width, sometimes steep and narrow, broad, and winding.   It contains large barracks for foot soldiers, and, near its easterly extremity, the Cattle-market, one of the most interesting sights of Glasgow.   It occupies 30,000 square yards, and is admirably and even elegantly laid out, for its especial objects.   The tower of St. John's Church is the most prominent feature in this part of the city, which, exhibiting no other objects of peculiar interest to a stran-ger, we shall return from this hasty sally, and proceed due north, up the ancient avenue of the High Street, which may be considered as the backbone of the skeleton of the old city.

The buildings in this fine old street are many of them venerable from their antiquity ; but the presence of new ones on every side, indicates the rapid disappearance of the ancient characteristics of this part of the city.   On every side, numerous *closes*, or narrow lanes, appear teeming with population, and alive with the hum and stir of active life. They are inhabited chiefly by the lower classes, and, in many of them, as well as in those in the Saltmarket and Bridgegate, the inmates are densely wedged together, which circumstance co-operating with other fatal causes, has tended to foster the elements of contagious diseases, and to lower the aver-age duration of life of the poorer classes in the city.   Pro-ceeding up the street, and passing one or two inferior streets, there is on the right, a long range of venerable monastic-looking buildings, with a fine stone balcony in front. These are the buildings of the University, the external aspect of which harmonizes well with the grave purposes to which they are devoted. In the first of the three inner courts, there is a fine old staircase, much admired for its stately elegance. The buildings are old, and imposing in their appearance, but some of the older portions, having been taken down a few years ago, have been replaced by others of a character wholly foreign to the original style, thus marring the harmony, and disturbing the uniformity and propriety of the structure. Behind is the Hunterian Museum, a splendid edifice of the Grecian character.

It is understood that the College grounds and buildings have been, or are about to be purchased, by a railway company, for a terminus, and the College is to be rebuilt in a fine situation to the west of the city.

A little above the College is Duke Street, a fine opening to the east, and containing the City and County Bridewell, a large and striking mass of buildings in the old Saxon style of Architecture.* The High Street becomes here rather steep and narrow, with a considerable curve, and is called the Bell of the Brae. Here, in the year 1300, a severe action took place betwixt the English, commanded by Percy and Bishop Beik, and the Scots, by the Scottish champion—Wallace; in which the former were defeated with the loss of their commander. Within these thirty years, this part of the High Street contained the oldest and most curious-looking buildings in the city, but almost the whole of these ancient tenements have been pulled down, and replaced by others of the most ordinary character. At the top of this ascent, on the right, is the

---

* This establishment is justly celebrated for the superior excellence and economy of its arrangements and management. It contains ample accommodation and means of classification for nearly 300 prisoners, by whose labour its expenses are almost wholly defrayed. Each prisoner, it is calculated, costs the community no more than £1, 10s. per annum, so judicious is the system pursued.

Drygate, and on the left the Rottenrow; both of them very old streets, and still exhibiting sundry venerable-looking buildings, the relics of their ancient grandeur and importance. A few yards further we reach a large open space, containing in front, the Infirmary, a large and elegant building, of a composite character of architecture, and light and airy in appearance; and a little to the right, the huge mass of the Cathedral at once arrests and detains the eye of the stranger. Having already in the historical and introductory matter, briefly noticed this noble relic of antiquity, we shall merely observe farther, that it is surrounded by a vast churchyard, in which the bones of many generations rest from their labours; besides this, it contains a great many rich and ancient monumental tombs of the worthies of the old city, and the grave dignitaries of church and state in the days of other times.—The Glasgow Infirmary, including the recent additions made to it for a Fever Hospital, is a very large building. The extent of its accommodation may be inferred from the fact, that 6272 patients were admitted during the year 1837-1838. It bears a high character, not merely for the matured excellence of its arrangements, but the superior character of its medical school.* A building, in the worst possible taste, stands a little to the right of these two fine specimens of ancient and modern architecture, which is the Barony Church. Betwixt this eye-sore and the wall of the Cathedral burying-ground, which is lined with ancient sepulchral monuments, a narrow path conducts to the Bridge of Sighs, so called from its affording access to the new Glasgow Necropolis, anciently called the Fir Park, and believed to have been one of the dark retreats of the Druids. With a fine bold arch, the bridge spans the brawling rivulet, called the Molendinar Burn, which, after being collected into a small dam or lake, dashes briskly over an artificial cascade down a steep ravine, imparting a character of life and cheerfulness to a spot consecrated to the most solemn associations. The

---

* Its affairs are managed by twenty-five Directors, ten of whom are elected by the subscribers of two guineas a-year; the others are elected by the various public bodies of the city. The Members for the city are also *ex officio* Directors.

bold and rocky eminence which forms the Necropolis shoots suddenly up to the height of from 200 to 300 feet, forming, with its fine shrubberies, a noble background to the Cathedral. A splendid gateway, in the Italian style, appears in front, and the entire surface of the rock, bristling with columns, and every variety of monumental erection, some of them peculiarly happy and chaste in style, is divided into walks. The fine statue of Knox on the summit, and one erected to the memory of Mr. William M'Gavin, with the monument to the late Rev. Dr. Dick of Glasgow, are particularly conspicuous, and will instantly attract the eye of the stranger.* It is said to be intended ultimately to carry a tunnel through the hill from south to north, and to form galleries and chambers in the solid rock, so as to form a vast crypt, in addition to the cemetery above. From the summit, 250 feet above the level of the Clyde, the Great Reformer just mentioned looks grimly down on one of the most striking scenes that can well be imagined. The huge mass of the venerable Cathedral, surrounded by the crumbling remains and memorials of twenty-five generations, stands still and solemn at his feet, like the awful Genius of the Past; whilst the vast city stretches away in long lines and perspectives in every direction, intersected by the broad and brimming Clyde, and the uplands of Lanarkshire and Renfrewshire, with the Dumbartonshire and Argyleshire hills, forming a noble frame to the picture.† Descending from this elevated site, we shall retrace our steps down the High Street, and, striking to the right, enter George's Street, a broad and handsome opening, but, with the exception of the buildings of Anderson's University,

* Since these were erected, a marble statue of the late Mr. Charles Tennant of St. Rollox has been placed in the grounds, and a splendid mausoleum is in course of erection to the memory of Major Monteith, which, from the rich and florid style of its workmanship, and its bold imposing look and situation, will form one of the most striking objects in this noble garden of the dead.

† A little to the west of the Cathedral is the Asylum for the Blind, an establishment of great merit in its arrangements. The inmates are employed in various ways, and manufacture articles of use or ornament to a considerable extent, which are disposed of for the benefit of the institution. The new method of printing for the blind has been carried here to great perfection. Generally speaking, any respectable inn-keeper knows how to procure an order of admission for this and any other public institution in Glasgow.

which are respectable but plain in appearance, and the New
High School behind them, a large building, equally devoid
of architectural attraction, it offers no particular induce-
ment to the tourist to linger on its pavements, and he now
finds himself again in George's Square, ready, after brief
repose, for

WALK SECOND.*

TURNING to the right, and still continuing in George Street,
now called West George Street, which, after passing
round St. George's Church, continues its course for nearly
half a mile further, till it is lost in Blythswood Square,
the tourist enters Buchanan Street. Here it may be proper to observe, that four great lines of street run west
from Buchanan Street, parallel to each other, two of them
for nearly a mile in length—St. Vincent Street, West
George Street, Regent Street, and Bath Street. The first
and last named are the longest and finest. Turning north,
we shall follow the easy ascent of Buchanan Street, and
when at the top, we recommend a brief pause, to take a
hasty look behind. The eye courses down the long vista of
a spacious street, lined with handsome buildings, and in
the lower half crowded with a gay population, for we have
already mentioned that this is the Regent Street (London)
of Glasgow. It is finely terminated by St. Enoch's Church,
standing in the Square of that name; and beyond, in the
distance, the green slopes of the Renfrewshire uplands appear above the houses, giving a rich and half rural character to the view. A few yards further on, we reach Sauchie-

---

* This walk is coloured *yellow* on the Map.

hall Street, or road, at the corner of which stands a handsome pile of buildings, denominated the Cleland Testimonial, from having been built and presented to the eminent statist of that name, by his friends in Glasgow, on his retirement from the public service of the city, after having been for many years superintendent of public works. From this point, the lofty dome of the New Town's Hospital, or Poor's House, meets the eye. This is one of the largest and finest buildings belonging to the city of Glasgow. From an octagonal centre four wings diverge, of three storeys in height, and the style of the whole building is impressive and striking. Its accommodation is very extensive, and the grounds contain about four acres.* Sauchiehall Road is lined with handsome rows of houses, and is very broad for the first half of its length. As the tourist proceeds, he finds, on the left, various handsome streets, opening into it from the south, forming part of the new town, and chiefly occupied by the wealthier classes. On the right, an elevated ridge accompanies him, containing many handsome villas, and intersected with streets. This is called Garnet Hill, and should be specially visited by the picturesque tourist, as it commands a noble view from its summit. To the north and north-west, bold ranges of hills appear at a few miles' distance ; and, faintly looming on the horizon, the lofty peaks of the Argyleshire and Perthshire mountains are seen ; nearer, the masts of vessels on the Forth and Clyde Canal appear, in the basin at Port-Dundas, with a rich undulating surface, crowded with villas, private dwellings, and the tall chimneys of numerous public works. Returning to Sauchiehall Street, the tourist arrives at Woodside Crescent, and is struck with surprise at the number and elegance of the fine streets, rows, and terraces, intermixed with ornamental shrubberies, which attract his eye. This part of the suburbs

---

* This building, formerly a Lunatic Asylum, has lately been purchased by the directors of the Town's Hospital, for the accommodation of the poor of the city. A new Lunatic Asylum is now erected to the west of the city, for which purpose sixty-six acres of land have been obtained, to meet the fast-growing popularity of this estimable institution. This new Asylum is an enormous pile of building, in the Saxo-Gothic style, and being happily placed on a rising ground, arrests the eye of the traveller as he approaches from the west.

is the most recently built, and is at present the most fashionable quarter for what are called self contained houses.   In
this neighbourhood was formerly the Royal Botanic Garden, which was recently removed to the great Western
Road, about two miles from the city.   It occupies a fine
elevated situation, sloping down on the north to the waters
of the Kelvin, whilst, on the south, the New Observatory
stands out a conspicuous object, on a green swelling elevation of considerable height.   Public promenades occur every
week on the Saturday evenings of summer ; admission, a
sixpence, and at all times access can be had for the same
money.

Retracing our steps, we shall strike down the first opening on the right, into Elmbank Crescent, a very handsome
row of houses, but only half built.   Passing through a new
street just begun, called India Street, containing a few
very handsome buildings, in the stately but somewhat
stiff style of Louis the Fourteenth's time, the stranger
finds himself at the western extremity of St. Vincent Street,
here called Greenhill Place.   Proceeding citywards, along
this noble street, and ascending gradually, on the right is
Blysthwood Square, the buildings of which, from their lofty
position and elegant exterior, form one of the finest and
most prominent objects to the stranger approaching Glasgow from the west.   The view from this square, to the south
and west, is very fine, but on the north, it is intercepted by
the more commanding ridge of Garnet Hill.   Returning to
St. Vincent Street, the stranger finds himself descending
gradually, with elegant masses of building on each side, and
a noble street vista of great length before him.   On the left
is a handsome building, recently fitted up as a club-house,
but there being no particular object to detain the eye, we
shall suppose the tourist once more deposited in George's
Square, in the north-west angle of which this noble opening has its termination.

WALK THIRD.*

INGRAM STREET — ASSEMBLY ROOMS — OLD BRIDGE OF GLASGOW — POOR'S HOUSE — CATHOLIC CHAPEL — CUSTOM HOUSE — GORBALS CHURCH—CARLTON PLACE—WOODEN OR SERVICE BRIDGE—GLASGOW BRIDGE—VIEW FROM BROOMIELAW—HARBOUR—SHIPPING, STEAM-VESSELS, ETC.—SUBURBS OF LAURIESTON, TRADESTON, AND HUTCHESONTOWN—BARONY OF GORBALS—PAISLEY CANAL.

LEAVING George Square again, and proceeding down Queen Street on the left, the eye glancing along Ingram Street, rests on the fine portico of the Assembly Rooms,† standing boldly forward, with the grave old College steeple in the distance, looking demurely down on the bustle and animation of this great business thoroughfare. A splendid pile of building has recently been erected at the west end of this street, opposite to the Exchange, intended for the British Linen Company's Bank. This range of building forms one of the most striking objects in the city. Entering Argyle Street once more, and threading our way eastward, through the busy crowd, to the Stockwell, we request the stranger to dash with us down this avenue towards the river, and there being no objects of any note on the route, but those which have been already seen and commented on, we find ourselves on the Old Bridge of Glasgow. This bridge was built in 1345, and was the first stone bridge erected in Glasgow. It has been twice widened, and the last time in a very elegant and ingenious manner, by adding footpaths, supported by cast-iron frames of a tasteful character, from a design by the late Mr. Telford. It is about to be taken down and rebuilt, the deepening of the river rendering this

* This walk is coloured *green* on the map.
† The Assembly Rooms is one of the finest edifices in the city, taken in connexion with the buildings on each side, which are built on a plan harmonizing with it. The principal room is 80 feet long, 35 feet wide, and 27 in height, with a tastefully painted ceiling. Nearly opposite to the Assembly Rooms is the Union Bank of Scotland, recently erected, a fine building, though faulty in some of its details. The portico in front is surmounted by six colossal statues of allegorical personages.

necessary, as well as the interests of the river navigation.
Looking up the stream, the back and one side of the Jail
buildings are seen on the left, with the Green sloping beautifully down to the river.   The view downwards is still
finer : two bridges (the nearest, a very fine and perfectly
level one, of wood, from a design by Mr. Stevenson of Edinburgh) span the glittering waters of the river.   Next to
it, is the Catholic chapel, one of the most striking modern buildings in the Gothic style of architecture in the
kingdom.   It is very large, and elegantly fitted up, and is
officiated in by Bishop Murdoch and several Catholic
clergymen.   Beyond it a little way is the New Custom-
House, a respectable looking building.   On the left bank of
the river, the spire of the Gorbals Church breaks the uniformity of the outline in a pleasing manner, and two fine
masses of buildings, East and West Carlton Place, from
their simplicity, good taste, and happy elevation, confer a
peculiar dignity upon this part of the river vista. Proceeding along this noble street, Glasgow or Broomielaw Bridge,
designed by the late Mr. Telford, next demands the attention of the tasteful stranger.   It is one of the finest bridges
in Europe—500 feet in length, and sixty feet wide, being
seven feet wider than London Bridge.   It is cased with
Aberdeen granite, and consists of seven arches, whilst the
curve is so slight as scarcely to be observed.   It forms a
superb entrance to the city from the south, and from it
one of the finest river harbour views in the United Kingdom may be obtained.   To the south, a fine broad avenue
stretches away till it is lost in the country.   On the right
is the Broomielaw Street, at least a mile long, with a fine
ample margin to the river, and long ranges of covered sheds,
and other harbour appurtenances.   A noble basin, from
three to four hundred feet wide and about a mile in length,
with its range of quays, is before the eye, crowded with
vessels of every description, from eight hundred tons burden to the smallest coasting craft, whilst steam-vessels are
perpetually sending up clouds of smoke or steam, and dashing in or out with a startling velocity and noise.

Crossing the river,* the stranger will admire the spacious and elegant streets which, as he walks along, strike his eye. Portland Street is nearly a mile in length, very broad, and lined with handsome buildings. The population on this side of the river, is understood to be about 60,000, located in Laurieston, Tradeston, and Hutchesontown, all in the Barony of Gorbals, which is a dependency of Glasgow. The parliamentary constituency elect their own magistrates, by poll election, who must, however, be approved of by the Town Council of Glasgow. The terminus of the Ayr, Paisley, and Greenock Railway is on this side, close to Glasgow Bridge, and, half a mile to the south, is the basin of the Johnstone and Paisley Canal ; to which places light and swift passage-boats depart, almost every hour, during the summer. Arrived at the old bridge of Glasgow again, the stranger, before crossing, will probably cast one lingering look on the river, and noble view on either side, after which, retracing his steps up Stockwell Street, he may, if he please, return to George's Square, by Glassford Street, Ingram Street, and the Royal Exchange, thus passing through the most crowded and interesting business thoroughfares of the city.

* There are always several steam-vessels of the largest class lying in the river to get in their machinery, and there is a powerful crane, capable of raising thirty tons, for lifting the heavy boilers, &c. on board; a much larger one is preparing, expected to be the most powerful in Britain. Glasgow has attained great celebrity as a manufactory of marine steam-engines, and, indeed, of machinery of every description. The depth of water at the Broomielaw at spring tides is now from 14 to 16 feet, and it is proposed by the Trustees of the harbour and river, to deepen to the extent of 20 feet at neap tides, no obstacles existing, according to the report of the engineer, to prevent such a result being obtained. It is also intended to widen the river, for ten or twelve miles down, to from 300 to 400 feet wide, the width to increase downwards ; to bevel off the banks on either side, and to remove every other obstacle to the freedom of the navigation ; so that, in a few years, with wet docks, for which a large space of ground on the south side, immediately below the suburb of Tradeston, has recently been purchased, Glasgow will possess one of the most spacious and convenient harbours in the kingdom. From July 1837 to July 1838, 4600 sailing vessels of every description, arrived and departed from the harbour, with a tonnage of 214,471 tons ; and the steam tonnage on the river during the same period was 731,028 tons ; these latter vessels made 7850 trips in the same time. The revenue from the harbour and river in 1839 was £43,287, 16s. 10d. ; customs levied in 1839, £468,974, 12s. 2d. ; and post-office revenue, £47,527, 7s. 7d.

SEVENTH TOUR.

GLASGOW—BOTHWELL CASTLE AND BRIDGE—HAMILTON—LANARK—
FALLS OF CLYDE.

LEAVING Glasgow,* the tourist proceeds eastward, and passes Camlachie and Tollcross, where there are extensive coal and iron works. On the opposite side of the Clyde is the ancient royal burgh of Rutherglen, formerly a place of some importance, but now much reduced. In the church of Rutherglen, a peace was concluded between the Scotch and English, 8th February 1297. All along the sides of the road are numerous elegant villas. Five miles from Glasgow is Broomhouse. At this point, a new line of road has lately been opened up as far as the village of Uddingston, where the old road, which passes near the banks of the river, again joins it. A quarter of a mile beyond Broomhouse, the road crosses the North Calder Water by a new bridge. Half way between Broomhouse and Uddingston, the Edinburgh road, by Holytown and Whitburn, branches off to the left. A little to the right from this point, a bridge has lately been thrown across the Clyde, uniting the parishes of Bothwell and Blantyre. A little farther on is the village of Uddingston, situated on an eminence, commanding a delightful view. A short way beyond, on the right, are the magnificent ruins of

BOTHWELL CASTLE.

This noble structure is built of red freestone, and consists of a large oblong quadrangle, flanked, towards the south, by two huge circular towers, and covering an area of 234 feet in length, and ninety-nine feet in breadth. The origin

* There is another road from Glasgow to Hamilton on the other side of the Clyde, by Rutherglen, but it is by no means so interesting as the route described.

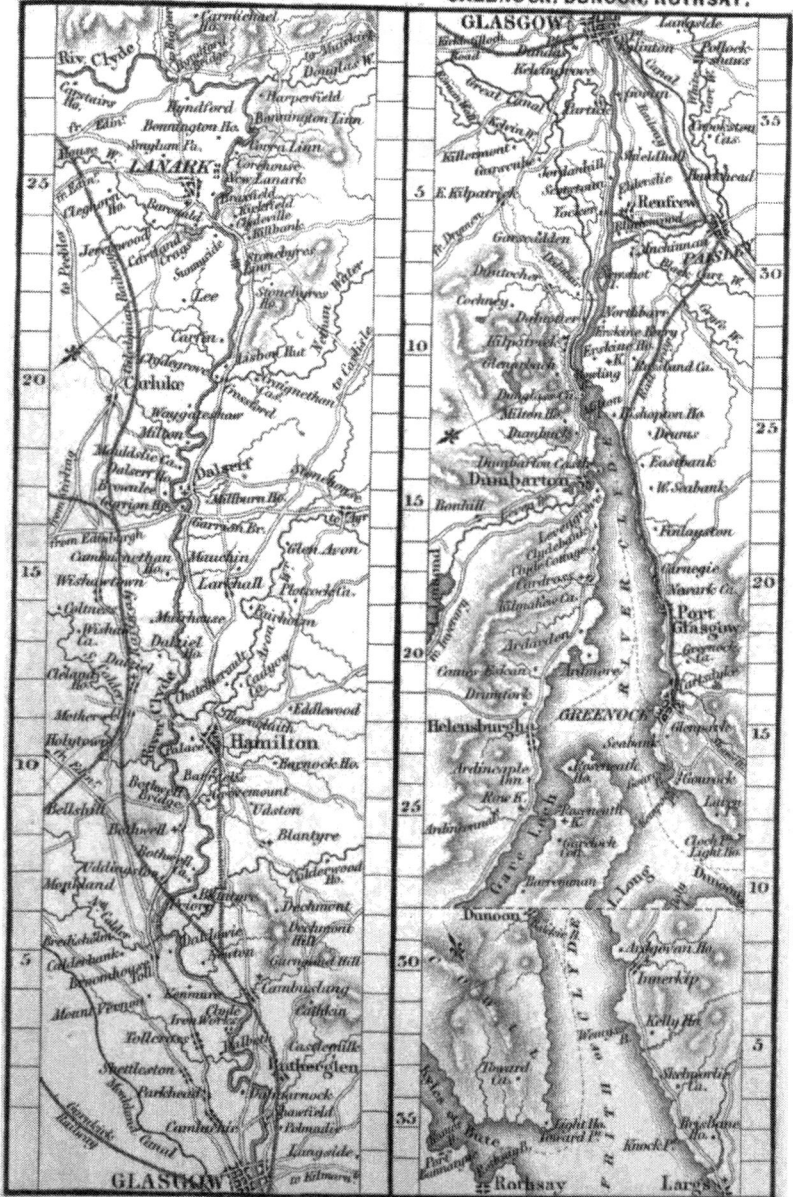

SEVENTH TOUR.
GLASGOW to HAMILTON, LANARK, & THE FALLS OF CLYDE.

EIGHTH TOUR.
GLASGOW, DUMBARTON, HELENSBURGH, GREENOCK, DUNOON, ROTHSAY.

Edinburgh. Published July 1 1846 by Adam & Charles Black, 27 North Bridge.

of the castle is unknown, and its name was unheard of, until the time of Wallace, when it is said to have belonged to Sir Andrew Murray of Bothwell, who, with Lord William Douglas, was the first nobleman to join the Scottish hero in the assertion of his country's independence, and the last to forsake him after the failure of his patriotic attempt. After Murray's outlawry, his estate of Bothwell was forfeited, and conferred by Edward I. on Aylmer de Valence, second Earl of Pembroke, commander of his forces in Scotland.* In this fortress a number of the English nobility took refuge after the battle of Bannockburn, but were speedily obliged to surrender. Bruce bestowed Bothwell Castle on Andrew Murray, who had married that monarch's sister. It next came into the possession of Archibald the Grim, Earl of Douglas, who married the granddaughter of Andrew Murray. After the forfeiture of the Douglases in 1445, it was successively possessed by the Crichtons, John Ramsay, a favourite of James III., and the Hepburns, Earls of Bothwell. After the forfeiture of the infamous nobleman of that name, it passed through several hands, till it at last reverted to the noble family of Douglas. The present residence of Lord Douglas is a plain mansion, standing on a beautiful lawn, near the old castle. It was built by the young Earl of Forfar, who was killed at the battle of Sheriffmuir.† The scenery around

---

* See part of the ballad in allusion to this, next page.

† "In the autumn of 1799, when on a visit to Lord Archibald Douglas at Bothwell Castle, Sir Walter Scott commenced the following beautiful ballad, which, notwithstanding its incompleteness, we shall here transcribe, for the additional interest it throws on the romantic associations already connected with this beautiful spot.

" If chance, by Bothwell's lovely braes
    A wanderer thou hast been,

P   Or

Bothwell Castle is remarkably splendid, and is adorned with luxuriant natural wood. The Clyde here makes a beautiful sweep, and forms the fine semicircular declivity called Bothwell Bank, celebrated in Scottish song. The following interesting anecdote, quoted from a work entitled " Verstegan's Restitution of Decayed Intelligence," printed at Antwerp in 1605, is a proof of the antiquity of at least the air to which the song of " Bothwell Bank" is sung :—" So fell it out of late years, that an English gentleman, travelling in Palestine, not far from Jerusalem, as he passed

Or hid thee from the summer's blaze
    In Blantyre's bowers of green,

Full where the copsewood opens wild
    Thy pilgrim step hath staid
Where Bothwell's towers, in ruin piled,
    O'erlook the verdant glade;

And many a tale of love and fear
    Hath mingled with the scene
Of Bothwell's banks that bloom'd so dear,
    And Bothwell's bonny Jean.

O, if with rugged minstrel lays
    Unsated be thy ear,
And thou of deeds of other days
    Another tale wilt hear,

When all beneath the spreading beach
    Flung careless on the lea,
The Gothic muse the tale shall teach
    Of Bothwell's sisters three.

Wight Wallace stood on Decmont head,
    He blew his bugle round,
Till the wild bull in Cadyow wood
    Has started at the sound.

St. George's cross o'er Bothwell hung,
    Was waving far and wide,
And from the lofty turret flung
    Its crimson blaze on Clyde;

And rising at the bugle blast
    That mark'd the Scottish foe,
Old England's yeomen muster'd fast,
    And bent the Norman bow.

Tall in the midst Sir Aylmer rose,
    Proud Pembroke's Earl was he,
While "———

Lockhart's Life of Scott, vol. i.

through a country town, he heard, by chance, a woman sitting at her door dandling her child, to sing, *Bothwell Bank, thou blumest fair.* The gentleman hereat wondered, and forthwith, in English, saluted the woman, who joyfully answered him, and said, she was right glad there to see a gentleman of our isle; and told him that she was a Scottish woman, and came first from Scotland to Venice, and from Venice thither, where her fortune was to be the wife of an officer under the Turk; who being at that instant absent, and very soon to return, she entreated the gentleman to stay there until his return. The which he did; and she, for country sake, to show herself the more kind and bountiful unto him, told her husband, at his homecoming, that the gentleman was her kinsman; whereupon her husband entertained him very kindly, and, at his departure, gave him diverse things of good value." Leyden makes the following allusion to this story, in his Ode on Scottish music :—

> " And thus the exiled Scotian maid,
>   By fond alluring love betray'd,
>   To visit Syria's date-crown'd shore,
>   In plaintive strains that soothed despair,
>   Did ' Bothwell's Banks, that bloom so fair,'
>   And scenes of earlier youth deplore."

Directly opposite to Bothwell Castle, on the south bank of the Clyde, are the ruins of Blantyre Priory, situated on the brink of a perpendicular rock.

Proceeding onwards, at the distance of a mile and a half, the tourist reaches Bothwell village and church. The old church, part of which is still standing, is the remains of an ancient Gothic fabric, cased all over with a thin coating of stone. Within its walls, the unfortunate Robert Duke of Rothesay, who was afterwards starved to death by his uncle the Duke of Albany, in Falkland Palace, was married to a daughter of Archibald the Grim, Earl of Douglas.

At a little distance in front, the tourist crosses the Clyde by Bothwell Bridge, the scene of the famous battle which took place in 1679, between the Royal forces, under the Duke of Monmouth, and the Covenanters. The Royal army

moved towards Hamilton, and reached Bothwell-moor on
the 22d of June. The insurgents were encamped chiefly in
the Duke of Hamilton's park, along the Clyde, which separated the two armies. Bothwell Bridge was then long and
narrow, having a portal in the middle, with gates, which the
Covenanters shut and barricadoed with stones and loads of
timber. This important post was defended by 300 of their
best men, under Hackston of Rathillet and Hall of Haugh-
head. The more moderate of the insurgents waited upon
Monmouth, to offer terms, and obtained a promise that he
would interpose with his Majesty in their behalf, on condition of their immediately dispersing themselves, and yield-
ing up their arms. The Cameronian party, however, would
accede to no terms with an uncovenanted king, and, while
they were debating on the Duke's proposal, his field-pieces
were already planted on the eastern side of the river, to
cover the attack of the foot-guards, who were led on by
Lord Livingstone, to force the bridge. Here Hackston maintained his post with zeal and courage, nor was it until all
his ammunition was expended, and every support denied
him by the general, that he reluctantly abandoned the important pass. When his party were drawn back, the Duke's
army, with their cannon in front, slowly defiled along the
bridge, and formed in line of battle as they came over the
river. The Duke commanded the foot, and Claverhouse
the cavalry. It would seem that these movements could not
have been performed without at least some loss, had the
enemy been serious in opposing them. But the insurgents
were otherwise employed. With the strangest delusion that
ever fell upon devoted beings, they chose these precious
moments to cashier their officers, and elect others in their
room. In this important operation, they were at length
disturbed by the Duke's cannon, at the very first discharge
of which, the horse of the Covenanters wheeled and rode off,
breaking and trampling down the ranks of the infantry in
their flight. Monmouth humanely issued orders to stop the
effusion of blood, but Claverhouse, burning to avenge his
defeat, and the death of his cornet and kinsman, at Drum-
clog, made great slaughter among the fugitives, of whom 400

were slain. These events are thus described in *Clyde*, a poem by Wilson, reprinted in *Scottish Descriptive Poems*, edited by Dr. Leyden, Edinburgh, 1803 :—

> " Where Bothwell's Bridge connects the margin steep,
> And Clyde below runs silent, strong, and deep,
> The hardy peasant, by oppression driven
> To battle, deem'd his cause the cause of Heaven ;
> Unskill'd in arms, with useless courage stood,
> While gentle Monmouth grieved to shed his blood ;
> But fierce Dundee, inflamed with deadly hate,
> In vengeance for the great Montrose's fate,
> Set loose the sword, and to the hero's shade
> A barbarous hecatomb of victims paid."*

Many of the fugitives found shelter in the wooded parks around Hamilton Palace.

Great changes have now been made on the scene of the engagement. The gateway, gate, and house of the bridge-ward were long ago removed. The original breadth of the bridge was twelve feet ; but, in 1826, twenty-two feet were added to its breadth, the hollow which once lay at the Hamilton extremity was filled up, and an alteration was also made in the road, at the other end. The open park in which the Covenanters were posted, is now changed into enclosed fields and plantations, and the moor upon which the royal army advanced to the engagement, is now a culti-vated and beautiful region.

The level grounds, which stretch away from Bothwell Bridge along the north-east bank of the river, once formed the patrimonial estate of Hamilton of Bothwellhaugh, the assassin of the Regent Murray.

A mile and a half beyond Bothwell Bridge, and ten miles and a half from Glasgow, the tourist enters the town of

HAMILTON,

the capital of the Middle Ward of Lanarkshire. Hamilton is a burgh of regality, dependent on the Duke of Hamilton ; it contains about 6000 inhabitants, of whom a considerable

---

* See notes to the ballad of " The Battle of Bothwell Bridge," in the Border Minstrelsy. The reader cannot but remember the spirited description given of this engagement in the novel of Old Mortality.

number are engaged in weaving.   The town has been much
improved by the recent erection of a new bridge, called
Cadzow Bridge, opening into a street of the same name. The
principal object of attraction, in this vicinity, is Hamilton
Palace, the seat of the Duke of Hamilton, which stands on
a plain between the town and the river.   It is a magnificent
structure, and has been greatly enlarged and improved by
the present Duke.   Its interior is extremely splendid, and
contains a magnificent collection of paintings, supposed
to be the best in Scotland.   The most celebrated of these
is *Daniel in the Lions' Den*, by Rubens.*   Among other
curiosities, Hamilton Palace contains the carbine with which
Bothwellhaugh shot the Regent Murray.

Near Hamilton is the river Avon, a tributary of the
Clyde.   The vale which this stream waters is adorned with
gorgeous old wood, and several ancient and modern mansions, the most famous of which is Cadyow or Cadzow Castle,
the ancient baronial residence of the family of Hamilton,
situated upon the precipitous banks of the Avon, about two
miles above its junction with the Clyde.   It was dismantled
in the conclusion of the civil wars, during the reign of the
unfortunate Mary.   The situation of the ruins, embosomed
in wood, darkened by ivy and creeping shrubs, and overhanging the brawling torrent, is romantic in the highest
degree.   In the immediate vicinity of Cadyow is a grove
of immense oaks, the remains of the Caledonian forest,
which anciently extended through the south of Scotland,

---

* On this splendid picture Wordsworth has composed the following sonnet :—
  " Amid a fertile region, green with wood
    And fresh with rivers, well doth it become
    The ducal Owner, in his palace-home
    To naturalize this tawny Lion brood ;
    Children of Art, that claim strange brotherhood
    (Couched in their den) with those that roam at large
    Over the burning wilderness, and charge
    The wind with terror while they roar for food.
    Satiate are *these ;* and still—to eye and ear ;
    Hence, while we gaze, a more enduring fear !
    Yet is the Prophet calm, nor would the cave
    Daunt him—if his companions now be-drowsed,
    Outstretched and listless, were by hunger roused :
    Man placed him here, and God, he knows, can save."

from the Eastern to the Atlantic Ocean. Some of these trees measure twenty-five feet and upwards in circumference, and the state of decay in which they now appear, shows that they may have witnessed the rites of the Druids. The whole scenery is included in the magnificent park of the Duke of Hamilton. The famous breed of Scottish wild cattle, milk-white in colour, with black muzzles, horns, and hoofs, are still preserved in this forest. They were expelled about 1760, on account of their ferocity, but have since been restored.* The following description of their habits is abridged from an article, by the Rev. W. Patrick, in the Quarterly Journal of Agriculture :—

"I am inclined to believe that the Hamilton breed of cattle is the oldest in Scotland, or perhaps in Britain. Although Lord Tankerville has said they have 'no wild habits,' I am convinced from personal observation, that this is one of their peculiar features. In browsing their extensive pasture, they always keep close together, never scattering or straggling over it, a peculiarity which does not belong to the Kyloe, or any other breed, from the wildest or most inhospitable regions of the Highlands. The white cows are also remarkable for their systematic manner of feeding. At different periods of the year their tactics are different, but by those acquainted with their habits they are always found about the same part of the forest at the same hour of the day. In the height of summer, they always bivouac for the night towards the northern extremity of the forest; from this point they start in the morning, and browse to the southern extremity, and return at sunset to their old rendezvous; and during these perambulations they always feed *en masse.*

"The bulls are seldom ill-natured, but when they are so, they display a disposition more than ordinarily savage, cunning, pertinacious, and revengeful. A poor bird-catcher, when exercising his vocation among the 'Old Oaks,' as the park is familiarly called, chanced to be attacked by a savage bull. By great exertion he gained a tree before his assailant made up to him. Here he had occasion to observe the habits of the animal. It did not roar or bellow, but

SCOTTISH WILD OX.

* See notes to the ballad of Cadyow Castle, in the Border Minstrelsy.

merely grunted, the whole body quivered with passion and savage rage, and he frequently attacked the tree with his head and hoofs. Finding all to no purpose, he left off the vain attempt, began to browse, and removed to some distance from the tree. The bird-catcher tried to descend, but this watchful Cerberus was again instantly at his post, and it was not till after six hours' imprisonment, and various bouts at 'bo-peep' as above, that the unfortunate man was relieved by some shepherds with their dogs. A writer's apprentice, who had been at the village of Quarter on business, and who returned by the 'Oaks' as a 'near-hand cut,' was also attacked by one of these savage brutes, near the northern extremity of the forest. He was fortunate, however, in getting up a tree, but was watched by the bull, and kept there during the whole of the night, and till near two o'clock next day.

"These animals are never taken and killed like other cattle, but are always shot in the field. I once went to see a bull and some cows destroyed in this manner—not by any means for the sake of the sight—but to observe the manner and habits of the animal under peculiar circumstances. When the shooters approached, they, as usual, scampered off in a body, then stood still, tossed their heads on high, and seemed to snuff the wind; the manœuvre was often repeated, till they got so hard pressed, (and seemingly having a sort of half-idea of the tragedy which was to be performed,) they at length ran furiously in a mass, always preferring the sides of the fence and sheltered situations, and dexterously taking advantage of any inequality in the ground, or other circumstances, to conceal themselves from the assailing foe. In their flight, the bulls, or stronger of the flock, always took the lead; a smoke ascended from them which could be seen at a great distance; and they were often so close together, like sheep, that a carpet would have covered them. The cows which had young, on the first 'tug of war,' all retreated to the thickets where their calves were concealed; from prudential motives, they are never, if possible, molested. These and other wild habits I can testify to be inherent in the race, and are well known to all who have an opportunity of acquainting themselves with them."

Sir Walter Scott has made Cadyow Castle the subject of the following magnificent ballad, the perusal of which must gratify every lover of poetry and of historical recollections :—

" 'Tis night—the shade of keep and spire
  Obscurely dance on Evan's stream;
And on the wave the warder's fire
  Is chequering the moonlight beam.

Fades slow their light; the east is grey:
  The weary warder leaves his tower;
Steeds snort; uncoupled stag-hounds bay,
  And merry hunters quit the bower.

The draw-bridge falls—they hurry out—
  Clatters each plank and swinging chain,
As, dashing o'er, the jovial rout
  Urge the shy steed, and slack the rein.

First of his troop, the chief rode on;
  His shouting merry-men throng behind;
The steed of princely Hamilton
  Was fleeter than the mountain wind.

From

From the thick copse the roe-bucks bound,
  The startled red-deer scuds the plain,
For the hoarse bugle's warrior-sound
  Has roused their mountain haunts again.

Through the huge oaks of Evandale,
  Whose limbs a thousand years have worn,
What sullen roar comes down the gale,
  And drowns the hunter's pealing horn ?

Mightiest of all the beasts of chase,
  That roam in woody Caledon,
Crashing the forest in his race,
  The Mountain Bull comes thundering on !

Fierce, on the hunter's quiver'd band,
  He rolls his eyes of swarthy glow,
Spurns, with black hoof and horn, the sand,
  And tosses high his mane of snow.

Aim'd well, the chieftain's lance has flown ;
  Struggling in blood, the savage lies ;
His roar is sunk in hollow groan—
  Sound, merry huntsmen ! sound the *pryse!* [*]

'Tis noon—against the knotted oak
  The hunters rest the idle spear ;
Curls through the trees the slender smoke,
  Where yeomen dight the woodland cheer.

Proudly the chieftain mark'd his clan,
  On greenwood lap all careless thrown,
Yet miss'd his eye the boldest man,
  That bore the name of Hamilton.

' Why fills not Bothwellhaugh his place,
  Still wont our weal and woe to share ?
Why comes he not our sport to grace ?
  Why shares he not our hunter's fare ? '—

Stern Claud replied, with darkening face,
  (Grey Paisley's haughty lord was he,)
' At merry feast, or buxom chase,
  No more the warrior wilt thou see.

' Few suns have set since Woodhouselee
  Saw Bothwellhaugh's bright goblets foam,
When to his hearth, in social glee,
  The war-worn soldier turn'd him home.

' There, wan from her maternal throes,
  His Margaret, beautiful and mild,
Sate in her bower, a pallid rose,
  And peaceful nursed her new-born child.

' O change accursed ! past are those days ;
  False Murray's ruthless spoilers came,
And, for the hearth's domestic blaze,
  Ascends destruction's volumed flame.

' What sheeted phantom wanders wild,
  Where mountain Eske through woodland
Her arms enfold a shadowy child— [flows,
  Oh, is it she, the pallid rose ?

' The wilder'd traveller sees her glide,
  And hears her feeble voice with awe—
" Revenge," she cries, " on Murray's pride !
  And woe for injured Bothwellhaugh ! " '

He ceased—and cries of rage and grief
  Burst mingling from the kindred band,
And half arose the kindling chief,
  And half unsheathed his Arran brand.

But who, o'er bush, o'er stream and rock,
  Rides headlong with resistless speed,
Whose bloody poniard's frantic stroke
  Drives to the leap his jaded steed ?

Whose cheek is pale, whose eye-balls glare,
  As one some vision'd sight that saw ;
Whose hands are bloody, loose his hair ?—
  'Tis he ! 'tis he ! 'tis Bothwellhaugh !

From gory selle [†] and reeling steed
  Sprung the fierce horseman with a bound,
And, reeking from the recent deed,
  He dash'd his carbine on the ground.

Sternly he spoke—' 'Tis sweet to hear
  In good greenwood the bugle blown,
But sweeter to Revenge's ear
  To drink a tyrant's dying groan.

' Your slaughter'd quarry proudly trode,
  At dawning morn, o'er dale and down,
But prouder base-born Murray rode
  Through old Linlithgow's crowded town

' From the wild Border's humbled side
  In haughty triumph marched he,
While Knox relax'd his bigot pride,
  And smiled the traitorous pomp to see.

' But can stern Power, with all his vaunt,
  Or Pomp, with all her courtly glare,
The settled heart of Vengeance daunt,
  Or change the purpose of Despair ?

' With hackbut bent,[‡] my secret stand,
  Dark as the purposed deed, I chose,
And mark'd, where, mingling in his band,
  Troop'd Scottish pikes, and English bows.

' Dark Morton, girt with many a spear,
  Murder's foul minion, led the van ;
And clash'd their broad-swords in the rear
  The wild Macfarlanes' plaided clan.

' Glencairn and stout Parkhead were nigh,
  Obsequious at their regent's rein,
And haggard Lindesay's iron eye,
  That saw fair Mary weep in vain.

' Mid pennon'd spears, a steely grove,
  Proud Murray's plumage floated high ;
Scarce could his trampling charger move,
  So close the minions crowded nigh.

' From the raised visor's shade his eye,
  Dark-rolling, glanced the ranks along,
And his steel truncheon, waved on high,
  Seem'd marshalling the iron throng.

' But yet his sudden'd brow confess'd
  A passing shade of doubt and awe ;
Some fiend was whispering in his breast,
  " Beware of injured Bothwellhaugh ! "

                                           ' The

---

[*] The note blown at the death of the game.
[†] Saddle. A word used by Spenser, and other ancient authors.   [‡] Gun cocked.

> The death-shot parts—the charger springs—
> Wild rises tumult's startling roar !
> And Murray's plumy helmet rings—
> Rings on the ground to rise no more.
>
> ' What joy the raptured youth can feel,
> To hear her love the loved one tell,—
> Or he who broaches on his steel
> The wolf, by whom his infant fell !
>
> ' But dearer to my injured eye,
> To see in dust proud Murray roll ;
> And mine was ten times treble joy
> To hear him groan his felon soul.

> ' My Margaret's spectre glided near :
> With pride her bleeding victim saw ;
> And shriek'd in his death-deafen'd ear,
> " Remember injured Bothwellhaugh ! "
>
> ' Then speed thee, noble Chaterherault !
> Spread to the wind thy banner'd tree !
> Each warrior bend his Clydesdale bow—
> Murray is fallen, and Scotland free.'
>
> Vaults every warrior to his steed ;
> Loud bugles join their wild acclaim—
> ' Murray is fallen, and Scotland freed !
> Couch Arran ! couch thy spear of flame ! ' "

Opposite Cadyow is Chatelherault, built by the Duke of
Hamilton, without regard to interior comfort, as a representation of the beautiful edifice on the so called estate and
dukedom in France, anciently possessed by his Grace's
ancestors.*

Leaving Hamilton, the tourist proceeds in a south-
easterly direction, and, at the distance of half a mile,
crosses the Avon. On the opposite bank of the Clyde is
Dalziel House, (General Hamilton,) surrounded by fine
plantations, giving an imposing effect to the landscape.
The views now obtained of the river and the surrounding
scenery are extremely fine. About a mile beyond Avon
Bridge, the road strikes off the Carlisle road, leading towards Douglasdale, and gradually descending towards the
margin of the river. On the opposite bank is Cumbus-
nethan, (R. Lockhart, Esq.,) a fine castellated mansion,
seated on a beautiful lawn, partly shaded by splendid lime
trees. This district, which has earned the name of " The
Orchard of Scotland," or "The Fruit Lands," is eminently
worthy of its appellation, presenting, as it does, " one un-
interrupted series of grove, garden, and orchard—a bil-
lowy ocean of foliage, waving in the summer wind, and
glowing under the summer sun." During spring, the luxuriance of the blossom, and during autumn, the teeming
abundance of the fruit, contribute to render this one of the
most delightful drives in Scotland. Six miles from Hamil-

* The banks of the south Calder, which lie at no great distance from Hamilton,
are extremely romantic, and adorned with a number of fine seats, the most
remarkable of which are Wishaw Castle, (Lord Belhaven,) Coltness, (Henry
Holdsworth, Esq.,) Murdieston, (Admiral Sir A. Inglis Cochrane,) Allanton,
(Sir Henry Steuart, Bart.) &c.

ton, the Edinburgh road to Ayr crosses the Clyde at Garrion Bridge, which derives its name from a seat of Lord Belhaven's, in the immediate vicinity. A mile beyond, is the delightful bower-like village of Dalserf, celebrated for its excellent orchards. On the left is Dalserf House, (Lieut. Campbell,) and, on the right, Millburn House, (Watkins, Esq.) On the opposite bank of the river is Brownlee, (Harvie, Esq.,) and the stately mansion of Mauldslie Castle, the seat of the last Earl of Hyndford.* A little farther on is Milton-Lockhart, (Captain Lockhart, M.P.,) a handsome edifice in the Tudor style, standing on a fine promontory, with delightful sloping banks and gardens ; and Waygateshaw, (Steel, Esq.,) once the residence of the notorious Major Weir and his sister, condemned for witchcraft in the seventeenth century. Two miles and a half beyond Dalserf, the tourist crosses the river Nethan, at Nethanfoot, by a bridge. On the right, near the junction of the Nethan and the Clyde, are the ruins of the Castle of Craignethan, or Draphane, situated on a single rock, overhanging the former stream. Craignethan appears to have been, at one time, a most extensive and important fortress. It was the seat of Sir James Hamilton, called the Bastard of Arran, a man noted for his sanguinary character, in the reign of James V. ; and here Queen Mary lodged for a few days, after her escape from Lochleven. Craignethan has furnished the author of "Old Mortality" with his description of Tillietudlem.† It is now the property of Lord Douglas. The scenery around the castle exhibits a striking mixture of the sublime and beautiful. A short way beyond, on the north bank of the river is Carfin House, (Nisbet, Esq.,) and, soon after, the road enters the plantations of Stonebyres, (Monteith, Esq.) The channel of the river now

* Robert Bruce granted ten merks sterling out of his mills at Mauldslie for the purpose of keeping a lamp constantly burning upon St. Machute's tomb at Lesmahagow. The lamp was kept burning till the Reformation.

† "One morning, during his visit to Bothwell, was spent on an excursion to the ruins of Craignethan Castle, when the poet expressed such rapture with the scenery, that his hosts urged him to accept, for his lifetime, the use of a small habitable house, enclosed within the circuit of the ancient walls."—Lockhart's Life of Scott, v. i., p. 307.

becomes rugged and confined, and the banks more precipitous ; and, in a short time, the tourist reaches THE FALL
OF STONEBYRES, the first of

THE FALLS OF THE CLYDE,

in approaching from the west.*. The river here makes
three distinct falls, being broken by two projecting rocks.
The scene is uncommonly magnificent.†

Passing, on the left, Sunnyside Lodge, (A. Gillespie, Esq.,)
and, on the right, Kirkfield, (Steel, Esq.,) and other elegant
villas, the tourist, at the distance of a mile from the fall of
Stonebyres, crosses the Clyde by an ancient bridge of three
arches, and soon after reaches

LANARK,‡

a royal burgh, and the county town of Lanarkshire, situated
at the distance of twenty-five miles from Glasgow, and
thirty-two from Edinburgh. The population of the burgh
at last census was 4818. Lanark is a town of no great
importance in itself ; till lately, it was extremely dull, but
the extension of the cotton-works in its neighbourhood,

---

* The approach is by a path laid out by the well known Robert Owen.

† An interesting spectacle is afforded by the efforts of the salmon, during the
spawning season, to surmount this obstacle to their further progress. It is
scarcely necessary to say that these efforts are quite unavailing.

‡ It is said that the burgh of Lanark was till very recent times so poor that
the single butcher of the town, who also exercised the calling of a weaver. in
order to fill up his spare time, would never venture upon the speculation of killing
a sheep till every part of the animal was ordered beforehand. When he felt
disposed to engage in such an enterprise, he usually prevailed upon the minister,
the provost, and the town-council to take shares ! but when no person came
forward to bespeak the fourth quarter, the sheep received a respite till better
times should cast up. The bellman or *skellyman*, as he is there called, used often
to go through the streets of Lanark with advertisements such as are embodied
in the following popular rhyme :—

> Bell-ell-ell !
> There's a fat sheep to kill !
> A leg for the provost,
>   Another for the priest,
> The bailies and deacons
>   They'll tak the neist ;
> And if the fourth leg we cannot sell,
> The sheep it maun leeve and gae back to the hill !
>   CHAMBERS' *Rhymes of Scotland*, p. 140.

and t
consi
to the
for st
inn, t
tion,
in La
glori
and
nity,
the l
to tl
A
the
by
T
hoo
Ho
the
l
sh
L
it,
R
b
it
d
o
tl
a

e
t
w
y
c
t
n
c
e

!

and the erection of several good public buildings, have considerably improved its appearance ; while its vicinity to the Falls of Clyde, makes it a favourite place of resort for strangers during the summer months. The principal inn, the Clydesdale Hotel, is equal, in point of accommodation, to any provincial establishment in Scotland. It was in Lanark that the Scottish hero Wallace commenced his glorious exertions to free his country from a foreign yoke, and tradition points out a number of localities in the vicinity, identified with his name and exploits.* A statue of the hero is placed in a niche, above the principal entrance to the parish church.

About a quarter of a mile to the east of the town, are the ruins of the very ancient church of Lanark, surrounded by the parish burying-ground.

There are a number of handsome seats in the neighbourhood of Lanark, the most splendid of which are Carstairs House, the seat of Henry Monteith, Esq., and Lee House, the seat of Sir Norman Macdonald Lockhart, Bart.

In visiting the Falls of Clyde from Lanark, the tourist should at once proceed to the uppermost, called BONNINGTON LINN, two miles from Lanark. A romantic path leads to it, through the grounds of Bonnington House, (Sir Charles Ross.) Above this cataract the river moves very slowly, but all at once it bends towards the north-east, and throws itself over a perpendicular rock of about thirty feet, into a deep hollow or basin. A dense mist continually hovers over this boiling caldron. Immediately below the first fall, the river hurries along with prodigious rapidity, boiling and foaming over its narrow and rocky channel. The banks

---

* Here "Wallace had many frays with Englishmen; but his first serious exploit, according to the Minstrel and general historical tradition, was the killing of young Selby, the son of the English constable of Dundee. Wallace was walking along the street, sprucely dressed in green, when Selby, a swaggering youth, came up to him with three or four companions. 'Abide, Scot,' he cried ; 'who grathed you, I would like to know, in so gay a weed ; an Irish cloak on your back, a Scots whittle in your belt, and rough rulzions on your feet, were fitter for your kind to wear. I will have that knife from you.' He made a step as if to take the knife, when Wallace drew it, grasped him by the collar, and ran it into him. Ere he could be seized by Selby's companions he escaped."—*Lowe's Edinburgh Magazine,* vol. i.

are very steep, and, at one point, the river struggles through
a chasm of not more than four feet, where it may be stepped
over.   Half a mile below Bonnington Linn is CORRA LINN,
the grandest of the falls, where the river takes three distinct leaps, making altogether a height of about eighty-four
feet.   The best view of this magnificent fall, is from the
semicircular seat on the verge of the cliff opposite.   There
is also a rustic staircase, leading to the bottom of the Falls,
partly formed of wood, and partly cut out of the solid rock,
from which the cataract has a very magnificent effect.
Above is a pavilion, erected in 1708, by Sir James Car-
michael, then of Bonnington, which commands a fine view,
and which is fitted up with mirrors, so arranged as to give
the cataract the appearance of being precipitated upon the
spectator.   Upon a rock above the fall, on the opposite side
of the river, is the old Castle of Cora ; and, to the right of
this castle, is Cora House, the seat of George Cranstoun,
Esq., half hid by trees.

About half a mile below Corra Linn is the celebrated
village of New Lanark, originally established in the year
1783 by the benevolent David Dale of Glasgow, father-in-
law of Robert Owen.   The inhabitants, who amount to
about 2500, are exclusively engaged in cotton-spinning.

In Bonnington House are preserved two relics of Sir
William Wallace, a portrait of the hero, and a very curious
chair on which he is said to have sat.

No traveller should leave this district without visiting
Cartland Crags on Mouse Water, about a mile west from
Lanark.   The stream flows through a deep chasm, apparently formed by an earthquake, instead of following what
seems a much more natural channel a little farther to the
east.   The rocky banks on both sides rise to the height of
about 400 feet.   A few years ago a bridge was thrown
across this narrow chasm, consisting of three arches of the
height of 128 feet.   At a little distance below is a narrow
old bridge, supposed to be of Roman origin.   On the north
side of the stream, a few yards above the new bridge, is a
cave in the face of the rock, termed "Wallace's Cave,"

which is pointed out by tradition as the hiding-place of that hero after he had slain Haselrig the English Sheriff.

About a mile and a half westward from Lanark, on the south side of the Mouse, is the ancient house of Jerviswood, the seat of the illustrious patriot who was murdered under the forms of law during the infamous government of Charles II. The attainder of Jerviswood was reversed by the Convention Parliament at the Revolution. On the opposite bank of the stream, situated amidst extensive plantations, is Cleghorn, the seat of Allan Elliot Lockhart, Esq., of Borthwickbrae.

About three miles below Lanark, on the north bank of the Clyde, is Lee House, the seat of Sir Norman Macdonald Lockhart, Bart. It is a fine mansion, lately modernized in the castellated style, and contains a good collection of pictures. Here is kept the famous Lee Penny, the use made of which by Sir Walter Scott, in his splendid tale of " The Talisman," must be familiar to every reader. The following curious extract is given in a note to that tale :—

" Quhilk day, amongst the referries of the Brethren of the Ministry of Lanark, it was proponed to the Synod that Gavin Hamilton of Raploch had pursueit an Complaint before them against Sir James Lockhart of Lee, anent the superstitious using of an Stone, set in silver, for the curing of deseased Cattle, q^{lk} the said Gavin affirmed could not be lawfully usit, and that they had deferrit to give ony decisioune thairin till the advice of the Assemblie might be had concerning the same. The Assemblie having inquirit of the manner of using thereof, and particularly understood, be examination of the said Laird of Lee, and otherwise, that the custom is only to cast the stone in some water, and give the deceasit Cattle thereof to drink, and that the same is done without using any words, such as Charmers and Sorcerers use in their unlawful practices ; and considering that in nature thair are many things seen to work strange effects, whereof no human wit can give a reason, it having pleast God to give to stones and herbs a speciall vertue for healing of many infirmities in man and beast, advises the Brethren to surcease thair process, as therein they perceive no ground of Offence, and admonishes the said Laird of Lee, in using of the said stone, to take heid that it be usit hereafter with the least scandal that possibly maybe. Extract out of the Books of the Assemblie, holden at Glasgow, and subscribed at their command. —M. ROBERT YOUNG, Clerk to the Assemblie at Glasgow."

In the grounds of Lee there is a huge oak tree, which is
so completely hollowed out by age that it can hold half a
dozen individuals standing upright.

The tourist may proceed from Lanark to Edinburgh (32
miles) by West Calder, Calder House, (Lord Torphichen,)
Mid-Calder, Dalmahoy, (Earl of Morton,) &c. For a description of this route see Itinerary.

EIGHTH TOUR.

₊ There are two sets of steamers which ply down the Clyde; both proceed,
in the same way to Gourock. From Gourock, the one keeps the left side and
continues its route by way of Largs and Millport to Arran or Ardrossan, the
other takes the right side by way of Dunoon to Rothesay and Lochgilphead.
This division is therefore adopted in the present route.

The steamers for Largs and Millport, Dunoon and Rothesay, sail from Glasgow almost every hour during the summer months, but those which continue
their course *all the way* either to Arran, Ardrossan, or Lochgilphead, not oftener
than once every day.

A chart of this Tour will be found facing page 232, and an Itinerary of the
Glasgow and Greenock Railway, of which the tourist may perhaps avail himself,
at the end of the volume.

GLASGOW—DUMBARTON—PORT-GLASGOW—HELENSBURGH—
GREENOCK.
I. GOUROCK—LARGS—MILLPORT—ARRAN—ARDROSSAN.
II. GOUROCK—DUNOON—ROTHESAY—LOCHGILPHEAD—OBAN.

STARTING from Broomielaw in one of the steamboats which
ply on the river, a few minutes' sail brings the passengers
to the mouth of the Kelvin, a stream celebrated in Scottish
song. The village on the left is Govan. On both sides of
the river there is a series of pleasant suburban villas.
About two miles below Govan, on the same side of the river,
is Shieldhall, A. Johnston, Esq. On the right, Jordanhill,
James Smith, Esq. A little farther down the river, and on

the same side, is Scotstoun, the seat of Miss Oswald. On
the left is Elderslie House, the seat of Archibald Speirs,
Esq.; and about a mile farther down is Blythswood House,
the seat of Archibald Campbell, Esq. Between the two last
mentioned places is Renfrew Ferry, where a near view may
be obtained of the ancient burgh of Renfrew. The appearance of the town is mean and antiquated. In the neighbourhood, Somerled, Thane of Argyle and Lord of the Isles,
who had rebelled against Malcolm IV., was defeated and
slain in the year 1164. The barony of Renfrew was the
first possession of the Stuart family in Scotland. It gives
the title of Baron to the Prince of Wales. The collected
waters of the two Carts and the Gryfe flow into the Clyde
at Inchinnan, about a mile below Renfrew. Near Inchinnan
Bridge, the Earl of Argyle was taken prisoner in 1685. On
the left, near the river, is the old mansion-house of Erskine,
anciently the seat of the Earls of Mar, and latterly of the
Blantyre family. Robert, eleventh Lord Blantyre, who
perished accidentally in the commotions at Brussels, in
1830, erected the new princely mansion which crowns the
rising ground a little farther down. The tourist is now
half-way between Glasgow and Greenock. The river has
expanded greatly, and assumed the appearance of a lake,
apparently closed in front. The lofty heights on the right
are the Kilpatrick Hills, and the village in the narrow
plain between them and the river is Kilpatrick, supposed
to have been the birth-place of St. Patrick, the tutelar
saint of Ireland. The little bay in front of Kilpatrick is
Bowling Bay. Near Bowling Inn may be perceived the
mouth of the Great Junction Canal, which unites the east
and west coasts of Scotland, by means of the Firths of Forth
and Clyde. At a short distance below, on the right, is the
little promontory of Dunglass Point, the western termination of Antoninus' Wall or Graham's Dyke, with the ruins
of Dunglass Castle, formerly the property of the Colquhouns
of Luss, but now belonging to Buchanan of Auchintorlie.
On this spot, a monument has lately been erected to the
late Henry Bell, who introduced steam-navigation on the
Clyde. On the left, in the distance, are seen the church

Q

and manse of Erskine ; Bishopton House, (Lord Blantyre) ; Drums, (Captain Darroch.) On the opposite side are Milton Island, Milton House, and Printworks, (Mitchell, Esq.) ; Dumbuck House, (Colonel Geils) ; at the foot of Dumbuck Hill (*Hill of Roes*) Garshake, (Dixon, Esq.,) ; Chapel Green and Silverton Hill. But by far the most prominent object is the rock of

DUMBARTON,

which rises suddenly from the point of junction of the Leven and Clyde, to the height of 560 feet, measuring a mile in circumference, terminating in two sharp points, one higher than the other, and studded over with houses and batteries. Previous to his being sent to England, Wallace was confined for some time in this castle, the governor of which was the infamous Sir John Menteith, who betrayed him. The highest peak of the rock is still denominated " Wallace's Seat," and a part of the castle " Wallace's Tower." In one of the apartments, a huge two-handed sword said to have belonged to that hero, is still shown. At the union of Scotland with England, this was one of the four fortresses stipulated to be kept up ; and, accordingly, it is still in repair, and occupied by a garrison.* Opposite

---

* During the wars which desolated Scotland in the reign of Queen Mary, this formidable fortress was taken in the following remarkable way, by Captain Crawford of Jordanhill, a distinguished adherent of the King's party :—" He took advantage of a misty and moonless night to bring to the foot of the castle-rock, the scaling ladders which he had provided, choosing for his terrible experiment the place where the rock was highest, and where, of course, less pains were taken to keep a regular guard. This choice was fortunate ; for the first ladder broke with the weight of the men who attempted to mount, and the noise of the fall must have betrayed them, had there been any sentinel within hearing. Crawford assisted by a soldier who had deserted from the castle and was acting as his guide, renewed the attempt in person, and having scrambled up to a projecting ledge of rock where there was some footing, contrived to make fast the ladder, by tying it to the roots of a tree, which grew about midway up the rock. Here they found a small flat surface, sufficient, however, to afford footing to the whole party, which was, of course, very few in number. In scaling the second precipice, another accident took place :—One of the party, subject to epileptic fits, was seized by one of these attacks, brought on perhaps by terror while he was in the act of climbing up the ladder. His illness made it impossible for him either to ascend or descend. To have slain the man would have been a cruel expedient, besides that the fall of his body from the ladder

to Dumbarton Castle, on the left is West Sea Bank; and beyond the Leven, on the right, is Leven Grove, the seat of the Dixons of Dumbarton. Two miles farther, on the left, is Finlayston, formerly the family mansion of the Earls of Glencairn, now the seat of Graham of Gartmore; on the right, are Clyde Bank and Clyde Cottage. Approaching Port-Glasgow, we reach the Castle of Newark, which, after having belonged, in succession, to a branch of the Maxwells and to the Belhaven family, is now the property of Lady Shaw Stewart. PORT-GLASGOW was founded in 1668, by the merchants of Glasgow, for the embarkation and disembarkation of goods; but since the river was deepened, its importance has much declined. On the opposite shore of the Clyde are the remains of an ancient castle, believed to have been that of Cardross, in which Robert Bruce breathed his last. For several miles the shore is thickly studded with villas, among which are Ardarden House, Ardmore House, Camis-Eskan, Kilmahew Castle, and Drumfork House, all on the right side of the Firth. Three and a half miles from Dumbarton is the Kirk of Cardross, with its little attendant village. Five miles further along the shore, the beautiful sea-bathing village of HELENSBURGH occupies a sheltered situation at the opening of the Gare Loch. It was founded about fifty years ago by Sir James Colquhoun. A mile to the westward is the pleasant inn of Ardincaple; and a mile and a half further are the village and kirk of Row, which is the parish church of Helensburgh. The promontory opposite to Helensburgh, between the Gare Loch and Loch Long, is occupied by the mansion and beautiful grounds of Rosneath, a seat of the Argyle family. This palace, built in the Italian style, occupies the site of a fine old castle, which was burnt down in 1802. After a sail from Glasgow of about two hours and a half, the steamer reaches the large and populous seaport of

might have alarmed the garrison. Crawford caused him, therefore, to be tied to the ladder; then all the rest descending, they turned the ladder, and thus mounted with ease over the belly of the epileptic person. When the party gained the summit they slew the sentinel ere he had time to give the alarm, and easily surprised the slumbering garrison, who had trusted too much to the security of their castle to keep good watch. This exploit of Crawford may compare with any thing of the kind which we read of in history."

GREENOCK,

which occupies a narrow stripe of level ground stretching along the shore, while streets extend over the rising
ground behind. Close upon the quay stands the Custom-
house, an elegant and commodious building.   There are also
several fine buildings towards the west end of the town.

The situation of Greenock, with the mountains of Argyleshire and Dumbartonshire rising on the opposite side, is
very fine.   Whin-hill, the rising ground at the back of the
town, commands a noble prospect, and the view from the
quay is perhaps the finest commanded by any seaport in the
kingdom.   In the admirably managed factory of the Shaws-
water Cotton Spinning Company, is the largest water-wheel
in Britain, measuring 70 feet in diameter. Its majestic
revolutions are fitted to impress the spectator with feelings
of admiration and awe.   This town was the birth-place of
Watt ; its population in 1841 was 36,936.   Leaving Greenock, the steamer makes direct for Kempock Point, passing

many villas on the shore, the residences of the merchants and other inhabitants of the town. About three miles below Greenock, occupying both sides of Kempock Point, is situated the pretty village of GOUROCK. It commands a noble sea-view, and the walks along the shore towards the Cloch are very beautiful.

I. GOUROCK—LARGS—MILLPORT—ARRAN—AND ARDROSSAN.*

About a quarter of a mile off shore, the Comet steamboat was run down by the Ayr steampacket, October 21, 1825, when upwards of fifty individuals found a watery grave. Two miles further along this coast, is the old ruin of Leven Tower, crowning a fine eminence. About three miles below Gourock, the coast bends to the south at the Cloch Light-house, one of the most important beacons on the Clyde. A little below stands Ardgowan, the seat of Sir R. M. Shaw Stewart, Bart. A short way farther on, at the bottom of a small bay, is the little sequestered village of Innerkip, one of the most delightful watering-places on the west coast. Two miles farther on is Kelly House, the seat of Robert Wallace, Esq. M.P. The counties of Renfrew and Ayr are here divided by Kellyburn. About a mile and a half further on is Skelmorlie Castle, a seat of the Earl of Eglinton. The next promontory is Knock Point, on rounding which we pass Brisbane House (Sir T. M°D. Brisbane,) and come in sight of the beautiful picturesque village of Largs. The battle of Largs, between the Scottish army and that of Haco, King of Norway, in which the latter was defeated with great slaughter, took place in 1263, on a large plain upon the seashore to the south of the village. Steering between the Gt. Cumbray island and the mainland, the steamer passes, at a short distance from Largs, Kelburne Castle, (Lord Kelburne) embosomed in trees, and two or three miles further on, halts at the sequestered village of Fairlie, from which it crosses to Millport, a beautiful sea-bathing village

* For the continuation of the route from Gourock to Rothesay and Lochgilp-head, see page 262.

lying in a sheltered bay at the south-east corner of the Great Cumbray Island.*

TOUR ROUND ARRAN.

Passing between the southern point of the Island of Bute, and the Little Cumbray,† the towering heights of Arran burst upon the view. Presenting their full dimensions from the shore to their summits, and being congregated together in one stupendous group, few scenes can be more magnificent and impressive than these mountains. " Many are bare precipices from their very foundations ; and the greater number raise their naked tops to the sky in stupendous pyramids and spires of rough granite, appearing to the beholder as if they had but yesterday been upheaved from their primitive beds, below the bottom of the ocean.' ‡

The steamer makes a halt at Corrie, a small village which derives its name from the remarkable corrie or valley on the hill immediately behind it ; and while it skirts along the shores of the island, which teem with the picturesque and beautiful, the tourist is favoured with

---

* From Millport, another steamer leaving Glasgow at a different hour, proceeds to Ardrossan. Sailing between the Little Cumbray and the coast of Ayr, it passes Hunterston (Robert Hunter, Esq.,) and about four miles further on, reaches the ruins of Portincross Castle, situated on the edge of a rocky promontory called Fairlie Head. This castle is said to have been used as a temporary residence by the first Stewart Kings, on their way to Brodick in Arran, and Dundonald in Kyle. Its situation is singularly wild and picturesque, and the view it commands, in which the island of Arran forms the most striking feature, is beautifully varied and extensive. On doubling Fairlie Head, and keeping the coast for about five miles, we reach the seaport town of Ardrossan. Of late years the streets have been laid out on a regular plan, with commodious buildings, and it is now a regular sea-bathing resort. Excellent baths have been constructed, which attract a number of visitors, and there is one expressly for the use of the poor, for which no charge is made. It has a safe and spacious harbour, and a population of about 3500. From Ardrossan there is a daily steamer to Arran, during the summer months, and the railway affords the tourist an opportunity of reaching Ayr, or of returning to Glasgow, in a short space of time.

† " Where Cumbray's isles with verdant link
       Close the fair entrance of the Clyde ;
       The woods of Bute, no more descried,
       Are gone."
                          (LORD OF THE ISLES, *Canto V.*)
‡ *Statistical account of Scotland.*

an advantageous view of Goatfell from the sea, although from the similarity of contour in many of the surrounding peaks, it is not, at first sight, so easily distinguished. The steamer now rounds Merkland Point, and enters the beautiful bay of Brodick, where tourists generally disembark. There is a comfortable little inn at the village, where guides may be engaged for ascending Goatfell, and vehicles for visiting the places of interest throughout the island.

Arran forms part of the county of Bute, is 20 miles in length, by from 8 to 11 in breadth, and contains a superficial area of 165 square miles, or 105,814 acres, of which about 14,431 are cultivated. With the exception of a few farms, the whole island belongs to the Duke of Hamilton. Its population in 1841 was 6181.

The island is chiefly distinguished for its geological interest and the beauty of its scenery. " Although," observes Dr. Macculloch, " in every sense, a hilly island, its character is in this respect unequal, and in the northern and southern halves strongly contrasted. The high and serrated forms of the northern division are peculiarly striking ; presenting a rugged mountainous character unequalled in Scotland, except by the Cuchullin hills in Skye. These mountains are also exceedingly elegant in their outline ; and though not attaining to quite 3000 feet of elevation, yet, from their independence, and from their rising immediately out of the sea, their alpine effect is equalled by that of very few mountainous tracts in Scotland, of even much greater altitude. The southern hilly division is a tame undulating land without features, and there are not many parts which are strictly level, except in the Machrie Glen, on the west side, and on the shores of Brodick Bay. Though the shores are generally rocky, and commonly steep, they rarely rise into cliffs; but in most places the hills spring at once from the sea, leaving, however, a narrow belt of flat and green land in many places, which forms a natural road of communication nearly all round the island, agreeable, alike for its beauty, and for the access it affords to the various picturesque scenes of the island, which are chiefly found on its sea margin."

The scenery about Glen Sannox, extending southwards to the two bays of Brodick and Lamlash, is that which will chiefly engage the attention of the traveller. Its characteristic features are beautifully described by Sir Walter Scott, in the " Lord of the Isles," when Father Augustine is sent by Lord Douglas with a message to Bruce from Lochranza, " across the hills to Brodick Bay."

> " Through birchen copse he wander'd slow,
> Stunted and sapless, thin and low ;
> By many a mountain stream he pass'd,
> From the tall cliffs in tumult cast,
> Dashing to foam their waters dun,
> And sparkling in the summer's sun,

Round his grey head the wild curlew
In many a fearless circle flew.
O'er chasms he passed where fractures wide
Crav'd wary eye and ample stride ;
He cross'd his brow beside the stone,*
Where Druids erst heard victims groan,
And at the cairns upon the wild,
O'er many a heathen hero piled."

There are only four roads in Arran. The first makes the circuit of the island, the second cuts through its centre from Blackwater foot to Brodick, the third crosses its southerly part from Bein na Carrigan to Lamlash, and the fourth connects the latter two together from Glen Scoradail to Clachan Glen. Confining ourselves to the first of these, we shall continue the route round the island, diverging only occasionally from the beaten track, when any object sufficiently attractive, either inland or to the sea-shore, shall induce us to do so.

From its situation, and the many objects of interest and beauty in its immediate vicinity, we shall commence with Brodick Bay, a beautifully curved plain, girt with a beach of sand and ornamented with neat cottages and villas, flourishing plantations, and cultivated fields, which, as they retire inwards, are met by the wildly contrasting valleys of Glenrosa, Glensheraig, and Glencloy. To the north is Brodick Castle, while Goatfell rises majestic in the rear.

Brodick Castle, beautifully situated on an eminence surrounded by waving plantations, remained in ruins until the year 1845, when its noble proprietor, the Duke of Hamilton, completed, with great good taste, its reconstruction on the model of the ancient fortress. At the time of the memorable interregnum when Edward I. was endeavouring to crush the spirited efforts of Wallace and Bruce for the independence of their country, it was taken and held by the English under Sir John Hastings. It did not, however, remain long in their possession ; " for James, Lord Douglas, who accompanied Bruce to his retreat in Rachrin, seems in the spring of 1306 to have tired of his abode there, and set out accordingly, in the phrase of the times, to see what adventure God would send him. Sir Robert Boyd accompanied him ; and his knowledge of the localities of Arran appears to have directed his course thither. They landed in the island privately, and appear to have laid an ambush for Sir John Hastings, the English Governor of Brodick, and surprised a considerable supply of arms and provisions, and nearly took the castle itself. . . . . When they were

---

* "The Isle of Arran, like those of Man and Anglesea, abounds with many relics of heathen, or probably Druidical superstition. There are high erect columns of unhewn stone, the most early of all monuments, the circles of rude stones, commonly entitled Druidical, and the cairns or sepulchral piles, within which are usually found urns enclosing ashes.

joined by Bruce, it seems probable that they had gained Brodick Castle. At least tradition says that from the battlements of the tower he saw the supposed signal fire on Turnberry nook."*

After the settlement of the Scottish crown by Bruce, the castle of Brodick, as well as the greater part of Arran, was the property of the High Steward of Scotland, who, by failure of male-heirs to Bruce, succeeded to the throne under the title of Robert II. In 1455, it was stormed and levelled to the ground by the Earl of Ross, who had espoused the cause of the Earl of Douglas against his sovereign. Its next possessor was Sir Thomas Boyd, a court favourite, who married King James I.'s eldest sister, who received from that monarch the earldom of Arran as her marriage dowry. On the disgrace of the Boyds, Sir Thomas was divorced from his royal spouse, and the princess's hand, with her earldom of Arran, bestowed upon Lord Hamilton, in whose hands, with the exception of a few interruptions, it has remained until this day.

Goatfell, which forms so prominent a feature in the aspect of the island, is 2959 feet high, and rises immediately behind Brodick Inn, from which a footpath, to the east of Cnocan Burn,† conducts the tourist for a considerable way upwards, to a mill-dam. Having gained this point, without descending into the valley which runs along the bottom of the principal peak, and keeping well upon the ridge to the right, the remaining part of the ascent, (which is by far the most difficult,) will be easier accomplished than by any other way. Wild though the mountain is, its ascent is by no means so difficult as it appears to be, and with the aid of a guide can be accomplished in the space of two hours. The view from the summit on a clear day, amply repays the labour of reaching it. " The jagged and spiry peaks of the surrounding mountains, the dark hollows and deep shady corries into which the rays of the sun scarcely ever penetrate, the open swelling hills beyond, the winding shores of Lochfine, and the broad Firth of Clyde studded with its peaceful and fertile islands, the rugged islands of Argyleshire, the gentle curves of the hills of the Western islands," and the blue shores of the Green Isle, " their outlines softened in the distance, form a scene of most surpassing grandeur and loveliness."‡

Deep embosomed between the lofty mountains Goatfell and Ben Noosh, lies the beautiful valley of Glenrosa, celebrated for the impressive character of its scenery. Delightful excursions can also be made to Glensheraig and Glencloy, which are both in the immediate

---

*˙ Lord of the Isles.

† The best geological route is by the bed of this stream.

‡ Ramsay's Geology of the Island of Arran, a hand-book which will be found of great use to those who wish to become practically acquainted with the geological phenomena of the island.

vicinity of Brodick. In Glencloy are the remains of an ancient fort, which tradition points out as having afforded shelter to Bruce's partisans, who had arrived in Arran before himself, while Brodick Castle was in the possession of the English ; and at the head of the glen there are also the remains of a Druidical circle.

About five miles from Brodick, in the middle of a beautiful semi-circular bay, lies the neat little village of Lamlash. Sheltered by the Holy Island—an irregular cone 900 feet high—this bay forms an excellent harbour for the accommodation of ships of all sizes, while its surrounding scenery cannot be beheld without delight by all lovers of the picturesque.

The Holy Isle was once the site of an ancient cathedral, said to have been founded by St. Molios, a disciple of St. Columba, who not considering the discipline of Iona sufficiently rigid, retired for greater seclusion, to this lonely isle, whence he carried the light of Christianity among the Pagan inhabitants of Arran. The cave in which the saint resided is still to be seen on the sea-shore. In the interior of it there is a shelf of rock said to have been his bed, and on the roof a Runic inscription, mentioning his name and office. He is said to have died at the advanced age of 120 years, at Lochranza, where he spent the latter part of his life, and where his remains still repose in the burying-ground at Clachan. Retiring behind the village of Lamlash are Glens Alaster and Meneadmar, at the head of which may be seen the remains of an ancient Druidical sepulchral cairn, measuring 200 feet in circumference. It is believed to cover the ashes of those who fell in a battle fought upon the spot, as on removing some of the stones, several stone coffins were found buried underneath. At the southerly point of the bay, about 3 miles from Lamlash, is King's-cross Point, whence Robert Bruce is said to have embarked for the coast of Carrick. On the other side of the Point is Whiting Bay, and a mile from Learg-a-Beg is the valley of Glen Ashdale, where there are two beautiful cascades, one above a hundred, the other above fifty feet high. When the stream is swelled by rains, one may pass dry between the larger cascade and the rock over which it falls.

From Learg-a-Beg, a splendid range of lofty precipices occupies the shore to the ruins of Kildonan Castle. " Like the Benan cliffs, the place is still and solitary. A rough and difficult footpath forms the only track beneath the cliffs ; and as the tourist warily winds along, he will hear no sound save the dash of the breaking waves, the shrill cries of the waterfowl, and the incessant cawing of the rooks, which float in airy circles round the verge of the overhanging cliffs."* Opposite Kildonan Castle is the small island of Pladda, with its lighthouse. About a mile further on, to the north-east of

---

* Ramsay's Geological Tour in Arran.

the farm of Auchinlew, a most picturesque waterfall called Eeiss-a-Mor dashes over a lofty precipice into a magnificent amphitheatre of perpendicular cliffs. On the north side of the road, before coming to Benan, a stream descends in a fine cascade from a ravine above, to the depth of about seventy feet. On the coast, between Benan-head and the Torlin Water, situated among a vast range of columnar cliffs, called the Struye Rocks, there is a huge cavern, called the Monster's Cave, measuring 110 feet long, 40 feet broad, and 80 high. After crossing the Torlin Water, we reach Lag, where there is a small inn. About a mile from the inn, a road strikes off to the right hand, crossing the island, through Glen Scoradail, to Lamlash. Continuing along the coast, the road crosses Sloadridh Water, along the base of a mass of rounded hills, called Leac-a-Breac, and reaches Kilpatrick, where there is a cave, called the Preaching Cave. About a mile from the road, at Blackwaterfoot,* is the basaltic promontory of Drumidoon, near which there are a number of water-worn caves, one of which, called the King's Cave, is famed for having been the residence of the patriot Bruce on his first arrival in the island. On the wall at the entrance are inscribed the letters M. D. R.; and at the southern extremity is still to be seen a rudely cut hunting-scene, said to have been executed by the fugitive monarch, as a representation of his own condition when this lonely cavern was the place of his abode. It is 114 feet long, 44 broad, and 47½ high. Some of the other caves are equally large; one is called the King's Kitchen; another his cellar; and a third his stable. The hill above the caves is called the King's Hill, from its connexion with Bruce. At the northern side of this hill, on the farm of Tormore, are the remains of a very perfect and interesting Druidical circle, called Sindhe choir Thionn, or Fingal's Cauldron-seat. To one of these stones, pierced through with a hole, Fingal tied his favourite dog Bran. The road now continues along the coast, crossing the Mauchrie† and Iorsa waters. From this to Loch Ranza, the only objects of particular interest are, a solitary mountain tarn in the silent recesses of Beinn Mhorroinn, the most picturesque lake in the island, lying in a deep hollow, called Corrie an Lochan; and on the road at North Thunder-

---

* The remains of a large cairn or tumulus are to be seen here; but, owing to the large number of stones which have been carried away, it is now very much diminished in size. To the north of it, there is another, said to mark the spot where Fingal held his court of justice.

† The pass over the river Mauchrie is "renowned for the dilemma of a poor woman, who, being tempted by the narrowness of the ravine to step across, succeeded in making the first movement, but took fright when it became necessary to move the other foot, and remained in a posture equally ludicrous and dangerous, until some chance passenger assisted her to extricate herself. It is said she remained there some hours."—*Note to Lord of the Isles.*

gay, where there are two remarkable masses of contorted schist, which have fallen from the cliff upon the shore. Continuing along the shores of Catacol Bay, and passing the glen of the same name, the road turns round Choillembor Point, and brings us at length to " Fair Loch Ranza," where

> " Wreaths of cottage-smoke are upward curl'd
> From the lone hamlet, which her inland bay
> And circling mountains sever from the world."—

It is about a mile in length, and, during the fishing-season, is a place of great resort, 300 boats sometimes lying at anchor in the bay at the same time.*

The ruins of Loch Ranza Castle stand upon a small peninsula near the entrance of the Loch. This castle is not heard of until the year 1380, when it is enumerated among the Royal Castles, as a hunting seat of the Scottish sovereigns. The roof having fallen in, it is now fast falling into decay. Near this, in the burying ground of Clachan, are interred the remains of good St. Molios, who died here at the advanced age of 120. The figure of the saint is sculptured on his tombstone, which is said to have been brought from Iona. The ruins of the convent of St. Bride, celebrated in the " Lord of the Isles," as the lonely abode of the maid of Lorn, occupied a site near the castle :—

> "In that lone convent's silent cell,
> The lovely Maid of Lorn remain'd,
> Unnamed, unknown, while Scotland far
> Resounded with the din of war ;
> And many a month and many a day,
> In calm seclusion wore away."

---

* Sir Walter Scott, in his fourth canto to the " Lord of the Isles," gives the following beautiful description of the view on Bruce's approach to Loch Ranza, from the Island of Rachrin, where he had lain concealed :—

> " Now launch'd once more, the inland sea
> They furrow with fair augury,
> 　And steer from Arran's isle.
> The sun, ere yet he sunk behind
> Ben Ghoil, ' the Mountain of the Wind,'
> Gave his grim peaks a greeting kind,
> 　And bade Loch Ranza smile.
> Thither their destined course they drew ;
> It seem'd the isle her monarch knew,
> So brilliant was the landward view,
> 　The ocean so serene ;
> Each puny wave in diamonds roll'd
> O'er the calm deep, where hues of gold
> 　With azure strove, and green.
>
> The hill, the vale, the tree, the tower,
> Glow'd with the tints of evening's hour,
> 　The beech was silver sheen ;
> The wind breathed soft as lover's sigh,
> And oft renewed, seem'd oft to die,
> 　With breathless stop between.
> O who, with speech of war and woes,
> Would wish to break the soft repose
> 　Of such enchanting scene !
> 　　*　　*　　*
> To land King Robert lightly sprung,
> And thrice aloud his bugle rung
> With note prolong'd and varied strain,
> Till bold Ben Ghoil replied again."

But now unfortunately all trace of this interesting place is completely swept away. There is a small inn here for the accommodation of travellers. To the back of the loch is Ben Ghoil, and the two beautiful glens, Chalmadael and Eeis na bearradh. At the head of the latter glen is a small loch called Loch Davie. The road runs along the southern shore of Loch Ranza, and leaving the coast strikes through the former of these glens to Corrie. Diverging, however, from the road, a two miles' walk from Loch Ranza along the coast, will bring the tourist to Scriden, the most northerly point of Arran. Here a most striking scene presents itself. The cliffs having given way, and rolled down the hill, have fallen in confused masses on the shore, rendering it necessary, in following the line of coast, to climb over the rocks by a rough and winding passage. Near the summit of the hill there is a chasm, not more than a yard broad, and so deep, that the bottom is lost in darkness. The edge being covered with heath, the aperture is so much hidden that the utmost caution should be used in approaching it. There are also many similar rents of a smaller size on the same mountain. Near Scriden point, is the Cock of Arran, a large stone on the beach, forming a well known landmark for seamen. Formerly, when viewed from the sea, it resembled a cock crowing ; hence its name. Having been decapitated, however, it is now deprived of this distinguishing feature. A mile from the Cock, are the grey ruins of some deserted saltpans, which, standing, as they do, amidst a scene of solitude on the unfrequented shore, lend an additional charm to the still and lonely landscape. About two miles from Sannox, the eye of the traveller is suddenly arrested by a scene as imposing as it is unexpected, known by the name of the Fallen Rocks. An immense cliff of old red sandstone, which overhung the brow of the hill, seems suddenly to have given way, and the entire slope is covered with huge irregular masses of rock, hurled from above in the wildest and most tumultuous confusion. It is not known when this fall occurred ; but there is a tradition, that the noise of the descent was heard in the Isle of Bute. About a mile from the Fallen Rocks we regain the road at North Glen Sannox, and a short way further on, the famed Glen Sannox is presented to the view. This beautiful glen is separated from Glen Rosa by a rocky ridge, and is surrounded by high hills on all sides—to the north by Suithi Fheargus, or Fergus' Seat;* to the south by the steep conical hill Ciodhua Oigh,

---

* There is a tradition, that when Fergus the First made a survey of his kingdom, he visited Arran in the course of his wanderings; and that he might at once obtain a view of the island, the monarch and his attendants climbed this lofty hill, when, to refresh themselves after the fatigue, they sat down to dine. Hence the name.

or the Maiden's Breast; while it is closed, to the east, by lofty Cir Mhor and Ceum na Cailleach, or the Carlin's Step. This glen is admitted by almost all to be the finest in the island, and is justly characterized by MacCulloch as " the sublime in magnitude and simplicity, obscurity and silence." As the traveller pursues his lonely path, he is ever induced to pause and gaze around him in silent admiration of the wild and desolate scene. No sound of man strikes his ear, save the tramp of his own footsteps; and no sign of life is heard but the distant bleating of the moorland sheep, or the wild shriek of the eagle, soaring above his eyrie in Ciormhor. Reluctantly retracing our steps, and gaining the road, after proceeding a short way, we observe, between the road and the sea, two large boulders of granite, which have rolled down from the neighbouring heights; after passing these we are not long of reaching Corrie, where there is a small inn. At a short distance from Corrie, there is a small cascade, formed by the Locherim Burn; and further on, another more conspicuous, called the White Water, dashes down the mountain side, presenting one unbroken line of white and sparkling foam. Passing Maolden Hill, and turning Merkland Point, we again come in sight of our head-quarters at Brodick, having completed the circuit of the island.

II. GOUROCK—DUNOON—ROTHESAY—LOCHGILPHEAD.

Returning to Cloch Point, straight opposite on the coast of Argyle, stands Dunoon, a sea-bathing village, very much frequented during the summer months. The Castle of Dunoon is an interesting relic of antiquity. It was once a royal residence, and a strong fortress. The hereditary keepership of this castle was conferred by Robert Bruce on the family of Sir Colin Campbell of Loch Awe, an ancestor of the Duke of Argyle. It was the residence of the Argyle family in 1673, but from the commencement of the eighteenth century was allowed to fall into a state of ruin, and nothing but a wall now remains. An extensive and beautiful prospect is commanded from its site. At a short distance from Dunoon is the Holy Loch, surrounded by steep and picturesque hills. On its eastern shore is situated the little village of Kilmun, where may be still seen the ruins of the Collegiate Church, founded, in 1442, by Sir Duncan Campbell of Loch Awe, ancestor of the

Argyle family. Here the Argyle family have their burying-place. On leaving Dunoon, the steamer skirts along Bawkie Bay. The peninsula of Cowal ends a few miles lower at Toward Point, where there is a light-house, besides a large modern edifice, Toward Castle, the seat of Kirkman Finlay, Esq. On the neighbouring height, on the right, are seen the venerable ruins of Toward Castle, the ancient seat of the Lamonts. Turning Toward Point, we enter Rothesay Bay, and in a short time reach the pleasant town of ROTHE-SAY. The town consists of several neat streets, and the views to be obtained of the neighbouring coasts, from various elevated points around it, are extremely beautiful. The ancient royal castle of Rothesay, the favourite residence of Robert III., is one of the finest ruins in Scotland. It was burned down by the Earl of Argyle in 1685. The closet in which Robert III. died is still pointed out. Rothesay gave the title of Duke to the eldest son of the Scottish kings, as it still does to the heir-apparent of the British crown. The western side of the Bay of Rothesay commands a noble view of the entrance to the Kyles of Bute, the crooked strait which divides Argyleshire from Bute, and the mouth of Loch Strevin, with the shores of Cowal. About two miles from Rothesay, the steamboat passes Port Bannatyne, a beautiful village encircling the bottom of Kames Bay. In the immediate vicinity stands Kames Castle, an old fortified mansion still inhabited. Between Rothesay and Kilchattan Bay stands Mount Stewart, the seat of the Marquis of Bute, surrounded by fine woods. Etterick Bay, on the west side of the island, is often visited on account of its picturesque scenery. After passing the mouth of Loch Strevin, the channel rapidly narrows. Between the ferry and the entrance of Loch Ridden, it is contracted by four islands. The passage, though narrow and intricate, is exceedingly interesting. Leaving the entrance to Loch Ridden, on the right, the steamer emerges into the open space between Ard Lamont Point on the mainland, and Etterick Bay in Bute, from which the heights of Arran are seen to great advantage. On entering Loch Fyne, the steamer passes on the left the islet of Inchmarnock, with the ruins of a chapel, and soon after another islet, called Slate Island. On the left is the wild and rugged peninsula of Cantire, joined to South Knapdale by a very narrow isthmus, formed by the western and eastern Lochs of Tarbet. These two salt-water lakes or bays, into the eastern of which we now enter, encroach so far into the land, and the extremities come so near each other, that there is not a mile of land to divide them. Bruce on his way from Rachrin is said to have drawn his bark across this isthmus.

> " Up Tarbet's western lake they bore,
> Then dragg'd their bark the isthmus o'er,
> As far as Kilmconnel's shore,
> Upon the eastern bay."*

In the immediate vicinity is the Castle of Tarbet, now in ruins. Here the Earl of Argyle kept his troops previous to his unsuccessful descent upon the Lowlands in 1685. Leaving Tarbet, and pursuing our course northward, we pass Barmore Island, and shortly after come in sight of the village of Lochgilphead, and the extremity of the Crinan Canal. This canal, which was formed to save doubling the Mull of Cantire, is only nine miles in length, but has no fewer than fifteen locks. On entering the canal, a good view is obtained of Lochgilphead and Kilmory, the seat of Sir John Ord. Two miles from the sea-lock, on the left, is Oakfield, after which the canal passes through an extensive tract of marshy uninteresting country. Passing the village of Bellanach, we enter the Bay of Crinan. Upon the right is the modernized Castle of Duntroon, (Malcolm, Esq.,) and northward, on the same side, Loch Craignish, a fine arm of the sea, intersected by a chain of beautiful little islands, covered with ancient oak-trees. The steamboat proceeds through the Dorishmore, or Great Gate, between the point of Craignish, and one of the chain of islets just mentioned. Iona and Islay are now in sight. On the south are the

* Lord of the Isles. Canto IV.

shores of Knapdale, and to the north the islands of Sh'una and Luing, with Loch Melfort opening to the right. Two miles from the Point of Luing is Blackmill Bay, opposite to which is the island of Lunga. Three miles further north is the slate islet of Balnahuay, and farther to the west the Garveloch Isles. The Sound of Cuan runs between the northern extremity of Luing and the island of Seil. The length of this beautiful and diversified passage is about three miles. On the west side of Seil is the circular islet of Easdale, celebrated for its slate quarries. After passing Easdale and the point of Ardincaple, Loch Feochan opens on the right, and a distinct view of the broad-shouldered and double-peaked Ben Cruachan is obtained. To the north is the Island of Kerrera, with the ruins of Gylen Castle occupying its southern point. This island forms a natural break-water to the Bay of Oban. At the head of this bay is situated the pleasant and thriving village of Oban. The high cliffs on the north side of the bay command one of the finest views in Scotland. They terminate in a rocky promontory, surmounted by Dunolly Castle, an ivy-clad square keep, the ancient seat of the M'Dougals of Lorn, whose representative resides here in Dunolly House.*

* "The view from Dunolly Castle is as varied as striking. Umbrageous mountains arise behind in various rocky ranges—

'Shade above shade, a woody theatre
Of stateliest view.'

Strange gigantic masses of rock, each with its own wild legend, lie scattered between the higher terrace and the shore, and resemble dismantled turrets, or portions of ruined castles, rather than natural shapes of stone. But the seaward aspect (and the projecting promontory is almost sea surrounded) forms the noblest feature of the scene. To the west the mountains of Mull, and the opening of the lengthened Sound, with portions of Kerrera and the Maiden Island, almost at our feet :—north-westwards the green Lismore, backed by bolder ranges of the misty Morven, with the Linnhé Loch receding into the far distance; while the lofty heights of Appin and Barcaldine rise behind the bright broad bosom of Loch Etive, which, opening almost beneath the castle's northern bounds, ascends far inland, laving the base of many a mighty mountain, till it retires a 'shy Winander' behind the dark gigantic masses of Ben Cruachan. To the south are countless isles, nameless or hard to name, but all most fair to look upon on a beautiful summer morning, their mingled craggy rocks and sunny verdure encompassed by that interlacing sea. These, and other features, though

R

A little to the north of Dunolly stands the Castle of Dunstaffnage, " an irregular four-sided building, placed upon a
rugged mass of conglomerate rock, the sides of which have
been partially picked away so as to produce a more precipitous
descent beneath the walls.   Its circumference is said to be
about 400 feet, and the battlements are still high and of
tenacious strength."   In consequence of its having been
occasionally possessed by the early Scottish Kings, Dunstaffnage Castle is ranked as one of the royal palaces of
Scotland.   From this ancient seat of royalty, it is said, the
Coronation stone, now in Westminster Abbey, was transferred by Kenneth II. to Scone.

NINTH TOUR.

GLASGOW—INVERARY—LOCH AWE—DALMALLY—TAYNUILT—OBAN.

THE tourist has his choice of several routes to Inverary.
He may proceed by Loch Lomond, or by Loch Long, to
Arroquhar, and thence, by Cairndow, to Inverary—or by
Loch Goil and St. Catharine's—or by Rothesay, Tarbet, and
Lochgilphead.

Supposing him to take the first route, he proceeds by
steamboat to Dumbarton, and thence to the foot of Loch
Lomond, where he embarks in a steamboat, and sails fourteen miles northward, to Tarbet, on its west side.   From

in themselves fixed as the earth's foundations, assume in truth an ever-changing
aspect, as the beholder with mild benignant eye stands gazing from the lonely
battlements, or ranges the wooded heights and varied hollows of these romantic
grounds."—WILSON's *Voyage round the Coasts of Scotland*, vol. i. p. 151.

this point to Arroquhar, on the shore of Loch Long, is a delightful walk of about half an hour, across the isthmus which lies between Loch Lomond and Loch Long. The inn of Arroquhar is twenty-two miles from Dumbarton. Loch Long is an arm of the sea, about twenty-four miles in length. In 1263, the Norwegians, who invaded Scotland, and were ultimately defeated at Largs, sailed up this loch with a fleet of sixty vessels, ravaging the country on all sides, and, on reaching the head of the loch, they drew their boats across the isthmus into Loch Lomond, and committed the same depredations on its shores. Near the head of Loch Long is a fantastic peak, called Ben Arthur or the Cobbler, from its grotesque resemblance to a shoemaker at work. Arroquhar was formerly the seat of the chief of the clan Macfarlane, it is now the property of Sir James Colquhoun of Luss. Starting from the inn at this spot, the tourist winds round the head of Loch Long, and crossing the water of Taing, enters Argyleshire. The road now skirts the western shore of Loch Long, till within a few yards of Ardgarten House, (Campbell, Esq.) where it turns to the right, and enters the vale of Glencroe—a desolate but magnificent glen about six miles in length, guarded on the right by the bold and fantastic peak of Ben Arthur. A steep path conducts the traveller to the summit of the pass, where there is a stone seat, with the inscription, " Rest and be thankful."* The road now gradually descends, passing, on the

---

* On this resting-place Wordsworth has composed the following sonnet:—

" Doubling and doubling with laborious walk,
  Who, that has gain'd at length the wish'd-for Height,
  This brief, this simple way-side Call can slight,
  And rest not thankful ? Whether cheer'd by talk
  With some loved friend, or by the unseen hawk
  Whistling to clouds and sky-born streams, that shine
  At the sun's outbreak, as, with light divine,
  Ere they descend to nourish root and stalk
  Of valley flowers. Nor, while the limbs repose,
  Will we forget that, as the fowl can keep
  Absolute stillness, poised aloft in air,
  And fishes front, unmoved, the torrent's sweep,—
  So may the Soul, through powers that Faith bestows,
  Win rest, and ease, and peace, with bliss that angels share."

left, a small sheet of water, called Loch Restal, and enters
the lonely valley of Glenkinglas. Passing through this solitary vale, at the distance of about three miles, the tourist
is gladdened with a view of Loch Fyne. The road now
passes, on the right, the farm-house of Strowan, and on the
left, Ardkinglass, (Callander, Esq.) and shortly after reaches
the inn of Cairndow, (thirty-six miles from Dumbarton,)
where there is a ferry across Loch Fyne. Crossing the
ferry, the distance to Inverary is six and a half miles. If
the tourist should prefer to go round by the head of the
loch, the distance is nine and a half miles.

The second route to Inverary leads the tourist up Loch
Goil, which branches off from Loch Long. The peninsular
group of rugged mountains which separate them is called
Argyle's Bowling Green. The shores are bold and magnificent. On the margin of the loch are situated the ruins
of Carrick Castle, an ancient seat of the Dunmore family.
From Loch Goil Head a road leads through a wild valley,
called Hell's Glen, to St. Catharine's, a distance of seven
miles, whence the tourist may proceed across Loch Fyne
(four miles) to Inverary.

By the third, and much the longest route, the tourist
proceeds to Rothesay, then through the Kyles of Bute, and
into the long arm of the sea called Loch Fyne. (See page
264.)

INVERARY,

the county town of Argyleshire, stands at the lower end of
a small bay, where the river Aray falls into Loch Fyne. It
was erected into a royal burgh, in 1648, by Charles I. while
he was a prisoner in Carisbrook Castle. An obelisk has
been erected in a garden beside the church, to commemorate the execution of several gentlemen of the name of
Campbell, who suffered here in 1685, for their opposition
to Popery. The population of Inverary is about 1000 or
1100. Its staple trade is the herring fishery—the herrings of Loch Fyne being celebrated for their superior excellence. Large sums of money have been laid out by the
Dukes of Argyle in improving and adorning the town and

neighbourhood. Inverary unites with Oban, Campbelton, Irvine, and Ayr, in electing a member of Parliament.

INVERARY CASTLE

The most interesting object in this vicinity is Inverary Castle, the seat of the Duke of Argyle. The edifice was commenced by Duke Archibald, in 1748, after a plan by Adam. It is built of chlorite-slate, and consists of two storeys and a sunk floor, flanked with round overtopping towers, and surmounted with a square winged pavilion. In the Hall are preserved about 100 muskets, which were "out in the forty five," and in one of the rooms is some very beautiful tapestry, which the old lady who exhibits it, states to have been "made by the goblins, wha' are a' dead now." The mansion contains nothing else of peculiar interest to strangers. The view from the hill of Duniquoich is very fine, and the rides and the walks through the grounds are extensive and picturesque.*

From Inverary a road leads through Glen Aray, to Loch

---

* "Embarked on the bosom of Loch Fyne, Captain Dalgetty might have admired one of the grandest scenes which nature affords. He might have noticed the rival rivers Aray and Shiray, which pay tribute to the lake, each issuing from its own dark and wooded retreat. He might have marked on the soft and gentle slope that ascends from the shores, the noble old Gothic castle, with its varied outline, embattled walls, towers, and outer and inner courts, which so far as the picturesque is concerned, presented an aspect much more striking than the present massive and uniform mansion. He might have admired those dark woods which, for many a mile, surrounded this strong and princely dwelling, and his eye might have dwelt on the picturesque peak of Duniquoich, starting abruptly from the lake, and raising its scathed brow into the mists of middle sky, while a solitary watch-tower, perched on its top like an eagle's nest, gave dignity to the scene by awakening a sense of possible danger." — *Legend of Montrose.*

Awe, a distance of nine miles.   After leaving the pleasure-
grounds round Inverary Castle, the tourist will find little
to attract his attention till he reaches the head of the glen,
and begins to descend towards Cladich, when the beautiful
expanse of Loch Awe breaks upon his view.   Loch Awe is
about twenty-four miles in length, and varies from one and
a half to two and a half in breadth.   The mingled grandeur
and beauty of the scenery are scarcely equalled in Britain.

Loch Awe is surrounded by lofty mountains of a rude and
savage aspect, the highest of which (Ben Cruachan) rises
to the height of 3400 feet, while its base, which reaches to
Loch Etive, occupies an area of twenty square miles.   Its
towering proportions give a striking character to the scenery at the eastern extremity of Loch Awe.   The sloping
banks of the lake are richly clothed with natural wood.   The
river Awe flows from its northern side, and pours its waters
into Loch Etive at Bunawe.   The gully or hollow, known
by the name of the *Brender*, through which the river flows,
is exceedingly grand.   There are about twenty-four little
islands in Loch Awe, some of them beautifully crowned
with trees.   On one of these islets, (Inishail, or the Beautiful Isle,) are the ruins of a small nunnery of the Cistercian
order.   It was suppressed at the Reformation, and its possessions were erected into a temporal lordship in favour of
Hay, Abbot of Inchaffray, who abjured the Roman Catholic
faith.   The old churchyard in this island contains a number of ancient tomb-stones, curiously carved.   The Mac-
Arthurs formerly inhabited the shores of Loch Awe, opposite
the island, and numerous stones in the churchyard bear the
names of individuals of that ancient race.   On Innes Fraoch,
or the Heather Isle, are the ruins of an ancient castle of
the chief of the MacNaughtons.   This isle was the Hesper-
ides of the Highlands, and is fabled to have derived its
name from Fraoch, an adventurous lover, who, attempting
to gratify the longing of the fair Meyo for the delicious
fruit of the isle, encountered and destroyed the serpent by
which it was guarded, but perished himself in the conflict.
The point of land which runs into the lake immediately beyond the village of Cladich, is called Innistrynich, or the

Island of the Druids, and is the property of Mr. M'Allister of Innistrynich, who is an extensive proprietor on the opposite shore of the lake. The island of Fraoch, with the contiguous lands, were granted, in 1267, to Gilbert Mac-Naughton, by Alexander III. The MacNaughtons formed part of the force of MacDougal, Lord of Lorn, when he attacked Robert Bruce at Dalrigh, near Tyndrum. It is stated by Barbour, that MacNaughton pointed out to the Lord of Lorn the deeds of valour which Bruce performed in this memorable retreat, with the highest expressions of admiration. " It seems to give thee pleasure," said Lorn, " that he makes such havoc among our friends."—" Not so, by my faith," replied MacNaughton; " but be he friend or foe who achieves high deeds of chivalry, men should bear faithful witness to his valour; and never have I heard of one who, by his knightly feats, has extricated himself from such dangers as have this day surrounded Bruce." The Mac-Naughtons, an ancient Highland tribe, are supposed to have derived their origin from one Naughton, a distinguished warrior in the reign of Malcolm IV., who received various grants of lands from the Lord of Lochers, as a reward for the services which he rendered to him in his wars with the M'Dougals of Lorn. It is said by Buchanan of Auchmar, that " the ancestors or chiefs of this surname are reported to have been, for some ages, thanes of Loch Tay, and also to be possessed of a great estate betwixt the south side of Loch Fyne and Lochers, parts of which are Glenera, Glenshira, and Glenfine." The chief of the clan, in the reigns of Charles I. and II., was Sir Alexander MacNaughton, a stanch royalist. At the Reformation, he was knighted, and received a liberal pension, as a reward for his services. His circumstances, however, became embarrassed, and the family estates were seized by his creditors for debts, it is said, no way equivalent to their value. His great-grandson was a custom-house officer on the east coast.

At the eastern extremity of Loch Awe, at the base of Ben Cruachan, the conjoined waters of two rivers, the Strae and the Orchy, descend from their respective glens, and empty themselves into the lake. On a slightly elevated neck of

land at the head of the lake, where the Orchy flows into it,
stand the ruins of the celebrated castle of KILCHURN, or
more properly Coalchuirn.   The great tower is said to have
been erected in 1443, by the lady of Sir Colin Campbell,
the Black Knight of Rhodes, second son of Sir Duncan
Campbell of Loch Awe, ancestor of the Argyle family.   Sir
Colin acquired by marriage a considerable portion of the
estates of the family of Lorn, and was the founder of the
powerful family of Breadalbane.   He was absent on a cru-
sade when his lady erected this noble pile, which (says Macculloch), " in the Western Highlands at least, claims the
pre-eminence, no less from its magnitude and the integrity
of its ruins, than from the very picturesque arrangements
of the building."   For the pencil of the artist few finer subjects can be found in Scotland than these ruins present.   So
late as 1745, Kilchurn was garrisoned by the King's troops,
and all the exterior and greater part of the interior walls
are still entire.*

* Our space will not admit of our quoting the whole of Wordsworth's fine
Address to Kilchurn Castle, but we give the introductory part of the poem and
the prose extract with which it is prefaced.
   " From the top of the hill a most impressive scene opened upon our view,—
a ruined castle on an island, (for an island the flood had made it,) at some distance from the shore, backed by a cove of the mountain Cruachan, down which
came a foaming stream.   The castle occupied every foot of the island that was
visible to us, appearing to rise out of the water,—mists rested upon the mountain side, with spots of sunshine; there was a mild desolation, in the low
grounds, a solemn grandeur in the mountains, and the castle was wild, yet
stately—not dismantled of turrets—nor the walls broken down, though obviously a ruin."—*Extract from the Journal of my Companion.*
          " Child of loud-throated War ! the mountain stream
          Roars in thy hearing : but thy hour of rest
          Is come, and thou art silent in thy age ;
          Save when the winds sweep by, and sounds are caught
          Ambiguous, neither wholly thine nor theirs,
          Oh ! there is life that breathes not : powers there are
          That touch each other to the quick in modes
          Which the gross world no sense hath to perceive,
          No soul to dream of.   What art thou, from care
          Cast off—abandon'd by thy rugged Sire,
          Nor by soft Peace adopted ; though, in place
          And in dimension, such that thou mightst seem
          But a mere footstool to yon sovereign Lord,
          Huge Cruachan, (a thing that meaner hills
                                                  Might

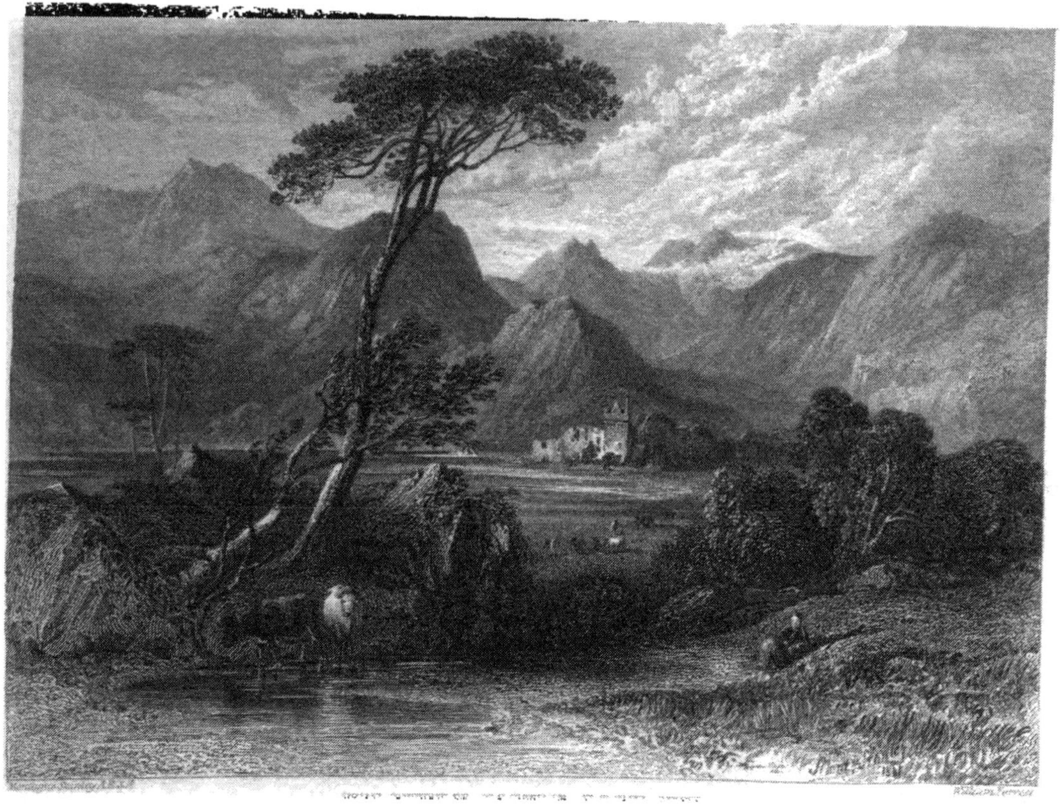

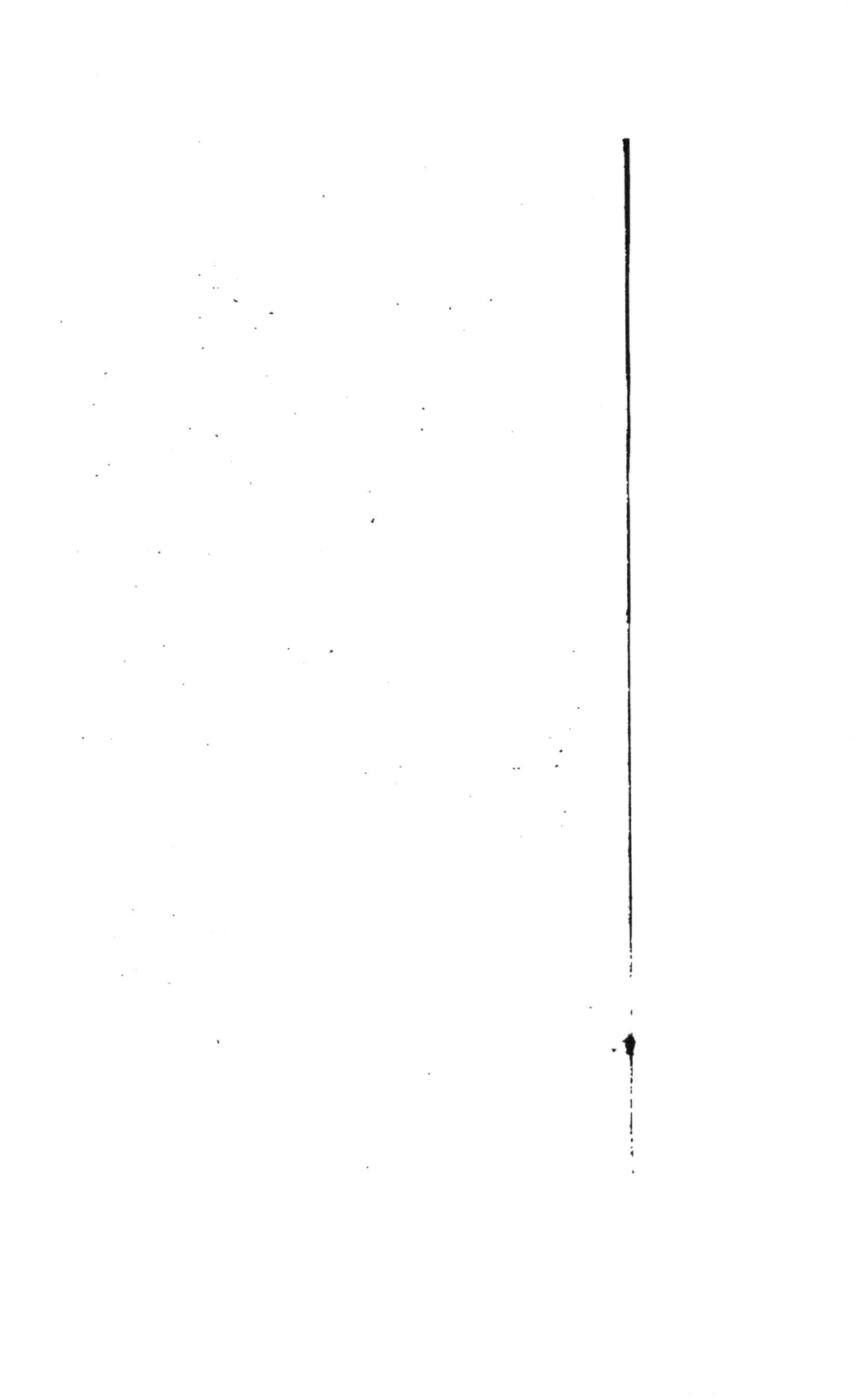

There is a good inn at Dalmally, near the head of the lake, and from it there is a beautiful view of the vale of Glenorchy. The old church of Glenorchy is of great antiquity, and the churchyard contains many ancient gravestones. The road from Dalmally to Taynuilt passes the new church of Glenorchy, and makes a long circuit round the head of the lake. Pedestrians may shorten the distance and pleasantly diversify their journey by crossing the lake in a boat. Two miles from Dalmally, we cross the river Strae, which descends from Glenstrae on the right. The whole of this district was at one time possessed by the Clan-Gregor, but they have long been deprived of all their possessions around Loch Awe, and may now say, in the words of the poet—

" Glenorchy's proud mountains, Coalchuirn and her towers,
    Glenstrae and Glenlyon no longer are ours,
        We're landless, landless, Gregalich !"*

In later times, this district fell into the hands of the Campbells, and often afforded them shelter in times of danger. " It's a far cry to Lochow," was the slogan of the clan, indicating the impossibility of reaching them in these

Might crush, nor know that it had suffer'd harm ;)
Yet he, not loth, in favour of thy claims
To reverence, suspends his own ; submitting
All that the God of Nature hath conferr'd,
All that he holds in common with the stars,
To the memorial majesty of Time
Impersonated in thy calm decay !"

* " In the early part of the 17th century, a young man of the name of Lamont, travelling from Cowal, in Argyleshire, to Fort-William, fell in with the son of a chieftain of the Clan Macgregor, resident in Glenstrae, while on a shooting excursion. Having adjourned to a public-house, a dispute arose, which terminated in a scuffle, in which Macgregor was mortally stabbed. Lamont instantly escaping, was closely pursued. Descrying a house, he sped thither for shelter : unquestioned, the host assured him of protection. Those in pursuit coming up, communicated the startling intelligence that the fugitive was the murderer of the eldest son of the family. Macgregor, however, faithful to his word, conducted the young man to Loch Fyne, and saw him safe across. His clemency and magnanimity were not without their recompence. Not long after, the Clan-Gregor were proscribed ; when Lamont received the aged chieftain to his house, and, by every act of kindness to him and his relatives, sought to supply the place of him of whose support he had been the means of bereaving them."—*Anderson's Guide to the Highlands.*

remote fastnesses. Passing the farm-house of Corry, the road now skirts the tremendous base of Ben Cruachan, and leaving behind the majestic lake, descends the course of the foaming and rapid river Awe. The rocks and preci- pices which stoop down perpendicularly on the path, ex- hibit some remains of the wood which once clothed them, but which has, in later times, been felled to supply the iron furnaces at Bunawe. The whole of this pass is singu- larly wild, particularly near the bridge which has been thrown across the impetuous river. Here was fought the celebrated battle between Robert Bruce and John of Lorn, chief of the M'Dougals, in which that warlike clan were almost destroyed. The bridge of Awe is the scene of Sir Walter Scott's beautiful tale of the Highland Widow.* Proceeding onwards about two miles, a view is obtained of Loch Etive, and the little village of Bunawe. Crossing an old bridge, and passing the church of Muckarn on the right, the tourist reaches the Inn of Taynuilt, on the south side of Loch Etive, twelve miles distant from Dalmally. About a mile to the north is the village of Bunawe, where there is a ferry across Loch Etive, and an extensive iron furnace, which has been wrought since the middle of last century, by a Lancashire company. The portion of Loch Etive above Bunawe, possesses a high degree of simple and sequestered grandeur. Bunawe is the point from which the ascent to Ben Cruachan can be best effect- ed. The prospect from the top of the mountain is re- markably extensive and interesting. Leaving Taynuilt, the road, at the distance of four miles, descends to the shore of Loch Etive, beautifully fringed with wood. On

* The following description is given of the spot where her cottage stood :— " We fixed our eyes with interest on one large oak, which grew on the left hand towards the river. It seemed a tree of extraordinary magnitude and picturesque beauty, and stood just where there appeared to be a few roods of open ground lying among huge stones, which had rolled down from the mountain. To add to the romance of the situation, the spot of clear ground extended round the foot of a proud-browed rock, from the summit of which leaped a mountain stream in a fall of sixty feet, in which it was dissolved into foam and dew. At the bot- tom of the fall, the rivulet with difficulty collected, like a routed general, its dis- persed forces, and, as if tamed by its descent, found a noiseless passage through the heath to join the Awe "

the north side of the Loch, about three miles from Taynuilt,
are seen Ardchattan House, and the ruins of Ardchattan
Priory, covered with luxuriant ivy, and o'ercanopied by
trees. The Priory, where Robert Bruce held a Parliament,
was built by John MacDougal in the thirteenth century,
and was burnt by Colkitto during Montrose's Wars. In
the distance are seen the dark mountains of Mull and
Morven, and the green island of Lismore. The latter is
entirely composed of limestone. Three miles farther is
Connel Ferry, where, from the narrowness of the passage,
and a reef of sunken rocks, a very turbulent rapid is occasioned at particular states of the tide. In the immediate
vicinity, antiquaries have placed the apocryphal Pictish
capital of Beregonium. There is also a vitrified fort.
Two miles beyond Connel Ferry, at the entrance of Loch
Etive, are the ruins of Dunstaffnage Castle. They occupy
the summit of a perpendicular rock near the extremity of
a low peninsular flat projection from the southern shore.
Dunstaffnage was inhabited by the MacDougals till 1448,
when it was taken by Bruce after his victory at the Pass
of Awe. It is now a royal castle, the Duke of Argyle being
hereditary keeper. From Dunstaffnage, the celebrated
stone on which our Scottish monarchs used to be crowned
was transported to Scone, whence it was removed to England by Edward I., and is now deposited beneath the
coronation chair in the chapel of Edward the Confessor, in
Westminster Abbey. At a little distance from the castle
is a small roofless chapel, where one of the Scottish kings
is said to have been buried. Three miles from Dunstaffnage is the pleasant thriving village of OBAN, situated at
the head of a fine bay. From the heights in the neighbourhood, magnificent sea views may be obtained ; and the
road which skirts the shore to the southward is overhung
by romantic cliffs. In the vicinity is Dunolly Castle, the
ancient fortress of the MacDougals of Lorn, situated on the
point of a rocky promontory, at the northern extremity of
the bay. Near it is Dunolly House, inhabited by the representative of that once powerful family.*

* "Nothing can be more wildly beautiful than the situation of Dunolly. The
ruins are situated upon a bold and precipitous promontory overhanging Loch

TENTH TOUR.

_____

OBAN TO SKYE.

Tourists visiting Skye generally start from Glasgow by
steamer, or if they have previously reached Oban by either
of the routes described in the Eighth and Ninth Tours,
they may embark from that village when the steamer
touches there.

Supposing Glasgow to be the starting point, the route as
far as Oban will be found already described in the Eighth
Tour. Proceeding from the finely sheltered bay of Oban,
with the island of Kerrera on our left, the Castle of Dunolly
will be observed proudly seated on a rugged steep. For a
description of this Castle we refer the reader to the end of

Etive, and distant about a mile from the village and port of Oban. The principal part which remains is the donjon or keep; but fragments of other buildings, overgrown with ivy, attest that it had once been a place of importance, as
large, apparently, as Ardtornish or Dunstaffnage. These fragments enclose a
court-yard, of which the keep probably formed one side; the entrance being
by a steep ascent from the neck of the isthmus, formerly cut across by a moat,
and defended, doubtless, by outworks and a drawbridge. Beneath the castle
stands the present mansion of the family, having on the one hand Loch Etive,
with its islands and mountains, on the other two romantic eminences tufted
with copsewood. There are other accompaniments suited to the scene; in
particular, a huge upright pillar or detached fragment of that sort of rock called
plum-pudding stone, upon the shore, about a quarter of a mile from the castle.
It is called *Clachna-eau,* or the Dog's Pillar, because Fingal is said to have used
it as a stake to which he bound his celebrated dog, Bran. Others say, that when
the Lord of the Isles came upon a visit to the Lord of Lorn, the dogs brought
for his sport were kept beside this pillar. Upon the whole, a more delightful
and romantic spot can scarce be conceived; and it receives a moral interest from
the considerations attached to the residence of a family once powerful enough
to confront and defeat Robert Bruce, and now sunk into the shade of private
life. It is at present possessed by Patrick MacDougall, Esq., the lineal and undisputed representative of the ancient Lords of Lorn. The heir of Dunolly fell
in Spain, fighting under the Duke of Wellington—a death well becoming his
ancestry."—*Lord of the Isles.*

For a description of the view from Dunolly Castle, the reader is referred to
the *footnote,* p. 265.

the Eighth and of the Ninth Tours. Rounding the point of
Kerrera the steamer stretches across the Sound of Mull.
On approaching the entrance of the Sound, soon after leaving Lismore Lighthouse, we pass the " Lady's Rock,"
where Maclean of Duart exposed his wife at low water to
be drowned by the returning tide. His cruelty was disappointed by some fishermen, who, hearing her cries,
rescued her from her impending fate, and restored her to
her friends. A little onwards we reach Duart Castle, now
the property of Campbell of Possil, and on the opposite
side, projecting from the Morven shore, are the ruins of the
Castle of Ardtornish, in former times a chief residence of
the Lords of the Isles. The steamer next passes the opening of Loch Aline, and four miles beyond it the Castle of
Aros may be observed on the leftward shore. The wild
situations of these fortresses, and their limited accommodation, afford a striking contrast to the spacious castles of
the south. They are supposed to date their origin from
the period of the prostration of the Norwegian power,
when Haco, King of Norway, was defeated at the battle of
Largs, and when many of the island chieftains assumed an
independent sway.

Proceeding onwards, we pass upon the Morven shore the
estate of Drimnin. On the Mull side, the coast is high
and precipitous, and finely clothed with natural wood.
Passing Drumfin House, seated on a lofty terrace, and surrounded by extensive plantations, the steamer next reaches
Tobermory, where it generally anchors for the night, but
sails in the morning so early as to make it imprudent to
sleep on shore, even although the accommodation were
more inviting than it is. Upon leaving the bay of Tobermory, and crossing the mouth of Loch Sunart—which extends twenty miles among the hills to the eastward—the
steamer begins to feel the full swell of the Atlantic. To
the westward are the islands of Coll and Tiree. The
heaviest sea throughout the voyage will be felt in doubling
Ardnamurchan Point, and a stiff breeze from the westward
is, at this point, apt to poison the pleasures of the picturesque. The steamer then touches at Faskadle, and after-

wards passes the mouth of Loch Moydart, into which the
fresh waters of Loch Shiel discharge themselves by the
river of the same name. On a rocky promontory on the
shore of Loch Moydart, stand the ruins of Castle Tyrim,
an ancient stronghold of Clanranald, burned by its proprietor in 1715, before he set out to join the Earl of Mar,
prior to the battle of Sheriffmuir. This act of arson he
resorted to, that the castle might not fall into the hands
of his hereditary enemies, the Campbells, during his absence. The barren promontory on which the castle stands,
and a small wooded island near it, are the last remaining
territorial possessions of Clanranald.

On the left may be seen the islands of Eig, Rum, and
Canna, and further northward the Cuchullin (*pron.* Coolin,)
hills of Skye rear their storm-shattered summits to the
clouds. On the mainland will be observed the fine rugged
outline of the Moydart hills. Pursuing our voyage, we
pass in succession Loch Aynort, Loch Nuagh, and Arasaig
Point, (at the last of which passengers are landed,) and
enter the sound of Sleat. Armadale Castle, the seat of
Lord Macdonald, "Lord of the Isles," the largest proprietor in Skye, will be seen occupying a fine situation on a
gentle slope, about a quarter of a mile from the shore. It
is surrounded on all sides by thriving plantations, which,
with the woods of Dunvegan in the district of Kilmuir,
may be said to form the whole woodland scenery of the
island.

Having passed on the mainland side the outlets of Loch
Morrer and Loch Nevish, the ruins of Knock Castle, in
Skye, may be discerned seated on a rocky promontory
projecting into the sea. The steamer next passes the
mouth of Loch Hourn, another of those arms of the sea
by which the western coast of Scotland is so much indented. The whole mountains around Loch Hourn are
lofty and picturesque, sweeping down in grand lines
towards the water's edge. Guarding the mouth of the loch
stands the lofty Ben Screel, a mountain of very noble outline. The tourist will be aided in distinguishing it by the
accompanying woodcut.

Approaching Khyle Rhea, a view may be obtained, on the right, of the church and ruined barracks of Bernera, built as a military station to maintain the authority of the Hanoverian Government among the Celts. A strong current prevails at Khyle Rhea, which makes it necessary for vessels to avail themselves of the tide in passing the strait. On either side of the ferry, there is an inn—an acceptable shelter in such a country, although the internal comforts are not of the highest order. Passing the narrows, the steamer reaches Loch Alsh—another arm of the sea—which, at its upper extremity, divides into the lateral branches of Loch Loung and Loch Duich. At the head of Loch Alsh, between the two subsidiary branches, stand the ruins of Eilan Donan Castle, the ancient stronghold of the Mackenzies of Kintail, built, in the time of Alexander II., as a defence against the Northmen. Passing Castle Moil, we reach the harbour of Kyle-Akin, with a substantial pier, built by Lord Macdonald and the Parliamentary Commissioners. The steamer shortly after reaches Broadford, a scattered village, from which the access to the Spar Cave, Loch Coruisk, and the Cuchullin Mountains—the objects for which Skye is chiefly visited—is easier than from

any other landing place at which the steamer touches.   In
reaching these objects, and terminating the day's journey by
walking through Glen Sligachan, the tourist must be prepared to endure considerable fatigue ; for unless he invades
the hospitality of some of the few inhabitants of the district, he has no resting-place between Broadford and Sligachan Inn.   The toil of the journey makes it also desirable that he should start early in the morning of a long
summer's day, with a sufficient supply of provisions, and a
flask of whisky—the latter to be reserved for use where it
will most be required, in passing through Glen Sligachan.

The first object to be visited is the Spar Cave of Strathaird ; and as candles must be carried from Broadford to
light its recesses, the tourist may provide himself with
these at the Inn.   Perhaps he may also be inclined to hire
a pony or a cart to carry him the first stage of his journey,
and thus diminish the fatigues of the day.   Having made
all the preliminary arrangements, he proceeds along the
river side towards Torrin, a small cluster of cottar-houses
six miles to the westward of Broadford.   Five miles from
Broadford, at a short distance from the road side, upon the
right, he passes the house of the minister of Strath.   Nothing
of picturesque interest occurring to arrest his progress, a
two hours' walk along an excellent road brings the tourist to
Torrin, where a boat must be engaged to carry him to the
cave.   The distance will take four oars two hours' rowing.
On the right will be observed Blabhein, (*pron.* Blaven) which
contends with the Cuchullins for the honour of being the
highest mountain in Skye, and is little inferior to them in the
wildness of its scenery ;* and, at a short distance from the
shore, is Kirkibost, the residence of Dr. Macalister, whom

* The ascent of Blaven may be made either from Broadford or Sligachan,
but in neither case should it be attempted without a guide; for not only is it
beset with dangerous and impracticable crags and precipices, but it is peculiarly
liable to be suddenly enveloped in the mists which ascend from the low ground
or from the sea.   From either of the two places named, the tourist may devote
an entire day to the ascent and the return homewards, although, with a concur-
rence of every favourable circumstance, and with great powers of enduring
fatigue, it might be possible to include it with the excursion to the Spar Cave,
Coruisk, and Glen Sligachan.

many a benighted traveller has to thank for the kindly
shelter of his hospitable roof. Next passing the farm-house
of Kilmarie, and coasting along the rocky shore, the boat
at length reaches the mouth of the celebrated Spar Cave of
Strathaird, where the tourist disembarks to explore its recesses. A description of the interior in the Notes to the
"Lord of the Isles" will be so much more acceptable to
our readers than any original account we could supply,
that we reprint it in an abridged form, with such slight
variations or additions as the present state of the Cave
appears to require. The entrance lies through an opening
in the rock-bound shore, and at first the appearance is rude
and unpromising; but an advance of a few yards unfolds
the splendour of the scene, the roof, floor, and walls appearing to be sheeted with marble, partly smooth, partly rough
with frostwork and rustic ornaments, and partly seeming
to be wrought into statuary. The floor, which forms a
steep ascent, may be fancifully compared to a sheet of
water, which, while it rushed whitening and foaming down
a declivity, has been suddenly arrested and consolidated by
the spell of an enchanter. At the summit of the ascent,
the cave opens into a splendid gallery, adorned with dazzling
crystallizations, and finally descends with rapidity to the
brink of a pool of beautifully limpid water, which forms
the internal boundary of the cave. The groups of combined figures, projecting or embossed, by which the pool is
surrounded, are exquisitely elegant and fanciful, and might
indeed give hints to the statuary by their singular and
romantic disposition. There is scarce a form or group on
which active fancy may not trace figures or grotesque ornaments, which have been gradually moulded in this cavern
by the dropping of the calcareous water hardening into
petrifactions. Many of these fine groups have either been
wholly destroyed, or grievously defaced, by the Vandalism
of that class of tourists who cannot rest satisfied without
bearing away a fragment of every thing they contemplate,
be it the lava of a volcano, or the monument of a martyr.
The smoke of the torches and candles has also sullied the
purity of the crystallizations; but mutilated and dimmed

s

though they be, there is yet beauty enough left amply to
reward the enterprise of the tourist, and the enthusiasm of
the lover of Nature.

EYE SKETCH OF THE CUCHULLIN HILLS.

Leaving the Cave, and rounding Strathaird Point, the
tourist enters the Bay of Scavaig, where a scene of the
wildest sublimity opens upon his eye. The wild and romantic forms of the Cuchullin Hills, looming through the
mist in which they are generally more or less enveloped,
rear their grisly summits to the clouds, while columnar
and needle-pointed rocks shoot abruptly from the bosom of
the deep, forming together a scene of grandeur and of
desolation altogether unequalled in any other part of the

British Isles. To reach the upper end of Loch Scavaig, at the nearest point to Loch Coruisk, will occupy the tourist about three hours from the time of leaving the Spar Cave. In the bosom of the majestic solitude before him, and only about a quarter of a mile from the landing-place, reposes the far-famed Loch Coruisk. It is approached along the course of the brawling stream which discharges the superfluous waters of Loch Coruisk into Loch Scavaig. Pursuing this track, the shores of that "dread lake" expand to the eye, and there are few who will not concur in the exclamation of the Bruce, when the deep, dark, and solemn sheet of water stretches before him :

> "St. Mary ! what a scene is here !
> I've traversed many a mountain strand
> Abroad and in my native land,
> And it has been my lot to tread
> Where safety, more than pleasure led ;
> Thus many a waste I've wandered o'er—
> Clombe many a crag—cross'd many a moor—
> But, by my halidome,
> A scene so rude, so wild as this,
> Yet so sublime in barrenness,
> Ne'er did my wandering footsteps press,
> Where'er I happ'd to roam."*

"The margins of the lake are composed of vast sloping rocks and gigantic stones, and these hard and herbless masses rise ridge above ridge till they blend with the higher sides and summits of the mountains, seen only partially through the racking clouds, and seeming, so unexpectedly do they appear at times above you, as if in the very act of rolling downwards. The pervading colour is an ashy brown, and there is not only a vastness, but an air of volcanic desolation about them, which we have not seen elsewhere equalled. The loftier portions of all these mountains are extremely jagged and precipitous, rising here and there into gigantic pinnacles and spires, the smallest points of which, however, would crush to atoms all the cathedrals in the earth. But the sides and bases are in many parts composed of vast rounded or tabular masses of equal-sur-

* Lord of the Isles, Canto iii., stanza xiii.

faced rock, steeply inclined, indeed, but slightly gra-
nulated, so as to render walking, with due attention, easy.
At least we found it so.   Sir Walter Scott seems to have
viewed them as more sudden in their ascent from the lake
than they really are; for he describes the Cuillen mountains as rising 'so perpendicularly from the water edge, that
Borrowdale, or even Glencoe, is a jest to them.'   But, in
truth, their lower portions are not precipitous, as there
are various rocky platforms between the lake and the lofty
mountain steeps, and it is these forlorn and sloping flats
which constitute a pervading character of this desolate
scene.   Still they are steep enough, in all conscience, and
whether they are or not, why should a worm of the earth
gainsay the feelings of the great Magician ?"*

* Wilson's *Voyage round the Coasts of Scotland*, vol. i., page 218.
For the small eye-sketch of Coruisk and the Cuchullins, introduced into the
text, we are indebted to Professor Forbes of Edinburgh University.   It was
sketched by the Professor, in the course of his scientific researches, without
any pretension to geometrical accuracy, to give a general idea of the disposition of the hills and valleys of the district; and is appended to a paper on the
topography and geology of the Cuchullin Hills, and on the traces of ancient
glaciers which they present, contributed to the *Edinburgh Philosophical Journal.*
To this paper, in No. 79 of the *Journal,* the scientific reader is referred for the
most satisfactory description which has yet been published of the physical features of this portion of Skye.   The humbler objects of the present work admit
of our availing ourselves only of the following brief extract :—

"The mountainous part of Skye, between Broadford and Loch Brittle (a
distance of eleven miles,) comprises two very distinct groups of hills, as distinct
in arrangement and external form as in geological composition.   The group of
the Red Hills (to the east) is distinguished by rounded forms, consisting of a
group of dome-shaped masses crowded together; and composed of a kind of
syenite, in which felspar predominates.   The Cuchullin range constitutes a more
connected chain of craggy peaks, whose fantastic outlines, in certain positions,
may perhaps vie with any in the whole world.   They may be compared to those
of the granite mountains of Dauphiné ; and one part, in particular, resembles
the Montagne de la Grave, aptly likened, by M. Elie de Beaumont, to "a gigantic nut-cracker, menacing heaven with its open jaws." This group, as we shall
see, is more compact and less straggling than the other ; its colour, too, is in
singular contrast, varying from brown to deep green on the one side, to purple
on the other, particularly after rain.   Its composition is principally of hyper-
sthene rock, which was discovered here by Dr. Macculloch, of which the excessive
toughness, and its resistance to every kind of external action, whether from violence or from weather, gives much propriety to the name.   The mountain of
Ben Blaven stands beyond the proper limit of the Cuchullins, but in form, and
evidently also in composition, it must be classed with them.
"The appearance of the Red hills, as first seen after passing the Kyles of

At the head of the lake is a quiet, grassy plain, through which the crystalline stream by which the Loch is fed meanders on its mission. The serene beauty of the spot presents a refreshing contrast to the sterile grandeur around, but when a storm brings down the floods foaming from the mountain sides, the gentle stream swells into a mighty torrent, and sweeps the plain with resistless fury.

The circuit of the lake, as Mr. Wilson observes, is by no means so difficult, as the description of Sir Walter Scott, and the distant aspect of the margin would lead the tourist to suppose. It must, however, be admitted that the *Stron-na-Stree*, on the eastern side, does rise very precipitately. The walk round cannot much exceed three miles; but the fatigue of the journey, and the length of time taken to accomplish it, make it equal to at least five miles over a good road. The lake abounds with trout, and their flavour and condition satisfied the present writer that they at least are not sufferers from the general sterility around them. The eagle may often be seen tracing its sublime circles above the serrated peaks of the Cuchullins, and the red deer—joint-heir of the wilderness—sometimes forsakes his mountain fastnesses to browse on the plain at the head of the lake.

The description of Loch Coruisk and the scenery around it, is one of the noblest passages in the Lord of the Isles. To those tourists who have not provided themselves with a copy of that poem as a companion on their tour, the quotation cannot fail to be acceptable.

*   *   *

—— rarely human eye has known
A scene so stern as that dread lake,
With its dark ledge of barren stone.
Seems that primeval earthquake's sway
Hath rent a strange and shatter'd way
   Through the rude bosom of the hill,

And that each naked precipice,
Sable ravine, and dark abyss,
   Tells of the outrage still.
The wildest glen, but this, can show
Some touch of Nature's genial glow;
On high Benmore green mosses grow,
And heath-bells bud in deep Glencroe,

Skye, recalls, in almost every detail, the groups of *Puys* of Auvergne. The absence of craters does not altogether destroy the analogy; for such mountains as Ben na Cailleach and Glamich may be perfectly compared to the Puy de Dome which has no proper crater, and of which the form is attributed to the pasty consistence of the matter during ejection, without so great an explosive force as to clear an open vent through it. The Cuchullins, as has been said, recall granitic forms, but invested with a blackness and sterility which, taken as a whole, even few active volcanoes present."

And copse on Cruchan-Ben ;
But here,—above, around, below,
　On mountain or in glen,
Nor tree, nor shrub, nor plant, nor flower,
Nor aught of vegetative power,
　The weary eye may ken.
For all is rocks at random thrown,
Black waves, bare crags, and banks of stone,
　As if were here denied
The summer sun, the spring's sweet dew,
That clothe with many a varied hue
　The bleakest mountain-side.

And wilder, forward as they wound,
Were the proud cliffs and lake profound.
Huge terraces of granite black
Afforded rude and cumber'd track ;
　For from the mountain hoar,
Hurl'd headlong in some night of fear,
When yell'd the wolf and fled the deer,

Loose crags had toppled o'er ;
And some, chance-poised and balanced, lay,
So that a stripling arm might sway
　A mass no host could raise,
In Nature's rage at random thrown,
Yet trembling like the Druid's stone
　On its precarious base.
The evening mists, with ceaseless change,
Now clothed the mountains' lofty range,
　Now left their foreheads bare,
And round the skirts their mantle furl'd,
Or on the sable waters curl'd,
Or on the eddying breezes whirl'd,
　Dispersed in middle air.
And oft, condensed, at once they lower,
When, brief and fierce, the mountain shower
　Pours like a torrent down,
And when return the sun's glad beams,
Whiten'd with foam a thousand streams
　Leap from the mountain's crown.

If the tourist has brought a guide from Torrin, or if any of the boatmen are qualified to act in that capacity, he may at once strike across from the head of the loch to Glen Sligachan, by the wild pass known by the name of Hart-o-Corry. If he has no guide, and is not of an adventurous disposition, he must re-embark and be landed at Camasunary, where he will be directed to the footpath conducting to Sligachan Inn. The distance from Camasunary to Sligachan is at least eight miles, and the footpath (if the rude track merits the name) is so rough, that it will occupy three or four hours to perform the journey. On the left the pedestrian passes two sheets of water, called Loch-na-Creach and Loch-na-Nain, and on his right he will perceive the precipitous side of Ben Blaven, the mountain referred to in a former page. Pursuing his route, he will observe upon the left the opening of Hart-o-Corry, and at this point he has the most striking view of the Cuchullins he will command throughout the journey. Of the numerous peaks of the Cuchullins, Scuir-na-Gillean (*the rock of the young men*) is generally regarded as the highest. As far as is known, the summit of this mountain was first reached by Professor Forbes in 1836, accompanied by a local guide who had made many previous unsuccessful attempts both alone and with strangers.* Its height was computed by Professor Forbes,

---

* The name of this guide is Angus Macintyre, and strangers who propose to scale the giddy heights should secure his services. He may be heard of at Sligachan Inn.

by barometrical observations in 1845, and was found to be between 3200 and 3220 feet. Bruch-na-Fray is considered by the same authority to be about forty feet lower. Scuir-na-Banachtich, (*the smallpox rock*), a very acute summit of the western range, appears to the eye as elevated as Scuir-na-Gillean itself, and there is yet no evidence that it is not so. Ben Blaven is also a competitor for the honour of ranking first in altitude, and when it is considered that its less acuminated form is calculated to diminish its apparent height, we think it not improbable that it may make good its title. With the single exception of Glencoe, there is nothing on the mainland of Scotland comparable with the magnificent scene at this point of Glen Sligachan. The hills in both glens do not much differ in height, and in sterility they are nearly equal; but in the romantic gran-deur of their forms, chiefly of their summits, the palm must be assigned to the Cuchullins over the hills of Glencoe. In the latter, however, there is a closer proximity of the hills to the spectator, and although the poet has sung that " distance lends enchantment to the view," we incline to believe that the near approach of these mountain masses gives them additional impressiveness.

Following the course of the river that waters this deso-late valley, the tourist will reach Sligachan Inn, and although its accommodation is of a humble order, the shelter of its roof will be most welcome after the toils of the day. Should he wish to push on to Portree, a distance of nine and a half miles, a vehicle or ponies may be engaged at the Inn. The road presents no feature of any interest, and it is therefore of little consequence whether it is tra-velled by day or by night. There is an excellent road the whole way.

Portree, the capital of Skye, is situate on a steep acclivity at the side of the loch of the same name, the bay of which forms a fine land-locked natural harbour, spacious enough to contain several hundred sail. The entrance to the har-bour is surrounded by bold headlands, forming the com-mencement of a noble range of coast scenery extending northward to the Point of Aird. The Inn affords good accommodation, and branches of the National Bank of Scotland, and of the North of Scotland Bank, are established in the village. At Portree the tourist may avail himself of the steamer to return to Glasgow, for he has now been conducted through by far the most interesting scenery of Skye. Should he desire to extend his tour to Trotternish, Vaternish, and Sleat, we shall furnish a few rapid notes to assist his progress.

PORTREE—PRINCE CHARLES'S CAVE—THE STORR—QUIRAING—POINT OF AIRD—DUNTULM CASTLE—DUNVEGAN CASTLE—BRACADALE—SLIGACHAN—SCONSER—BROADFORD—KHYLE AKIN—ISLE ORONSAY —ARMADALE CASTLE.

The fine cliff scenery extending northward along the coast makes it desirable that a boat should be engaged at Portree for the first stage of the tourist's progress. Four miles from Portree, close upon the water's edge, is a cave in which Prince Charles lay for a time concealed.

The interior presents the same richly wrought natural rock-work as adorns the cave at Strathaird, while the exuding lime-water which produces the stalactites has hardened over the entrance into a variety of graceful forms of a rich cream colour, " intermingled with the lichen-covered rock, and interwreathed with long festoons of ivy leaves of the freshest green." The ruthless hand of the spoiler here, as at Strathaird, has destroyed many of the finest stalactites. Three miles further along the coast, and about a mile and a half from the shore, is the rocky pyramidal peak called the Storr. If the tourist land here he must pursue his way over the moor to Stanchel, which is sixteen miles distant from Portree, and about eight from Storr. But to perform this journey a guide is indispensable, for the track is scarcely discernible by any eye but that of a native. From the farm-house of Stanchel

QUIRAING

is distant about a mile and a half. This remarkable scene, the boast of Trotternish, and upheld by the natives of this portion of Skye as quite equal in interest to anything in the island, is a mile and a half or two miles from Stanchel. The mountain, among the rocky barriers of which it is enclosed, is about 1000 feet in height, sloping by a declivity towards the west, but presenting north-eastwards a front of rugged precipices, varied by huge uprising columns of basalt and massy fragments of fluted rock. In other parts large spaces forming concave sections present themselves to view, ribbed by fissures and projecting seams, between which in moist weather (which is seldom wanting) streamlets descend in lengthened silvery streaks. Quiraing itself consists of a verdant platform covered with an even and unvarying turf of the finest grass, and of sufficient extent (observes the martial spirit of its Highland pastor) to contain six or seven regiments of soldiers. To readers unversed in military affairs, it may be more intelligibly described as 100 paces long by 60 broad. It is studded all round with massive columns of rock, rising up in lofty peaks, more or less acuminated, and separated by deep chasms, rendering them for the most part inaccessible. On approaching the great inlet to the platform, the passage is much obstructed by heaps of stones and rubbish, the detritus of the fractured cliffs during the waste of ages.

> " But through the dark and through the cold,
> And through the yawning fissures old,
> Let tourist boldly press his way
>
> Right through the quarry ; and behold
> A scene of soft and lovely hue !
> Where blue and grey, and tender green,
> Together make as sweet a scene
> As ever human eye did view.

very majestic, and, from the sea, have a very magnificent effect.
They are thus described by Mr. Wilson:—" The cliffs immediate to
the sea were formed of gigantic prisms, of such large proportions
as to resemble the towers of castles grouped together, each being
several yards in diameter. Above these, and farther back, were
some of the loftiest columns of the more ordinary thickness, we had
yet observed. On the whole, the basaltic or columnar scenery of the
north of Skye exceeds, in the lofty grandeur of its ranges, whatever
Staffa or the Giant's Causeway can produce, although the angular
forms of the two latter are more minutely finished and symmetrical."
A mile and a half from Killmaluack, we reach Duntulm Castle, the
ancient residence of the Macdonalds, seated on a high, rocky, and
almost sea-girt point. Three miles further, on the left, stands Kilmuir Church, in the burying-ground of which, Flora Macdonald, the
faithful companion of the fortunes of Prince Charles, is interred.
The marble slab which was inlaid in her tombstone has been broken
and carried off piecemeal by the same class of ruthless destroyers
whom we have already had occasion to denounce in our description
of the caves at Strathaird and Portree. Two miles further, on the
right hand side of the road, is Monkstadt House, the residence of
Hugh Macdonald, Esq., one of the most extensive farmers in Skye.
The fertile valley extending to the north of the house is the bed of a
lake which has recently been drained, the ground thus acquired
being cultivated with the crooked spade peculiar to the agriculture
of Skye. Mr. Macdonald is the grandnephew of Flora Macdonald,
and possesses the habit-shirt worn by Prince Charles when disguised
in female apparel. Three miles and a quarter from Monkstadt the
tourist reaches Uig, a village of cottar farms at the head of the bay
of the same name. The whole land around the bay is laid out in
cultivated stripes, upon which is raised the produce which forms
the chief subsistence of the inhabitants. This scattered hamlet contains a population of about 600. A few small vessels generally enliven the bay. From Uig all the way to Portree, the road possesses
no interest beyond what is conferred on it by the view across Loch
Snizort, with its islands and bold rocky coast. Six miles from Uig
is Kingsborough, the residence of Donald M'Leod, Esq., the most
extensive farmer on Lord Macdonald's estate. If the tourist can
here find the means of crossing the loch to Tayinlone Inn in Lyndale, he will save seven miles of a dreary road: if not, he must pursue his way till he passes Snizort Church, beyond which, 8½ miles
from Uig, he reaches Cain-sail-eyre, a thatched public house of a very
abject order. Portree is distant from this point 6¾ miles. Pursuing
the road round Loch Snizort, for about 3 miles, we reach the farm-
house of Skebost, and 4½ miles further, passing a small plantation,
we arrive at Tayinlone Inn in Lyndale. The road now lies through
a dreary moorland, uncheered by any object of interest till the

traveller reaches Dunvegan,* a distance of 11½ miles. The branch
road to Dunvegan leads off the main road between the 9th and 10th
milestones from Tayinlone.

DUNVEGAN CASTLE,

the family seat of Macleod of Macleod, stands upon a rock near the
shore of a small bay, surrounded by woods of considerable extent,
to which additions have recently been made. Though the general pile
is imposing from its size and situation, the modern alterations made
to improve it as a family residence, have somewhat impaired its dignity as a stronghold. The most ancient portion is said to have been
built in the ninth century. Among the antiques preserved in Dunvegan, the most remarkable are the fairy flag, the horn of Rorie
More, and a chalice or drinking cup of oak, mounted with silver.
The last is said to have been part of the spoil taken from an Irish
chief called Nial Glundubh, (*Niel of the Black Knees.*) The date in
the inscription is much effaced, but it appears to be 993. The only
mountains of any considerable elevation in this district of Skye are
the Greater and Lesser Helvel, commonly called Macleod's Tables,
from the perfectly level nature of their summits. Their height is
1700 feet.

The next stage of the tourist's journey is Struan in Bracadale, a
slated public house 11¼ miles from Dunvegan.† The road skirts
Loch Bracadale, and in ascending from Struan the bay presents a
pleasing prospect. Half way between Struan and Sligachan the
road to Talisker branches off to the right. The scenery of Talisker
is highly romantic, and its soil particularly fertile. The commanding forms of the Cuchullins are again rising before us, as we approach Sligachan, which is 13¾ miles from Struan. Passing on the
right the lofty conical hill called Ben Glamich, and proceeding along
the shores of Loch Sligachan for 3½ miles, we reach Sconser
Inn. From Sconser to Broadford the road first skirts Loch Ainort

* Should the tourist desire to extend his researches into Vaternish, he strikes
off the Dunvegan road at Fairy Bridge. Four miles from Fairy Bridge, Stein,
a small village of slated houses, will be observed close by the water edge. The
fertility of this spot, with its small garden farms, is a cheering contrast to the
sterile wilderness through which the traveller has passed to reach it. The house
of Major Macdonald, the principal proprietor of Vaternish, is about a mile
further along the road, which extends to Vaternish Point.

† At Struan, a boat may be engaged by those who wish to see Macleod's
Maidens, three naked basaltic pillars, shooting abruptly from the sea off the
western horn of Loch Bracadale. The highest is 200, and the other two about
100 feet in height. There was at one time a fourth pillar, but it yielded to the
action of the storms and the waves, and has now disappeared in the deep.

The bay of Talisker is seen to the best advantage by approaching it by water;
and the tourist proceeding to Sligachan, by landing at Talisker shortens his journey by three miles.

and then the Sound of Scalpa, making a distance of 12 miles. The hillside by Scalpa Sound has a pleasant feathering of hazel and birch.

From Broadford the tourist may proceed either to Khyle Akin (8½ miles,) Khyle Rhea (12 miles,) or Isle Oronsay (12 miles.) None of the roads possesses much interest. At Khyle Akin an attempt was made, under the auspices of the late Lord Macdonald, to establish a seaport town, but the scheme entirely failed of success. It possesses, however, a respectable inn, and about a dozen good slated houses. Close to the village are the ruins of Castle Moil.

At Isle Oronsay there is a small steam-boat inn, and a commercial establishment has been founded there by the judicious enterprise of Mr. John Elder. The place derives its name from a small island, which lies so close upon the Skye coast as to form a convenient natural harbour.

Pursuing the route along the coast a road is passed on the right leading to Ord.* We next reach Knock farm on the left, and immediately adjoining it, on a rocky promontory projecting into the sea, are the ruins of Knock Castle. The country in this neighbourhood, it will be observed, presents an appearance of much higher cultivation than that through which we have hitherto passed. About two miles from Knockfin is Ostaig, the pleasant residence of Captain Macdonald, and a mile further is Armadale Castle, the seat of Lord Macdonald, and the chief mansion-house in the island. It is seated on a gentle slope, with a well-dressed lawn in front, and surrounded by woods of considerable extent. The chief ornament of the interior is a large window of painted glass in the staircase, executed at an expense of £1000, representing Somerled of the Isles, the founder of the family, who flourished in the twelfth century. The figure is in full Highland costume, armed with sword, battle-axe, and targe.

A mile and a half from Armadale Castle, is Ardvasar, a small hamlet, from the pier of which passengers can have a boat to or from the steamer. The public-house here is of a very humble kind, but the tourist who has walked over Skye may contrive to spend a night in it, for there is no other accommodation to the Point of Sleat.

* Ord is 4½ miles distant from this point. The part of the road nearest Ord lies through a pleasant valley, the sides of which have a covering of alder and of birch.

ELEVENTH TOUR.

GLASGOW TO INVERNESS, BY THE CALEDONIAN CANAL.

TOURISTS generally proceed to Oban by Lochgilphead and the Crinan Canal. There are two routes by land from Oban to Fort-William; the coast line by Connel Ferry and Appin, which is the shorter of the two, and the other by Taynuilt, Dalmally, and Glencoe. Loch Linnhe, bounded on the one hand by the craggy knolls of Appin, and on the other by the purple hills of Morven, is the commencement of that chain of salt and fresh water lakes formed into the Caledonian Canal, and presents on both sides scenery of a most romantic character. Opposite to the upper extremity of the island of Lismore, Loch Creran branches off into Lorn. The first mansion to the north of this Loch is Airds, the seat of Sir John Campbell; next is the ruin of Castle Stalker; Appin House, (Downie of Appin,) next occurs; and after that, at the mouth of Loch Leven, Ardshiel, (Stewart, Esq.) From Ballachulish Ferry on Loch Leven, noted for its slate quarry, the West Highland road penetrates the savage vale of Glencoe.* Coran Ferry, nine miles from Fort-William, divides Loch Linnhe from Loch Eil. Fort-William, and the contiguous village of Maryburgh, stand on a bend of Loch Eil, near the confluence of the river Lochy. The fort, erected in the reign of William III., is provided with a bomb-proof magazine, and barracks to accommodate about 100 men. Maryburgh is a village of about 1500 inhabitants, and contains two inns. BEN NEVIS,

* On certain days the steamer lands the passengers for Glencoe at Ballachulish Ferry. When this is not done, they must land at Coran Ferry, from which the distance to Ballachulish is four miles. A cart, said by its owner to have springs, may be hired from one of the boatmen at a charge of one shilling per mile, to carry on tourists to Ballachulish.

THE CALEDONIAN CANAL.

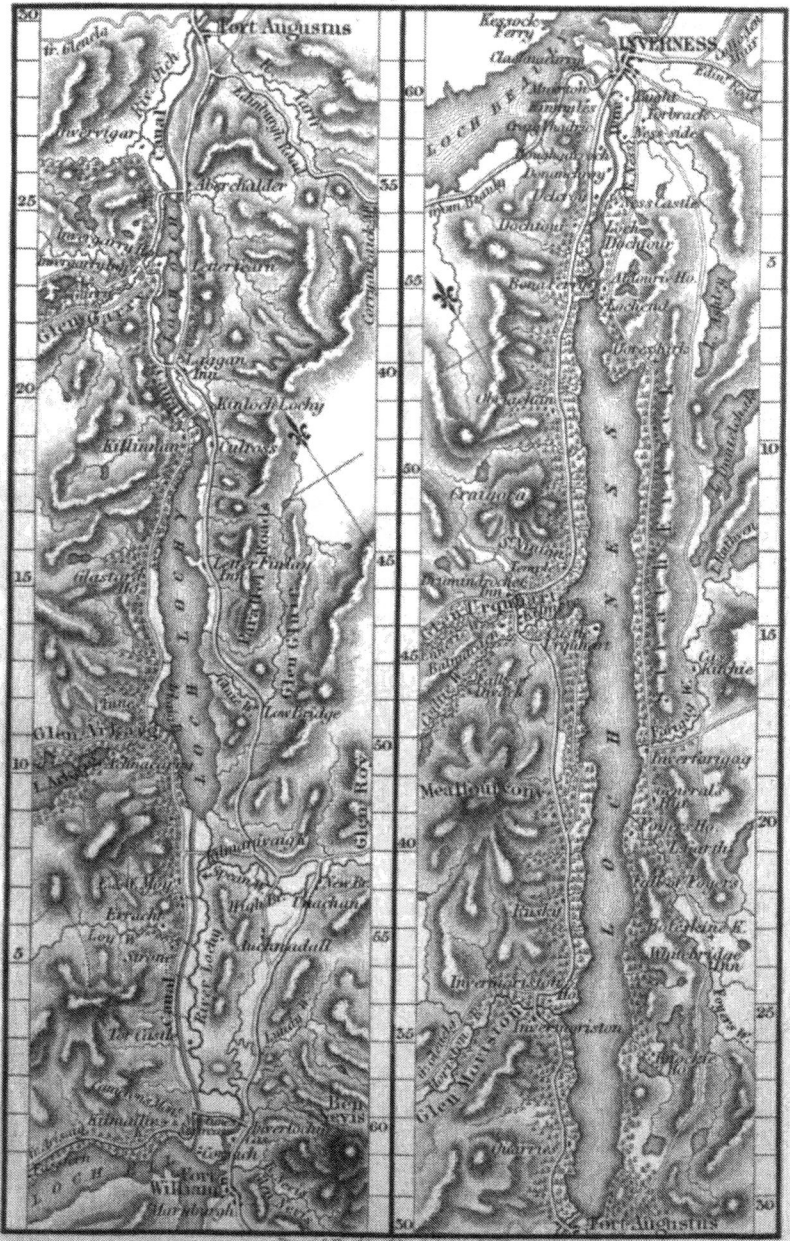

till lately considered the highest mountain in Scotland, is one of the most striking features of this neighbourhood. It rises 4416 feet above the mean level of the sea, and its circumference at the base, which, upon one side, is almost washed by the sea, is supposed to exceed twenty-four miles. " Its northern front consists of two grand distinct ascents, or terraces, the level top of the lowest of which, at an elevation of about 1700 feet, contains a wild tarn or mountain lake. The outer acclivities of this the lower part of the mountain are very steep, although covered with a short grassy sward, intermixed with heath ; but at the lake this general vegetable clothing ceases. Here a strange scene of desolation presents itself. The upper and higher portion seems to meet us, as a new mountain shooting up its black porphyritic rocks through the granitic masses, along which we have hitherto made our way, and, where not absolutely precipitous, its surface is strewed with angular fragments of stone of various sizes, wedged together, and forming a singularly rugged covering, among which we look in vain for any symptoms of vegetable life, except where round some pellucid spring the rare little Alpine plants, such as Epilobium alpinum, Silene acaulis, Saxifraga stellaris and nivalis, which live only in such deserts wild, are to be found putting forth their modest blossoms, amid the encircling moss. The eagle, sallying from his eyry, may greet the approach of the wanderer, or the mournful plover, with plaintive note, salute his ear ; but for those birds of the mountain the rocky wilderness were lifeless and silent as the grave ; its only tenants the lightnings and the mists of heaven, and its language the voice of the storm."* A terrific precipice on the north-eastern side makes a sheer descent from the snow-capped summit of not less than 1500 feet. The tourist who is so fortunate as to ascend the mountain in a favourable state of the atmosphere, is rewarded with a prospect of remarkable extent and grandeur. Ben Lomond, Ben Cruachan, Ben More, Ben Lawers, Schehallion, and Cairngorm, rear their gigan-

* Guide to the Highlands and Islands of Scotland, by George Anderson and Peter Anderson, Esquires.

tic heads around, while other peaks, scarcely less aspiring, extend in countless number and infinite variety of form and character, to the extreme verge of the horizon.* Two miles from Fort-William stands the old Castle of Inver-lochy, (lately enclosed and ornamented with evergreens and shrubs,) near which Montrose, in 1645, achieved one of his easiest and most decisive victories. He attacked the Campbells by surprise, and with a sacrifice of only three of his men, slaughtered or drowned upwards of 1500 of Argyll's forces. A few years since, a quantity of bones were dug up on the scene of this sanguinary rout where so many fell to deck a single name. Between Inverlochy and Fort-William, the country has an aspect of stern and rugged sublimity. Hills rise over hills of all shapes and sizes, and of various hues, from the deep distant blue to the hard weather-beaten grey and dark-wooded green. A high range of lime-stone rocks in Glen Nevis (remarkable for the splendour of its scenery (forms a magnificent panorama of mountains, especially when lighted up by the setting sun. About three miles from the sea, on the river Lochy, are the ruinous walls of Tor Castle, the ancient seat of the Clan-Chattan. From Loch Eil to Loch Lochy the distance is eight miles. At Corpach are three locks, and, a mile beyond, a series of eight locks, called Neptune's Staircase. Each lock is 180 feet long, 40 broad, and 20 deep. Here there is a comfort-able inn established, called Bannavie Inn, at which tourists

* " The ascent of Ben Nevis usually occupies three hours and a half from the base of the mountain, and the descent rather more than half that time. Some travellers go up at night, that they may enjoy the sunrise ; by doing so, they run a great risk of being disappointed, as in the morning the view is generally ob-scured by mists, and only occasional glimpses can be caught of the glorious pro-spect, which is generally clearest from mid-day to six o'clock in the evening. It is imprudent for a stranger to undertake the ascent without a guide, and one can always be procured about Fort-William for seven or eight shillings. The inex-perienced traveller, also, may be the better of being reminded to carry with him some wine or spirits (which, however, should be used with caution,) wherewith to qualify the spring water, which is, fortunately, abundant, and to which he will be fain to have frequent recourse, ere he attain the object of his labours. It is customary to ascend the hill on the northern side. By making a circuit to the eastward beyond Inverlochy Castle, the traveller can proceed as far as the lake on the back of a Highland pony."—*Anderson's Guide to the Highlands*, p. 268.

will be as well accommodated as at Fort-William. Passing the farms of West and East Moy, the steamer, two miles farther, enters Loch Lochy, which is ten miles in length, by about one in breadth ; near the west end there is a fine bay, called the Bay of Arkaig, at a short distance from which is the mansion of Cameron of Lochiel, chief of that clan.

Between Loch Lochy and Loch Oich, is the village of Laggan. The distance between the two lochs is nearly two miles. Loch Oich is about three and a half miles long by half a mile broad, and forms the summit level of the Caledonian Canal. Near the mouth of the river Garry, which discharges itself into this loch, are the ruins of Invergarry Castle, the ancient gathering-place of the clan Macdonell. In front is a small islet with green trees, and behind, a high mountain, called *Craig an phitich,* or the Rock of the Raven, an appellation which formed the war-cry, and is still the motto of the chiefs of Glengarry.

From Loch Oich, the steamboat descends to Loch Ness, by eight locks ; the distance between the lochs being five and a half miles. At the south-western extremity of the latter, and close upon the edge of the water, stands Fort Augustus. It was built shortly after the Rebellion of 1715. In form it is quadrangular, with four bastions at the corners. The barracks contain accommodation for about 300 men, but only six privates and a sergeant are now kept in the place.

Loch Ness is nearly twenty-four miles in length, and averages a mile and a quarter in breadth. In many places it is of great depth—about 130 fathoms—and, from the uniformity of temperature maintained by this depth of water, the lake never freezes. The character of its scenery, though highly interesting, is not so varied and striking as that through which we have already conducted the tourist.

A short distance from Fort Augustus, we pass the mouth of Glenmoriston, and the beautifully situated mansion of James Murray Grant, Esquire, the proprietor. A few miles further, on the right, are Foyers House and the mouth of the river Foyers, where the steamer generally

T

stops to afford passengers an opportunity of viewing the celebrated fall.

This famous cataract consists of two falls, of which the lower is by far the more imposing. The upper fall is about thirty feet high, twice broken in its descent; a bridge of one arch—an aerial-looking structure—being thrown over the chasm. It is seen to the best advantage from the channel of the river below the bridge. After pursuing its impetuous course for about a quarter of a mile, the stream makes its descent in a sheet of spray of dazzling whiteness into a deep and spacious linn, surrounded by gigantic rocks. The cavity of the fall is lined with a profusion of shrubs and plants, nursed by the perpetual spray. The height of this fall is variously stated, but it cannot be less than sixty feet. The banks on either side are diversified with the birch and the ash, and an undergrowth of copsewood, with those stupendous chasms and rocky eminences which confer additional grandeur on such a scene. "The Fall of Foyers," says Professor Wilson, "is the most magnificent cataract, out of all sight and hearing, in Britain. The din is quite loud enough in ordinary weather; and it is only in ordinary weather that you can approach the place from which you have a full view of all its grandeur. When the Fall is in flood—to say nothing of being drenched to the skin—you are so blinded by the sharp spray smoke, and so deafened by the dashing, and clashing, and tumbling, and rumbling thunder, that your condition is far from enviable, as you cling, 'lonely lover of nature,' to a shelf, by no means eminent for safety, above the horrid gulf. In ordinary Highland weather—meaning thereby weather neither very wet nor very dry—it is worth walking a thousand miles for one hour to behold the Fall of Foyers."* About two and

---

* Dr. E. D. Clarke, who visited this fall, declared it to be a finer cascade than Tivoli, and, of all he had seen, inferior only to Terni. The following lines were written by Burns upon the spot on September 5, 1787 :—

    "Among the heathy hills and ragged woods,
    The roaring Foyers pours his mossy floods,
    Till full he dashes on the rocky mounds,
    Where through a shapeless breach his stream resounds,
    As high in air the bursting torrents flow,
    As deep recoiling surges foam below,

a half miles from this, on the left, are seen the ruins of Castle Urquhart, often noticed in the annals of the earlier Scottish monarchs, and which was the last to surrender to Edward the First. Further notice of this fine ruin will be found in our Fifteenth Tour. Glen Urquhart, which recedes behind the castle, is a beautiful Highland vale, containing many gentlemen's seats; and, at the mouth, there is a good inn called Drumindrochet. Glen Urquhart chiefly belongs to the Earl of Seafield. At the Ferry of Bona, eight and a half miles from Drumindrochet, the steamer enters Loch Dochfour by a narrow channel about a quarter of a mile in length. On the margin of Loch Dochfour, stands Dochfour House, the elegant mansion of E. Baillie, Esq. At the foot of the lake the steamer again enters the canal, and proceeds to Muirton, from whence there is a descent by four locks to the capacious basin of the canal, at the end of which there are two other locks, opening from the Beauly Firth.

The Caledonian Canal was finally opened in October 1822. The whole distance from the Atlantic to the German Ocean is sixty and a half miles, of which thirty-seven and a half are through natural sheets of water, and twenty-three cut as a canal. The present depth of water is fifteen feet, but it is proposed to deepen it to seventeen feet, according to the original plan; also to increase the efficiency of the works, and to place steam-tugs on the lakes. These improvements having been suggested to the Lords of the Treasury by Sir Edward Parry, and Mr. Walker, engineer, are now in course of progress. The estimated expense of the operations is £200,000, towards which the sum of £155,000 has already been voted by Parliament. A contract has been entered into for the execution of the engineering works, amounting to £136,000, which will occupy a period of three years from their commencement in October

Prone down the rock the whitening sheet descends,
And viewless echo's ear, astonish'd, rends.
Dim-seen, through rising mists and ceaseless showers,
The hoary cavern, wide-surrounding, lowers;
Still through the gap the struggling river toils,
And still below the horrid caldron boils."

1843. The passage of the navigation from sea to sea is
necessarily interrupted during their progress; but parts of
the canal are kept open, and made available for the local
traffic. The lakes are still traversed by the Glasgow
steamers.

For a description of Inverness, and the objects of interest
in its neighbourhood, we refer to the Fourteenth Tour.

TWELFTH TOUR.

STAFFA AND IONA.

TOURISTS wishing to proceed to Staffa usually leave Glasgow
in a steamboat for Oban, where in the summer and autumn
months, a vessel is kept for the accommodation of strangers
wishing to visit this far-famed spot.

After leaving Oban, the steamer passes Kerrera, a narrow
rugged island, forming a natural breakwater to the bay of
Oban. It was here that Alexander II. died on his expedition in 1249, and here Haco, king of Norway, met the island
chieftains, who assisted him in his ill-fated descent on the
coast of Scotland. Upon the south point of the island are
the ruins of the Danish fort, Gylen. The boat now approaches Lismore,* a fertile island about nine miles in
length and two in breadth. In ancient times it was the
residence of the bishops of Argyle, who were frequently
styled "Episcopi Lismorienses." Leaving Lismore on the
right, the steamer enters the Sound of Mull, and passes the
Lady Rock, visible only at low water, on which Maclean of
Duart exposed his wife, a daughter of the second Earl of
Argyle, intending that she should be swept away by the
returning tide; but she was fortunately rescued by some of

* *Leosmore,* that is, "the Great Garden."

her father's people, who were passing in a boat. Maclean gave out that she had died suddenly, and was allowed to go through the ceremonial of a mock funeral, but was shortly afterwards put to death by the relations of his injured wife. This incident has been made the subject of one of Joanna Baillie's dramas—the "Family Legend." On the brink of a high cliff, on the shore of Mull, is Duart Castle, formerly the seat of the chief of the warlike and powerful clan of the Macleans. The steamer now sails along through a narrow but deep channel. On the left are the bold and mountainous shores of Mull, on the right those of that district of Argyleshire called Morven, successively indented by deep salt water lochs running up many miles inland. To the south-eastward, arise a prodigious range of mountains, among which Ben Cruachan is pre-eminent, and to the north-east is the no less huge and picturesque range of the Ardnamurchan Hills. Many ruinous castles, situated generally upon cliffs overhanging the ocean, add interest to the scene. In fine weather, a grander and more impressive scene, both from its natural beauties, and associations with ancient history and tradition, can hardly be imagined. When the weather is rough, the passage is both difficult and dangerous, from the narrowness of the channel, and in part from the numerous inland lakes, out of which sally forth a number of conflicting and thwarting tides, making the navigation perilous to open boats. The sudden flaws and gusts of wind which issue, without a moment's warning, from the mountain glens, are equally formidable ; so that, in unsettled weather, a stranger, if not much accustomed to the sea, may sometimes add to the other sublime sensations excited by the scene, that feeling of dignity which arises from a sense of danger. Opposite to Duart, on the coast of Morven, are the ruins of Ardtornish Castle,

> " Where turret's airy head,
> Slender and steep, and battled round,
> O'erlook'd, dark Mull ! thy mighty Sound,
> Where thwarting tides, with mingled roar,
> Part thy swarth hills from Morven's shore."*

---

* Lord of the Isles. *Opening Canto.*

" The situation is wild and romantic in the highest
degree, having on the one hand a high and precipitous
chain of rocks overhanging the sea, and, on the other,
the narrow entrance to the beautiful salt water lake,
called Loch Aline, which is in many places finely fringed
with copsewood. The ruins of Ardtornish are not now
very considerable, consisting chiefly of the remains of an
old keep or tower, with fragments of outward defences.
But, in former days, it was a place of great consequence,
being one of the principal strongholds which the Lords of
the Isles, during the period of their stormy independence,
possessed upon the mainland of Argyleshire." Above the
Castle of Ardtornish, is Ardtornish House, (Gregorson, Esq.)
Another residence of the Island Kings' next meets the eye
in the Castle of Aros, in Mull, a powerful rock-built fortress,
situated about half-way from either end of the Sound.* A
short way beyond, on the Morven coast, is Killundine Castle.
Holding on towards the head of the Sound, the steamer,
seven miles beyond Aros, reaches Tobermory, (the well of
our Lady St. Mary,) the only village of any note in Mull.
It was founded in 1788, by the British Fishery Company,
and is finely situated at the head of the inner recess of a
well protected bay. In the immediate vicinity is Drumfin,
the splendid mansion of Maclean of Coll. This romantic
spot is well worthy the notice of the tourist. Quitting
Tobermory, we enter Loch Sunart. Seven miles from
Tobermory, on the Ardnamurchan coast, is the Castle of
Mingarry, which

> "——— sternly placed,
> O'erawes the woodland and the waste."

The ruins, which are tolerably entire, are surrounded by a
very high wall, forming a kind of polygon, for the purpose
of adapting itself to the projecting angles of a precipice
overhanging the sea, on which the castle stands. It was
anciently the residence of the MacIans, a clan of Macdonalds, descended from Ian or John, a grandson of Angus

* From the village of Aros there is a road which leads across the island to
Loch-na-Keal, and thence to Laggan Ulva, where there is a place of embarkation for Staffa and Iona.

Og, Lord of the Isles. Rounding the point of Callioch, the last promontory of Mull, we find ourselves moving freely on the bosom of the Atlantic, and at the same moment, if the weather is fine, the islands of Mull, including the Trishnish Isles, Tiree, Coll, Muck, Eig, and Rum, burst on the view, and, far to the north-west, the faint outlines of South Uist and Barra.* In fine weather the light-house lately erected on Skerryvore Rock may also be seen. It is a granite column 150 feet in height, and has been erected at great cost and hazard by the Commissioners of the Northern Light-houses, from the design of Alan Stevenson, Esq., engineer to the Board.

Staffa is about eight miles distant from the western coast of Mull. It is of an irregular oval shape, and about three-fourths of a mile in length, by half a mile in breadth. The most elevated point is toward the south-west, where the rock attains an elevation of about 144 feet. The first cave approached is the Clam or Scallop-shell Cave, on one side of which the basaltic columns appear bent like the ribs of a ship, while the opposite wall is made up of the ends of horizontal columns, resembling the surface of a honeycomb. This cave is 30 feet in height, and 16 or 18 in breadth at the entrance, its length being 130 feet. Next occurs the noted rock Buachaille, or the Herdsman, a conoidal pile of columns about 30 feet high. From this spot the pillars extend in one continued colonnade along the whole face of the cliff to the entrance of Fingal's Cave, by far the most impressive and interesting object in the island. The best and most recent description of this far-famed cave, is contained in Mr. James Wilson's "Voyage round the Coasts of Scotland and the Isles." We therefore extract the following passage for the benefit of our readers, recommending the work itself

---

* " The shores of Mull on the eastward lay,
  And Ulva dark and Colonsay,
  And all the group of islets gay
    That guard famed Staffa round.
  Then all unknown its columns rose,
  Where dark and undisturbed repose
    The cormorant had found." †

† Lord of the Isles. Canto iv., stanza x.

to their attention, as the most interesting and comprehensive
account of the coast scenery of Scotland which has hitherto
appeared.

"Fingal's Cave is indeed a most magnificent example of
nature's architecture. A vast archway of nearly 70 feet in
height, supporting a massive entablature of 30 feet additional, and receding for about 230 feet inwards,—the entire
front, as well as the great cavernous sides, being composed
of countless complicated ranges of gigantic columns, beautifully jointed, and of most symmetrical though somewhat
varied forms,—the roof itself exhibiting a rich grouping of

overhanging pillars, some of snowy whiteness from the calcareous covering by which they have become encrusted,—
the whole rising from and often seen reflected by the ocean
waters,—forms truly a picture of unrivalled grandeur, and
one on which it is delightful to dwell even in remembrance.
How often have we since recalled to mind the regularity,
magnitude, and loftiness of those columns, the fine o'erhang-
ing cliff of small prismatic basalt to which they give sup-

port, worn by the murmuring waves of many thousand years, into the semblance of some stupendous Gothic arch,

"Where thro' the long-drawn aisle and fretted vault,"

the wild waters ever urge their way,—and the receding sides of that great temple, running inwards in solemn perspective, yet ever and anon, as ocean heaves and falls, rendered visible in its far sanctuary, by the broad and flashing light reflected by the foaming surges sweeping onwards from below! Then the broken and irregular gallery which overhangs that subterranean flood, and from which, looking upwards and around, we behold the rich and varied hues of red, green, and gold, which give such splendid relief to the deep and sombre-coloured columns—the clear bright tints which sparkle beneath our feet, from the wavering yet translucent sea—the whole accompanied by the wild yet mellow and sonorous moan of each successive billow, which rises up the sides, or rolls over the finely-formed crowns of the lowlier and disjointed pillars: these are a few of the features of this exquisite and most singular scene, which cannot fail to astonish the beholder."

> " Where, as to shame the temples deck'd
> By skill of earthly architect,
> Nature herself, it seem'd would raise
> A Minster to her Maker's praise !
> Not for a meaner use ascend
> Her columns, or her arches bend ;
> Nor of a theme less solemn tells
> That mighty surge that ebbs and swells,
> And still, between each awful pause,
> From the high vault an answer draws,
> In varied tone prolong'd and high,
> That mocks the organ's melody.
> Nor doth its entrance front in vain
> To old Iona's holy fane,
> That Nature's voice might seem to say,
> ' Well hast thou done, frail Child of clay !
> Thy humble powers that stately shrine
> Task'd high and hard—but witness mine !' "*

The Boat Cave, and Mackinnon's, or the Cormorant's

* *Lord of the Isles*, c. iv., st. x.

Cave, are two others of less extent and beauty, which are usually visited after Fingal's Cave.*

Iona or Icolmkill, celebrated as an early seat of Christianity, is about nine miles to the south of Staffa. "In any other situation," says Dr. Macculloch, "the remains of Iona would be consigned to neglect and oblivion; but connected as they are with an age distinguished by the ferocity of its manners and its independence of regular government; standing a solitary monument of religion and literature, such as religion and literature then were, the mind imperceptibly recurs to the time when this island was 'the light

IONA.

of the western world,' 'a gem in the ocean,' and is led to

* Professor Wilson, with Scott's description probably present to his fancy, speaks of "the pealing anthem of waves in the Cave-Cathedral of Staffa," an expression of rare felicity and beauty.

Among the numberless poetical offerings made to the glories of the place, we must content ourselves with the fine Sonnet of Wordsworth.

"Thanks for the lessons of this spot—fit school
For the presumptuous thoughts that would assign
Mechanic laws to agency divine;
And measuring heaven by earth, would overrule
Infinite power. The pillar'd vestibule,
Expanding, yet precise, the roof embow'd,
Might seem design'd to humble man, when proud
Of his best workmanship by plan and tool.
Down-bearing with his whole Atlantic weight ·
Of tide and tempest on the Structure's base,
And flashing to that Structure's topmost height,
Ocean has proved its strength, and of its grace
In calms is conscious, finding for his freight
Of softest music some responsive place."

contemplate with veneration its silent and ruined structures. Even at a distance, the aspect of the cathedral, insignificant as its dimensions are, produces a strong feeling of delight in him who, long coasting the rugged and barren rocks of Mull, or buffeted by turbulent waves, beholds its tower first rising out of the deep, giving to this desolate region an air of civilization, and recalling the consciousness of that human society, which, presenting elsewhere no visible traces, seems to have abandoned these rocky shores to the cormorant and the sea-gull." Iona is nearly three miles in length, and one in breadth. The origin of the celebrity of this island* is to be traced to its having become, about the year 565, the residence of Columba, an Irish Christian preacher. The monastery became, in subsequent years, the dwelling of the Cluniacenses, a class of monks who followed the rule of St. Bennet. At the Reformation, Iona, with its abbey, was annexed to the bishopric

* The following splendid and well known passage records the emotions excited in the breast of Dr. Johnson by the prospect of Iona :—" We were now treading that illustrious island which was once the luminary of the Caledonian regions, whence savage clans and roving barbarians derived the benefits of knowledge, and the blessings of religion. To abstract the mind from all local emotion would be impossible, if it were endeavoured, and would be foolish if it were possible. Whatever withdraws us from the power of our senses—whatever makes the past, the distant, or the future, predominate over the present, advances us in the dignity of thinking beings. Far from me and from my friends be such frigid philosophy as may conduct us indifferent and unmoved over any ground which has been dignified by wisdom, bravery, or virtue. That man is little to be envied whose patriotism would not gain force upon the plain of Marathon, or whose piety would not grow warmer among the ruins of Iona." Wordsworth has composed the following sonnet upon landing at Iona :—

" How sad a welcome! To each voyager
Some ragged child holds up for sale a store
Of wave-worn pebbles, pleading on the shore
Where once came monk and nun with gentle stir,
Blessings to give, news ask, or suit prefer,
Yet is yon neat trim church a grateful speck
Of novelty amid the sacred wreck
Strewn far and wide. Think, proud philosopher !
Fallen though she be, this Glory of the west,
Still on her sons the beams of mercy shine ;
And ' hopes, perhaps more heavenly bright than thine,
A grace by thee unsought and unpossest,
A faith more fix'd, a rapture more divine,
Shall gild their passage to eternal rest.' "

of Argyle, by James VI., in the year 1617.   The celebrated
ruins consist of a cathedral, a nunnery, and St. Oran's
chapel.   The latter, which appears to be the most ancient
of these ecclesiastical remains, is of small extent (60 feet
by 20) and rude architectural style, and was probably built
by the Norwegians.   It contains some tombs of different
dates, and there are many carved stones in the pavement.
The chapel of the nunnery is the next in the order of antiquity ; it is in good preservation ; the roof has been
vaulted, and part of it still remains.   The nuns were not
displaced at the Reformation, but continued a long time
after that event, to live together.   They followed the rule of

St. Augustine. The
Cathedral Church
of St. Mary is the
principal   edifice.
Its form is that of
a cross, the length
being about 160
feet and the breadth
24. "Whatever may
be its actual age
it now possesses
enough of ' hoar
antiquity' to throw
an air of solemn
grandeur over the
general aspect of
the   scene,   and
produces,   indeed,
a most imposing
effect, with its mas-
sive square tower
rising to the height of 70 feet above the lonesome graves,
the grassy verdure of its foundations almost washed by the
murmuring sea, at this time flowing gently between the
lowlier shores of the Sacred Island, and the stern and rocky
coast of the opposing Mull."*   Most families of distinction

* WILSON'S *Voyage round the Coasts of Scotland*, vol. I., p. 138.

in the Highlands had burying-places here, and many erected votive chapels in different parts of the island. On the west side of Martyrs' Street is Maclean's Cross, a beautifully carved pillar, and one of the 360 stone crosses which are said to have once adorned the island; but about the year 1560, they were thrown into the sea by order of the Synod of Argyle. Iona contains 450 inhabitants, and is the property of the Duke of Argyle.

> "Homeward we turn. Isle of Columba's cell,
> Where Christian piety's soul-cheering spark
> (Kindled from Heaven between the light and dark
> Of time) shone like the morning-star,—farewell !"

THIRTEENTH TOUR.

An Itinerary of this Tour will be found at the end of the Volume.

GLASGOW—PAISLEY—KILMARNOCK—ARDROSSAN—AYR—AND THE LAND OF BURNS, BY THE GLASGOW AND AYRSHIRE RAILWAY.

THE prospectus of the Railway between Glasgow and Ayrshire was issued in the spring of 1836; operations were commenced about the middle of May 1838; several portions of the line were opened at different periods; and the entire line between Glasgow and Ayr was opened on the 12th of August 1840.

The station-house at Glasgow is situate on the west side of Bridge Street, Tradestone, and very near the "Glasgow Bridge." On leaving Glasgow, the tourist passes an immense number of cotton and silk manufactories, iron-works, and other establishments of a similar kind, together with a succession of elegant villas, belonging to the wealthy merchants and manufacturers connected with the city. About

half way between Glasgow and Paisley the ruins of Crookston Castle are to be seen on an eminence overhanging the
south bank of the White Cart. This Castle was at one time
the property of the Stewarts of Lennox, and here Queen
Mary resided, when receiving the addresses of Darnley.
It is now the property of Sir John Maxwell of Pollock.
Proceeding onward, the train reaches

PAISLEY STATION,

seven miles from Glasgow, 33 from Ayr. The large manufacturing town of Paisley is situated on the banks of the
White Cart. It is a place of great antiquity, and owes its
first existence to a religious establishment founded here,
about the year 1160, by Walter Stewart, the ancestor of
the royal family of Scotland. The progress of the town
was slow, and it was not until towards the close of last
century that it assumed any appearance of importance.
The original manufactures of Paisley were coarse checked
linen cloth and checked linen handkerchiefs, and these were
succeeded by fabrics of a lighter and more fanciful kind.
About the year 1760, the manufacture of gauze was introduced into Paisley, in imitation of the manufactures of
Spitalfields. The experiment met with remarkable success,
and the immense variety of elegant and richly ornamented
fabrics which were issued from this place, surpassed all
competition. The gauze trade now employs but few hands,
and shawls of silk and cotton, plaids, scarfs, chenille and
Canton crape shawls and handkerchiefs, silks, and Persian
velvets, are at present the staple manufactures of the town.

Among the most interesting objects in Paisley, the Abbey
Church occupies a prominent place. This magnificent
building, which was dedicated to St. James and St. Mirren,
suffered severely at the Reformation, and its immense revenues became the prey of several of the nobility. The chancel, which is now used as a parish church, still remains
entire, along with the window of the northern transept.
Attached to its south side is a small but lofty chapel, which
possesses a remarkably fine echo, and contains a tomb, surmounted by a recumbent female figure, usually supposed to

represent Marjory, daughter of Robert Bruce, and wife of
Walter Stewart, founder of the abbey. This lady, who was
mother of Robert Second, the first of the Stewart sovereigns, was killed by a fall from her horse, at a place in the
neighbourhood of Paisley. The buildings connected with
the abbey are the property of the Marquis of Abercorn, the
representative of Claud Hamilton, the last abbot, and first
temporal superior of Paisley, referred to in Sir Walter
Scott's ballad of Cadyow Castle, as

" Stern Claud ——————
Grey Paisley's haughty lord."

The population of the town, in 1841, amounted to 60,487.
It returns one member to the House of Commons. A short
distance from Paisley, the line passes on the left the straggling village of Elderslie. Here, near the turnpike road,
is the oak in which, according to tradition, Sir William
Wallace, the " Knight of Elderslie," concealed himself from
the English troops. Elderslie House, which stands at a short
distance, appears to be of later erection than the era of the
hero. About three miles from Paisley is JOHNSTONE STA-
TION. The town of JOHNSTONE is situated on the banks of
the Black Cart. It is a thriving seat of the cotton manufacture, and contains a population of about 5900. In the
vicinity of the town, to the west, is Milliken House, the seat
of Sir W. M. Napier, Bart. Farther, to the north-west, is
Houston House, A. Speirs, Esq., M.P., Lord-Lieutenant of
the county of Renfrew. A short way farther on is the village of Kilbarchan, containing a population of 3612. The
superiors of this village, in ancient times, were the Sempills
of Beltrees, a family in which poetical talent was long hereditary. Sir James Sempill, ambassador to England in 1599,
wrote the satire of " The Packman and the Priest." His
son, Robert Sempill, was the author of the poem entitled
" The Life and Death of the Piper of Kilbarchan." Francis,
the son of this poet, wrote the well-known songs, " Maggie
Lauder," and " She rose and loot me in." A few years ago, a
statue of Habbie Simpson, the piper above-mentioned, was
affixed to the steeple of the Town-Hall. After leaving the

Howood station, the line runs through a rich strath, celebrated
for its beautiful scenery.   On the right are the extensive
and highly ornamented pleasure-grounds of Castle Semple,
the seat of Colonel Harvey.   On the left, above the public
road to Beith, are the ruins of Elliston Tower, formerly the
seat of the Sempill family.   Fifteen and a half miles from
Glasgow, is LOCHWINNOCH STATION.   The village of this
name is situated on the side of Castle Semple Loch, near
the bottom of a range of hills.   The population amounts
to about 3000.   At a short distance to the west of the village is Barr Castle, supposed to have been built in the
fifteenth century.   In the vicinity is Barr House, (W. Mac-
Dowell, Esq.)   Castle Semple Loch, which is about a mile
in length, contains three wooded islets, on one of which
are the remains of a fortalice erected, in ancient times,
by Lord Sempill.   About two and a quarter miles from
Lochwinnoch, and seventeen and three quarters from Glasgow, is BEITH STATION.   The town of BEITH contains a
population of about 6000.   In the vicinity of the town are
the ruins of Giffen Castle, formerly a possession of the
Eglinton family.   A little farther on we perceive, near the
river Garnock, the remains of the ancient castle of Glen-
garnock, the property of the Earl of Glasgow, and the beautiful sheet of water called Kilbirnie Loch, extending about
two miles in length, and half a mile in breadth.   Nineteen
and a half miles from Glasgow we reach KILBIRNIE STA-
TION.   The village of Kilbirnie is situated on the banks
of the Garnock, at the distance of about a mile and a half
to the right.   Two miles farther on, at the distance of
twenty-two miles from Glasgow, is DALRY STATION,
from which a branch line strikes off to the left to KILMAR-
NOCK, a thriving manufacturing town, pleasantly situated
upon an almost level plain, surrounded by pleasing scenery.
It is distinguished for its manufacture of worsted shawls,
Brussels and Venetian carpets, boots, shoes, and some other
articles ; and its success in these manufactures has raised
it to the rank of the principal town in Ayrshire for size,
wealth, and population.   According to the last census, the
population amounted to 17,844.   Within a mile north of the

town, stand the ruins of Dean Castle, once the residence of the Earls of Kilmarnock. Eight and a half miles from Kilmarnock, and twenty-three and a half from Glasgow, is STEWARTON. The thriving village of DALRY is situated on an eminence, and nearly surrounded with the waters of the Garnock, Rye, and Caaf. It contains 4326 inhabitants, who are chiefly employed in weaving. Returning to Dalry, and proceeding onwards, we reach, about fourteen miles from Ayr, and twenty-six from Glasgow, KILWINNING STATION, where, on the right a branch of the railway leads to the towns of SALTCOATS and ARDROSSAN, the former being about four miles distant, and the latter about five and a half miles. About 200 years ago, Saltcoats was inhabited by only four families, who gained their livelihood by making salt. It now contains 4000 inhabitants, including seamen. The town of Ardrossan, which of late has attained considerable celebrity as a watering place, is of recent origin, and its rise is owing chiefly to the public-spirited exertions of the Eglinton family. It possesses an excellent harbour, for which it was indebted to the late Earl of Eglinton, who laid out an enormous sum of money on the undertaking, without the satisfaction of having completed what had been so much an object of his solicitude. The undertaking has now been accomplished by the present Earl. *
Kilwinning † signifies the cell of Winning, and derives

* Steamboats ply regularly from Ardrossan to Glasgow, Fleetwood, Arran, and Belfast. Communication by the railways to and from Glasgow and Ayr, and the intermediate towns, takes place five times a-day. During the summer, the steamer to Arran plies daily.

† At the distance of about a mile from Kilwinning stands Eglinton Castle, the splendid mansion of the Earl of Eglinton and Wintoun, towards which public attention was recently directed by the tournament which was held in its vicinity in September 1839.—The castle was built about forty years ago, and is surrounded by extensive pleasure-grounds. The family of Montgomery is of Norman origin, and the first of the name that settled in Scotland was Robert de Montgomerie, who obtained from Walter, the High Steward of Scotland, a grant of the barony of Eaglesham, in the county of Renfrew. In the fourteenth century, Alexander de Montgomerie acquired the baronies of Eglinton and Ardrossan, by marriage with Elizabeth, daughter and sole heiress of Sir Hugh de Eglinton. At the famous battle of Otterbourne, fought in 1387, Henry Percy, the renowned Hotspur, was taken prisoner by Sir Hugh Montgomery, and, for

its name from the circumstance of a saint named Winning having resided here in the eighth century.   Hugh
de Moreville, lord of Cunningham, in 1107, founded
here an abbey for monks of the Tyronensian order, dedicated to Saint Winning, the ruins of which still
exist.   The greater part of this splendid edifice was
destroyed at the Reformation, and a grant of it was
made to the Earl of Glencairn ; but the temporalities
were erected in 1603, into a lordship in favour of Lord
Eglinton.   A party of freemasons, who came from the continent to assist in the building of this monastery, were the
first to introduce freemasonry into Scotland, and by means
of the establishment of lodges, the knowledge of their mysteries was diffused over the rest of the country.   Kilwinning is also distinguished as a seat of archery, a company
of archers having been organized here in 1488.   They have
a custom of shooting annually for a prize at the popinjay
or popingo, a practice described in the tale of Old Mortality.
The population of Kilwinning is 3772.   Proceeding onward,
should the atmosphere be clear, the tourist will obtain on
the right, a view of the Island of Arran, with its lofty and
precipitous mountains.   The line next crosses the Garnoch,
which here forms the boundary betwixt the parishes of
Kilwinning and Irvine.   A little farther on, it crosses the
river Irvine* by an elegant bridge of six arches, and reaches

his ransom, built the castle of Penoon or Polnoon, in Renfrewshire, which is
still the property of the Eglinton family.   In 1488, the representative of the
family was raised to the peerage, by the title of Lord Montgomery, and in
1507-8, Hugh, the third baron, was created Earl of Eglinton.   In 1582, Robert,
the first Earl of Wintoun, married Lady Margaret Montgomery, eldest daughter
of Hugh, third Earl of Eglinton, and the third son of that marriage, Sir Alexander Seton of Foulstruther, was adopted into the family, and became sixth
Earl of Eglinton.   The direct line of the Wintoun family having failed, the
present Earl of Eglinton was, in January 1841, served heir to the title of Earl
of Wintoun.   The late Earl, Hugh, was created a British peer, by the title of
Baron Ardrossan.   Archibald William, the present and thirteenth Earl, was
born 29th September 1812, and succeeded to the titles and estates on the death
of his grandfather Hugh, 14th December 1819.

* Here, while Wallace was on a visit to his uncle at Riccarton, occurred the
famous incident of his killing three English troopers, and putting two to flight
with no other weapon than his pout-staff or fishing-rod.

IRVINE STATION, twenty-nine and a half miles distant from Glasgow, and ten and a half miles from Ayr. Irvine is a royal burgh of considerable antiquity ; and a monastery of Carmelite or White Friars was founded here in 1412. There are 124 vessels belonging to the port, which employ 1000 seamen. Irvine unites with Ayr, Campbelton, Inverary, and Oban, in returning a member to Parliament. The population in 1840 was 10,779. Irvine is remarkable for having been the temporary residence of Burns, and the birth-place of James Montgomery the poet, and John Galt the novelist. After leaving Irvine, a view is obtained, on the left, of the remains of the ancient castle of Dundonald, standing on an elevated position, about two miles distant. The situation of this castle, on the top of a beautiful hill, is singularly noble. It was the property of Robert Stewart, who, in right of his mother, Marjory Bruce, succeeded to the Scottish throne under the title of Robert II. Here he wooed and married his first wife, the beautiful Elizabeth Mure of Rowallan, and here he died in 1390. This castle gives the title of earl to the noble family of Cochrane. The estate passed into the hands of the Earl of Eglinton in the beginning of last century ; but the castle, along with the hill on which it stands, and five roods of adjoining land, still belong to the Earl of Dundonald. In the vicinity of Dundonald Castle are the remains of an ancient church, dedicated to the Virgin, called Our Lady's Kirk. James IV., in passing through this part of his kingdom, uniformly made an offering at this Kirk, generally giving fourteen shillings at a time. About four and a half miles from Irvine, and six miles from Ayr, is TROON STATION, with the village of the same name, situated on the right, at the distance of about half a mile. The Duke of Portland is superior of this place, and under his patronage it has attained to considerable importance. It is a well-frequented watering place, and carries on a large coasting trade. The line now passes very near the sea ; and in the course of a short time we observe, on the left, Fullarton House, a seat of the Duke of Portland, situate on a spacious lawn, and

surrounded, except in front, with extensive woods.   Three
miles onward is MONKTON STATION, and village, and a mile
farther, the small burgh of Prestwick ; a little beyond it,
the ruins of Kingscase, a charitable institution, endowed
by King Robert Bruce ; and, at the distance of forty miles
from Glasgow, reaches the town and station of

AYR,

the county town and a royal burgh, situate at the mouth of
the river of the same name.   Ayr is a very ancient town,
and was erected into a royal burgh by William the Lion.
It contains a number of handsome public buildings, and
many of its shops and dwelling-houses may vie in elegance
with those of the metropolis.   The river Ayr divides Ayr
Proper from Newton and Wallacetown.   The river rises on
the border of the county, at the eastern extremity of the
parish of Muirkirk, and after a course of about thirty miles,
falls into the sea at this place.   It is crossed here by two
bridges, respectively termed the Auld and New Brigs, and
noticed under these denominations by Burns, in his poem
of " The Twa Brigs."   The Auld Brig is said to have been
built in the reign of Alexander III. (1249-1285) by two
maiden sisters of the name of Lowe, whose effigies were consequently carved upon a stone in the eastern parapet, near
the south end of the fabric.   It is stated by tradition, that
before the erection of this bridge, a ford, about two hundred
yards farther up, called the Doocote Stream, afforded the
best passage which is to be had across the river in this
quarter.   The new bridge was erected in 1788, chiefly
through the exertions of Provost Ballantyne, the gentleman
to whom Burns dedicated the poem of " The Twa Brigs."
The " Dungeon Clock," alluded to in the poem, was placed
at the top of an old steeple in the Sandgate, which was
taken down in 1826.   The " Wallace Tower" was a rude
old building, which stood in the eastern part of the High
Street, at the head of a lane named the Mill Vennel.   It
was in this tower, according to tradition, that Wallace was
confined.   Having become ruinous, it was taken down in

1835, and a Gothic structure erected on its site, containing at the top the clock and bells of the dungeon steeple, and ornamented in front by a statue of Wallace, executed by Mr. Thom, the well-known self-taught sculptor. Another statue of " Scotia's ill-requited chief" was placed about thirty years ago by a citizen of Ayr, on the front of a dwelling-house, which occupies the site of the ancient court-house of Ayr, supposed to have been that in which, according to Blind Harry, the Scottish lords were treacherously hanged. The fort of Ayr was built by Oliver Cromwell, in 1652, upon a level piece of ground between the town and the sea. A few fragments of the ramparts still remain, together with an old tower, which formed part of St. John's Church, founded in the twelfth century. Cromwell inclosed this church within the walls of his citadel, and turned it into an armoury, but, as a compensation to the inhabitants, he gave £150 towards the erection of the present Old Church of Ayr, on the site of a Dominican monastery, remarkable in history as the place where Robert Bruce held the Parliament which settled his succession. The only memorial now existing of this monastery is in the name of a spring called the Friar's Well, which runs through the churchyard into the river. The Old Church still contains the same seats and galleries with which it was originally fitted up.

At the north-eastern angle of the fort, close upon the harbour, is supposed to have stood the ancient Castle of Ayr, built by William the Lion. The Cross of Ayr, an elegant structure in the form of a hexagon, which stood where Sandgate Street meets High Street, was removed when the New Bridge was built in 1788.

The population of the burgh of Ayr, within the Royalty, amounted, in 1841, to 7035.

About two and a half miles to the south of Ayr, overhanging the sea, is the old castle of Greenan, of which mention is made in a charter granted towards the end of the twelfth century, in the reign of King William the Lion.

DUNURE CASTLE stands about five miles farther along the

coast, round the heads of Ayr, and not far from the mouth of the Doon. Dunure is now a tall empty tower, occupying a commanding situation on this rugged coast. It appears

to have been the first mansion of any consequence possessed by the family of Kennedy, and was the place where, in 1570, Gilbert, fourth Earl of Cassillis, confined Allen Stewart, Commendator of the Abbey of Crossraguel; and, in order to prevail upon him to surrender his lands, roasted him before a slow fire, till pain obliged him to comply. This castle, which has been in ruins since the seventeenth century, now gives a territorial designation to a branch of the family of Kennedy, the present representative of which is T. F. Kennedy, Esq., formerly Member of Parliament for the Ayr district of burghs.

COLZEAN, or COLYEAN CASTLE, the principal seat of Archibald Marquis of Ailsa, and twelfth Earl of Cassillis, is situate about three miles farther along the Carrick coast, and about two miles from the village of Kirkoswald. This magnificent and picturesque mansion was built in 1777 by David tenth Earl, on the site of the old House of the Cove, erected about the middle of the sixteenth century by Sir Thomas Kennedy, second son of Gilbert Earl of Cassillis. It stands upon the verge of a great basaltic cliff overhanging the sea, and presents along the verge of a precipice "a range of lofty castellated masses, with windows in a Gothic taste, a splendid terraced garden in front, a bridge of approach and offices in corresponding style at a little distance to the left, the whole covering an area of four acres, and conveying a most imposing impression of baronial dignity, affluence, and taste." The interior of the castle contains an extensive and valuable collection of arms and armour.

The Kennedys have long held a prominent place among the aristocracy of Ayrshire. According to the old rhyme,

> " 'Twixt Wigton and the town o' Ayr,
> Port-Patrick and the Cruives of Cree,
> Nae men need think for to bide there,
> Unless he court wi' Kenedie."

This powerful race was first ennobled, in 1466, by the title of Lord Kennedy ; in 1510 they attained the dignity of Earls of Cassillis ; and, in 1831, Archibald the twelfth and present Earl, was created Marquis of Ailsa. The main line of the Cassillis family became extinct in 1759, and the title and family estates became the inheritance of Sir Thomas Kennedy of Colzean, who accordingly became ninth Earl of Cassillis. He was descended from Sir T. Kennedy, who was assassinated near the town of Ayr, May 12th, 1602, by Kennedy of Bargeny, at the instigation of Mure of Auchindrane, a deed which has been made the subject of a drama by Sir Walter Scott.

Directly underneath the castle are the Coves of Colzean, six in number. According to popular report, they are a favourite haunt of fairies, and are known to have afforded shelter, after the revolution, to Sir Archibald Kennedy of Colzean, who acquired an unenviable notoriety as a *persecutor*, during the reigns of Charles II. and James VII.

Colzean and the Cove are thus alluded to by Burns, in his "Halloween :"

> " Upon that night when fairies light,
>   On Cassillis Downan's dance,
> Or ower the lays in splendid blaze,
>   On sprightly coursers prance,
> Or for *Colzean* the route is ta'en
>   Beneath the moon's pale beams,
> There up the *Cove*, to stray and rove,
>   Among the rocks and streams,
>   To sport that night."

TURNBERRY CASTLE,

> " Where Bruce once ruled the martial ranks,
>   And shook the Carrick spear,"

stands a few miles to the south of Colzean.   It was in the twelfth and thirteenth centuries " the principal house in Carrick, and the seat of a powerful race of native chiefs, derived from Fergus, Lord of Galloway, and designated Earls of Carrick, who possessed the supreme influence in this mountainous region previous to the rise of the Kennedies."   In 1271, Robert Bruce, son of the Lord of Annandale, married the widowed Countess of Carrick, to whom the earldom had descended.   From this union sprung Robert Bruce, King of Scotland, who, if not born in Turnberry Castle, must have spent many of his youthful years in it.   It was in the neighbourhood of this place that a fire, accidentally kindled, was mistaken by the hero for an appointed signal, and caused him to cross the sea from Arran to Carrick, to attempt the deliverance of his country. On landing, the mistake was discovered, but he nevertheless determined to proceed with the enterprise ; and though he was not immediately successful in his exertions for the liberation of Scotland from the English yoke, he was never again forced to leave the country till this object was attained.   This incident has been related both by Barbour, and by Sir Walter Scott, in the " Lord of the Isles."   The latter thus describes the appearance of the " ruddy signal" kindled on Carrick shore :—

" As less and less the distance grows,
  High and more high the beacon rose ;
  The light, that seem'd a twinkling star,
  Now blazed portentous, fierce, and far.
  Dark-red the heaven above it glow'd,
  Dark-red the sea beneath it flow'd ;
  Red rose the rocks on ocean's brim
  In blood-red lights her islets swim,
  Wild scream the dazzled sea-fowl gave,
  Dropp'd from their crags on plashing wave.
  The deer to distant covert drew,
  The black-cock deem'd it day, and crew.
  Like some tall castle given to flame,
  O'er half the land the lustre came.
    *   *   *   *
  Wide o'er the sky the splendour glows,
  As that portentous meteor rose;
  Helm, axe, and falchion glitter'd bright,
  And in the red and dusky light
  His comrade's face each warrior saw,
  Nor marvell'd it was pale with awe.
  Then high in air the beams were lost,
  And darkness sunk upon the coast." *

" The only tradition now remembered of the landing of Robert Bruce in Carrick, relates to the fire seen by him from the isle of Arran. It is still generally reported and religiously believed by many, that this fire was really the work of supernatural power, unassisted by the hand of any mortal being ; and it is said, that for several centuries the flame rose yearly on the same hour of the same night of the year on which the king first saw it from the turrets of Brodick Castle; and some go so far as to say, that if the exact time were known it would be still seen. That this superstitious notion is very ancient, is evident from the place where the fire is said to have appeared being called the Bogle's Brae beyond the remembrance of man.

" The top of the rock on which Turnberry is built is about eighteen feet above high-water mark. The ruin, rising between forty and fifty feet above the water, has a majestic appearance from the sea. Around the Castle of Turnberry

* *Lord of the Isles*, c. v., st. 13, 14.

was a level plain of about two miles in extent, forming the
Castle Park. There could be nothing more beautiful than
the copsewood and verdure of this extensive meadow before
it was invaded by the ploughshare."*

Turnberry is still enumerated (under the denomination
of Carrick) among the royal palaces of Scotland. It is now
the property of the Marquis of Ailsa.

Within sight of Turnberry, and not more than a mile
from it, is the farm of Shanter, formerly the residence of
Douglas Graham, the original of "Tam o' Shanter."

At a short distance is the village of Kirkoswald, at which
Burns attended school for some months, in the nineteenth
year of his age. In the churchyard of this village two of
his characters (Tam o' Shanter and Souter Johnny) are interred.

AILSA CRAIG, a huge rock, which rises sheer out of the
sea, presents a striking appearance from this shore. Its
nearest distance to land is about ten miles from the coast
near Girvan. It is 1103 feet in height, and about two miles
in circumference at the base. The ruins of a tower, of three
storeys, are to be seen perched upon it. It is the property
of the Marquis of Ailsa, who takes his title as a British Peer
from it. Its principal productions are solan geese, goats,
and rabbits, and it is let at £30 per annum. Ailsa Craig
is noticed by Burns in his song of "Duncan Gray."

BURNS' MONUMENT & COTTAGE, ALLOWAY KIRK, AND THE BRIG OF DOON.

Burns' Monument is 2¾ miles south of Ayr, 5¾ miles
from Maybole, 36¾ miles from Glasgow by the Turnpike,
and 42¾ by the Railway. Following the road from Ayr, a
short distance from the town, there is a hill called Barn-
weil, which is said to have derived its name from the circumstance, that Wallace, on leaving Ayr, after having, in
revenge for the treacherous slaughter of his friend, set
on fire the barns in which the English soldiery were inclosed, paused on this spot to look back upon the conflagra-

* Notes to canto v. of the Lord of the Isles.

tion, and remarked, " The Barns o' Ayr burn well." There is good reason, however, to doubt the accuracy of this traditionary etymology, and it is more likely that the name is of Celtic origin, and is descriptive of the nature of the ground. In the neighbourhood of Kirk Alloway are the various localities mentioned in " Tam o' Shanter's" route. At the distance of about one hundred and fifty yards from a bridge, called Slaphouse Bridge, is

> " The Ford,
> Where in the snaw the chapman smoor'd."

About one hundred yards from the " Ford," and about twenty from the road, in the plot of ground behind the house occupied by Roselle gamekeeper, is

> " The meikle stane,
> Whare drunken Charlie brak 's neck-bane."

Passing on the left the beautiful mansion of Roselle, (Archibald Hamilton, Esq. of Carcluie,) the tourist, at the distance of about two miles from Ayr, reaches the cottage where Burns was born on the 25th of January 1759. The original erection was a *Clay Bigging*, consisting of two apartments, the kitchen and the *spence*, or sitting-room. The cottage was built on part of seven acres of ground, of which Burns' father took a perpetual lease from Dr. Campbell, physician in Ayr, with the view of commencing business as nurseryman and gardener. Having built this house with his own hands, he married, in December 1757, Agnes Brown, the mother of the poet ; and, having been engaged by Mr. Ferguson of Doonholm, as his gardener and overseer, he abandoned his design of forming a nursery, but continued to reside in the cottage till 1766. On removing to Lochlee he sold his leasehold to the Corporation of Shoemakers in Ayr, to whom the house and ground still belong. The house is now occupied as an ale-house. In the interior of the kitchen is shown a recess, where stood the bed in which the Poet was born. This bedstead may now be seen at Brownhill Inn, near Thornhill, Dumfries-shire.

About a mile and a half to the south-east of the cottage, on an eminence, stands the farm of Mount Oliphant, which

William Burns rented on leaving the cottage at Whitsun-tide 1766.

Proceeding towards Burns' Monument, we perceive in a field a single tree, enclosed with a paling, the last remnant of a group which covered

> " The cairn
> Where hunters fand the murder'd bairn."

The position of the " cairn," and also of the " ford," at a distance from the highway, is accounted for by the fact, that the old road from Ayr, by which the Poet supposed his hero to have approached Alloway Kirk, was to the west of the present line.   We now reach

> " Alloway's auld haunted kirk."

This interesting building has long been roofless, but the walls are pretty well preserved, and it still retains its bell at the east end.   The woodwork has all been taken away to form snuff-boxes and other memorials of this celebrated spot.

In the area of the kirk, the late Lord Alloway, one of the Judges of the Court of Session, was interred ; and near the gate of the churchyard is the grave of Burns' father, marked by a plain tombstone, a renewal of the original stone, which had been demolished and carried away in fragments.   " The churchyard of Alloway," says Mr. Robert Chambers, " has now become fashionable with the dead as well as the living.   Its little area is absolutely crowded with modern monuments, referring to persons, many of whom have been brought from considerable distances to take their rest in this doubly consecrated ground."

A few yards to the west of Alloway Kirk, a well trickles down into the Doon, where formerly stood the thorn on which

> " Mungo's mither hang'd hersel."

A few hundred yards from the kirk is the " Auld Brig" of Doon, which figures so conspicuously in the tale of Tam o' Shanter.   The age of the structure is unknown, but it is evidently of great antiquity.   The " New Bridge" which

has been built since the time of Burns, stands about a
hundred yards below the Old. The tasteful cottage between the Kirk and the Bridge belongs to Mr. David Auld,
to whom the admirers of the Ayrshire bard are deeply indebted for the unwearied zeal and fine taste which he has
displayed in adorning the grounds of the Monument.
Close. beside the end of the bridge is a neat inn for the
accommodation of tourists. Directly over the bridge stands
the beautiful Monument of Burns, the foundation-stone of
which was laid on 25th January 1820. The project of
erecting this monument originated with the late Sir Alexander Boswell of Auchinleck. It was designed by Thomas
Hamilton, Esq., architect, Edinburgh, and cost upwards of
£3300. The grounds around it measure about an acre and
a rood, and are very tastefully laid out. In a circular
apartment on the ground-floor there are exhibited several
articles appropriate to the place,—various editions of the
Poet's works, a snuff-box made from the woodwork of Alloway Kirk, a copy of the original portraits of Burns by
Naysmith, &c., and the Bibles given by Burns to his Highland Mary. The possessor of these interesting relics having
emigrated to Canada in 1834, they were purchased by a
party of gentlemen in Montreal for £25, and forwarded to
the Provost of Ayr, to be presented in their name to the
trustees for the Monument. This was accordingly done on
the 25th of January 1841, the anniversary of the Poet's
birth-day. From the base of the columns, a remarkably
splendid view is obtained of the surrounding scenery. In
a small grotto at the south side of the enclosed ground are
shown the two far-famed statues of Tam o' Shanter and
Souter Johnnie by Mr. Thom of Ayr.

The Doon, to which the writings of Burns have given
such celebrity, takes its rise in a lake of the same name,
about eight miles in length, which is situated at the junction of the counties of Ayr and Kirkcudbright. The Doon
has a course of eighteen miles, throughout which it forms
the boundary between the districts of Carrick and Kyle.
The scenery of the Ness Glen, through which the river runs
immediately after issuing from the lake, is remarkably

woody and picturesque, and is a favourite resort of *picnic*
parties. Colonel M'Adam of Craigengillan, with a praiseworthy liberality, allows visiters to pass through his grounds
on their way to the Loch from Dalmellington. On a small
island, near the upper extremity of Loch Doon, are the
ruins of an ancient castle of considerable strength, which
figured in the wars between England and Scotland during
the time of Robert Bruce. Sir Chrystal Seton, that hero's
brother-in-law, took refuge in this fortress after the defeat
at Methven, June 1306. When the castle was surrendered
to the English, Sir Chrystal was taken, and barbarously put
to death at Dumfries, by command of King Edward.

TARBOLTON, COILSFIELD, &c.

William Burns, on the death of his landlord, Provost
Ferguson, removed from Mount Oliphant, in 1777, to Lochlee, situate in the parish of Tarbolton, and about three miles
from the village of that name. While residing in this farm,
Burns established a Bachelor's Club in Tarbolton, in the
latter part of the year 1780 ; and here, in 1783, he was ini-
tiated into the mysteries of freemasonry. About two hundred yards north of the village, on the road leading to
Galston, lies the scene of "Death and Dr. Hornbook."
"Willie's Mill," alluded to in the poem, was the Mill of
Tarbolton, situated on the Faile, about two hundred yards
east of the village, and was called by the name used in the
poem, in consequence of its being then occupied by William
Muir, a friend of the Burns family.

About half a mile from Tarbolton stands the mansion-
house of Coilsfield, designated by Burns "the Castle o' Montgomery," from its being in his time the residence of Colonel
Hugh Montgomery, afterwards Earl of Eglinton. Here
Mary Campbell, Burns' "Highland Mary," lived in the
humble capacity of a dairymaid. In this neighbourhood,
near the junction of the rivulet Faile with the Ayr, was
the scene of the parting which the poet has described in
such exquisite terms. In the anticipation of her marriage
with Burns, Mary resolved to pay a visit to her relations
in Argyleshire. Previous to her departure, she met her

lover on a Sunday in May, and at their parting, "standing one on each side of a small brook, they laved their hands in the stream, and, holding a Bible between them, pronounced a vow of eternal constancy." This was their last meeting. In returning from her visit of filial duty, Mary Campbell fell sick and died at Greenock. This event produced an indelible impression on the mind of Burns, and he has given utterance to his feelings in some of the finest and most touching verses he has ever written. That "noblest of all his ballads," as the Address to "*Mary in Heaven*" has justly been designated, was composed at Ellisland, in 1789, on the anniversary of the day on which he heard of the death of his early love. According to the account given by Mrs. Burns to Mr. Lockhart, "Burns spent that day, though labouring under a cold, in the usual work of his harvest, and apparently in excellent spirits. But as the twilight deepened, he appeared to grow 'very sad about something,' and at length wandered out into the barnyard, to which his wife, in her anxiety for his health, followed him, entreating him in vain to observe that frost had set in, and to return to the fireside. On being again and again requested to do so, he always promised compliance —but still remained where he was, striding up and down slowly, and contemplating the sky, which was singularly clear and starry. At last Mrs. Burns found him stretched on a mass of straw, with his eyes fixed on a beautiful planet, 'that shone like another moon,' and prevailed on him to come in. Immediately, on entering the house, he called for his desk, and wrote exactly as they now stand, with all the ease of one copying from memory, the sublime and pathetic verses—

"Thou lingering star, with lessening ray,
　　That lovest to greet the early morn,
　Again thou usherest in the day
　　My Mary from my soul was torn.

O, Mary! dear departed shade,
　　Where is thy place of blissful rest?
See'st thou thy lover lowly laid,
　　Hear'st thou the groans that rend his breast," &c.

" This," observes Mr. Carruthers in his 'Highland Notes,'
" is the most beautiful and touching passage in all Burns'
life.   His after loves were of the earth, earthy, but his
passion for Highland Mary was as pure as it was fervent
and lasting.   It dawned upon him at the most susceptible
period of life ; it let in enchantment upon scenes and objects which he had previously looked upon with coldness or
aversion — it gave a fine tone of humanity to his whole
moral being.   Let us not admit the dictum of Byron, that
' the cold in clime are cold in blood,' since in peasant life,
among the woods of Ayr, was nursed, in solitude and obscurity, a passion as deep, and thrilling, and romantic, as the
loves of Tasso or Petrarch, and immeasurably beyond those
of Sidney and Waller.   Sacharissa and the fair ones of
Arcadia must yield to the dairymaid of Montgomery
Castle."*

According to unvarying tradition, Coilsfield derives its
name from " Auld King Coil," who is supposed to have left
his name to this whole district of Ayrshire, as well as to
the rivulet of Coyl and the parish of Coylton.   He is said
to have been overthrown and slain in this neighbourhood,
in a bloody battle with Fergus King of Scots.   This state-
ment receives some countenance from the fact, that in May
1837, several urns, and a stone grave containing some bones,
were dug up in a circular mound near Coilsfield, where,
according to unvarying tradition, the remains of " Auld
King Coil" were deposited.   Burns alludes to this tradition
in his poem of " The Vision."

> " There where a sceptred Pictish shade,
> Stalk'd round his ashes lowly laid,
> I mark'd a martial race portray'd
>   In colours strong ;
> Bold, soldier-featured, undismay'd
>   They strode along."

* The Highland Note-Book, or Sketches and Anecdotes, by R. CARRUTHERS,
a small volume of narrative and descriptive pieces of much merit and interest,
evincing throughout not only an intimate acquaintance with local history and
tradition, but a fine appreciation of the beautiful and sublime in natural scenery,
and a picturesqueness of style well fitted for the subjects.

The "martial race," here referred to, are the Montgomeries. Coilsfield is now the property of the Earl of Eglinton, grandson of the gentleman who possessed it in Burns' time.

MAUCHLINE, MOSSGIEL, &c.

On the death of William Burns, his widow and family removed to Mossgiel, a farm about a mile north of Mauchline, which the poet and his brother Gilbert had taken some months before the death of their father. Here Burns lived during the period of his life extending from his 25th to his 28th year, and here he wrote his principal poems. The *spence* of this farm-house is the scene described in the opening of *The Vision*, and in the *stableloft*, where he slept, many of his most admired poems were written. Mauchline, which "appropriated a large share of the notice of the poet during his residence at Mossgiel," lies about nine miles from Kilmarnock, and eleven from Ayr. It is situated on the face of a slope, about a mile from the river Ayr, and contains upwards of 1300 inhabitants. Mauchline was the scene of the *Holy Fair*, and of the *Jolly Beggars*, and here dwelt John Dow, Nanse Tinnock, "Daddy Auld," and other characters who figured conspicuously in the poet's writings. The churchyard was the scene of the *Holy Fair*, but the present church is a recent substitute for the old barn-like edifice which existed in Burns's time. Near the church is the *Whitefoord Arms* Inn, where Burns wrote, on a pane of glass, the well-known amusing epitaph on the landlord, John Dow. Nearly opposite the churchyard gate is the house of "Auld Nanse Tinnock," bearing over the door the date 1744. "It is remembered," says Mr. Chambers, "that Nancy could never understand how the poet should have talked of enjoying himself in her house three times a-week,—' the lad,' she said, ' hardly ever drank three half-mutchkins under her roof in his life.'" The cottage of *Poosie Nansie*, the scene of the "Jolly Beggars," is also pointed out. Close behind the churchyard is the house in which Mr. Gavin Hamilton, the early friend of

x

Burns, lived. In this house is shown the room in which
Burns composed the satirical poem entitled "The Calf."
This room is farther remarkable as the one in which the
poet was married.

The scenes of some of Burns's most admired lyrics are to
be found on the banks of the Ayr, at a short distance from
Mauchline. The "Braes of Ballochmyle," the scene of his
beautiful song entitled "The Lass o' Ballochmyle," are
situated at the distance of about two miles from Mossgiel,
and extend along the north bank of the Ayr, between the
village of Catrine and Howford Bridge. They form part of
the pleasure-grounds connected with Ballochmyle House,
the seat of Claud Alexander, Esq. Ballochmyle was at one
time the property of the Whitefoords, an old and once
powerful Ayrshire family. Colonel Allan Whitefoord, one
of the members of this family, was the original of the
character of Colonel Talbot, described in the novel of
Waverley. Another of them, Caleb Whitefoord, "the best
natured man, with the worst natured muse," has been im-
mortalised by Goldsmith in a postscript to his witty poem
entitled "Retaliation." Sir John Whitefoord, the representative of the family in the time of Burns, having been
forced to part with his estate in consequence of declining
circumstances, Burns wrote some plaintive verses on the
occasion, referring to the grief of Maria Whitefoord, now
Mrs. Cranstoun, on leaving the family inheritance :

> " Through faded groves Maria sang,
>   Hersel' in beauty's bloom the while,
> And aye the wild-wood echoes rang,
>   Fareweel the braes of Ballochmyle.
>
> Low in your wintry beds, ye flowers,
>   Again ye 'll flourish fresh and fair;
> Ye birdies dumb in withering bowers,
>   Again ye 'll charm the vocal air;
>
> But here, alas ! for me nae mair
>   Shall birdie charm or floweret smile;
> Fareweel the bonnie banks of Ayr—
>   Fareweel, fareweel, sweet Ballochmyle."

Ballochmyle was purchased by Claud Alexander, Esq.; and shortly after that gentleman had taken possession of the mansion, his sister Miss Wilhelmina Alexander, a famed beauty, walking out along the braes one evening in July 1786, encountered Burns, with his shoulder placed against one of the trees. The result was, that the poet, during his homeward walk, composed the well-known song entitled " The Lass of Ballochmyle." The spot where Miss Alexander met the poet is now distinguished by a rustic grotto or moss-house, ornamented with appropriate devices; and on a tablet in the back there is inscribed a fac-simile of two of the verses of the poem, as it appeared in the holograph of the author. Near Ballochmyle is the manufacturing village of Catrine, at one time the seat of Dr. Stewart, and of his son, the celebrated Professor Dugald Stewart. To them Burns alludes in the following stanza in " The Vision :"

> " With deep-struck reverential awe,
> The learned sire and son I saw,
> To Nature's God and Nature's law
> They gave their lore ;
> This all its source and end to draw,
> That to adore."

Between the villages of Tarbolton and Mauchline stands the mansion of Barskimming, occupying a romantic situation on the banks of the Ayr. The scenery of the river at this spot is remarkably beautiful. Barskimming, and its late proprietor, Lord President Miller, are thus alluded to in the above-mentioned poem :—

> " Through many a wild romantic grove,
> Near many a hermit-fancied cove,
> Fit haunts for friendship or for love;
> In musing mood,
> An aged judge I saw him rove,
> Dispensing good."

Barskimming is now the property of Sir William Miller of Glenlee, Bart., only son of Lord Justice-Clerk Miller, and a retired judge of the Court of Session.

A short distance farther up the river, at the point where the Lugar joins the Ayr, is the spot where Burns composed the poem entitled " Man was made to mourn."

FOURTEENTH TOUR.

EDINBURGH TO INVERNESS BY KINROSS—PERTH—DUNKELD—
BLAIR-ATHOLL.

LEAVING Edinburgh by the Queensferry Road, the tourist crosses the Water of Leith by Dean Bridge, a superb edifice of four arches, each ninety feet in span. Below, on the right, is St. Bernard's Well. On the left stands the village of the Water of Leith ; and at a short distance are two buildings of great elegance—the Hospital endowed by John Watson, W.S., for the maintenance and education of destitute children, and the new Orphan Hospital, opened in 1833. The road now passes the new Episcopal Chapel, on the left, and on the right Dean House, Craigleith House, and Craigleith Quarry, from which the stone employed in building the New Town of Edinburgh was chiefly procured. At a short distance to the left are Ravelston, (Lady Murray Keith,) and Craigcrook, (Lord Jeffrey.) About four miles from Edinburgh stands Barnton House, (W. R. Ramsay, Esq.) A mile farther on, the tourist crosses the Almond by Cramond Bridge, and passes, on the right, Newhall, (Scott Moncrieff, Esq.) On the shore is the village of Cramond, and the entrance to Dalmeny Park, (Earl of Rosebery.) The banks of the river Almond in this neighbourhood are very beautiful, and the scenery about the old bridge of Craigiehall is romantic. Passing in succession Dalmeny Kirk, a little to the left,

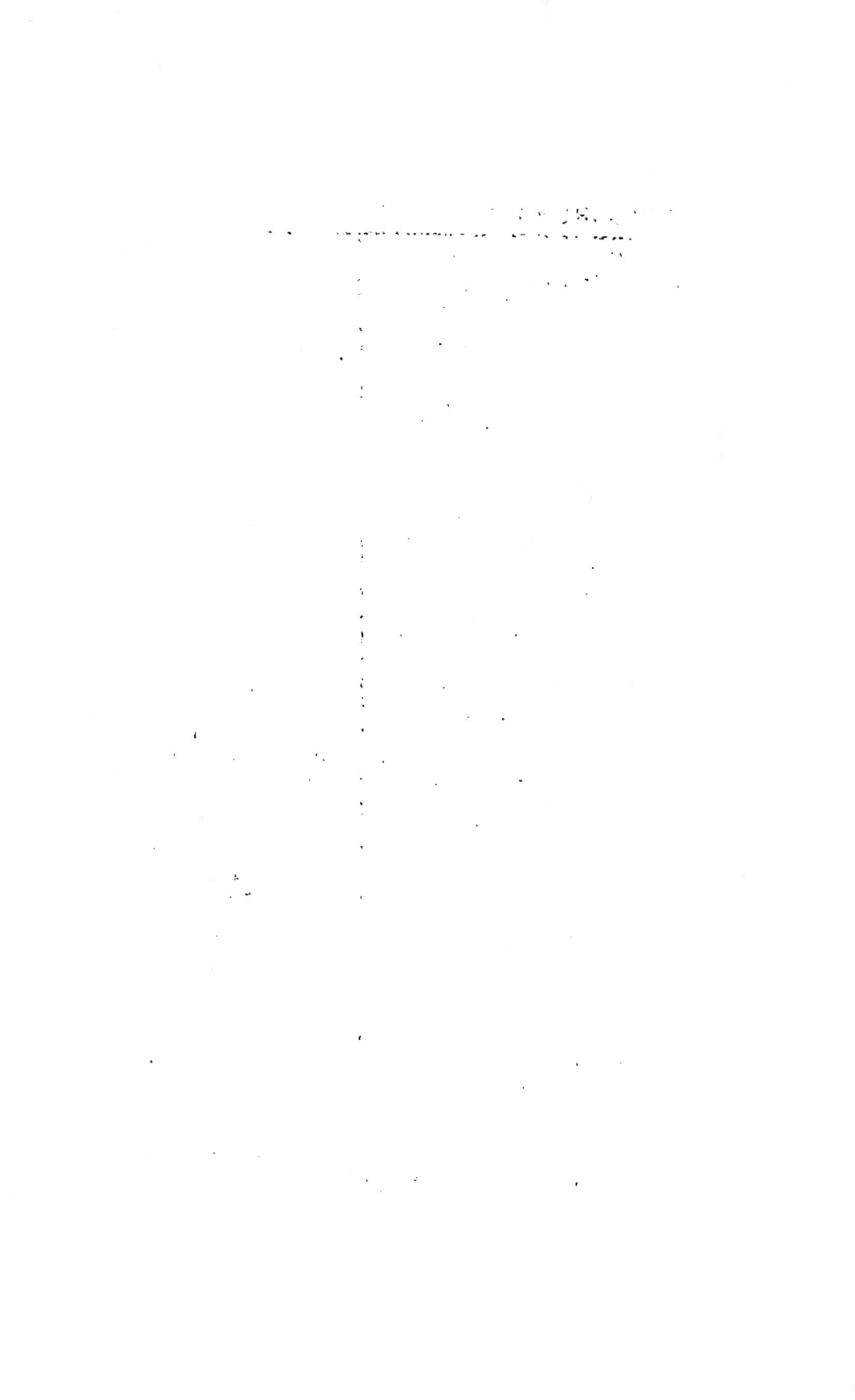

EDINBURGH, KINROSS, PERTH, DUNKELD, BLAIR ATHOLL.

Edinburgh. Published July 1. 1846 by Adam & Charles Black 27 North Bridge

seven and a half miles, and Newhalls or Ha's Inn, eight miles from Edinburgh, you enter South Queensferry, which was erected into a royal burgh by Malcolm Canmore, and derived its name from Margaret his queen. Here are some ruins of a monastery of Carmelite Friars, founded in 1330. On the left is Dundas House, (G. H. Dundas, Esq.,) and a little to the south, the ruins of Dundas Castle, a building of great antiquity, which has been in the Dundas family upwards of 700 years. The ferry across the Forth belonged, before the Reformation, to the Abbot of Dunfermline, and was at that period sold by his orders to a joint stock company.* Three miles west from Queensferry stands HOPETOUN HOUSE, a building of great splendour, and possessing a delightful prospect. In the narrow strait at Queensferry, there is the little island of Inch Garvie, on which a fort was established during the last war. On this island, previous to the reign of Charles II., the principal state prison was placed. Upon a promontory, on the northern coast, stands the small village of North Queensferry. It is remarkable as the place where Oliver Cromwell first encamped on crossing the Forth, in 1651. On this promontory, which is called the Cruicks, there is a lazaretto, where goods landed on this part of the coast, from tropical climates, have to pass quarantine. In the immediate neighbourhood is Rosyth Castle, a huge square tower, situated close by the sea. It was the ancient seat of the Stuarts of Rosyth, a branch of the royal family, from which Oliver Cromwell is said to have descended. The bay between the Cruicks and Rosyth Castle is called St. Margaret's Hope, from the circumstance of the Princess Margaret, sister of Edgar Atheling, afterwards consort of Malcolm Canmore, having been wrecked there in her flight from England, immediately after the Norman conquest.

Two miles beyond North Queensferry, the road enters

* The agent appointed to dispose of the ferry divided it into sixteen shares, and offered the same for sale. The project was immediately successful; the shares were eagerly purchased ; the agent continued to sell as long as he found persons willing to buy ; and, scandalous to relate, there is evidence still in existence that he actually sold eighteen sixteenth shares of the Queensferry passage.

A short distance to the east of Inverkeithing, and close upon the shore, stands Donibristle House, a seat of the Earl of Moray. (See Fifth Tour, pp. 177–78, *note*.) The tourist now passes, in succession, on the right, Fordel (Colonel Mercer,) Lochgelly (Earl of Minto,) and Lochore (Sir W. Scott.) A short way to the left, on the old road, is the Kirk of Beith, six miles from Inverkeithing; two and a half miles beyond that, Maryburgh, the birth-place of the two brothers Adam, the celebrated architects, and, farther on, Blair-Adam (Sir Charles Adam.) The road crosses the Kelty Water, and shortly after the Gairney at Gairney Bridge, where the poet Michael Bruce once taught a small school; and, twenty-seven miles from Edinburgh, the tourist enters

KINROSS,

the capital of the county of that name, pleasantly situated on the banks of Loch Leven. Kinross House (Sir Graham Montgomery,) erected in 1685, stands on the edge of the lake. The promontory on which it stands was once occupied by a stronghold, long the residence of the Earls of Morton. By far the most interesting object in the neighbourhood of Kinross is the lake, on the banks of which the town is situated. Loch Leven is well worthy of a visit from

ingly done. It is to be regretted that the bad taste displayed in the erection, has, in a great measure, marred the beauty of the design. In clearing away the ruins of the ancient choir, the tomb of Robert Bruce, who was buried here in 1329, was discovered. The skeleton of the illustrious monarch was found entire, together with the lead in which his body was wrapt, and even some fragments of his shroud. He was reinterred with much state by the Barons of the Exchequer, immediately under the pulpit of the new church. In the area of the church is shown a large marble slab, broken into three pieces, said to be the tombstone of Queen Margaret; also six large flat stones, affirmed to mark the graves of as many kings. The remains of the Abbey are very extensive, but it is generally asserted that the original buildings were much more so. The Fratery still retains an entire window, much admired for its elegant and complicated workmanship. Beneath the Fratery there were six and twenty cells, many of which still remain. The celebrated Ralph Erskine, one of the founders of the Secession Church, was, for a number of years, minister of Dunfermline. The tourist ought to ascend the old steeple of the church, from which a very extensive and magnificent prospect may be obtained. Dunfermline has greatly increased within the last thirty years, and is now distinguished by its activity in the manufacture of linen.

the Crown. The pennon of the ruthless baron is displayed by one of his attendants, as a signal for the boat, while he himself blows "a clamorous blast on his bugle." Queen Mary escaped from the castle, May 2, 1568, through the aid of young Douglas, and is said by general tradition to have gone ashore on the lands of Coldon, at the south side of the lake, whence she was conducted, by Lord Seton, to Niddry Castle in West Lothian. The keys of the Castle, which were thrown into the lake at the time of her escape, were recently found by a young man belonging to Kinross, who presented them to the Earl of Morton. Loch Leven is celebrated for the excellence of its trout. The rich taste and bright red colour, are derived chiefly from small crustacea and shell-fish upon which they feed. The silver grey trout is apparently the original native of the loch, and, in many respects, the finest fish of the whole. The *char* or *geily trough*, rivalling in richness and flavour the best specimens of this kind, have of late years disappeared ; and an attempt made in April 1843, by Sir W. Jardine and Mr. James Wilson, to obtain them by deep water fishing, proved unsuccessful.* At the eastern extremity of the loch, there are some remains of the monasteries of Portmoak and Scotland's Well. The little sequestered village of Kinneswood, situated on the north-east shore of Loch Leven, was the birthplace of Michael Bruce, the poet. The house in which he first saw the light is still pointed out. His poem on Loch Leven Castle, his ballad of Sir James the Rose, and his verses in anticipation of his own death, are much admired. He died at the early age of twenty-one, before his poetical genius arrived at maturity. The river Leven flows from the lake on the east side, and pursues an easterly course to the Firth of Forth. The vale of the Leven is beautiful, and is ornamented with the woods around Leslie, the seat of the Earl of Rothes. About two miles from Kinross, is the vil-

---

* The level of the loch has lately been reduced 4½ feet, by means of a deep cut at the eastern extremity, conveying the water to the river, a portion of the former channel of which is now dry : 750 acres of land have thus been gained from the loch, but this has been effected at so great an outlay, that the value of the land barely covers the expense of the works which were necessary to reclaim it.

by the ancient Romans with the exclamation *"Ecce Tiber !*
Ecce Campus Martius !" The Tiber rather than the Tay is
the gainer by this comparison. The Tiber at Rome is
much narrower than the Tay at Perth; its waters are
muddy and sluggish, and its banks tame, dirty and unclad
with trees. The Tay, on the contrary, is here 500 feet in
breadth, its stream deep—but of crystalline purity, and
although it forms a broad and beautiful sheet of water, it
is not stagnant, but flows with a perceptible current. Its
eastern bank rises rapidly, and for more than a mile exhibits
an almost unbroken line of villas, which are seen peeping
through partial openings in the masses of willows, limes, and
sycamores, which cover the acclivity down to the water's
edge. The fertile Carse of Gowrie,—the Firth of Tay, with
the populous town of Dundee,—the city of Perth, and the
beautiful valley of Strathearn, bounded by the hills of
Menteith, are all distinctly seen from this eminence. Pen-
nant calls this view " the glory of Scotland."

PERTH,

an ancient royal burgh, and one of the handsomest towns
in Scotland, is beautifully situated on the west bank of the
Tay, at the distance of forty-four miles from Edinburgh.
It occupies the centre of a spacious plain, having two
beautiful pieces of public ground called the North and
South Inches extending on each side of it.

A splendid bridge of ten arches and 900 feet in length,
built in 1772, leads across the Tay to the north. Perth,
or, as it used to be called from its church, St. Johnstoun,
boasts of a high antiquity, and has been the scene of many
interesting events. On account of its importance and its
vicinity to the royal palace of Scone, it was long the metropolis of the kingdom before Edinburgh obtained that distinction. Here, too, the Parliaments and national assemblies were held, and many of the nobility took up their residence. Perth contains several beautiful streets and terraces, and a number of fine public buildings. The oldest of
these is St. John's Church, the precise origin of which is
unknown. It has undergone various modifications, and is

tender as king. The Inches are two beautiful pieces of ground, each about a mile and a-half in circumference, affording agreeable and healthy walks to the inhabitants, and delightfully variegated with trees. On the North Inch there took place, in the reign of Robert III., that singular combat between the Clan-Kay and Clan-Chattan, which Sir Walter Scott has introduced with so much effect into his novel of the Fair Maid of Perth. The town is surrounded on all sides with the most beautiful and picturesque scenery, and the interesting objects in the neighbourhood are so numerous, that it would require a volume to notice them all. The summits of the hills of Moncreiffe and Kinnoull, to which the access is easy by carriage roads, are well worthy of a visit—the former, in particular, no tourist should omit visiting, as it affords one of the finest prospects in Scotland. At the foot of Kinnoull Hill, lies Kinfauns Castle, from which every visiter returns delighted with the natural and artificial beauties both in and around it. Scone Palace (noticed below) will amply repay the trouble of a visit; and so will Dupplin Castle, the seat of the Earl of Kinnoull, situated about five miles west of Perth. The Dupplin Library is well known for its collection of rare and valuable editions of the classics, and the woods around the castle are magnificent. Lynedoch, also, is a favourite excursion, chiefly on account of the graves of Bessy Bell and Mary Gray, which are situate on the romantic banks of the Almond. According to the census of 1841, the population of Perth, within the Parliamentary boundary, was 18,281. On the occasion of the Queen's visit, Perth honourably distinguished itself by the admirable arrangements made by its civic authorities, for the reception of Her Majesty.

Leaving Perth by the North Inch, the tourist passes on the left Few House, (Nicol, Esq.,) and Tulloch Printfield ; and, at the distance of two and a-half miles from Perth, on the opposite side of the Tay, he will observe Scone Palace, the seat of the Earl of Mansfield, who represents the old family of Stormont. It is an immense modern building, in the castellated style, occupying the site of the ancient palace of the kings of Scotland. Much of the old furniture

aid of these courageous peasants, who were armed only with
a yoke, the Scots obtained a complete victory. In commemoration of this circumstance, the crest of the Hays has
for many centuries been a peasant carrying a yoke over his
shoulder. The plain on which the battle was fought is now
used as a bleachfield. A mile in advance the road crosses
the fine trouting streams of Ordie and Shochie.* A little
farther on, a road turns off to the right to the Linn of
Campsie, where the Tay forms a magnificent cascade, and
the village of Stanley, famous for its extensive spinning-
mills. The tourist next passes, on the left, the ruins of a
residence of the family of Nairn, and the Mill of Loak ; and
nine miles from Perth, enters the village of Auchtergaven.
Three miles farther on the tourist passes Murthly Castle
(Sir Wm. Drummond,) a magnificent but unfinished edifice,
and a short way north of it, the old castle of Murthly. In
the immediate neighbourhood is Birnam Hill, 1580 feet
above the level of the sea, and Birnam Wood, so famous
for its connexion with the fate of Macbeth. The ancient
forest has now disappeared, and been replaced by a few
trees of modern growth. From the summit of the hill a
magnificent prospect is commanded of the vale of the Tay,
and of the extensive woods which environ Dunkeld.† The
traveller now passes the village of Little Dunkeld,‡ crosses
the river and enters

* Perth suffered from a nocturnal inundation of the Tay in the year 1210,
and it is predicted that it will again be destroyed in a similar manner :—
      " Says the Shochie to the Ordie,
         ' Where shall we meet ?'
       ' At the cross o' Perth,
         When a' men are fast asleep.' "
                             Popular Rhyme.
† Birnam Inn is a comfortable and well-frequented establishment, where the
wants of tourists are equally well supplied as at the inns in Dunkeld.
    ‡ " O what a parish, what a terrible parish,
        O what a parish is that of Dunkell !
    They hae hangit the minister, drown'd the precentor
    Dung down the steeple, and drucken the bell !
    Though the steeple was down, the kirk was still stannin',
        They biggit a burn where the bell used to hang ;
    A stell-pat they gat, and they brew'd Hieland whisky,
        On Sundays they drank it, and rantit and sang."
                               Old Song.

and converted into a place of worship by the late Duke of
Atholl, at an expense of £5000. The new church is handsomely fitted up. In the vestry there is a statue in armour,
of somewhat rude workmanship, which was formerly placed
at the grave of the notorious *Wolf of Badenoch*, who burned
the cathedral of Elgin. The early history of this establishment is obscure, but it is understood that there was a
monastery of the Culdees here, which David I. converted
into a bishoprick, A.D. 1127. Among its bishops were
Bishop Sinclair, celebrated for his patriotic exertions in the
reign of Robert Bruce, and Gawin Douglas, famous for his
poetical talents. Immediately behind the cathedral, stands
the ancient mansion of the Dukes of Atholl. A magnificent new mansion was commenced by the late Duke, but
his death, in 1830, has suspended the progress of the building. At the end of the cathedral are the first two larches
introduced into Britain. They were originally brought
from Switzerland in 1737, and placed in flower-pots in a
green-house, but are now upwards of ninety feet high,
measuring fifteen feet in circumference, at three feet from
the ground. The walks through the policies of Dunkeld
have been pronounced, by the late Dr. E. Clarke, to be
almost without a rival. The larch woods alone cover an
extent of 11,000 square acres; the number of these trees
planted by the late Duke of Atholl being about twenty-
seven millions, besides several millions of other sorts of
trees. The tourist returns from the policies to Dunkeld by
the village of Inver, in which the small thatched house
long occupied by Neil Gow, the celebrated musician, may
be seen. An old wooden press, said to have belonged to
him, forms part of the furniture of the present tenant.
Dunkeld, it will be remembered, was among the places
visited by Her Majesty in 1842, on which occasion the festivities were on a scale of great splendour. The royal tent
stood on the lawn to the east of the cathedral.

From the base of Craigvinean, a long wooded eminence
projects, across which a path leads to Ossian's Hall, situated
beside a cataract formed by a fall of the Braan. This is
generally esteemed the greatest curiosity of Dunkeld. A

Y

be obtained from the cottage of Dr. Fisher, situate upon an eminence at the east end of the bridge. The proprietor politely allows strangers to enter his ground, in order to enjoy the prospect.

ABERFELDY—KENMORE—TAYMOUTH CASTLE—KILLIN—LOCHEARN-HEAD—COMRIE—CRIEFF.

THE tourist who wishes to survey the beautiful scenery of Kenmore and Killin, may either proceed to Blair Atholl, and thence to Kenmore, distant, by the common road, twenty-eight miles—over the hills, twenty miles—or he may adopt the route by Logierait and Aberfeldy. If he prefers the former, shortly after leaving Blair Atholl he reaches a chasm in the hill on the right hand, through which the little river Bruar falls over a series of beautiful cascades. These falls were formerly unadorned by wood; but, in consequence of the poetical address, written by Burns, entitled "Humble petition of Bruar Water," the Duke of Atholl has formed a plantation along the chasm. The river makes three distinct falls, the lowest of which forms an unbroken descent of 100 feet. The shelving rocks on both banks, the depth of the chasm, and the roughness of the channel through which the stream rushes, add greatly to the sublimity and interest of the scene. From these falls the tourist may either proceed by the common road, or over the hill on the south side of the vale, to Tummel Bridge and Inn. The scenery around this spot is extremely beautiful. In the midst of it stands Foss, the seat of —— Stewart, Esq. From the Bridge of Tummel there is a road which leads through a gloomy and mountainous country to Loch Rannoch. This lake is about ten or eleven miles in length, and two and a half in breadth, and is surrounded by lofty mountains covered with forests. In the neighbourhood is the steep mountain Schehallion, 3550 feet high, which afforded shelter to Robert Bruce after the battle of Methven. Leaving the Bridge of Tummel, an Alpine road of seven or eight miles in length leads to Strath Tay. The ruins of a high square keep, called Garth Castle, occupying a narrow rocky promontory at the confluence of two rivulets, form a prominent object in the landscape. The stream runs in deep perpendicular channels, and the dell is richly wooded, and so deep that the roaring of the waters can scarcely be heard. The view from the confined channel of the burn, over-canopied by slanting trees, is peculiarly impressive; and the whole scene presents a striking combination of beauty and terror. The tourist now descends along the edge of a deep and wooded dell, bordered by sloping cultivated ground, and, passing Coshieville Inn, reaches Fortingal, as the

ingly confined, that the trees in some places unite their branches
from the opposite sides. The lowest fall consists chiefly of a series of
cascades formed by a small tributary rivulet pouring down the east
side of the dell. The next series consists of a succession of falls,
comprising a perpendicular height of not less than a hundred feet.
The last and highest cascade is a perpendicular fall of about fifty
feet. Here the traveller may cross the dell by means of a rustic
bridge, and return to the inn by a varied route. Opposite Aberfeldy
the Tay is crossed by one of General Wade's bridges. About a mile
in advance, on the north side, stands Castle Menzies, (*pron. Meengis,*)
the seat of Sir Neil Menzies, the chief of that name, erected in the
sixteenth century. It stands at the foot of a lofty range of rocky
hills, and is surrounded by a park filled with aged trees, among
which are some planes of extraordinary size. Weem Castle, the
former seat of the family, was burned by Montrose. About a mile
farther is Balfrax, (Marquis of Breadalbane,) and about a mile beyond, the Lyon water joins the Tay. Six miles from Aberfeldy the
tourist reaches the beautiful little village of Kenmore, situated at the
north-east extremity of Loch Tay. It consists of an inn, with good
accommodation, and fifteen or sixteen houses, neatly white-washed,
some of them embowered in ivy, honeysuckle, and sweet-briar. The
most remarkable object in the vicinity of Kenmore, is

TAYMOUTH CASTLE,

the princely mansion of the Marquis of Breadalbane, with its much
admired environs. The castle is a magnificent dark-grey pile of four
storeys, with round corner towers, and terminating in an airy central
pavilion. Its interior is splendidly fitted up, and it contains one of
the best collections of paintings in Scotland. The most striking
feature in the edifice is the grand staircase. The pleasure-grounds
are laid out with great taste, and possess a striking combination of
beauty and grandeur. The hills which confine them are luxuriantly
wooded and picturesque in their outlines, and the plain below is
richly adorned with old gigantic trees. The view from the hill in
front of the castle is reckoned one of the finest in Scotland. On the
right is Drummond Hill, and behind it the lofty Ben Lawers, with
Ben More in the remote distance. On the left, two hills, partially
wooded, rise from the water, one above another. In the foreground
a portion of the lake is seen, with the village and church of Kenmore, and to the north of them, a light bridge spans the Tay, immediately behind which is the little wooded island of Loch Tay, with
the ruins of a priory founded by Alexander I., whose Queen, Sybilla,
lies interred here.* The scene is thus described in an impromptu of
Robert Burns, who visited the spot in August 1787.

* The last residents in this priory were three nuns, who, once a-year, visited
a fair in Kenmore, which, owing to that circumstance, is still called "Holy
Women's Market."

THE QUEEN PLANTING THE SCOTCH FIR. TAYMOUTH.

visible by their own volcanic-looking flames. To all these blazing and sparkling wonders, the intense darkness of the night gave additional effect. At ten o'clock, a salute from the battery announced the commencement of the fireworks, which were produced in the highest style of pyrotechnical art. Their display took place upon the sloping lawn that hangs towards the base of the hill, directly across the park in front of the house. There were many honest citizens of London present, who had seen the glories of Vauxhall, and who declared that they were all utterly extinguished by those of this single night at Taymouth. The dancing took place on two platforms in front of the Castle, the manly forms and energetic action of the Highlanders being exhibited to striking advantage by a blaze of torch-light.

Many were the whimsical scenes that occurred in Kenmore, Aberfeldy, and the hamlets and the houses of the surrounding districts, on this memorable occasion, from the crowds of strangers that besieged them for beds. Every floor was covered with shakedowns, and for each of these a charge of from ten shillings to a sovereign was made ; and many were glad to content themselves with a chair to sit up in. The scramble for food next morning was no less than it had been for beds, and many who had never tasted porridge in their lives before, seized upon the wooden bicker that contained it, and were fain to gobble it up with the help of a horn spoon. It was pleasant to see, however, that all these inconveniences were borne with good humour, every one declaring that a sight of the glories of Taymouth would have been cheaply purchased by deprivations and hardships of tenfold greater magnitude. And, indeed, they were glories, such as, when taken together with the magnificence of the natural theatre where they were exhibited, are scarcely to be paralleled. The revelries at Kenilworth, in honour of Elizabeth, were sufficiently gorgeous ; but rich as is the district in which they took place, it can no more be compared, in point of romantic effect, with that of the bold wooded mountains, the variegated plains, and the sparkling streams of Taymouth, than the homely countenance and ascetic expression of the Queen, who was a guest there, can be thought of in comparison with the lovely face that shed its smiles that night on all within the noble castle of the Marquess and Marchioness of Breadalbane.*

Leaving Kenmore and Taymouth, the tourist proceeds along the shores of the Loch to Killin, which is sixteen miles distant at the

---

* The above description of the festivities at Taymouth is abridged from Sir Thomas Dick Lauder's " Memorial of the Royal Progress." We lament that limited space has rendered it necessary for us to condense the picturesque and glowing style of the distinguished author, but the force of circumstances has made this Procrustean process unavoidable.

on one of which is the tomb of the Macnabs. From the upper end of the lower island there are three bridges across the stream. "Killin," says Dr. Macculloch, with some exaggeration, "is the most extraordinary collection of extraordinary scenery in Scotland—unlike every thing else in the country, and perhaps on earth, and a perfect picture gallery in itself, since you cannot move three yards without meeting a new landscape. A busy artist might here draw a month and not exhaust it. * * * Fir-trees, rocks, torrents, mills, bridges, and houses, under endless combinations, produce the great bulk of the middle landscape, while the distances more constantly are found in the surrounding hills, in their varied woods, in the bright expanse of the lake, and the minute ornaments of the distant valley, in the rocks and bold summit of Cailleach, and in the lofty vision of Ben Lawers, which towers, like a huge giant, to the clouds—the monarch of the scene. On the north side of Loch Tay, and about a mile and a half from the village of Killin, stand the picturesque ruins of Finlarig Castle, an ancient seat of the Breadalbane family. The castle is a narrow building of three storeys, entirely overgrown with ivy, and surrounded by venerable trees. Immediately adjoining is the family vault. The following anecdote of the olden times is related by the Messrs. Anderson in their excellent Guide to the Highlands: "On the occasion of a marriage festival at Finlarig, in years gone by, when occupied by the heir-apparent, intelligence was given to the company, which comprised the principal youth of the clan, that a party of the Macdonalds of Keppoch, who had just passed with a drove of *lifted* cattle, had refused to pay the accustomed *road* collop. Flushed with revelry, the guests indignantly sallied out and attacked the Macdonalds on the adjoining hill of Stronoclachan, but, from their irregular impetuosity, they were repulsed, and twenty young gentlemen left dead on the spot. Tidings of the affray were conveyed to Taymouth, and a reinforcement arriving, the victors were overtaken in Glenorchy, and routed, and their leader slain."

On leaving Killin the tourist proceeds up Glen Dochart and passes, on the right, the mansion house of Achlyne, a seat of the Marquis of Breadalbane. A little beyond, at a place called Leeks, a road strikes off to Crianlarich Inn, from which the tourist may either go by Tyndrum and Dalmally to Inverary, or he may descend Glenfalloch till he reach the head of Loch Lomond. The traveller now enters Glen-Ogle, a narrow and gloomy defile, hemmed in by the rocky sides of the mountains, which are here strikingly grand, rising on the one side in a succession of terraces, and on the other in a steep acclivity, surmounted by perpendicular precipices. Among these wild cliffs the eagle has built her nest for many years. At the distance of eight miles from Killin, is the little village of Lochearn-Head, with a good inn. From this point the tourist may turn southwards by Balquhidder, the burial-place of Rob Roy, and proceed through the wild pass

very causes, aiding to confer upon Loch Earn a character entirely its own."

There is a road on each side of the lake, but the southern route is to be preferred. About a mile and a half from the inn, we come to Edinample, an ancient castellated mansion belonging to the Marquis of Breadalbane. There is also a beautiful waterfall here, immediately below the road, formed by the Ample, a mountain stream, which pours in two perpendicular torrents over a broad rugged rock, and uniting about midway, is precipitated again over a second precipice.* The road now passes through continuous woods of oak, larch, ash, and birch. The view to the south is closed up by the huge Ben Voirlich, (*i. e.* the Great Mountain of the lake,) which rises to the height of 3300 feet. About midway between Lochearnhead and the east end of the lake is Ardvoirlich, (Robert Stewart, Esq.,) the Darlinvaroch of the *Legend of Montrose*.† The landscapes

---

* After passing along the bridge, a footpath will be observed on the left, leading to the best points of view below the fall.

† "During the reign of James IV., a great feud between the powerful families of Drummond and Murray divided Perthshire. The former being the most numerous and powerful, cooped up eight score of the Murrays in the kirk of Monavaird, and set fire to it. The wives and children of the ill-fated men, who had also found shelter in the church, perished by the same conflagration. One man, named David Murray, escaped by the humanity of one of the Drummonds, who received him in his arms as he leaped from amongst the flames. As King James IV. ruled with more activity than most of his predecessors, this cruel deed was severely revenged, and several of the perpetrators were beheaded at Stirling. In consequence of the prosecution against his clan, the Drummond, by whose assistance David Murray had escaped, fled to Ireland, until, by means of the person whose life he had saved, he was permitted to return to Scotland, where he and his descendants were distinguished by the name of Drummond Eirinch, or Ernoch, that is, Drummond of Ireland; and the same title was bestowed on their estate.

"The Drummond-Ernoch of James the Sixth's time was a king's forester in the forest of Glenartney, and chanced to be employed there in search of venison about the year 1588, or early in 1589. The forest was adjacent to the chief haunts of the MacGregors, or a particular race of them, known by the title of MacEagh, or Children of the Mist. They considered the forester's hunting in their vicinity as an aggression; or perhaps they had him at feud, for the apprehension or slaughter of some of their own name, or for some similar reason. This tribe of MacGregors were outlawed and persecuted, as the reader may see in the Introduction to Rob Roy; and every man's hand being against them, their hand was of course directed against every man. In short, they surprised and slew Drummond-Ernoch, cut off his head, and carried it with them, wrapt in the corner of one of their plaids.

"In the full exultation of vengeance, they stopped at the house of Ardvoirlich, and demanded refreshment, which the lady, a sister of the murdered Drummond-Ernoch, (her husband being absent,) was afraid or unwilling to refuse. She caused bread and cheese to be placed before them, and gave directions for more substantial refreshments to be prepared. While she was absent with this

LOCHEARN-HEAD

Tay to Loch Earn, surprised the banditti by night, and put them all to the sword. In commemoration of this event, the Macnabs assumed for their crest a man's head, with the motto, " Dreadnought."

At the east end of Loch Earn stands the neat little village of St. Fillans. It was formerly a wretched hamlet, known by the name of Portmore, but through the exertions of Lord and Lady Willoughby D'Eresby, on whose ground it stands, it has become one of the sweetest spots in Scotland. It derived its name from St. Fillan, a celebrated saint who resided in this place. He was the favourite saint of Robert Bruce, and one of his arms was borne in a shrine by the Abbot of Inchaffray at the battle of Bannockburn. On the summit of a hill in this neighbourhood, called Dun Fillan, there is a well consecrated by him, which even to this day is supposed to be efficacious for the cure of many disorders. The St. Fillan Society, formed in 1819, holds an annual meeting in this place for athletic sports and performances on the bagpipe, and confers prizes on the successful competitors. These games are usually attended by great numbers of persons of condition, male and female, from all parts of the Highlands. The valley of Strathearn, which extends from this place nearly to Perth, contains many fine villas and wooded parks, and is celebrated for its beauty and fertility. Leaving St. Fillans, the road winds along the banks of the Earn, through groves of lofty trees, presenting here and there broken glimpses of the ridges of the neighbouring mountains. About two miles and a half from Loch Earn, we pass the mansion of Duneira, the favourite seat of the late Lord Melville, with its picturesque grounds and delightful pleasure walks. It is now the property of Sir David Dundas, Bart. A little farther on, Dalchonzie (Skene, Esq.,) and Aberuchill Castle* (Major Drummond,) are seen on the right; and, five miles and a half from St. Fillans, the tourist enters the village of Comrie, pleasantly situated on the north bank of the Earn, at its confluence with the Ruchill. Comrie is remarkable for the earthquakes with which it has occasionally been visited for a number of years. It is by many supposed to have been the scene of the dreadful battle between Galgacus and Agricola. Half a mile south of the village are the remains of a Roman Camp. Close to the village stands Comrie House (Dundas, Bart.,) on the east side of which the Lednock Water flows into the Earn. On the summit of a hill called Dunmore, a monument seventy-two feet in height has been erected to the memory of the late Lord Melville, overhanging a turbulent little stream called the " Humble Bumble." At the foot of Dunmore, there is a place called the " Devil's Caldron," where the Lednock, at the farther extremity of a long, deep, and narrow chasm, is precipitated into a dark and dis-

* Aberuchill was built in 1602, and was the scene of many sanguinary battles between the Campbells and Macgregors.

This ancient "keep" was visited by her Majesty on her tour through the Highlands, on which occasion a splendid pavilion was erected for the dining hall, the accommodation within the building being but limited.   Immediately in front of the principal face of the castle lie the matchless flower-gardens of Drummond, known by repute to every florist in the kingdom.

North from Crieff, on the road to Amulree, is Monzie Castle (pronounced *Monee*,) Campbell, Esq., situate amidst splendid scenery. The paintings and armoury are well worthy of attention.   Leaving Crieff for Perth, we pass in succession Fern Tower (Lady Baird;) a mile beyond this Cultaquhey (Maxton, Esq.,) then Inchbraikie (Major Græme,) and next, on the right, Abercairney, (Major W. M. Stirling.)   Farther on is the village of Foulis, and a mile beyond this are the ruins of the Abbey of Inchaffray, founded in 1200 by an Earl of Strathearn and his Countess, and the abbot of which carried the arm of St. Fillan at the battle of Bannockburn.   A mile farther on, the road passes Gorthy, (Mercer, Esq.,) and shortly after enters the plantations of Balgowan, the seat of the late Lord Lynedoch.   A little farther, the road passes on the right Tippermalloch, (R. Smythe, Esq.,) and, between six and seven miles from Perth, enters the village of Methven, containing a population of about 2000.   In the immediate neighbourhood stands Methven Castle, (R. Smythe, Esq.)   Near Methven, Robert Bruce was defeated, June 19, 1306, by the English, under the command of Aymer de Valence, Earl of Pembroke.   About two miles and a half from Perth, the road passes the ancient castle of Ruthven, the scene of the memorable incident known in Scottish history by the name of the *Raid of Ruthven.*   The name of the building has been changed to Huntingtower, and it is now converted into a residence for workmen.   A short distance to the north is Lynedoch Cottage, within the grounds of which is Burn Braes, a spot on the banks of Brauchieburn, where Bessie Bell and Mary Gray

—————————"biggit a bower,
And theekit it ower wi' rashes."

Dronach Haugh, where these unfortunate beauties were buried, is about half a mile west from Lynedoch Cottage, on the banks of the river Almond.*   Over their supposed grave is placed a stone with

* The common tradition is, that Bessie Bell and Mary Gray were the daughters of two country gentlemen in the neighbourhood of Perth, and an intimate friendship subsisted between them.   Bessie Bell, daughter of the Laird of Kinnaird, happened to be on a visit to Mary Gray, at her father's house of Lynedoch, when the plague of 1666 broke out.   To avoid the infection, the two young ladies built themselves a bower in a very retired and romantic spot called the Burnbraes, about three-quarters of a mile westward from Lynedoch House, where they resided for some time, supplied with food, it is said, by a young gentleman of Perth, who was in love with them both.   The disease was unfor-

surrounded by wooded hills, forming a most romantic and attractive scene.* Proceeding onward, at the distance of a mile, the traveller enters the celebrated pass of KILLIE-CRANKIE, which stretches for the space of a mile or more along the termination of the river Garry. The hills which, on both sides, approach very near, are covered with natural wood, and descend in rugged precipices to the deep channel of the river. At the bridge over the Garry, near the entrance of the pass, a road leads on the left to the districts of the Tummel and Rannoch. The north end of this pass is the well-known scene of the battle fought, in 1689, between the Highland clans under Viscount Dundee, and the troops of King William, commanded by General Mackay. A stone is pointed out at Urrard House, on the right, which marks the spot where Dundee received his death-wound.†

* On the estate of Faskally, upon the high ground about a mile from Pit-lochrie, on the road from Dunkeld, is a pretty little waterfall called the Black Spout.

† "Dundee," says Sir John Dalrymple, "flew to the Convention, and demanded justice. The Duke of Hamilton, who wished to get rid of a trouble-some adversary, treated his complaint with neglect; and in order to sting him in the tenderest part, reflected upon that courage which could be alarmed by imaginary dangers. Dundee left the house in a rage, mounted his horse, and with a troop of fifty horsemen, who had deserted to him from his regiment in England, galloped through the city. Being asked by one of his friends who stopped him, where he was going? he waved his hat, and is reported to have answered, ' Wherever the spirit of Montrose shall direct me.'"—*Memoirs*, &tc edit. vol. i. p. 287. Dundee immediately proceeded to collect the army with which he fought the battle of Killiecrankie. This incident has been commemorated by Sir W. Scott in the following spirited song :—

"To the Lords of Convention, 'twas Clavers who spoke,
Ere the King's crown go down, there are crowns to be broke,
So each cavalier, who loves honour and me,
Let him follow the bonnet of Bonnie Dundee.

Come, fill up my cup, come, fill up my can,
Come, saddle my horses, and call up my men;
Come, open the West Port, and let me gae free,
And it's room for the bonnets of bonnie Dundee.

Dundee he is mounted, he rides up the street;
The bells are rung backward, the drums they are beat;
But the Provost, douce man, said, Just e'en let him be;
The town is weel quit of that deil of Dundee.
Come, fill up, &c.

z

son, Esq.,) &c. Passing Lude, (M'Inroy, Esq.,) the road descends into the valley, and crosses the river at the Bridge of Tilt, where there is a neat village and an excellent inn. The beauties of Glen Tilt, and the Falls of Fender, formed by a burn falling into the water of Tilt, will amply repay a visit. A little farther on, the road reaches the village and inn of Blair, the latter commodious and well conducted ; and, in the neighbourhood, the noble old castle of Blair, now called Atholl House, the ancient residence of the Dukes of that name. It is a long narrow building of three storeys. It was formerly much higher, and a place of considerable strength, but was reduced in height in consequence of the attacks of the Highlanders in 1716. In September 1844, Her Majesty sojourned for nearly three weeks at Blair Castle, visiting the falls of Bruar, the pass of Killiecrankie, the falls of Tummel, and the other picturesque scenery with which the neighbourhood abounds. Blair is celebrated for its noble old woods.

In the immediate neighbourhood there are many interesting waterfalls. Three miles to the westward are those of Bruar. The streamlet makes several distinct falls, and rushes through a rough perpendicular channel above which the sloping banks are covered with a fir plantation formed by the late Duke of Atholl, in compliance with the request of Burns in the well-known " Petition." And now, according to the poet's wish,—

" lofty firs and ashes cool,
The lowly banks o'erspread,
And view deep-bending in the pool,
Their shadow's watery bed !

since by the late Mr. M'Pherson of Belleville, the tourist reaches the farm-house of Pitmain, where he will enjoy an extensive view of the valley of the Spey, and of the high black rock of Craig Dhu, the rendezvous of the M'Phersons. Badenoch was anciently the possession of the great family of the Comyns who ruled here during the reigns of the early Scottish sovereigns. The remains of many of their numerous fortresses are still visible. The vast possessions of this family were forfeited on account of the part which they took in the wars between Bruce and Baliol. Badenoch now belongs to various proprietors, the principal of whom are James Evan Baillie, Esq., of Kingussie and Glenelg, (now owner of the greater part of the old Gordon estates,) Cluny Macpherson, Sir George Macpherson Grant of Ballindalloch, and Mackintosh of Mackintosh. A mile beyond Pitmain are the village and inn of Kingussie (the latter a handsome new building erected by Mr. Baillie,) opposite to which, on the other side of the Spey, are the ruins of Ruthven Barracks, destroyed by the Highlanders in 1746. On the same mount once stood one of the castles of the Comyns. It was at this place that the Highlanders reassembled to the number of 8000 two days after their defeat at Culloden, and here they received from Prince Charles the order to disperse. About two miles distant, on the north side of the Spey, is Belleville, the seat of Macpherson, the translator of Ossian, a native of the district, who died here in 1796, now occupied by his daughter, Miss Macpherson. It stands on the site of the ancient castle of Raits, the principal stronghold of the Comyns. A little farther on, a view is obtained of Invereshie, the seat of Sir George Macpherson Grant of Ballindalloch, on the south bank of the Spey of Loch Insh, through which the river passes, and of some of the highest of the Grampians. A short way beyond is Kinrara, the favourite seat of the late Duchess of Gordon, and now the property of the Duke of Richmond. The high rocky crag on the north banks of the Spey is Tor Alvie. On its eastern brow is a rustic hermitage, and at the other

off. Here are relics of a Roman encampment, of which the lines are still discernible.

strath.—" From its swelling base and rifted precipices the
birch trees wave in graceful cluster, their bright and lively
green forming a strong contrast in the foreground to the
sombre melancholy hue of the pine forests, which in the
distance stretch up the sides of the Cairngorms."* At
Aviemore a road leads along the banks of the Spey to
Grantown and Castle Grant, one of the residences of the Earl
of Seafield. The road now leaves the Spey, and at the
Bridge of Carr, eight miles from Aviemore, crosses the Dul-
nain ; near this place another road strikes off on the right to
Grantown. The country around is barren and uninteresting, but some burnt stumps sticking above the moor, and a
few hoary and stunted pine trees are still to be seen, the
solitary remains of those immense forests which once covered
the surface of the country. The road now passes through
the deep and dangerous pass called Slochmuicht, (the boar's
den or hollow,) which was the favourite haunt of banditti
even so late as near the close of last century. Four miles
from the Bridge of Carr it re-inters Inverness-shire ; and
two miles farther on crosses the rapid river Findhorn. The
banks of the Findhorn are in general highly romantic, but
at this spot they are by no means interesting.

In the month of August 1829, the province of Moray,
and adjoining districts, were visited by a tremendous flood.
Its ravages were most destructive along the course of those
rivers which have their source in the Cairngorm Mountains. The waters of the Findhorn and the Spey, and their
tributaries, rose to an unexampled height. In some parts
of their course these streams rose *fifty feet* above their
natural level. Many houses were laid desolate, much agricultural produce was destroyed, and several lives were lost.
The woodcut in our text represents the situation of a boat-
man called Sandy Smith, and his family, in the plains of
Forres. " They were huddled together," says the eloquent
historian of the Floods, " on a spot of ground a few feet
square, some forty or fifty yards below their inundated
dwelling. Sandy was sometimes standing and sometimes
sitting on a small cask, and, as the beholders fancied,

* ANDERSON's *Guide to the Highlands*, p. 81.

afterwards recovered the boat under circumstances almost miraculous, and finally succeeded in rescuing Sandy and his family from their perilous situation.

After crossing the Findhorn, the road passes Corybrough House (Campbell Smith, Esq.,) and a short way beyond reaches the Inn of Freeburn, about nine miles from Bridge of Carr. Near it are the house and plantations of Tomatin (Duncan Macbean, Esq.) The small estate of Free is the property of John Mackintosh, Esq. of Holm. All the rest of the adjoining lands, on the north side of the Findhorn, belong to the Mackintosh estate. Three miles and a half beyond this, on the right, is the castle of Moy, the ancient residence of Mackintosh, the chief of the Clan-Chattan, a confederation of the clans Mackintosh, Macpherson, and others of less consequence. It stands on an island in the midst of a small gloomy lake, called Loch Moy, surrounded by a black wood of Scotch fir, which extends round the lake, and terminates in wild heaths, which are unbroken by any other object as far as the eye can reach. Near the southern end of the lake is a small artificial islet of loose stones, which the former chiefs of Moy used as a place of confinement for their prisoners. On the largest island, a handsome granite obelisk, seventy feet high, has been erected to the memory of the late Sir Æneas Mackintosh, Bart., chief of the clan. On the west side of Loch Moy are the church and manse of Moy, and at the head of the lake, Moy Hall, the family residence of Mackintosh of Mackintosh. Here is preserved the sword of Viscount Dundee, and a sword sent by Pope Leo X. to James V., who bestowed it on the chief of Clan-Chattan, with the privilege of holding the king's sword at coronations. Leaving Loch Moy, the road enters Strathnairn, and passes for three miles through a bleak and heathery plain till it crosses the river Nairn, called in Gaelic *Kis-Nerane*, or the Water of Alders. Six miles from Inverness the road passes, on the right, Daviot House, the residence of Æneas Mackintosh, Esq., (brother of Mackintosh of Mackintosh.) Here are the remains of the ancient castle of Daviot, founded, it is said, by David Earl of Crawford, who, by his marriage

donian Hotel and the Union Hotel. The town carries on a respectable trade with London, Leith, and other places ; and a regular communication by steam is kept up between Inverness, London, Leith, and Glasgow. The tonnage of all the shipping belonging to the port is about 4300 tons, and the number of vessels sixty. In 1841, the population of the parish amounted to 15,308, that of the town alone being 11,575. It unites with Forres, Nairn, and Fortrose, in electing a member of Parliament.

Inverness is a town of great antiquity, but the exact date of its origin is unknown. On an eminence to the south-east of the town stood an ancient castle, in which it is supposed that Duncan was murdered by Macbeth. It is highly probable that Macbeth had possession of this castle, and it is certain that it was destroyed by the son of the murdered king, Malcolm Canmore, who erected a new one on an eminence overhanging the town on the south. This latter edifice continued for several centuries to be a royal fortress. It was repaired by James I., in whose reign a Parliament was held within its walls, to which all the northern chiefs and barons were summoned, three of whom were executed here for treason. In 1562, Queen Mary paid a visit to Inverness, for the purpose of quelling an insurrection of the Earl of Huntly. Being refused admission into the castle by the governor, who held it for the Earl, she took up her residence in a house, part of which is still in existence. The castle was shortly after taken by her attendants and the governor hanged. During the civil wars this castle was repeatedly taken by Montrose and his opponents. In 1715, it was converted into barracks for the Hanoverian soldiers, and in 1746, it was blown up by the troops of Prince Charles Stuart, and not a vestige of it now remains. On the site of this ancient edifice, a handsome castellated building has been erected, from a design by Mr. Burn, architect, consisting of the Court House, County Buildings, &c. On the north side of the town, near the mouth of the river, Cromwell erected a fort at an expense of £80,000. The stones employed in its construction were procured from the monasteries of Kinloss and Beauly, and the Grey-

ture of the ground rendered it peculiarly unfit for the movements of the Highland army, against cavalry and artillery.
According to the general accounts, about 1200 men fell in
this engagement. The number killed on both sides was
nearly equal.

The victory at Culloden finally extinguished the hopes
of the house of Stuart, and secured the liberties of Britain;
but the cruelties exercised by the Duke of Cumberland on
his helpless foes have stamped his memory with indelible
infamy; and there are few who will not join in the sentiments expressed in the concluding stanza of Burns' pathetic
song on the battle of Culloden.

> " Drummossie muir, Drummossie muir,
>   A waefu' day it was to me,
> For there I lost my father dear,
>   My father dear and brethren three.
>
> " Their winding-sheet the bluidy clay,
>   Their graves are growing green to see,
> And by them lies the dearest lad
>   That ever blest a woman's e'e.
>
> " Now wae to thee, thou cruel Duke,
>   A bluidy man I trow thou be,
> For monie a heart thou hast made sair,
>   That ne'er did wrang to thine or thee."*

* On the road leading from the battle-field to Inverness, there is an old farm-
steading with trees about it, like a small laird's dwelling. On the day succeeding the battle, the body of a youth of the better class was carried here shrouded
in a plaid: "My darling! my darling!" said the pitiful matron, to whom the
stranger's corpse was brought, "some mother's heart is lying with thee." It
was her own son, whom she fancied safe away with her relations in Glen Urquhart. The following beautiful and pathetic song, of which Culloden is the
scene, has never before (as far as we are aware) been in print. It was written,
we believe, by a young man of the name of Blair, belonging to Dunfermline.

> " Again the lav'rock seeks the skies,
>   And warbles, dimly seen,
> And summer views wi' sunny joys
>   Her gowanny robe o' green.
> But, ah! the summer's blythe return,
>   In flowery pride array'd,
> Nae mair can cheer this heart forlorn,
>   Nor charm the Highland maid.

near this place, Cawdor Castle, (erected about the year
1400,) which has still its moat and drawbridge, tower and
" donjon keep," as in the days of antiquity. It is the most
perfect specimen now remaining of the old feudal fortress.
Some ancient timber trees (which attracted the admiration
of Dr. Johnson himself,) surround the castle, and the scenery of the neighbourhood is wild and romantic.

A delightful excursion may be made to the little town of
Beauly, situated at the head of the firth which bears its
name, twelve miles north-west from Inverness. It has been
justly said that there are not many rides of a more various
and animating kind than that from Inverness westward to
Beauly. Leaving Inverness, the tourist crosses the Caledonian Canal. The beautiful wooded hill in front is Craig
Phadric, and the turreted mansion close by the road, embowered among trees, is Muirton, the seat of Mr. Huntly
G. Duff. The road now passes on the right the basin and
village of Clachnaharry,* and enters on the Aird, the richest and most beautiful district in Inverness-shire, and the

---

* Clachnaharry derives its name (Clach-na-herrie, or the Watchman's Stone)
from the rough impending rocks to the westward, where, in the days of blackmail and reavers, a watchman used to be stationed to give notice of the approach of the Highland clans from Ross or the west coast. On the highest pinnacle of the rock a column was erected by the late Major Duff of Muirton, to
commemorate a sanguinary engagement fought here between the Munroes of
Foulis and the Clan-Chattan. It is thus described by Mr. Anderson in his *Historical Account of the Family of Fraser*, p. 54. " The Munroes, a distinguished tribe of Ross, returning from an inroad they had made in the south of Scotland, passed by Moyhall, the seat of Mackintosh, leader of the Clan-Chattan ; a
share of the booty, or road-collop, payable to a chief for traversing his dominions,
was acceded to ; but Mackintosh's avaricious spirit coveting the whole, his proposal met with contempt, and Mackintosh summoned his vassals to extort compliance. The Munroes pursuing their journey, forded the river Ness, a little
above the island, and dispatched the cattle they had plundered across the hill of
Kinmylies to Lovat's province. Their enemy came up to them at the point of
Clachnahayre, and immediately joined battle ; the conflict was such as might
have been expected from men excited to revenge by a long and inveterate en-
mity. Quarter was neither sought nor granted ; after an obstinate struggle,
Mackintosh was killed. The survivors of this band retraced their steps to their
own country. John Munro, tutor of Foulis, was left for dead upon the field ;
his kinsmen were not long of retaliating. Having collected a sufficient force,
they marched in the dead of the night for the Isle of Moy, where the chief of
the Mackintoshes resided. By the aid of some planks which they had carried
with them, and now put together, they crossed to the isle, and glutted their
thirst for revenge by the murder or captivity of all the inmates."

magnificent view is obtained of the village of Beauly, traversed by the broad winding river, the village and the old
priory, Beaufort Castle, and other mansions, embosomed in
woods, and in the distance the rugged heights of Strathglass and Glenstrathfarrar.

Crossing the ferry, the tourist reaches the inn and village
of Beauly, worthy of its name,—Beau-lieu, *beautiful place.*
Close by the village, on the brink of the river, are the ruins
of the priory founded by John Bisset of Lovat, in 1230, and
peopled at first by monks from France, belonging to the
order of Valliscaulium, a reform of the Cistercians. Only
the walls and nave and transepts of the chapel now remain.
The internal area is used as a burying-place by the Clan-
Fraser, the Chisholms, and other families in Strathglass.
The north aisle belongs exclusively to the Mackenzies of
Gairloch. The priory is overshadowed by some fine old
trees, which have a pleasing effect.

The tourist while in this district, may visit Dingwall, nine miles
north from Beauly, and the scenery around Strathpeffer. On quitting Inverness-shire, the road at Beauly enters Ross-shire by a flat
dull tract called the *Muir of Ord*, once the scene of the clan battles
of the Frasers, Macleods, and Mackenzies, now distinguished for its
large cattle-markets. About three miles farther on, the tourist
reaches the banks of the Conon, a stream flowing through a beautiful
valley, richly studded with mansion-houses, woods, hamlets, and
farms. On the left is Highfield (Gillanders, Esq.,) beyond it Fair-
burn (Fowler of Raddery,) and in the centre of the plain, Castle
Brahan, the seat of the Right Hon. J. Stewart Mackenzie of Seaforth, an imposing structure, with charming grounds.[*] Some de-

* Brahan Castle was built by Kenneth, the founder of the clan of the Mackenzies. The father of Kenneth, an Irishman, of the house of Geraldine, married the only daughter and heiress of *Coinneach Grumach, i. e.* "Kenneth the
morose," chief of the clan Mathieson. Kenneth was named after his grandfather, and given up as heir-apparent to his management. According to clan
traditions, Coinneach Grumach was assassinated through a perfidious plot of
the chief of Glengarry, with whom he was at feud about the lands of Lochalsh.
At the same time, nearly the whole of his clan were murdered by the Macdonalds in cold blood in their beds. Young Kenneth alone escaped through the
affection and fidelity of his nurse. At a royal hunting match, held in Kintail
by Alexander III., the King, having been accidentally separated from his attend-

Leaving Strathpeffer, the road leads us to the banks of the Conon, passing by the church and manse of Contin, standing on an island of the river, embowered among trees and shrubs, and Coul House, the mansion of Sir George S. Mackenzie, Bart., the principal proprietor of this fine woodland district. A little to the east of Contin village, the fine streams of the Conon and the Garve or Blackwater unite. At the church of Contin, the Parliamentary Road from Dingwall is joined by the other branch from Scuddel Bridge before noticed.* Exactly opposite the inn of Contin rises the shapely and graceful hill of Tor Achilty, lightly sprinkled with birches and pines, and young oak copses. From this spot a road strikes off to the west, which leads past Loch Achiltie and Comrie to Strathconon, and the Falls of the Conon. Passing Craigdarroch, a lovely villa lately purchased by Sir George S. Mackenzie, and now occupied by Horatio Ross, Esq., of Rossie, the tourist reaches Loch Achiltie, " the most enchanting small lake in Great Britain," one of those exquisitely beautiful spots, where, if

" Art ere come, 'tis with unsandall'd feet."

" It is literally embosomed among hanging glades, and shrubby crags, and birchen knolls, rising in every light, graceful, and fanciful form, which, however, come not so near as to trouble or dim its bright loveliness there where it reposes

" ' A mirror in the depths of sylvan shelves,—
So fair a spot of earth, you might, I ween,
Have deem'd some congregation of the elves,
To sport by summer-moons, had shaped it for themselves.' "

Loch Achiltie is about three miles in circumference, its margin is broken into caves, islets, and promontories, luxuriantly clothed with trees, shrubs, and herbage, while in the extreme distance tower the "aërial or hazily empurpled summits" of Scuirvullin in Strathconon. The road skirts the northern shore, and, leading past a series of little lochs, at the distance of two miles, enters the soft meadow holms of Comrie, and the sweet valley of Scatwell, watered by the combined streams of the Conon and Meig. The former river descends

donald, and married another lady, a daughter of Lord Lovat. The clan, in revenge for the injured honour of their chieftain, Macdonald, laid waste the lands of the Mackenzies. It is said they were challenged by the latter to meet them on the spot, and the combat which ensued was most desperate. A thousand of the islesmen are said either to have been killed or drowned in the river Conon while attempting to escape. This conflict is generally known as the battle of Blar-na-Parc."

* Contin is only sixteen or eighteen miles distant from two points where the Edinburgh and London steamers touch,—Invergordon, on the Cromarty Firth, and Kessock Ferry, opposite Inverness. From Kessock a coach (*the Caberfae*) proceeds in summer to Dingwall every afternoon through the Black Isle.

manse, and are best viewed from it. The falls themselves are of no great consequence, " but the whole scene—the full river toiling through the deep tortuous chasm, and escaping in smooth lapses—the rough rocky steeps, and hanging woods and green margins—is beautiful and striking." It used to be a favourite sport to catch the salmon at this place,· as they struggle to ascend the river over the rocky ledges ; and it is said that the Lords Lovat of the olden time, by a particular contrivance, made the salmon leap into a boiling kettle which was kept suspended over the bank. On the opposite side of the river, close by the saw-mills, are the ruins of the old church and the deserted manse of Kiltarlity.

A little below the falls, on the right bank of the river, is Beaufort Castle, the seat of Lord Lovat, the chief of the Clan-Fraser. Castle Downie, the old seat of the Lovats, was destroyed in 1746, and the present is but an inferior structure. The grounds, however, are finely laid out, and the spot ornamented with some large and venerable trees. A fortress was erected here in the twelfth century, by the powerful family of Bisset. The possessions of this family extended over the Aird, and a great part of Stratherrick and Abertarff on Loch Ness ; but being implicated in the rebellion of Donald, Lord of the Isles, their estates were bestowed on the Frasers, who emigrated to the north from Peebles and Tweeddale about the year 1296. Castle Downie was besieged by Edward I. in 1303, and also by Oliver Cromwell, who blew up the citadel.

About three miles above the church and falls of Kilmorack, there is another succession of falls, at a place called " the Drhuim," where the valley has narrowed to a gorge, and completely shut out the view of firth and champaign. " The hilly banks, luxuriantly wooded, are lofty and steep, and high pyramids of rock, in every fantastic shape, shoot up like glaciers from the choked though wide-spread bed of the river, which here boils and chafes in fury, and there, when its rage is spent, sleeps in dreamy dark pools among the banks of the loveliest moss and freshest verdure, as if mustering its force for another fierce encounter.

" The broad rocky bed of this powerful river, in which

by the stream whose name it bears. In ancient times large pine forests stretched along the valley up to the summits of the hills. These have long ago been destroyed, but the sides of the glen are still fringed with beautiful birch trees. A fine road has lately been made through what is termed Chisholm's Pass, which passes along some splendid mountain scenery. About fifteen miles from Struy Bridge, the tourist reaches the elegant mansion-house of Guisachan, the seat of William Fraser, Esq. of Colbockie. The grounds are in a high state of cultivation, and their luxuriant vegetation is very unlike what we might have expected in such a remote district. The scenery around is uncommonly magnificent. The distance from Guisachan, through Glen Affrick to Dornie in Kintail, is only a forenoon's journey. The route lies along a series of lochs through a hoary primeval pine forest. The scenery is of a kindred nature to that of the Trosachs, but greatly surpasses it in wildness, grandeur, and extent.

Until the Parliamentary road was opened through Glen Moriston, and by Cluny into Glen Sheil, this was the principal route from Inverness and Ross-shires into Kintail and the surrounding parts of the west coast.*

There are various roads which lead across the hills from Strathglass into Urquhart and Glen Moriston.

* It may be easily believed that no one was permitted in those days to enter Kintail whose visits were not perfectly acceptable to the natives. "When the estates of the Earl of Seaforth were forfeited, after the Rebellion of 1715, and the foolish attempt at invasion which succeeded it in 1719, it was found quite impracticable for the Government to collect any rents in Kintail. A Mr. Ross, the first gentleman sent to make the attempt, was attended by a select party of soldiers, whom the Kintail men—to save them the needless trouble of coming through Glen Affrick, on a bootless errand—met at Lochan Cloigh, in the heights of Strathglass, where an admonitory bullet, sent from an overhanging thicket, grazed the neck of the collector of his Majesty's exchequer. He, however, was a Highlander, though a Whig: and he gallantly advanced three or four more miles, when his son was fired at from another ambuscade, and mortally wounded. The *soldiers* became alarmed, and their leader capitulated, and retreated as wise as he came. Another attempt to enter Kintail next rent-time, made by a more northerly route, was met in the same manner: the military leader was wounded and forced to return. Yet all this while the rents were duly collected among the devoted tenantry of Seaforth—the Macraws of Kintail, and, by some means or other, duly transmitted to France to the forfeited Earl, by a Donald Murchison, the memory of whose military and business talents,

House (Evan Baillie, Esq.,) surrounded by fine parks and magnificent trees. A monumental pillar has lately been erected, near the house, to the memory of the late proprietor, Evan Baillie, Esq., who was at one time M.P. for Bristol, and died in his native glen at the advanced age of ninety-five. Nearly opposite, in a sequestered bay which forms the narrow eastern extremity of Loch Ness, is Aldourie, the seat of W. F. Tytler, Esq., where Sir James Mackintosh was born, and in the immediate neighbourhood of which he spent several years of his childhood. For the first few miles along the shores of Loch Ness, the hills are bare and very steep. They are called Craig Derg, or the Red Rocks, from their reddish tint. The inhabitants of these *braes* were formerly noted for smuggling whisky. About fifteen miles from Inverness, Glen Urquhart opens up from the lake. This glen, which has been pronounced the fairest, the richest, and the most splendid in its beauty among Scotland's glens, is about ten miles in length, and is luxuriantly wooded. At the mouth of the glen there is an excellent inn called Drumindrochet. In the centre of the vale there is a small but very pretty lake, having the mansions of Lakefield, Lochletter, and Sheuglie, scattered around its borders. About two miles from the inn, a small burn falls over a lofty ledge of rock forming the falls of Divach. A small bay runs up from the loch for about two miles into the valley, receiving the united waters of the Coiltie and Enneric. On the western promontory of this bay are the ruins of the castle of Urquhart, rising finely over the dark waters of the loch, which, at this point, is 125 fathoms in depth. It appears to have been once a strong and extensive building. In 1303 it was besieged and taken by the troops of Edward I. In 1509, it fell, along with the barony of Urquhart, into the hands of the chief of the Clan-Grant, and it still continues in the possession of that family, who have a residence in it called Balmacaan. The road from Drumindrochet to Invermoriston—thirteen miles—is one of remarkable beauty. It is cut in the mountain side, plunging into hollows and climbing sharp acclivities, sometimes bordering the loch, part of the Great Glen. Glen Garry, which opens upon Loch Oich, is a charming valley, abounding in the most fascinating scenery. " Less splendid than Glen Urquhart, less diversified than Glen Moriston, it has, in its beautiful Loch Garry, and its endless succession of birch-clad knolls and eminences, and, above all, in the magnificence of the mountain vista to the west, a character quite peculiar." In the birch-woods which adorn this romantic glen the trees have attained a size and luxuriance equal to the finest of the pines of Rothiemurchus, or the beeches of Atholl. Near the mouth of the Garry, and close to the loch, are the ruins of the ancient castle of Invergarry, situated on a rock. It was burnt by the Duke of Cumberland after the Rebellion of 1745. In the immediate neighbourhood of the castle is Invergarry House, lately the residence of the chief of the Macdonells, who, in 1839, sold his estate of Glenquoich to ·Edward Ellice, Esq., and emigrated, along with a considerable part of his clan, to Australia. Invergarry Inn, one of the best in the Highlands, which stands a little way up the glen, is about seven and a half miles from Fort-Augustus, and about the same distance from Letterfinlay Inn on the banks of Loch Lochy. A little way from Invergarry Castle is a small monument erected by the late Colonel Macdonell of Glengarry over the " well of seven heads," commemorating the summary vengeance inflicted by a former chief of Glengarry, " in the swift course of feudal justice," on the perpetrators of the foul murder of the Keppoch family. This eccentric chief was the original of the character of Fergus M'Ivor, who occupies such a prominent place in the novel of Waverley. The distance between Lochs Oich and Lochy is about two miles. In 1544 Kinloch Lochy was the scene of a bloody encounter between the Frasers and a much superior force of the Macdonalds of Clanranald. On account of the heat of the weather, the combatants threw off their coats and fought in their shirts, whence the battle received the name of " Blar-na-leine," or " the Field of Shirts." Lord Lovat and his eldest son, together with most of the principal gentlemen of the clan, were slain in this engagement. Fourteen miles from Fort-Augustus, on the south side of

numerous observations made upon them they have been
proved to be perfectly horizontal or level; and although
geologists are still divided in opinion as to their origin, they
are generally supposed to be the vestiges of ancient lakes.
Proceeding onward, the road opens upon the river Lochy,
and, keeping along its banks, the tourist reaches the ruins
of Inverlochy Castle, about two miles distant from Fort-
William. It consists of four large towers, the western and
southern of which are nearly entire. Inverlochy is supposed to have been built by the powerful family of Comyn.
It was the scene of a bloody engagement, during the reign
of James I., between Donald of the Isles and the Earls of
Mar and Caithness, in which the latter were defeated, and
the Earl of Caithness slain. Here also, in 1645, the Marquis of Argyle was defeated with great slaughter by the
Marquis of Montrose. This engagement is described at
great length in the "Legend of Montrose."

A mile and a half from Inverlochy Castle, the tourist
reaches

FORT-WILLIAM,

situated at a bend of Loch Eil, twenty-nine miles from
Fort-Augustus, and sixty-one from Inverness. The fort
was erected in the reign of William III., from whom it derived its name. It contains a bomb-proof magazine, and the
barracks are intended to accommodate ninety-six private
soldiers, with the proper number of officers. In 1715, and
again in 1745, the Highlanders besieged it, but without
success. The adjacent village of Maryburgh, named in
honour of Queen Mary, contains a population of about 1500
persons, who are for the most part engaged in the herring
fishery. There are two respectable inns in the village.
The celebrated mountain, Ben Nevis, which rises from the
plain to the east of Fort-William, having been already
minutely described in the Tenth Tour, demands no additional notice in this place.*

* Glen Roy, in which are the Parallel Roads described in the preceding page,
is about sixteen miles distant from Fort-William, where gigs and other vehicles
may be engaged by tourists. There is an inn at the bridge of Spean, and another
at the bottom of the glen, where horses can be put up.

Treachtan, from which issues the wild stream of Cona, celebrated by Ossian, who is said to have been born on its banks. On both sides of this river the hills shoot up perpendicularly to a tremendous height, casting a deep gloom on this wild vale, calculated to strike the traveller with the deepest awe. At the head of the glen the disposition of the mountains becomes peculiarly grand and impressive. Their magnitude, form, and colour, all contribute to the greatness of the effect. In the huge clefts of their rocky and blackened summits, wreaths of snow may be seen all the year round, and the scream of the eagle, and the roar of the mountain torrents are the only sounds heard in " the waste howling wilderness." From one end of the vale to the other only one solitary farm-house is to be seen.* The well-known massacre of Glencoe, which casts so deep a stain on the character of King William and his ministers, happened at the north-west end of the vale. At the farthest extremity of Glencoe is the rugged mountain of Buchael Etive, and on the opposite side of the road is the steep ascent called *The Devil's Staircase,* by which pedestrians may proceed to Fort-William.† Proceeding onward through a barren district, the tourist arrives at King's House Inn, distant twenty-eight miles and a half from Fort-William. The road then crosses a tedious hill called the Black Mount ; and, nine and a half miles from the King's House, reaches Inverouran, on the banks of Loch Tulla. Two miles beyond this, the road crosses the river Orchy, which

---

* As a piece of perfectly wild mountain scenery, Glencoe has no superior that I know of. In the Alps there are many ravines and valleys immensely larger, but I am not aware of any which has better claims to attention in all that relates to the fantastical disposition of barren rocks of great magnitude tossed indiscriminately about by the hand of Nature."—*Captain Basil Hall's Patchwork,* vol. ii., p. 268.

† The distance from King's House Inn to Fort-William by the Devil's Staircase is about 23 miles. From the excessive roughness and steepness of a part of the first half of the road, it can be travelled only by pedestrians. The Staircase diverges from the main road at a small cluster of shepherd's houses, called Altnafedh, where it may be well to obtain a guide for the first two miles, the road being scarcely distinguishable among the rocks and loose stones which surround its tract. The only house where any refreshment can be obtained, is one of a very humble order, about twelve miles from Altnafedh, where drovers are accustomed to lodge on their way from the north.

account given in Barbour, three of the strongest among Lorn's followers resolved to rid their chief of this formidable foe. "They watched their opportunity until Bruce's party had entered a pass between a lake (Loch Dochart probably,) and a precipice, where the King, who was the last of the party, had scarce room to manage his steed. Here his three foes sprung upon him at once. One seized his bridle, but received a wound which hewed off his arm ; a second grasped Bruce by the stirrup and leg, and endeavoured to dismount him, but the King, putting spurs to' his horse, threw him down, still holding by the stirrup. The third taking advantage of an acclivity, sprung up behind him upon his horse. Bruce, however, whose personal strength is uniformly mentioned as exceeding that of most men, extricated himself from his grasp, threw him to the ground, and cleft his skull with his sword. By similar exertion he drew the stirrup from his grasp, whom he had overthrown, and killed him also with his sword as he lay among the horse's feet."

brated by Sir Walter Scott in the following song, entitled "THE BROOCH OF LORN," supposed to be sung by the bard of Lorn at his chieftain's request :—

" Whence the brooch of burning gold,
    That clasps the chieftain's mantle-fold,
    Wrought and chased with rare device,
    Studded fair with gems of price,
    On the varied tartans beaming,
    As, through night's pale rainbow gleaming,
    Painter now, now seen afar,
    Fitful shines the northern star ?

" Gem ! ne'er wrought on Highland mountain,
    Did the fairy of the fountain,
    Or the mermaid of the wave,
    Frame thee in some coral cave ?
    Did, in Iceland's darksome mine,
    Dwarf's swart hands thy metal twine ?
    Or, mortal-moulded, comest thou here,
    From England's love or France's fear ?

" No ! thy splendours nothing tell
    Foreign art or faëry spell,
    Moulded thou for monarch's use,
    By the overweening Bruce,
    When the royal robe he tied
    O'er a heart of wrath and pride ;
    Thence in triumph wert thou torn
    By the victor hand of Lorn !

" When the gem was won and lost,
    Widely was the war-cry toss'd !
    Rung aloud Bendourish fell,
    Answer'd Douchart's sounding dell,
    Fled the deer from wild Teyndrum,
    When the homicide, o'ercome,
    Hardly 'scaped with scathe and scorn,
    Left the pledge with conquering Lorn.

" Vain was then the Douglas brand,
    Vain the Campbell's vaunted hand,
    Vain Kirkpatrick's bloody dirk,
    Making sure of murder's work ;
    Barendown fled fast away,
    Fled the fiery De la Haye,
    When this brooch, triumphant borne,
    Beam'd upon the breast of Lorn.

" Farthest fled its former Lord,
    Left his men to brand and cord,
    Bloody brand of Highland steel,
    English gibbet, axe, and wheel,
    Let him fly from coast to coast,
    Dogg'd by Comyn's vengeful ghost,
    While his spoils, in triumph worn,
    Long shall grace victorious Lorn !"
            Lord of the Isles, canto ii., stanza II,
                and Notes.

lighthouse on this island is a work of great neatness, and the machinery by which the lights revolve, is very interesting. From the middle of the Firth, a fine view is obtained of the city of Edinburgh, with the harbours of Leith, Newhaven, and Granton, and the coast of Fife, thickly studded with towns. In allusion to this striking characteristic of Fife, King James VI. is said to have likened it to "a grey cloth mantle with a golden fringe." A little to the west is Burntisland, nearly opposite is the inn of Pettycur,* and a little farther east is the royal burgh of Kinghorn,† which gives the title of Earl to the Earls of Strathmore. About half a mile west of the town is a precipice called the King's Woodend, where Alexander III. was thrown from his horse and killed, 19th March 1285-6. Below Kinghorn is a square tower, the remains of Seafield Castle. A short way farther on is the "lang town of Kirkaldy," a royal burgh of great enterprise and trade. Its streets are extremely irregular, narrow, crooked, ill-paved, and dirty. Dr. Adam Smith, author of the "Wealth of Nations," was a native of this town. Balwearie, in the neighbourhood, was the birth-place of Sir Michael Scott, the famous wizard immortalized in the Lay of the Last Minstrel. The ruins of the old tower of Balwearie are still to be seen. On a rising ground behind Kirkaldy is Raith House, the handsome seat of Colonel Ferguson, M.P. for the Kirkaldy burghs. The situation is commanding, and the pleasure-grounds are extensive and very beautiful. At a short distance is Dunnikier House, the seat of Lady Oswald. To the east of Kirkaldy is Ravenscraig Castle, the property of the Earl of Rosslyn, situated upon a rock overhanging the sea. It has been in the possession of the St. Clair family since the reign of James III., and was entire and habitable till the time of

---

* Pettycur is supposed to have derived its name (pètit corps) from the landing of a small body of French troops during the regency of Mary of Guise.

† The parish church of Kinghorn is without a spire. This, and some other circumstances, supposed to be characteristic of the town, have given rise to the following couplet :—

"Here stands a kirk without a steeple,
A drucken priest, and a graceless people."

he returned next day with a sufficient force, and captured the whole band. A short way farther east are the ruins of Macduff's castle, said to have been built by Macduff, created Thane of Fife about the year 1057. A mile farther down is Buckhaven, a curious antique fishing village, inhabited by a most extraordinary race, supposed to be the descendants of the crew of a vessel from the Netherlands, which was wrecked near this place in the reign of Philip II. They were severely ridiculed more than a century ago in a celebrated satirical pamphlet called the "History of the College of Buckhaven, or the Sayings of Wise Willie and Witty Eppie," well known to the book-stall collectors of pamphlets and broadsides. Buckhaven is, however, a place of considerable wealth. A mile farther on is the small village of Methill, and, at the distance of another mile, the thriving village of Leven, situated at the mouth of the river of the same name, which issues from Loch Leven. Though it has a course of only twelve miles, it receives an immense number of tributary streams. The principal of these are enumerated in the following rhyme:—

> Lochtie, Lochrie, Leven, and Orr,
> Rin a' through Cameron Brig bore.

Leven contains about 1200 inhabitants, who are principally engaged in weaving linen. A short way in the interior is Durie House (C. M. Christie, Esq.) The steamer is now in Largo Bay, familiar to every Scotsman from the allusion made to it in the fine old song, "Weel may the boatie row." In the centre of the bay is the village of Lower Largo, the birth-place of Alexander Selkirk, whose singular adventures form the groundwork of Defoe's charming novel of "Robinson Crusoe." The chest and cup which he used on the uninhabited island are still in possession of his family, and the gun with which he killed his game, now belongs to Major Lumsden of Lathallan. Upper Largo was the birth-place of Sir Andrew Wood, the celebrated Scottish Admiral, who received the barony of Largo from James IV. as a reward for his services at sea against the English.

built in the reign of Charles I. A fine view is obtained
here of North Berwick Law, the Bass, and the coast of East
Lothian. About a mile farther down the coast stands Kil-
renny, another royal burgh, with a population of about
1500. The next town to the east is Crail, a venerable and
decayed burgh, formerly a place of considerable importance, but now greatly diminished. It contains about 2000
inhabitants. It was in the church of Crail that John Knox,
on the 29th of May 1559, preached a sermon against popery,
which so inflamed the populace, that they immediately
rose, and, in a very short time, demolished all the churches
in Crail, Anstruther, and the adjacent towns along the
coast. Crail was famous for its *capons*, a kind of dried
haddocks prepared by a peculiar mode of cookery.* The
well-known Archbishop Sharpe was at one time minister of
this parish. About a mile to the east of Crail is the East
Neuk of Fife, which gives name to a popular Scottish air.
Beyond this promontory is the Carr Rock, on which there
is a beacon of iron, after rounding which the coast stretches
away towards the north-west, forming the extensive bay
called St. Andrew's Bay. At the bottom of this bay, on a
ridge of rock projecting into the sea, stands the ancient
city of

* " Next from the well-air'd ancient town of Crail,
    Go out her craftsmen with tumultuous din;
  Her wind-bleach'd fishers sturdy-limb'd and hale;
    Her in-kneed tailors garrulous and thin;
  And some are flush'd with horns of pithy ale;
    And some are fierce with drams of smuggled gin;
  While, to augment his drouth, each to his jaws
  A good Crail capon holds, at which he rugs and gnaws."
                                              Anster Fair.

There is a strange old song called " Crail Town," of which the following are
the introductory stanzas:—
              " And was you ere in Crail toun?
                Igo and ago;
              And saw ye there Clerk Dishington,
                Sing from igon ago.
              His wig was like a doukit hen,
                Igo and ago;
              The tail o't like a goose pen,
                Sing irom igon ago," &c.
It appears to have served as a model for Burns' lines on Captain Grose

although it has been exposed to the weather for so many centuries, it still remains quite entire and unimpaired. The chapel to the east of the tower, which was the principal one, still remains ; but of a small chapel to the west, which formerly existed, there is now no trace. The cathedral was founded in the year 1159 by Bishop Arnold, but it was not finished till the time of Bishop Lamberton, who completed it in 1318. This magnificent fabric, the work of several ages, was demolished in a single day by an infuriated mob, excited by a sermon of John Knox against idolatry, preached in the parish church of St. Andrews.* It was an edifice of great extent, the length being 350 feet, the breadth 65, and the transept 180 feet. The eastern

* This event is graphically described by Professor Tennant in his poem entitled " Papistry Stormed; or the Dinging Doun o' the Cathedral." We may give a short extract as a specimen of the poem :—

" I sing the steir, strabash, and strife,
    Whan bickarin' frae the towns o' Fife
Great bangs o' bodies, thick and rife,
        Gaed to Sanct Andro's town ;

" And wi' John Calvin in their heads,
    And hammers in their hands, and spades,
Enraged at idols, mass, and beads,
        Dang the Cathedral down.

" I wot the bruilzie then was dour,
    Wi' sticks, and stanes, and bluidy clour,
Ere Papists unto Calvin's power
        Gaif up their strongest places ;

" And fearfu' the stramash and stour
    Whan pinnacle cam down, and tow'r,
And Virgin Marys in a shower
        Fell flat, and smash'd their faces,

" The copper roofs that dazzlit heaven,
    Were frae their rafters rent and riven,
The marble altars dasht and driven,
        The cods wi' velvet laces ;

" The siller ewers and candlesticks ;
    The purple stole and gowden pyx ;
And tunakyis and dalmatycks
        Cam tumbling frae their cases.

" The devil stood bumbazed to see
    The bonnie cosie byke where he
Had cuddlit mony a century,
        Rip't up wi' sic disgraces.

one, and, turning them out of the castle, without violence, tumult, or injury to any other person, inflicted on Beaton the death he justly merited. The conspirators were immediately besieged in this castle by the regent, Earl of Arran ; and although their strength consisted of only 150 men, they resisted his efforts for five months, owing more to the unskilfulness of the attack than the strength of the place, for in 1547, the castle was reduced and demolished, and its picturesque ruins serve as a landmark to mariners."*

The University of St. Andrews—the oldest establishment of that nature in Scotland—was founded in 1411 by Bishop Wardlaw. It consisted formerly of three colleges :—1. St. Salvator's, which was founded in 1458 by Bishop Kennedy. The buildings of this college formed an extensive court or quadrangle about 230 feet long, and 180 wide, and a gateway surmounted by a spire 156 feet high. On one side is the church, on another what was the library of St. Salvator's, the third contains apartments for students, the fourth is unfinished. The buildings connected with this college have fallen into a state of decay, and a grant was made by Parliament for erecting a new structure. One half of the proposed buildings for the United College have been erected, but the rest of the funds appointed to complete the works having unfortunately been diverted to another purpose, the structure remains incomplete. 2. St. Leonard's College, which was founded by Prior Hepburn in 1532. This is now united with St. Salvator's, and the buildings sold and converted into private houses. 3. New, or St. Mary's College, which was established by Archbishop Hamilton in 1552, but the house was completed by Archbishop Beaton. The buildings of this college have lately been repaired with great taste.

In the United College the languages, philosophy, and the sciences are taught. St. Mary's, which stands in a different part of the town, is reserved exclusively for theology. The classes and discipline of the two colleges are quite distinct, each having its respective Principal and

---

* *Encyclopædia Britannica*, seventh edition, vol. iii., p. 121.

church, the college church, an episcopal, free church, secession, independent, and baptist chapel, and a new chapel
in connexion with the established church, which was
opened in August 1840. The parish church is a spacious
structure, 162 feet in length, by 63 in breadth, and is large
enough to accommodate 2500 persons. It contains a lofty
monument of white marble, erected in honour of Archbishop Sharpe, who, in revenge for his oppressive conduct,
was murdered by some of the exasperated Covenanters.
On this monument is a bas relief representing the tragical
scene of the murder. To the north is situated the college
church, which belongs to the united college of St. Salvator
and St. Leonard. It was founded in 1458 by Bishop Kennedy, and contains a beautiful tomb of its founder, who
died in 1466. It is a piece of exquisite Gothic workmanship, though much injured by time and accidents. About
the year 1683, on opening this tomb, six highly ornamented silver maces were discovered, which had been concealed
there in times of trouble. Three of these maces are still
preserved in the university, and one was presented to each
of the other three Scottish universities. The top has been
ornamented by a representation of our Saviour, with angels
around, and the instruments of his passion ; with these are
shown some silver arrows with large silver plates affixed to
them, on which are inscribed the arms and names of those
who were victors in the annual competitions of archery,
which, after having been discontinued for half a century,
were again revived in 1833. Golf is now the prevailing
game in St. Andrews. It is played on a piece of ground
called the Links, which stretches along the sea-shore to the
extent of nearly two miles. A considerable number of golf-
balls are manufactured in St. Andrews. Besides the consumption of the town, about 9000 are annually exported to
various other places.

The trade of St. Andrews was once very considerable.
The shipping of the port now consists of a few vessels employed in the coasting trade. The harbour is guarded by
piers, and is safe and commodious ; but it is difficult of access, having a narrow entrance, and being exposed to the

and machinery. Ship-building is also carried on to a considerable extent. Although the depression of trade materially affected all these departments of enterprise for several years, the year 1844 has been distinguished by very general commercial prosperity.

The grandest and most important feature of Dundee is its harbour, with its magnificent wet docks, built and in progress, and a number of spacious quays, patent slip, graving dock, &c., spreading along the margin of the Tay, and terminated on the west by the Craig Pier, which is exclusively appropriated to the use of the ferry. These splendid works up to April 1845 have cost about £550,000. An elegant building has been erected for the Custom House and Excise Office, with premises for the accommodation of the Harbour Trustees, and officers connected with the establishment. The number of vessels belonging to the port in December 1844 was 326, their tonnage being 50,901. Of these a few are employed in the whale fishery, and many of them in the Baltic and American trade. In the London trade, besides a number of schooners, there are three splendid steam vessels, of 300 horse power, each of which was built at an expense of upwards of £20,000.

The streets are for the most part narrow and irregular, except in the modern portions of the town. The market place, or High Street, is a spacious square, 360 feet long by 100 broad, from which diverge the Nethergate, Seagate, Overgate, and Murraygate, the principal streets, which run from east to west, nearly parallel to the river. Castle Street leads from the south-east end of the High Street to the new docks on the south, and contains, among other neat buildings, an Episcopal chapel and a theatre. At the south-east corner is an elegant building in the Grecian style, erected for an exchange and reading-room. On the south side of the market-place or square stands the Town Hall, surmounted by a steeple, and having piazzas below; it was built in 1743. Opposite to this building is a spacious new street, named Reform Street; at the north end of which, and fronting the Town Hall, is an elegant edifice, in the Grecian style of architecture, for an academy and public

with the proposed great lines centering in that city, so that Dundee will have the advantage of unobstructed railway communication with all parts of the kingdom.

Dundee was in ancient times fortified with walls; but of its walls or gates, no traces now remain, except the Cowgate Port, from which Wishart the martyr is said to have preached to the people during the plague of 1544. At the period of the Reformation, it was the first town in Scotland which publicly renounced the Roman Catholic faith : and so zealous was the spirit of its Protestantism, that it acquired the name of " *the second Geneva.*" In 1651, the town was sacked, with circumstances of revolting cruelty, by General Monk ; and so great was the amount of plunder, that each of his soldiers is said to have received £60 sterling as his share. According to tradition, the indiscriminate carnage which took place on this memorable occasion was continued till the third day, when a child was found sucking the breast of its murdered mother.

About twelve miles east from this part of the coast is the famous BELL ROCK,* or Inch Cape Rock, which, from a very remote period, has been the cause of numerous shipwrecks. The top of the rock only being visible at low water, one of the abbots of Aberbrothock attached to it a framework and a bell, which, being rung by the waves, warned mariners to avoid the fatal reef. A tradition respecting this bell has been embodied by Dr. Southey in his ballad called "Ralph the Rover." A famous pirate of this name is said to have cut the bell from the frame-work " to plague the Abbot of Aberbrothock," and some time after to have received the just punishment of his malice by being shipwrecked on the spot. An elegant lighthouse, 115 feet high, has now been erected by the Commissioners of the Northern Lighthouses at an expense of £60,000. It is one of the most prominent and serviceable beacons on the Scottish shores, and has been the means of preventing innumerable

* The Bell Rock is 24 miles east of Dundee Harbour, 12 from the Bucy of Tay, 12 from Arbroath, and 12 from Fifeness.

Leaving Arbroath, at the distance of two miles and a half, is Carlinheugh Bay, and a short way further on, Ethie House, the seat of the Earl of Northesk. About a mile be-

rose, bespattered and blinded with mire, and mistaking the Earl for the offender, ran him through the body. He was tried for the crime, and narrowly escaped the gallows. On a mount to the north of the town was the castle in which King Malcolm resided, and his queen lived in a nunnery which stood on a small artificial island near the north side of the loch. In the steeple of Forfar is preserved a curious instrument, called " the Witches' Bridle," which was placed on the head of the miserable creatures burnt in Forfar for the imaginary crime of witchcraft, and acted as a gag to prevent their cries during the dreadful process of incremation. There are a number of pleasant anecdotes connected with Forfar, but it is somewhat curious, as has been noticed by Chambers, that they all refer to drinking or to public-houses. The legal gentlemen of this town, indeed, are characterized as the "drucken writers of Forfar." Their tippling habits are finely illustrated by an anecdote of the late Earl of Strathmore. The town is a good deal annoyed with a lake in its neighbourhood, which the inhabitants have long had it in contemplation to drain, and which would have been drained long ago but for the expensiveness of such an undertaking. At a public meeting held some years ago for the discussion of this measure, the Earl said, that he believed the cheapest method of draining the lake would be, to throw a few hogsheads of good mountain dew into the water, and set the *drucken writers* of Forfar to drink it up.*

The chief magistrate of Forfar, in the time of King James VI., kept an alehouse. His Majesty, in the course of his first journey to London, having been entertained with great splendour by the mayor of an English town, who, in honour of the occasion, kept open house for several days, some of the courtiers hinted that such examples of munificence must be very rare among the civic dignitaries of Scotland. " Fient a bit o' that are they," cried the King; " the provost o' my burgh of Forfar, whilk is by nae means the largest town in Scotland, keeps open house a' the year round, and aye the mae that comes the welcomer."

It was in Forfar that the famous case occurred which led to the decision that no charge could be made for a stirrup-dram. A brewster-wife in Forfar, previous to the Restoration, having one day "brewed a peck o' maut," and set it out to the door to cool, a neighbour's cow passing by drank the whole browst. The injured ale-wife had recourse to the law for satisfaction, when it was decided, that as, by the immemorial custom of the land, nothing is ever charged for a standing-drink, otherwise called a *deoch-an-dorras*, or stirrup-dram, the defendant ought to be absolved from the charge in dependence, seeing that she swallowed the browst standing, and at the door.

Forfar is situated in the beautiful valley of Strathmore, which gives title to the noble family of Lyon. The seat of this family, the celebrated castle of Glammis, stands near the village of the same name, about five miles and a-half south-west of Forfar. It is situated in the midst of a park, one hundred and sixty acres in extent, and containing a considerable number of fine old trees. The castle is an edifice of great antiquity, and has a princely and antique ap-

---

* Chambers' Rhymes of Scotland, p. 117. Picture of Scotland, vol. ii., p. 220.

river expands into a spacious basin which forms a sort of
road-stead to the port. At high water, it has a peculiarly
striking and beautiful effect. The South Esk is crossed by
a very magnificent suspension bridge, the distance between
the points of suspension being 432 feet. Montrose is a remarkably neat town, and carries on a considerable trade.
It'has been connected with a number of interesting and important events in Scottish history. From this place Sir
James Douglas embarked in 1330 on a pilgrimage to the
Holy Land, carrying along with him the heart of Robert
Bruce. It was the birth-place of the celebrated Marquis of
Montrose. It was the first port made by the French fleet
in December 1715, with the Chevalier St. George on board;
and that personage embarked at the same place 14th February 1716, having spent the previous night in the house
in which Montrose was born. The principal public buildings are the town-hall, the parish church, the Episcopal
chapel, the public schools, the academy, the lunatic asylum, and the office of the British Linen Company. In
1841, the population of Montrose, within the Royalty, was
13,552.*

About four miles and a half from Montrose, the North
Esk joins the ocean, and immediately behind it commences
Kincardineshire or the Mearns. The scenery along the
coast is peculiarly desolate. Passing the fishing village of
Milltown, and the manufacturing village of Johnshaven,

* Eight miles west from Montrose is the ancient royal burgh of Brechin,
romantically situated on the banks of the South Esk. In ancient times there
was an abbey of Culdees in this place, and a bishoprick was established here by
David I. in 1150. On the edge of a precipitous bank descending towards the
river, stood the Cathedral, a stately Gothic fabric, but its architectural symmetry has of late been almost entirely destroyed by the wretched taste displayed
in repairing it as a modern place of worship. Brechin contains one of those
round towers, which, like that of Abernethy, is "with great probability ascribed
to the Picts, although antiquarians are divided in their opinion concerning
them. The tower of Brechin is a circular column, of great beauty and elegance,
80 feet high, with a kind of spire or roof 23 feet more, making the whole height
103, while the diameter is 16 feet." Brechin Castle, the ancient seat of Lord
Panmure, stands on a precipitous rock in the immediate neighbourhood of the
town. It underwent a siege of twenty days, in 1303, from the English army
under Edward I., and only surrendered on Sir Thomas Maule, its brave governor, being killed.

of Kinneff, by Mrs. Granger, the wife of the minister of
that parish. At the Restoration, all the persons connected
with this affair were amply rewarded. Ogilvy was made a
baronet ; the brother of the Earl Marischal was created
Earl of Kintore ; and Mrs. Granger was rewarded with a
sum of money. During the reign of Charles II. Dunnotar
was used as a State prison, for confining the Covenanters.
It was dismantled soon after the Rebellion of 1715, on the
attainder of its proprietor, James Earl Marischal. "The
battlements, with their narrow embrasures, the strong
towers and airy turrets, full of loop-holes for the archer
and musketeer ; the hall for the banquet and the cell for
the captive, are all alike entire and distinct. Even the
iron rings and bolts that held the culprits for security or
torture, still remain to attest the different order of things
which once prevailed in this country. Many a sigh has
been sent from the profound bosom of this vast rock—
many a despairing glance has wandered hence over the
boundless wave—and many a weary heart has there sunk
rejoicing into eternal sleep."*

About a mile and a half from Dunnotar is the seaport
of Stonehaven, situated in the bottom of a bay at the mouth
of a stream called the Carron. It has a safe and commodious harbour, and contains a population of upwards of 2000.
The tract of country which extends between Stonehaven
and Aberdeen is remarkably bleak and sterile, presenting,
for the most part, barren eminences, and cold swampy moor-
lands. Within the last four years, however, a few neat houses
have been erected along the roadside. The only object
worthy of notice is the fishing village of Finnan, remarkable
for the dried fish called Finnan Haddocks.† At the north-

* A Summer Ramble in the North Highlands.

† In a very amusing and well-written work, entitled "The Book of Bon Accord: or a Guide to the City of Aberdeen," we find the following glowing apo-
strophe to these far-famed fish :—"FINNAN, *magnum et venerabile nomen!*
'To abstract the mind from all local emotion,' says the moralist, 'would be impossible if it were endeavoured, and would be foolish if it were possible. Far
from me and from my friends be such frigid philosophy. That man is little to
be envied whose patriotism would not gain force upon the plain of *Marathon,*'
or whose appetite would not grow keener among the huts of *Finnan.* Its un-
lettered sages will impart wisdom which will be vainly sought in elaborate dis-

by the Dee, which the tourist crosses by a fine old bridge
of seven arches, erected about three centuries ago, by
Bishop Dunbar. In the days of the Covenant, this bridge
was the scene of more than one tough contest between
hostile parties. In 1842 its breadth was nearly doubled,
by an addition made to one of its sides. The facing of the
side upon which the addition was made, having been removed at the commencement of the work, and afterwards
restored to its original position, the character of the structure remains unimpaired by the improvement. A drive of
a mile through the western suburbs of the city, which boast
many elegant private buildings, brings the traveller to one
extremity of Union Street, terminating, at the other, in
Castle Street, and presenting a vista which is generally and
justly admired, whether regard be had to the spacious dimensions of the street itself, the beauty and regularity of
the buildings which line it on each side, the splendour
of many of its shops, or the bustle which constantly enlivens
it. The three chief inns of the city are situated in it, in
any of which, not to mention the attractions of the minor
hostelries, the stranger will be comfortably accommodated.
Curiosity will probably first direct his steps toward Castle
Street, the *Plde* of the city. Here he will find the Town
House, a plain but commodious building, of date 1730. It
contains the Town Hall, Council Chamber, &c., to which
ready access may be obtained. The hall is a spacious
apartment, and contains one or two good paintings, three
superb lustres, and some other matters worthy of inspection.
The Council Chamber contains a fine head by Jameson.
On the east end of the Town House is a square tower, of
ancient date, which has been recently faced up with granite
in a very tasteful style. It is surmounted by a spire 120
feet high, of singularly elegant proportions. Contiguous to
the tower, on the east, are the new offices of the North of
Scotland Banking Company, a fine building in the Grecian
style, of beautifully dressed granite. The principal entrance is under a curved portico, supported by granite
columns of the Corinthian order, the capitals being executed with a delicacy and precision hitherto deemed un-

cemetery, which is separated from the street by a very beautiful façade of the Ionic order. The West Church is a building in the Italian style, containing a fine monument, in white marble, to the memory of a lady, executed by Bacon, at an expense of £1200 : a curious monumental plate of brass, commemorative of the death of Dr. Duncan Liddel, founder of the professorship of Mathematics in Marischal College ; and a stone effigy of Sir Robert David-son, Provost of Aberdeen, who fell at Harlaw in 1411. The East Church is a modern building, in the Gothic style, deservedly much admired. The churches are separated by Drum's Aisle, so called from its being the burial-place of the ancient family of that name. It formed the transept of the original church of St. Nicholas, a fabric of the twelfth century. The only part of the old structure is the central tower, in which hang the bells. The original date of the great bell, Laurence, which weighs 40,000 lbs., is 1352. In the churchyard reposes the hallowed dust of the poet of " The Minstrel," of Principal Campbell, the learned Blackwell, and Dr. Hamilton, the well known author of the work on the National Debt. Part of Union Street is carried over a deep ravine, by means of a magnificent bridge, consisting of one arch of 130 feet span, 44 feet in breadth, and 50 feet above the surface of the ground below. It is built of dressed granite, and surmounted with a cornice, parapet, and balustrades. It cost £13,342. Westward of the bridge, at some distance, are situated the Public Rooms. In beauty of architecture, and splendour of internal decoration, they are inferior to none in the kingdom. The banqueting-room contains a portrait of the late Duke of Gordon, by Lawrence, and another of Provost James Hadden, by Pickersgill. To these has been added another, by the latter artist, of the Hon. Captain Gordon, who has, for many years, represented the county in Parliament. The other public buildings which particularly merit the attention of the stranger, are the New Infirmary, the Lunatic Asylum, Gordon's Hospital, the New Female Orphan Asylum, the Institution for the Blind, the New Hall of the Society of Advocates, the Trades' Hall, and Marischal

in the city many extensive manufactories of flax, cotton, wool, and iron, which employ an aggregate number of hands, amounting to about 14,000. We would particularly recommend to the stranger a visit to Banner Mill, one of the most extensive and best arranged cotton manufactories in the kingdom. There are various other branches of commerce and trade successfully prosecuted in the city, the extent of which may be inferred from the fact, that the tonnage of all the vessels actually arriving in the port is about 210,000 tons. Large steamers ply regularly between it and London, Leith, and Hull. The adoption of steam navigation has been of the greatest advantage to the city and county, and particularly to the agriculturist. Cattle are thus shipped in large numbers, and at all seasons, for the London market. The accommodation for passengers is excellent. In the course of three or four days may the care-worn denizen of the metropolis escape from its din and dust, to "the land of the mountain and the flood," there to inhale its invigorating breezes, enjoy the splendid sports offered by its heaths and streams, and admire the magnificent scenery of "dark Lochnagar." The population of the city within the Parliamentary boundary, according to the census of 1841, was 62,900. It is a city of high antiquity, its earliest charter extant being one granted by William the Lion in 1179. Previously to that early period, however, it was a place of comparative importance, and enjoyed, for so remote an age, a rather extensive commerce. At a subsequent period, it stood high in the favour of "The Bruce," who bestowed on it many important privileges, and a large extent of lands in its vicinity, in consequence of the devotion shown by its inhabitants to his cause. The history of Aberdeen exhibits it participating largely in the successive vicissitudes of the times; but, under all circumstances, its inhabitants have generally been distinguished for their loyalty, prudence, and enterprise.

Old Aberdeen, which is situated about a mile to the north of the city, contains the Cathedral and King's College, both of which will amply reward a visit. The nave of the former is used as the parish church, and is in excellent repair.

Aberdeenshire and Banffshire. Its total course is about sixty-one miles. It is a much less rapid river than the Dee, and flows, for a considerable part of its course, through rich valleys. About a mile from Old Aberdeen, the Don is crossed by the " BRIG OF BALGOWNIE," celebrated by Lord Byron in the tenth canto of Don Juan.

" As ' auld lang syne' brings Scotland, one and all,
  Scotch plaids, Scotch snoods, the blue hills and clear streams,
The Dee, the Don, Balgownie's Brig's black wall,
  All my boy-feelings, all my gentler dreams,
Of what I then dream't cloth'd in their own pall,
  Like Banquo's offspring ;—floating past me, seems
My childhood, in this childishness of mind :
  I care not—'tis a glimpse of ' Auld lang syne.' "

"The Brig of Don," adds the poet in a note, " near the Auld Town of Aberdeen, with its one arch, and its black deep salmon stream below, is in my memory as yesterday. I still remember, though perhaps I may misquote, the awful proverb which made me pause to cross it, and yet lean over it with a childish delight, being an only son, at least by the mother's side. The saying as recollected by me, was this, but I have never heard nor seen it since I was nine years of age :—

" ' Brig of Balgownie, black's your wa',
    Wi' a wife's ae son, and a mare's ae foal,
    Doon ye shall fa' ! ' "

The bridge was built by Bishop Cheyne, in the time of Robert Bruce, and consists of one spacious Gothic arch, which rests on a rock on each side.*

* From Aberdeen a very interesting tour may be made up the Dee to Ballater and Castleton of Braemar. The district of country which this route gives the tourist an opportunity of visiting is peculiarly wild, exhibiting scenes of savage grandeur unsurpassed in any part of Scotland.

Although Aberdeen is made the starting point in this excursion, we shall advert, in our progress, to other routes by which the various interesting spots mentioned in it may be reached, without passing through Aberdeen.

standing on a steep precipice overlooking the sea. This fortress was destroyed in 1594, when James VI. marched

must have been combined in the construction of works so gigantic on such a spot. The whole of this neighbourhood bears traces of ancient and long-forgotten conflict. There are many minor fortifications and camps, and the peasantry frequently turn up flint spear and arrow heads of exquisite proportion and finish, remnants of an ancient and partial civilization, that must have passed away long before the commencement of Scottish history.

At the tenth mile is the house or castle of Drum, (Alex. Irvine, Esq.) boldly looking out from a noble hill slope among scattered forest trees. The most remarkable part of the building is the old keep or donjon, a massive square tower, with rounded corners, which looks as if it had been built to give battle to earthquakes. The walls are twelve feet thick, and thus, though the outside circumference is considerable, the interior merely consists of a small gloomy vaulted chamber in each floor. The family of Drum is of considerable antiquity, and great fame in local history. It is the subject of a multitude of traditions, the more striking of which concern a long deadly feud with the Keith family, and the great battle of Harlaw. A little beyond the tenth mile are Mains of Drum Inn and Drumoak Church and Manse. Opposite the eleventh mile-stone there is, on the south bank of the river, the House of Durris, (Anthony Mactier, Esq.) and a little farther on the Kirk of Durris, or, as it is pronounced in the vicinity, Dores. On the north side of the river, and between it and the road, is Park House, (A. Kinloch, Esq.) a somewhat more dapper and villa looking edifice than the majority of the Deeside buildings. About the 15th mile, Crathes Castle, (Sir Robert Burnett of Leys, Bart.) looks majestically forth from a sloping mass of thick woodland. It is one of those old Flemish buildings which, rising as it were from a solid root and stem, becomes, as it ascends, broken into a varied picturesque cluster of turrets, chimneys, and peaked gables. There are, unfortunately, some modern additions sadly out of keeping with the picturesque character of the older part. Here, as at Drum, there is abundant traditionary lore, both in prose and song.*

* Of the latter, there is a somewhat humorous ballad, called " The Baron of Leys," in which a hopeful heir of the family, having got inveigled in some foreign liaison, is represented as mystifying the object of his affections on the subject of his identity, by successively representing himself as the proprietor of very grotesque and unreasonable names. The dialogue proceeds thus :—

" Some ca's me this, some ca's me that,
    Whatever may best befa' me ;
But when I'm in Scotland's King's high court,
    Clatter-the-speens they ca' me.

2 D   " O waes

their present habitation, a collection of low houses forming
a quadrangle, one side of which is built on the very verge

A little more than a mile beyond Banchory, on the south bank, is
the modern castellated mansion of Blackhall, (Colonel Campbell,) a
parkish looking place, with a long wide avenue, bordered by magnificent trees. On the north bank is Inchmarlo, (D. Davidson, Esq.)
About a mile farther on is Woodend Cottage, peeping from a
plantation sloping finely to the Dee. At the 24th mile is the Brig of
Potarch, where the old south and north road, still used by drovers,
crosses to the Cairn o'Mont, Fetter Cairn, and Brechin.* The Dee
where it is spanned by this bridge, is hurried between two rocks,
which leave a space only of twenty feet for its ample waters. According to Mr. James Brown's Guide Book—of which anon—a caird, or
gipsey, called John Young, pursued for murder, escaped, by leaping
this wild chasm.† Twenty-six miles from Aberdeen is the village of
Kincardine O'Neil, where we could not have wished the traveller
better fortune than to find the worthy Mrs. Gordon still presiding
over her well-conditioned inn, venerable in the administration of hospitalities, from which the profuseness and cheapness seemed to remove
all mercenary character. Mrs. G. has, we understand, retired from
her important duties ; and we doubt not her successor will feel a stimulus in the ambition to rival so distinguished a predecessor. This
remote locality is connected with one of the most remarkable incidents in Scottish history. The pursuit and death of Macbeth, transferred by Boece, and the other fabulous annalists whom Shakspeare
read, to Perthshire, took place according to the earlier and more
credible chroniclers, in the vicinity of Kincardine. Wynton says,

> " And ower the mownth thai chast hym than
> Til the wode of Lunfanan.
>   *   *   *
> This Macbeth slewe thai there
> Into the wode of Lunfanan,
> And his hewyd thai strak off thare,
> And that wyth thame fra thair thai bare
> Til Kynkardyn, quhare the King
> Till thare gayne come made byding."

If any one wishes to experiment on a really old-fashioned Scottish country
inn, equally unknown to tourists and commercial travellers, we would recommend him to the hostel of Cutties-Hilloc on this road, should it still remain the
respectable relic of former hospitality which we remember it to have been but
a few years ago.

† Young was a man of many feats in Aberdeenshire story, and is the same
to whom was attributed the bold practical joke of releasing all the prisoners in
the jail of Aberdeen, (himself included,) and placarding the door with the ad-
vertisement " ROOMS TO LET."

which remain where the soft parts have been washed away, have assumed the appearance of old Gothic towers. In this neighbourhood is that wonder of nature, the BULLER OF

exchanging courtesies with those he meets. Nor, however humble may be the peasant who says "a fine day," and perhaps offers his "sneeshun mull," will much servility be found in his deportment. There is, in fact, an independence of demeanour in these worthy fellows, which, backed by their energetic accent, has a somewhat repulsive appearance to strangers ; yet, from the genuine kindness met at every turn, wherever there is an opportunity to call it forth, such a feeling must soon disappear. The hospitalities of the Deeside peasantry are, however, by no means of the kind which would generally be called refined in high life. As an illustration of their courtesies, it is said that a weary pedestrian from Aberdeen, who had lost his way, and was kindly provided with a night's lodging, was not a little astonished in stepping out of bed to find himself up to the knees in water—the night had been rainy. On appearing before his entertainers, in a pitiable plight, and representing to them that such an inroad of the element in such a quarter was an uncommon event, which required some peculiar explanation, he met the excuse justificative in these terms, " Oh, man, you surely forgot to look for the stappin' stons."

To the north of the Muir of Dinnet lies the district of Cromar and the village of Tarland. The highest summit in this direction is the Hill of Morven, round, and somewhat flat in its outline ; and a glimpse is just caught from the road of a pretty sedgy sheet of water, called the Loch of Kinnord. The monotony of the progress through the dreary muir is gradually relieved by the opening prospect of the hills, which rise, terrace above terrace, like mounds thrown up for an audience of Titans. Highest of all, a long gracefully waving outline, bending on either side from a sharp peak, characterises the mountain monarch of the district, Lochnagar. If the atmosphere be clear, the line of precipice which constitutes its eastern wall may be seen from summit to base, clear and smooth ; but most generally it suits not the monarch to unveil his fearful beauties, and a mass of black cloud hovers round his summit, within whose mysterious folds proceeds the manufacture of elemental wrath. As the traveller approaches closer to the base of the series of mountain terraces, he perceives a little fertile plain reposing beneath their huge shadows, and edged by the clear waters of the Dee. When the eye is sufficiently accustomed to the large masses by which it is surrounded to detect minuter objects, a small spire may be seen rising very distinct from the plain, round it curls a light smoke, indicative of the dwelling of human beings, and finally, rows of small houses, like so many

around the top which in one place is only two feet wide, with a monstrous precipice on either side. In the side of

by a fine stone bridge, which being destroyed by the floods of 1829, has been replaced by a structure partly of wood. The ostensible object of the Ballater visiters (the medicinal wells) are at a spot called Pananich, about two miles to the east, on the south side of the river. Their virtues are long famed in Highland tradition, and bring multitudes from the far off hills to partake of their healing influence; and if the water, unadulterated by any artificial admixture, produced all the joviality that may be witnessed among the groups that sometimes congregate round the brinks of the wells in a sunny evening, it would probably acquire a still more extensive reputation.

From Ballater there are many pleasing detours. The first task of the visiter is invariably to climb Craigendarroch (the rock of oaks), a steep round knob, about the height of Arthur Seat, *i. e.* 800 feet, and rising right up from the village. Its celebrity consists in a rather uncommon qualification to be applied to a hill—its smallness. It is, in fact, the lowest hill in the vicinity that one can get satisfactorily to the top of; and it is many a one's sole premises for the satisfactory conclusion of being "able to say" he has climbed a Highland hill. It is, in this respect, a valuable appendage to Ballater; but it is not without its own merits: the view is magnificent, and few so wide and varied can be purchased with so small an expenditure of climbing. Immediately at its foot is Ballater Cottage, belonging to Mr. Farquharson. To the north, Craigendarroch is separated from a loftier ridge of rock by a precipitous chasm called " The Pass of Ballater." Another rocky hill, about four miles from the village, is frequently scaled, not so much for its own intrinsic merit, perhaps, as because Byron said of it,

> " When I see some dark hill point its crest to the sky,
> I think of the rocks that o'ershadow Culbleen."

From like associations, the farm-house of Ballatrich on the south side

rious that some of the steeples of Aberdeen are timber as well as the Ballater steeple—from which they differ in no respect except that they are covered with lead, and have clocks, which it must be confessed Ballater steeple has not. Nevertheless, for all that, it is as excellent a steeple as any body need wish to look at, and if not covered with lead, is so curiously painted, that it looks just as well as if it were real stone. Indeed, many of those who now scoff at it, at first mistook it for stone. As for other things with which Aberdeen people taunt the Ballaterians—saying that they have no fine streets, or noble buildings, or stately bridges, such as Aberdeen has, we can show hills and mountains, and woods and valleys, and rocks and lochs, with which Aberdeen has nothing to compare, and which every one will allow are much better worth looking at than any streets, bridges, or buildings any where in the whole world, not to speak of Aberdeen. So much for the comparison which has been made between Ballater and Aberdeen."

natural wall of the Buller, which is at least two hundred feet high. Rounding the promontory of Buchanness,—the

Brechin. One more object of interest to be mentioned before we leave Ballater is the Burn of the Vat, so termed from its perforating diagonally a huge natural well of perpendicular rock. The visiter creeps through the channel of the burn by a narrow stony orifice, and looks up astonished through this Barclay-and-Perkins looking freak of nature to the clear heavens, with nothing to interrupt the circular smoothness of the rocks but some birch trees in invisible fissures, that hang from the height like little tendrils.

There are two roads from Ballater up the Dee, one on the north, the other on the south bank—the former is generally preferred. It will be remarked, that the mile-stones on it, (where any happen to remain,) calculated direct from Aberdeen by the old road through the pass, make no allowance for a divergence of a mile and a half at Ballater. Sweeping round Craigendarroch, the water of Gairn is crossed at a point about equidistant from Aberdeen with Ballater. About a mile farther on, on the north side, is Craig Youzie (the rock of firs,) a round knob, something like Craigendarroch. About the forty-fifth mile is a pristine Highland Clachan, not yet brushed up by tourists, called the Micras. Rather more than a mile farther on is Abergeldie Castle (M. F. Gordon, Esq.,) with an old turreted square tower and some modern additions of various dates,—a formidable place in the reaving days, when it was held that

> " He should take who had the power,
> And he should keep who can."

Hitherto the traveller will have observed the birch trees thickening as he proceeds, and here he will find them at their climax of dense luxuriance and beauty, covering almost every spot, save where the broad river sweeps along the bottom of the glen, or the hills carry their broken rocky heads to the clouds. Abergeldie owes no good turn to Burns, who finding it worthily possessed of the old air of "the Birks of Abergeldie," with the despotism of genius, transferred its leafy honours, without a moment's warning, to his nearer neighbour Aberfeldy. About a mile farther on are two localities respectively bearing the expressive denominations of " The Thief's Pot " and "The Gallow's Hill." These classic spots are held sacred to the memory of that great effort of political subordination and martial affection which prompted the high-souled Highland spouse to say to her rebellious husband, " Get up, John, and be hanged, and dinna anger the laird ;" but, as in the case of other heroic acts, Deeside is not without competitors for this honour.

Between the forty-eighth and forty-ninth mile are the kirk, manse, and school of Crathie, on the north side, and the old mansion of Balmoral, belonging to the Earl of Fife, lately fitted up as a shooting

the principal whale-fishing port in the kingdom. It possesses a highly accessible, safe, and commodious harbour,

down into the Dee. The Castletown is in its pristine state as an old
Highland village, the capital of the Strath. It has few if any new
lodging-houses for health-seeking citizens ; but it has two excellent
inns for the tourist, where he may be positively on occasion saturated
with venison and grouse. In the close vicinity are the remains, little
beyond the foundation, of the old Castle, where the Earl of Mar
raised the standard of rebellion in 1715. However adventurously
disposed, the traveller should take up his central position in Braemar, as, without crossing the great mountain barriers to the basins
of the Tay or the Spey, he will find no other home near the wild
scenery of the higher Grampians. It may be mentioned that it is
by no means necessary that the journey to Braemar from the south
should be made *via* Aberdeen and along Deeside. From Dunkeld
or Blairgowrie it may be easily reached through Spital of Glenshee,
where there is a good inn. The distance from Blairgowrie to Braemar by this route is about thirty-five miles—viz., Brig O'Cally,
(where there is an inn,) six miles ; thence to Spital, fourteen miles ;
thence to Braemar, fifteen miles. By another and wilder road, Braemar may be reached through Blair-Athol, by following the Tilt to its
source, and descending the streams that run to the Dee. The distance is estimated at twenty-eight miles from Blair-Athol.

To begin with the smaller objects of interest near Braemar : About
four miles east, on the declivity of the dusky pine forest of Ballach-
bowie, is seen a white streak, which forms the cataract of the Garra-
walt. It is easily approached by drives constructed along the natural
terraces of the forest banks. There is here a considerable supply of
water rolling over a bank of great height, which, though not perpendicular, gives a thundering and foamy torrent ; but, as a cataract, it is rather deficient in interest, from its not disgorging itself
into one of these black cauldrons, which give a mysterious, frightful,
and characteristic feature to most of the Highland falls. It has a
rustic bridge, and a fog-house to make it " tural lural" as the cockney said when he tried to utter " truly rural" with his mouth full of
strawberries. Between three and four miles west of Braemar, there
are two other waterfalls, one on the south, the other on the north
side of the river. The former is termed Corramulzie,—exactly the
sort of spot where old painters send fawns to sleep in hot days. It
is a deep gash in the rock, narrow and precipitous, but having all its
asperities softened off by the profusion of birches and creeping plants
with which it is matted. The fall (which one often forgets, for it has
so little of the terrible in it, though of considerable height, and very
steep,) slides down pearly white through a winding slit in the rock,
where its gentle surface is in close companionship with the tender

head in the disguise of a sailor, on his fruitless expedition
to Scotland in 1715. Eighteen miles north from Peterhead

ties, as to give a perfectly wintry aspect to the higher shaded glens.
Down the sides of these mountains there are several cataracts of
great height and no small bulk. But the scenery is not without its
softer features. Many of the most rugged are relieved by the gentle
weeping birch. Glen Lui, one of the entrance avenues from Deeside
to this lonely district, presents a wide plain of green turf as bright
and almost as smooth as a shaven lawn, while a pellucid stream rip-
ples through it over yellow sand, or among sedges and waterflowers,
as gentle and modest as if it could not have come roaring down just
ten minutes before from the black precipices of Ben-muich-dhui.
The old weather-beaten pines are a curious feature of some of these
glens. By Deeside, the trees, lofty and grand as many of them are,
have more an air of good keeping about them ; they are more park-
like. In Glen Quoich and Glen Derry, they are scarred by centuries
of contest with the mountain storms. Some are bowed to the earth,
others twisted round and round like the horn of a sea-unicorn, and
others stripped bare still stand erect, like mammoth skeletons set on
end. On the lower declivities of the hills, and on the skirts of the
forest land, may be occasionally seen those noble troops of red-deer,
which, since the days of sheep farming and black cattle, are scarcely
to be found elsewhere in the Highlands, in their ancient glory. By
Deeside you may see a shy stag or so looking down on you from a
bank ; but even there the air is tainted to their nice senses ; it is in
Glen Lui or Glen Derry that they congregate in droves ; and though
they seldom approach very close to the wanderer, he will frequently
see their graceful forms and stately antlers on the edges of the
heights between him and the setting or rising sun.

To see all the characteristic portions of this wild district, the ad-
venturer should make two or three detours from Braemar, unless he
can manage to sleep on the heather, and so take the stages successively. One special object of attention should be Loch A'an. The
best means of reaching it is by proceeding up the Glen Lui already
mentioned, and at the point where the glen diverges into two others,
following that to the right, Glen Derry. When the head of this glen
is reached, the mound must be ascended, and then descended on the
other side by the stream, the Alt-dhu-lochan, which runs towards
the Spey, the mound forming the water-shed between the Straths of
Dee and Spey. After descending a considerable way, and winding to
the left among precipitous banks, Loch A'an is reached, a sheet of
water about two miles long, bedded in the precipices of Ben-muich-
dhui and Ben a'an, which rise in varied and grotesque forms to the
height of from 1000 to 1500 feet. Loch A'an may be reached by following the Quoich instead of the Lui, and crossing the water-shed,

the construction here, during last war, of a large harbour for the reception of ships of war. The old castle of Fraserburgh, which is now converted into a lighthouse, stands on Kinnaird-head, about a mile north of the town, and is a picturesque object seen from the sea. Twenty-one miles from Fraserburgh is the royal burgh of BANFF, the capital of the county which bears its name. It is an old-fashioned, but clean and neat town, containing about 3000 inhabitants. At the distance of a mile, on the opposite bank of the Deveron, is the modern village and seaport of Macduff. In the immediate neighbourhood is Duff House, the magnificent mansion of the Earl of Fife, surrounded by extensive plantations. The park is fourteen miles in circumference. About a century ago Banff was the scene of the execution of a noted robber, named Macpherson, whose "farewell" has been made the subject of a spirited song by Burns.

About seven miles from Banff is Portsoy, a small irregularly built town, with a thriving port. A few miles farther is the royal burgh of Cullen, where the Queen of Robert Bruce died, and was buried in the eastern aisle in the old church. Behind the town is Cullen House, the splendid mansion of the Earl of Seafield. It contains a valuable collection of paintings. The other towns round the coast are Garmouth, a neat modern town on the left bank of the Spey; Burghead, a thriving seaport with a considerable trade in ship-building and herring fishing; Nairn, a royal burgh, and capital of the county. After leaving Aberdeen, the Orkney steamer does not touch at any intervening place till it reaches Wick, a royal burgh, and the county town of Caithness. It is a thriving town, and is the principal seat of the herring-fishery in the north of Scotland.

After leaving Wick, the steamer proceeds to Kirkwall, the principal town in the ORKNEY ISLANDS. The Orkney and Shetland Islands lie in two groups to the north of Scotland, and form between them a county which returns a member to Parliament. The former, which are the most southerly, are separated from the county of Caithness by the Pentland Firth, which is about six miles broad. Their number is estimated at sixty-seven, of which twenty-seven

is only 500 feet in length, and 170 broad, and rises abruptly from the sea to the height of 160 feet. The communication with the coast of Bressay is maintained by strong ropes stretched across, along which a cradle or wooden chair is run, in which the passenger is seated. It is of a size sufficient for conveying across a man and a sheep at a time. The purpose of this strange contrivance is to give the tenant the benefit of putting a few sheep upon the Holm, the top of which is level, and affords good pasture. The animals are transported in the cradle, one at a time, a shepherd holding them upon his knees in crossing.

" The temptation of getting access to the numberless eggs and young of the sea-fowl which whiten the surface of the Holm, joined to the promised reward of a cow, induced a hardy and adventurous fowler, about two centuries ago, to scale the cliff of the Holm, and establish a connexion by ropes with the neighbouring main island. Having driven two stakes into the rock and fastened his ropes, the desperate man was entreated to avail himself of the communication thus established in returning across the gulf. But this he

ITINERARY.

I. EDINBURGH.—GALASHIELS.—MELROSE.—JEDBURGH.—51 Miles.

ON RIGHT FROM EDIN.	From Jed.	EDINBURGH.	From Edin.	ON LEFT FROM EDIN.
		Leave Edinburgh by Newington.		
Grange House, Sir Thos. Dick Lauder, Bart.	49	Powburn.	2	
	48	Libberton vill. & Kirk.	3	
In the neighbourhood is Roslin Castle and Chapel.	47	Gilmerton.	4	Eldin, —— Clerk, Esq.
	45	Lasswade.	6	Melville Castle, Lord Melville.
Hawthornden, once the seat of Drummond the Poet ; under the house are several curious caves.	43	🏛 cr. South Esk.	8	Newbattle Abbey, Marquis of Lothian.
		Dalhousie.		Powder Mills, the oldest in Scotland.
Dalhousie Castle, Earl of Dalhousie, an ancient seat modernized.	42	Kirkhill vill. & Kirk.	9	
	39¾	Fushie Bridge.	11¼	Ruins of Borthwick Castle, with Borthwick Kirk. The Castle is very entire, and was inhabited for a short time in 1567 by Queen Mary and Bothwell.
Arniston, —— Dundas, Esq.	38	Middleton.	13	
Heriot House.	31	Crookston.		
Heriot Kirk and Manse.		🏛 cr. Heriot Water.		
Bowland, —— Walker, Esq.	27	🏛 cr. Crookston Wat.		
		Gala bank Inn.	24	
		Torsonce Inn.	25	Crookston House, —— Borthwick, Esq.
Torwoodlee and Fernielie, —— Pringle, Esq.	25½	Stow vill.	25½	Pirn, —— Tait, Esq.
Galashiels is separated from this line of road by the Gala, which joins the Tweed about a mile below.	20½	Buckholm Farm. Laudhopeburn House.	30½	
Gala House, —— Scott, Esq.		Langhaugh.		Langlee House, —— Bruce, Esq.
Across the river may be seen Abbotsford, the seat of Sir Walter Scott.		🏛 cr. Allan Water.		Pavillion, L. Somerville. The vale of the Allan is supposed to be the " Glendearg" of the Monastery.
Melrose Abbey, the finest specimen of Gothic architecture in Scotland.	15	🏛 cr. Tweed. Darnick vill.		
In St. Boswell's Village a great annual fair is held on the 18th of July for horses, cattle, sheep, &c.	13 10	MELROSE. Eildon vill.	36	Near Melrose are the Eildon Hills, on which are the remains of Roman Camps.
Ancrum House, Sir Wm. Scott, Bart.	3	Newton, Dryburgh. St. Boswell's.	38 41	Dryburgh Abbey is beautifully situated on the left bank of the Tweed. Sir Walter Scott was interred here. Farther down the Tweed is Mertoun, the seat of Lord Polwarth.
Near Ancrum the Battle of Lilliards Edge was fought in 1545, where a body of English troops, under Lord Evers and Sir Brian Latoun, were completely defeated by the Earl of Angus.	2	Ancrum, where the Ale joins the Teviot. Teviot Bridge. 🏛 cr. Teviot. Bonjedward. 🏛 cr. Jed Water. JEDBURGH.	48 49 51	Near Ancrum the Roman road from York to the Firth of Forth passes.

Jedburgh is situated on the west bank of the Jed, in the midst of a country beautifully wooded. It is a royal burgh of very ancient erection, and was one of the chief Border towns, and a place of considerable importance before the Union. After that period its trade was, in a great measure, destroyed ; it has now, however, greatly revived. The remains of the Abbey form the principal object of curiosity in Jedburgh. It was founded either in 1118 or 1147, and, after various damages in the course of the Border wars, was burnt by the Earl of Hertford in 1545. It is a magnificent ruin, and is considered the most perfect and beautiful specimen of the Saxon and early Gothic in Scotland. Part of the west end is fitted up as a parish church. The Castle of Jedburgh, situated on an eminence at the town head, was a fortress of very great strength. The ground is now occupied by a Jail. The environs of Jedburgh abound in rich woodland scenes. Some remains of the famous ancient forest are to be seen in the neighbourhood of the half ruined castle of Ferniehirst, belonging to the Marquis of Lothian, and the original seat of his ancestors, the Kers. Jedburgh contains above 4000 inhabitants, and joins with Haddington, North Berwick, Dunbar, and Lauder, in electing a member of Parliament.

III. EDINBURGH.—SELKIRK.—HAWICK.—LONGTOWN.—85¾ Miles.

ON RIGHT FROM EDIN.	From Longtown	For the space between Edinburgh and Galashiels, 30½ miles, see No. 1.	From Edin.	ON LEFT FROM EDIN.
		A new road from Galashiels to Selkirk was formed in 1829, now crossing the Tweed and Ettrick by two handsome bridges. It leaves the old road at Crosslee toll-bar, three miles from Galashiels.		
A little above Yair is Ashiestiel, formerly the residence of Sir W. Scott.	53	Whitebank.	29	
		cr. Gala Water.		
Near Selkirk is Bowhill, a seat of the Duke of Buccleuch.	50	cr. Tweed at Yair Bridge.	32	
	49	Sunderland.	33	Sunderland Hall, Plomer.
Philiphaugh, a plain to the north of the junction of the Ettrick and Yarrow, was the scene of the famous battle between the army of the Marquis of Montrose, and a body of horse commanded by General Leslie, in which the former was completely defeated.	46	cr. Ettrick Wat. and enter SELKIRK.	39¼	Selkirk is a royal burgh, containing a population of 1800. A band of Selkirk burgesses behaved with great gallantry at Flodden. A standard was taken by them, which is still preserved by the corporation. A great business in shoemaking was formerly carried on. The electors of Selkirk vote with those of the county.
		Immediately beyond Selkirk, pass the Haining, —— Pringle, Esq.		
	41	cr. Ale Water.	44¼	
Wool, Scott, Esq.	40½	Ashkirk.	44¾	Sinton, Scott, Esq.
Thirlestane, Lord Napier.				
Wilton House, across the Teviot.	34½	Wilton Kirk.	50¼	
Near Hawick, on the banks of the Teviot, stands Branxholm Castle, belonging to the Duke of Buccleuch, and the chief scene of the Lay of the Last Minstrel.	34	cr. the Teviot, and enter HAWICK.	50¾	Population, 4970; a remarkably active manufacturing town, chiefly producing hosiery. Votes with the county.
		Junction of Borthwick and Teviot.		
	32	cr. the Teviot.	52¾	Goldiland's Tower, celebrated in Border ballads.
Here Johnny Armstrong and his men were hanged by the summary justice of James V.	26	Carlinrig Ch. in ruins.	58¾	On the heights where the counties of Roxburgh and Dumfries meet.
	22	Mosspaul Inn.	63½	
Mickledale, Beatty, Esq.	16	Ewes Kirk.	69½	
Langholm Lodge, a minor seat of the Duke of Buccleuch.		cr. Ewes Bridge.		
	11¼	Langholm vill.	73¾	Broomholm, —— Maxwell, Esq.
	9½	cr. Esk River.	75½	The banks of the Esk are here romantically beautiful.
Near Hollows is Gilnockie Tower, the ruined stronghold of Johnny Armstrong.	8	Hollows vill.	77	
		cr. Canobie Wat.	78	
	6	Canobie vill.	79	
		Scots Dyke toll-bar,	81½	
	3½	Where English ground commences.		Across the Esk is Netherby, the beautiful seat of Sir James Graham.
	2¼	Kirk Andrews.	82½	
		cr. the Esk, and enter LONGTOWN.	85¾	

NORTH BRITISH RAILWAY.—*Continued.*

ON RIGHT FROM EDIN.	From Berwick.	DUNBAR TO BERWICK.	From Edinr.	ON LEFT FROM EDIN.
Dunbar station. Famous for its historical associations.	29		29	**Dunbar station.** Dunbar Castle, where Black Agnes, (Countess of March,) signalized herself. (See page 152.)
Chesterhall, (J. Henderson, Esq.)				Broxmouth Park, a seat of the Duke of Roxburgh. Barryhill, (Capt. Sandilands.) East Barns village.
Ruins of Innerwick Castle. On the other side of the Glen is Thornton Tower, the former the fortalice of a Hamilton, and the latter of a Hume.				Skateraw. Thornton Loch.
Dunglass House, (Sir John Hall,) embosomed amid beautiful plantations. **Cockburnspath sta.**	21		37	Bitsdean. **Cockburnspath sta.**
Ancient tower of Cockburnspath, the property of Sir John Hall of Dunglass. Tunnel.				Peas Bridge, 123 feet high, and 300 feet long. In former times was an important pass. Oliver Cromwell described it as a place "where one man to hinder another is better than twelve to make way."
Grant's House sta. Road from Dunse.	16¼		41¼	**Grant's House sta.** Renton Inn. South Renton. Greenwood. Houndwood. Houndwood House, (Mrs. Coulson.)
Reston station. From which there are coaches to Dunse.	11¼		46¼	**Reston station.** Coldingham, near the sea, with the ruins of a priory celebrated in Border history. Near Coldingham is St. Abb's Head and Fast Castle, the wolf's crag of "the Bride of Lammermoor," (see page 156.)
Ayton station.	7¼		50¾	**Ayton station.** Ayton village on the banks of the Eye, and Ayton House, (Mitchell Innes, Esq.) Burnmouth, a romantic little fishing village, formerly a frequented haunt of the smuggler.
Ruins of Lamberton Kirk, where Margaret, daughter of Henry VII., was married by proxy to James IV., a marriage which ultimately led to the union of the crowns. Berwick, situated on a gentle declivity, is a well built town, with spacious streets, and is surrounded by walls, which only of late ceased to be regularly fortified. **Berwick station.**			58	Beautiful view of the sea. Berwick Castle, so celebrated in early history, is now a shapeless ruin. **Berwick station.**

VI. EDINBURGH.—LINLITHGOW.—FALKIRK.—STIRLING.—35¼ MILES.

ON RIGHT FROM EDIN.	From Stirling.	EDINBURGH.	From Edin.	ON LEFT FROM EDIN.
		Leave Edinr. by west end of Prince's Street.		
Corstorphine Hill, richly wooded and studded with gentlemen's seats and villas.	33¾	Coltbridge.	1	
	33¼	cr. Water of Leith.	2	
	31¼	Corstorphine vill.	4	On the right bank of the Almond, before crossing the bridge, is a rude monument, called the Cat-stane, commemorative of a battle fought in 995.
	27¾	cr. Almond Water, and enter Linlithgowshire.	7½	
	26¼	Kirkliston vill.	9	Ruins of Niddry Castle, where Queen Mary first slept after her escape from Lochleven.
At Winchburgh, Edward II. first halted after his defeat at Bannockburn.	23¾	Winchburgh vill.	11½	
		cr. Union Canal.		
	22¼	Three-Mile-Town.	13	
Champfleurie, Johnston of Straiton.		cr. Haugh-burn.		Linlithgow Bridge was the scene of a battle fought between the Earls of Arran and Lennox in the minority of James V.
Linlithgow, a town of great antiquity. In its streets the Regent Moray was shot. The palace is the chief object of interest. In it Queen Mary was born. The church is a fine specimen of Gothic architecture.	18¼	LINLITHGOW.	16¾	
	17¼	cr. Avon by Linlithgow Bridge and enter Stirlingshire.	18	Callander House, Forbes, Esq., formerly the seat of the Earl of Kilmarnock.
	14	Polmont vill.	21¼	Falkirk, an ancient town, celebrated for a defeat sustained in its neighbourhood by Wallace, in a battle with Edward I. Also the scene of an engagement between the rebel and the royal armies in 1746, when the latter was defeated. The town has now acquired a more peaceful celebrity, by its trysts or cattle markets. At a short distance from the village of Bannockburn, is the field of Bannockburn, where Robert Bruce, with 30,000 men, defeated Edward II. with 100,000. At Milton, in the same neighbourhood, is the scene of James Third's assassination after his defeat at Sauchie.
		cr. Castle Water.		
	13¼	Lauriston.	21¾	
		cr. Burn Water.		
	10¾	FALKIRK.	24	
	10¼	cr. under Canal.	25	
A mile from Camelon the Carron Iron Works are easily distinguishable by the smoke and flames.	9¼	Camelon vill.	26	
		cr. Carron Water.		
	8¼	Larbert.	27	
At Torwood stood the tree in which Wallace used to conceal himself when hard pressed by his enemies. Here Mr. Cargill, in 1680, excommunicated King Charles II. the Duke of York, and the Ministry.	6¼	Torwood.	29	
	1¾	Bannockburn vill.	33½	
		cr. Bannockburn.		
	1	St. Ninian's vill.	34¼	
		STIRLING.	35¼	

The central and original part of Stirling bears an appearance rather antique than elegant, but there are several good streets, and a great number of neat villas in the outskirts. The church is a handsome old Gothic fabric, and includes two places of worship called the East and West Churches. The former was erected by Cardinal Beaton, the latter by James IV. in 1494. The celebrated Ebenezer Erskine, founder of the Secession Church, was for some time minister of the West Church.

The most conspicuous object in Stirling is the Castle. It was a favourite residence of the Scottish monarchs, and a stronghold of great importance. Many events of historical interest are associated with this fortress. Here James II. murdered William Earl of Douglas for refusing to withdraw himself from a rebellious association with other Scottish nobles; in revenge for which the friends of Douglas burnt the town. Here also James IV. was born, and James V. crowned. The prospect of the surrounding country from the castle is magnificent, combining every element of beauty and of grandeur. A visit to Demyat, one of the Ochils, will amply repay the labour of the tourist, as this hill commands one of the noblest views any where to be met with.

VIII. EDINBURGH.—MID CALDER.—STRATHAVEN.—GALSTON.— KILMARNOCK.—AYR.—72 Miles.

ON RIGHT FROM EDIN.	From Ayr.	EDINBURGH. Leave the city by Princes St.	From Edin.	ON LEFT FROM EDIN.
Near Merchiston Ho., Walker, Esq.	69½	Gorgie Mills. cr. Wat. of Leith.	½	Dalry House, Walker, Esq.
Saughton Hall, Baird, Bart.	66	Loanend. Long Hermandston vill.	6	
Saughton, Watson, Esq.	64			Riccarton, Sir James Gibson-Craig, Bart.
	63½	Addiston. } Earl of Dalmahoy. } Morton. cr. Gogar Burn.	7½	
Hatton, Captain Davidson ; formerly a residence of the Lauderdale family.	63 61¾	Burn Wynd Inn. Wester Cocksiedean. East Calder.	9 10¼	
The Church of Mid Calder is a fine specimen of an old parochial place of worship in the Gothic style. The father of Archbishop Spottiswoode officiated here, being Minister of Calder.	60	MID CALDER. From Mid Calder proceeds also the southern line of road to Glasgow. See No. XIV. cr. Almond Wat.	12	Close to Mid Calder is Calder House, the seat of Lord Torphichen, where John Knox preached, and where the only authentic portrait of him exists. The scenery around Mid Calder is of a very romantic description.
	55½	West Calder vill. Here commences an extensive moor, unenlivened by any object of interest. At length, after passing near the extensive iron work of Shotts, the road begins to descend by the minor vale of Calder into the valley of the Clyde.	16½	
A new road leads from this to Strathaven, crossing the Clyde by the Garion Bridge ; another road, somewhat less direct, leads by Hamilton. The former is used by the stage coaches to Ayr.	44 43 42	Allanton, Lady Seton Stuart. Bonkill. Newmains Inn. On left of Garion Bridge the vill. of Dalserf. Stonehouse vill.	28 29 30	The road now passes over a long tract of moorish land, enlivened only by the towering form of Loudon Hill, where Ayrshire is entered. The more direct road to Ayr from this point, leads by Fail and St. Quivox, saving two miles. Kilmarnock is eminent as a seat of various branches of woollen manufacture. It now rivals Kidderminster in the manufacture of carpets. The cotton manufacture has also been introduced with marked success, and the town now produces shawls, gauzes, and muslins of the finest quality. The external appearance of Kilmarnock is very pleasing.
Wallace's Cairn, marking the scene of a conflict between that hero and a party of English.	32 22 21	STRATHAVEN. Priestland. Darvel vill.	40 50 51	
A mile and a half to the right is Drumclog, the scene of the battle of that name, in May 1679, in which Claverhouse was defeated by the Covenanters. Loudon Castle, the magnificent seat of the Marquis of Hastings.	17 12 11	Newmills vill. GALSTON. KILMARNOCK. cr. Irvine Water, and pass through	55 60 61	
		Riccarton vill.		
	7	Symington Kirk.	65	
	4	Monkton vill.	68	
	2¾	Priestwick vill.	69¼	
		AYR.	72	

X.—EDINBURGH.—QUEENSFERRY.—INVERKEITHING.—KINROSS.—PERTH.—44 MILES.

ON RIGHT FROM EDINB.	From Perth.	EDINBURGH.	From Edinb.	ON LEFT FROM EDINB.
		Leave Edinburgh by Queensferry road.		The old road passes between John Watson's Hospital, and the Orphan Hospital; both buildings of great elegance.
St Bernard's Well. Dean House, Sir J. Nisbet. Craigleith Park, Bonar, Esq. Craigleith Quarry.		cr. Water of Leith by Dean Bridge, a superb edifice of four arches, each 90 feet in span.		Ravelston, Lady Murray Keith. Craigcrook, Lord Jeffrey.
Barnton, W. R. Ramsay, Esq.	40	Barnton.	4	Craigiehall, Hope Vere, Esq.
Village of Cramond on the shore to the right.	39	cr. Almond by Cramond Bridge.	5	Dalmeny Kirk.
Dalmeny Park, Earl of Rosebery.		Hawes Inn.		
A little to the south are the ruins of Dundas Castle, a building of great antiquity, which has been in the Dundas family upwards of 700 years.	35	QUEENSFERRY. Cross Ferry.	9	Queensferry was erected into a royal burgh by Malcolm Canmore, and derived its name
	33¼	North Queensferry Inn.	10¼	from Margaret his Queen, sister of Edgar Atheling. Here are the ruins of a monastery of Carmelite Friars, erected in 1330.
Donibris House, Earl of Moray. Donnibrissel House was the scene, in 1592, of the murder of the Earl of Moray by the Marquis of Huntly. This melancholy event is commemorated in the ballad of "The bonnie Erle of Moray."	31½	INVERKEITHING. Crossgates.	12½	A very ancient royal burgh, erected, it is said, by William the Lion. The bay is large and safe. Great quantities of coal and salt are annually exported here. Population, 3189.
	27		17	
Fordel, Colonel Mercer.	25	Cowden Beath Inn.	19	
Lochgelly, Earl of Minto.		cr. Orr.		Kirk of Beath.
Lochore, Sir Walter Scott.		cr. Kelty Water.		Maryburgh, the birth-place of the two brothers Adam, the distinguished architects.
		Benarty Hill.		Blair-Adam, Sir C. Adam.
	19	Gairney Bridge hamlet.	25	
	17	KINROSS. Population, 2017.	27	
Burleigh Castle.	15	Milnathort.	29	
Kinross is situated on the beautiful banks of Lochleven. Lochleven Castle, remarkable for its great antiquity, and as being the place where Queen Mary was imprisoned. The trout produced in Lochleven are of acknowledged excellence.	11½	Damhead Inn.	32½	The road now enters Glenfarg, a beautiful little valley, enclosed by the Ochils. To the right Abernethy, the capital of the Pictish kingdom.
	4	Bridge of Earn. Moncrieffe Hill, On whose shoulder the traveller first comes in sight of Perth.	40	In the neighbourhood of Bridge of Earn is Pitcaithly Well, celebrated for its medicinal waters.
		PERTH.	44	

Perth is one of the handsomest and most ancient towns in Scotland. It is beautifully situated on the west bank of the Tay, having the spacious plains of the North and South Inches extending on each side. On account of its importance, and its vicinity to the royal Palace of Scone, it was long considered the capital of Scotland, before Edinburgh acquired that distinction. Here, too, the Parliaments and national assemblies were held, and many of the nobility took up their residence. A splendid bridge of ten arches, and 900 feet in length, leads across the Tay to the north. Perth contains several beautiful streets and terraces, and a number of splendid public buildings. It is peculiarly rich in objects of historic and picturesque interest. Of Gowrie House, the scene of a well known mysterious incident in Scottish history, most unfortunately not a vestige remains. In Blackfriars Monastery, which once stood at the north side of the town, James I. was assassinated by a band of conspirators. The principal and oldest public building is St John's Church, in which the demolitions of the Reformation commenced, in consequence of a sermon preached by John Knox.

XII. PERTH.—DUNKELD.—BLAIR ATHOLL.—INVERNESS.—112 Miles.

ON RIGHT FROM PERTH.	From Inverness	PERTH. Leave Perth by the North Inch.	From Perth.	ON LEFT FROM PERTH.
Balhousie.	109½	Palace of Scone.	2½	Tulloch Printfield.
Luncarty Bleachfield, near which is the scene of the battle of Luncarty, between the Scots and the Danes.	109	cr. Almond Wat.	3	Earl of Mansfield. Feu House,—Nicol, Esq. Near Birnam Hill and Birnam Road.
	106	cr. Shochie Wat.		The walks through the policies of Dunkeld are upwards of 50 miles.
Near Stanley Mills, celebrated for their enormous wheels, and the Linn of Campsie.	103	New Inn.	6	
	100	Auchtergaven vill.	9	
		Murthly Castle.	12	
Another road parts off directly east to Blairgowrie. The present route passes for some miles along the east bank of the Tay.		—— Stewart, Bart.)		From this point a road proceeds by the west side of the river to Logierait, and thence by Aberfeldy to Kenmore.
	98	Little Dunkeld. cr. the river Tay. DUNKELD. Dunkeld Ho., Duke of Atholl.	14	Eight miles above Dunkeld the united waters of the Tummel and Garry fall into the Tay.
Dunkeld is a place of great antiquity, and was at one time the capital of ancient Caledonia. One of the principal objects of curiosity here, is the ruined Cathedral. It must have been a fine pile of building. The architecture is partly Gothic, partly Saxon.	93	Dowally Kirk. Near Dalguise Ho., Stewart, Esq.	19	The site of Faskally is of a peculiarly romantic character. It stands at the junction of three deep and confined valleys, and is encircled on all sides by diverging mountains.
	92	Kinnaird House. Logierait, where Prince Charles kept the prisoners whom he had taken at Prestonpans.	20 22½	
The road now enters the pass of Killiecrankie, a narrow glen, at the bottom of which runs the Tummel water.	90¾	Moulinearn Inn. Faskally, Butter, Esq.	28	In front, on the ascent to Urrard House, is the scene of the battle of Killiecrankie, fought July 26, 1689, between the Highlanders under Dundee, and the forces of King William under Mackay, the former being killed, and the latter defeated.
	84	Lude, M'Inroy, Esq.	30½	
	81½	cr. the Tilt Wat.	33	
The vale of the Tilt is celebrated for its fine scenery, and for geological wonders. At the Bridge of Tilt is an excellent inn.	77	BLAIR ATHOLL.	35	
The noble old Castle of Blair, (Duke of Atholl,) is in the neighbourhood.		The road now passes through a wild Alpine territory, almost to Inverness.		
About two miles from Blair Atholl, the road crosses the Bruar, where that river makes a series of cascades, which enjoy extensive celebrity.	69½	Dalnacardoch Inn. Dalnaspidal. cr. Edendon Wat. Enter Inverness-shire.	42½	From Dalwhinnie the mountain of Benalder may be seen, situated on the north side of Loch Ericht.
	67½	Drumochter Forest.	44½	
Near Etrish there is a beautiful waterfall.	56½	Dalwhinnie Inn. In front is Ben Chruben.	55½	Here a road parts off by Laggan and Garvamore, and over the difficult hill of Corriarrack to Fort Augustus.
Across the Spey, ruins of Ruthven Castle and Barracks, destroyed by the Highlanders in 1746.	50	Etrish. cr. Truim Wat.	62	From Pitmain may be seen the rocky barrier of Craig Dhu towards the west, the gathering-place of the M'Phersons.
Across Spey, Invereshie, Sir Geo. M'Pherson Grant of Ballindalloch.	46	Bridge of Spey. Newton of Benchar.	66 66½	
Rothiemurchus, Sir J. P. Grant.	43½	Pitmain.	68½	Belville, the seat of M'Pherson, the translator of Ossian, now possessed by Miss M'Pherson.
	42	Kingussie Kirk & vill.	70	
Opposite Aviemore is Cairngorm Hill.	37	Kincraig, Built on the site of an ancient monastery.	75	
Near Moy Hall, M'Intosh of M'Intosh. Here Prince Charles Stuart was nearly taken by surprise in February 1746.	20½	Aviemore Inn. cr. the Dolnain.	91½	Inverness is a royal burgh of the first reformed class, joining with Forres, Fortrose, and Nairn in electing a Member of Parliament. Population 14,324. Inverness is considered the capital of the Highlands, being the only town of importance beyond Aberdeen.
	13	Freeburn Inn.	99	
	6	Daviot Kirk.	106	
		INVERNESS.	112	

XIV.—DUNDEE, NEWTYLE, CUPAR-ANGUS RAILWAY, 15 MILES,
With Branch to Glammis.

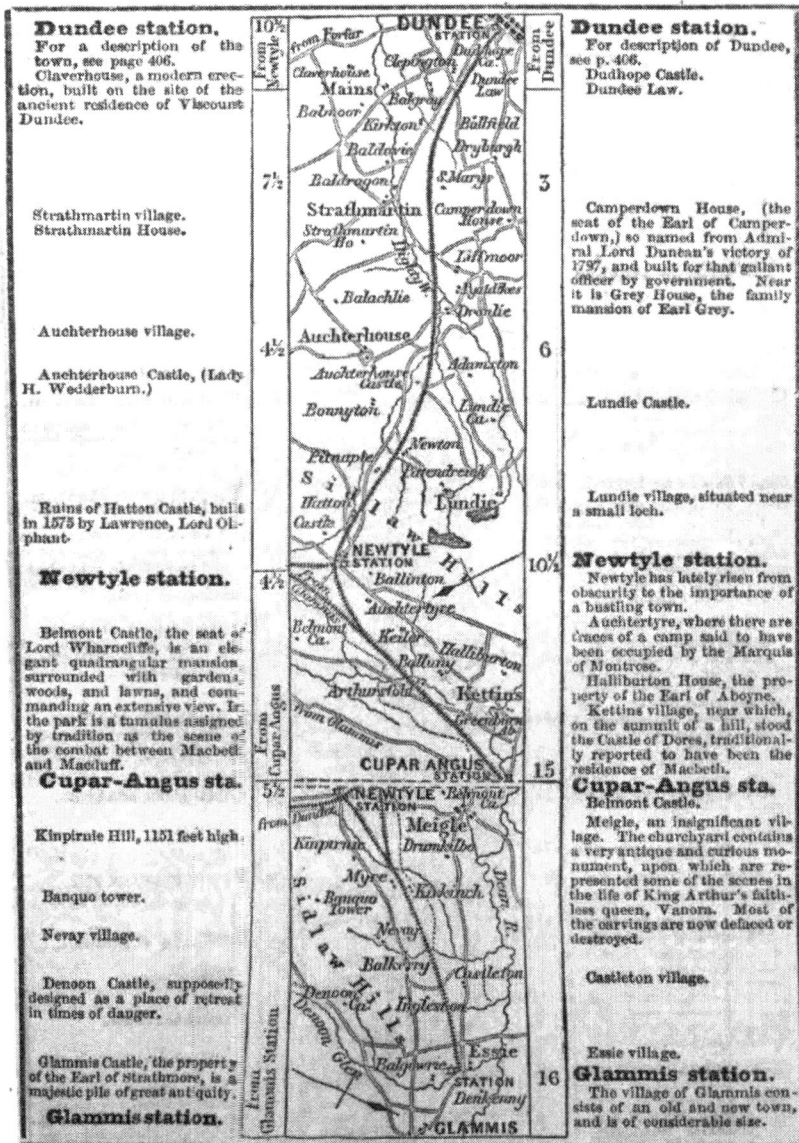

Dundee station.
For a description of the town, see page 406.
Claverhouse, a modern erection, built on the site of the ancient residence of Viscount Dundee.

Strathmartin village.
Strathmartin House.

Auchterhouse village.

Auchterhouse Castle, (Lady H. Wedderburn.)

Ruins of Hatton Castle, built in 1575 by Lawrence, Lord Oliphant.

Newtyle station.

Belmont Castle, the seat of Lord Wharncliffe, is an elegant quadrangular mansion surrounded with gardens, woods, and lawns, and commanding an extensive view. In the park is a tumulus assigned by tradition as the scene of the combat between Macbeth and Macduff.

Cupar-Angus sta.

Kinpruie Hill, 1151 feet high.

Banquo tower.

Nevay village.

Denoon Castle, supposedly designed as a place of retreat in times of danger.

Glammis Castle, the property of the Earl of Strathmore, is a majestic pile of great antiquity.

Glammis station.

Dundee station.
For description of Dundee, see p. 406.
Dudhope Castle.
Dundee Law.

Camperdown House, (the seat of the Earl of Camperdown,) so named from Admiral Lord Duncan's victory of 1797, and built for that gallant officer by government. Near it is Grey House, the family mansion of Earl Grey.

Lundie Castle.

Lundie village, situated near a small loch.

Newtyle station.
Newtyle has lately risen from obscurity to the importance of a bustling town.
Auchtertyre, where there are traces of a camp said to have been occupied by the Marquis of Montrose.
Halliburton House, the property of the Earl of Aboyne.
Kettins village, near which, on the summit of a hill, stood the Castle of Dores, traditionally reported to have been the residence of Macbeth.

Cupar-Angus sta.
Belmont Castle.
Meigle, an insignificant village. The churchyard contains a very antique and curious monument, upon which are represented some of the scenes in the life of King Arthur's faithless queen, Vanora. Most of the carvings are now defaced or destroyed.

Castleton village.

Essie village.
Glammis station.
The village of Glammis consists of an old and new town, and is of considerable size.

XVI. EDINBURGH.—MID CALDER.—KIRK OF SHOTTS.—HOLYTOWN—GLASGOW.—44 MILES.

ON RIGHT FROM EDIN.	From Glasgow.	EDINBURGH.	From Edin.	ON LEFT FROM EDIN.
		For a description of the road from Edinburgh to Mid Calder, see No. VII.		
	32	Howden.	12	
	29	Kirk Livingston.	15	
		Cowsland.		
	26¾	Seafield.	17¼	
	25¼	Blackburn.	18¾	
	25	Lathbrae.	19	
	24	Swan Inn.	20	
Polkemmet House, Baillie, Bart.; remarkable for the quantities of game in the neighbourhood.	23	Whitburn vill.	21	
	22	Half-way-house.	22	
	19	Badweather.	25	
	17	Kirk of Shotts Inn.	27	Here the traveller is on the highest ground between the Forth and Clyde in this direction.
	13¾	Newhouse Inn.	30¼	
Lachup House, Robertson, Esq. Woodhall, Campbell of Shawfield.	11	HOLYTOWN, Where a road turns off to Hamilton.	33	
		cr. Shirle Water.		
Tollcross Ho., Dunlop, Esq.	9	Bellshill vill.	35	
	2¾	cr. Calder Wat.	41¼	One mile to the left, are the Clyde Iron Works, where 12,500 bars of iron were produced in 1835, a greater amount than the aggregate production of any other work in Scotland.
Jeanfield, Finlayson, Esq.		Tollcross vill.		
Newlands and Borrowfield Houses, Hozier, Esq.	1½	Parkhead.	42½	
		Camlachie.		
		GLASGOW.	44	

XVII. EDINBURGH.—LINLITHGOW.—FALKIRK.—CUMBERNAULD.—GLASGOW.—46¾ MILES.

ON RIGHT FROM EDIN.	From Glasgow.	EDINBURGH.	From Edin.	ON LEFT FROM EDIN.
Larbert Ho., Stirling, Bart.		For a description of the road between Edinburgh and Falkirk, see No. V.		
Dunipace, Spottiswoode, Esq.		Camelon.	26	
Underwood House.		Cumbernauld Inn.		
Knowhead Ho., Patrick, Esq.		cr. Bonny Wat.		Merchiston Hall.
Castle Cary House. Cumbernauld House, Admiral Fleming.	14¼	CUMBERNAULD.	32½	Woodside Ho., Russell, Esq.
		cr. Logie Water.		Bankhead Ho., Cuthill, Esq.
Dunbeath Tower in ruins, once the property of the Kilmarnock family.	9¾	Bedlay Inn.	37	Mayothill Ho., Graham, Esq.
	8¼	Christon vill.	38½	Frankfield Loch.
Frankfield Ho., Millar, Esq.	4¼	Frankfield House.	42½	Kennyhill Ho., Stewart, Esq.
Rosemount Ho., Millar, Esq.	2¾	Provan Mill.	44	Whitehill Ho., Graham, Esq.
Garnkirk, Sprott, Esq.		cr. Monkland Canal.		Dunchattan and Cudbear Manufactories.
Riddry Park, Miss Provan.		GLASGOW.	46¾	Broom Park.

XIX. EDINBURGH.—KIRKALDY.—CUPAR.—DUNDEE.—ARBROATH.—STONEHAVEN.—ABERDEEN.—109¼ MILES.

ON RIGHT FROM EDIN.	From Aberdeen.	EDINBURGH. Newhaven to Pettycur by steam-boat.	From Edin.	ON LEFT FROM EDIN.
	100¼	Kinghorn.	9	
At the east end of the town Ravenscraig Castle in ruins, formerly the seat of the family of St. Clair.	98¼	KIRKALDY.	11	An ancient royal burgh. Population of the parish 2579.
	97¼	Pathhead vill.	12	
	95¼	Galatown.	14	
	89¾	Plasterer's Inn.	19½	Raith, Robert Ferguson, Esq.
Near Markinch Kirk, where General Leslie, the leader of the Covenanting army, lies interred.		cr. Leven Wat.		Leslie House, Earl of Rothes.
	87¼	New Inn	22	Balbirnie, Gen. Balfour.
Cults Kirk. Cults Manse, the birth place of Sir David Wilkie, R.A.	85¼	Kettle vill.	24	On left, two miles distant, bye-road to Perth, Falkland, and Falkland Palace.
	84¼	Pitlessie.	25	
		cr. Eden Wat.		Rankeillour, Maitland M'Gill Crichton, Esq.
The Mount, the patrimonial estate of Sir David Lindsay, is about four miles to the west of Cupar, but no old building exists at the place.	79¼	CUPAR.	30	Crawford Priory, Earl of Glasgow.
	76	Dairsie Kirk.	33¼	
	75½	Osnaburgh vill.	33¾	Cupar is a handsome town, of modern and thriving appearance. The Town Hall and County Hall are elegant buildings. An eminence at the east end of the town was the site of a fortress of considerable importance, of which no trace now exists.
	72¼	St. Michael's Inn.	37	
	69¼	Newport, Where embark in a steam-boat, and cross the Tay to	40	
Dundee is the chief seat of the linen manufacture in Britain, and one of the most prosperous towns in the empire. The principal objects are the Town Hall, Exchange Reading Rooms, (open to strangers,) Academy, the Howf or Burying Ground, the Tower of the old Church, and the Law, from which a most extensive view is to be seen.	67¼	DUNDEE.	42	
	65¼	cr. Dighty Wat.	44	
	54¼	Muirdrum vill.	55	Near Cupar, in ruins, Airdit Ho., Stewart, Esq.
		Panbride Kirk.		
		cr. Elliot Wat.		Fintry, Graham, Esq.
	50¼	ARBROATH.	59	The most interesting object in Arbroath is the venerable ruins of the Abbey. It was founded by William the Lion, who is interred here.
	44¼	Chance Inn.	65	
		cr. Lunan at Lunan Kirk.		
		cr. South Esk to		The rock on which the Bell Rock Lighthouse is founded, is about 12 miles from the shore at Arbroath
Ethie, Earl of Northesk.	37½	MONTROSE.	71¾	
The road, for some miles, passes near the sea coast.		cr. North Esk.		
	32¼	St. Cyrus Kirk.	77	Montrose is a remarkably neat, and even handsome town. The river is crossed by a fine suspension bridge.
Kaim of Mathers, Adam.	28¼	Johnshaven.	81	
Ruins of Dunnotar Castle. Dunnotar was built by an ancestor of the Marischal family about the time of the contest between Bruce and Baliol. Before the use of fire arms, it was considered as almost impregnable, and was used as the deposit of the Regalia of Scotland, to preserve them from the English army under Cromwell, in 1651.	24¼	INVERBERVIE.	85	
		cr. Bervie Wat.		Aberdeen is a large and elegant city of great antiquity, possessing many handsome streets and splendid public buildings. The large proportion of eminent Scotsmen who have been produced in this city, is very remarkable, and can only be attributed to the presence of its Universities. In Old Aberdeen are to be seen the remains of the Cathedral. The scenery in the neighbourhood is remarkably interesting.
	15	STONEHAVEN.	94¼	
		cr. Carron and Cowie Waters.		
	11	Muchals House.	98¼	
		cr. Dee, and enter		
		ABERDEEN.	109¼	

INVERNESS to THURSO—*Continued.*

ON RIGHT FROM INVERN.	From Thurso.		From Invern.	ON LEFT FROM INVERN.
The road from Tain to Dornoch is a very singular one. The distance between the two towns, straight across the firth, is only four miles.	125 123	TAIN. On right Meikle Ferry of Dornoch, which, if adopted, cuts off 19 miles of road.	47 49	Tain is an irregularly built town, with several new and handsome houses. It is situated on the margin of the Dornoch Firth. The ancient church of Tain was collegiate, and dedicated to St. Duthus. James IV. performed pilgrimage to the shrine of
The Castle of Lochlin is a remarkable building; it has stood 500 years. Sir George M'Kenzie, (popularly denominated *The Bloody M'Kenzie*,) King's Advocate in the reign of Charles II., was born there. Bonar Bridge is a strong and magnificent structure, composed of iron. It cost £14,000. Near Creich Church is an obelisk, eight feet by four, erected in memory of a Danish chieftain. Here, on the summit of a hill, which juts out into the firth, is a noted vitrified fort, called Dun Creech.	122 115 114½ 112½ 100¾ 97¾ 95	Edderton Kirk. West Fearn. Kincardine Inn. cr. Firth of Dornoch, by Bonar Bridge. Bonar Inn. Clashmore Inn. Dornoch. cr. Loch Fleet, By a stupendous mound, built to dam out the sea—Cost £9000. The Cathedral was fitted up by the late Duchess-Countess of Sutherland, at an expense of £6000, as the parish church.	50 57 58½ 59¾ 71¼ 74¼ 77	this Saint, to whose honour several churches were at different times built in this place. Near Fearn, there are the ruins of an abbey of great antiquity, founded by the first Earl of Ross. Patrick Hamilton, an abbot of this place, was the first who suffered in this country for the Reformed religion. Near the abbey is a high square column, covered with Saxon characters. Skibo Castle, G. Dempster, Esq. Ospisdale, D. Gilchrist, Esq. Dornoch is one of the most miserable of our royal burghs. It is nevertheless, the county town of Sutherland, and formerly was the seat of the bishopric of Caithness.
From Golspie, all the way to Brora, the road is skirted with neat cottages, surrounded with shrubberies and covered with honeysuckle. Brora is one of the new villages built by the Duke of Sutherland. It is situated at the mouth of the river Brora, which descends from a vale of the most romantic and savage character.	86¾ 83 82 80½ 77 71¼	Golspie vill. Brora. Kirk of Clyne. Kinkradwell. Loth Kirk. Helmsdale.	85¼ 89 90 91 95 100¾	Dunrobin Castle, the seat of the Duke of Sutherland, occupies an eminent site upon the shore, a little beyond Golspie, and is surrounded by some fine old wood, besides extensive modern plantations. It is said to have been founded in the 13th century by one of the earliest Earls of Sutherland. About a mile farther on, between the road and the beech, stands one of those unaccountable relics of antiquity, called Picts Houses. Adjoining Helmsdale, are the ruins of a romantic old castle, once the seat of an extensive proprietor of the name of Gordon.

XXI. GLASGOW.—PAISLEY.—GREENOCK.—LARGS.—KILWINNING.—AYR.—72 MILES.

ON RIGHT FROM GLASGOW.	From Ayr.	GLASGOW.	From Glasgow.	ON LEFT FROM GLASGOW.
		Leave Glasgow by the New Bridge, and pass through Tradestown.		
	70		2	Parkhouse, Walkinshaw, Esq.
	69		3	
Paisley, a celebrated seat of manufacturing industry.	64¼	PAISLEY.	7¾	Cardonald, Lord Blantyre.
Placing the factories out of view, the most interesting object of curiosity in Paisley is the Abbey church, which	61	Johnston vill. where cr. Black Cart River.	11	Crookston Castle in ruins. A place deriving interest from its connexion with Queen Mary.
is still a magnificent and impressive object. Attached to its south side there is	58½	Kilbarchan vill.	13½	
a small chapel, where it is said Marjory, daughter of King Robert Bruce, was interred. This chapel possesses a remarkably fine echo.	58	Bridge of Weir; where cr. Gryfe Water.	14	A thriving village, engaged in the cotton manufacture. The course of the Gryfe, to its junction with the Cart, is a tract of beautiful
	53¾	Kilmalcolm vill.	18¾	scenery.
Greenock is a large and populous town, the first seaport in Scotland. The	49¼	Port Glasgow.	22¾	A populous sea-port erected by the merchants
situation of Greenock is remarkably beautiful. The	46½	GREENOCK.	25½	of Glasgow, as an appropriate place for the shipping of goods. On the
principal branches of its commerce have reference to the East and West Indies,	43½	Gourock.	28½	shore, at a little distance to the east, is situated the deserted Castle of Newark,
the United States, and British America. The Custom House is a beautiful building. There is also an elegant Exchange.	40½	Innerkip vill.	31½	formerly a place of great strength.
	38½	cr. Kelly Water.	33½	Near Innerkip, Ardgowan, Shaw Stewart, Bart.
	32¾	cr. Nodle Water.	39¼	and Kelly, Wallace, Esq.
Largs stands on a beautiful plain, surrounded by	32	LARGS.	40	Brisbane Ho., Brisbane, Bart.
mountains on the land side. Near this place, in	29¾	Fairley.	42¼	Kelburn Ho., Earl of Glasgow.
1263, in the reign of Alexander III., was fought the battle of Largs between the Scots and Danes.		cr. Rye Water.		Fairley Castle in ruins.
	26¼	West Kilbride.	46¾	Near ruins of Ardrossan Castle. The Harbour of
A few miles to the north of Ardrossan, stands the	20	Ardrossan.	52	Ardrossan possesses advantages superior to all
ruined Castle of Portincross, rendered memorable	18½	Saltcoats.	53½	the other harbours in the Frith of Clyde.
by the frequency of the visits of the first Stuart	14	KILWINNING.	58	Eglinton Castle, Earl of Eglinton; a splendid
sovereign to it. Its situation on a bare rock projecting into the sea, is		cr. Garnoch Wat.		structure.
singularly wild and picturesque.	11	Irvine.	61	Irvine was the birth-place of John Galt, and James Montgomery, the poet.
Kilwinning is remarkable as the first settlement of Free Masons in Scotland.	3	cr. Irvine Water. Monkton.	69	Burns was, for a short time, engaged in business in Irvine as a flax-dresser.
		AYR.	72	

Ayr is a handsome old-fashioned town, skirted with modern streets of considerable elegance. It dates as a royal burgh from 1202, and was the scene of several remarkable exploits of Sir William Wallace. Many of the localities of Ayr and its vicinity are rendered interesting by their association with the life and poems of Burns. The poet was born in a clay-built cottage, about two miles and a half from the town. At a little distance are the ruins of Alloway Kirk, the Auld Brig of Doon, Burns' Monument, &c.

XXIII. GLASGOW AND GREENOCK RAILWAY.

GLASGOW—PAISLEY—PORT-GLASGOW AND GREENOCK.—22¾ Miles.

* Steamboats in connexion with this Railway ply between Greenock, Dunoon, Rothesay, Helensburgh, Row, Gairlochhead, Largs, Millport, Ardrossan, and Arran.

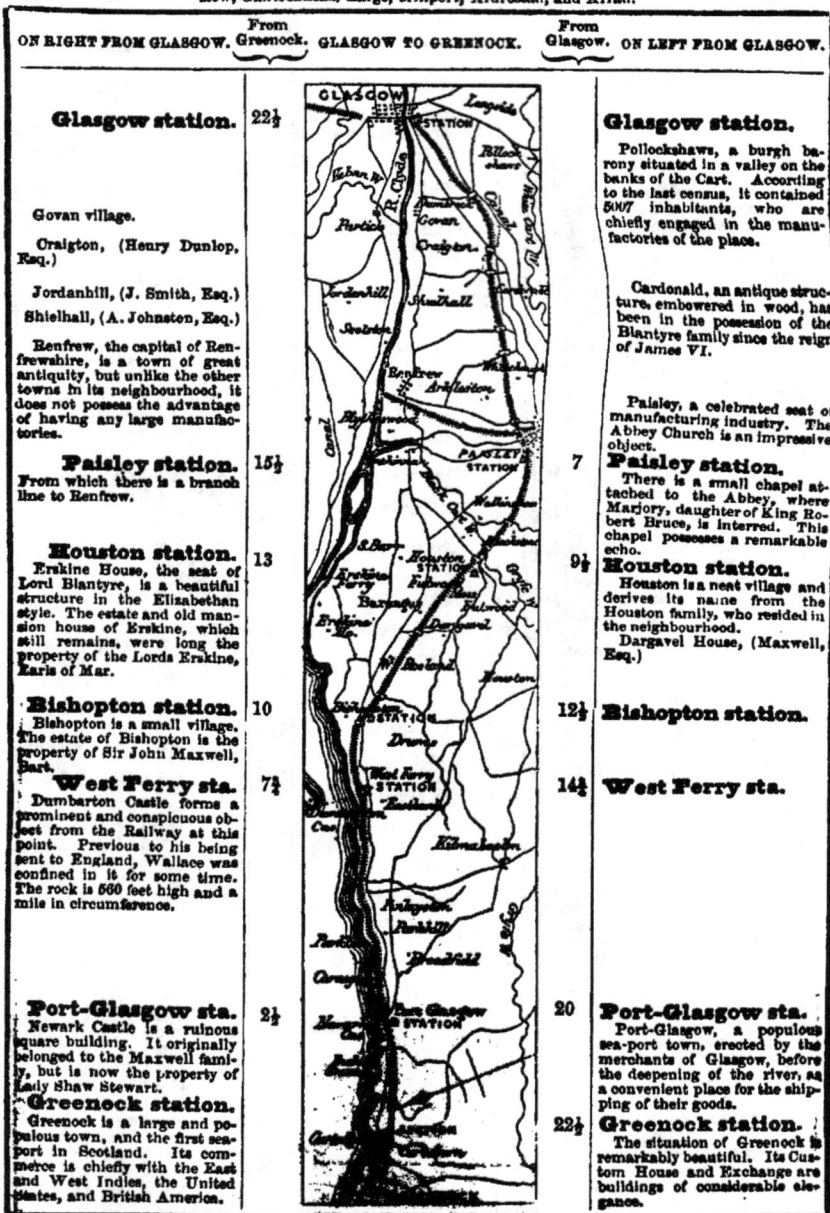

ON RIGHT FROM GLASGOW.	From Greenock.	GLASGOW TO GREENOCK.	From Glasgow.	ON LEFT FROM GLASGOW.

Glasgow station. 22¾

Govan village.

Craigton, (Henry Dunlop, Esq.)

Jordanhill, (J. Smith, Esq.)
Shielhall, (A. Johnston, Esq.)

Renfrew, the capital of Renfrewshire, is a town of great antiquity, but unlike the other towns in its neighbourhood, it does not possess the advantage of having any large manufactories.

Paisley station. 15½
From which there is a branch line to Renfrew.

Houston station. 13
Erskine House, the seat of Lord Blantyre, is a beautiful structure in the Elizabethan style. The estate and old mansion house of Erskine, which still remains, were long the property of the Lords Erskine, Earls of Mar.

Bishopton station. 10
Bishopton is a small village. The estate of Bishopton is the property of Sir John Maxwell, Bart.

West Ferry sta. 7½
Dumbarton Castle forms a prominent and conspicuous object from the Railway at this point. Previous to his being sent to England, Wallace was confined in it for some time. The rock is 560 feet high and a mile in circumference.

Port-Glasgow sta. 2½
Newark Castle is a ruinous square building. It originally belonged to the Maxwell family, but is now the property of Lady Shaw Stewart.

Greenock station.
Greenock is a large and populous town, and the first sea-port in Scotland. Its commerce is chiefly with the East and West Indies, the United States, and British America.

Glasgow station.
Pollockshaws, a burgh barony situated in a valley on the banks of the Cart. According to the last census, it contained 5007 inhabitants, who are chiefly engaged in the manufactories of the place.

Cardonald, an antique structure, embowered in wood, has been in the possession of the Blantyre family since the reign of James VI.

Paisley, a celebrated seat of manufacturing industry. The Abbey Church is an impressive object.

Paisley station. 7
There is a small chapel attached to the Abbey, where Marjory, daughter of King Robert Bruce, is interred. This chapel possesses a remarkable echo.

Houston station. 9½
Houston is a neat village and derives its name from the Houston family, who resided in the neighbourhood.
Dargavel House, (Maxwell, Esq.)

Bishopton station. 12½

West Ferry sta. 14½

Port-Glasgow sta. 20
Port-Glasgow, a populous sea-port town, erected by the merchants of Glasgow, before the deepening of the river, as a convenient place for the shipping of their goods.

Greenock station. 22¾
The situation of Greenock is remarkably beautiful. Its Custom House and Exchange are buildings of considerable elegance.

XXV. GLASGOW.—AYR.—MAYBOLE.—GIRVAN.—PORTPATRICK.—94 Miles.

ON RIGHT FROM GLASGOW.	From Portpat.	GLASGOW. Glasgow to Ayr, see No. XIX.	From Glasgow.	ON LEFT FROM GLASGOW.
The native cottage of Burns, his monument, the old bridge of Doon, and other objects deriving interest from the life and writings of the poet.	60¼ 59	Alloway Kirk. cr. Doon by new Bridge, and skirt along Brown Carrick Hill.	33½ 35	Blairston, Cathcart. Maybole is a burgh of barony, and obtained its privileges in 1516. It carries on a woollen manufacture to a considerable extent. The Mansion House of the Cassilis family is the finest surviving specimen of the twenty-eight winter seats of noble and baronial families formerly existing in Maybole. It is said to have been the residence of the repudiated Countess of Cassilis, whose story was the subject of the well known ballad of Johnny Faa. Burns received part of his education in Kirkoswald. Girvan, a place of considerable antiquity, situated at the mouth of Girvan Water, the banks of which abound in fine scenery, and in fine seats. Carleton Castle, ruins, Cathcart, Bart. Stinchar Castle ruins, an ancient seat of the Kennedys of Bargany. Such is the irregularity of the rivulet which runs through Glenapp, that the road crosses it at least half a dozen of times within the extent of half a dozen miles. Near Stranraer, Castle Kennedy and Culhorn, Earl of Stair. Stranraer is a thriving and handsome seaport town, uniting with Wigton, New Galloway, and Whithorn, in returning a Member to Parliament. In the centre of it stands a tall strong edifice, originally a castle. There are several seats in the neighbourhood adorned with all the charms of nature and of art. Dunskey Castle ruins, finely situated on a very high rock overhanging the sea.
	56	Grange House. Torrence, M'Micken, Esq.	38	
Crossraguel Abbey, founded in 1244; part of the cloisters remain, and the Abbot's house is entire. The last Abbot was famed for his disputation with John Knox. The ruin is preserved with great care.	51¼ 49	MAYBOLE. Population 6287. Ruins of Crossraguel Abbey.	42½ 45	
Some miles to the right of Kirkoswald, is Colzean Castle, the splendid mansion of the Marquis of Ailsa. It is built on the brink of a perpendicular precipice; under it are the celebrated caves of Culzean, penetrating 200 feet into the rock.	47 41	Kirkoswald. Chasel House. cr. Girvan Wat.	47 53	
On the coast, the ruins of Turnberry Castle, a seat of Robert Bruce when Earl of Carrick.	39	Girvan vill. The road now keeps close by the coast for many miles.	55	
The village of Ballantrae is situated close to the mouth of the Stinchar water, and picturesquely overhung by the ruins of an old castle. It was formerly a great haunt of smugglers. It has a good sea and salmon fishery.	36½ 34 26½	Ardmillan. Crawford, Esq. Carleton Bay. Ballantrae vill. cr. Stinchar Wat.	57½ 60 67½	
View of the beautiful Bay of Lochryan, celebrated in the fine old pathetic ballad, entitled "The Lass of Lochryan."	24 16½ 15	Glenapp, A romantic glen. Enter Wigtonshire. Cairn.	70 77½ 79	
Portpatrick is a thriving town of considerable size. The channel between Great Britain and Ireland is here only 21 miles across. Portpatrick possesses an excellent harbour and reflecting lighthouse.	9 6	Stranraer. Population 3320. Lochan's Bridge. PORTPATRICK.	85 88 94	

XXVII. GLASGOW.—DUMBARTON.—TARBET.—TYNDRUM.—FORT WILLIAM.—103 Miles.

ON RIGHT FROM GLASGOW.	From Fort Will.	GLASGOW.	From Glasgow.	ON LEFT FROM GLASGOW.
		Leave Glasgow by Anderston.		
		cr. Kelvin Water.		
Cranston Hill, Houldsworth, and numerous other villas, belonging to the wealthy citizens.	99½	White Inch.	3½	
Jordanhill, Smith, Esq.	93½	Kilpatrick vill.	9½	Dalnottar.
Dumbarton is one of the four fortresses stipulated by the articles of Union to be kept up, and accordingly is still in repair, and occupied by a garrison.	92	Dunglas Castle ruins.	11	Near the termination of the Forth and Clyde Canal.
	88½	DUMBARTON.	14½	
		cr. Leven Water.		Levenside, Ewing.
Cordale Ho., Stirling, Esq. Bonhill, Smollet, Esq. Balloch Castle Stutt. Loch Lomond is on the right for many miles.	86½	Renton vill.	16½	Near Smollet's monument, and Dalquhurn House, where he was born.
	85	Alexandria.	18	Broomley, Miss Alston. Tillichewen Castle.
	84	Lower end of L. Lomond.	19	Woodbank, Miss Scott. Bellretiro, Miss Rowet.
Cameron Ho., Smollet, Esq.	82	Arden, Buchannan.	21	Glen Fruin was the scene of a bloody conflict between the M'Gregors and Colquhoun in 1602.
Rossdow, Colquhoun, Bart.	78	cr. Fruin Water.	25	
Luss is beautifully situated; the waters of the Luss run through it, and fall into Loch Lomond.	76½	Luss vill. and Inn.	26½	For crossing Loch Lomond to Rowardennan, where the ascent to Ben Lomond is usually commenced.
	72½	Inveruglas Ferry.	30½	
	68½	Tarbet Inn.	34½	Three miles above Tarbet is a small wooded island called Inveruglas, and about two miles farther, another called Eilan ; on each of which are the ruins of a stronghold of the family of Macfarlane.
Nearly opposite Inveruglas Island, in a hollow above a small cascade, are the ruins of Inversnaid Fort, an old military station, chiefly designed to keep the Clan Gregor in check.		Keep along the side of Loch Lomond.		
	65	Across the loch is Inversnaid Mill.	38	
	60	Head of Loch Lomond.	43	
	58	Auldtarnan Inn.	45	
About half way between Crianlaroch and Tyndrum, there is a linn in the river called the Pool of St. Fillan's, which is to this day not unfrequently the scene of the observance of a degrading superstitious rite. Here St. Fillan, so noted in the Highlands for works of piety and sacred gifts, is said to have lived.	57	Glenfalloch, Campbell.	46	On the right a road proceeds to Killin.
	52	Proceed up Glenfalloch to Crianlaroch.	51	
		Take to the left up Strathfillan.		Strathfillan was the scene of a battle of Robert Bruce.
	47	Tyndrum Inn.	56	Tyndrum Ho., Marquis of Breadalbane.
	38	Inverouran Inn.	65	Between Inverouran and King's House, the road crosses a lofty hill called the Black Mount. From the top an extensive view is obtained of the Moor of Rannoch, the largest tract of the kind in Scotland.
In the neighbourhood of Ballachulish, is a cavern of so difficult access, that nobody of late has ventured to explore it.	28½	Mountainous scenery to King's House Inn.	74½	
	26	Foot of the steep road to Fort William, called the Devil's Staircase.	77	Glencoe is famous for its singularly wild Alpine scenery, and the historical event connected with it. The massacre of Glencoe in King William's reign, took place at the northwest end of the vale.
		Enter Glencoe.		
	14½	Ballachulish Inn.	88½	Maryburgh contains about 1500 inhabitants, and two respectable inns.
So called from the tradition of Patrick, a Danish Prince, having been drowned here.	13	The Ferry of Calas-ic Phatric.	90	It contains a bomb-proof magazine, and the barrack is calculated to accommodate 96 men. The fort was besieged in 1745-6 by the Camerons, but without success. It is now almost in a state of disuse.
Fort William is situated on the shore of Loch Eil, at the distance of about two miles from the termination of the canal of Corpach. It was erected in the reign of William III. for the purpose of keeping down the Jacobite clans of the west.	11	ONICH.	92	
	7½	Coran Ferry across Loch Eil.	95½	
	½	Maryburgh.	102½	
		FORT WILLIAM.	103	

XXIX. ABERDEEN.—BANFF.—CULLEN.—ELGIN.—FORRES.—NAIRN.—INVERNESS.—126 MILES.

ON RIGHT FROM ABERD.	From Inver.		From Aberd.	ON LEFT FROM ABERD.
		Leave Aberdeen, and pass for several miles along the bank of the Inverury Canal.		
Persley, Hadden, Esq. Woodside, Kilgour, Esq. Waterton, Pirie, Esq. Parkhill, Skene, Esq.		Dyce vill.	6	Hilton, Johnston, Bart. Kirkhill, Bannerman, Esq. Fintry House, Forbes, Bart. Kinmundy, E. of Aberdeen. Elrick House, Burnett, Esq.
		cr. the Don.		Straloch, Ramsay, Esq. Barra, Ramsay, Esq.
Tillygreig, Harvey, Esq.		New Macher Kirk.	9	Fingask, Elmslie, Esq. Tulloch, Kilgour, Esq.
Pittrichie, Milne, Esq.	111	Leithfield.	14½	
Udney Castle, Col. Udney. Kilblein, Manson, Esq.	108	Old Meldrum vill.	18	
Haddo House, Earl of Aberdeen.		Meldrum Ho., Urquhart, Esq.		
	101½	Fyvie Kirk.	24½	
	99½	Fyvie Castle, Gordon of Fyvie, on the right.	26½	Fyvie Castle is a princely looking building, beautifully situated on a small eminence in the centre of a large amphitheatre
	95½	Towie,	30½	of fine grounds, skirted with woods on the heights around, and the river winding through the centre.
Hatton Castle, Duff, Esq.		The native place of the father of Barclay de Tolly, i.e. Towie, the Russian general.		Gask, Earl of Fife.
"When ye're at the Brig o' Turay, Ye're half-way between Aberdeen and Elgin o' Murray."		cr. Turriff Water.		
		Muiresk, Spottiswood, Esq. Laithers, Stuart, Esq.		
Delgatty Castle, Earl of Fife, a mile from Turriff; not seen from the road.	93	Turriff. Pronounced Turay. Forglen House, Abercromby, Bart., about a mile from Turriff.	33	
Craigston Castle, Urquhart, Esq.	91½ 88	On the left Montblairy, Morison, Esq. and Eden, Duff, Esq.	35½ 38	Banff, the county town, is agreeably situated on the side of a hill at the mouth of the river Deveron. It was founded by Malcolm Canmore in 1163.
Forglen Church on the north side of the river Deveron.		cr. King Edward.		There have been large additional piers built to the harbour here, but, owing to the sandy bottom, the bar is often much
	79	cr. Deveron River, and enter BANFF.	47	filled up.
				On the left on entering the town is Duff House, the elegant mansion of the Earl of Fife.
Between Boyndie and Portsoy are the ruins of Boyne Castle, Earl of Seafield, once the finest seat in the North of Scotland, but destroyed in the civil war.	75½	New Kirk of Boyndie.	50½	Durn Park, Gordon, Esq.
		cr. Boyne Streamlet by of Broadlie.		Durn, Earl of Seafield.
Along this line of road the Earls of Fife and Seafield, and the Duke of Richmond, are the chief proprietors.	70	Portsoy, A small irregularly built town, with a thriving port; population 2000.	56	Glasshaugh, Abercromby, Esq.
From Banff to Fochabers (26 miles) the road passes at no great distance from the sea-coast.	65	CULLEN, A royal burgh in the Elgin district, population 1593.	61	Birkenbog, Abercromby, Bart. Cullen House, Earl of Seafield, a large and venerable building. The grounds are fine.
Near village of Buckie.	61	Letterfourie, Gordon, Bart.	65	Cairnfield, Gordon, Esq.
Near village of Port Gordon.	52	Fochabers vill.	74	On the right from Aberdeen, and at the back of Fochabers, is Gordon Castle, Duke of Richmond; a magnificent mansion,
Speymouth Kirk. The royal burgh of Elgin is an old fashioned and impressive place.		cr. Spey River, enter Morayshire.		erected by Alexander Duke of Gordon, who died in 1827. The ancient seat of the family was
The remains of the Cathedral form the chief object	48	Urquhart vill.	78	Huntly Castle, now in ruins; near it Huntly Lodge, Duchess of Gordon.
of attraction in Elgin. It was founded in 1224 by the Bishop	46	Kirk of St. Andrews.	80	
of Moray. The great tower fell in 1711. The Cathedral, when entire, was exactly a model of Lichfield. Elgin has been much improved of late years by the erection of various public buildings.	43	ELGIN Joins with Banff, Cullen, Inverury, Kintore, and Peterhead, in electing an M.P.; population 4500.	83	

TABLE OF THE DISTANCES

OF THE PRINCIPAL TOWNS IN SCOTLAND FROM EACH OTHER AND FROM LONDON, GENERALLY CALCULATED BY THE MAIL ROADS.

		DISTANCE FROM LONDON
Aberdeen	EDINBURGH	509
Arbroath	109 Aberdeen	501
Ayr	60 49 Arbroath	468
Banff	77 177 185 AYR	564
Berwick-on-Tweed	134 45 94 269 Banff	546
Campbelton	56 164 115 189 309 Berwick-on-Tweed	357
Cupar Fife	177 270 222 60 388 323 Campbelton	529
Dumbarton	30 79 80 107 194 85 181 Cupar Fife	432
Dumfries	56 130 105 47 195 118 108 81 Dumbarton	410
Dundee	71 180 131 69 240 166 205 101 98 Dumfries	385
Elgin	43 67 17 116 111 96 191 18 89 114 Dundee	434
Falkirk	109 68 99 206 34 294 231 130 240 119 Elgin	561
Glasgow	34 137 84 66 159 79 166 54 97 98 157 Falkirk	415
Greenock	44 143 100 83 175 99 183 74 14 72 97 93 Glasgow	380
Haddington	66 165 122 46 175 121 111 96 19 84 105 195 44 Greenock	418
Hamilton	17 126 77 84 171 33 184 47 75 88 60 196 41 67 Haddington	375
Inverary	37 146 97 88 188 92 184 66 28 61 80 184 99 11 83 Hamilton	381
Inverness	104 169 135 163 307 159 73 108 46 132 106 278 108 88 60 54 Inverary	456
Jedburgh	157 104 138 196 75 213 306 126 148 208 136 413 146 296 138 181 111 Inverness	549
John o' Groat's	47 156 107 98 201 33 999 71 108 78 100 216 71 89 111 46 78 149 Jedburgh	554
Kelso	814 235 294 306 905 369 380 894 970 305 294 179 977 993 815 831 804 966 181 961 John o' Groat's	700
Kirkcudbright	43 152 108 190 213 32 990 73 101 83 86 218 67 57 109 36 90 147 900 147 900 Kelso	564
Lanark	99 208 159 64 263 185 115 199 119 97 149 996 191 98 180 116 95 157 995 109 991 112 Kirkcudbright	595
Montrose	81 140 91 51 195 96 52 68 74 199 96 35 47 48 14 85 127 64 318 69 68 Lanark	575
Paisley	72 27 181 149 83 197 210 42 119 143 99 98 113 184 89 128 187 136 119 966 115 171 Montrose	464
Perth	58 151 108 84 183 107 157 89 9 90 91 181 81 6 10 69 19 54 170 97 301 95 166 Paisley	407
Port Patrick	40 88 89 94 195 95 159 92 65 111 59 139 45 61 93 57 73 86 114 87 978 88 189 191 Perth	438
Stirling	188 949 199 135 304 958 188 60 108 103 78 173 958 119 89 111 150 98 149 951 135 389 196 55 90 Port Patrick	481
Thurso	35 116 72 60 145 40 128 47 34 89 61 145 11 97 49 59 89 90 195 78 195 97 85 35 84 116 Stirling	447
Wick	816 926 918 994 986 971 907 905 907 995 900 906 974 179 964 800 889 819 811 973 138 342 19 388 904 810 973 906 959 389 Thurso	708
Wigton	105 214 165 60 566 106 98 185 97 65 143 966 191 63 95 192 84 148 945 188 404 188 81 70 176 83 144 97 116 405 385 Wick	697
Carlisle	99 90 111 951 925 98 180 189 109 97 195 961 116 9 117 109 84 155 949 63 386 63 68 74 164 100 188 190 110 405 307 194 Carlisle	591

☞ The names of the various towns are arranged at each end of the line of figures, and the angle where the perpendicular and horizontal lines meet, gives the distance of the respective towns from each other.

NO PASSAGE THIS WAY

THE OPINIONS OF THE PRESS

ON THE

STOPPING OF THE HIGHLAND PASSES.

EDINBURGH:
PRINTED FOR THE ASSOCIATION FOR THE PROTECTION OF
PUBLIC RIGHTS OF ROADWAY IN SCOTLAND.

[*Price One Penny, or 5s. per* 100.]

ADVERTISEMENT.

THE object of the Association in printing the following documents, is to subject the matters to which they relate to that wholesome publicity from which powerful individuals, in remote districts, are too apt to be exempt. The solitary traveller across a thinly peopled district, or the humble peasant passing by the old accustomed path to visit his relatives in the next glen, if compelled by the owner of the soil to make a circuit of thirty miles, is in a far different position from the individual on whom a like hardship is attempted to be imposed in the midst of a populous neighbourhood. In both cases, it is true that the law is open to the party injured; but it is often but a poor protection to his rights to tell a solitary individual that he is at liberty to commence expensive proceedings. The great protection of the poor against the rich is, that in the face of day, and under the eye of public opinion, the latter will not venture to infringe on legal rights, knowing that the elements of their own power and greatness depend on the sacredness and efficiency of the laws. In taking such means as they could readily find for bringing this discussion under public notice, the Association beg to say, that they

THE OPINIONS OF THE PRESS

ON THE

STOPPING OF THE HIGHLAND PASSES

---

1. *Blackwood's Magazine.**

WE have observed with great pain, that a far too exclusive spirit has of late manifested itself in certain high places, and among persons whom we regard too much to be wholly indifferent to their conduct.   This very summer the public press has been indignant in its denunciation of the Dukes of Atholl and Leeds—the one having, as it is alleged, attempted to shut up a servitude road through Glen Tilt, and the other established a cordon for many miles around the skirts of Ben-Muich-Dhui, our highest Scottish mountain. We are not fully acquainted with the particulars; but from what we heard, it would appear that this wholesale exclusion from a vast tract of territory is intended to secure the solitude of two deer-forests.   Now, we are not going to argue the matter upon legal grounds—although, knowing something of law, we have a shrewd suspicion that both noble lords are in utter misconception of their rights, and are usurping a sovereignty which is not to be found in their charters, and which was never claimed or exercised even by the Scottish Kings.   But the churlishness of the step is undeniable, and we cannot but hope that it has proceeded far more from thoughtlessness than from intention.   The day has been, when any clansman, or even any stranger, might have taken a deer from the forest, a tree from the hill, or a salmon from the river, without leave asked or obtained : and though that state of society has long since passed away, we never till now have heard that the free air of the mountains, and their heather ranges, are not open to him who seeks them. Is it indeed come to this, that in bonny Scotland, the tourist, the botanist, or the painter, are to be debarred from visiting the loveliest spots which nature ever planted in the heart of a wilderness, on pretence that they disturb the deer!   In a few years we suppose Ben Lomond will be preserved, and the summit of Ben Nevis remain as unvisited by the foot of the traveller as the icy peak of the Jungfrau.   Not so, assuredly, would have acted the race of Tullibardine of yore.   Royal were their hunting gatherings, and magnificent the driving of the Tinchel; but over all their large territory of Atholl, the stranger might have wandered unquestioned, except to know if he required hospitality.   It is not now the gate which is shut, but the moor; and that not against the depredator, but against the peaceful wayfaring man. Nor can we as sportsmen admit even the relevancy of the reasons which have been assigned for this wholesale exclusion.   We are convinced, that in each season not above thirty or forty tourists essay the ascent of Ben-Muich-Dhui; and of that number, in all probability, not one has either met or startled a red

---

* Although posterior in date of publication to many of the notices which follow it in this collection, precedence is given to this article, as it affords a lively and able sketch of the general character of the contest, and supplies in some measure the place of an Introduction.

Leeds, the lessee of Mar Lodge, and the extreme impertinence of his keepers.
Instead of being allowed to take the shortest way, the tourist is compelled to
take a long, tedious, and circuitous route up Glen Derry.   Even here he is
constantly assailed by keepers impressing careful advances and still longer
rounds.   This is a most annoying proceeding, which no guide dare gainsay
when "the Duke is down."   The advice I give to tourists is to disregard all
injunctions whatever, whether from innkeeper or gamekeeper, guide or grand
Duke, and proceed boldly up Glen-lui-beg by the shortest, best, and accustomed way.   There is no right whatever to prevent this.   It is an exercise
of public right, established by immemorial usage, and expressly encouraged
by the late Earl of Fife, the proprietor.   If the tourist meets with any insult
or injury, it is to be hoped he will be spirited enough to resent it, and to
punish it in a proper manner.   In these secluded glens oppression may
silently and ruthlessly crush the poacher and the poor hospitable harbourer
of the poacher.   The same submissive deference cannot surely be expected
from travellers.

3. *The Scotsman.*

SHUTTING OF HIGHLAND PASSES

In a late article on the Game-laws, we alluded to the circumstance that
some of the English gentlemen who had become proprietors or lessees of sporting districts in the Highlands, were attempting to prohibit tourists from
passing through these waste lands to visit our mountain scenery.   On more
particular inquiry, we find that such an attempt has been made in Glen-lui-
beg, one of the valleys which descend to the Dee, in Aberdeenshire, and the
principal means of entrance to the wild and majestic scenery of the Cairngorm mountains.   The tourist is now liable to be stopped at the entrance
of the pass by keepers who say they are acting under the instructions of
an English Duke, who is the lessee of the ground under the Earl of Fife.
The other day, a young Englishman, seeking to vary his university studies
by enjoying a ramble amongst the wildest features of our Highland scenery,
after having passed unquestioned wherever the original Highland proprietor
continued owner of the soil, felt a pang of shame and indignation, that the
first inhospitable and invidious act he encountered should come from the
hands of a countryman of his own—a patrician of the boasted land of freedom.   The guides in the neigbourhood have been intimidated, and refuse to
conduct strangers through the forbidden ground.   We have already stated
that we question the legality of such a proceeding.   We know no law of
trespass to protect waste unenclosed grounds; nothing which enables the
owner of the soil to exclude the public from it, unless he reclaim it from
nature by enclosing it, or applying it to productive purposes.   The law is
somewhat reasonable—more so than grasping individuals would wish it to be;
and before the soil is held sacred from intrusion, the law demands that the
owner shall appropriate it to a useful or ornamental purpose.   The *stet pro
ratione voluntas* is not, and should not, be authority for stopping the pedestrian on a barren heath; he should be warned from intrusion by those signs
of ownership which mark the landlord's appropriation of the soil to his own
use.   If he sees none of this, to subject him to any penalty as an intruder is
to catch him in a trap.   No human being will ever be brought to feel that
he is committing the same offence in walking across the pathless heathy
desert, as if he were treading down broccoli or dahlias.   At this moment
several thousand tourists are loose over the land.   They are climbing Ben
Nevis or Ben Lomond—they are rambling among the braes of Glencoe or the
banks of Loch Katrine.   Are these all trespassers, liable to pay some heavy

Notwithstanding its many attractions, a small portion only of the annual shoal of northern tourists reaches this wilderness. The journey involves hardships, for which your systematic sight-seer, who goes to noted places of easy access, "to say he has been there," is not prepared. The waste separates the nearest dwellings by distances of about thirty miles from each other; there are no roads through it; and the pedestrian must tread the narrow footpaths, or scramble over the rocks with his staff and wallet, prepared, when night overtakes him, to spread a couch for himself, and repose on nature's most fragrant bed—tufts of newly plucked heather. That any one visiting such wilds should be interrupted, has heretofore never entered into the dreams of man. Such an occurrence is totally inconsistent with the habits and notions of the Scottish people. They have not advanced far enough in civilisation to exhibit the exclusive spirit of proprietorship in the howling wilderness. Where nature is roughest and wildest, the human heart is all the more warm and open; and the pedestrian never contemplates the Highland gentleman's distant shooting lodge, save as a place where, if hunger and fatigue should overtake him, he will meet with a warm reception. To apply a law of trespass to these wild regions, would indeed have something in it ludicrous; it would be like finding a powdered porter to warn you off an iceberg in Nova Zembla, or a glacier of the Jungfrau.

So stood matters when his Grace the Duke of Leeds became the tenant from the Earl of Fife of Glen-lui-beg, a long uninhabited valley, which forms the entrance avenue to the valleys of the Cairngorm Mountains from the south-east. His Grace has been pleased to call the wild tract he occupies a deer forest, and to decree that it shall not be polluted by human footsteps without his consent. Accordingly, at the gorge of the glen, the pedestrian is stopped by his Grace's keepers; and if he yield to their oppression, he must travel round to a distant entrance pass in another district of the country, or give up his sojourn among the Cairngorm Mountains. Can this meet with its parallel elsewhere in the world? Do any of those petty German Princes whom we love to ridicule as small despots, insult nature's worshippers by blocking up mountain scenery? Does the King of Sardinia station keepers on Mount Blanc, or has the unpopular King of Hanover extended his despotism to stopping tourists on the Harz? Well, but it will be said the parallel must fail—this English Duke is an owner, not a monarch: his right is of a very different class from that of any king or ruler. If he chooses to be illiberal and exclusive, may he not do what he likes with his own? May he not, if it suits his fancy, count his savage mountain ravine as safe from intrusion, as if he had spread on it a lawn with gravel walks and built a park gate? And may he not enforce such his decree? We doubt it very much; and as his Grace has certainly not studied the customs and national character, we suspect he is as far from conforming with the laws of the people he has gone among. We have it on pretty good authority, that there is no law to protect unfenced desolate ground, not laid out for any productive purposes, from intrusion, in Scotland; and that whoever traverses such spots is only responsible by an action for whatever damage he may do. Laws arise from the customs of a people and the state of their country; and it would plainly, in a country of which so large a proportion is barren heath, have only been putting a power of capricious annoyance in the hands of individuals, to give them the right of appealing to a strict law of trespass. It would come under the reproach of that attempt in international law which was crushed by Lord Stowell; the establishment of a paper blockade, without a sufficient armament to enforce it.

We cannot help in these remarks referring to the Duke of Leeds with freedom, because it is in his Grace's name that the obnoxious act is done. He may, however, be ignorant of the zeal with which he is served. The

own heather—who seeks the hill for health or exercise, not shooting in a close-walled paddock, with a band of music, and bright eyes to stimulate him, but breasting the crags or scouring the moor—is not to be pitied if he never rejoices in the sight of a distant antler, from morning grey till dewy eve. His comfort will be to hear that some of the "annual shoal of northern tourists" were "awa' up the glen before him." His philanthropy and patriotism should at once beat high within his bosom while he reflects with pleasure that some adventurous sight-seer, deserting his lean "Rosinante," whom repeated Sunday excursions in the park have crippled for a while, has been "happy yet" in the exercise of his free and independent rights of spoiling the sport for which others have to pay.

I must leave the writer in the *Examiner* to explain the poetical vagaries of his description, such as "most fragrant bed of nature," "tufts of newly plucked heather," "howling wilderness," "powdered porters," &c., as well as his axiom, that "where nature is roughest and wildest, the human heart is all the more warm and open," with this remark, that I fear he is a man of sedentary habits, more given to imagine than to behold. As for "the King of Sardinia and Mount Blanc," or "the unpopular King of Hanover and the Hartz," I have only to say, that I believe no one rents a deer forest from one or the other.

So far from being infected by a "paltry, invidious, and grasping spirit," the Scottish Nimrods are generally hospitable and kind. No one would be stopped in their glens, if the traveller would take the trouble of sending to the forester, or asking leave of the proprietor, so that he might not be unconsciously the cause of spoiling a whole day's amusement, which I think no one would desire. I remember, last year, a gentleman coolly walking down Glen Tilt, and driving every deer out of it, when Lord Glenlyon was endeavouring to show sport to his friends. The traveller intended no harm, yet he did irreparable mischief, and this, had he given notice, or applied beforehand, might have been avoided.

With regard to the Duke of Leeds, he has been at Mar Lodge long enough to be perfectly acquainted with the manners and customs of the people, and it is believed that he has "studied the national character," as his Grace and the Duchess are fond of identifying themselves with their temporary tenancy, and delight to exchange the grandeur of Hornby for the granite of the Grampians. His Grace always appears at the Braemar and Athole gatherings "all plaided and plumed in his tartan array," with a score of stout gillies at his back, armed with swords, shields, and partisans. The Duchess also does a world of good in the neighbourhood, having mainly contributed to build a Catholic chapel, and supporting many poor and helpless persons.

In conclusion, I have only to say that the public, in my opinion, very often interfere, guided by vague reports, where they have no business; and in these days it seems not as if every one had a right to do what they like with their own, but as if no one had any right to do anything.—I am, Sir, your obedient servant,   LEATHERSTOCKING.

ENCROACHMENTS ON PUBLIC RIGHTS.

(From the same.)

An intelligent correspondent has favoured us with the following reply to "Leatherstocking's" defence of the Duke of Leeds. We insert it thus prominently, not from any wish to give the one side an undue advantage, but because we think the subject is of very great importance, and imperatively calls for public attention.

Sir,—I have just read with much interest the letter of your correspondent "Leatherstocking," vindicating the Duke of Leeds for attempting to close up the path to

regular procession over the walks to which the community can establish a right.

While the Earl of Fife's aristocratic tenant is endeavouring to shut out the public from barren moors and glens, the noble Earl is showing a very different example in the north. The *Elgin Courier*, which reached us last night, says:—

The Right Hon. the Earl of Fife has conceded, in the handsomest manner possible, a request made by the ladies of Elgin, for *a new walk* through the fine plantation of larches which fringe the river on the north side; to connect with and extend *that* which his Lordship formerly gave them through his beautiful Oak-wood. This boon is of exceeding value to the ladies, and the whole community of Elgin; opening as it does a new source of healthful recreation, vigour, and happiness, to the lisping infancy, the aspiring youth, and the fading age of our good town These two walks thus united, and brought as it were, by the proposed bridge, to our very doors, will furnish a round of three miles under the shelter of the richest foliage, affording also many fine and interesting views. * * * To commemorate that kindness of heart, urbanity of manners, which have always distinguished his Lordship's conduct to the people of Elgin, this new walk will be for ever designated—"LORD FIFE'S WALK."

TO THE EDITOR OF THE MORNING HERALD.

Sir—Permit me to request the publication of the enclosed letter to the Editor of the *Examiner*.—Your most obedient, GRANTLEY F. BERKELEY.

To the Proprietor of the *Examiner*.

Dear Fonblanque—So long as the *Examiner* is written under the motto you have selected as your watch-word, I cannot think that any letter addressed to you, reminding you of the colour under which you select to sail, will be deemed unfairly obtrusive on your editorial capacity, or unpleasant to you as coming from your personal friend.

We have known each other many years; we agree on some political points; but on the subject of the Game-laws we are opposed to each other, perhaps only in the means by which we desire to obtain a similar result.

It appears to me that while you are amusing yourself in your yacht, there oftentimes creeps into the *Examiner* a style of article wide of the intention of your motto, and differing much from your usual method. An article in your last number, headed, "English Game Preservers in Scotland," and attacking the Duke of Leeds, is the one with which it is my present purpose to deal.

In the article I complain of, you say, that the fact "of an uninhabited portion of Scotland, where the Highlands of Aberdeenshire and Inverness-shire meet, called the Cairngorm Mountains," being preserved by his Grace of Leeds as a deer forest, whence "sight-seers" and strangers are excluded, "strongly evinces the paltry, invidious, grasping spirit of those whom Blackstone has so well denominated 'Little Nimrods.'"

Now, when "the pen, that mighty instrument of little men," is thus wielded in a sweeping and uncharitable charge against a great body of English sportsmen, for the most part composed of the middling class of proprietors, and of men of funded fortunes renting manors, it would be well, in the first instance, to ascertain if, according to the set phrase of your motto, you were "truly standing upon the dangerous precipice of telling unbiassed truth," or whether, in the language of the amusement of which you are so fond, you have not in this instance lost your steerage way, and become for a time but as a log upon the water, telling, in fact, no truth at all. You charge us, for I never shrink from taking upon myself all the responsibilities of an "English game preserver," with a spirit paltry, invidious, and grasping, because we, or one of us, retiring from the thronged haunts of men, choose to benefit a Scotch proprietor by renting his otherwise uselessly wild rocks and heather—amusing ourselves with a sport at once manly, grand, and

upon such vague merits as those he puts forth in this article. Before a public contributor to a paper presumes to condemn a man, or a body of men, on motives with which he cannot be conversant, being ignorant of surrounding circumstances, he should take the trouble to examine the sources of his information, and be prepared, if necessary, to give the name and date of his authority. If he cannot do this, he will have to exclaim—and your contributor of the objectionable article will have to exclaim—with Shakspeare's *Dogberry*, in *Much ado about Nothing*, "Masters, remember that *I am* an ass, though it be not written down!"—Yours faithfully,

GRANTLEY F. BERKELEY.

Beacon Lodge, Sept. 8, 1846.

ENGLISH GAME PRESERVERS IN SCOTLAND.

To A. Fonblanque, Esq., Connaught Square.

Dear Fonblanque—Though *you* find fault in your letter of the 16th with the method of my address, I will not now adopt a more formal one, being governed *by no hostile feeling to you individually.* It has of late been the constant custom of a portion of the press to rail at *the amusements* of the aristocracy and gentry, and to deny them, even in retirement, the privilege of privacy.

For this reason I have, for some time, looked out to catch one of our assailants, and though expecting at first to hook but a minnow of the literary shallows, I am the better pleased in that I have caught the Triton. You will pardon me, then, for using the gaff, and landing you high and dry on the rock of my position!

You gentlemen, who pass your time in writing *under cover* of the anonymous "*We*," concerning everything and everybody, are, I find, *morbidly sensitive* when, by accident, *your own names and affairs* come to be publicly mentioned! Lawyers are afraid of law proceedings, physicians of physic, far more than other people, but the fright of a newspaper editor, upon being made the subject of newspaper comment, *is even yet more remarkable!* The terror of Jack Ketch, when condemned to be hanged, is the only really parallel passage *in the annals of professional cowardice.*

I am anxious that both you and the public, whom you weekly address, should draw *a wholesome moral from your own feelings* upon the occasion of my letter, addressed to you through the *Morning Post,* &c. You, I hope, may, under the influence of a fellow feeling, learn to be less bitter and more charitable, while your friends, the public, may form a more accurate estimate than they usually do, *of the true dimensions of the formidable* "WE."—Faithfully yours, GRANTLEY F. BERKELEY.

Let the following parallel passages speak for themselves:

HIS GRACE THE DUKE OF LEEDS, WITH *no alias.*

The Duke of Leeds being fond of sporting, rents in the wilds of Scotland a *primeval deer forest,* of the Earl of Fife, for which he pays a rental of twelve hundred a year. At an additional and heavy expense he employs keepers to protect it. Before any strangers are permitted to *trespass by the private passes, there being several highways through the property, commanding views of the scenery,* it is required of them that they should ask permission, and give their names.

In this proceeding the Duke of Leeds,

THE EDITOR OF THE *Examiner, alias* MR. A. FONBLANQUE.

Mr. A. Fonblanque, *alias* the editor of the *Examiner,* is *also* "fond of sporting." His business lies in the stalking of men under the shield and disguise of that cloak of darkness, the powerful and mysterious "*We.*"

His private amusement, his "*sport*" is in sailing on the sea in a hired yacht.

Mr. Fonblanque having, in the pursuit of his weekly occupation, and in his character of editor of the *Examiner, unfairly attacked the Duke of Leeds* (as well as all other gentlemen who choose to preserve

" The truth is this. . I rent the Mar Forest of Lord Fife, and have done so for many years. The stock of deer has always been large, and I *am bound in honour to the proprietor to take every care* that the forest is not spoiled by the diminution of their number.

" The interests of the forest *depend on quiet*, and total absence from all disturbance. An incautious intruder might be the means of sending several hundred head of the best deer out of the forest, *to return no more*. There are three roads through the Mar Forest, enough for all purposes of sight-seeing, &c. If indiscriminate trespass was permitted, any person, under pretence of sight-seeing, might purposely drive the deer out of bounds, when they might be killed by other people. &c.—Most truly yours,

(Signed)   " LEEDS."

6. *The Scotsman.*

Mr. Grantley Berkeley having thought fit to publish a letter from the Duke of Leeds, in which his Grace vindicates his conduct regarding the closing of Glen-lui-beg, we reprint it, both because it is fair to hear what his Grace may have to say, and because the letter will put an end to any doubts in the public mind that the interdict on entering these wilds is so extensive and severe as it was stated to be by ourselves and others.

[Here his Grace's letter is inserted.]

We would have thought it cruel to be the first to give publicity to such a document; but as the writer's own friend has thought otherwise, we may be pardoned for giving it a little more publicity. The taste which suggested the simile from the dog kennel is exactly on a level with the grammar in which it is expressed. There might be a suspicion of affectation in a remark suggesting the inference that his Grace is unacquainted with one of the finest writers of the age, but the truly Mrs. Gamp-like elliptical style in which the ignorance is expressed—" I conclude he is a gentleman "—attests the sincerity of any profession that fine literature has not been among the writer's studies. It is as convincing as that celebrated part of a sentence in which a noble lord commenced his disavowal of the authorship of a clever pamphlet,—" I hereby scartify." Really the state of education among our ducal population is a melancholy subject.

7. *The Morning Chronicle.*

A queer compilation of letters, with which Mr. Grantley Berkeley has obliged a contemporary journal, was printed in yesterday's *Chronicle*. Mr. Fonblanque, the Honourable Grantley Berkeley, and his Grace the Duke of Leeds are the contributors to this miscellany, of which Mr. Berkeley is the editor. A controversy has been carried on between these gentlemen for some weeks past.

In the first place, there appeared in the *Examiner* newspaper, on the 5th of September, some complaints regarding the present condition of the valley of Glen-lui-beg, in Scotland, rented by the Earl of Fife to his Grace the Duke of Leeds. This vast district is occupied by his Grace as a deer forest. To stalk deer—as those familiar with the sport by experience or written works are aware—it is necessary that the horned animals should be visited but by few of the human race. The deer must have many thousands of acres to range, the huntsmen be but one or two. So delicate is the scent of the deer, as described in Mr. Scrope's amusing work, that even a half dozen Dukes would disturb them, and their Graces would find an utter destruction of pastime between the wind and their nobility. Thus a man (if we may be per-

Ketch when condemned to be hanged is the only really parallel passage in *the annals of professional cowardice.*" The words are dear Grantley's, and the italics, and the style, and the grammar, and the happy elegant confusion, and the apt metaphor, and the graceful propriety of simile too. You see how men of noble descent write. This is a gentleman beyond our degree. There is a peculiar grace and charm about him. He belongs to "the aristocracy and gentry." Only a person of his exalted lineage could think of comparisons so polite. Perhaps had he been a *roturier,* dear Grantley would not have published dear Fonblanque's private note. Such communications are generally not sent to newspapers. It did not appear that the public necessities required that the confidential note should be confided to all England— but who knows best? the "aristocracy and gentry" of course. Also, it seems curious that Mr. Grantley Fitzhardinge Berkeley, complaining of the anonymous "We" in newspapers, should straitway address the newspaper editor, of whose publication he complains.

And now, the Duke's champion having done his worst, the Duke himself appears.

[Here his Grace's letter is repeated as above.]

Very good. Keep the deer, as your Grace is bound in honour to your Grace's landlord; let tourists go what way you will for the purpose of sight-seeing, &c.; disregard the vain clamours that are made against your Grace; let your Grace wrap yourself up in your Grace's virtue, and disregard "the productions of a pack of curs"—(Cur me querelis exanimasti.) O, your Grace! what a gracious and genteel style of writing your Grace possesses! " the productions of a pack of curs who yelp at a distance."

But why say to Mr. Grantley Berkeley, " *As you wrote to the Editor of the* Examiner *as your friend,* I conclude he is a gentleman." Did your Grace never hear that gentlemen wrote for the press, or of the *Examiner* newspaper, before? While the *Examiner* made all England laugh and think, was your Grace, above doing either, engaged in the solitary sports of the Cairngorm Mountains, the only man or Grace ignorant of such a journal? Does your Grace know the difference between the writing of a gentleman and that of an ass? Does your Grace conclude that, because a person knows Mr. Grantley Berkeley, therefore he is a gentleman, and that learning and wit and genius go for nothing without the knowledge of that consummate worthy? A man may be a duke, and have no genius nor learning nor wit. A man may be a duke, and be a fool. A man may be at the head or the tail of the aristocracy of the Red Book, and ignore the press with Leeds's stupendous dulness, or assail it with Berkeley's delicate raillery. But when your Grace is as forgotten in death, as your Grace has been in your Grace's gracious life, and when " dear Grantley" is as extinct as the victims of that Jack Ketch who is present to his elegant mind, it may happen that the name of the Editor of the *Examiner* may be known for something besides his yacht, and—who knows ?—historically he may turn out to be the noble gentlemen's equal in birth, and breeding, and honesty, as he is their superior in other qualities of a gentleman.

8. *The Glasgow Argus.*

THE SHUTTING UP OF HIGHLAND PASSES.

We are glad to see that the illegal attempt of the Duke of Leeds to shut up the pass to Glen-lui-beg amid the Cairngorm Mountains, has excited so much attention throughout England and Scotland. There has been a growing disposition for some years, on the part of great Highland proprietors, and the English sportsmen to whom they let their shootings, to exclude the people

". The other day" (it is added) " a young Englishman seeking to vary his university studies, by enjoying a ramble amongst the wildest features of mountain scenery, after having passed unquestioned, wherever the original Highland proprietor continued owner of the soil, felt a pang of shame and indignation that the first inhospitable act he encountered should come from the hands of a countryman of his own—a patrician of the boasted land of freedom. The guides in the neighbourhood have been intimidated, and refuse to conduct strangers through the forbidden ground." Now, if it will be any relief to the wounded feelings of the ingenuous young Englishman in question, we can positively assure him, that the novel taboo he complains of,— one more arbitrary, barbarous, and wanton, than any of the South Sea Islands ever knew, is by no means peculiar to his own countrymen, but is largely participated in by the " original Highland proprietors," whom he deems exempt. We may mention, for example, that according to our information, Glen Tilt, justly reckoned amongst the grandest and most beautiful of Highland Glens, and affording the only direct communication betwixt the wide districts of Atholl and Deeside, has been laid under a similar interdict against the passage of tourists and way-farers, by Lord Glenlyon. It is, indeed, too true, that the system, as yet only in its beginnings, is rapidly extending throughout the Highlands ; and unless it is checked by some very marked expression of public indignation, or is put down by the strong arm of the law, it seems probable that in a few years hence, the general community will be unable to gain any more intimate acquaintance with Highland scenery, or to inspire more of the healthful breezes of the hills, than they may catch, as they are whirled rapidly along the dusty turnpikes. We observed some year or two ago, the formation of an association in Edinburgh having in view the patriotic object of protecting common rights and privileges by all legal means, against the grasping appropriation of landed aristocrats. If still in vigorous life and action, here is a noble field for its exertions, and one in which it will earn the cordial approbation and support of the whole community. There cannot be a doubt that the taboo is entirely illegal. There is not a glen nor hill within the whole circuit of the Highlands over which there has not existed from time immemorial an undisputed use of public way, and proof of the unchallenged existence of such a usage for forty years, is sufficient to constitute a perpetual and indefeasible right of servitude. It needs, therefore, but somebody like the association in question, or even some resolute and public spirited individual, to step into the breach, and have the question fairly tried, and the law declared, to put an end at once to the march of encroachment.

* * * * * * *

Before we leave this subject we should like to drop just a hint or two as to the Atholl estates. Throughout all their wide limits the taboo system reigns in full and unrelenting rigour. Woe to any heedless piscatory disciple of the gentle Izaak, who shall dare to drop a line or cast a fly into the waters of loch or stream on the whole domain without the counter-sign of the authorities ! Over the hills and in the woods, the taboo is equally omnipotent—the earth and the waters are clutched in its relentless grasp, only the free air of heaven has escaped its fetters, and that the denizens of Atholl may happily still breathe without the sanction of its lord. But we will not trust ourselves to write more upon such a theme. We will only recommend such of our readers as may wish to obtain a correct apprehension of the sort of system pursued upon some Highland estates, to go and live upon them for a time, and glean from among the people themselves the chapter of their experiences.

It may be well, however, that we advert, before we close, to one privilege

Our attention has been recalled to these aggressions by a gigantic attempt on the part of the Duke of Leeds to shut up an immense district of country, which, from time immemorial, has been patent to " nature's worshippers," and which contains some of the grandest, most romantic, and most beautiful scenery in Scotland. In a late number, we copied from the *Examiner* an able article on this subject, which we hope will have the effect of stimulating some inquiry into it. We confess we have heard of this attempt with some alarm. If successful, and if it be imitated by other Highland proprietors, the inhabitants of Scotland, and of the island generally, will be deprived of one of their most delightful and healthy recreations; and foreigners, who may be anxious to visit our miniature *Mount Blancs*, must in future be content to restrict their excursions to the low countries, and to tell their wondering friends when they go home, that, in the ancient and free kingdom of Caledonia, the " high places" are all reserved for the high people. A sad pass this for an enlightened nation, in the most palmy time of its civilisation, to be brought to! The outlets to the Highland hills used to be looked to by all descriptions of toil-worn beings, as affording happy escapes for a time from the cares of business or the drudgery of a profession; and we should look upon the shutting up of any of these outlets as little less than a national calamity. Are we indeed doomed to see Ben-Muich-Dhui and Ben Nevis guarded henceforth by a cordon of gamekeepers from the footsteps of all who are not connected with their princely possessors? We say with *Punch*—

" He who the traveller denies
. On Nature's charms to feast his eyes,
Behaves like an ungracious churl—
Not like a noble Duke or Earl."

It is time that the public should inquire for themselves how this matter stands; whether indeed these barren mountains can be preserved as if they were orchards, wheat fields, or flower gardens, and the " red heather" be in future to bloom only for its wild inhabitants and their privileged destroyers; or whether, more happily, immemorial usage has conferred upon the public a right to seek health, amusement, and delight among these majestic recesses. The *Examiner* says,—" We have it on pretty good authority that there is no law to protect unfenced desolate ground, not laid out for any productive purpose, from intrusion in Scotland." We hope that the *Examiner's* authority is good. Proprietors of late have been drawing their lines around us very rapidly; and we are sorry to say that not one, but several attempts have been made successfully, in cases more or less analogous to that alluded to, to exclude the public from pursuits which were once open to them, and to indulge in which they certainly have hitherto been in the belief that they had an unchallengeable right. Anglers especially have been pretty roughly handled; and streams and rivers, which have been patent to them for ages, are now as strictly preserved for the lord of the manor and his friends, as his pheasant covers and his deer parks. In the present state of the law, no one knows where he can throw a line without running the risk of being pulled up for a trespass, or, what is as disagreeable, being insulted by a surly gamekeeper with a cudgel or a gun in his hand, and a dog at his heels. We repeat that we do not take upon ourselves to say how far these attempts may be consistent with law; but, certainly it is highly desirable that there should be some settled law or understanding on the subject. If it be true that Lord Fife, or his lessee, may lawfully guard the Cairngorm Mountains from the intrusion of the tourist, lest he should scare the game of noble sportsmen, the sooner the fact is known the better, that people may save themselves from the humiliation and disappointment of being turned off his lordship's grounds as tres-

11. Punch.

DR. SYNTAX TO MR. PUNCH.

Good *Mr. Punch*—the public's friend—
To you this note I'm led to send,
In hopes it may, perchance, induce
Your notice of a great abuse.
You are aware, my friend grotesque,
How much I love the picturesque:
My last excursion in these islands
Was to the famous Scottish Highlands.
To Glen-lui-beg my way I bent,
Which leads to the magnificent
Scenery of the Cairngorm Mountains,
Hard by the Dee's romantic fountains.
I reached the Pass conducting to
This highly celebrated view,
When, lo! to my exceeding wrath,
A keeper did obstruct my path.
" My man! (quoth I) explain, I pray,
Wherefore you thus arrest my way ?"
Quoth he, " 'T is by the Duke's command,
Who rents this piece of sporting land
Under my Lord The EARL OF FIFE."
" This is unpleasant! on my life,
(Said I) a disappointment keen!
Here all this weary way I've been,
And, now I've reached the wished-for spot,
To see it I am suffered not !"
" Hech! (said the man) I dinna ken,
The Duke he's bid us close the Glen."
" Friend, (I replied) were you His Grace,
Thus much I'd tell you to your face:
He who the traveller denies
On nature's charms to feast his eyes,
Behaves like some ungracious churl—
Not like a Noble Duke or Earl.
Nor is it a sagacious aim
Thus strictly to preserve your game;
For thus the general indignation
You'll rouse against its preservation."—
So having said, I turn'd my back,
And homeward bent my weary track.

DOCTOR SYNTAX.

POSTHUMOUS RENOWN.—The Duke of Leeds has closed Glen-lui-beg, the Duke of Atholl Glen Tilt, against the tourists. Long live both their Graces! But should anything happen to either of them, how appropriate to him will be the simple epitaph—" Stop ! Traveller."

12. *The Examiner.*

HIGHLAND PASSES.

The notice which our northern contemporaries have taken of our remarks on the attempt to close up Glen-lui-beg, in the Cairngorm Mountains, shows

attempted to exclude the public from Richmond Park. It was part of the royal domains attached to the residence of one of the princesses, and seclusion was peculiarly desirable. The public, however, had for generations enjoyed a right of way through the park, and a brewer of Richmond took up the subject. He brought an action against the royal family, and he gained it, compelling them to throw down the obnoxious barriers. This was done in the face of royalty, and with respect to finely cultivated grounds—and can a subject be more powerful in the case of waste lands untenanted by aught save grouse and deer? We do not believe he can. The plea put forth for the Duke of Leeds is, that he pays a large price for his shooting grounds, and that, if pedestrians are permitted to enter them, their value is deteriorated. This may be a good plea as respects his Grace, but it does not either apply to the proprietor or the public. A common right cannot be so disposed of. The point to be tried is, whether shooting grounds are to be held more sacred than cattle ranges or sheep walks, and whether the public are to be debarred from those approaches to our mountain scenery which have hitherto been open to all as a source of national pride and enjoyment. The Duke of Leeds is described as having " a score of stout gillies at his back, armed with swords, shields, and partisans," and if some determined wayfarer, bent on exploring the Cairngorm precipices, or crossing to Atholl, be turned back, the result will in all likelihood be an assault, and a subsequent appeal to the law. Funds for the latter could be easily procured throughout the kingdom. The scene-hunter, the geologist, and the botanist, would all make common cause in defending the right of way; for if the Duke of Leeds be successful, and Mar Forest be shut up, other cases will soon follow; exclusion will become the order of the day; and the grandest scenery of Scotland will soon be an exclusive appanage of the wealthy and titled sportsman.

Paragraph from an unknown quarter.

The motto of the Duke of Atholl is,—" Furth fortune and fill the fetters." This sentence, which has puzzled many distinguished antiquaries, has lately been discovered to be a corrupt version of an exclamation frequently used by his Grace in reference to foot passengers in Glen Tilt,—" Furth footman and fell the footers."

14. Tait's Magazine.

The idea of treating his waste districts of country as an English proprietor would his lawn and gravel walks, and attempting to preclude access to them, never would have occurred to a Highland chief in his most despotic moments. An English Duke, however, having become the tenant of the wild mountain district at the head of the Dee, deeming that he can conduct his field sports with more success and more satisfaction to himself if the wild waste which calls him occupant be surrounded by a legal cordon excluding it from intrusive footsteps as securely as if it were a walled garden, has made a new law for himself, and instructed his keepers to stop people who are found crossing this wilderness. The glen principally watched is the Glen-lui-beg, the natural passage towards Ben-Muich-Dhui, the centre of the Cairngorm range, the highest mountain in Britain, and for abundance of summer snow, precipices, and cataracts, the most worthy of a visit. As the interruption of the passenger over uncultivated and unfenced wilds is a new thing in Scotland, it has not yet received the sanction of any law, and till it has done so, must be held illegal. If any bill, perhaps in the form of an Act, " to interpret" some Game Act, should be brought in to extend the

and lairds may obtain for their wastes, provided they can give them the character of unapproachableness. A few rich English lessees may, by judiciously blocking up the passes as the Highlanders did of old, shut up the whole of our mountain ranges from intrusion. It is true they must have new law to put this new restriction on the liberty of the people. But such restrictions have occasionally been created when they were required to serve very worthy and beneficial purposes. The law of copyright is a restriction for the benefit of literature; the law of patents is a restriction for the encouragement of invention. It remains to be seen whether deer-stalking be considered a pursuit so ennobling, and so valuable to the community, that new restriction on personal freedom, not needed by graziers and others who raise the ordinary food of man, shall be made for its special encouragement and protection.

15. *Chambers' Journal.*
SHUTTING UP OF THE HIGHLAND GLENS.

A very large portion of the north-west of Scotland consists of wild mountain tracts, full of picturesque beauty, little intersected by roads, and for the most part many miles distant from any of the Lowland towns. A hundred years ago this Alpine region afforded subsistence to a thinly scattered Celtic population; but modern improvements have for the most part sent the Highlanders adrift, and many of them have found a home in Canada, where they are infinitely more comfortable than in the sterile glens of their forefathers. In the place of a human, a sheep population has been generally introduced into the Highlands; and where this is found not to *pay*—that being the great thing now-a-days—a population of deer, grouse, blackcock, and other game has been cultivated, for the sake of autumnal sportsmen. An English or Scottish Lowland estate usually consists of a few thousand acres, laid out in well-fenced fields. A Highland estate extends probably over twenty miles of country, and includes many tall frowning hills, deep valleys and ravines, lakes, waterfalls, and brown heathy moors—the whole unenclosed, and lying pretty much in the condition it has done ever since the creation. In the old times, these wastes were the domain of the chiefs of clans—Macdonnells, Macleods, Macgregors, Mackays, Grants, and so forth. In some cases, descendants of these heroes still possess and draw a rental from them; and in others they have passed, by purchase or inheritance, into the hands of English noblemen and gentlemen. There has latterly been something like a mania among Englishmen for buying Highland properties; and if it continue much longer, the lairds of the old stock will be as much adrift as their expatriated clansmen.

The cause of the odd-looking mania to which we refer is a love of "sport;" for which, as is well known, Englishmen will go great lengths, and do very mad things. Satiated with shooting pheasants and other half-civilised game in English preserves, and longing for novelty, off set troops of wealthy southerns to buy, or at least rent, Highland estates, where battues can be carried on upon a great and enlivening scale. Such old Highland lairds as still call their estates their own, are usually glad to have dealings with these wanderers—at least their Edinburgh agents are—and bargains are made of a kind which would very much astonish the Fergus M'Ivors of former days. It is stated that in Perthshire alone shootings are let to the extent of £10,000 annually, and altogether the money squandered every year on game rents in the Highlands is probably £40,000. While this traffic is gratifying to the lairds, it is equally satisfactory to the scattered sheep farmers and hangers-on of the wilderness; for they contrive to pick up considerable sums of money from the sportsmen-tenants for petty services and provisions. With all this, however, no one can find any fault, and it is only to be lamented that a number of these settlers from the south so conduct themselves, as to render their tenantries a nuisance to the country. Their insatiable and selfish love of sport

MEETING OF THE ASSOCIATION FOR PROTECTING THE PUBLIC RIGHTS OF ROADWAY.

(From the Scotsman, 26th June 1847.)

A Meeting of the Directors of this Association was held in the Council Chambers yesterday—the Lord Provost in the chair.

It will be recollected that the Association was formed about two years ago, for the purpose of protecting the rights of roads and bye-paths which remain uninvaded, and of opening up such as may yet be regained, and that it was resolved to carry it on agreeably to the following rules or constitution :—

1. The Association shall be denominated—"Association for the Protection of Public Rights of Roadway in Scotland."

2. The object of the Association shall be to preserve or recover for the public use, such legal rights of way, as are either in danger of being interrupted, or of being permanently lost to the public in consequence of interruptions already in existence.

3. The Association shall consist of all persons, wheresoever resident, who shall contribute to its funds an annual subscription of ten shillings or upwards ; each subscriber being entitled to be present at, and to take part in, the general meetings of the Association.

4. The business of the Association shall be managed by a President, three Vice-Presidents, twenty-four or more Directors, Treasurer, and Secretary, who shall meet as often as necessary, and who shall have power to appoint Committees of their own number, and to adopt whatever measures may appear advisable for carrying out the objects of the Association.

5. The Association shall hold general meetings, at such times as may appear necessary.

The office-bearers who were elected at the time the Association was formed, and who have since been chosen, are as follows :—

The Right Hon. the LORD PROVOST—*President.*

Sir Thomas Dick Lauder Bart.
 W. Gibson-Craig, Esq., M.P. } *Vice-Presidents.*
 James Gray, Esq., Princes Street,

[Here follow the names of the Directors.]

The LORD PROVOST, on taking the chair, said,—I regret that we have not been able to open up any of the pathways that have been shut up by proprietors. At the same time we have not been altogether inattentive to our duty. We have been making investigations and taking precognitions, so that we will now be better prepared to proceed than we were at this period last year. I think the fact that we do not proceed rashly will give the public confidence in the Association, and will induce them to consider that, when we do commence operations, it is with a vigorous and determined resolution to carry whatever we take up to a successful issue. I may mention that, during this very week, a gentleman from England called upon me for the purpose of ascertaining the name of the agent for the proprietor of Glen Tilt. He was going to make a tour of the Highlands, in company with some ladies ; and, as he did not wish to be insulted or stopped while viewing the beautiful scenery of that romantic locality, he was desirous of receiving, before setting out, a written permission from the Duke of Atholl's man of business. I was unable to satisfy him on that point ; but I conceive that it would be proper

TO TOURISTS.

BLACK'S GUIDE BOOKS AND TRAVELLING MAPS.

NEW EDITIONS.

*" They are really the best books of the sort that have been published. * * * We can sincerely recommend them all to our readers, with a caution, not to commence their journey without them, as their possession will save them both time and money."*—HOOD'S MAGAZINE.

" Without the pretension of a tutor, dictating what he shall admire, the traveller will find these books very pleasing, intelligent, and instructive companions, giving him the exact knowledge he requires at the exact time that he needs it; and very useful, not only to the professed tourist, but to any person who has at any time occasion to journey from his residence in any direction, and who desires to know something more than the mere names of the places he visits."—BRITANNIA.

*" We have looked carefully through the volumes. They are admirably 'got up;' the descriptions are accurate, and remarkably clear and comprehensive. We have seldom examined books better 'edited.' * * Altogether, this series of works is of immense value to tourists."*—ART-UNION.

---

1. *Guide-Book for England.*

BLACK'S PICTURESQUE TOURIST AND ROAD BOOK OF ENGLAND AND WALES; Containing a General Travelling Map, with the Roads and Railways distinctly laid down; besides Sections of the more important Districts on an enlarged scale, and Engraved Charts of Roads, Railroads, and Interesting Localities. In a closely printed and portable volume. *Price* 10s. 6d.

" A carefully executed work, prettily illustrated, with useful Maps."—*Athenæum.*
" The characteristics of 'Black's Picturesque Tourist of England and Wales' are, a more compact and handy form, a more modern style of letterpress, getting up, and illustration, with a very moderate price."—*Spectator.*
" A decided improvement upon the old Road-Book."—*John Bull.*

---

2. *Guide-Book for Scotland.*

BLACK'S PICTURESQUE TOURIST OF SCOTLAND; Containing an accurate Travelling Map; Engraved Charts of Roads, Railroads, and Interesting Localities; Plans of Edinburgh and Glasgow; numerous views of the Scenery on Wood and Steel; and a copious Itinerary. *Fifth Edition*, corrected and improved. In a handsome portable volume. *Price* 8s. 6d.

" A comprehensive, intelligent, and well-arranged Guide-Book. We have been furnished with an incidental proof of the remarkable accuracy of the Charts and Descriptions, in the personal testimony of a pedestrian, who has traversed a considerable space, book in hand."—*Spectator.*
" As nearly as possible what a Guide-Book ought to be—sensible, concise in its information, with that touch of poetry which is no less indispensable in such a haunted land than details of distances and historical facts, but which requires sound taste in its introduction."—*Athenæum.*

7. *Travelling Map of England.*

BLACK'S ROAD AND RAILWAY TRAVELLING MAP OF ENG-
LAND AND WALES, Carefully compiled from the Maps of the
Ordnance Survey, and beautifully engraved by SIDNEY HALL; with all the
ROADS, RAILROADS, and other TOPOGRAPHICAL Information required by the
TOURIST OR TRAVELLER on BUSINESS. Size, 32 inches by 22½. In a neat
Portable Case. *Price 4s. 6d.*

" A beautifully executed Map of England and Wales, which, after careful observation
and reference, we can characterize as being among the most correct ever issued."—*Mining
Journal.*

    ** A SMALLER MAP OF ENGLAND AND WALES. *Price 2s. 6d.*

8. *Voyage round Scotland.*

A VOYAGE ROUND THE COASTS OF SCOTLAND, AND THE
ISLES. By JAMES WILSON, F.R.S.E., M.W.S., &c. Author of the
Treatise on Angling in " The Rod and the Gun." In two volumes post 8vo,
with 20 Etchings, and numerous Woodcuts. *Price 21s.*

" Two of the most charming volumes we have had under our notice for a long time. They
describe scenery round which the imagination loves to linger, and of which no description can
be fatiguing."—*Court Journal.*

" Written in a flowing and animated style."—*Edinburgh Review.*

9. *Tales of the Highlands.*

HIGHLAND RAMBLES, AND LONG LEGENDS TO SHORTEN
THE WAY. By Sir THOMAS DICK LAUDER, Bart. Author of " An
Account of the Morayshire Floods," " Lochandhu," " Wolfe of Badenoch,"
&c. &c. In two volumes, 8vo. With Seven illustrative Etchings, by W.
Dyce, Esq. *Price 21s.*

" We heartily recommend these volumes to all tourists to the ' Land of the Mountain and
the Flood,' who are now setting forth on their delightful trip."—*Bentley's Miscellany.*

" Full of legend, full of adventure, full of interest."—*Athenæum.*

" Sir Thomas evinces an intense sympathy with our Highland landscapes, people, and traditions."—*Inverness Courier.*

" Admirable, and admirably narrated. . . . Full of the true perceptive feeling of the
beautiful in nature."—*Dublin University Magazine.*

10. *Sketches of the Highlands.*

THE HIGHLAND NOTE-BOOK; or, SKETCHES AND ANEC-
DOTES. By R. CARRUTHERS, Inverness. Small 8vo. *Price 4s.*

" The present volume is more than usually interesting, as giving us glimpses into Macbeth's
country, the mountain and moorland fastnesses in which the young Chevalier's Rebellion was
closed, and the district swept by the Morayshire floods made classical ground by the delightful
narrative of Sir Thomas Dick Lauder."—*Athenæum.*

" A clever little volume. Everywhere we find vivacity and rich allusion, to which is added
in the Highland Scenes a poetical feeling for nature in her grander and wilder moods."—
Chambers's Journal.

CPSIA information can be obtained
at www.ICGtesting.com
Printed in the USA
LVHW021518310323
743151LV00003B/92

9 781015 448841